THE SOCIAL ENVIRONMENT AND HUMAN BEHAVIOR

A DIVERSITY PERSPECTIVE

MAGALY QUERALT

Florida International University

ALLYN AND BACON

Boston   London   Toronto   Sydney   Tokyo   Singapore

Executive Editor: *Karen Hanson*
Managing Editor: *Judy Fifer*
Vice-President, Publisher: *Susan Badger*
Editorial Assistant: *Susan Hutchinson*
Executive Marketing Manager: *Joyce Nilsen*
Editorial-Production Service: *Lynda Griffiths, TKM Productions*
Composition Buyer: *Linda Cox*
Manufacturing Buyer: *Megan Cochran*
Cover Administrator: *Linda Knowles*
Cover Designer: *Suzanne Harbison*

Library of Congress Cataloging-in-Publication Data

Queralt, Magaly.
    The social environment and human behavior : a diversity
perspective / Magaly Queralt.
        p.   cm.
    Includes bibliographical references and index.
    ISBN 0-02-397191-6
    1. Social systems.   2. Human behavior.   3. United States--Social
conditions--1980-   4. Pluralism (Social sciences)--United States.
5. Minorities--United States--Social conditions.   I. Title.
HM51 .Q48   1995
306--dc20   95-11989
                                                                              CIP

Printed in the United States of America
10 9 8   05 04 03 02 01

Photo Credits:
p. 1: Will Faller; pp. 57, 72, 82, 91, 94, 112, 127, 141, 167, 187, 204, 221, 232, 238, 310, 343, 358, 364,
387, 393, 395, 406: Robert Harbison; p. 89: United Nations High Commissioner for Refugees (R. Manin,
photographer); pp. 136, 202, 259, 330: John Coletti; p. 184: North Wind Picture Archives; p. 307:
Stephen Marks.

To my father and mother

Contents

PREFACE

This book has been written with attention to the 1992 Curriculum Policy Statements for Baccalaureate and Master's Degree Programs of the Council on Social Work Education (CSWE) in the area of human behavior and social environment (HBSE). Within social work programs, it is suggested that it be used during the first semester of a two-semester HBSE curriculum, with the second semester to be dedicated to the study of individual development and behavior through the life course.

A central objective of *The Social Environment and Human Behavior* is to give balanced attention to the social contexts within which people function—families, small groups, organizations and institutions, communities, societies, and cultures. In accordance with the book's subtitle, *A Diversity Perspective*, the book gives prominence to factors such as culture/ethnicity, socioeconomic status, race, gender, and sexual orientation. The thorough and up-to-date knowledge base provided about the social environment and about diverse cultural groups will prove useful to anyone working and living in a multicultural society. This knowledge is of critical importance to those considering a career as human service practitioners.

This work is the culmination of 27 years of professional experience in the human services, including over 20 years developing and teaching graduate and undergraduate social work courses in HBSE. Written with awareness of and sensitivity to practice issues, *The Social Environment and Human Behavior* communicates in a simple and straightforward manner the enormous range of current knowledge about the social environment necessary for the culturally competent beginning practitioner in the human services. It assumes a *minimum* background of knowledge in the social and behavioral sciences such as that normally derived from college introductory courses in sociology and psychology.

ORGANIZATION OF THE BOOK

The Social Environment and Human Behavior: A Diversity Perspective examines in detail major social system influences on human development and behavior—culture, society, social class, community, organization, small group, and family. Careful consideration is given throughout the book to the impact of gender, race, ethnicity, and sexual orientation. The subject matter is presented according to the sequence I usually follow in teaching undergraduate and graduate social work HBSE courses and is intended to be covered in one semester of instruction. Some instructors may prefer to follow a different topical arrangement to fit their curricular needs. This can be done easily, as the chapters can be studied independently of one another, except for Chapter 1, which should be read first.

The book's comprehensiveness and depth of coverage make possible to use in both graduate and undergraduate programs, with instructors emphasizing different topics at these two levels of instruction in accordance with the unique curricular designs of their academic programs. Depending on the level of preparation students

Curriculum Policy Statements on HBSE for Baccalaureate and Master's Degree Programs in Social Work Education

The following sections are pertinent to human behavior and social environment from the Curriculum Policy Statements for Baccalaureate and Master's Degree Programs in Social Work Education, approved by the Board of Directors of the Council on Social Work Education (CSWE) on July 19, 1992, to become effective June 1995:

HUMAN BEHAVIOR AND SOCIAL ENVIRONMENT
BACCALAUREATE PROGRAMS

B6.7   Programs of social work education must provide content about theories and knowledge of human bio-psycho-social development, including theories and knowledge about the range of social systems in which individuals live (families, groups, organizations, institutions, and communities). The human behavior and the social environment curriculum must provide an understanding of the interactions between and among human biological, social, psychological, and cultural systems as they affect and are affected by human behavior. The impact of social and economic forces on individuals and social systems must be presented. Content must be provided about the ways in which systems promote or deter people in the maintenance or attainment of optimal health and well-being. Content about values and ethical issues related to bio-psycho-social theories must be included. Students must be taught to evaluate theory and apply theory to client situations.

MASTER'S PROGRAMS

M6.9   The professional foundation must provide content about theories and knowledge of human bio-psycho-social development, including theories and knowledge about the range of social systems in which individuals live (families, groups, organizations, institutions, and communities). The human behavior and social environment curriculum must provide an understanding of the interactions between and among human biological, social, psychological, and cultural systems as they affect and are affected by human behavior. The impact of social and economic forces on individuals and social systems must be presented. Content must be provided about the ways in which systems promote or deter people in the maintenance or attainment of optimal health and well-being. Content about values and ethical issues related to bio-psycho-social theories must be included. Students must be taught to evaluate theory and apply theory to client situations.

Source: Council on Social Work Education, Alexandria, VA. Reprinted by permission.

bring to the course and the level of instruction (graduate or undergraduate), instructors may want to assign or skip some sections and to use supplementary sources. The references provided at the end of each chapter, particularly those under the heading Suggestions for Further Reading, provide a good source of additional up-to-date sources. In some programs, the material on cultures and on nondominant groups may be covered in a separate course on "minorities." Similarly, the chapters that provide the theoretical and conceptual background on small groups, organizations, and communities may be used in practice (methods) courses in those programs that have taken this required content out of the HBSE sequence and have included it in the practice methodology course(s) on groups, organizations, and communities.

To enhance and reinforce student learning, each chapter begins with an outline, uses frequent examples and occasional illustrations, and concludes with a glossary of key terms and concepts, a list of references, a list of suggestions for further reading, and a list of journals in each of the major topical areas. An accompanying Instructor's Manual/Test Bank is available to instructors.

The Social Environment and Human Behavior: A Diversity Perspective covers the social, cultural, and economic contexts of human behavior. Chapter 1 introduces the postmodern, diversity, and eclectic emphases of the book and its conceptual and theoretical bases, and it explores the role of empirical research in the knowledge-building process. Chapter 2 covers the concept of culture and various acculturation issues. It also examines some of the central values of the Euro-American (mainstream) culture and of major other cultures in the United States, including the African-American, Latino, Asian/Pacific-American, and Native-American (American-Indian) cultures, the culture of American Jews, and the cultures of gays and lesbians. Chapter 3 explores the societal context with focus on the U.S. social class system and on poverty. Chapter 4 continues the study of social stratification with emphasis on race, ethnicity, gender, and sexual orientation and on the causes and consequences of discrimination and oppression. The focus of attention in the second part of Chapter 4 is on the current situation of women, African Americans, Latinos, Asian/Pacific Americans, American Indians, and gays and lesbians in the United States.

Chapter 5 concentrates on the study of U.S. local communities, Chapter 6 focuses on organizational behavior, and Chapter 7 examines behavior in small groups. All three chapters explore how these social systems influence and are influenced by their participants and by the external environment. They analyze basic structures and processes across groups, organizations, and communities and the commonality of challenges faced by women, African Americans, Latinos, and other nondominant group members functioning within these social systems.

Chapter 8 examines families from different theoretical perspectives with emphasis on the structural-functional and developmental approaches. The second half of the chapter concentrates on contemporary forms of family organization, such as one-parent families, remarriage families, and gay and lesbian families. Chapter 9 focuses on families belonging to nondominant racial/ethnic groups, such as African-American, Latino, Asian/Pacific-American, and American-Indian families.

GENERAL APPROACH

Even though the field of human behavior and social environment is nearly boundless, there is an identifiable core of essential knowledge about the social environment that students should master in preparation for generalist practice in a diverse society. This book presents this knowledge base in a coherent framework. It draws from the current literature in the social and behavioral sciences and on the insights, concepts, theories, and empirical research findings that best help to understand and assess the sociocultural realities confronted by clients.

Because there is presently no one theory capable of explaining all aspects of the social environment, *The Social Environment and Human Behavior* is not based on any single theoretical orientation. Instead, the book's diversity perspective emphasizes close attention to culture, gender, socioeconomic status, race, ethnicity, and sexual orientation. The approach is ecosystemic, multidimensional, eclectic, post-

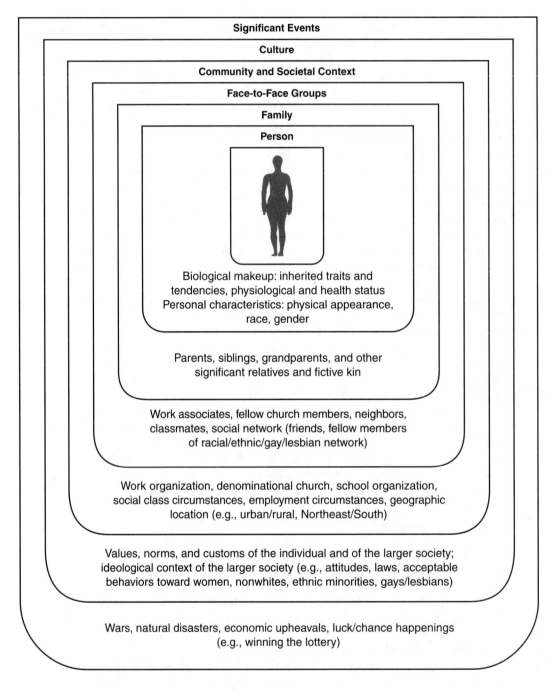

Significant Events

Culture

Community and Societal Context

Face-to-Face Groups

Family

Person

Biological makeup: inherited traits and tendencies, physiological and health status
Personal characteristics: physical appearance, race, gender

Parents, siblings, grandparents, and other significant relatives and fictive kin

Work associates, fellow church members, neighbors, classmates, social network (friends, fellow members of racial/ethnic/gay/lesbian network)

Work organization, denominational church, school organization, social class circumstances, employment circumstances, geographic location (e.g., urban/rural, Northeast/South)

Values, norms, and customs of the individual and of the larger society; ideological context of the larger society (e.g., attitudes, laws, acceptable behaviors toward women, nonwhites, ethnic minorities, gays/lesbians)

Wars, natural disasters, economic upheavals, luck/chance happenings (e.g., winning the lottery)

Forces That Shape Human Behavior

modern/constructivist, and empirical. The approach is ecosystemic because (1) it stresses the importance of attending to contextual factors in the study of human behavior and (2) it puts emphasis on the transaction between person and environment and on the interrelatedness and interdependence of all factors affecting human behavior/development and the environment.

The book's approach is multidimensional because it systematically considers all potential areas of environmental influence—social/political, cultural, and socioeconomic—within various contexts, including the larger society and culture, the community, the organization, the small group, and the family. The approach is eclectic because it draws on any theory, observation, insight, or empirical research finding that helps to explain the system under study, as long as the explanatory constructs are compatible with the ethical principles and values of the social work profession and allied human service professions. It is postmodern/constructivist because it emphasizes human diversity and flexibility and the role of individual perception in the construction of reality. Finally, it is empirical because of its emphasis on knowledge substantiated by observation and careful empirical research—commodities that are in short supply in the study of women and members of nonmainstream groups.

ACKNOWLEDGMENTS

I came to the United States as a refugee in 1959. The United States and its people have been very good to me. I offer this book as a small contribution to the host society that has given me the opportunity to create for myself a meaningful and productive life.

I completed my university studies in the United States in part with the help of scholarships and fellowships and assistance provided by my place of employment. Friends who are members of the mainstream group made me feel at home from the start. I remember fondly the Smith family who invited me to live with them and opened their hearts to me while my parents went to Puerto Rico for a few years, looking for a way to get reestablished. Their daughter, Dottie Smith, has remained a good friend through the years and read parts of this book's manuscript.

Shortly after arriving in the United States, I met Yvonne Bacarisse, social worker *par excellence*. The child of an immigrant mother and a father born in New Orleans, Yvonne was a first-rate socialization agent and translator of the U.S. culture. This life-long dear friend introduced me to the field of social work and to Florida International University (FIU), where we have worked together in the School of Social Work for over 20 years.

Many people have contributed to this book in different ways. My loving mother provided the nurturance that laid the foundation for my love of teaching and learning and taught me the joy of sharing with others. My father modeled the precision and organizational skills that served me well in the process of researching and writing this book. Rachel B. Marks, my mentor and dear friend, gave me much encouragement during my doctoral studies and patiently read and criticized several of my doctoral papers and my dissertation. To her I owe a good part of my ability to write simply and clearly. My discussions with thousands of students who have taken my courses over the years also have helped me to select from the boundless subject matter of human behavior and social environment the most essential concepts. Their comments and questions in class have been invaluable to me.

In relation to the writing of this book, I would like to express my appreciation to several people for their contributions. My dear friends and colleagues, Yvonne Bacarisse and Ann Dryden Witte, read portions of the manuscript and provided insightful comments. I am also grateful to the panel of reviewers selected by the publisher who provided many helpful suggestions and comments: Amanda S. Barusch, University of Utah; Kia J. Bentley, Virginia Commonwealth University; M. Diane Calloway, Utah State University; Leon W. Chestang, Wayne State University; William Downs, State University of New York at Buffalo; Paul A. d'Oronzio, University of South Florida; Judith I. Gray, Ball State University; Nancy R. Hooyman, University of Washington; Elizabeth D. Hutchison, Virginia Commonwealth University; Nancy P. Kropf, University of Georgia; Donald D. Mowry, University of Wisconsin–Eau Claire; Phylis J. Peterman, Rutgers University; David Royse, University of Kentucky; and Lacey M. Tillotson, Southern University. Scott Briar, former Director of the School of Social Work, and Allan Rosenbaum, former Dean of the School of Public Affairs and Services at FIU, supported this effort by approving my requests at various points for a reduced faculty appointment to concentrate on this writing project. Roberta Rothschild was my guardian angel at the dean's office. She made sure that I received some student assistance throughout the project. Tina Fain and Sharon Danski did a fine job tracking down a lot of the sources from the library and helped in innumerable other ways. In addition, I would like to acknowledge the assistance of Abigail Hoskins, Linda Visaggi, and Rod Ellis. Finally, I would like to thank the editorial staff at Allyn and Bacon and TKM Productions.

CHAPTER 1

THEORETICAL, CONCEPTUAL, AND EMPIRICAL FOUNDATIONS

This book examines the many social contexts that influence our behavior—culture, society, social class, community, organization, small group, and family—with attention to the role played by our race, ethnicity, gender, and sexual orientation. One of its unique features is the centrality it accords to the experiences of members of nondominant groups, particularly women, the poor, African Americans, Latinos, gays and lesbians, Asian/Pacific Americans, and Native Americans.

Knowledge about the unique situation and life experiences of nondominant group members is essential for human service practitioners because these individuals—especially women, people of color, and the poor—constitute a large proportion of the clientele of most social service agencies. Specifically in the field of social work, an understanding of the life situation of these social groups is of critical importance because the profession has made a commitment to serving the poor and the oppressed in our society.

This chapter discusses the general perspective of the book, particularly its emphasis on human diversity and its eclectic approach, and examines the dual role of theory and empirical research in the development of a knowledge base for human behavior and social environment (HBSE).

A DIVERSITY PERSPECTIVE

One important aspect of this book's perspective is the emphasis on human diversity and on an **ethnocultural approach** (Lister, 1987). Accordingly, the book provides knowledge about the life experiences of a variety of social groups, including knowledge about each group's cultural values, family patterns, strengths, problems, and other unique experiences. In addition, this book will assist you in understanding the impact of powerlessness, discrimination, and oppression on people's lives. The objective is to help you attain the insights that are necessary for **culturally competent** professional practice—that is, practice congruent with the behavior and expectations that members of each distinctive cultural group recognize as appropriate (Green, 1982).

The diversity perspective also stresses insight derived from the concepts of "dual perspective" (Norton, 1978), "biculturalism" (De Anda, 1984), "ethclass" (Gordon, 1964; Devore & Schlesinger, 1991), and "cultural pluralism" (Kellen, 1956; Herskovits, 1972). The concept of **dual perspective** teaches us that members of most nonmainstream cultural groups, while sharing many commonalities with members of the mainstream group, differ in their need to live simultaneously in two or more "worlds"—the mainstream culture and their own culture(s). This requires that such individuals learn to negotiate these different contexts, each with its unique language, values, beliefs, lifestyles, and behavioral expectations.

Biculturalism refers to the relative ease with which a person is able to move back and forth between cultural systems—usually the person's culture of origin, which provides nurturance or support, and the mainstream culture, which provides access to economic and other types of sustenance. In a multicultural society such as the United States, members of nonmainstream groups must develop a certain degree of bicultural competence in order to survive and succeed. The next chapter will explore some of the major variables that facilitate or hinder the process of bicultural socialization.

Ethclass is a concept that denotes the dual influence of ethnicity (*eth*) and socioeconomic status (*class*) on people's lifestyles, values, and life chances. It reminds us that an individual's life chances, lifestyles, and behaviors vary not only on the basis of the person's ethnic background but also depending on the individual's social class membership. Specifically, this means that socioeconomic status must always be taken into consideration when considering the effects of ethnic group membership. For example, the lifestyle and behavioral style of a suburban upper-middle-class African American would be substantially different from the lifestyle and behavioral style of an African American inner-city public project dweller who is a high school dropout, notwithstanding the fact that both are African Americans.

Cultural pluralism is a viewpoint emphasized in this book that respects the cultural differences that exist among various social groups and recognizes the strengths and merits of each group's culture. It stresses the right of each group to retain its culture, language, and way of life. Additionally, cultural pluralism emphasizes the responsibility of all social groups to participate in and contribute to the mainstream society and to develop communication skills in the common language of the United States—the English language.

In sum, this book's diversity perspective affirms the worth and validity of all social groups. It also emphasizes the importance for human service practitioners of acquiring knowledge and understandings about the total life experiences of members of dominant and nondominant groups that make up our diverse society.

On the Use of Racial and Ethnic Labels

In talking about various racial and ethnic groups, it is necessary to use certain designations so that authors and readers communicate clearly. Few of the descriptor terms used to refer to specific racial/ethnic groups are entirely satisfactory. The choices made by the author to be used in this book are presented here; not everyone will agree with the selections made, however.

For the sake of consistency in labeling, we will refer to all racial and ethnic group members in the United States as "hyphenated Americans," such as African Americans, Irish Americans, Italian Americans, Mexican Americans, and Japanese Americans. This term is useful to differentiate between individuals who reside in the United States and their counterparts in their countries of origin, such as the Africans residing in Africa, the Irish in Ireland, the Italians in Italy, the Mexicans in Mexico, and so on. In the case of Puerto Ricans, those residing in the United States will be referred to as mainland Puerto Ricans, whereas their counterparts in the island will be called Puerto Ricans, to follow the conventional way in which the two groups are usually differentiated.

In this book, we will use the term *African American* to refer to those blacks born in the United States whose ancestors originally came

Box 1.1

About Men

Coloring Lessons

BY DAVID UPDIKE

It was the big annual fair at Shady Hill, a private school nestled away in one of our city's finer neighborhoods. Though October, it was warm and the ash gray clouds were giving way to soft, swelling shapes of blue. There were lots of kids already, their parents working the various concessions—apple bobbing and doughnut biting, waterballoon throwing at a heckling buffoon—all ploys to harvest money for the school's scholarship fund.

It seemed like the perfect event to bring an almost-4-year-old to, but my son, Wesley, was dragging on my arm, nervously surveying the scene. Getting tired of pulling him, disappointed that he was not having more fun, I stopped finally, kneeled down and asked him what was the matter.

He hesitated, looked around, chewing on his sleeve. "Too many pink people," he said softly. I laughed, but Wesley failed to see the humor of it and kept peering out through the thickening throng. "Too many pink people," he repeated. But along with my laugh came a twinge of nervousness—the parent's realization that our apprehensions are not entirely unfounded and that racial awareness comes even to 3-year-olds. I suspected, half wished, that his state of unhappiness had less to do with too many "pink" people than with too many people.

And we had taught him to use "pink" in the first place, in preference to the more common adjective used for people of my complexion. For my wife, we had opted for "brown" because that's the color she actually is: Wesley was learning his colors, after all, and it seemed silly and misleading to be describing people by colors they clearly are not.

The issue had arisen at his first day care—predominantly African-American—from which he had returned one day and asked whether he really was "gray." We told him no, he wasn't gray, more brown, but a lighter, pinker shade than his mother.

A few months later he came home from his new day care, this time predominantly European-American, and asked, "Mommy, are we brown?"

"Yes," she said. "Why?"

"Melissa said we're b_____."

'She did?"

"Yeah."

The whole question caused me to wonder what these two words, b_____ and w_____—so frequently used and so heavily laden with historical and social baggage—actually mean. I looked in a dictionary: the lighter of the two, I learned, is "the color of pure snow…reflecting nearly all the rays of sunlight, or a similar light…."

The other means "lacking hue and brightness; absorbing light without reflecting any of the rays composing it…gloomy, pessimistic or dismal… without any moral light or goodness."

I am not the color of pure snow, and my wife and son reflect a good deal of light; they seem much closer in the spectrum to brown, "a dark shade with a yellowish or reddish hue." In any event, perhaps my problem with the two words is that they are, in the spectrum and in people's minds, absolutes and polar opposites, absorbing light or reflecting it but admitting no shades in between except gray—the pallor of the recently departed on the mortuary slab, blood drained from their earthly vessel.

All of which is likely to raise the hackles ("hairs on a dog's neck that bristle when the dog is ready to fight") of the anti-politically-correct thought police, who are fed up with all this precious talk about what we should call one another. They resist African-American—too many syllables, so hard to say—though they seem to be comfortable with Italian-American.

Let me enrage them further by suggesting that w_____ may also have outlived its usefulness in describing people, and that we should take up European-American, instead, in keeping with the now-accepted Native, Asian- and African-American. Or maybe just plain "pink" will do, the color even the palest of us turn when push comes to shove and we reveal our humanity—when angry, say, or while laughing or having sex or lying in the sun, trying to turn brown.

W_____ and b_____ are colors no one really is, monolithic and redolent with historical innuendo and social shading, and the words encourage those of us who use them—everyone—to continue to think binary terms, like computers. I am not suggesting the terms be abandoned, tossed onto the scrap heap of language with other discarded words—just that they are used too easily and often and should be traded in, occasionally, for words that admit that issues of race and ethnicity are more complicated than these monosyllables imply. Try not saying them, once or twice, and see how it feels. And if you are teaching a child his or her colors, you might want to adopt a vocabulary that holds true for skin tones and for crayons.

But at the fair, things were improving slowly. I had, with misgivings, pointed out to Wesley that I am "pink," like some of his cousins and grandparents and uncles and aunts and school friends, and that it's not nice to say there are "too many" of us.

We walked around, mulling all this over, and I bought us a doughnut. We went into a gym and looked at old sports equipment, and I fought the temptation to buy something. We went outside again into the soft yellow sunlight and found happiness at a wading pool where, using fishing poles with magnets dangling from the lines, you could catch plastic fish with paper-clip noses. He caught a few and we traded them for prizes he then clutched tightly in his small, strong hands.

But he was still tired, and when I suggested we go home, he nodded and started to suck his thumb. I picked him up and carried him, and as we approached the gate he triumphantly called my attention to a "brown boy" with a baseball hat, who was just then coming in.

Again, his observation elicited in me a vague discomfort, and I wondered if we couldn't get away from all this altogether. But how?

"Wesley," I finally offered. "Do you have to call him 'brown boy'? Why don't you just say, 'That tall boy' or 'the boy with the blue hat' or 'the boy in the green sweatshirt'?" He mulled over my suggestion, but then rejected it.

"No," he said firmly. "He's brown."

---

from any of the African nations. This is currently the designation preferred by members of this group, given that the word *African* incorporates the cultural identity of United States-born blacks that the term *black* leaves out. At times, the term *black* is used if it is not clear that the information provided refers exclusively to African Americans. For example, practically all the data collected by the U.S. Bureau of the Census pertain to blacks in the United States, not just African Americans. This means that it encompasses Bahamians, Jamaicans, Haitians, and all other blacks living in the United States, not just African Americans.

Strictly speaking, the term *African American* is broader in scope than its common usage indicates, as it applies to any individual of African origin on the American continent, including Canadian blacks, Mexican blacks, Central and South American blacks, black Caribbean islanders such as black Cubans, Haitians, Jamaicans, and Bahamians, and even African whites (e.g., South Africans) who have migrated to the United States. However, we will NOT be using the term *African American*

in this broadly encompassing way since it is not customary to do so in the United States.

The hyphenated-American designation is probably acceptable to most members of non-mainstream ethnic groups in the United States (U.S. Hispanics say, call us "Americans," 1992), but it is not entirely satisfactory. This is because some individuals believe that the hyphenation denotes some degree of marginality in the society as long as mainstream Americans (e.g., Anglo Americans, German Americans, French Americans) continue to be referred to as "Americans." For instance, some may argue that the term *Mexican American* denotes that the individual is neither fully Mexican nor fully American but something in between (Asamoah, Garcia, Ortiz Hendricks, & Walker, 1991). Now that mainstream Americans are increasingly referred to in the literature as "Euro Americans," it is becoming evident that even the uniform use of the hyphenated-American designation will not eliminate the so-called pecking order, as some hyphenated Americans continue to be seen by some people as "more American" than others. These are the nuances in labeling that we need to be sensitive to in practice so that we refer to clients by the racial or ethnic label of their choice, not by the label used by a particular author (such as the author of this book) or by a particular social agency.

The term *minority* has become objectionable in some professional circles because it can be perceived as connoting a *lessened* status (Asamoah et al., 1991). This designation also can be misleading when applied to women, as they constitute the majority, not the minority, of the U.S. population, or to various racial and ethnic groups that have become the majority population in some localities. Consequently, the old dichotomy *majority/minority group* is referred to in this textbook as **dominant/nondominant** group (Folb, 1988). These latter designations, although not satisfactory either because they also denote higher and lower status, at least more clearly convey the fundamental difference between the two groups, which is not a matter of size but of power, dominance, and control of resources.

When appropriate, we will use the term **people of color** (Hopps, 1987) to refer to nonwhites. For example, all black persons, regardless of their specific ethnic backgrounds, are people of color, as are all Asian/Pacific Islanders and American Indians. Mexican Americans and mainland Puerto Ricans (the two largest Latino ethnic groups in the United States) are conventionally classified as people of color because a substantial proportion of these groups' members are of mixed racial background. However, a good number of Mexican and Puerto Rican individuals in the United States are of white European (usually Iberian Spanish) ancestry. Other nonmainstream ethnic groups in the United States have a large proportion of whites. For example, among Latinos residing in the United States, Cubans, Argentinians, and Chileans, to mention a few groups, are predominantly of white European background. It would be inaccurate to refer to members of these ethnic groups collectively as people of color.

We will use the term *Latino* to refer to Spanish-speaking persons born in Latin America or in one of the Caribbean islands or to U.S. natives whose Spanish-speaking ancestors came from Latin America or the Caribbean. Whenever possible, we will avoid using the term *Hispanic* (meaning from Spain) because often it is applied inappropriately. Some Latin Americans and Spanish-speaking Caribbean Islanders are Native Indians from the Americas and many are *mestizos*—that is, part Native American Indian and part Hispanic. Others are of African descent or partly of African descent. Still others are of Portuguese, German, Scandinavian, or Italian extraction, to mention a few possible national origins. Given the variety of extractions, it becomes clear that a good number of Latin Americans or Spanish-speaking Caribbean Islanders in the United States are not Hispanic or are only partly Hispanic. More importantly, some may resent being labeled Hispanic because conquistadors or colonists from Spain vanquished or enslaved their ancestors (Asamoah et al., 1991, p. 13). To call such people Hispanics would be about as inaccurate as calling African Americans "Anglos."

Given the preceding considerations, practitioners are cautioned to restrict their use of the term *Hispanic* to those individuals who consider themselves to be Hispanic. The term *Latino* is less sensitive, and, therefore, usually a more acceptable designation when the various groups must be aggregated under one category. However, like the term *Hispanic*, the word *Latino* is an umbrella designation encompassing people from many countries in Central America, South America, and the Caribbean who have very little in common other than the Spanish language. As such, the term ignores important cultural and demographic differences. This is probably the reason why a recent national survey revealed that two-thirds of Hispanics/Latinos in the United States prefer to be called by national-origin labels such as Cuban American, Mexican American, Dominican, or just plain American rather than Latino (Gonzalez, 1992; U.S. Hispanics say, call us "-Americans," 1992). Exactly the same tends to be true of Asian/Pacific Islanders in the United States (e.g., Chinese Americans, Japanese Americans, Korean Americans, and so on) who are frequently lumped under the *Asian* designation even though these national groups have little in common with one another.

ECLECTIC EMPHASIS

To encompass the vast reservoir of social and behavioral science knowledge that social work and other human service students must master to become competent practitioners, a HBSE book must almost by necessity be **eclectic.** This means that it must offer insights derived from a wide variety of theoretical perspectives and it must encourage readers to take from the various schools of thought and practice the best they can offer to understand and treat clients (Siporin, 1980). From a humanistic ethical value base, this book emphasizes the eclectic approach.

Some so-called purists may question the wisdom of suggesting an eclectic approach because it may encourage some practitioners to mix philosophically inconsistent theories. Although eclecticism may lead to some philosophical or theoretical inconsistencies, it is up to the practitioner to decide the extent to which he or she is willing to compromise ideological purity and sometimes even to use in complementary fashion what some might consider "rival" approaches in order to obtain maximum insight and understanding and to offer the highest level of assistance to clients.

POSTMODERN, SOCIAL CONSTRUCTIVIST EMPHASIS

Postmodernism, which has found expression recently in a variety of fields besides the social sciences (e.g., literature, art, philosophy, and architecture), is probably one of the most significant multidisciplinary intellectual developments in recent years (Ritzer, 1992). The diversity/eclectic emphasis of this book is part of the postmodern tradition that places a great deal of emphasis on the importance of respecting and celebrating differences among people. This perspective is highly compatible with the purposes of the social work profession.

Unlike the "modern world" created by the industrial revolution that stressed standardization and mass production, the "postmodern world" (the world of the 1980s and beyond) is much more diverse and fluid (constantly changing). Accordingly, the postmodern point of view rejects absolutism and objectivism and stresses the importance of pluralism, eclecticism, relativism, and flexibility (Laird, 1993). It stresses the limitations of old theories tied to the industrial era and emphasizes the need to search for new paradigms (Kellner, 1990). It values diverse ideas and theoretical perspectives. In short, the postmodern perspective considers any attempt to objectify and standardize knowledge and to develop all-encompassing theories and major organizing principles as misguided and inconsistent with current realities.

Constructivism is an old concept newly adopted by postmoderns that stresses that reality is shaped by the perceptions of each individual. In other words, there is no such thing as an "objective reality" of being a poor person, a pregnant teenager, a homeless person, a woman, a homosexual, an old person, a drug addict, a welfare recipient, a Chinese American, a ghetto resident, or a single parent. The meaning of such experiences is perceived differently by each individual experiencing them (Fisher, 1991).

Constructivism emphasizes that reality is mediated or constructed by each person or other social system such as a family or work organization on the basis of a unique set of experiences. Consequently, each individual or social system has a different assumptive world and experiences a different "truth." That is *not* to say that no two people or families are alike in any way. On the contrary, there are many similarities, consistencies, and regularities in the ways people experience and interpret reality. For example, many African-American families are likely to show similarities in the ways they use language and in their values, customs, rituals, beliefs, and approach toward the mainstream society. This is because they share a common cultural background and a common history and may have undergone similar experiences such as poverty, racism, and discrimination (Fleck-Henderson, 1993).

The postmodern/constructivist perspective of this book demystifies theories and limits their authority by treating them as explanations constructed by individuals with the power to define meanings at a given time in history, usually males from the dominant group in the society. Such individuals are likely to have developed insights consistent with the "realities" they have experienced. The knowledge base derived from these theories may or may not help us understand the realities of life for women or for people who have experienced different social circumstances, such as the poor. If the theories were developed in the past, they may not explain present social circumstances.

This book treats empirical research with much respect as an important source of knowledge; however, in typical postmodern/constructivist fashion, it does not treat it as the ultimate or most authoritative source of knowledge. Systematic empirical research can be of narrow applicability if it explores primarily the issues of interest to the dominant group such as when it is based on data collected from samples made up primarily of white males or middle-class participants. Research can even serve as "oppressor" if it sets itself up as "the standard" for gaining legitimate knowledge and discounts or disqualifies the validity of other more qualitative ways of knowing, such as accounts of "lived experience" or participant observation reports (Saleebey, 1992, pp. 23–24).

Some people within the postmodern movement have emphasized the need for theories, research reports, or any other writings (often referred to as *texts* or *narratives*) to be "deconstructed" (Lyotard, 1984; Brown, 1987; Harvey, 1989). Specifically, **deconstruction** of a text means to pick it apart in order to dig out the things it ought to have said or the issues it should have addressed but didn't and to uncover the biases inherent in what it says. This is a very demanding task, as it requires that we become familiar with the social, historical, and political circumstances under which the text was written to uncover its biases and to elicit the voices the text may have marginalized or suppressed. Typically, these are the voices of women and other nondominant group members whose experiences may have been ignored by the writer or researcher (Sands & Nuccio, 1992; Stephens, 1994). Although deconstruction is by no means one of the goals of this book, it nevertheless attempts to assess, when possible, the extent to which various mainstream theories and empirical reports take into consideration or ignore the experiences of women and other nondominant group members.

ETHICAL EMPHASIS

Knowledge alone will not make you a good human service practitioner or researcher unless you conduct your professional practice in an ethical manner. In particular, the social work profession puts emphasis on certain humanistic values and democratic principles embodied in the Code of Ethics of the National Association of Social Workers (NASW) (see the Appendix at the end of this chapter). This book affirms and reinforces the importance of *treating all human beings* with dignity and respect and in accordance with the values and principles delineated in the NASW Code of Ethics. These values include:

- Fairness, justice, and equality
- Respect, acceptance, understanding, and sensitivity toward others, regardless of race, gender, ethnicity, social class status, sexual orientation, age, or any other personal attribute
- Responsibility to reduce and prevent discrimination and oppression
- Responsibility to provide equal access to services, resources, and opportunities, irrespective of the client's race, gender, ethnicity, social class standing, sexual orientation, age, or any other personal attribute
- Responsibility to work to improve the societal resource allocation process so that there is less inequality, to improve social conditions, and to make social institutions more humane and responsive to human needs, especially the needs of the poor and disadvantaged
- Respect for the individuality, freedom, autonomy, and self-determination of all clients and for their right to participate actively in their own helping process
- Responsibility for staying abreast of current scientific and professional information relevant to the services one offers
- Responsibility to be honest and truthful and to keep information provided by the client private and confidential

One major objective of this book, by providing extensive coverage of human diversity issues, is to help you, the reader, evolve in your ability to value others outside your own social group, to develop a better appreciation of the infinitely variable circumstances of people's lives, and to become more accepting, nonprejudiced, nondiscriminating, and nonjudgmental. Hopefully, as a result of reading this book, you will grow in your ability to refrain from passing judgment (whether it be about unmarried mothers, welfare recipients, illegal immigrants, gays and lesbians, abusive parents, or others) and from imposing your values on other people.

As you develop a pluralistic perspective, you are likely to grow in your ability to appreciate the importance of other ethical principles, such as self-determination or the right for clients to make their own choices and decisions. Also, as you grow in knowledge about the effects of discrimination and oppression, you are likely to become sensitized to the special needs of those who are poor and disadvantaged, such as many children and women in the United States. As a human service professional, it will be your responsibility to facilitate their access to opportunities and programs and to work toward making the society and its institutions more humane and responsive to people's needs.

In our everyday professional practice, ethical principles often conflict, pushing us to make choices among them. For example, at some point you are likely to have to choose between the duty to keep the information your client has provided private and confidential and the social duty to reveal that this individual intends to cause serious harm to others or has already caused harm. For instance, a client may reveal that he intends to kill his boss or that she is having unprotected sex with someone who does not know she has acquired immune deficiency syndrome (AIDS). If one of your clients seems intent on committing suicide, you may have to decide between supporting his or her autonomy/self-determination and protecting the person's life. Without question, the protection of human life takes precedence over other ethical considerations such as the right to privacy and confidentiality; consequently, when it conflicts with other values, it is appropriate to give it priority above all else (Loewenberg & Dolgoff, 1992, p. 60). In the case of the client who intends to harm others or who has already caused harm, probably you would want to do anything within your power to convince the person to tell others. However, if your client

IT WAS ON THAT FIRST PARENTS DAY THAT MRS. KARNEL BEGAN TO SUSPECT HER VALUES-CLARIFICATION CLASS WAS HEADED FOR TROUBLE!

Source: Chuck Asay, *Colorado Springs Gazette Telegraph.* Reprinted by permission of the *Colorado Springs Gazette Telegraph.*

refuses, you may want to consult with the legal adviser in your agency so that you may act in a socially responsible and legally appropriate manner.

It may be more difficult to resolve value conflicts when life is not at stake. One way of approaching such conflicts is to reflect about the relative importance of various ethical principles and to rank them in order of priority. This is a difficult task, even for ethicists. Loewenberg and Dolgoff (1992) have devoted a whole book to the discussion of ethical conflicts and their suggestions as to how to go about resolving them. They have suggested that, next in importance to the protection of life, social workers rank issues pertaining to equality and inequality, then those that have to do with autonomy and freedom, quality of life, and, finally, privacy, confidentiality, and full disclosure (p. 60). You may want to reflect about this suggested set of priorities and work

out your own ethical framework for practice as you encounter a wide diversity of human situations and problems throughout this book.

As you read this book, you are also encouraged to reflect about your personal attitudes, values, and goals and to compare them against those of the profession you have chosen to determine how suitable your perspective seems to be. In the process, you may come face to face, for example, with the fact that you habitually avoid social contact with black or white people, or that you are annoyed when people around you speak in a language other than English, or that you have trouble being friendly and accepting with someone who is gay or lesbian, or that you do not treat women as men's equals. Perhaps you feel that you would be unable to be accepting and nonjudgmental toward a child molester, a person with AIDS, or a crack addict, to mention just a few of the possible people with whom you are likely to work.

We all have biases of one sort or another; however, as human service professionals, we have the obligation to act in an accepting, nonjudgmental manner and to treat all clients equitably. Sometimes practitioners remain unable to overcome some of their biases. For example, someone may be unable to accept those who sexually abuse children or who commit violent acts. It is perfectly acceptable to step aside and let another colleague deal with such clients. However, if, after completing this book, you still have multiple biases and remain unable to make any progress in overcoming them, it would be wise to think carefully about your career choice.

CAPITALIZING ON STRENGTHS

Interventions tend to be more effective if they build on the resourcefulness of clients, as much as possible. In practical terms, this means that, in assessing your clients, it is wise to focus on their strengths as well as on their problems and deficits.

You will likely be more effective in assisting your clients to overcome deficits and to deal with their problems if you help them construct a better life for themselves by discovering and using their strengths and by reaching out for resources available to them in their environments. This is the essence of **empowerment**—helping people discover the power and energies within them, their families, and their communities and assisting them to take active part in the decisions that shape their worlds (Saleebey, 1992, p. 8).

If you focus too much on the deficits, problems, weaknesses, disorders, and other negative attributes of your clients, you may end up having negative expectations about their ability to deal with their problems. In turn, this may cause your clients to perceive themselves negatively and to act in accordance with your expectations (Saleebey, 1992). This is the well-known problem of the *self-fulfilling prophecy*.

CONCEPTUAL/THEORETICAL AND RESEARCH BASES

This book draws from a variety of theoretical and empirical sources because there is no HBSE theory that is comprehensive enough to explain all the subtleties and complexities of the social environmental context of human behavior. In the following section, we will examine the role of theories and research in the development of a knowledge base. Then we will take a detailed look at the major theories that form our conceptual base for the study of the social environment. Following this, we will consider several criteria useful in the evaluation of theories. Finally, we will conclude the chapter by reviewing the major types of research that contribute to the construction of a HBSE knowledge base.

Building a Knowledge Base: The Place of Theories and Research

Some people have little respect for theories. They say, "Oh, it is *only* a theory," meaning it is a hunch or a guess, not fact. It is true that theories that are not supported by evidence are pure speculation, yet they may offer insightful and compelling explanations of phenomena. Notwithstanding this, some people prefer to pay attention to the evidence, unadorned by interpretations or explanations. They say, "Just give me the facts." Yet, if observation and fact finding are not driven or guided by some conceptual framework or theory, these activities may wander aimlessly, producing a disorganized conglomerate of data. Hence, theories are needed, but they should be tested by research. At the same time, research should be anchored in some theory. The two go hand in hand.

We may be getting ahead of ourselves because at this point we have not defined the word *theory*. A **theory** is a collection of related statements or propositions that attempt to describe, explain, or predict a particular aspect of experience. For example, you may believe that parents treat their boys and girls differently and that, by doing so, they cause them to engage in sex-role playing. Such belief may be one of the propositions that form part of a more encompassing theory you may have concerning the relative influence of heredity and environment on personality traits. Perhaps your more general theory concerning gender differences may be that traits are primarily acquired through the socialization process rather than inherited.

If we were to restate a theoretical proposition in observable and measurable terms, we would create a hypothesis (Cloninger, 1993). Specifically, a **hypothesis** is an "educated guess" about the possible relationship between two or more variables (Kornblum, 1991, pp. 35–36). For example, starting with the belief that frustration causes aggression, one might come up with several specific hypotheses, such as: Married men who lose their jobs (a frustrating experience) will be more likely to physically abuse their wives than those who are employed. Or, starting with the idea that the level of welfare dependency in a community is related to its rate of unemployment, one might hypothesize that the higher the rate of unemployment, the greater will be the proportion of people on the welfare rolls. By translating theoretical propositions into hypotheses, we restate them in operational terms (i.e., terms that are measurable and testable), and, by so doing, we can test if they are consistent with the evidence.

As you can see, ideally theories and research should be very closely related. Theories may be initially based on casual observations, intuition, or speculation. But as they get refined and translated into specific hypotheses, they serve to guide our research efforts. Similarly, research is important because it allows us to test the validity of our beliefs and theories. Sometimes research confirms a hypothesis, providing support for the theory from which it was derived, whereas other times it disconfirms the hypothesis, and the theory from which it was derived must be modified to account for

the unexpected findings. The relationship between theory and research can be seen in Figure 1.1. Reality is often different from the ideal, however. Many times, theories persist even though they are not tested, and data are often gathered without the research effort being guided by any particular theory.

Theoretical Bases of Knowledge about the Social Environment and Human Behavior

As previously noted, there is no grand theory capable of explaining the subtleties and complexities of the social environmental contexts of human behavior. However, a large number of theories of limited or "special" scope have been developed to explain smaller subsets of observations and empirical findings. You will come across many of these theories throughout this book.

This section will discuss several of the major wide-scope theories about the social environment, even though most would not score well on the criteria for evaluating theories that will be examined in a later section of this chapter. To be sure, most of these theories do not have a strong empirical foundation. In fact, even if researchers wanted to test them, it is not clear how they would do it because their conceptual base is difficult to operationalize—that is, to restate in observable and measurable terms. These classic theories—including structural functionalism, conflict theory, ecosystems theory, symbolic interactionism, role theory, and social exchange theory—are given less importance today than in years past; yet, they have contributed important insights that have sharpened our understanding of human behavior and social environment. This section will also consider the main tenets of feminist theory, which is crucial because it reminds us of the importance of including the perspectives and experiences of women and other nondominant groups in all theoretical and empirical efforts. The collective legacy of ideas contributed by the theories to be examined provides a

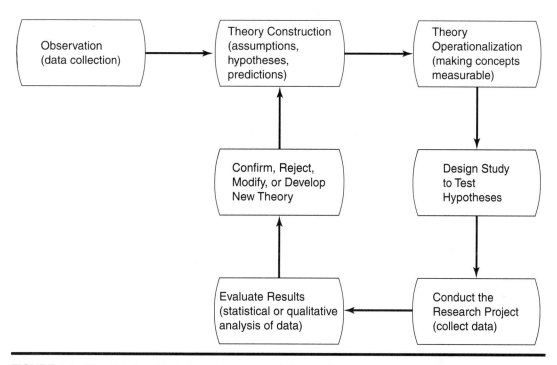

FIGURE 1.1 The Relationship between Theory and Research

powerful conceptual base for the study of the social environmental context of behavior.

Structural Functionalism

Structural functionalism was for many years the dominant theory in sociology; however, it has lost a great deal of its former prominence (Ritzer, 1992). Among its leading proponents were Talcott Parsons (1951), Robert Merton (1968), and Emile Durkheim (1964). This theory throws light on the relationship of the various components of society (e.g., families, schools, work organizations), particularly in terms of the functions they fulfill, including adaptation, goal achievement, pattern maintenance, and integration. This conceptualization of social systems along functional lines is one of the important legacies of structural functionalism and of Talcott Parsons in particular.

Adaptation refers to the way in which various subunits of a system and the system as a whole change in order to better fit the require-

ments of the environment and how they change the environment to better fulfill system needs. *Goal achievement* consists of defining and meeting the goals the system sets for itself and regulating the means by which to achieve system goals. *Integration* refers to the regulation of the interrelationship of component parts of the system. Finally, *pattern maintenance* has to do with the way the social system and its component parts keep the system in equilibrium.

According to Parsons, the economy is the subsystem of the society primarily in charge of facilitating adaptation to the environment. It accomplishes this function by providing a labor market and systems of production, allocation, and distribution. The political system has primary responsibility for goal attainment. It fulfills this function by pursuing social objectives and mobilizing people and resources toward meeting them. The family and the schools are mainly in charge of pattern maintenance. They do this through the socialization process by which they pass on to children the cultural norms and values of the society. The integration function is performed by the community through the development of laws, rules, and procedures that regulate interrelationships (Ritzer, 1992).

One of the better-known aspects of structural functionalism is the theory of stratification developed by Davis and Moore (1945). According to this theory, which has had much influence on sociological thinking, a social class system is necessary for a society to survive. In particular, the theory suggests that in order for the society to fill its important positions with individuals who have the appropriate credentials and expertise, it must properly reward those who are trained and qualified to assume those jobs. The rewards must be financial as well as in terms of social status and prestige so that competent individuals will be motivated to make the necessary sacrifices to take on these responsibilities.

To some extent, the argument of the functionalists seems reasonable. If the society rewarded its members equally for all the jobs to be done, from the most responsible and demanding to the simplest, it might have a hard time recruiting for the hardest jobs. However, the rationale for a social class system fails to explain why certain social positions are unrewarded even though they are critical while others are overly rewarded even though less critical. Mothers, for example, traditionally have not received compensation for the care and socialization of their children and have enjoyed little status in the society by virtue of playing the child-care role, even though it is an essential one. Similarly, garbage collectors, teachers, and nurses are paid less than movie stars or professional athletes even though most people would agree that the former perform a more vital job for the society than the latter.

One must also look closely at the structural-functional argument that there is a scarcity of people with the ability and credentials to fill high-level positions and therefore a small group of very talented people must be highly rewarded. Although high levels of expertise are not in large supply in the United States today, thus making the argument valid on the surface, the scarcity of highly skilled people largely has been created by the power elite to protect their interests. They have done this by erecting and maintaining barriers to talent development, such as poverty, inferior public education in poor areas, racial and ethnic discrimination, and the ideology of sex roles and motherhood, which has kept women from fully realizing their potential. This has made it difficult for many able children to get the education they need to prepare for complex and essential societal roles in various fields such as medicine and engineering). In addition, the power elite often erects other educational barriers to limit the talent pool, such as highly selective admission to elite professional education programs, limited financial aid for higher education, and licensing examinations that control the flow of people admitted to various professions. If the society chose to cultivate the self-realization and talent of all its people, there would be an ample supply of people to fill all social positions, and none would have to be excessively remunerated. In such a society, socioeconomic differences would exist, but they would be much less marked than those in the United States today.

Merton (1968), another structural functionalist, made several important contributions to the functional analysis of social systems. Three will be briefly reviewed here: the concept of dysfunction as opposed to function, the need to conduct functional analyses not only at the societal level but at other levels such as within families and groups, and the conceptualization of deviant behavior as motivated by the desire for material success.

According to Merton, we should look at subunits of society such as communities, organizations, groups, and families in the same manner we look at society as a whole—that is, in terms of how well they fulfill their basic functions. He suggested that social structures do not always serve a useful or adaptive function. Sometimes they produce negative consequences or are dysfunctional, at least for some subunits of the system. Hence, systemic dysfunctions should be considered as well as those that are adaptive. To give you an example, slavery served useful functions for white southern plantation owners by supplying them with cheap labor and by giving them social status vis-à-vis those who did not own slaves. However, slavery was dysfunctional for the African-American families that suffered it and for the economy of the South, which remained tied to agriculture and unprepared for industrialization. Similarly, large families and early marriages were adaptive in an agrarian economy prior to the mechanization of agriculture because many hands were needed to work in the fields. But, once agriculture became mechanized, large families became dysfunctional because their members had difficulty finding employment and therefore were likely to be poor (Kornblum, 1991).

Dysfunctions sometimes persist in social systems because, although a particular structure may be dysfunctional for one part of the system, it may be adaptive for another part of the system with the power to preserve the dysfunction (Merton, 1968). Discrimination, for example, has been dysfunctional for U.S. society and for women and members of other nondominant groups because it keeps many people underproductive and their talents underdeveloped and because it fosters social conflict. Yet, it continues to exist because it is beneficial to the power structure controlled by white males (Ritzer, 1992).

Merton (1968) also contributed the important idea that deviant behavior is at least partly motivated by the U.S. cultural emphasis on material success. He noted that the poor and uneducated have adopted the cultural value of material success, just like the rest of society. But they have slim chances of achieving financial success by legal means. Consequently,

some of the poor and uneducated turn to alternative and sometimes illegal ways of making money, such as drug dealing, prostitution, gambling, and theft.

Structural functionalism has been criticized for its conservative bias. This is because traditionally it has placed emphasis on maintaining the normative order of society through norms and values, and it has paid limited attention to the social benefits of conflict. Structural functionalism also has been blamed for legitimizing the privileged position of the elite by suggesting, through the theory of social stratification, that they deserve the rewards they get. In addition, proponents of this theory often have assumed mistakenly that the ideology, values, and norms of the dominant group should be normative for society. The theory has also been faulted for conceptualizing social change mainly as an evolutionary process of **differentiation** into more adaptive units with increased capacity to perform their functions (Parsons, 1966, p. 22) rather than as a process usually fraught with conflict. Finally, structural functionalism has been blamed for its highly abstract and ambiguous concepts that are very difficult to operationalize and test. In the mid-1980s, an effort was made by Alexander and Colomy (1990) to revive the theory, under the name of *neofunctionalism*, to address its weaknesses and to broaden its scope. However, neofunctionalism has made few inroads (Ritzer, 1992). Notwithstanding these limitations, structural functionalism has contributed important insights that help us to better understand social systems.

Social Conflict Theory

Conflict theory reminds us that social conflict plays a central role in social life and, therefore, its sources and dynamics must be understood. This theory is particularly useful in the analysis of the relationship between dominant and nondominant groups in our society.

Social conflict theory was developed in the 1950s and 1960s in large part as a reaction to structural functionalism. It was heavily influenced initially by the writings of Karl Marx, who viewed social life as a continuous struggle between oppressors and the oppressed; however, it is no longer tied to Marxism. What conflict theory shares with Marxism is the notion that those in the upper strata of society use certain ideologies and tactics as weapons to maintain their positions of power and dominance and to deprive and exploit labor (Cox, 1959).

A couple of concrete examples will help to clarify this point. Social conflict theory suggests that the power elite in the United States has cultivated and encouraged the ideology of racism and prejudice to keep workers of different racial and ethnic backgrounds divided and fighting over jobs. This simple tactic has prevented them from uniting to fight oppressive labor conditions. Similarly, this perspective proposes that the dominant group uses the ideology of meritocracy (i.e., the notion of an open society in which anyone with ability who works hard can move to the top) and to justify their privileged status to make the poor feel inadequate and responsible for their failure to succeed (Jeffries & Ransford, 1980).

According to the conflict perspective, the dominant group often uses its power to promote its own interests at the expense of the poor and the working class. From time to time, however, it is forced to share some of the wealth of the nation with labor to prevent social unrest (Lenski, 1966; Lenski et al., 1991). The dominant group does this by buying off workers with limited concessions (Dahrendorf, 1959, 1968). These concessions include things such as civil rights laws, equal employment opportunity laws, minimum wage laws, unemployment compensation, health care benefits, sick leave, aid to families with dependent children, food stamps, low-income housing, and Medicaid.

Because concessions by the dominant group are never adequate, social conflict erupts from time to time. This conflict often leads to needed social changes (Dahrendorf, 1959). Thus, conflict theory posits that conflict is a natural and inevitable outcome of human interaction and considers it one of the most important processes in social life (Collins, 1975). To be sure, social systems are characterized more by power struggles, coercion, domination, dissension, and even chaos than by the harmony, cooperation, and integration emphasized by structural functionalism.

Conflict is not necessarily bad, as it can have positive consequences (Coser, 1956). For example, conflict with an outside group can foster intragroup cohesiveness. Specifically, the long-standing conflict between African Americans and Euro Americans in the United States has served, in part, to foster solidarity and a sense of common identity among African Americans (Himes, 1973). Conflict can also improve communication, as it provides a medium to air misunderstandings so that they can be clarified and worked out. This can lead to needed change. Consequently, it is healthier to allow conflict to surface and run its course than to suppress it.

The Ecosystems Perspective

Most fundamentally, the **ecosystems perspective** is a way of thinking and organizing knowledge that emphasizes the interrelatedness and interdependency of social phenomena. The ecological base stresses the importance of the person-in-context unit of study, the transactional nature of human interaction, and the continuous process of adaptation or accommodation between individuals and their environments. The systems perspective provides a language that is useful in describing many shared properties of social systems, whether they be families, groups, organizations, communities, or even society as a whole. Both perspectives are congruent with the value base of the social work profession. This section begins by examining separately the conceptual base of these two streams of knowledge.

The Ecological Perspective. Basically, **human ecology** refers to the study of the continuing transaction between people and their

environments and the accommodations that they mutually make. In the human services, the ecological perspective suggests that the source(s) of a system's difficulties may be located anywhere within the system, its environment, or both. This view suggests that the psychological, emotional, and behavioral problems people experience are not necessarily the result of individual pathology, as the medical model would emphasize, but may be due to dysfunctions located anywhere in the ecosystem surrounding them. This perspective, elucidated and adapted to the field of social work by Carel Germain, underscores the need for a comprehensive assessment of person and situation and for intervention that encompasses individual, familial, interpersonal, institutional, societal, and cultural systems.

Several important contributions from the ecological perspective—including the concepts of transaction, adaptation, stress, coping, niche, and habitat—will now be discussed.

Transaction. Perhaps the most basic principle formulated by human ecologists is that people and their physical-social-cultural environments form an integrated **ecosystem** in which each influences the others.[1] In other words, people are engaged in continuous transactions with one another and with the physical, social, and cultural systems in their environments. Each influences one another continually and reciprocally (Dubos, 1968; Germain & Gitterman, 1987, p. 489).

To illustrate the concept of transaction, consider the child socialization process within the Scull family. Mr. and Mrs. Scull have been teaching their three children appropriate behaviors and values. In the process of rearing and socializing the children, they have become more responsible, more giving and loving, more willing to sacrifice, more patient, and more sensitive to the needs of others than they used to be. The Sculls are having much influence on their children, but the children are also having considerable impact on Mr. and Mrs. Scull. In technical terms, we may say that **transaction** involves a circular feedback process (Maruyama, 1968) whereby cause becomes effect (e.g., the Sculls, in the process of rearing their children, are being affected by them) and effect becomes cause (e.g., the children are acting as change agents in relation to their parents). This process of reciprocal causality or mutual influence may be negative as well as positive. A harshly punitive father may generate a great deal of hostility and resentment in his son. In turn, the son may rebel against his father, causing the father to become even more abusive toward him.

The ecological concept of transaction enlarges the focus of attention of the practitioner from the individual viewed in isolation to the person-in-environment context. Accordingly, it shifts the emphasis in assessment from identifying individual causal factors to looking at the interrelationship of all elements in the situation—intrapersonal, interpersonal, and environmental.

The emphasis on transactions among systems highlights the importance of the practitioner's "boundary" roles, such as enabler, broker, mediator, cultural translator, advocate, and guardian. These contextual roles, which you will explore and play in your methods courses and in your field practice, are as important for practitioners as the more conventional role of conferee or person with whom clients discuss their problems (Pardeck, 1988; Chau, 1991).

Adaptation. **Adaptation,** another fundamental principle of human ecology, consists of the continuous process of mutual accommodation between an active and evolving human being and the ever-changing settings within which the person functions. Social systems—families, groups, organizations, and communities—are also continually involved in a process of adaptation or mutual accommodation with the larger contexts in which they are embedded (Bronfenbrenner, 1989).

The achievement of a good adaptive balance between system and environment requires continuous transaction, negotiation, and compromise as well as the willingness and ability to make personal or environmental changes (Hartmann, 1958; Germain & Gitterman, 1980, 1987). For instance, an automotive worker who is about to become unemployed because her manufacturing plant is scheduled to be closed may adapt by enrolling in a computer course that she thinks will prepare her for reentry into the labor force because she has heard that jobs dealing with computers are available. Similarly, a student who wants to go on a field trip with his classmates must adapt to the situation by showing good behavior in class to make sure that his teacher does not ground him for misbehaving. In these two illustrations, individuals make personal adaptations to meet environmental demands or to seize environmental opportunities.

Sometimes, instead of making personal adaptations, people choose to modify the environment to make it better fit their needs and goals. For example, the Parent-Teacher's Association at a local school might decide to sponsor the creation of an after-school program to ensure the children's safety and involvement in constructive activities after school while the parents are at work.

Stress and Coping. Two additional transactional concepts adopted by human ecologists are stress and coping. In their continuous transactions with the environment, people continually face stress generated by many different forces. **Stress** consists of feelings of tension or strain that arise when a system perceives an imbalance between the demands it faces and its capacity to meet these challenges.

To cope with the stress, the system makes adaptations such as engaging in problem solving or managing negative emotions and attitudes such as anger, depression, or helplessness (Germain & Gitterman, 1987; Monat & Lazarus, 1991). For example, when the only provider in a family loses his or her job, the family's general well-being is threatened by worry that there will not be enough money to buy food or pay the rent. This causes considerable stress. If the head of the family is able to cope successfully with the challenge of unemployment by actively searching for a new job and collecting unemployment compensation and if the family finds creative ways of stretching its resources, keeping expenses to a minimum, and maintaining a positive emotional attitude, the family will likely enhance its sense of efficacy and competence. If the family is unsuccessful, however, stress is likely to increase and the family is apt to become more vulnerable to breakdown.

Niche and Habitat. People live in particular regions of the social environment. These are called *niches.* An ecological **niche,** according to Bronfenbrenner (1989, p. 194), is a particular region of the environment where a person fits that is favorable or unfavorable to his or her development. The favorableness or unfavorableness of a specific niche depends on the nature of its "social address," such as socioeconomic status, level of education, occupation, family size, rural or urban residence, one-parent or two-parent family, and so on. The favorableness or unfavorableness of niches is also determined by personal characteristics such as race, ethnicity, nationality, gender, age, sexual orientation, and disability status. By way of illustration, a white Anglo-American pregnant teenage dropout from a large, one-parent, poor family living in a housing project and receiving welfare occupies a considerably less favorable niche than the teenage daughter of an African-American professional couple who is attending a private boarding school.

Besides occupying a specific niche, each social system inhabits a particular habitat. **Habitat** refers to the social system's physical environment and setting, including its climate, geographic terrain, degree of crowding, noise level, level of pollution, and other physical aspects of the environment such as the quality of dwellings, density (e.g., big buildings versus detached homes), urban layout, availability of night lighting and transportation, and the level of public hygiene. Like niches, habitats range from highly favorable to extremely hostile or adverse in terms of providing or denying the material and psychosocial resources necessary for people to fulfill their basic needs. For example, in a poor neighborhood, housing may be improperly located in relation to public transportation or transportation may be lacking altogether. This would seriously limit access to work, shopping, and health care. The quality of life may also be limited in poor neighborhoods by crowding, dirty streets, dilapidated housing, and the lack of nearby libraries, museums, parks, or recreational centers (Germain, 1985, p. 41).

The Open Systems Perspective.

Systems theory became popular in the 1960s as a possible successor to structural functionalism, which had come under attack particularly by conflict theorists. Combining a variety of ideas from several fields such as cybernetics, information theory, economics, and operations research, systems theory yielded a more dynamic assessment of the social world than structural functionalism. However, after the initial excitement and impetus, the theory has experienced few additional developments and has generated limited research (Ritzer, 1992).

Social systems theory has been given considerable prominence in the field of social work. Alex Gitterman, for example, is known for his applications of this theory to practice situations. The theory remains popular in the field because its conceptual base is highly compatible with generalist practice, as it elucidates the many areas of commonality among individuals, families, groups, organizations, communities, and society as a whole and emphasizes the interrelationship between people and their environments. Consequently, social systems theory will be examined here in considerable detail. This section looks at the concepts of system, system structure, system dynamics, hierar-

chical organization of systems, hierarchical constraints, steady state, conflict, boundaries, interface, energy, input, feedback, output, throughput, entropy, negative entropy, and differentiation.

System.   A **system** may be defined as a whole composed of transacting parts. **Social systems,** specifically, are human collectives such as families and other small groups, social organizations and institutions, communities, and societies.

Systems may be open or closed. **Open systems** maintain an active exchange with their environments through a permeable boundary that permits energy and information to flow in and out. By definition, all living systems are, to some extent, open to their environments. For example, most families are open systems, to various degrees, because they typically interact with many parts of their environments such as friends, neighbors, co-workers, schoolmates, merchants, health care providers, and so on. **Closed** (or nearly closed) **systems** have impermeable or nearly impermeable boundaries that isolate them from their environments and allow very little or no energy and information to pass through. An inanimate object such as a chair, for example, is a closed system. A family of recluses would be a nearly closed system.

The component parts of a social system are in continuous transaction; thus, what happens to one part affects all other parts. For example, if a single mother becomes temporarily disabled by severe depression, her children may be unfed or unkempt, her performance at work may slip, and her parent may have to move in with the family to keep the household going.

Because many parts of a system affect many others, we must look at the whole system to understand what is happening to any of its parts. If we take a reductionist stance (e.g., if we look only at the "problematic" part(s) of the system), we may "miss the point." Suppose that a young boy is referred to you by the school because he is acting out in class. Following an ecosystems approach, you would want to learn about the child's medical history, family situation, classroom situation, teacher, classmates and peers, and the neighborhood and community in which he lives. You would probably want to see the child in action within the family and in the classroom. Certainly, you would not want to work with the child without involving the family and the teacher. Another practitioner with a more analytic (reductionist) philosophy might decide to work only with the boy since he is the one presenting the problem, and might not be interested in involving in the intervention anyone else in the child's immediate environment.

System Structure.   The **structure** of a social system consists of the regularities observed within it—that is, the enduring patterns of relationship among the system's elements (Blau, 1975; Greif & Lynch, 1983). Such relational patterns are primarily determined by constantly changing roles, positions, and norms.

Roles, or the parts each person plays within the system, are probably the most critical structural elements. Roles are derived from the functions the system is expected to perform. For example, the role of direct practitioner played by Mr. Johnson at the Family Center (the local family and children's services agency) incorporates many functions necessary in order for the agency to fulfill its social service mission. Specifically, in his role as practitioner, Mr. Johnson is expected to conduct intake interviews, write psychosocial histories, conduct individual and group intervention sessions, participate in periodic supervisory conferences, be a team member, attend and contribute to staff meetings, chair the community relations committee, make referrals to other agencies as appropriate, and make home visits. This is the way the role of practitioner has been defined at the agency. However, people seldom play their roles exactly as stipulated. For example, Mr. Johnson has not conducted a single group session, has not had a single supervisory conference, and

has not participated in any team effort in over a year.

Norms are expected ways of behaving in specific situations. To continue with the preceding example, the Family Center includes a number of positions, such as agency director, personnel and budget officer, unit supervisors, and direct practitioners. Each of these positions requires the incumbent to play a variety of roles, such as the roles attached to the position of direct practitioner delineated in the previous paragraph. These roles are expected to be carried out in accordance with the normative expectations of the agency, its funding sources, and the community and societal context in which the agency operates. For example, Mr. Johnson is expected to conduct himself in accordance with the values and ethics of the social work profession, dress appropriately, refrain from smoking in the office, record interviews and psychosocial histories immediately after each session, make home visits accompanied by another worker, attend staff meetings, work one evening per week, and so on. These are some of the normative expectations attached to the position he holds at the agency.

System Dynamics.   As noted in the section on structural functionalism, social systems perform certain functions; that is, they are involved in some sort of activity, sometimes goal directed, sometimes integrational, sometimes maintenance oriented, and sometimes adaptational in nature (Parsons, 1961). These activities keep the system's component parts engaged in continuous exchanges among themselves and with the environment.

Consider the Gomez family. Its members—father, mother, two young children, and maternal grandmother—are often involved in *goal-directed* activities. To support the family, Mr. Gomez works as a mechanic and Mrs. Gomez works as an office clerk. Mrs. Gomez's mother, Doña Dora, cooks, takes care of the house, and looks after the children after school. At night, Mr. Gomez helps the children with their homework while Mrs. Gomez washes the dishes and grandma relaxes by watching TV.

To stay together in relative peace and harmony (*integration* function), family members try to be sensitive to one another's needs and wants and to accommodate one another. For example, Mr. and Mrs. Gomez give the children permission to play with neighborhood friends and to watch their favorite TV programs every day after completing their homework, and each child is allowed to invite a friend to spend the weekend at home once a month. After dinner, grandma has exclusive right to the TV set for an hour to watch her favorite *novelas* (soaps) in Spanish. After helping the children with their homework, Mr. Gomez goes out to the porch to chat with his neighbor or to smoke a cigar. Nobody in the family would dare to interfere with that evening routine, which he enjoys a great deal. Mr. Gomez also has first right to the TV set whenever there is a baseball game on. On Sundays, Mrs. Gomez sleeps late until it is time to get ready for the noon Mass at the nearby Catholic Church. In the afternoon, the family goes out together to places sometimes chosen by the parents and sometimes suggested by the children.

The adults in the Gomez family also try to maintain the family's distinctive character (*maintenance* function) by teaching the children norms of behavior and values and by acting and expecting their children to act in accordance with family traditions and societal expectations. For instance, Mr. Gomez tries to be a good father, husband, sexual partner, and positive role model by working responsibly, being affectionate with his wife and children, trying to keep his wife sexually satisfied, helping the children with their homework, paying his taxes, being honest and truthful, and sharing some of the chores around the house. The children are expected to speak Spanish at home, to get good grades at school, and to go to Catechism instruction and Mass on Sundays.

The Gomez family is also constantly adapting to the external environment (*adaptation* function). For example, Mrs. Gomez always responds promptly to any school request for a conference concerning the children, and Mr. Gomez tries to be accommodating in relation to requests from his boss to work overtime while at the same time trying to fulfill his responsibility to pick up the children after school.

Hierarchical Organization of Systems. Systems are composed of subsystems or subunits. A **subsystem** is a system nested within a larger system. Instead of using the terms *system* and *subsystem*, some people prefer to refer to the larger system as the **suprasystem** and to its subsystems as **systems.** The Gomez family, for example, exists within a community suprasystem that includes many different individuals, groups, institutions, and organizations with which the family is actively connected, such as close friends and neighbors, the children's school, the parents' workplaces, health care providers, recreational groups, their parish church, and so on. The Gomez family is also made up of various subsystems; for example, Mr. and Mrs. Gomez are part of the spouse subsystem, they and Doña Dora (Mrs. Gomez's mother) form the parental subsystem, and the children constitute the sibling subsystem. A hierarchy of social systems is depicted in Figure 1.2.

Bronfenbrenner (1989, pp. 226–230) delineated four levels of social systems: microsystem, mesosystem, exosystem, and macrosystem, as shown in Figure 1.3. As his ecological theory of human development gains ascendancy, the terms are becoming increasingly used today. The **microsystem** includes all the immediate face-to-face contexts in which people function in their everyday lives, such as the family, kin and peer groups, school, and workplace. The **mesosystem** comprises the linkages and other processes taking place between two or more face-to-face settings in which a person participates. For example, for the Gomez children, one aspect of the mesosystem would be the relations between their family and the schools they attend.

World Community

U.S. Society

Local Community

Neighborhood

Face-to-Face
Groups

Family

Individual

FIGURE 1.2   Hierarchy of Social Systems Surrounding the Individual

The **exosystem** consists of the linkages and other processes taking place between two or more social settings, including at least one setting that does not ordinarily contain the person or persons who are the unit of attention but in which events occur that influence such individuals. For the Gomez children, the relations between their school and the local school board are part of the exosystem, as are the relations between their parents and their parents' workplaces. The children do not participate in the school board or in their parents' workplaces, but both social units have profound influences on the quality of the children's schooling and of their lives. For example, if the mother were suddenly given a night shift at work, the children's home lives would change considerably.

The **macrosystem** consists of the larger societal and cultural circumstances experienced by the individual, depending on factors such as the person's race, gender, socioeconomic status, ethnic background, place of birth, religion, sexual orientation, and rural or urban place of residence. Some people have been raised in an environment that is different from that in which they currently reside. Both the original and current environments form their macrosystem because both have influenced them (Bronfenbrenner, 1989, p. 237). Such distinction is particularly important for people who have experienced transplantation from one environment to another (e.g., immigrants and refugees) or people who must negotiate two cultures on a regular basis (e.g., those from nonmainstream racial, ethnic, or sexual orientation groups). The Gomez family, for example, is influenced greatly by the Mexican-American working-class culture of Los Angeles (where they

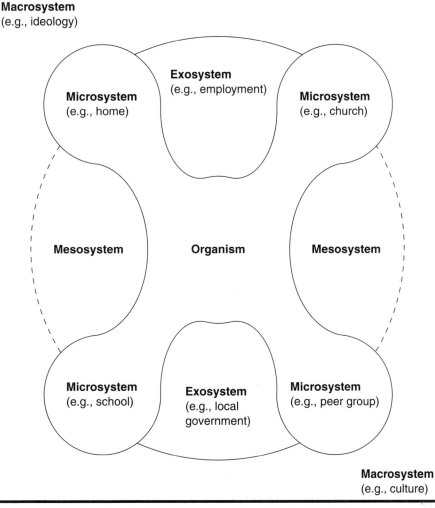

Macrosystem
(e.g., ideology)

Macrosystem
(e.g., culture)

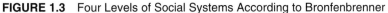

FIGURE 1.3 Four Levels of Social Systems According to Bronfenbrenner

Source: Reprinted with permission from Garbarino, James et al. *Children and Families in the Social Environment,* 2nd Edition. (New York: Aldine de Gruyter) Copyright © 1992 Walter de Gruyter, Inc., New York.

reside), the culture of Mexico (where the grandmother and the parents were born and raised and where many friends and relatives reside), by the U.S. mainstream culture, and by the Catholic heritage. These are key elements in their macrosystem.

The individual is also a system although not a *social* system because the person system does not have the requisite minimum of two members necessary for social exchange to take place. As a system, the person system has biological and psychological subsystems, each composed of still other subsystems. The biological subsystem, for example, is divided into the circulatory system, the digestive system, the nervous system, the endocrine system, and others. Psychological subsystems include memories, thoughts, dreams, fantasies, emotions, and other mental constructs.

Hierarchical Constraints.   Systems are constrained or restricted in action by the rules of their suprasystems, according to the principle of **hierarchical constraints** (Martin & O'Connor, 1989). For example, the Family Center referred to earlier is partly funded by the United Way and also receives funds from federal and state grants. Consequently, it must follow many federal, state, and United Way guidelines, which significantly restrict the agency's ability to act autonomously. These are important hierarchical constraints that the agency must observe.

The children in the Gomez family are similarly constrained by family rules. For example, they are required to bathe and be ready for dinner by 7:00 P.M., they must go to bed no later than 10:00 P.M., they must keep the volume down when they play music, and they are not allowed to talk on the phone for more than 10 minutes at a time.

Steady State.   Still another characteristic of open systems is the tendency to keep some sort of balance between maintenance/stability (i.e., keeping the system going more or less as usual) and change. This adaptive relationship with the environment is known as **steady state** (von Bertalanffy, 1968, pp. 156–160). Steady state should not be confused with **homeostasis** or equilibrium. Steady state is an open systems concept that presupposes that disequilibrium is normative and that systems and environments are constantly transacting and dealing with change. In contrast, the concept of homeostasis or equilibrium should be restricted to less open systems such as the human body or an air conditioning system that must maintain a steady temperature or stable functions such as blood pressure or pulse rate. When these functions depart from their normal level, such as when the body temperature rises, the body automatically institutes certain processes, such as increased perspiration, to bring the temperature back down to its homeostatic level of around 98.6 degrees.

Change is critical for a social system to maintain a steady state. That is, to survive, the system must be willing and able to make changes or adaptations, even to transform itself completely when necessary, in order to meet environmental challenges or to benefit from environmental opportunities. For example, due to a recent influx of immigrants and refugees, the socioeconomic and ethnic composition of the neighborhood surrounding the Family Center has changed in the past five years from primarily native-born middle-class Italian American to immigrant Latino working class.

To respond to the demographic changes that threatened the survival of the Family Center as previously constituted, the director began to hire Spanish-speaking personnel every time someone retired or left the agency. She also instituted an intensive in-service training program aimed at teaching agency personnel basic Spanish language skills and acquainting them with Latino cultures. These changes helped the agency to maintain a steady state and to remain viable despite major changes that took place in the surrounding community.

To maintain a steady state, sometimes it is necessary to bring about changes in the external environment or suprasystem to make it more responsive to the system's needs. Consider the options of a business enterprise located in a deteriorating community with a rising crime rate. One alternative to enhance its survival potential would be to contribute to improve job opportunities for community folks by offering job training and scholarships for at-risk teenagers and unemployed persons in the community. Another possibility would be to become actively involved with community residents in their crime-stopping efforts and in cleaning up and beautifying the neighborhood.

At the personal level, coping strategies are often necessary to maintain a steady state. For instance, faced with the challenge of having to make a class presentation, a shy student may become excessively anxious and throw her system off balance. To return to a steadier state, she may decide to engage in extensive preparations, to rehearse her presentation in front of her best friend or in front of her mother to get over her stage fright, to meditate, to do breathing exercises, or if nothing calms her down, she may decide to take a mild tranquilizer prescribed by her physician before the presentation.

Sometimes, major changes are necessary or desirable to keep a steady state. For instance, in order to survive, an organization may have to reinvent or completely transform itself. Faced with emergent technology, business organizations many times must change gears rapidly or risk failure. In the 1990s, for example, a good number of major U.S. business organizations have had to change radically to survive as their technologies became threatened by new technological advances. Couples must sometimes change radically in the way they relate to one another if they want their relationship to survive. Societies must sometimes institute major reforms (i.e., end apartheid, universal health care) if they want to remain viable.

Are the radical changes that systems must sometimes undergo to survive encompassed by the structural functional dialectic of stability/change denoted by the concept of steady state? It is difficult to say. Liberals may insist that steady state is too conservative a concept that does not allow for the fundamental or radical changes that systems must sometimes undergo. Perhaps this is so, technically speaking. Practically speaking, however, one may retain the concept of steady state because it is useful, as long as one acknowledges that to keep a steady state, major reforms are sometimes necessary.

Conflict. As previously noted, social systems are normally and routinely exposed to **conflict** and need not avoid it in order to maintain a steady state. In fact, conflict often has a good effect because it forces people to clarify their positions and this may lead to a better understanding.

However, excessively high levels of conflict can be detrimental, such as when there is continuous in-fighting or disharmony. Yet, even highly conflicted systems are not necessarily doomed. Some are able to change substantially to achieve a more harmonious balance. Consider the case of a couple who had a long, stormy relationship. When everyone expected them to break up, the couple underwent some significant experience—perhaps religious or therapeutic—and thus established again a positive relationship.

Boundaries. All systems have external **boundaries**—that is, separating lines that enclose them so that they can be distinguished from the rest of the environment or from other systems. Systems also have internal boundaries that divide their subsystems. Boundaries are important because they protect systems and subsystems from unwanted outside interference. For example, a private university may set up a gate at the entrance to the library to limit access to those who are currently enrolled. Within the Gomez family, boundaries are sometimes drawn verbally by statements such as "Keep out of this" or "It's none of your business." In this manner, Mr. and Mrs. Gomez sometimes exclude their children or Doña Dora from certain private conversations.

Sometimes boundaries are clearly visible, such as the skin separating the body from the environment. Sometimes they are not so evident. For example, a family boundary is not necessarily demarcated by the exterior walls of a particular house because sometimes its members live separately. Thus, one cannot always determine who belongs and who does not belong to a particular family by looking at the composition of a specific household.

Boundaries change as the systems they enclose change and evolve. Universities, for example, expand their boundaries every time they develop a new institute or degree program. Similarly, family boundaries expand when the couple has a child or adopts one, and they contract when the family loses a member due to a child moving out, separation, divorce, or the death of one of its members.

Interface. All open systems interact with other systems. The actual exchange, sometimes direct and sometimes through representatives, constitutes the **interface.** For example, Carlitos, one of the Gomez children, was referred recently by his school to the Family Center because he was misbehaving in class. The interface between the Gomez family and the Family Center consisted of the interactions (face to face and by telephone) between Mrs. Gomez and her mother, Doña Dora, with Mrs. Fantini, the family practitioner, and Ms. Manos, the secretary at the agency. Figure 1.4 illustrates this interface.

Because interfaces occur at the point where two or more boundaries intersect, they must be cooperatively maintained by the systems involved. For instance, when Mrs. Gomez and

Carlitos did not show up for their first appointment, Mrs. Fantini called their home in the evening and spoke to Mrs. Gomez. They were able to determine that there had been a misunderstanding. Ms. Manos, the secretary, had called to set up the appointment and Doña Dora, who answered the phone, wrote down the wrong date. Having clarified the situation, Mrs. Fantini immediately gave Mrs. Gomez a new appointment. Had Mrs. Fantini made no effort to contact the family and had they shown up the wrong day at a time when she was unable to see them, the agency intervention might not have taken place because the interface was negative on both sides. Suppose that Ms. Manos, who was cordial in her telephone conversation with Mrs. Gomez's mother, had instead been short and discourteous. Doña Dora might have been turned off by the secretary's negative attitude, and the family might have decided to cancel the agency appointment because they had experienced a negative interface.

Energy. Systems need **energy** to perform their functions. This energy can be produced within or it can be imported from the outside. Individuals, for example, derive part of their energy from the food they eat and from the oxygen they breathe. This energy, in turn, is used for many processes such as circulation, thinking, walking, talking, working, and so on. People also derive considerable energy from the information, guidance, love, emotional support, and material resources they get from the environment.

Input. All open systems import resources from their environment to carry out their functions. This incoming energy is referred to as an input. Specifically, an **input** is anything that the system or subsystem gets from its suprasystem or from another system or subsystem, whether it be food, raw materials, personnel or other human resources, money, information, love, support, communication, or any other thing that flows in. For instance, the salaries that a couple makes constitute an important type of family

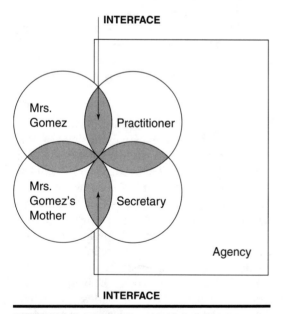

FIGURE 1.4   Illustration of Initial Interface between the Gomez Family and the Family and Children's Agency

input. Emotional support from friends and relatives represents still another input.

Feedback. The concept of feedback was borrowed by systems theorists from the field of cybernetics to explain how a system maintains a steady state and grows even under conflictual circumstances. **Feedback** is a special form of input consisting of information about a system's performance to guide its continuing operation. All systems need feedback to stay on course. This feedback may come from within the system or from the environment (see Figure 1.5). For example, at the Family Center, the director keeps an open-door policy and encourages employees and clients to drop in to see her about any problems or to make suggestions or express their opinions about any matters concerning the agency or the community. The agency also receives feedback from external entities such as its funding sources, former clients, and other organizations and institutions (e.g., the schools) with which it works closely. A **feedback loop** consists of the return of feedback to the system, which helps to maintain the steady state (von Bertalanffy, 1968).

Negative feedback or negative information is important because it lets the system know that it has deviated from its course. By so doing, it enables the system to get back on track (Miller, 1955; Katz & Kahn, 1969; Grief & Lynch, 1983). Suppose that as part of your first practicum at a social agency you are assigned to work with a client with high cholesterol and diabetes on his weight problem. Suppose that the two of you develop a plan aimed at bringing his weight down by about three pounds per month and that at the end of the first month he weighs two pounds more than when the intervention started. Knowing that he is further away from the goal than he was when he came to see you initially is important negative feedback because it tells both of you that the intervention is not working and therefore needs to be changed.

Positive feedback is equally important because it reinforces the system by letting it know that it is on the correct path toward a goal. Suppose now that, instead of gaining weight, your client actually lost two pounds in a month. This loss is not enough to meet the goal of three pounds that you two had established, but it is movement in the right direction. As a result of receiving this positive feedback, you are unlikely to alter the intervention plan in any major way because it is basically working, and your client is likely to feel satisfied that he is making progress.

Output. **Output** is anything that a system sends out or exports to the environment or to other systems. It may be people, products, information, communication, support, attention, responses to stimuli, or anything else. Often this output is translated into some form of energy that comes back to the system and reactivates its cycle of activities (Katz & Kahn, 1969).

The work that you do is one of your outputs. Hopefully, it provides you with important inputs such as a salary, recognition, college credit, personal satisfaction, or other reinforcements that motivate you to continue working. When the Gomez family completed the intervention at the Family Center, they became the agency's output. In turn, if Carlitos was doing better after the agency intervention than before, the Gomez's probably would recommend the agency to other parents in the community and the boy's school teacher and principal would also be more likely to refer other children with similar difficulties to the agency. Referrals from satisfied clients and school teachers are among the inputs that generate the energy necessary for the agency to keep going. Similarly, one day when the Gomez children become independent of their parents and move away from home to live somewhere nearby (as the parents hope), they will become the family's output. Mr. and Mrs. Gomez will derive a great deal of satisfaction from seeing their children

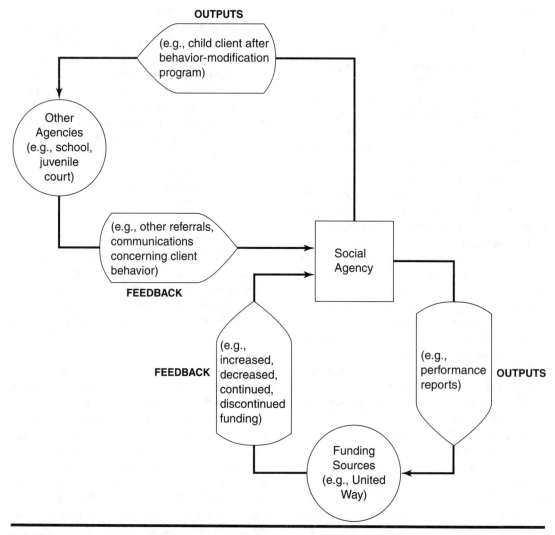

FIGURE 1.5   Illustration of Environmental Feedback

successfully on their own, and this satisfaction will give them the energy to adjust to not having the children at home anymore.

Like individuals and families, organizations and communities produce many outputs. For example, your city or county government provides you with police and fire protection and water and sewage services, maintains your streets and night lighting, runs the schools children attend, provides various social services, and so on. The more successful these outputs

are, the greater the likelihood that you and other taxpayers will be willing to be taxed at a rate that keeps the city or county input/output process going.

Systems need to maintain a favorable input/output balance to have sufficient energy to function effectively while continuing to grow and develop. When outputs exceed inputs, the system's steady state is threatened. In other words, if more energy flows out of the system than comes in, the system will eventually become depleted or its functioning will be impaired in some way. For instance, if a social agency terminates more clients than it takes in, eventually it will lose its funding for lack of a clientele. Similarly, a single father who engages in exhausting physical labor to make the minimum wage and comes home to take care of his two small boys is likely to exhaust his energies and collapse if he does not get some support, relief, or reinforcement from some source.

Throughput. All open systems act on and transform their inputs into outputs. This process is referred to as **throughput** (Katz & Kahn, 1969; Greif & Lynch, 1983). For example, when you eat, your digestive system receives food and, through the process of digestion (its throughput), converts the food into energy. In a helping relationship, the intervention is the throughput. The client (the central input to the relationship) undergoes the intervention (throughput) and is thus transformed into an output of the relationship when the intervention is completed.

Entropy. Still another characteristic of open systems is their natural tendency to lose vitality and move toward disorganization and death. This process is known as **entropy.** Due to the entropy that inexorably sets in, each of us can be absolutely certain that some day we will die, no matter how regularly we exercise, or how much we watch our diets, cholesterol levels, or blood pressure. Similarly, even though a family name can be passed on from generation to generation, individual families cease to exist when all their members either leave the family for various reasons, such as to form their own families, or die. Sometimes systems reach entropy prematurely. For instance, some teenagers die of drug overdoses, and couples sometimes break up shortly after getting married.

Some social systems do not appear to be entropic, at least not for a very long time. Some universities were founded hundreds of years ago and still continue to function with vitality.

The Roman Empire lasted for centuries before it declined and ceased to exist, and the Catholic Church has been around continuously for two millennia. Some businesses have been in continuous operation much longer than any person can aspire to live.

Although some social systems are very durable, others become entropic almost from the start. Entropy results whenever a system expends or exports more energy than it is able to generate or import. For instance, some social agencies close their doors shortly after they begin to operate because their funding is discontinued. Small communities sometimes disintegrate quickly when their main source of employment closes down or moves elsewhere.

Negative Entropy and Differentiation. Von Bertalanffy (1950, 1968) has observed that although closed systems move toward increasing deterioration, most living things behave differently: They grow and develop before they begin to decline. This very important process of growth and development is called in the language of systems theory **negative entropy** or *negentropy.* As noted earlier, it requires that the system import more energy than it exports to maintain enough vitality to discharge its functions while continuing to grow and evolve.

As systems grow and develop, they become more highly differentiated. From a social systems perspective, **differentiation** (von Bertalanffy, 1950) is the tendency of a system to become more complex and specialized in function as it develops. For example, due to differentiation, the human fetus is a more complex organism than the human embryo, adults have more complex personalities than small children, and relationships develop more and more aspects as they become more long-standing and intimate.

Symbolic Interactionism
Still another theory that has enriched the knowledge base about the social environment and human behavior is symbolic interactionism.

This theory has contributed the idea that subjective perceptions and personal meanings greatly influence people's actions. According to **symbolic interaction theory** (Blumer, 1969; Mead, 1934), social acts have no inherent meaning other than the meaning people attribute to them. Consequently, different actions will have different meanings for different individuals, depending on the perceptions, values, beliefs, attitudes, and norms they have acquired through the lifelong process of socialization.

According to symbolic interaction theory, human beings do not merely respond or react to the actions of others or to environmental stimuli but choose which stimuli to attend to and which to ignore and assign meanings or interpret these events or stimuli. Then, after assessing the situation, they take action (Mead, 1938).

People interact with others based on their subjective understanding of situations, what they want to do or think they need to do, and their perception of what others expect them to do. As they transact with others, they receive feedback as to how well or poorly they are doing as far as meeting their expectations. Based on their interpretation of this information, they adjust their behaviors. The concept of the *looking-glass self* helps to elucidate parts of this feedback process. By the looking-glass self, Cooley (1902) meant the ability to see ourselves through the eyes of others. Beginning in childhood, we learn to take the role of the other—that is, to put ourselves in the shoes of another person, to imagine how they perceive us, to wonder what judgment they are likely to pass about us, and to develop a feeling of pride or shame as a result (Miller, 1981). By assuming another person's perspective, we learn to anticipate possible consequences of our intended actions and to modify our behavior in accordance with the predictions we make.

Symbolic interactionism is particularly relevant to the process of communication because people are constantly conveying a great deal of information, not always intentionally, through language and other means of expression such as gestures, voice tone, dress, and body movements. The communication process will be explored in Chapter 7.

The concept of **labeling,** developed by Erving Goffman (1959, 1961, 1974), is an important derivative of symbolic interactionism with implications for the human services. Many clients seen by practitioners have been assigned various labels, such as *mental patient, school dropout, criminal offender, learning disabled,* or *child abuser*. According to Goffman, once given a label, individuals often act in accordance with the label's expected roles, thus significantly altering their behavior and eventually their self-concepts and fates.

Symbolic interactionism has been criticized for its disinterest in gathering empirical evidence for its propositions and for the vagueness of its concepts, which are almost impossible to operationalize. In addition, it has paid little attention to the influence of larger social structures, insisting that what matters are the immediate situations in which people interact (Ritzer, 1992). Notwithstanding these limitations, the insights contributed by symbolic interactionism concerning the process of human interaction are substantial.

Role Theory

The basic ideas for another theory that has contributed much to the understanding of how the individual is linked to social systems were borrowed from the world of the theater by various social scientists, most notably Goffman (1959). Specifically, role theory is a derivative of structural functionalism and symbolic interactionism.

A **role** is a set of expectations people share concerning behaviors to be performed as part of a specific social position. In the theater, the term is used to refer to the part an actor plays. Although actors must enact their roles in prescribed ways, they are allowed flexibility to offer their own interpretations of a role. However, if they diverge too much from the script, the rest of the cast may find itself unable to adapt. Similarly, the roles that we play in various positions in life are influenced not only by the expectations that accompany such positions but by our own ideas of how we should behave as occupants of such positions. In that sense, we make or create our roles rather than just play them according to the script (Heiss, 1981), but there are limits to the flexibility we are allowed in role making. For example, a teacher who consistently fails to show up for class because he does not consider meeting with students to be part of his role as teacher is likely to lose his teaching job.

We play many different roles during the course of our lives—son, daughter, brother, sister, friend, student, lover, husband, wife, father, mother, laborer, manager, teacher, or religious minister, to mention a few. These are learned through observation, modeling, and reinforcement as part of the process of socialization. Each person plays multiple roles. For example, a short-order cook may alternately act as stepmother, lay minister, wife, daughter, lover, student of social work, friend, daughter-in-law, and repairperson.

Because we play multiple roles, often simultaneously, we sometimes have difficulty meeting their demands. Two types of role strain are particularly common: role conflict and role overload. When we find that the behaviors associated with one role we must play are incompatible with those associated with other roles we must also play, we suffer **interrole conflict.** For example, people often feel torn between their job responsibilities and their commitment to their families. **Intrarole conflict** results from opposing demands from a single role or from having mixed feelings about it. Frequently this happens when the role occupant has a different interpretation of the role than others who have a say in the way the role is to be performed. For instance, a mother may see nothing wrong with putting her six-month-old baby in day care so she can return to her full-time job, but her in-laws may disapprove of this

action and make her feel guilty about it. **Role overload** occurs whenever we try to play too many roles at the same time. For example, if you tried to hold a full-time job and go to school full time, you might not be able to cope with the simultaneous demands of these roles.

Social Exchange Theory

Social exchange theory was influenced considerably by rational choice theory developed in the field of economics and by the radical behaviorism of psychologist B. F. Skinner. Its leading exponents are George Homans (1961), Peter Blau (1964), and John Thibaut and Harold Kelley (1959). This theory has yielded important insights about the social environment and human behavior, particularly about the ways in which people conduct their relationships. Specifically, social exchange theory assumes that human relations are based on self-interest and therefore are similar to economic activity: People make decisions concerning their relationships on the basis of a cost-benefits analysis of various contemplated courses of action.

A basic assumption of social exchange theory is the principle of *distributive justice* (Homans, 1961), also called *fair exchange* (Blau, 1964) or *reciprocity.* This means that most people expect to get out of a relationship something roughly equivalent in value to what they put into it. If the costs exceed the actual or potential benefits, people are likely to abandon the relationship.

To be sure, the assessment of what constitutes a "fair exchange" is very subjective and varies a great deal from person to person. This is because people have different conceptions of the value of things they give and receive, such as affection, knowledge and advise, money, gifts, companionship, approval, respect, emotional support, peace and quiet, cooperation, attention, stimulation, challenge, control, dependence, and submission. People also have divergent standards concerning giving and receiving, their responsibility to give in a particular situation, or the ability or responsibility of others to reciprocate. For example, charitable, generous, and compassionate people (those who are highly altruistic) may find it rewarding to give to others with little expectation of getting anything in return. Most ordinary people, however, would prefer their relationships to be more balanced or symmetrical. Another dimension of fair exchange is time: Even those strongly motivated by self-interest generally do not expect to be "paid back" immediately; some may patiently wait for months or even years to get their fair share out of a relationship. Eventually, however, most people expect to "collect" in some way.

According to social exchange theory, people stay in social situations as long as they perceive that they are getting a fair-enough deal. However, when exchanges are imbalanced, such as when one party consistently and over the long run gets more out of a relationship than the other, the relationship becomes exploitative, and the disadvantaged party, feeling unfairly treated, is likely to abandon it. Sometimes relationships persist even though they appear to be imbalanced. It may be that the party that makes most of the contributions to the relationship is getting "contributions" from the other party that outsiders may not perceive as part of what makes the relationship "balanced." For example, a person who needs to exercise power or control over others may be willing to support financially someone else who offers submission and dependency, even if the other has little else to offer (Ritzer, 1992).

Some people remain in relationships even though they are treated unfairly because they think they have no better alternative (Thibaut & Kelley, 1959, Kelley & Thibaut, 1978) or because they fear the consequences of leaving. For example, a battered wife may continue to live with a husband that abuses her as long as she believes that staying with him is better for the children or for herself than having to survive on a minimum-wage job or on welfare or as long as she feels that he will seriously hurt her if she attempts to leave.

Social exchange theory explains altruistic behavior when it is motivated by self-interest, such as when people behave kindly and generously primarily because it makes them feel good about themselves or in order to attract attention or win "browny points." Yet, at least occasionally, people appear to be motivated by kindness, compassion, generosity, humanitarianism, or tenderness without any apparent self-interest or ulterior motive (Schwartz, 1993; Wakefield, 1993). Social exchange theory cannot explain such purely altruistic behavior.

Feminist Theory

Feminist theory is vital to the study of human behavior and social environment because, unlike any other theory we have examined, it looks at the world from a woman-centered perspective with the aim of incorporating the female point of view into our conceptual base (Lengermann & Niebrugge-Brantley, 1992). Most other social theories have failed to take into account the viewpoints and experiences of women. Another important contribution of feminist theory has been to raise society's level of awareness of how men traditionally have oppressed women and denied them equal opportunities.

Throughout history, women have been forced to play roles that are less privileged and more subordinate to men's roles. Relegated to inferior positions in life, their point of view and their experiences have been largely ignored. To be sure, not all women have been invisible and unequal to the same extent; those in favorable social locations (e.g., white women of European extraction, those of high socioeconomic status, and those well educated) have been less affected, but nonetheless subordinated and less privileged vis-à-vis similarly situated men.

The feminist perspective stresses that most of the knowledge people have about human behavior and the social environment reflects the experiences and insights of white men. Until recently, these mostly-male accounts were assumed to be universally descriptive of human experience. Now, scholars recognize that there is a whole other set of actors out there, including women and other subordinate or oppressed groups, whose experiences have been ignored to a large extent. Consequently, our understandings of behavior and environment need to be reworked (Lengermann & Niebrugge-Brantley, 1992).

Feminists suggest that the relationship of men and women must be understood as one of unequal power, specifically one of traditional subjugation and oppression of women by men. They emphasize that women have gotten and continue to get fewer material and social rewards from society such as monetary pay for their work, social status, power, and opportunities for self-actualization than the men who share their same social position. They suggest that men have accomplished this subjugation of women by keeping them tied down to the private sphere where they have made them bear the lion's share of "endless rounds of demanding, mindless, unpaid, and undervalued tasks associated with housework, child care, and the emotional, practical, and sexual servicing of men" (Lengermann & Niebrugge-Brantley, 1992, pp. 325–326).

According to radical feminists, women have been subjugated by men principally through the ideology of patriarchy, which traditionally has given men, as heads of the family, the right to dominate and control women. The ideology of patriarchy has been maintained with the help of cultural values that complement it, such as the idealized view of women as primarily mothers, wives, and homemakers. In addition, male dominance has been maintained by a host of societal practices that keep women dependent on men for support such as low wages, unpaid homemaking and child care labor at home, and violent behavior against women when they have "gotten out of line" (Nes & Iadicola, 1989; Lengermann & Niebrugge-Brantley, 1992, p. 337). All these values and social practices have limited women's opportunities for self-realization and have denied the society the full range of female talent.

Radical feminists point out that men are not the only oppressors in the society. Some women in the United States and throughout the world contribute to the continuing oppression of women by celebrating and reinforcing the traditional patriarchal values that have served to entrap them. In addition, some white European women, in particular, have oppressed other women, usually women of color, by discriminating against them or by employing them under conditions that have denied these women their dignity or that have prevented them from making a decent living. Thus, radical feminists and young feminists stress the importance of confronting all oppressive practices, such as racism, discrimination, poverty, and environmental pollution, including those perpetrated by women and by nondominant group men against women (Frye, 1983). Many young feminists now welcome men into their ranks to help in the fight against oppression (Schrof, 1993).

The feminist agenda for improving the situation of women is:

1. To help women to get rid of unproductive sex-role playing such as submissiveness, passivity, and dependency and to adopt a behavioral style that is appropriate and adaptive for specific situations rather than based on sex-role stereotypes
2. To identify sexist and racist practices that have denied women full access to the resources of the society, such as steering and tracking practices in the schools and discrimination and harassment in the labor market and workplace, and to work collectively to overcome these barriers and move toward equality
3. To raise the consciousness of the society and of women about the negative effects on women of the patriarchal system and the need for women to reclaim control over themselves (Nes & Iadicola, 1989)

Evaluating Theories

Given the large number of existing theories about the social environment and human behavior, the most important of which we have examined here, how can their relative merits be evaluated? That is, how are we to decide what makes one theory better than another? This section will consider briefly six major criteria that may be employed to assess the relative merits of various theories: parsimony, comprehensiveness, inclusiveness, relevance to practice and to everyday life, testability and empirical support, and predictive power. Ideally, we would like the theories we turn to for insights to fulfill these requirements, but the reality is that the existing theories concerning the social environment or human behavior fall short of fulfilling some of these requirements. This does not mean that we should disregard them, particularly if there are no other theories capable of shedding equal or better understandings or insights. What the shortcomings of currently available theories suggest is that we should treat them as tentative explanations, not as absolute truths.

Parsimony

Brevity, simplicity, and internal consistency are strengths to which every theory should aspire. In other words, a good theory explains phenomena—be it societal dynamics; community, group, or family structure or processes; human behavior or development; or whatever else—simply and straightforwardly without being overly simplistic. To be sure, theories about complex phenomena (e.g., society, organizations, or families) cannot be so simple that they fail to account satisfactorily for the intricacies of such phenomena, but they should not be any more complicated than necessary. They should also use the least possible number of propositions and assumptions to explain or predict whatever they set out to explain or predict with a minimum of internal inconsistencies. In short, a theory that provides an unnecessarily exotic or complex explanation of an event that can be explained in simpler terms is undesirable. For instance, if you hear hoofbeats as you walk down the street, your first theory should be that there is a horse trotting around, not a giraffe (Peterson, 1992, p. 67).

Comprehensiveness

A good theory is comprehensive—that is, it encompasses and explains a variety of phenomena, not just a handful of observations. Generally, the wider the range of experiences that a theory can explain, the more powerful and useful it is. Yet, it would be unreasonable to expect a theory to account for all aspects of the phenomenon under consideration, particularly if it is as broad and complex as a society or community or human behavior. Hence, a good theory is comprehensive but selective. It concentrates on central and important issues, not on every little detail.

Inclusiveness

Another characteristic of a good theory is inclusiveness. This means that it is based on a wide range of observations. Consider, for example, a theory that attempts to explain some aspect of human behavior. The criterion of inclusiveness requires that the theory be based on observations of people of diverse backgrounds—male as well as female, and people of different races, socioeconomic and ethnic backgrounds, educational levels, sexual orientations, and so on.

A good theory of human behavior and social environment does not address and explain exclusively the social situations, experiences, and developmental issues pertinent to or of interest to white middle-class males of European extraction. It also explains the unique developmental experiences and social situation of women and other nondominant group members in the society (Zerbe Enns, 1989). Theories that are based mainly on observations of a homogeneous group of people, such as white, middle-class Euro-American males, are applicable to this group only until research with other social groups confirms their wider scope.

All of the existing major theories about the social environment or human behavior and development would be considered deficient, to various degrees, on this standard of inclusiveness. This does not mean that we should throw them away and start anew. It would be unwise to ignore the valuable insights a particular theory has to offer simply because it was developed largely on the basis of observations of certain people in specific social, cultural, historic, and economic circumstances. It does mean, however, that most theories need to be tested using more diverse samples of the population and that some aspects of these theories may need to be revised or reconceptualized to make them applicable to females, African Americans, the poor, gays, lesbians, or other nondominant group members.

Although social scientists give verbal recognition to the importance of broadening their theories and making them more inclusive by conducting research with members of nondominant groups, action has been lagging. For instance, a review of mainstream psychological journal articles published between 1970 and 1989 (articles appearing in six of the journals of the American Psychological Association) showed a declining representation of research on African Americans. In addition, many of the publications on African Americans were found to be lacking in methodological rigor and confounded the effects of race and social class. Few studied African Americans of various socioeconomic backgrounds independently of other racial/ethnic groups (Graham, 1992). This marginalization of African Americans in mainstream psychological research as well as the even more marked marginalization of other racial/ethnic groups in the United States is a very serious and limiting concern in the field of human behavior.

Part of the reason for the dearth of research on nondominant groups may be that social scientists shy away from conducting socially sensitive research because they fear that any controversial findings may shatter their careers (Graham, 1992). If so, this value conflict is significantly interfering with the development of the social science knowledge base. Another reason may be that research and scholarly writing on nondominant groups traditionally has been accorded low status within the academic community, which continues to be dominated by white males; therefore, few researchers want to spend energies in ways that will not be fully rewarded.

Relevance to Practice and to Everyday Life

A theory about the social environment or human behavior needs to be practical and useful and not just an ivory-tower intellectual exercise. Specifically, it should help us to better understand some social system or life situation and how these may affect various people and it should help us to deal more effectively with the problems our clients confront.

A practical theory of human behavior and social environment is one that helps us to understand ourselves and that is relevant to the understanding of the individuals and families we encounter and the problems they are likely to present. Practical theories help us to understand the groups in which we participate and those that we conduct as practitioners, our workplaces and those organizations with which we may be called on to work, the communities and neighborhoods in which we live as well as those with which we may work, and our multicultural society and the diverse social groups that are part of it.

Testability and Empirical Support

A good theory is supported by evidence derived from systematic observations and empirical research. This requires that its concepts and propositions be stated clearly so that they can be operationalized or translated into hypotheses that can be put to the test. Then, if the empirical data collected confirm the theory's propositions, we can have more confidence in the theory because it has been tested and confirmed. If the data collected are contradictory, the theory must be modified to accommodate the new empirical evidence. Most of the existing theories about the social environment, particularly macro-theories and mezzo-theories, have generated little research. Such theories, insightful as they may be in describing and explaining aspects of the social environment, are more properly called ideologies than theories (Peterson, 1992).

Predictive Power

Good theoretical propositions have predictive power; that is, they not only describe or explain behavior *ex post facto* (retrospectively) but they also help us anticipate or predict how people will behave in future occasions. Consider, as an example, a theoretical proposition, widely confirmed by research, that is part of radical behavioral theory and that helps to predict innumerable human and animal responses: When an organism emits a response and this response is followed by reinforcement, the organism will emit the response more frequently than if it is not followed by reinforcement. Based on such a proposition, you would be able to predict the behavior of all kinds of people in widely different circumstances. For example, if a little girl's parents gave her the attention she craved when she misbehaved, even if this attention were in the form of scoldings, you could predict that she would misbehave more often.

The Place of Observation and Research in the Knowledge-Building Process

As noted, although the theories and perspectives examined here contributed many significant insights to the study of the social environment and human behavior, they have not generated a great deal of knowledge vis-à-vis other possible sources of knowledge. Observation and empirical research, many times not directly linked to any of the preceding theories, have played a large role as sources of information in the field of HBSE. This section will discuss how observation and empirical research contribute to building the knowledge base in this field.

The Scientific Method

In general terms, the **scientific method** may be described as an attitude of objectivity in thinking and a belief that ideas should be supported by empirical evidence (e.g., systematic data collection such as through observation, surveys, or interviews). For social scientists, following the scientific method means that they cannot simply sit back and philosophize about the dynamics of social systems or human behavior. Even if they can produce brilliant ideas in this manner, they have a responsibility to search for evidence that their ideas provide accurate descriptions and explanations of the real world. This requires that social scientists follow certain accepted methods of data collection and research design and that they institute proper controls.

Conventionally, to follow the scientific method means that if you want to study some aspect of the social environment or human behavior, you should start by reviewing the literature to see what others who have previously studied the same phenomenon have found and by selecting a theoretical framework that offers some explanation for the phenomenon in which you are interested. This helps to define the problem more sharply and to formulate better research questions or hypotheses to guide your study. You must then select an appropriate research design to collect and analyze information to provide evidence for or against your hypotheses. Many designs are possible, such as participant observation, surveys, correlational studies, time series studies, and experiments. Most research designs require that you draw a representative sample from the population of interest, that you use established methods of collecting and analyzing the data, that you employ valid and reliable instrumentation, and that you control extrinsic factors that might influence the results. If your findings contradict the theoretical framework, the theory may have to be modified to account for the new results. The final step in the process, following the scientific method, is to write a report about your study and findings so that others may be able to compare their results with yours, thus advancing the knowledge base.

Types of Research

Observational Methods. A good way to gather evidence about human behavior and the social environment is to observe people in their natural surroundings—for example, observing children at home with their parents, on the playground, or in the classroom, and carefully recording what happens. In doing this, however, the observer must guard against bias or the tendency to distort the observation to fit his or her hypotheses. That is why it is better to have a neutral third person doing the observations, not the theorist/researcher.

A disadvantage of observation as a method of data collection is that, just by being there, the observer may cause the study participants to behave differently than they would otherwise. This is called the **Hawthorne effect.** It reminds us that paying attention to people, in and of itself, may have a measurable effect on them. A good way to make the observation less obtrusive is to videotape it, particularly to leave the equipment on location for a long time so that the study participants get used to it and forget that it is there.

Sometimes the observer collects information while participating with the subjects under study. This method is called **participant observation.** For example, to gain insight into life in a low-income neighborhood, the researcher may decide to move into the neighborhood and spend some time living there as a resident. In this manner, the data can be collected less obtrusively because the researcher is considered part of the scene. However, in many circumstances it would be dishonest for the observer to withhold information as to his or her identity or purpose. For example, if the study intruded into people's personal lives or illegal behaviors (e.g., if it explored alcohol consumption patterns, drug dealing, prostitution, homosexual acts, and so on), it would be unethical for the researcher to gather information under cover.

A major technique used to gather data unobtrusively is to collect information from reports provided by a large number of public agencies in the United States or from newspapers, books, or television, to mention but a few possible sources of data. For example, the U.S. Bureau of the Census provides a great deal of information pertinent to the study of the social environment and human behavior, which will be considered throughout this book.

Observations are easier to make in the laboratory than in natural settings because in the laboratory it is easier to control the variables to be studied. But the problem with this method of data collection is that people often do not behave in a contrived lab situation as they would in real life. Consequently, the observations made under lab conditions may have little applicability to life outside the lab.

Surveys. A great deal of information about the social environment and human behavior is collected by **surveying** people about their experiences, behaviors, and attitudes. The public is constantly bombarded with the results of surveys/polls taken by the media and the press such as the CBS News/*New York Times* Poll and the Harris and Gallup Polls and by reports of various professional and research organizations such as the National Opinion Research Center and the Institute for Social Research at the University of Michigan. By continually surveying the public, these organizations keep us informed about the mood of the nation on various issues of public concern and policy, such as abortion, conservation of the environment, immigration, child care, social welfare, health maintenance, guns, defense spending, and so on. In addition, research-oriented surveys collect data about people's life experiences and activities. If the sample on which the survey is based is carefully chosen (e.g., a random sample versus a volunteer or convenience sample), the sample size is adequate, and the response rate is sufficiently high, the results may be generalized to the entire population in the United States or to a particular subset, depending on the nature of the sample taken.

The data collected through large-sample surveys is customarily made available by researchers after their own studies have been analyzed and reported so that other social scientists may reanalyze them. If the data base was collected with the help of taxpayers' money, researchers are obligated to release it after a reasonable period of time. Many such subsequent studies using "canned data," commonly referred to as *secondary analyses*, yield a great deal of human behavior and social environment knowledge.

Perhaps the most ambitious of all the surveys taken in the United States is the decennial census of population conducted by the U.S. Bureau of the Census that asks information from every member of the society about personal characteristics such as age, sex, racial, and ethnic background; employment status; occupation; income; living arrangements; family structure; marital status; fertility; educational attainment; welfare dependency; and many other factors. This national census, conducted every 10 years, is constitutionally mandated for the purpose of allocating seats in the House of Representatives, but the demographic information it gathers is used in a variety of ways by social scientists, policy makers, and social program planners, among others. This information is updated monthly by smaller sample surveys conducted by the census bureau called current population surveys (CPSs), which are published throughout the year.

Most surveys are conducted by administering a questionnaire in writing, by telephone, or face to face. One problem with this method of data collection is that the results may not always be accurate because of response bias (e.g., the study participants may have forgotten the facts of the situation or may distort their answers to make them more acceptable) or nonresponse bias (e.g., some people may not respond to the survey, causing the sample not to be representative of the population under study). In addition, sometimes results are affected when the sex, race, language, or ethnic background of the participants and interviewers are different.

Correlational Studies. **Correlational studies** are another important source of information about the social environment and human behavior. They provide information about whether or not two or more variables are related in such a way that if one varies, the other does too. Correlations may be positive or negative. A *positive correlation* indicates that as one variable changes in one direction, the other variable also changes in the same direction. A *negative correlation* means that the variables vary inversely; that is, as one changes in one direction, the other changes in the opposite direction. For example, suppose you believed, as many people do, that TV violence makes people aggressive. To operationalize this theory with respect to children, you might develop the hypothesis that the more aggressive/violent acts children watch on TV, the more aggressive/violent behavior they will display in their play. To test this hypothesis, you might count the number of violent/aggressive acts in the TV programs watched by a group of children and you might also observe the children at play to record the number of times they engage in violent/aggressive acts in a set period of time. If you were to find the two variables to be positively correlated—that is, that the children who watched the highest number of violent programs also showed the largest number of aggressive acts at play—you might be tempted to conclude that TV violence causes children to become more aggressive. But, as you shall see shortly, you can't make such generalization because correlation is not evidence of causation.

Many correlational studies concerning human behavior and the social environment explore the possible consequences of *natural* events to which people have been exposed. For example, a researcher may compare the behaviors, traits, or family backgrounds of children who have been sexually abused, of teenage alcohol abusers, of young adults raised by lesbian mothers, of pregnant teenage girls, or of individuals whose homes were destroyed by an earthquake with those of similarly situated individuals who did not have these experiences. Clearly, the researcher cannot go out and cause children to be sexually molested, or teenagers to drink excessively, or ask some mothers to take up lesbianism. Therefore, the researcher would have to find people who have had these experiences and enlist them to participate in the study, matching them with others similar in as many ways as possible except in terms of having had the experience under consideration. For instance, for the study comparing young adults raised by lesbian mothers versus those raised by heterosexual mothers, the measure selected might be the percent who chose same-sex partners versus opposite-sex sexual partners. In the study comparing those whose homes were destroyed by an earthquake versus those whose homes were not destroyed, the dependent variable might be the incidence of major depression or of post-traumatic stress disorder a year later. And so on.

Although correlational studies provide much information about the relationship between various human behavior and social environmental factors, generally they cannot unambiguously ascertain cause-effect relationships. For instance, going back to the study of the relationship between TV violence and aggression, the fact that you found a highly significant positive correlation between TV violence and children's aggression during play

would not necessarily mean that TV violence caused the children to be aggressive. It might be that the relationship goes the other way around; for example, aggressive children might be more likely to choose to watch violent TV programs. Or a third cause might be responsible for both: Perhaps aggressive parents teach their children to behave aggressively and to choose violent TV programs by modeling these behaviors.

Experimental Studies. Much of the knowledge we have about the social environment and human behavior has been derived from observation, surveys, and correlational studies. Such studies are important to explore relationships among variables and to generate hypotheses for further research, but none is capable of establishing causation unambiguously. Only **experiments** allow us to investigate cause-effect relationships by manipulating one variable to observe and measure changes in another variable. Yet, to date, only a small fraction of our HBSE knowledge has been derived from experimentation. Let us return to the issue of TV violence and its relation to children's aggression. If your goal was to determine if TV violence causes aggression in children, as indicated by your original theory, you would do better to set up an experiment rather than to measure the correlation between the two variables.

In your experiment, the *independent variable*—that is, the variable that is manipulated to cause an effect on another variable—would be the specific TV program that is shown to the children participating in the study. You could have one group of children (the *experimental group*) view a program in which the actors behaved violently or aggressively and another group (the *control group*) view a program containing no violence. Your *dependent variable*, the variable that you observe and measure, would be the number of aggressive acts exhibited by the children at play after watching the TV program. To make sure that all other factors capable of influencing the results are *controlled*, you would need to assign the children on a random basis to the experimental or control groups; in this manner, any other variables that might influence the results would be randomly distributed and thus equalized.

A contrived study, such as the one just described, is called a *laboratory experiment*. Many lab studies are conducted by researchers at universities, using college students as participants because they are readily available. Although the results of such experiments may provide useful preliminary evidence and hypotheses for further study, the results obtained by testing such a select group of participants are seldom generalizable to other groups in the U.S. society.

An experiment conducted outside the laboratory is called a *field experiment*. This type of experiment is frequently set up to compare the effects of different interventions. Typically, the researcher will have two or more groups of people exposed to two or more different interventions. Sometimes there will also be a control group of people who experience no intervention. For example, the interventions might be infant day care provided in centers versus infant day care provided in private homes, provision of job training for prisoners versus no provision of job training, or police arrest versus counseling versus taking no action following an incident of domestic violence. If the researcher is able to institute appropriate controls—for example, by randomly assigning participants to the interventions—any significant difference between the groups under study on the dependent measure(s) would be attributable to the interventions.

Field experiments involving an unplanned intervention or an abrupt social change of some sort are called *natural experiments*. The independent variable would be the unplanned interventions (e.g., identical twins who happened to be reared together versus those who happened to be reared apart) or the abrupt change (e.g., discontinuation of public assistance to women

having a third child in a particular state or a sudden cut of federal funds for abortion). The dependent variable would be the effects on the participants assessed by whatever objective measures you choose to use. For instance, in the case of identical twins reared together versus those reared apart, we might be interested in looking at the degree of concordance in the incidence of extreme shyness or gay/lesbian behavior among both sets of twins.

In natural experiments, as in natural correlational studies, one cannot manipulate the independent variable nor can one randomly assign the study participants to the experimental or control conditions. Because of the lack of experimental control, one cannot make strong statements about cause-effect relationships. However, consistent results by a large number of studies using sound research methods would give researchers confidence about the findings.

Time Series Studies: Cross-Sectional versus Panel/Longitudinal Studies. **Cross-sectional studies** aim to identify developmental changes or changes occurring over time in people by comparing different groups of people of different ages or developmental levels on a one-time measure or measures (e.g., religiosity, conservatism/liberalism, or mental flexibility/rigidity). The advantage is that one does not have to wait until the same group of people grow up to obtain the same results. The problem is that such data are derived from different cohorts of people, not from measuring the same persons over a long period. Because each age cohort may have experienced a different set of historical, cultural, and educational circumstances, any differences found between the groups may be reflective of sociohistorical factors and not of any personal developmental changes.

Sometimes a group of people are asked the same set of questions or their traits are measured again and again over a period of several years to determine how their behavior, attitudes, or way of thinking has changed over time. Such studies are referred to as *panel stud-*

ies or **longitudinal studies.** Although they are better than cross-sectional studies in their ability to reflect personal/developmental changes experienced over time, they are not without drawbacks. Specifically, longitudinal studies take a long time to complete and during that time the theories that generated them may have become obsolete or may have lost significance. Also, because they take so long to complete, the researcher may lose track of many of the study participants over the years. Furthermore, such studies are representative of one age cohort only (e.g., those who started kindergarten in 1952). These individuals experienced a unique set of sociohistorical circumstances different from those experienced by older or younger people; consequently, their personal/developmental experiences may not be representative of any age group other than their own.

Sequential designs may be the best solution to time series studies in the sense that they combine features from cross-sectional and longitudinal designs. Specifically, by focusing on multiple samples of participants of different ages and by following them up over time, sequential studies are better able to separate developmental changes from cohort effects.

Research Ethics

Having reviewed the major methods of building an empirical knowledge base, we conclude this chapter by turning once again to the all-important subject of ethics. The need to maintain ethical standards in the conduct of empirical research has led to the codification of research ethics in most major professional and scientific fields. The ethical codes developed are usually congruent with the ethical standards set by the federal government for all federally funded research and include the following principles and values:

- Maintenance of honesty, integrity, and objectivity in all aspects of the study. Research results often affect the lives of many people; therefore, the researcher should be scrupulously honest, straightforward, and accurate.
- Respect for the participants' right to dignity, privacy, confidentiality, and informed consent. No research study should in any way embarrass or demean the participants. To preserve anonymity and confidentiality, individual responses should be securely protected and findings should not be shared with anyone except in aggregate form so that the answers cannot be traced to individual respondents. The decision to participate in the study should be made by potential participants voluntarily on the basis of accurate information about the study provided by the researcher in advance.
- Protection of the participants from harm, physical or mental. It is the responsibility of the researcher to make sure that the study participants suffer no negative consequences of any kind. In some cases, this may require counseling or debriefing after the study to correct any possible short-term or long-term effects of participation.
- Disclosure of all sources of support for the study. The researcher should clearly specify all funding sources or entities that contributed any resources to the study or to the researcher. This is very important, particularly when there may be a conflict of interest of which research consumers should be aware.
- Acknowledgment of the work contributed by all those who collaborated in the study. The work contributed by each author should be acknowledged so that readers know who was responsible for what. People not included as authors but who provided significant help in any aspect of the study, such as those who made substantial comments on early drafts of the paper or who gave help with the research design or statistical analysis, should be given credit.

ENDNOTE

1. This is reminiscent of the concept of the lifespace in Kurt Lewin's field theory (1951), which greatly influenced the thinking of human ecologists.

GLOSSARY

Adaptation: The continuous process of mutual accommodation between person and environment.

Biculturalism: The ease with which a person can move back and forth between two cultural systems.

Boundary: A separating line, visible or invisible, that encloses a system so that it can be distinguished from its environment or from other systems. Also, internally, a separating line that divides the system's subsystems. Boundaries are important because they protect systems and subsystems from unwanted outside interference.

Closed System: A system that has no exchange with its environment, such as a piece of furniture.

Conflict: When a person or group engages in behavior that another individual or group perceives as interference with the attainment of one of its goals.

Constructivism: A postmodern perspective that emphasizes that there is no such thing as "objective reality." Instead, all reality is mediated or constructed by each person or other social system such as the family based on the person's or system's unique experiences. This means that each person or system has a different assumptive world and the "truth" must be considered relative to context and to historical time.

Coping: Dealing with stress by making certain adaptations, by engaging in problem solving, or by managing negative emotions and attitudes such as anger, depression, and helplessness.

Correlational Study: A research study designed to provide information about whether two or more variables are related in such a way that if one varies, the other does too. Correlations may be positive or negative.

Cross-Sectional Study: A research study designed to identify changes occurring over time by comparing the one-time responses of different groups of people at different points in their development.

Cultural Competence: The ability to conduct one's professional work in a manner that is considered appropriate by members of a distinctive cultural group.

Cultural Pluralism: Respect for cultural diversity with recognition of the strengths and merits of each group's culture and support of each group's right to retain its culture.

Deconstruction: To pick apart a writing in order to dig out the things it ought to have said but didn't or the issues it should have addressed but didn't and to uncover the biases inherent in what is actually said.

Differentiation: The tendency of systems to become more complex, elaborate, and specialized in function as they develop.

Diversity Perspective: As used in this book, a perspective that supports the right of each noncultural group in society to retain its culture and stresses its responsibility to participate and contribute to the mainstream culture. It emphasizes the importance of acquiring knowledge about the various cultural groups that constitute our diverse society, understanding the bicultural experience, the problems of discrimination and oppression, the vicissitudes of migration, and the challenges of acculturation.

Dominant Group: The social group in power in the society; the group that controls major social institutions and resources and makes the major decisions—the "establishment."

Dual Perspective: A concept that states that members of most nonmainstream groups live simultaneously in two or more cultures—the dominant culture of the society and their own culture(s)—and must negotiate these different worlds, each with its own set of values, beliefs, lifestyles, and behavioral expectations.

Dynamics: Goal-directed, integrational, maintenance, or adaptational activities in which social systems are involved.

Eclectic Approach: Taking from the various schools of thought and practice the best insights they can offer to better understand and treat clients.

Ecosystem: An integrated system composed of people and their physical-social-cultural environments in which each part of the system shapes every other part.

Ecosystems Perspective: A conceptual framework composed of ecological theory and systems theory that emphasizes the interconnectedness and interdependency of social phenomena. Because it is value free as well as free from theoretical commitment, this framework can accept diverse contributions of knowledge from a wide range of psychological, social psychological, and sociological theories used by helping professionals.

Emergent Characteristics: Those unique properties of systems that distinguish them from their component parts and that give them a character of their own different from the characteristics of their individual components.

Empowerment: Helping people to discover the power and energies within them, their families, and their communities and assisting them to take an active role in the decisions that define their worlds.

Energy: The fuel that makes it possible for systems to perform their functions. Individuals, for example, derive part of their energy from the food they eat, the oxygen they breathe, and the information, support, resources, and communication they get from the environment.

Entropy: The natural tendency of open systems to lose vitality and to move toward disorganization and death.

Ethclass: A concept that stresses the fundamental role played simultaneously by social class membership and ethnicity in influencing lifestyles, life chances, and problems of living.

Ethnocultural Approach: A teaching or interventive approach that considers the total experiences of each racial, ethnic, or cultural group, including knowledge not only about the effects of powerlessness, discrimination, and oppression but also about each group's cultural values, family patterns, beliefs, strengths, unique conditions (physical, psychoemotional, or situational), and life-course experiences. The objective is to equip students with the comprehensive understandings necessary for culturally competent practice.

Exosystem: Linkage and other processes taking place between two or more settings, including at least one setting that does not ordinarily contain the person or persons who are the unit of attention, but in which events occur that influence processes within the immediate settings that contain that person. For instance, the relations between a child's school and the state board of education.

Experiment: A type of research designed to investigate cause-effect relationships by manipulating one variable to observe and measure changes in another variable and by controlling all other factors, usually by random assignment of study participants to the experimental situations.

Feedback: A special form of input consisting of information about a system's performance to guide its continuing operation.

Feedback Loop: The return of feedback to a system serving to maintain its steady state or to institute some change, depending on whether it is positive or negative.

Habitat: A social system's physical environment and setting, including such things as physical aspects of the community, climate, terrain, degree of crowding, noise level, and level of pollution.

Hawthorne Effect: By paying attention to people (i.e., simply by observing them), a researcher may have a measurable effect on their performance or behavior. Because of this problem, good research requires that observations be made as unobtrusively as possible.

Hierarchical Constraints: Systems and subsystems are constrained or restricted in action by the rules of the larger systems to which they belong.

Homeostasis: The tendency of closed or nearly closed systems to maintain equilibrium and, when this balance is disrupted, to attempt to restore it.

Human Ecology: The study of the continuing transaction between people and their environments and the accommodations that they mutually make.

Hypothesis: An educated guess about the possible relationship between two or more variables stated in observable and measurable terms.

Input: Anything that a system or subsystem imports or receives from the outside, whether it be food, raw materials, information, human resources, money, or communication.

Interface: An exchange, sometimes direct and sometimes through representatives, between two systems.

Interrole Conflict: Role strain experienced when one finds that the behaviors associated with a role one person must play are incompatible with those associated with other roles that must also be played.

Intrarole Conflict: Role strain resulting from opposing demands from a single role. Frequently this happens when the role occupant has a different interpretation of the role than others who have a say in the way the role is performed.

Labeling: A process of assigning descriptive or diagnostic labels to individuals, such as *mental patient, criminal offender,* or *child abuser.* Once given a label, individuals often act in accordance with the label's expected roles, thus significantly altering their behavior and eventually their self-concepts and fates.

Longitudinal Study: A research study consisting of asking a group of people the same set of questions or measuring them on the same trait(s) several times over a period of several years to determine the changes that have taken place over time. Also known as a panel study.

Macrosystem: The societal and cultural context, including the belief and value systems, lifestyles, social and economic resources, hazards, and life chances of the cultures within which an individual was raised and within which he or she currently lives.

Mesosystem: Linkages and other processes taking place between two or more face-to-face settings, all containing the individual or individuals who are the focus of attention (e.g., the relations between a family and the church they attend).

Microsystem: The immediate face-to-face context, such as the family, workplace, kin group, or peer group.

Negative Entropy: Also known as *negentropy,* the process of growth and development that precedes decline in living systems. It requires that a system import more energy than it exports to be able to discharge its functions while continuing to grow and evolve.

Negative Feedback: Information that a system has deviated from its course.

Niche: A region in the social environment that is especially favorable or unfavorable to the development of an individual. The quality of a social niche is influenced by various factors, such as nationality, race, ethnic group membership, socioeconomic status, gender, age, and sexual orientation.

Nondominant Group: A social group that has low standing in the stratification system of the society and that is the recipient of inequitable and inferior treatment.

Norms: Rules or standards that regulate behavior.

Open System: A system that maintains an active exchange with its environment, such as a healthy family.

Output: Anything that a system sends out or exports to the environment or to other systems. It may be people, products, information, communication, a response to a stimulus, or anything else.

Participant Observation: A data-collection method in which the researcher joins the group to be observed and participates as a member.

People of Color: Members of a nonwhite racial group in the United States, such as African Americans, Asians, or Native Americans.

Positive Feedback: Information that a system is on the correct path toward its goal.

Postmodernism: A perspective that places emphasis on diversity and on the importance of respecting and celebrating differences among people. It stresses the limitations of old theories tied to the industrial period and emphasizes the need to search for new paradigms.

Role: A pattern of behavior expected of an individual occupying a specific social position, such as teacher or parent.

Role Conflict: Role strain experienced when there is a discrepancy between what others expect one to do and what one wants to do or thinks one should do.

Role Overload: Role strain felt when one tries to play too many roles at the same time.

Role Strain: Difficulty meeting the demands of the roles one plays.

Scientific Method: A principle that requires that ideas such as theories or hypotheses be validated by evidence derived from observation or other forms of empirical research.

Sequential Designs: Time series studies of human behavior that combine features from cross-sectional and longitudinal designs. Specifically, they focus on multiple samples of participants of different ages and follow them up over time, thus being able to separate developmental changes from cohort effects.

Social Conflict Theory: A sociological theory that considers conflict a natural and inevitable outcome of human interaction.

Social Exchange Theory: A social-psychological theory that assumes that human relations are motivated by self-interest and based on a cost/benefit analysis.

Social System: A system composed of people as members of various collectives, such as families and other groups, social organizations and institutions, and communities.

Steady State: A system's adaptive relationship with its environment whereby it keeps some balance between maintenance and change.

Stress: Internal strain or tension that arises within a system when it perceives an imbalance between the demands it faces and its capacity to meet these challenges.

Structural Functionalism: A prominent sociological theory that views society as a dynamic system of interconnected parts or structures, each performing certain tasks or functions.

Structure: A stable pattern of functioning that develops in a system as its members interact. Its most important components are positions, roles, and norms.

Subsystem: A system that is part of a larger system.

Suprasystem: A larger system that contains one or more systems within it.

Survey: A method of collecting data consisting of asking people questions through the use of interviews and questionnaires.

Symbolic Interaction Theory: A social-psychological point of view that stresses the importance of personal meanings, symbols, interpretations, and other internal processes in understanding the dynamics of situations.

System: A whole composed of transacting parts.

Theory: A collection of related statements or propositions that attempt to describe, explain, or predict a particular aspect of experience.

Throughput: The process by which open systems act on and transform their inputs into outputs.

Transaction: A continuous reciprocal exchange between systems in which each one influences and changes every other.

REFERENCES

Alexander, J. C., & Colomy, P. (1990). Neofunctionalism: Reconstructing a theoretical tradition. In G. Ritzer (Ed.), *Frontiers of social theory: The new syntheses* (pp. 33–67). New York: Columbia University Press.

Asamoah, Y., Garcia, A., Ortiz Hendricks, C., & Walker, J. (1991). What we call ourselves: Implications for resources, policy, and practice. *Journal of Multicultural Social Work, 1*(1), 7–22.

Berrien, F. K. (1968). *General and social systems.* New Brunswick, NJ: Rutgers University Press.

Blau, P. M. (1964). *Exchange and power in social life.* New York: Wiley.

Blau, P. M. (1975). Parallels and contrasts in structural inquiries. In P. Blau (Ed.), *Approaches to the study of social structure* (pp. 1–20). New York: Free Press.

Blumer, H. (1969). *Symbolic interaction: Perspective and method.* Englewood Cliffs, NJ: Prentice-Hall.

Bronfenbrenner, U. (1979). *The ecology of human development.* Cambridge, MA: Harvard University Press.

Bronfenbrenner, U. (1989). Ecological systems theory. *Annals of Child Development, 6*, 187–249.

Brown, R. (1987). *Society as text: Essays on rhetoric, reason and reality.* Chicago: University of Chicago Press.

Chau, K. L. (1990). A model for teaching cross-cultural practice in social work. *Journal of Social Work Education, 26*, 124–133.

Chau, K. L. (1991). Social work with ethnic minorities: Practice issues and potentials. *Journal of Multicultural Social Work, 1*(1), 23–39.

Cloninger, S. (1993). *Theories of personality: Understanding persons*. Englewood Cliffs, NJ: Prentice Hall.

Collins, R. (1975). *Conflict sociology: Toward an explanatory science*. New York: Academic Press.

Cooley, C. H. (1902). *Human nature and the social order*. New York: Scribner's.

Coser, L. A. (1956). *The functions of social conflict*. New York: Free Press.

Coser, L. A. (1967). *Continuities in the study of social conflict*. New York: Free Press.

Cox, O. C. (1959). *Caste, class, and race*. New York: Monthly Review Press.

Dahrendorf, R. (1959). *Class and class conflict in industrial sociology*. Stanford, CA: Stanford University Press.

Dahrendorf, R. (1968). *Essays in the theory of society*. Palo Alto, CA: Stanford University Press.

Davis, K., & Moore, W. E. (1945). Some principles of stratification. *American Sociological Review, 10*, 242–249.

De Anda, D. (1984). Bicultural socialization: Factors affecting the minority experience. *Social Work, 29*, 101–107.

DeHoyas, G., DeHoyas, A., & Anderson, C. B. (1986). Sociocultural dislocation: Beyond the dual perspective. *Social Work, 31*, 61–67.

Devore, W., & Schlesinger, E. G. (1991). Ethnic-sensitive social work practice (3rd ed.). New York: Macmillan.

Dubos, R. (1968). *So human an animal*. New York: Charles Scribner's Sons.

Durkheim, E. (1964). *The division of labor in society* (G. Simpson, Trans.). New York: Free Press.

Fisher, D. D. V. (1991). *An introduction to constructivism for social workers*. New York: Praeger.

Fleck-Henderson, A. (1993). A constructivist approach to "human behavior and the social environment I." *Journal of Teaching in Social Work, 8*(1/2), 219–238.

Folb, E. A. (1988). Who's got the room at the top? Issues of dominance and nondominance in intracultural communication. In L. A. Samovar & R. E. Porter (Eds.), *Intercultural communication: A reader* (5th ed., pp. 121–129). Belmont, CA: Wadsworth.

Frye, M. (1983). *The politics of reality: Essays in feminist theory*. Trumansburg, NY: Crossings Press.

Germain, C. B. (1973). An ecological perspective in casework practice, *Social Casework, 54*, 323–330.

Germain, C. B. (1985). The place of community work within an ecological approach to social work practice. In S. H. Taylor & R. W. Roberts (Eds.), *Theory and practice of community social work* (pp. 30–55). New York: Columbia University Press.

Germain, C. B., & Gitterman, A. (1980). *The life model of social work practice*. New York: Columbia University Press.

Germain, C. B., & Gitterman, A. (1987). Ecological perspective. In A. Minahan (Ed.), *Encyclopedia of social work* (18th ed., pp. 488–499). Silver Springs, MD: National Association of Social Workers.

Goffman, E. (1959). *The presentation of self in everyday life*. New York: Anchor.

Goffman, E. (1961). *Asylums*. New York: Anchor.

Goffman, E. (1974). *Frame analysis*. Cambridge, MA: Harvard University Press.

Gonzalez, D. (1992, November 15). What's the problem with "Hispanic"? Just ask a "Latino." *The New York Times*, p. E6.

Gordon, M. M. (1964). *Assimilation in American life*. New York: Oxford University Press.

Gordon, W. E. (1969). Basic constructs for an integrative and generative conception of social work. In G. Hearn (Ed.), *The general systems approach: Contributions toward an holistic conception of social work* (pp. 5–11). New York: Council on Social Work Education.

Graham, S. (1992). Most of the subjects were white and middle class: Trends in published research on African Americans in selected APA journals, 1970–1989. *American Psychologist, 47*, 629–639.

Green, J. W. (1982). *Cultural awareness in the human services*. Englewood Cliffs, NJ: Prentice-Hall.

Greif, G. L., & Lynch, A. A. (1983). The eco-systems perspective. In C. H. Meyer, (Ed.), *Clinical social work in an eco-systems perspective*. New York: Columbia University Press.

Hartmann, H. (1958). *Ego psychology and the problem of adaptation*. New York: International Universities Press.

Harvey, D. (1989). *The condition of postmodernity: An enquiry into the origins of cultural change*. Oxford: Blackwell.

Heiss, J. (1981). Social roles. In M. Rosenberg & R. H. Turner (Eds.), *Social psychology: Sociological perspectives* (pp. 95–129). New York: Basic Books.

Herskovits, M. J. (1972). *Cultural relativism: Perspective in cultural pluralism.* New York: Random House.

Himes, J. S. (1973). *Racial conflict in American society.* Columbus, OH: Merrill.

Homans, G. C. (1961). *Social behavior: Its elementary forms.* New York: Harcourt, Brace and World.

Hopps, J. G. (1987). Minorities of color. In A. Minahan (Ed.), *Encyclopedia of social work* (18th ed., pp. 161–171). Silver Springs, MD: National Association of Social Workers.

Jeffries, V., & Ransford, H. E. (1980). *Social stratification: A multiple hierarchy approach.* Boston: Allyn and Bacon.

Katz, D., & Kahn, R. L. (1969). Common characteristics of open systems. In F. E. Emery (Ed.), *Systems thinking: Selected readings* (pp. 86–104). Great Britain: Penguin.

Keeney, B. P. (1979). Ecosystemic epistemology: An alternative paradigm for diagnosis. *Family Process, 18,* 117–129.

Kellen, H. M. (1956). *Cultural pluralism and the American idea.* Philadelphia: University of Philadelphia Press.

Kelley, H. H., & Thibaut, J. W. (1978). *Interpersonal relations: A theory of interdependence.* New York: John Wiley & Sons.

Kellner, D. (1990). The postmodern turn: Positions, problems, and prospects. In G. Ritzer (Ed.), *Frontiers of social theory: The new syntheses* (pp. 255–286). New York: Columbia University Press.

Koestler, A. (1967). *The act of creation.* New York: Dell.

Kornblum, W. (1991). *Sociology in a changing world* (2nd ed.). Ft Worth: Holt, Rinehart and Winston.

Laird, J. (1993). Introduction. *Journal of Teaching in Social Work, 8*(1/2), 1–10.

Lengermann, P. M., & Niebrugge-Brantley, J. (1992). Contemporary feminist theory. In G. Ritzer, (Ed.), *Contemporary sociological theory* (3rd ed., pp. 308–357). New York: McGraw-Hill.

Lenski, G. (1966). *Power and privilege: A theory of social stratification.* New York: McGraw-Hill.

Lenski, G., Lenski, J., & Nolan, P. (1991). *Human societies: An introduction to macrosociology.* New York: McGraw-Hill.

Lewin, K. (1951). *Field theory in social science.* New York: Harper & Brothers.

Lister, L. (1987). Curriculum building in social work education: The example of ethnocultural content. *Journal of Social Work Education, 23,* 31–39.

Loewenberg, F. M., & Dolgoff, R. (1992). *Ethical decisions for social work practice.* Itasca, IL: F. E. Peacock.

Lyotard, J. F. (1984). *The postmodern condition.* Minneapolis: University of Minnesota Press.

Martin, P. Y., & O'Connor, G. G. (1989). *The social environment: Open systems applications.* New York: Longman.

Maruyama, M. (1968). The second cybernetics: Deviation-amplifying mutual causal processes. In W. Buckley (Ed.), *Modern systems research for the behavioral scientist* (pp. 304–313). Chicago: Aldine.

Marx, K., & Engels, F. (1969). *The Communist manifesto.* Baltimore: Penguin. (Original work published 1848)

Mead, G. H. (1934). *Mind, self and society: From the standpoint of a social behaviorist.* Chicago: University of Chicago Press.

Mead, G. H. (1938). *The philosophy of the act.* Chicago: University of Chicago Press.

Merton, R. (1968). *Social theory and social structure* (enl. ed.). New York: Free Press.

Meyer, C. H. (1973). Purposes and boundaries: Casework fifty years later. *Social Casework, 54,* 268–275.

Miller, D. (1981). The meaning of role-taking. *Symbolic Interaction, 4,* 167–175.

Miller, J. G. (1955). Toward a general theory for the behavioral sciences. *American Psychologist, 10,* 513–531.

Monat, A., & Lazarus, R. S. (1991). *Stress and coping: An anthology* (3rd ed.). New York: Columbia University Press.

Nes, J. A., & Iadicola, P. (1989). Toward a definition of feminist social work: A comparison of liberal, radical, and socialist models. *Social Work, 34,* 12–21.

Norton, D. (1978). *The dual perspective: Inclusion of ethnic minority content in the social work curriculum.* New York: Council on Social Work Education.

Pardeck, J. T. (1988). An ecological approach for social work practice. *Journal of Sociology and Social Welfare, 15,* 133–142.

Parsons, T. (1951). *The social system.* Glencoe, IL: Free Press.

Parsons, T. (1961). An outline of the social system. In T. Parsons, E. Shils, K. D. Naegele, & J. R. Pitts, (Eds.), *Theories of society: Foundations of modern sociological theory* (pp. 30–79). New York: Free Press.

Parsons, T. (1966). *Societies: Evolutionary and comparative perspectives.* Englewood Cliffs, NJ: Prentice Hall.

Peterson, C. (1992). *Personality* (2nd ed.). New York: Harcourt Brace Jovanovich.

Ritzer , G. (1992). *Contemporary sociological theory* (3rd ed.). New York: McGraw-Hill.

Rodway, M. R. (1986). Systems theory. In F. J. Turner & K. A. Kendall (Eds.), *Social work treatment: Interlocking theoretical approaches* (3rd ed., pp. 514–539). New York: Free Press.

Saleebey, D. (1992). *The strength perspective in social work practice.* New York: Longman.

Saleebey, D. (1993). *Notes on interpreting the human condition: A "constructed" HBSE curriculum, 8*(1/2), 197–217.

Sands, R. G., & Nuccio, K. (1992). Postmodern feminist theory and social work. *Social Work, 37,* 489–494.

Schrof, J. M. (1993, September 27). Feminism's daughters. *U.S. News & World Report,* pp. 68–71.

Schwartz, B. (1993). Why altruism is impossible…and ubiquitous. *Social Service Review, 67,* 314–343.

Siporin, M. (1980). Ecological systems theory in social work. *Journal of Sociology and Social Welfare, 7,* 507–532.

Stephens, M. (1994, January 23). Jacques Derrida. *The New York Times Magazine,* pp. 22–25.

Thibaut, J. W., & Kelley, H. H. (1959). *The social psychology of groups.* New York: Wiley.

U.S. Hispanics say, call us "-Americans." (1992, December 28). *Time,* p. 18.

von Bertalanffy, L. (1950). The theory of open systems in physics and biology, *Science, 111,* 23–29.

von Bertalanffy, L. (1968). *General systems theory: Foundations, developments and applications.* New York: George Braziller.

von Bertalanffy, L. (1974). General systems theory and psychiatry. In S. Arieti (Ed.), *American handbook of psychiatry* (Vol. 1) (2nd ed., pp. 1095–1117). New York: Basic Books.

Wakefield, J. C. (1993). Is altruism part of human nature? Toward a theoretical foundation for the helping professions. *Social Service Review, 67,* 406–458.

Zerbe Enns, C. (1989). Toward teaching inclusive personality theories. *Teaching of psychology, 16*(3), 111–117.

SUGGESTIONS FOR FURTHER READING

Barret, R. E. (1994). *Using the 1990 U.S. census for research.* Thousand Oaks, CA: Sage.

Brown, L. S. (1990). The meaning of a multicultural perspective for theory-building in feminist therapy. *Women and Therapy, 9*(1), 1–21.

Cowger, C. D. (1994). Assessing client strengths: Clinical assessment for client empowerment. *Social Work, 39,* 262–268.

Devore, W., & Schlesinger, E. G. (1991). *Ethnic-sensitive social work practice* (3rd ed.). New York: Macmillan.

Farganis, S. (1994). *Situating feminism: From thought to action.* Thousand Oaks, CA: Sage.

Greene, R. R. (1994). *Human behavior theory: A diversity framework.* Hawthorne, NY: Aldine.

Hollinger, R. (1994). *Postmodernism and the social sciences: A thematic approach.* Thousand Oaks, CA: Sage.

Loewenberg, F. M., & Dolgoff, R. (1992). *Ethical decisions for social work practice.* Itasca, IL: F. E. Peacock.

Pardeck, J. T., Murphy, J. W., & Choi, J. M. (1994). Some implications of postmodernism for social work practice. *Social Work, 39*, 342–346.

Philogene, G. (1994). "African-American" as a new social representation. *Journal for the Theory of Social Behavior, 24*(2), 89–109.

Pozatek, E. (1994). The problem of certainty: Clinical social work in the postmodern era. *Social Work, 39*, 396–402.

Saleebey, D. (1992). *The strength perspective in social work practice.* New York: Longman.

Smith, B. (1986). Some home truths on the contemporary black feminist movement. In N. Van Den Bergh & L. B. Cooper (Eds.), *Feminist visions for social work.* Silver Springs, MD: National Association of Social Workers.

Trickett, E. J., Watts, R. J., & Birman, D. (Eds.). (1994). *Human diversity: Perpectives on people in context.* San Francisco: Jossey-Bass.

Waters, M. (1994). *Modern sociological theory.* Thousand Oaks, CA: Sage.

Look for articles in the following journals:

Feminist Studies
Gender and Society
Journal of Multicultural Social Work
Signs
Sociological Theory
Symbolic Interaction

APPENDIX: CODE OF ETHICS OF THE NATIONAL ASSOCIATION OF SOCIAL WORKERS

As adopted by the 1979 NASW Delegate Assembly and revised by the 1990 and 1993 NASW Delegate Assemblies.

Sections I.B.3, I.B.4, II.F.4, III.J.12, and III.J.13, adopted by the 1993 Delegate Assembly, [went] into effect July 1, 1994.

This code is intended to serve as a guide to the everyday conduct of members of the social work profession and as a basis for the adjudication of issues in ethics when the conduct of social workers is alleged to deviate from the standards expressed or implied in this code. It represents standards of ethical behavior for social workers in professional relationships with those served, with colleagues, with employers, with other individuals and professions, and with the community and society as a whole. It also embodies standards of ethical behavior governing individual conduct to the extent that such conduct is associated with an individual's status and identity as a social worker.

This code is based on the fundamental values of the social work profession that include the worth, dignity, and uniqueness of all persons as well as their rights and opportunities. It is also based on the nature of social work, which fosters conditions that promote these values.

In subscribing to and abiding by this code, the social worker is expected to view ethical responsibility in as inclusive a context as each situation demands and within which ethical judgement is required. The social worker is expected to take into consideration all the principles in this code that have a bearing upon any situation in which ethical judgement is to be exercised and professional intervention or conduct is planned. The course of action that the social worker chooses is expected to be consistent with the spirit as well as the letter of this code.

In itself, this code does not represent a set of rules that will prescribe all the behaviors of social workers in all the complexities of professional life. Rather, it offers general principles to guide conduct, and the judicious appraisal of conduct, in situations that have ethical implications. It provides the basis for making judgements about ethical actions before and after they occur. Frequently, the particular situation determines the ethical principles that apply and the manner of their application. In such cases, not only the particular ethical principles are taken into immediate consideration, but also the entire code and its spirit. Specific applications of ethical principles must be judged within the context in which they are being considered. Ethical behavior in a given situation must satisfy not only the judgement of the individual social worker, but also the judgement of an unbiased jury of professional peers.

This code should not be used as an instrument to deprive any social worker of the opportunity or freedom to practice with complete professional integrity; nor should any disciplinary action be taken on the basis of this code without maximum provision for safeguarding the rights of the social worker affected.

The ethical behavior of social workers results not from edict, but from a personal commitment of the individual. This code is offered to affirm the will and zeal of all social workers to be ethical and to act ethically in all that they do as social workers.

The following codified ethical principles should guide social workers in the various roles and relationships and at the various levels of responsibility in which they function professionally. These principles also serve as a basis for the adjudication by the National Association of Social Workers of issues in ethics.

In subscribing to this code, social workers are required to cooperate in its implementation and abide by any disciplinary rulings based on it. They should also take adequate measures to discourage, prevent, expose, and correct the unethical conduct of colleagues. Finally, social workers should be equally ready to defend and assist colleagues unjustly charged with unethical conduct.

SUMMARY OF MAJOR PRINCIPLES

I. The Social Worker's Conduct and Comportment as a Social Worker

A. Propriety. The social worker should maintain high standards of personal conduct in the capacity or identity as social worker.

B. Competence and Professional Development. The social worker should strive to become and remain proficient in professional practice and the performance of professional functions.

C. Service. The social worker should regard as primary the service obligation of the social work profession.

D. Integrity. The social worker should act in accordance with the highest standards of professional integrity.

E. Scholarship and Research. The social worker engaged in study and research should be guided by the conventions of scholarly inquiry.

II. The Social Worker's Ethical Responsibility to Clients

F. Primacy of Clients' Interests. The social worker's primary responsibility is to clients.

G. Rights and Prerogatives of Clients. The social worker should make every effort to foster maximum self-determination on the part of clients.

H. Confidentiality and Privacy. The social worker should respect the privacy of clients and hold in confidence all information obtained in the course of professional service.

I. Fees. When setting fees, the social worker should ensure that they are fair, reasonable, considerate, and commensurate with the service performed and with due regard for the clients' ability to pay.

III. The Social Worker's Ethical Responsibility to Colleagues

J. Respect, Fairness, and Courtesy. The social worker should treat colleagues with respect, courtesy, fairness, and good faith.

K. Dealing with Colleagues' Clients. The social worker has the responsibility to relate to the clients of colleagues with full professional consideration.

IV. The Social Worker's Ethical Responsibility to Employers and Employing Organizations

L. Commitments to Employing Organizations. The social worker should adhere to commitments made to the employing organizations.

V. The Social Woker's Ethical Responsibility to the Social Work Profession

M. Maintaining the Integrity of the Profession. The social worker should uphold and advance the values, ethics, knowledge, and mission of the profession.

N. Community Service. The social worker should assist the profession in making social services available to the general public.

O. Development of Knowledge. The social worker should take responsibility for identifying, developing, and fully utilizing knowledge for professional practice.

VI. The Social Worker's Ethical Responsibility to Society

P. Promoting the General Welfare. The social worker should promote the general welfare of society.

THE NASW CODE OF ETHICS

I. The Social Worker's Conduct and Comportment as a Social Worker

A. Propriety—The social worker should maintain high standards of personal conduct in the capacity or identity as social worker.

1. The private conduct of the social worker is a personal matter to the same degree as is any other person's, except when such conduct compromises the fulfillment of professional responsibilities.
2. The social worker should not participate in, condone, or be associated with dishonesty, fraud, deceit, or misrepresentation.
3. The social worker should distinguish clearly between statements and actions made as a private individual and as a representative of the social work profession or an organization or group.

B. Competence and Professional Development—The social worker should strive to become and remain proficient in professional practice and the performance of professional functions.

1. The social worker should accept responsibility or employment only on the basis of existing competence or the intention to acquire the necessary competence.
2. The social worker should not misrepresent professional qualifications, education, experience, or affiliations.
3. The social worker should not allow his or her own personal problems, psychosocial distress, substance abuse, or mental health difficulties to interfere with professional judgment and performance or jeopardize the best interests of those for whom the social worker has a professional responsibility.
4. The social worker whose personal problems, psychosocial distress, substance abuse, or mental health difficulties interfere with professional judgment and performance should immediately seek consultation and take appropriate remedial action by seeking professional help, making adjustments in workload, terminating practice, or taking any other steps necessary to protect clients and others.

C. Service—The social worker should regard as primary the service obligation of the social work profession.

1. The social worker should retain ultimate responsibility for the quality and extent of the service that individual assumes, assigns, or performs.

2. The social worker should act to prevent practices that are inhumane or discriminatory against any person or group of persons.

D. Integrity—The social worker should act in accordance with the highest standards of professional integrity and impartiality.

1. The social worker should be alert to and resist the influences and pressures that interfere with the exercise of professional discretion and impartial judgement required for the performance of professional functions.

2. The social worker should not exploit professional relationships for personal gain.

E. Scholarship and Research—The social worker engaged in study and research should be guided by the conventions of scholarly inquiry.

1. The social worker engaged in research should consider carefully its possible consequences for human beings.

2. The social worker engaged in research should ascertain that the consent of participants in the research is voluntary and informed, without any implied deprivation or penalty for refusal to participate, and with due regard for participants' privacy and dignity.

3. The social worker engaged in research should protect participants from unwarranted physical or mental discomfort, distress, harm, danger, or deprivation.

4. The social worker who engages in the evaluation of services or cases should discuss them only for the professional purposes and only with persons directly and professionally concerned with them.

5. Information obtained about participants in research should be treated as confidential.

6. The social worker should take credit only for work actually done in connection with scholarly and research endeavors and credit contributions made by others.

II. The Social Worker's Ethical Responsibility to Clients

F. Primacy of Clients' Interests—The social worker's primary responsibility is to clients.

1. The social worker should serve clients with devotion, loyalty, determination, and the maximum application of professional skill and competence.

2. The social worker should serve clients with devotion, loyalty, determination, and the maximum application of professional skill and competence.

3. The social worker should not practice, condone, facilitate or collaborate with any form of discrimination on the basis or race, color, sex, sexual orientation, age, religion, national origin, marital status, political belief, mental or physical handicap, or any other preference or personal characteristic, condition or status.

4. The social worker should not condone or engage in any dual or multiple relationships with clients or former clients in which there is a risk or exploitation of or potential harm to the client. The social worker is responsible for setting clear, appropriate, and culturally sensitive boundaries.

5. The social worker should under no circumstances engage in sexual activities with clients.

6. The social worker should provide clients with accurate and complete information regarding the extent and nature of the services available to them.

7. The social worker should apprise clients of their risks, rights, opportunities, and obligations associated with social service to them.

8. The social worker should seek advice and counsel of colleagues and supervisors whenever such consultation is in the best interest of clients.

9. The social worker should terminate service to clients, and professional relationships with them, when such service and relationships are no longer required or no longer serve the clients' needs or interests.

10. The social worker should withdraw services precipitously only under unusual circumstances, giving careful consideration to all factors in the situation and taking care to minimize possible adverse effects.

11. The social worker who anticipates the termination or interruption of service to clients should notify clients promptly and seek the transfer, referral, or continuation of service in relation to the clients' needs and preferences.

G. Rights and Prerogatives of Clients— The social worker should make every effort to foster maximum self-determination on the part of clients.

1. When the social worker must act on behalf of a client who has been adjudged legally incompetent, the social worker should safeguard the interests and rights of that client.

2. When another individual has been legally authorized to act in behalf of a client, the social worker should deal with that person always with the client's best interest in mind.

3. The social worker should not engage in any action that violates or diminishes the civil of legal rights of clients.

H. Confidentiality and Privacy—The social worker should respect the privacy of clients and hold in confidence all information obtained in the course of professional service.

1. The social worker should share with others confidences revealed by clients, without their consent, only for compelling professional reasons.

2. The social worker should inform clients fully about the limits of confidentiality in a given situation, the purposes for which information is obtained, and how it may be used.

3. The social worker should afford clients reasonable access to any official social work records concerning them.

4. When providing clients with access to records, the social worker should take due care to protect the confidences of others contained in those records.

5. The social worker should obtain informed consent of clients before taping, recording, or permitting third party observation of their activities.

I. Fees—When setting fees, the social worker should ensure that they are fair, reasonable, considerate, and commensurate with the service performed and with due regard for the clients' ability to pay.

1. The social worker should not accept anything of value for making a referral.

III. The Social Worker's Ethical Responsibility to Colleagues

J. Respect, Fairness, and Courtesy—The social worker should treat colleagues with respect, courtesy, fairness, and good faith.

1. The social worker should cooperate with colleagues to promote professional interests and concerns.

2. The social worker should respect confidences shared by colleagues in the course of their professional relationships and transactions.

3. The social worker should create and maintain conditions of practice that facilitate ethical and competent professional performance by colleagues.

4. The social worker should treat with respect, and represent accurately and

fairly, the qualifications, views, and findings of colleagues and use appropriate channels to express judgements on these matters.

5. The social worker who replaces or is replaced by a colleague in professional practice should act with consideration for the interest, character, and reputation of that colleague.

6. The social worker should not exploit a dispute between a colleague and employers to obtain a position or otherwise advance the social worker's interest.

7. The social worker should seek arbitration or mediation when conflicts with colleagues require resolution for compelling professional reasons.

8. The social worker should extend to colleagues of other professions the same respect and cooperation that is extended to social work colleagues.

9. The social worker who serves as an employer, supervisor, or mentor to colleagues should make orderly and explicit arrangements regarding the conditions of their continuing professional relationship.

10. The social worker who has the responsibility for employing and evaluating the performance of other staff members, should fulfill such responsibility in a fair, considerate, and equitable manner, on the basis of clearly enunciated criteria.

11. The social worker who has the responsibility for evaluating the performance of employess, supervisees, or students should share evaluations with them.

12. The social worker should not use a professional position vested with power, such as that of employer, supervisor, teacher, or consultant, to his or her advantage or to exploit others.

13. The social worker who has direct knowledge of a social work colleague's impairment due to personal problems, psychosocial distress, substance abuse, or mental health difficulties should consult with that colleague and assist the colleague in taking remedial action.

K. **Dealing with Colleagues' Clients—The social worker has the responsibility to relate to the clients of colleagues with full professional consideration.**

1. The social worker should not assume professional responsibility for the clients of another agency or a colleague without appropriate communication with that agency or colleague.

2. The social worker who serves the clients of colleagues, during a temporary absence or emergency, should serve those clients with the same consideration as that afforded any client.

IV. The Social Worker's Ethical Responsibility to Employers and Employing Organizations

L. **Commitments to Employing Organization—The social worker should adhere to commitments made to the employing organization.**

1. The social worker should work to improve the employing agency's policies and procedures, and the efficiency and effectiveness of its services.

2. The social worker should not accept employment or arrange student field placements in an organization which is currently under public sanction by NASW for violating personnel standards, or imposing limitations on or penalties for professional actions on behalf of clients.

3. The social worker should act to prevent and eliminate discrimination in the employing organization's work assignments and in its employment policies and practices.

4. The social worker should use with scrupulous regard, and only for the purpose for which they are intended, the resources of the employing organization.

V. The Social Worker's Ethical Responsibility to the Social Work Profession

M. Maintaining the Integrity of the Profession—The social worker should uphold and advance the values, ethics, knowledge, and mission of the profession.

1. The social worker should protect and enhance the dignity and integrity of the profession and should be responsible and vigorous in discussion and criticism of the profession.
2. The social worker should take action through appropriate channels against unethical conduct by any other member of the profession.
3. The social worker should act to prevent the unauthorized and unqualified practice of social work.
4. The social worker should make no misrepresentation in advertising as to qualifications, competence, service, or results to be achieved.

N. Community Service—The social worker should assist the profession in making social services available to the general public.

1. The social worker should contribute time and professional expertise to activities that promote respect for the utility, the integrity, and the competence of the social work profession.
2. The social worker should support the formulation, development, enactment and implementation of social policies of concern to the profession.

O. Development of Knowledge—The social worker should take responsibility for identifying, developing, and fully utilizing knowledge for professional practice.

1. The social worker should base practice upon recognized knowledge relevant to social work.

2. The social worker should critically examine, and keep current with emerging knowledge relevant to social work.
3. The social worker should contribute to the knowledge base of social work and share research knowledge and practice wisdom with colleagues.

VI. The Social Worker's Ethical Responsibility to Society

P. Promoting the General Welfare—The social worker should promote the general welfare of society.

1. The social worker should act to prevent and eliminate discrimination against any person or group on the basis or race, color, sex, sexual orientation, age, religion, national origin, marital status, political belief, mental or physical handicap, or any other preference or personal characteristic, condition, or status.
2. The social worker should act to ensure that all persons have access to the resources, services, and opportunities which they require.
3. The social worker should act to expand choice and opportunity for all persons, with special regard for disadvantaged or oppressed groups and persons.
4. The social worker should promote conditions that encourage respect for the diversity of cultures which constitute American society.
5. The social worker should provide appropriate professional services in public emergencies.
6. The social worker should advocate changes in policy and legislation to improve social conditions and to promote social justice.
7. The social worker should encourage informed participation by the public in shaping social policies and institutions.

CHAPTER 2

U.S. CULTURES

America is not like a blanket—one piece of unbroken cloth, the same color, the same texture, the same size. America is more like a quilt—many pieces, many colors, many sizes, all woven and held together by a common thread.
—The Rev. Jesse Jackson ("The Fabric of a Nation," 1992)

Some readers may associate the word *culture* with refinement acquired through education as well as by reading and traveling widely, going to art museums, attending opera, ballet, and theater performances, eating exotic foods, and drinking vintage wines. Culture, however, is not restricted to these sophisticated aspects of living that are mostly part of the lives of upper- and upper-middle-class or highly educated people. The scope of culture is much broader, encompassing a society's or a group's entire way of life. That is, **culture** comprises all the customs, beliefs, values, knowledge, artifacts, and symbols (including language) shared by a social group.

Culture may be material or nonmaterial. **Material culture** encompasses people-made objects, such as cities, cars, articles of clothing, schools, churches, factories, books, paintings, computers, video recorders, vacuum cleaners, spacecraft, and so on. **Nonmaterial culture**, the kind in which we are interested, comprises all the human creations not embodied in a society's or group's physical objects, including its language, values and behavioral styles, beliefs, norms, customs, mores, and folkways (Light, Keller, & Calhoun, 1989, pp. 79–81; Robertson, 1989, p. 29).

Having absorbed more people from all over the world than any other country, the United States has become the most universal nation on earth (Wattenberg, 1991). Specifically, nearly 99 percent of the people in the United States come from places located all over the globe or are the descendants of people who originally came from somewhere else, voluntarily or involuntarily. Specifically, the U.S. population comes from all the western-European countries, Africa, Central America, South America,

the Caribbean islands, Canada, eastern Europe (including Russia and all the other states formerly part of the Soviet block), the Middle East, India, Asia, Australia, and the rest of the Pacific basin. As reflected by the 1990 census of population, only about 1 percent of the people in the United States—including American Indians, Eskimos, Aleutian Islanders, and native Hawaiians— can claim to be "native" in the sense that their ancestors have lived for all of recorded history in the area now known as the United States. But even these most native of U.S. citizens are believed to have migrated here from Asia. The United States, therefore, is a truly universal nation, and its history is one of immigration and diversity—racial, ethnic, and cultural.

As you prepare to become a social worker or other human service practitioner in this highly diverse society, it is essential that you increase your cultural competence—that is, your knowledge, understanding, and sensitivity to issues pertaining to human diversity—and your ability to work effectively with clients of different cultural backgrounds (Lum, 1986; Chau, 1990, pp. 124–125). To this end, this chapter will examine some of the major U.S. cultures, including the U.S. mainstream or Euro-American culture and the cultures of African Americans, American Indians, Latinos, Asian/Pacific Americans, American Jews, and gays and lesbians (see Figure 2.1). Cultures that coexist with the Euro-American culture in the U.S. share its values to various extents, but they also have their own distinctive values, customs, rituals, and lifestyles that set them apart from the mainstream group.

Unfortunately, culture has not been a well-established academic subject; consequently,

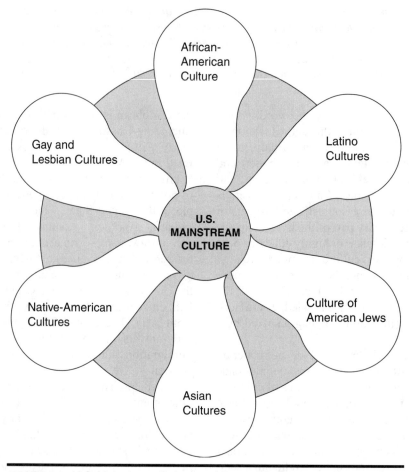

FIGURE 2.1   U.S. Mainstream Culture and Several Coexisting Nonmainstream Cultures

there has been little systematic research on it, compared to other areas of inquiry. This chapter integrates many of the research results that are available. However, much of the information included here about U.S. cultures was derived from qualitative sources of knowledge such as participant observation and descriptive accounts by practitioners and scholars, particularly sociologists, psychologists, social workers, historians, and anthropologists well versed in the various cultures and often members of each cultural group.

As you learn about U.S. cultural groups, you must be careful not to assume that each individual group member will show absolute compliance with his or her culture. People vary tremendously in the extent to which they adhere to the various cultures to which they belong, with the majority probably exhibiting some mixture of U.S. mainstream cultural values and behaviors and their other cultural traditions and behavioral styles. As a general rule, those of low socioeconomic status and limited education tend to remain closely tied (sometimes for several generations) to the traditional values and language of their racial or ethnic groups. This is because, with limited resources and education and perhaps limited ability to speak English, they often have little choice but to stay in racially or ethnically segregated, poor communities where their native language is spoken and where they may have a better chance of obtaining at least some subsistence-level employment. Although they are able to keep their original traditions, customs, and language alive in these racial/ethnic ghettos, they have limited opportunities to become acculturated to the mainstream. In contrast, individuals of higher socioeconomic status or those who are better educated and able to speak standard English tend to move away from the racial/ethnic neighborhoods to more integrated or mainstream communities. Consequently, they often show lesser degrees of adherence to their cultures of origin, especially when they also happen to be white and therefore able to blend in with the mainstream group.

In studying cultures, it is important not to overgeneralize or apply your knowledge stereotypically. Every person is unique and may behave in an entirely different manner than what you might expect given his or her cultural background. For example, regardless of the emphasis on familism in Latino cultures, your first Latino client may be detached and independent from her family. Your first African-American client may not practice any religion, regardless of the emphasis on religion or spirituality in the African-American culture.

Your first gay or lesbian client may be a right-wing conservative, regardless of the emphasis on liberalism in the gay and lesbian communities. In addition, you must guard against inadvertently making people act in accordance with your expectations of their cultural values. For example, if you assume that a Mexican-American friend will be late for engagements and you purposely show up late every time you have an appointment with this person, you are in fact setting up the situation so that he or she will fulfill your expectations. Similarly, if a practitioner communicates to an Asian-American client an expectation that he or she will show emotional restraint in accordance with traditional East Asian values, the person may feel obligated to act accordingly.

It is important to keep in mind that, like culture, socioeconomic status plays a very important role in influencing people's lifestyles, life chances, attitudes, and behaviors. Thus, as suggested by the concept of ethclass presented in Chapter 1 (Gordon, 1964; Devore & Schlesinger, 1991), cultural differences must always be interpreted in the context of specific social classes. This means that when interpreting behaviors cross-culturally, you must be careful not to attribute to culture characteristics that are primarily linked to social class. For example, poor people across different cultures tend to have limited education. In turn, deficient education is often associated with a higher than average rate of unemployment, intermittent employment, welfare dependency, family disruption, and one-parent families. It would be incorrect to attribute any of these characteristics that are primarily associated with poverty and lack of education to certain cultural groups (e.g., African Americans, mainland Puerto Ricans, or Native Americans) just because such groups happen to have a high incidence of poverty.

Finally, as you embark in this exploration of U.S. cultures, it is essential to stress that all human beings, regardless of racial or ethnic background or sexual orientation, are remarkably similar. They are similar because they share basic human needs and experiences. As you look at different cultural traditions, you must not lose sight of the fact that commonalities among culturally diverse people far outweigh differences.

BASIC ELEMENTS OF NONMATERIAL CULTURE

This section begins by examining some of the major components of nonmaterial culture, including values, norms, mores, folkways, and language (see Figure 2.2).

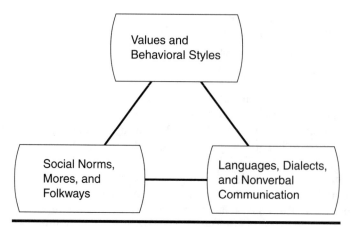

FIGURE 2.2 Basic Elements of Nonmaterial Culture

Values

Cultural **values** are socially shared notions about what is good, right, moral, or desirable, or, conversely, what is bad, wrong, immoral, or undesirable. Values color the way of life of a particular social group. For example, if a society values education, it is likely to provide mass education through a system of public schools and public universities. If it values population control, in all likelihood it will provide sex education and will make birth control devices widely available; perhaps it will also discourage excessive procreation through certain income tax disincentives or, in more repressive societies, through laws that prohibit people from having more than a certain number of children. In the same vein, if the society values democracy, it will likely keep an eye on groups that foster communist ideologies.

Social Norms

Social norms constitute another basic component of culture. They are widely shared rules or guidelines that develop in accordance with societal values and that prescribe appropriate behavior in general as well as in specific situations. Norms are generally supported by the use of sanctions (i.e., rewards for conformity and punishment for violation) usually applied informally by the group, such as family, friends, or co-workers.

Norms, as well as the values from which they are derived, vary from society to society and are often tied to societal resources. For example, because water has been plentiful in the United States, the norm of hygiene and personal grooming is to bathe frequently, generally everyday. However, people who live in desert areas of the world must conserve water; consequently, they would not be held to a "frequent bathing" norm. Similarly, it is not normative for Indians to eat beef, as cattle, especially cows, tend to be highly regarded and left undisturbed in India. This Hindu norm came into being because in India cows have always been necessary to produce milk and, above all, to bear the oxen that are essential for plowing the land in nonmechanized agricultural areas. In contrast, oxen are not needed for agriculture in the United States and there is no shortage of milk cows here; consequently, our norm of nutrition is to eat a varied diet, including beef. A growing number of people in the United States eat beef only occasionally, but they do it for entirely different reasons, such as fear of its high cholesterol content or of bacterial contamination arising from the unsanitary conditions at some slaughterhouses.

Norms not only vary cross-nationally but from group to group within the same society. For instance, in the United States, young teenagers are expected to refrain from having sex. Adults, however, are free to engage in sexual intercourse, at their own risk. Likewise, practicing Catholics are expected to attend Mass on Sundays, while Orthodox Jews are expected to observe the Sabbath. Norms also change from situation to situation. For example, at the theater or in church, people are expected to refrain from making noise, but they would not be expected to be quiet at a carnival or at a party. Similarly, you may be required to raise your hand to be recognized before speaking in class, but it would be unusual for friends to institute such rule when they are having a social conversation.

Mores and Folkways

Norms considered vital to the welfare of a society or group are called **mores**. Because they are important to society, mores are vigorously enforced. For example, the United States and most other societies have mores against incest, theft, and murder. People who violate these norms are likely to face stiff punishments, such as imprisonment or even the death penalty. To stress their importance, many mores are written into law; that is, they are enacted by the political body of the society and are enforced by its police and judicial powers.

In contrast, **folkways** are customs governing everyday behaviors and social conventions. Usually, folkways are enforced informally and may be violated without raising major concern. For example, you are not supposed to pick your nose or use foul language in public, but if you were to do so, nothing major would likely happen, although someone might raise an eyebrow, act disgusted, or make

a critical remark. You are unlikely to be officially penalized for engaging in such behaviors, however.

Language

Language refers to the verbal, nonverbal, and written symbols that enable people to communicate meanings and experiences, to talk about the past and the future, and to pass on their heritage from generation to generation. The language of each society expresses how its people perceive and understand the world and the things they have come to value, at least officially. For example, one can discern the level of sensitivity to gender issues in a particular society by the extent to which its language incorporates nonsexist words. Specifically, you may have noticed that as the United States struggles to become more accepting of females as equals, its language keeps adding more and more nonsexist terms. Thus, for example, there are no longer *mailmen* but *letter carriers*, and, in place of *policemen* and *firemen,* there are now *police officers* and *firefighters*.

The culture of a particular society influences its language, but language also influences culture by sharpening perceptions and directing attention to certain aspects of reality. This idea is known as the **linguistic-relativity hypothesis**, or Sapir-Whorf hypothesis (Sapir, 1929). For example, because snow is of critical importance to the Eskimos, their language includes many different terms to describe it. Having a large variety of terms for snow, Eskimos learn at a young age to distinguish subtle differences in the snow that surrounds them that non-Eskimos would not perceive. Transportation vehicles are probably just as critical in the U.S. culture as snow is to the Eskimos. Thus, many words have been created to refer to them. Having an extensive vocabulary to refer to such vehicles, we have become highly adept at recognizing a remarkable number of types, models, makes, and years. In sum, according to the linguistic-relativity hypothesis, when we look at the environment, we tend to perceive primarily the things for which we have words in our vocabulary. Those things for which we do not have words are more likely to pass unnoticed (Champion, Kurth, Hastings, & Harris, 1984, p. 38). More will be said about language, particularly its nonverbal aspects, when the communication process is discussed in Chapter 7.

THE ROAD TO ACCULTURATION

Having acquired a basic understanding of the concept of culture and what it encompasses, attention will now focus on two main acculturative possibilities—assimilation and biculturalism. The concept of assimilation and its appropriateness for a highly diverse nation such as the United States is discussed first.

Assimilation

Those who are **ethnocentric** judge people from other cultures by their own cultural standards rather than according to the norms and values of the other person's culture. Often, ethnocentrics also believe that their own culture and way of life are superior to others. Consequently, they tend to expect other people to speak their language and adopt their same values, customs, behavioral styles, moral standards, child-rearing practices, and marriage patterns. Such an attitude can generate conflict among diverse groups. Those who are ethnocentric often believe that assimilation is the best acculturative road for others to take. They feel that persons of different racial, ethnic, and cultural backgrounds living in the United States should adopt the U.S. mainstream culture and shed any vestiges of their original racial and ethnic cultures and native languages as soon as possible.

One problem with assimilation as an acculturation goal is that even in ideal circumstances, it takes place slowly. For example, on average, most white European immigrants who came to the United States took about three generations to become assimilated into the mainstream. Another problem is that assimilation implies that racial/ethnic cultures other than the U.S. mainstream culture are inferior since the emphasis is on discarding them. A third and perhaps the most fundamental problem with assimilation as an acculturation ideal for immigrants to the United States is that it has been beyond the reach of most people of color.

The Process of Assimilation

Assimilation is the process by which persons of diverse backgrounds slowly give up their original cultural identity and language and melt into another group, usually the core group of the host society. Gordon (1964) identified three stages in the assimilation process: cultural, structural, and marital.

Cultural Assimilation. **Cultural assimilation,** generally referred to as **acculturation**, consists of becoming able to function competently within a culture by developing an understanding of its value system and skill in behaving in accordance with the normative expectations of the culture. The person may actually adopt the norms, values, behaviors, and lifestyles of the mainstream culture as his or her own or simply develop competence in functioning within the culture. This degree of assimilation is potentially open to everyone in the United States, native born or immigrant. It does not require that members of the mainstream group accept the individual as one of their own—only that the person be able to function effectively within the mainstream culture. Of course, even this first level of acculturation may be difficult for the ghetto poor to attain because many are chronically isolated from the mainstream throughout their lives. In the case of immigrants, cultural assimilation or acculturation is generally attained by the second generation in the host country. By then, the native-born children of newcomers usually have learned to speak the mainstream language fluidly and with little if any accent and have learned the lifeways of the society. However, these individuals may also preserve their original culture and language, thus maintaining a separate identity as members of a distinct racial or ethnic group.

Structural Assimilation. To achieve **structural assimilation**, the second stage in the assimilation process, individuals must gain full acceptance and entrance into the primary groups and institutions of the mainstream group. This entails being able to enter into close friendships with members of the mainstream group and being able to attend school, work, reside, and enjoy leisure time side by side with the mainstream group as equals and full members of the society. Many **people of color** and gays and lesbians who are open about their sexual orientation have had difficulty reaching their level of assimilation into the U.S. mainstream because mainstream group members often exclude them, to various degrees, from their friendship circles, social clubs, private schools, and residential neighborhoods, and from high-level positions in work organizations, government, politics, and high-power civic, economic, and occupational networks.

Marital Assimilation. A still higher level of assimilation—**marital assimilation**—is attained by intermarriage with the mainstream group. Until recently, intermarriage was possible only among white ethnic groups. Specifically, intermarriage between whites and people of color was illegal in the United States until 1948 and remained so in 17 states until 1967 (Margolick, 1992). To this day, the vast majority of people of color are unable to marry into the mainstream group. A cultural group is not considered to be fully assimilated into the mainstream unless it has been structurally assimilated and unless there has been considerable intermarriage between its members and those of the dominant group. Thus, assimilation into the mainstream U.S. society remained an unattainable ideal in the 1990s for many non-white people and professed gays and lesbians.

Biculturalism

Assimilation into the Euro-American mainstream culture is not tenable as an acculturative objective. It not only forces everyone to conform to the same mold but it is an unrealistic goal to set for people who have been systematically excluded from full membership in this group. A more inclusive alternative is **biculturation**, based on the theory of cultural pluralism.

As noted in Chapter 1, the theory of **cultural pluralism** (Kellen, 1956; Herskovits, 1972) recognizes the strengths and merits of the cultures of all social groups and their importance as sources of identity and strength for their members. Thus, it supports each group's right to retain its customs, language, and values. However, to create a truly multicultural and pluralistic society, each social group in the United States must also be willing to support and conform to those values and practices deemed necessary for the survival of the society as a whole (Bennett, 1988, p. 37). For example, in the 1990s, some of the basic constituents of the U.S. macroculture critical to the survival of the nation as a whole (and therefore in need of support from every one of its social groups) were (1) the use of a common language as the *primary* language of the country (with English being the most practical and logical alternative); (2) acceptance of the idealized values of democracy, freedom, justice, and equality for all, values with which the United States has been traditionally identified; and (3) willingness to provide for the protection of the nation against outside aggression.

Hence, the sort of pluralism or multiculturalism affirmed in this book reinforces the right of each social group to retain its culture and identity, but it also expects every group to participate in and to contribute to the overall culture. If every group were to decide to go its separate way, the society would break apart and the United States would cease to be one nation.

Instead of dissolving or melting into the mainstream, the multicultural perspective suggests that members of most nonmainstream groups, native born or immigrant, can become part of a cultural "lumpy stew" or "tossed salad," participating in the mainstream culture while simultaneously retaining their distinctiveness. The acculturative objective from this perspective is to become **bicultural** or multicultural—that is, able to negotiate competently two or more cultures—the mainstream culture of the society and the individual's own culture(s)—each with its own set of values, beliefs, lifestyles, and behavioral expectations. The person does not need to gain full acceptance by the core societal group. He or she only needs to be protected from discrimination and to become skillful in functioning within the mainstream culture. Chestang (1976) noted that the push or motivation to become bicultural stems at least in part from the nonmainstream group member's need for certain inputs from the wider society in order to survive and prosper (e.g., employment, education, goods, and services), which forces him or her to gain some degree of competence in functioning within the mainstream.

Factors that Facilitate Socialization into a New Culture

Various factors play a role in determining the degree to which an individual is able to learn another culture. According to DeAnda (1984), these include the degree of similarity between the two cultures, the individual's physical appearance, the extent to which the person is able to speak the new language, the availability of socialization agents and positive corrective feedback, and the extent to which the individual's and the new culture's cognitive style and problem-solving approach are similar.

Before discussing DeAnda's conceptual framework, it is important to note that the degree to which people who belong to nondominant groups become bicultural is complicated by the effects of prejudice, discrimination, and oppression. For example, African Americans have had to contend not only with the task of learning to function within two cultures but also with the conflict of deciding the extent to which they want to participate in the cultural milieu of a people who have traditionally oppressed them. Their degree of motivation to do this has varied a great deal. In addition, like other nondominant group members, such as gays and lesbians and Latinos, they have had to learn coping strategies and adaptations to deal effectively with discrimination and oppression (Boykin & Toms, 1985).

Similarity between the Two Cultures. Socialization into another culture is easier if the individual's original culture and the culture the person is trying to learn are similar in the sense of overlapping considerably in terms of norms, values, customs, beliefs, behavioral styles, and so on. For example, the cultures of English-speaking Canada or England and the United States are very similar. Cultural similarity helps to explain why white European immigrants to the United States acculturated more rapidly than other immigrant groups, such as Latinos, and Asian/Pacific Americans, or indigenous groups, such as American Indians. The white European immigrants shared more values, customs, and behavioral patterns with the U.S. mainstream culture. In contrast, if the individual's own culture is highly dissimilar to the U.S. mainstream culture, such as in the case of people migrating from Cambodia or Iran, the process of biculturation is more lengthy and complex.

Similarity in Physical Appearance. In assessing bicultural potential, the role of physical appearance must also be considered. When a person looks quite different from members of a particular cultural group—perhaps because his or her skin color, facial features, or hair texture are different—socialization into this group is hindered. Similarities in physical appearance also made it easier for white European immigrants to "melt" into the U.S. mainstream group and to be given an "insider's" socialization.

Those who are physically different, such as African Americans, Asian Americans, Native Americans, or dark-skinned Latinos, are more likely to be treated as "outsiders."

Bilingualism. The person's ability to speak or learn to speak another language also plays a role in determining potential for biculturation. Specifically, the greater the English language proficiency of an individual, the more his or her socialization into the U.S. mainstream culture is facilitated and the easier it is for the person to function competently within the society. Conversely, the more limited the person's command of the language of the mainstream group, the more the process of biculturation is hindered. This applies not only to people whose native languages are not English but also to native-born English speakers whose cultural dialect differs significantly from standard English, such as speakers of "Black English." If their command of standard English is deficient, their ability to function within the mainstream culture is hampered.

Socialization Agents. Another variable that plays a role in determining bicultural potential is the availability of socialization agents. Bicultural socialization is facilitated when the person has access to socialization agents from both cultures, such as translators, mediators, or models. According to DeAnda (1984), *translators* are bicultural persons from an individual's own cultural group (e.g., friends, co-workers, fellow church members) who are willing to share their experiences with and knowledge of the mainstream culture to facilitate the person's acculturation. *Mediators* are individuals from the mainstream culture (e.g., teachers, co-workers, social workers, peers, mentors) who are willing to help the person in the socialization process. *Models* are people whose behavior the individual emulates to learn to act in concert with the normative expectations of the culture the individual is trying to learn.

Positive Corrective Feedback. The availability of positive corrective feedback also plays a role in determining the extent to which a person may be able to become bicultural. Although one can become acquainted with a particular culture simply by observing its members in action, corrective feedback is often necessary in order to fine-tune one's behaviors. Generally, the more available corrective feedback is, the higher the chances that a person's behaviors will conform to cultural expectations. In other words, biculturation is facilitated when there is someone available to provide feedback about the errors the individual has committed (such as in English pronunciation), to demonstrate more appropriate behaviors or responses, and to offer positive reinforcement. If only negative feedback is given, the recipient of this negative assessment is likely to become frustrated and to stop trying to emulate behaviors.

Two other determinants of bicultural potential, according to DeAnda (1984), are the cognitive style and problem-solving skills of the individual and the extent to which they are similar to the prevalent styles of the culture the person is trying to learn. For example, other things being equal, persons who think in analytical terms and who have good problem-solving skills will have an easier time becoming bicultural than those whose cognitive styles are nonanalytic or who do not have good problem-solving skills. This is because those with analytic and problem-solving skills will be better able to define the essential components of the socialization tasks they must accomplish and they will have a better repertoire of strategies to work on these tasks.

Other Factors. The acculturation potential of immigrants to the United States, in particular, and the speed with which they will be able to become bicultural is dependent on additional factors not mentioned by DeAnda (1984). These include the person's age at the time of immigration and his or her educational level, degree of motivation to learn the new culture, possession of certain personality traits, and prior exposure to the host culture (Kim, 1988). Specifically, older immigrants generally experience more difficulty in adjusting to a new culture and are slower in acquiring the new cultural patterns and learning the new language than younger immigrants. Education also facilitates acculturation because it increases the individual's capacity to deal with new learnings and challenges. Character traits such as sociability, willingness to take risks, perseverance, motivation to learn, open-mindedness, tolerance for ambiguity, and intellectual flexibility also tend to facilitate acculturation.

Finally, those who develop some familiarity with the U.S. mainstream culture prior to immigration, perhaps through previous travel or through the mass media, are likely to become bicultural sooner than those who have had no prior exposure to the host culture. Persons of higher socioeconomic status also tend to acculturate faster than those of lower socioeconomic status, probably because they are more likely to have lifestyles and values similar to those of the mainstream culture, to be better educated, and to have had prior exposure to the U.S. culture and its language.

Multiculturalism

The United States is a nation composed of immigrants of all races and nationalities. It also includes a small native-born population who are the descendants of indigenous Indian tribes originally conquered and subjugated by the colonists as well as a large population of descendants of Africans most of whom were originally brought in against their will as slaves. For such a highly diverse society, a multicultural/pluralistic acculturative mode seems more suitable than the melting pot/assimilatory standard that worked only for white immigrants of European extraction. Assimilation as an acculturation ideal marginalized, segregated, and disenfranchised nondominant groups members who had no chance of assimilating, particularly the

racially and ethnically different such as African Americans, Asian/Pacific Islanders, dark-skinned Latinos, and American Indians.

Although cultural pluralism is a more realistic standard for a heterogeneous nation such as the United States, it is not a panacea. It challenges those who do not belong to the U.S. mainstream to become competent in negotiating the Euro-American or mainstream culture. Cultural pluralism also requires a high degree of cultural knowledge and sensitivity on the part of the mainstream group. For the remainder of this chapter on U.S. cultures we take on the challenge of becoming more truly multicultural in our perspective.

THE U.S. MAINSTREAM CULTURE

The **mainstream culture** is the culture of the **dominant group** in the society—that is, the culture of the so-called establishment or group in control of major societal institutions and resources. In the United States of the 1990s, this was the culture of the white Euro-American middle-class composed primarily of native-born Anglo-Americans (i.e., descendents of immigrants from Great Britain—England, Scotland, or Wales), German Americans, and Irish Americans (see Table 2.1), as well as many other white native-born U.S. citizens of European extraction, such as Italian Americans, French Americans, American Ashkenazic Jews, Scandinavian Americans, and Polish Americans. Only recently has it become fash-

TABLE 2.1 Three Largest Mainstream Cultural Groups in the United States

ANCESTRY	POPULATION
German	57.9 million
Irish	38.7 million
Anglo	32.6 million

Sources: Based on "Portrait of America: A Time of Great Change and Growing Poverty," *The New York Times,* May 29, 1992, p. A12. Population figures taken from U.S. Bureau of the Census, 1990.

ionable to group people of such different ethnic backgrounds under the "European" umbrella, probably because white ethnics now realize, as the tide of Anglo dominance subsides, that by closing ranks under a broader umbrella they will be able to continue to exert major influence on U.S. society (Rubin, 1992). This section begins the study of U.S. cultures by examining this Euro-American culture in terms of its fundamental values.

In this section, we will examine the principal values that characterize the U.S. mainstream culture, including activity and work; achievement and success; individualism, freedom, and independence; efficiency and practicality; affluence, material comfort, and consumerism; competition; democracy; mobility; openness, directness, informality, egalitariansim, and equal opportunity; moralism; humanitarianism and generosity; self-fulfillment; perception of time as a valubale resource; and emphasis on progress, youth, and the future.

An increasing number of social scientists believe that the U.S. mainstream culture no longer has a core of clearly identifiable values because of its increasing diversity and the consequent diffusion of cultural traits (Abercrombie, Hill, & Turner, 1990). Undoubtedly, the component values of the U.S. mainstream culture are becoming more difficult to specify; yet there still is a set of values traditionally associated with "American culture." Keep in mind, however, that not every Euro-American of middle-class status subscribes to this traditional ideology that has always been more characteristically male than female (Wilkinson, 1992). It is equally important to understand that many individuals who are not middle class or who are not of European extraction, both immigrant and native born, have adopted the mainstream values to be discussed in this section to various extents. Many immigrants from nondominant racial and ethnic groups migrated to the United States precisely because they believed in and were attracted to the values that comprise the mainstream ideology and have embraced them

more thoroughly and enthusiastically than many Euro-Americans.

As we review the principal values that have traditionally defined the U.S. mainstream culture (Williams, 1970; Arensberg & Niehoff, 1964; Rokeach, 1973), it is important to note that many of these core values are *idealized* and that the reality is often contradictory. We should also note that the values the mainstream group holds for itself are not always the very same values they would want to see realized for nondominant groups.

Misunderstandings surrounding values are likely to arise when a Euro-American middle-class practitioner expects clients to behave in accordance with his or her ideology while clients perhaps subscribe to a different set of values. Therefore, it is important to recognize that the traditional mainstream ideology, which perhaps many of the readers share and have come to consider "second nature," is not universally accepted in the United States or in other parts of the world.

Activity and Work

The traditional Euro-American middle-class ideology places high value on activity and hard work. For example, you may have noticed that many people in the United States become uneasy, unhappy, or may even feel guilty unless they are doing something all the time. Keeping busy and "being on the go" are desirable in and of themselves. Of course, it is better to be busy doing something useful and productive rather than to be engaged in busywork. Some individuals even "play hard"—keeping a busy schedule even when they are on vacation. They seem to feel obligated to pack a great deal of activity into their vacation days even though they are off from work and supposedly resting.

The Euro-American traditional emphasis on hard work probably stems from the Puritan belief that "an idle mind is the devil's playground" (Hallman et al., 1983, p. 54). However, the Protestant Ethic, which valued work for its own sake, has less currency nowadays (Yankelovich, 1981; Wolfe, 1991). Now, many people value work as a means of attaining success and material comfort rather than as an end in itself. Many well-established Euro-American families express concern about their children not having the same work ethic and high drive as their parents and grandparents. The children of many recent immigrants seem more highly driven, in comparison.

Achievement and Success

The mainstream culture traditionally has valued personal achievement and success, particularly those accomplishments that lead to occupational advancement and affluence. "Fast-track" parents start early, "anxiously programming their tots for success" (Wilkinson, 1992, p. 30). Money is given respect and is commonly viewed as a symbol of success and personal worth. Those who are self-made and who have gone "from rags to riches" have been particularly admired. The meaning of success, however, has evolved through the years since the 1950s when it was more frequently defined by external and concrete symbols, such as the possession of luxury cars, fur coats, and expensive jewelry. Now, the definition of success is more flexible. Some people still seek externals to impress others, such as big homes, flashy cars, and designer clothes (Wilkinson, 1992), while others emphasize more personal types of success, such as autonomy (the freedom to make one's own decisions), self-expression, inner growth, and personal fulfillment (Yankelovich, 1984; Herdt, 1992; Riesman, 1992).

The middle class typically believes that with effort, hard work, and perseverance, one can attain success, surpass obstacles and difficulties, and solve problems. "We can do it" has been their traditional motto (Perry, 1992). You may have heard comments such as "Where there is a will, there is a way" or references to the "git-up-and-git" attitude of "Americans." The general belief is that one should not give

up, and if one fails, one should try again. Persistence is highly valued, and, for them, it has usually paid off. Recently, the intractability of various social problems—acquired immune deficiency syndrome (AIDS), drug abuse, crime, homelessness, and violence—and the realization that there is a limit to the amount of money the society can spend on these problems are having a dampening effect on the traditional mainstream "can-do" mentality of the mainstream culture.

People who have long suffered poverty and hardship as well as those whose ancestors were conquered, enslaved, or subjected to racism and oppression tend to be less optimistic than Euro-Americans because, given the experiences of their own cultural group, success is often beyond their reach. Many have learned to value endurance and acceptance of their limited circumstances rather than effort and perseverance. Some well-intentioned middle-class practitioners would like them to be better motivated, to have more initiative, to try harder, and to persevere in their pursuits. But some clients from nonmainstream groups may be resistant and evasive because, from their perspective, big efforts are costly in terms of personal investment of energy and usually do not pay. It takes time, sensitivity, understanding, and acceptance on the part of practitioners to get such clients to trust them enough to gather the courage to put forth effort at the risk of failing. If their clients are able to achieve some positive results, they are more likely to try again.

Individualism, Freedom, and Independence

The mainstream culture has traditionally stressed the importance of self-reliance, self-direction, and self-expression; the freedom to make choices and to lead one's life as one sees fit; as well as the consequent responsibility for one's actions. People like to do "their own thing," to be their own person, to think for themselves, to speak their minds, and to make their own decisions. This ideology of individualism was traditionally more characteristic of males than females (Potter, 1992b), although many females nowadays, particularly those who work outside the home, have embraced it to various extents.

As part of the emphasis on independence, late adolescents or young adults characteristically are expected to move away from their parents' homes, even if they are not married, and to start a life of their own. As they leave home, their parents are conditioned to view the "empty nest," even if it feels painful initially, as a mark of successful parenting (Tropman, 1989).

Outside the family, society also emphasizes personal freedoms. These include the freedom of speech and assembly, the freedom to conduct one's own private business enterprise, the freedom of religion, and political freedoms.

Bellah, Madsen, Sullivan, Swidler, and Tipton (1985) suggested that in recent decades American individualism has become more self-serving, with many people seeking primarily to maximize their own interests. You may have heard the question, What's in this for me? and if there is no clear personal advantage, you may have noticed that some people refuse to commit themselves or want to get "out." For example, if marriage no longer provides personal fulfillment, some people today want a quick divorce rather than to work at their marital problems. If work in a particular organization does not primarily satisfy their personal career goals, as opposed to the goals of the organization or the society, they want to move on to another job that better promotes their personal objectives. The author is in no way implying that one should stay in a bad marriage or in an unfulfilling job. The point being made is that some people seem to put too much emphasis on promoting their own agenda and much less on working together for the common good. Fortunately, this self-serving individualism appears to have reached a peak in the 1980s, and people now seem to be returning to a less extreme version balanced by greater commitment to others and to the environment (Yankelovich, 1981).

Individualism traditionally has been less valued by U.S. women and, as you will see later in this chapter, it is also less valued by most nonmainstream groups in U.S. society. For example, African-American, Latino, Asian-American, and Native-American cultures place a higher value on collectivism, cooperation, interdependence, group harmony, and mutual responsibility than on individualism (Markus & Kitayama, 1991). These are values many mainstream women have traditionally embraced.

Efficiency and Practicality

Members of the mainstream group are typically businesslike, down-to-earth, and practical people. They value technological innovations because these help to get things done quickly and efficiently. They usually prefer what is practical and useful over what is primarily intellectual, philosophical, spiritual, or mystical.

The traditional emphasis on practicality and efficiency has resulted in a tendency to concentrate on immediate problems and short-range goals rather than on longer-term consequences. In business and industry, the short-term, bottom-line mentality has put the United States at somewhat of a disadvantage in relation to other nations that have taken a longer-range perspective (e.g., Japan). This way of thinking, which favors immediate results, often has also resulted in a disregard of the environment, with business frequently dumping industrial wastes in sensitive areas, and in the contamination of the air with noxious chemicals—situations that increasingly threaten our health and that of future generations. To be sure, the United States is not the only or the worst environmental offender in the world.

Affluence, Material Comfort, and Consumerism

Since the Depression, the mainstream culture has put emphasis on the United States as a land of plentiful abundance and on the good life, material comfort, and consumerism (Potter, 1954; Packard, 1957). People value big houses, spacious cars, and all sorts of technological conveniences, such as computers, cellular phones, video recorders, and fax machines. They practically would not know how to get by without such staple everyday "necessities" as washing machines, clothes dryers, dishwashers, central air conditioners/heaters, microwaves, and cable television.

Shopping is a major leisure activity that has taken on the characteristics of a sport. Many people put considerable value on the material possessions they acquire (Seigel, 1992). The constant bombardment of advertising through the media reinforces a continuing desire for the latest in creature comforts. Thus, people "need" a variety of credit cards, and the easy availability of "plastic" leads many to incur high levels of personal debt and to save little money for emergencies and for retirement.

This ideology of affluence that has been so characteristic of the U.S. mainstream may be undergoing revision now that the economy has stopped expanding rapidly and the new generation coming of age is finding it increasingly harder to attain the same socioeconomic status as their parents (Newman, 1991). As more of the middle class experience the reality of downward mobility, dreams of the good life are being "downsized."

Competition

Together with capitalism, competition has been the fundamental principle and driving force behind the system of free enterprise that has been such an integral part of the U.S. culture. Accordingly, society has traditionally prepared its citizens from an early age, particularly the men, to compete in practically every area of their lives, whether it be in academics, sports, business, or even social relations. Euro-Anglo American

Some conformity to the work organization and expectations that the person will be a good "team player" are valued (Whyte, 1992), but usually within the framework of competition. Traditionally, women have placed greater value

on caring for others, connectedness, and cooperation rather than competition, and many other social groups such as African Americans, Latinos, American Indians, and Asian Americans have also put more emphasis on collectivism than Euro-American males. This may be one of the reasons why the United States appears to be growing less fiercely competitive (Yankelovich, 1981).

Democracy

Majority rule is widely accepted. Those who disagree with the majority normally remain willing to go along with the majority, as long as they think that the decision process was fair and that they will have the opportunity to promote their point of view and to carry the majority at another time (Tropman & Cox, 1987). The U.S. mainstream also puts emphasis on responsibilities that are part of the democratic system of governance such as active participation in community affairs and in the political process that elects representatives of the people to govern this nation.

Mobility

The mainstream group traditionally has been "on the move" (Pierson, 1992). In fact, their history has been one of continuous movement—movement to the United States from the British Isles and Europe, west to California, north to Alaska, over to Hawaii, and out to the moon and outer space (Hallman et al., 1983).

Upward mobility—or the desire to "get ahead," to search for new opportunities, and to maximize career development—has prompted many people to move frequently from one location to another. This high geographic mobility has left many without ready access to family members who may reside thousands of miles away. Mobility has also restricted the opportunity of many individuals to develop roots in one local community and to cultivate close and lasting friendships. In recent years, however, the

low cost of long-distance telephoning and air fares have made frequent communication and visitation more feasible.

Having limited opportunities to obtain companionship and emotional support from close relatives and intimate friends who often reside far away, many in the mainstream group have learned to substitute by "joining" groups and by practicing a less intimate form of sociability (Pierson, 1992). Accordingly, they may become involved in various organizations and associations and in social, recreational, and hobby clubs, as well as in a large variety of self-help groups. These associations tend to be transitory, usually lasting as long as they fulfill personal goals or as long as the person resides in a given locality. When the person moves elsewhere, he or she can join a new set of groups.

In recent years, the traditional mobility of the mainstream group has been declining, with a higher proportion moving within the same urban area from central city to the suburbs rather than across large geographic areas (Wolfe, 1991). This increasing residential stability may have salutary effects on the attachment to the local community and on the strength of emotional ties.

Openness, Directness, Informality, Egalitarianism, and Equal Opportunity

Members of the U.S. mainstream cultural group typically have simple, unaffected manners, dress casually, and are friendly, spontaneous, and informal in their interactions with others. They usually relate on a first-name basis and are open and straightforward in their communications. They like to meet problems head on and to put the cards on the table, so to speak (Hallman et al., 1983, p. 47). In contrast, people from many other countries are more formal in their relationships and deportment or may consider it more important to be polite than honest. Consequently, foreigners and people from other racial/ethnic groups in the United States are sometimes offended by the informality and directness (often considered excessive) of the typical mainstream Euro-American.

The mainstream group is also not particularly class conscious. In other countries, people from privileged groups are used to receiving more deference and subservience from others, and the rich tend to be more ostentatious.[1] In comparison, the mainstream group is fairly egalitarian in manners and, by and large, tends to treat others as equals without assuming a superior or deferent attitude (Lipset, 1992; Potter, 1992a). At least ideally, the mainstream group also subscribes to the principle of meritocracy. According to the ideology of meritocracy, people are supposed to be rewarded or given respect for actual achievements rather than because of any inborn qualities or family background. The reality, however, is that many people get ahead because of special connections, family pull, political pull, or the help of a mentor or sponsor, and not necessarily on the basis of sheer merit or competence (Tropman, 1989).

The U.S. core culture traditionally has put emphasis on fairness and equality of opportunity as an idealized goal; these ideals, however, have not been consistently practiced. That is, in principle it is believed that everyone should get a fair break and that each person should be given the opportunity to seek societal rewards and to strive for success (Silber, 1989; Lipset, 1990; Potter, 1992a). However, not until recently was equality extended to women and some other nondominant group members, such as African Americans, Latinos, and Native Americans. To do this, it has been necessary to pass laws prohibiting discrimination and to institute affirmative action programs that have given them greater access to educational and occupational opportunities. Yet, the use of affirmative action to give women and some other nondominant groups their fair share of equality often clashes with the mainstream/male ideology of merit and competition, and therefore frequently results in complaints of reverse discrimination. As of the mid-1990s, other social groups (e.g., gays and lesbians) were still denied full civil rights in the U.S. society.

Moralism

The U.S. mainstream culture has been more "puritanical," so to speak, than that of other advanced Western nations. People in U.S. society frequently moralize about the poor, welfare recipients, those who suffer from AIDS, gays and lesbians, prostitutes, alcoholics, criminals, ghetto dwellers, juvenile delinquents, and so on (Tropman, 1989). For instance, you may have heard comments that gays are immoral, that people are poor or commit crimes because they are not willing to work hard like the rest of us, and so on.

Another instance of mainstream "puritanism" is the insistence on holding public officials and candidates for public office to a higher standard of sexual behavior than the rest of the population. For example, regardless of job competence, in the mid-1990s, a U.S. public official risked losing political office if it were discovered that the person was having or had had an extramarital liaison or was gay or lesbian. In light of the personal shortcomings of many of the world's greatest leaders throughout history, few Europeans, for instance, would understand why people in the United States consider such private matters relevant if the person is otherwise competent and is doing a good job as a public official. Sometimes members of the U.S. mainstream are also quick to pass judgment on the morality of the customs of other societies with fundamentally different value standards instead of attempting to understand them.

Humanitarianism and Generosity

The United States is considered one of the most giving nations on earth. Historically, it has taken pride in being a haven for the downtrodden and the oppressed, even though its welcoming spirit seems to be wearing thin these days as a million or more immigrants continue to pour into this traditional land of opportunity every year.

The mainstream group traditionally responds promptly to calls for help and gives generously to those experiencing personal hardships or mass disasters. Typically, this humanitarianism is expressed in organized, institutional, and impersonal ways. For instance, those in the mainstream are more likely to make donations to organizations that help the needy (such as churches, the Red Cross, the Salvation Army, and other charitable institutions) than to give personal alms directly to the poor, as is customary in other less-advanced countries.

The genuine generosity and humanitarianism of the mainstream group is hard to reconcile with its continuing exploitation of and discrimination against legal and illegal immigrants, African Americans, Latinos, and other non-dominant group members, and its inattention to the plight of the nation's children. The mainstream group has come a long way in the sense that it officially condemns racial, ethnic, and gender discrimination (verbally perhaps more consistently than in practice), promotes human rights (sometimes more forcefully in relation to other countries than within the United States), and shows concern for the health, housing, living conditions, and economic situation of less fortunate members of the society (Tropman & Cox, 1987, p. 231). Up to the mid-1990s, the establishment had been considerably less inclined to extend full human rights to gays and lesbians and to condemn discrimination against them. It had also shown a lack of resolve to commit sufficient resources to improve the life chances of the nation's children.

Self-Fulfillment

A period of emphasis on duty, obligation, and responsibility lasted up to the 1950s. In the 1960s, however, as the antiestablishment student protests and civil rights movement got under way, a significant portion of the U.S. mainstream developed greater interest in seeking self-fulfillment and self-expression. Reich (1992) suggested that the salience of the African-American culture in society since the mid-sixties may have played a role in making the mainstream culture more expressive. At any rate, some Euro-Americans put emphasis on liberating themselves from commitments and role obligations and strived toward the attainment of greater self-awareness, pleasure, emotional fulfillment, expressiveness, a freer attitude toward sex, harmony with nature, and more sensitive relationships (Yankelovich, 1984; Reich, 1992). Beginning in the late 1970s and during the 1980s, segments of the mainstream group got carried away in the search for self-fulfillment and became increasingly egocentric and self-indulgent (Yankelovich, 1981; Bellah et al., 1985; Lasch, 1992). Known as the "me generation" (Wolfe, 1976), this group put emphasis on being "number one"—that is, on giving priority to their own needs and wants above everyone else's (Yankelovich, 1981). Some became self-serving, greedy, and less socially concerned (Astin, Green, & Korn, 1987; Astin, Korn, & Berz, 1990).

There are indications that this self-centeredness that afflicted some Euro-Americans recently peaked in the 1980s and is now on the wane, having proved itself largely unsuccessful in leading to greater self-realization or meaning in life. Thus, the struggle to attain self-fulfillment appears to have shifted to a higher ground. Pleasure has been redefined so that it now includes a greater concern with health, physical fitness, nutrition, sobriety, relational rather than recreational sex, and abstinence from drugs. The self-centeredness is still there, but it is modulated by greater discipline and self-restraint. In addition, more people are now putting emphasis on commitment as a means of attaining meaning and fulfillment in life. This includes commitment to closer and deeper personal relationships (not necessarily within the context of marriage), fidelity and romance, one's job or career, one's cultural group(s), the local community, self-expression and creativity, nature and preservation of the environment, historic preservation, social reform and service to others (Yankelovich, 1981; Herdt, 1992; Schaeffer & Lamm, 1992).

Perception of Time as a Valuable Resource

The mainstream group puts a premium on time, which they schedule, regulate, and measure exactly. Punctuality is very important because "time is money." Involvements in various aspects of life such as friendships and community or church-related affairs are often evaluated in terms of the time investments they require vis-à-vis the benefits they bring. Traditionally, the prerogative to consider time valuable has belonged to men more than to women since, until recently, the society has expected women to raise children, care for the sick and the elderly, offer emotional support to the family, and do most of the housework without regard for the heavy time investments these roles require or the cost to their personal or work lives (Sirianni & Walsh, 1991).

People with a rural, nonindustrial background, such as many recent immigrants and refugees, do not consider time as valuable a commodity as Euro-Americans; consequently, they are less likely to measure it exactly or schedule it precisely. As you will see later in this chapter, American Indians, Latinos, and African Americans are also, generally speaking, less concerned about being punctual than Euro-Americans.

The possibility for misunderstandings around the concept of time arises when a person who is not part of the U.S. mainstream is late or early for an appointment and the middle-class Euro-American practitioner interprets such behavior as indicative that the person lacks motivation or is resistant, impolite, or uninterested in help. The worker may get upset because the client seems to disregard the importance of the worker's valuable time. The client may be puzzled that the practitioner puts so much emphasis on time.

Emphasis on Progress, Youth, and the Future

In its short history since gaining independence in 1776, the United States experienced continuous growth and economic progress up to the early 1970s (with occasional interludes, such as the Depression of the 1930s). Consequently, the mainstream group became used to the idea of limitless progress (Williams, 1970, p. 468; Yankelovich, 1984). The societal accomplishments have been numerous—landing on the moon, many diseases conquered, the life expectancy dramatically increased, and infant mortality significantly reduced (at least for the babies of the mainstream group). In this land of plenty, parents were able to attain a higher standard of living than grandparents, and their children did significantly better than them. Industrial and technological progress has been staggering. Hence, the deeply ingrained tendency of the mainstream group became to look forward to the future with optimism rather than to reminisce about the past.

Since the late 1970s, it has become increasingly clear that the United States has paid a steep price for progress—damage to the environment and to the ozone layer due to industrial excesses, strains on the health care system and on the social security system due to an increasingly aging population resulting from the increase in the life expectancy, unprecedented traffic leading to gridlock in many urban areas due to the tremendous increase in cars, and so on (Lasch, 1992). As the pains of progress became clearer, there were also increasing signs that the uninterrupted period of economic prosperity might be coming to an end as the national debt soared, the economy became deindustrialized and more dependent on high-technological skills, and the supply of jobs for those with less education shrank. Given these new harsher realities, the mainstream's optimistic embracement of progress and the future may have to undergo some revision (Wolfe, 1991).

Given the traditional emphasis on progress and the future, the U.S. core culture has valued youth more highly than old age and has favored new and modern things over those that are old and traditional. This is because, in the experience of U.S. society, new things have been an improvement over those older and traditional. From that perspective, the aged often have not been appreciated for their wisdom and experience, as they are in some other parts of the world, and they have not been particularly respected, honored, or consulted. In fact, many people do not have the patience to listen to old folks and often dismiss them as senile.

Other societies, particularly those that had better times in the past than at present, have a different attitude toward the old and traditional. For them, old ways are tried and true, and newness has little value unless it is a real improvement over traditional ways. People in societies that have lost ground over the years may contrast the magnificence of their old buildings with the shabbiness of modern structures that begin to fall apart even before they are completed. In such cultures, the past is given emphasis, and old people are respected and consulted and acknowledged for their wisdom.

Many nonmainstream cultures in the United States (e.g., African-American, Latino, Asian-American, and Native-American cultures) value and respect the aged. Some members of these cultural groups might consider unacceptable a practitioner's suggestion that they put their elderly parent in a long-term care facility or nursing home because of the family disruption the old person may be causing and the extent to which home care drains their energies. It is important to appreciate the guilt some people might feel in taking such action and the rejection they might have to face from relatives and friends because doing so goes against the

cultural tradition of respecting and honoring the elderly and taking care of them within the family.

AFRICAN-AMERICAN CULTURE

One of the most longstanding cultures in the United States, the African-American culture combines elements from three main strands: the minority experience, West African cultural traditions, and U.S. mainstream culture. Specifically, African-American culture incorporates many coping strategies and adaptations developed primarily to ward off racism, discrimination, and oppression and to survive under economically deprived circumstances. It also includes many West African cultural traditions modified during the course of 300 years of contact with and exposure to the U.S. mainstream culture (Cole, 1970; Boykin & Toms, 1985).

The collective experiences of African Americans, including a shared history of slavery, economic deprivation, and institutionalized racism, coupled with an African heritage modulated by continuous exposure to the Euro-American culture, have resulted in a unique blend of cultural values as well as a strong feeling of connectedness and solidarity among the members of this cultural group. Notwithstanding this shared heritage, we must not lose sight of the fact that every African American is a unique individual in terms of the extent to which he or she shares the traditional values of the group, depending on factors such as education, socioeconomic status, age, rural/urban/suburban residence, and regional/geographic background (e.g., southerners versus northeasterners). Generally, younger, well-educated, middle- or upper-middle-class African Americans are likely to be conversant with the U.S. mainstream culture and to show in their behaviors, values, and lifestyles a blend of the two cultures. In contrast, less educated inner-city or rural folks, low-income persons, or those who are older are more likely to show a higher degree of adherence to traditional African-American cultural values and a lower level of acculturation to the mainstream culture.

This section examines major aspects of the African-American traditional culture. Family-related values and customs are covered in greater detail in Chapter 9. Demographic data describing the current situation of African Americans in the United States are provided in Chapter 4.

The Impact of Slavery

The historical experience of slavery has been critical in shaping the essence of the African-American people. It not only robbed them of many aspects of their cultural heritage, such as family life and use of their native languages, but it gave them a great capacity to endure pain and sorrow and remarkable strength to deal with adversity. However, it is important to know that not all African Americans share a history of slavery. The earliest African immigrants to the United States came as indentured servants, not slaves, and gained their freedom after working for a fixed number of years. Their children were free from the moment they were born. Early in the history of the United States, the descendents of some of these African immigrants became highly educated and attained considerable wealth (Sowell, 1978).

Although slavery obliterated many aspects of the African cultural heritage, it reinforced at least some African values. For example, in West Africa (the area from which most African slaves were imported to the United States), women were neither socially nor economically dependent on their husbands. Rather, they were socialized to earn their own way and not to expect their husbands to take care of them. In the United States, female slaves could not depend on male slaves for protection or economic assistance as white women depended on white men; consequently, slavery served to reinforce the African-American female slaves' equality vis-à-vis male slaves (Davenport & Yurich, 1991; Haile & Johnson, 1989).

Slaves were also allowed to retain certain nonthreatening elements of their cultures such as their music and dancing. This is probably an important reason why the African-American culture has traditionally had high regard for music and dance. In a society that tolerated and even appreciated their artistic creations while preventing them from expressing their abilities in many other ways, African Americans learned to express themselves through spirituals, the blues, jazz, soul, and "rap" as well as through dance (Smith, 1981; Jackson, 1986).

African-American Core Values

Extended Family

The extended-family kinship system is a fundamental part of the African heritage and a major source of social and emotional support. African Americans across all socioeconomic levels tend to maintain stronger kinship bonds than Euro-Americans (Hatchett & Jackson, 1993). These ties become especially evident in times of crisis, illness, celebration, or death. Particularly those who belong to the less mobile, lower socioeconomic group interact frequently with a broad range of blood-related and nonblood-related kin. These include grandparents, adult brothers and sisters, boyfriends and girlfriends, aunts and uncles, cousins, nieces and nephews, neighbors, boarders, preachers and deacons, and various friends considered to be part of the family.

Elderly members of the family are respected for the wisdom they possess, which comes from having been through many hardships, having overcome adversity, and having "learned how to keep on keepin' on" (White & Parham, 1990, p. 74). In addition, they have been respected as keepers of the oral literature inherited from their ancestors.

Communalism and Cooperation

In contrast to the U.S. mainstream culture that traditionally has favored competition and individualism, the African ideology values cooperation over competition, and interdependence over individualism and independence. Kin group members establish close, reciprocal relationships in which there is a mutual exchange of goods and services and help with child care and other problems of living. For example, an uncle may take his nephew in his home for a couple of years to get him away from bad influences in the neighborhood where the boy resides. In return, the boy's mother may put one of her brother's children through college or she may take in one of his children at a crisis point in the youngster's life. This mutual aid system has served African Americans well in an often hostile social environment.

Spirituality/Religion and the Church

Many traditional African Americans show a high level of spirituality—that is, respect for the transcending forces that may significantly affect them (Boykin & Toms, 1985). Spirituality, religiosity, and prayer have served this cultural group well as survival mechanisms and sources of strength. In addition, the music and verbal expressions that are part of church services have helped African Americans to release tensions and emotions (Jones, 1990).

African-American churches of various denominations have played a central role in their members' lives, not only by nourishing their souls but also by providing social services. Additionally, they have served a very important function as training ground for the development of leadership and political skills and therefore as vehicles for fostering self-esteem and a positive identity.

Death that is not violent or premature is generally perceived positively and taken as an occasion to celebrate that the person has completed his or her journey in this world. Traditionally, extended family and friends as well as church members come together at the funeral "to testify to the fact that the deceased has fought the battle, borne the burden, and finished the course" (White & Parham, 1990, p. 75). In short, those who attend the funeral come to say, "You did it well." Because of this generally positive attitude toward death, public celebration is sometimes part of the funeral and mourning process. For example, in New Orleans, many funerals, especially funerals for musicians and other artists, include a parade to the cemetery with a jazz band to get the deceased started on the next leg of his or her journey. After the funeral, it is customary for the participants to get together to eat and drink and talk about the good times they shared with the deceased.

Cultivating a Distinctive Personal Style

Spontaneity of expression is highly valued in the traditional African-American culture (Kochman, 1981, 1988). Accordingly, many people put emphasis on developing a distinctive personal style and on adding their personal touch or signature on the things they do.

Many people enjoy engaging in stylized and personalized behaviors. For instance, some of you may recall the elaborate handshakes of the 1960s and 1970s called "giving skin" that were used to show solidarity, power, and African-American identity. Inner-city youth, in particular, took great pleasure in the more elaborate hand, elbow, and hip movements that used to be referred to as "dapping." A popular hand gesture today is the "thumb grasp," which involves various ways of encircling the thumbs while the hands are grasped together. The "high five," often seen in sporting events, involves the mutual raising of right arms up in the air with the palms open while the two persons grasp or touch each other's palms. Still observable today is the rhythmic walking style, sort of like a walking dance (which used to be referred to as "bopping" in the 1960s and 1970s). Bopping was favored by some young African-

American males as a way of calling attention to themselves and showing off their masculinity and pride in self and race (Majors, 1991). These stylized ways of expressing one's individuality within the culture change from generation to generation, sometimes even from year to year.

Another example of the African-American taste for style is the way clothing and accessories are used as vehicles to make statements about oneself (Majors, 1991). For example, some people enjoy wearing flashy and flamboyant attire, jewelry, and other adornments, perhaps including hat and sunglasses (shades), to create a special image. Given the cultural emphasis on style, teenagers are often reluctant to remove all the paraphernalia they like to wear, as frequently required by the schools, because doing so destroys their especially-created image.

Another way of making a dramatic self-presentation is the cultural tradition of boasting and showing off, more common among lower socioeconomic groups, such as in showboating or grandstanding (or "styling out"). In contrast, Euro-Americans have a tradition of modesty and self-restraint (Kochman, 1981; McNeely & Badami, 1984). For instance, especially inner-city teenagers and young men may use superlatives to describe themselves or may make exaggerated claims about their capabilities and accomplishments. These boasts are not meant to be taken literally or seriously, as they are used primarily as a social lubricant to attract attention and to be amusing and entertaining.

Orality

African Americans place a great deal of emphasis on oral communication and use speech to convey deep meanings not possible to share in writing (Boykin & Toms, 1985). The elderly have traditionally functioned as the keepers of the oral literature inherited from their ancestors. This oral heritage includes parables, folk poetry, folktales, biblical stories, songs, and proverbs.

The traditional oral communication style, more readily observable among inner-city folks than among members of higher socioeconomic groups, is animated, high keyed, confrontational, and heated, in contrast to that of Euro-Americans, which generally tends to be more low key, dispassionate, impersonal, cool, and quiet (Kochman, 1981). Typically, speaker and listener following the African-American tradition engage in a great deal of back-and-forth verbal interaction. The listener acts as an echo chamber, validating, repeating, or affirming the speaker's message by sprinkling it with an occasional "amen," "right-on," "yeah, man," or "get out of here" in an interactive style that has been referred to as *call and response* (White & Parham, 1990, p. 64).

Traditional African-American speech is also characterized by a more spontaneous and improvised delivery, rhythmic pattern, musical tone, and variable intensity than that of Euro-Americans. It is also more likely to make use of rhymes, metaphors, and visual imagery (Jackson, 1986). Consider, for example, the use of rhyme in the following description by one African American of the experience of oppression: "We have been abused, misused, refused, and confused"; or the use of metaphor and visual imagery in Martin Luther King's statement: "Justice rolls down like water and righteousness like a mighty stream"; or the visual imagery in the following verbal description: "He jumped higher than five kites on a breezy day" (White & Parham, 1990, pp. 64–65).

Styles of Social Interaction

As a group, African Americans put a premium on emotional sensibilities and expressiveness (Boykin & Toms, 1985). Their traditional culture is people oriented and puts emphasis on personal/social relationships. Like Latinos, they often dislike the more impersonal way of relating that is characteristic of Euro-Americans, preferring instead a more personable, expansive, intense, and assertive style (Kochman, 1988).

Being personable, however, should not be confused with familiarity, particularly when it comes to addressing one another. Those who subscribe to the traditional culture expect to be treated respectfully—more so than the average Euro-American would (McNeely & Badami, 1984). For example, traditional African Americans prefer to be addressed by their last names rather than by their first names (even by other African Americans) and by any title they may have earned, such as judge, senator, doctor, or professor. The preference for formality in address within a society noted for its informality probably stems from the historical inequality to which African Americans have been subjected in their relations with the mainstream group. In the past, African Americans were expected to use titles and last names as a sign of respect when addressing persons of the white race, but whites customarily called them by their first names or, even worse, referred to them as "boy" or sometimes used still more disrespectful epithets.

Many young African Americans feel perfectly comfortable and unoffended when, in reciprocal social situations, Euro-Americans address them by their first name. However, it is appropriate to maintain the formal style of address when initiating a cross-cultural or interracial exchange or in situations involving unequal power; for example, when the authority figure or superordinate person (e.g., the job supervisor) is a member of the mainstream group and the subordinate (e.g., the employee) is African American. The same principle applies to interactions between social worker and African-American client; unless the client specifies otherwise, the social worker should address the client formally by the person's last name. Even in informal social situations, it is always more appropriate to address people, particularly those from a nonmainstream culture, by their last names and titles as a sign of

respect, unless they specifically suggest that their first names be used.

Social interaction among African Americans is often conducted at a more intense level than that which is usual among Euro-Americans. For example, when having a discussion, African Americans may display a higher level of energy and intensity and a more argumentative and confrontive style, on average, than Euro-Americans. However, this traditional "hot" style of relating is different from losing control. In the African-American culture, talking is talking, even when exchanging threats or insults. Fighting is something entirely different, involving the use of physical force. However, sheer intensity is sometimes threatening to Euro-Americans used to cooler and quieter interactions (Rich, 1974; Kochman, 1981; McNeely & Badami, 1984).

In interactions with white people, African Americans are sometimes distrustful and suspicious of the white person's motives and actions. This distrust is sometimes perceived by Euro-Americans as paranoia. Yet, the traditional African-American culture considers suspiciousness a necessary and healthy survival tactic in an often hostile social environment (Chestang, 1972; Triandis, 1976). Historically, as well as in the course of their own lives, many African Americans have had reason to question the motives of whites. Consequently, some may be slow to warm up to the Euro-American's attempts to be nice and friendly, or they may initially relate in an overly cautious or even unfriendly manner. For example, when a Euro-American stranger smiles, some black folks from the inner city may not return the smile. In fact, smiling may not be a good way for a Euro-American practitioner to attempt to establish rapport with low-income African-American clients who have not yet made up their minds that the worker can be trusted (McNeely & Badami, 1984). There are many individual differences, to be sure. Some inner-city folks are warm and friendly toward a white

person who is helpful and pleasant with them, even if the person is a total stranger.

Time is treated flexibly in social interactions, as compared to the greater stress on watching the clock and being punctual which is characteristic of the U.S. mainstream culture. This may be related to the African philosophy that assigns more value to events taking place in the present than to the future (Jones, 1991). Some African Americans consider the pressure of punctuality an impediment to social relations and to becoming involved in what is happening in the here and now (Jackson, 1986).

Nonverbal Aspects of Culture

Research has shown that African Americans, particularly when they are in the listening role or relating to an authority figure, tend to prefer a less continuous and intense level of eye contact than is customary for Euro-Americans (La-France & Mayo, 1976; Hanna, 1984). Traditionally, this low level of direct eye contact has been considered a sign of respectful attention.

Consequently, a Euro-American listener who establishes a high level of eye contact may be perceived by some traditional African Americans as aggressive or hostile, even though the individual may simply be trying to be courteous and attentive. At school, some children from traditional families may cast their eyes downward when their teacher speaks to them to show proper respect. Some teachers may misinterpret this respectful gesture as inattention or rudeness.

Like Latinos, African Americans tend to be more physically spontaneous and demonstrative and to engage in more touching behavior among themselves than Euro-Americans (Hanna, 1984; Jackson, 1986). Touching is common in social interactions among relatives and friends. However, the practitioner should not assume that touching is therefore acceptable in interactions with African-American clients. Physical contact is a sensitive issue that can lead to misunderstanding among people from different cultures. Therefore, it is best to refrain from touching unless one is absolutely sure that one is acting within acceptable and desirable parameters.

Contributions to U.S. Mainstream Culture

We cannot leave the subject of African-American culture without acknowledging some of its contributions to the U.S. culture. One major contribution has been the spearheading of the civil rights movement, which has had positive consequences for all nondominant groups. The women's rights movement also owes credit to the African-American culture, having evolved out of the abolitionist movement within which African-American women played important roles. Many early feminist demands—for example, the demand for women to have the right to own property and to engage in business—were influenced at least in part by the West African tradition of women's rights in these areas. These rights were first granted to American women in South Carolina, where the majority population was African American (Holloway, 1990).

Widely recognized by the U.S. mainstream are the contributions of African-American culture to "American" music, such as jazz, blues, spirituals, and syncopated rhythm, among other creations. Also well known are its culinary contributions. The heavy seasoning and spiciness characteristic of southern cooking and many dishes common in southern cuisine (e.g., fried chicken, gumbo, okra, and black-eyed peas) have African origins. African-American culture also has significantly influenced southern culture, including the distinctive enunciation of southerners, the musical quality of their speech, their use of terms of endearment, their formal but sincere courtesy, an emphasis on kinship relations, and respect for elders.

Many of the rituals of Pentecostal churches also show an African influence, including possession trances, drumming, and dancing. Even aspects of the cowboy culture of the "American West" closely resemble the patterns of Senegambian and Fulani cattle herders in Africa (Holloway, 1990).

Some African-American Contributors to U.S. Culture

African Americans have made important contributions to U.S. culture in practically all fields of endeavor. Exemplars in literature and poetry include Frederick Douglas, Phillis Wheatley, W. E. B. DuBois, James Baldwin, Ralph Waldo Ellison, Alex Haley, Alice Walker, Nikki Giovanni, and Maya Angelou. In the sciences are George Washington Carver, Charles Drew, Norbert Rillieux, Benjamin Banneker, Jan Earnst Matzeliger, Elijah McCoy, Granville Woods, Percy Julian, Ernest Everett Just, and, among the younger generation, physician Benjamin Carson and aeronaut/physician Mae Jemison. Among outstanding educators and scholars, are Booker T. Washington, Mary McLeod Bethune, E. Franklin Frazier, Thomas Sowell, William J. Wilson, Andrew Billingsley, Orlando Patterson, Henry Louis Gates Jr., Barbara Jordan, and Phyllis Wallace. Among civic, religious, and political leaders are Martin Luther King, Nat Turner, Harriet Tubman, Ida Wells, Malcolm X, Barbara Harris, Jesse Jackson, Shirley Chisolm, and Marian Wright Edelman. Other outstanding contributors include Thurgood Marshall of the Supreme Court, Nobel Prize winner for literature Toni Morrison, U.S. poet laureate Rita Dove, military leader and retired Chairman of the Joint Chiefs of the U.S. Military Colin Powell, media leaders Oprah Winfrey and Bill Cosby, film director Spike Lee, and business magnate Reginald Lewis.

NATIVE-AMERICAN CULTURES

According to the Bureau of Indian Affairs (1988), a **Native American** or **American Indian** (American Indians are divided as to which of these two terms they prefer) is a registered member of a Native-American/American-

Indian tribe or a person whose blood quantum is one-fourth or more Native American. This is an arbitrary definition imposed by the U.S. Congress with which American Indians do not necessarily agree (Sue & Sue, 1990). Some feel that only those who are of pure blood should be considered Native Americans; but others who are less than one-fourth Native American choose to identify with this part of their cultural heritage and to designate themselves as such. This is why, in counting the American-Indian population in the United States, the Bureau of the Census, unlike the Bureau of Indian Affairs, relies on self-identification. Anyone who claims to be an American Indian is accepted as such by the Census, regardless of blood quantum or tribal registration.

As members of several hundred different tribes scattered throughout the United States and as speakers of over 140 different languages, American Indians constitute a highly diverse social group. Some, particularly those who have lived on tribal reservations all their lives, are quite traditional in their ways and communicate primarily in the tribal language. Others, especially some of those born and reared in urban areas, have maintained little contact with their tribes and, consequently, they no longer understand or speak the tribal language and are highly acculturated to the U.S. mainstream. Most Native Americans fall somewhere along the continuum between these two extremes: They may not live on the reservation, and the tribal language may not be their primary language, but they manage to keep their cultural heritage alive to some extent. They do this by visiting relatives and friends on the reservation, by acquainting themselves with the tribal language at least so they can speak a few words and understand the language to some extent, and by attending American-Indian feasts, religious ceremonies, rodeos, and powwows.

This section will examine those American-Indian values, traditions, and customs shared by most of the tribes in the United States and

passed on from generation to generation almost entirely through oral myths and legends (as only the Cherokee developed a written language) (Locke, 1992). Although there is substantial consistency across tribes in terms of these customs and values, it is important to keep in mind that each tribe has a distinct culture and that each person is unique. (Additional traditional American-Indian values and customs specifically related to family life are discussed in Chapter 9. Demographic information is included in Chapter 4.)

Holism, Spiritualism, and Harmony

American Indians view the universe as a unified whole. From their perspective, the earth, the sky, humans, animals, and inanimate objects as well as mind, body, and spirit are interconnected and form part of the "hoop of life" (Heinrich, Corbine, & Thomas, 1990). Within the indivisible and continuous hoop of life, the soul is born and reborn, and some people can foretell the future since everything happens within the same cycle of time (Locke, 1992).

The cultures of the various tribes stress the importance of maintaining a harmonious relationship with nature, which is deeply respected as a reflection of God. The land is considered sacred; therefore, there is a strong belief that no earthly resource should be abused. Animals are treated with kindness and respect, and they are considered capable of wisdom and greatness (Richardson, 1981).

Health is seen as the result of being in harmony with the universe, whereas illness is considered the result of disruption in the balance of life. According to the Navajo, for example, feeling angry toward another person may cause illness; to restore harmony and health, one must give up the anger (Matheson, 1986).

Traditional Native-American cultures teach that everything in life has a spirit—the earth, the sky, animals, people, trees (living and dead), inanimate objects such as rocks and mountains, and even thoughts, feelings, and behaviors. From their perspective, it is not necessarily pathological to "feel," "see," or "hear" the spirits. In fact, it may be desirable in some circumstances. This is because it is believed that "visions" can throw light on the meaning and purpose of one's life and on the significance of certain events. In addition, it is not necessarily a sign of mental disorder for Native Americans to have certain extra-body experiences; this is because their cultures do not define the boundaries between entities as clearly as other cultures. Consequently, some believe that it is possible to become someone or something other than what one usually is, such as another person, an animal, or an inanimate object (Matheson, 1986).

One of the most important religious rituals facilitated by American-Indian traditional healers (*shamans, sakims*, or medicine makers) is the *Vision Quest*. Some human service practitioners refer to this ritual, with which most Native Americas are familiar, as a metaphor for explaining to their clients the processes of counseling and psychotherapy (Heinrich et al., 1990). Many American Indians consider the *Vision Quest* and other religious ceremonies and traditional healing practices a vital part of their spiritual lives and sometimes prefer them over modern forms of Western treatment.

Historically, the Vision Quest was a rite of passage for young boys as well as a ceremony of religious renewal for adult men. It is now used more broadly as a means of helping individuals to deal with difficult life transitions (Foster & Little, 1987). Typically, the person undergoing this ritual first goes into a sweat lodge to pray with the shaman and to purify the body and the spirit through perspiration. Then the individual goes to a remote and isolated area and stays alone without food for several days and nights while reflecting, praying, and searching for a vision to guide the future.

Extended Family

The traditional Native-American family is extended and forms part of a much larger group of families, or **clan,** that trace its descent to a common ancestor (Locke, 1992). The extended family includes up to second-degree relatives (e.g., aunts, uncles, and cousins) as well as non-kin, such as **namesakes** or role models. Generally, various members of the family or clan, not just the parents, share child-rearing responsibilities, which are usually carried out in a permissive manner without much use of punishment or guilt (Ho, 1987; Locke, 1992). Given this extended-family tradition, it is not unusual for children to live with various family or clan members rather than just with their parents. Within the clan as well as in the tribe, elders are honored and respected for their wisdom and experience and typically fill important positions on the tribal council (Lewis & Ho, 1989; Locke, 1992).

Collectivism, Giving, and Sharing

American Indians tend to see themselves as extensions of the tribe, the clan, and the family, all of which provide them with security and a sense of belonging. Their traditional cultures put the needs of tribe, clan, and family above those of the individual. Within this context, personal achievements and goals are valued if they benefit the tribe and the family group (Sue & Sue, 1990). Given the cultural emphasis on collectivism, Native Americans typically avoid competitive situations. Sometimes the children's reluctance to compete with their peers is misinterpreted by school teachers as a lack of motivation or intelligence (Ho, 1987).

Because their cultures stress the importance of working together and maintaining harmonious relationships, American Indians show a preference for making decisions by consensus rather than by majority vote, even if this requires long and arduous discussions to reach unanimity (Attneave, 1982). In the interest of maintaining harmony, the traditional cultures stresses the importance of being humble and modest, and children are taught not to use their names or the word *I* excessively (Ho, 1987).

Material goals and the accumulation of wealth are typically not highly valued. Just like Mother Earth shares its bounty with everyone, the traditional cultural belief is that giving is better than receiving and that one should share things with others. Specifically, one should keep only those things that can be used within a reasonable period of time and the rest should be given away to honor others and to spiritually cleanse oneself (Richardson, 1981; Matheson, 1986; Locke, 1992). Within this tradition, birthdays, for example, are occasions for the celebrant to give presents to the guests and to share his or her good fortune with those coming to celebrate.

Styles of Social Interaction

Native Americans typically speak softly, use a gentle handshake instead of a firm one, and are not physically demonstrative (Attneave, 1982; Everett, Proctor, & Cartmell, 1983). Their traditional cultures teach emotional restraint and self-control, observation rather than impulsive behavior, noninterference in the affairs of others, and avoidance of emotional outbursts. Thus, American Indians learn to be poised, aloof, and self-contained. Husbands and wives who behave traditionally rarely show emotion or affection toward each other in public.

Attitudes of resentment and suspicion toward Euro-Americans are common and understandable, given the treatment Native Americans received by European settlers. This included conquest and extermination, slavery, seizure of their lands, forced movement onto reservations, removal of their children from home to "civilize" them at boarding schools or to place them in non-Indian foster homes, and continuous oppression (Sue & Sue, 1990;

Locke, 1992). Thus, in working with members of this cultural group, Euro-American practitioners should not expect to be trusted until they have earned the client's respect. Similarly, it would be unrealistic for Euro-American practitioners to think that they can quickly and easily gain access to their clients' families. Such access is a privilege that must be earned. Table 2.2 succinctly shows a general comparison of the values of Native Americans and Euro-Americans.

Nonverbal Aspects of Culture

Low levels of eye contact are preferred, and too much staring is considered a sign of aggression or intrusion (Richardson, 1981; Lewis & Ho, 1989; Harrison, Wodarski, & Thyer, 1992). In some tribes, children are taught that it is disrespectful to look at an elder in the eye.

The cultural belief in relation to time is that it should not be scheduled rigidly because to do so disrupts the natural flow of things; instead, the person should be grounded in what is happening at the moment (Everett et al., 1983; Ho, 1987; Locke, 1992). This all means that traditional American Indians do not measure time exactly and are not characteristically punctual. Events begin when everyone is present and end when all business has been transacted.

Some American-Indian Contributors to U.S. Culture

Native Americans have made significant contributions to U.S. culture in many fields of endeavor. Among writers and poets are Paula Gunn Allen, Ella Carla Deloria, Gertrude S. Bonnin, Joy Harjo, Louise Erdrich, N. Scott Momaday, and Linda Hogan. In the sciences are Charles Alexander Eastman and Carlos Montezuma. Educators include Edward Pasqual Dozier and Charlotte Heth. Many have achieved prominence as civic leaders or political activists, such as Vice-President Charles Curtis (under Herbert Hoover), Dennis Banks,

TABLE 2.2 Comparison of Euro-American and Native-American Values

EURO-AMERICAN VALUES	NATIVE-AMERICAN VALUES
Mastery of nature	Harmony with nature
Future, progress, change	Present, following the old ways
Competition	Cooperation
Private property and accumulation of wealth	Sharing with others
Self-assurance, confidence, recognition	Modesty, humility, self-effacement
Use of resources	Conservation of resources
Time awareness	Time nonawareness
Impatience	Patience, acceptance
Emphasis on youth	Respect for age
Emphasis on the individual	Emphasis on the group, clan
Immediate family	Extended family, clan
Representative government	Face-to-face government
Analytic	Holistic
Outspoken	Silent
Social coercion	Permissiveness
Skeptical	Mystical
Logical	Intuitive
Religion as a segment of life	Religion as a way of life

The data used to prepare this table come in part from *Counseling the Culturally Different: Theory and Practice* (pp. 225–227) by D. W. Sue, 1981, New York: John Wiley & Sons. Copyright 1981 by John Wiley & Sons. Used by permission of John Wiley & Sons, Inc.

Box 2.1

Old Ways and New, in Harmony

BY ELIZABETH COHEN

Special to The New York Times

GALLUP, N.M. – Lighted by the blue and orange glow of a video monitor, Dr. Lori Cupp watched intently as she supervised another surgeon removing sections of a Navajo patient's diseased gallbladder through a tiny slit in the patient's navel.

In the high-tech world of the operating room, she often meets surgeons who view their skills as akin to auto mechanics: fixing things in need of repair. But for Dr. Cupp, who the Association of American Indian Physicians said is the first Navajo woman to become a surgeon, surgery is a powerful, spiritual experience.

"In the Navajo religion and culture, there is an emphasis on how you relate to everything around you," she said. "Everything has to be measured, weighed and harmonious. We call it nizhoni—walking in beauty—and I believe what I do as a surgeon fits into this philosophy. I know my actions directly alter the course of people's lives."

Not 10 minutes after leaving the operating room at the Gallup Indian Medical Center. Dr. Cupp, 34, a staff general surgeon, was on the road in her 10-year-old Mazda, its dashboard buried in pens, beepers, keys, paperwork and magazines. After a brief stop for a sandwich and a soda, Dr.

Cupp headed to Crownpoint, N.M., population 3,000. This is where she grew up and where she makes rounds these days at a hospital run by the Indian Health Service, a Federal program.

Dr. Cupp, who, graduated from Stanford University's medical school in 1990, found the inspiration to become a surgeon in her own home. Her father's mother, Grace Cupp, was a teacher and principal for 40 years at a Bureau of Indian Affairs school on the reservation. "I saw early that a woman could work at a job and make a difference in people's lives," Dr. Cupp said, adding that this was important in a world where there were virtually no professional role models: no Navajo doctors, no Navajo lawyers, no Navajo engineers. She believes that the Navajo culture itself, which is matriarchal, gives women a sense of power and independence, an asset in a medical specialty in which only 6 percent of the practitioners are women.

"My father's family was Navajo and my mother's is a blend of Western European cultures," she said. "I belong to the Dark Forest Clan or Bear People. I take my father's mother's clan."

Today, Dr. Cupp describes being an American Indian woman at Dartmouth, where she majored in psychology, sociology and Native American studies, as a challenge, although the college was chartered in 1769 by King George III of England to spread "Christian Knowledge among the Savages." Everywhere she looked, she was confronted with Dartmouth's mascot: a little red man with a tomahawk, headdress and loincloth.

Like other Americans abroad, the 35 Indian students on the Dartmouth campus banded together. Dr. Cupp said she enjoyed meeting Indians from all over the country, but she added, "I always felt a distance between myself and the non-Indian students at Dartmouth."

When she graduated and returned to New Mexico . . . her boss encouraged her to go to medical school. With the Indian Health Service paying for her education, she enrolled at Stanford, where she was one of three Indians in her class of 85 and the only Navajo.

Today, at a hospital where there are few women and no American Indians, let alone Indian women, in positions of authority, Dr. Cupp says she still feels vulnerable. When she first got her job in Gallup, she sensed prejudice from other members of the hospital staff.

"I used to hear rumors that I only finished at Stanford because I was a Native American," Dr.Cupp said. I did 1,100 operations at Stanford, and believe me, it wasn't because I was Native American. If you weren't any good, they would never let you perform so much surgery; you'd be too much of a liability from a malpractice standpoint."

Last spring, she was appointed to a National Institutes of Health task force on recruiting—and keeping—women as clinical research subjects. "Researchers don't like using women because their bodies are more complicated," she said. "They can be pre- or postmenopausal, pre- or postmenstrual. Hormonally, they are more complicated. The feeling is that because they are not included in research, they do not benefit from it."

It takes a subtle sensibility to treat people in a culture in which an owl's crossing your path can foreshadow tragedy. "If you were Navajo, I wouldn't even look at you," Dr. Cupp said. A direct gaze is considered insulting; so is touching the body and asking direct, personal questions.

By adapting what she learned in medical school to her own knowledge of Navajo ways, Dr. Cupp said, she has developed a method of treating Navajo people that lessens their uneasiness. "Now I know how to gauge a person's discomfort by asking a few questions at a time and asking them to only uncover that part of their body I need to see.

Dr. Cupp thinks most medical practitioners could benefit from an understanding of Navajo ways. She has encouraged the hospital to add a medicine man to perform healing ceremonies. She has also recommended that when a new medical center is built, it include a traditional Navajo round room for such ceremonies, known as sings. Dr. Cupp strongly believes that such steps not only show respect for the Navajo as a people but may also help in healing.

"I think for a lot of things, having a sing may be the best treatment—for example, for depression," she said. "But if I had a breast mass, I would want it surgically removed for a biopsy."

Source: "Navajo Surgeon and Pioneer" by Elizabeth Cohen, February 17, 1994, *The New York Times,* p. B1. Copyright © 1994 by The New York Times Company. Reprinted with permission.

Ivan Sidney, Wilma Mankiller, Alice Jemison, and Ned Hatathli.

NONMAINSTREAM IMMIGRANT CULTURES

Immigrants and Refugees

The term **immigrant** is generally used to refer to an individual who willingly migrates from one country to another, usually looking for better economic opportunities or a better life. **Refugees** are those forced to leave their countries out of fear of persecution due to their political opinions or actions, race, religion, sexual orientation, ethnic background, or membership in a particular social group (Berry, Kim, Mind, & Mok, 1987; National Association of Social Workers, 1990). The United States traditionally has admitted vast numbers of immigrants and refugees, compared to other countries. In fact, it has accepted more newcomers than any other nation on earth (Rumbaut, 1991). Just since 1950, about 20 million people have legally entered the United States as immigrants. With liberal immigration laws in effect since 1990, more than 1 million people are now arriving

annually (Harrison, 1992; Clark & Passel, 1993). An additional 2 to 3 million illegal immigrants were believed to be living in the United States in 1992.

It is important to keep in mind that even though the United States is the principal receiving country for the immigrants and refugees of the world, only 7.9 percent of the U.S. population in 1990 was foreign born, and many foreign born citizens had been in the United States for 20 or more years and were well established financially (U.S. Bureau of the Census, 1993a). This means that fears that new immigrants will take away jobs from the native-born population and that they will be an excessive burden on taxpayers are understandable but, for the most part, unfounded. Other nations, such as Australia and Canada, are able to do well despite the fact that the foreign born account for a much larger percentage of their population (Rumbaut, 1991). However, because many recent immigrants to the United States tend to gravitate toward certain urban areas with large concentrations of their own ethnic group (e.g., Southeast Asians and Mexicans to California, Cubans and Haitians to Miami), immigrants

Source: Toles © 1992. The Buffalo News. Reprinted with permission of Universal
Press Syndicate. All rights reserved.

and refugees can temporarily be a heavy burden on a few local communities.

Historically, immigrants have had an invigorating effect on the United States, even though the masses that have come to the nation's shores, on average, have had limited education and skills. Not all immigrants and refugees are uneducated or unskilled, however. In 1987, Rumbaut (1991) reported that 26.5 percent of immigrants and refugees entering the United States were high-status professionals, executives, or managers in their country of origin. In 1992, 38 percent of the new entrants were skilled workers or professionals (Huddle, 1993). At any rate, even though the majority of immigrants to the United States have been of humble origins, they have helped build a great nation. Some theorists speculate that the reason immigrants are typically "hardy" as a group is that the vicissitudes of migration act as a natu-

ral selection process, weeding out those who are less fit. Whatever the reason, many of the immigrants and refugees that have come to the United States have shown grit, ambition, determination, courage, vitality, and a great deal of productive energy. A large proportion of newcomers enthusiastically embrace U.S. mainstream values and work hard (frequently 10- to 12-hour days, six or seven days a week) to get established and to pursue the "American Dream."

Many immigrant newcomers, particularly those who are undocumented, take rock-bottom jobs that most U.S. citizens would be disinclined to consider except in dire circumstances. For example, they may work with hazardous chemicals in the agricultural fields, operate faulty or dangerous equipment in illegal sweatshops, wash and iron clothes at laundries, wash dishes at restaurants, and work as manual day

laborers or itinerant farm workers. Many of their employers, sometimes immigrant entrepreneurs themselves, profit by paying them low wages (without benefits) sometimes off the books. Other immigrants start by peddling merchandise in the streets, cleaning hotels, motels, hospitals, and offices, mowing lawns, or working as live-in maids or child-care workers for a fraction of the pay U.S. citizens would expect, or perform a variety of low-price home services, such as sewing, ironing, or cooking for others, washing cars, and doing manicures (Gonzalez, 1985; Sontag, 1992).

Based on the statistics they gather or review, most immigration scholars and economists believe, that immigrants, as a group, particularly long-term immigrants, are not a burden to U.S. society. This is because the majority eventually create more jobs and financial resources than they take and eventually pay as much or more than their proportionate share of local,

state, and federal taxes (Rumbaut, 1991; Clark & Passel, 1993). For example, a study by the Urban Institute found that although illegal immigrants cost their major destination states (Texas, Florida, and California) about $2 billion a year for schooling, medical services, and incarceration, legal and illegal immigrants generate a yearly surplus of about $25 to $30 billion for the nation from the income and property taxes they pay (Gibbs, 1994, p. 47).

Based on a review of recent studies of legal and undocumented immigration, Rumbaut (1991) concluded that immigration has "net economic benefits" for U.S. natives in terms of raising their salaries, increasing productivity and investment, and revitalizing declining sectors of the economy, such as light manufacturing, construction, and the garment industry. He noted that the influx of new low-cost immigrant manual labor pushes up native-born workers to supervisory positions. Also, Rumbaut noted that a significant portion of immigrants and refugees do not take away jobs from the native born because they work in businesses owned by other immigrants and refugees or they quickly become self-employed (e.g., Cubans, Chinese, Koreans). In addition, official records show that immigrants, compared to the native-born U.S. population, make less use of welfare services, such as Aid to Families with Dependent Children (AFDC), supplemental security income, food stamps, and Medicaid. This is because legal immigrants are restricted by law from receiving welfare during their first three years in the United States and undocumented immigrants do not qualify for welfare because of their illegal status. That leaves refugees as the only entrant group entitled to receive welfare, if they qualify, on the same bases as U.S. citizens (Rumbaut, 1991).

Notwithstanding all of the preceding data, some local economies in Texas, California, and Florida clearly spend more on public services to immigrant newcomers than what they collect from them in local taxes (Huddle, 1993). This is because, legally, states cannot deny anyone, documented or undocumented, access to public elementary and secondary education and to emergency health services, and these services are very costly. New immigrants are not the only groups that are a burden to some communities however. Native-born U.S. citizens cost some local economies more than what they pay in local taxes (Clark & Passel, 1993). One reality is indisputable: For a newcomer to the United States, the process of getting established and getting ahead is usually slow, taking most immigrants and refugees anywhere from eight to ten years to one generation. During this time, *some* newcomers are temporarily costly to the society, particularly in terms of education and health care.

Considering all the pros and cons discussed here, it appears to be in the interest of the United States to take in a reasonable number of *legal* immigrants and refugees each year, regardless of their race, nationality, socioeconomic status, or educational level. Although the number of entrants is not yet alarming, most immigration experts believe that the United States may have to put some restriction on the inflow of people. At between 1.0 million and 1.8 million immigrants per year, the nation was admitting newcomers in the early 1990s at a rate equal to or higher than that at which it absorbed them at the turn of the century (Booth, 1992; Goodman, 1992). The main difference between the new entrants and those who came at the turn of the century is that the majority of current immigrants and refugees do not come from Western or Eastern Europe but from the developing countries of the Third World, particularly Latin America and the Asian/Pacific basin (Rumbaut, 1991; Wattenberg, 1991). Hence, racial prejudice may account for some of the current resistance toward accepting newcomers. You should know, however, that the European newcomers at the turn of the century also encountered considerable resistance and prejudice, even though they were white.

Regardless of the extent to which prejudice drives the current resistance to newcomers, the number of immigrants arriving every year may have become too high for the society to absorb, particularly as long as the economy is growing at a sluggish rate. The problem with restricting immigration is that the process can easily become discriminatory; for example, should boat people with little or no education (most of whom happen to be people of color) be turned away? Should the society accept all the professionals that apply (a greater proportion of whom happen to be white)? This arrangement would be economically and technically advantageous for the society, but would it be a fair and just policy for a democratic nation to adopt?

Acculturation Issues

Immigrants have different levels of motivation or ability to learn the U.S. mainstream culture. For instance, an immigrant who has been in the United States for only a short period of time, perhaps 7 to 10 years, may be more accultur-ated than someone else of the same ethnic group born in the United States. Perhaps the first individual married a native-born U.S. citi-zen and totally submerged himself or herself in the new culture and language, whereas the sec-ond person's family always remained segre-gated in the ethnic community, limiting his or her ability to become more acculturated. As a rule of thumb, however, those who migrated recently—say, those who entered the United States in the last 10 years—are likely to show greater adherence to their traditional ethnic cul-tures and native languages than those who migrated one or more generations ago.

Some recent immigrants and refugees may not reflect in their behaviors and lifestyles the *traditional* values of their native cultures. This is because some cultures have been changing rapidly under the influence of modernization and industrialization (Gelfand & Fandetti, 1986). Consider many recent Korean immi-grants. Their traditional cultural values were forged during times when Korea was an agrar-ian society. With rapid industrialization, the cultural value system is changing dramatically. Consequently, a recent Korean immigrant to the United States may behave in ways that are quite different from what one would expect based on knowledge about traditional East Asian cultures.

As members of immigrant groups and their descendants become better integrated into the U.S. society and more acculturated into the mainstream, their ethnic cultures tend to lose primacy in their lives (Gelfand & Fandetti, 1986). Specifically, the longer a person's ancestors have lived in the United States, the less likely the individual's ethnic origin is to be reflected in terms of any specific beliefs, val-ues, customs, attitudes, languages, or behaviors (Longres, 1991). Particularly those descendants of immigrants who have been in the United States for three or more generations and who live outside the heavily ethnic ghettos and enclaves are unlikely to show a high degree of

adherence to their ethnic cultures or to be highly competent in the use of the native lan-guage of their ancestors. In fact, eventually some people even forget their immigrant past and the language of their ancestors and may even resent references by others to their "eth-nic" origins.

LATINO CULTURES

Although generally unrecognized, the Spanish heritage has been an integral part of U.S. life since the fifteenth century (Gann & Duignan, 1986; Sandoval & de la Roza, 1986). For exam-ple, the ancestors of some Spanish speakers in the Southwest came from Spain and settled in that area before the Pilgrims came to New England. Similarly, the nation's first non-Indian cities—St. Augustine (in the area named Florida by the Spaniards) and Santa Fe (in what is now New Mexico)—were founded by Span-ish colonists. However, most of the **Latinos** presently in the United States came after World War II from over 20 different Spanish-speaking nations in Central America, South America, and the Caribbean, each with its distinct cul-ture. The largest number have come from Mex-ico, Puerto Rico, and Cuba.

One common element among Latinos is the Spanish language, the second most widely spo-ken language in the United States today after English (U.S. Bureau of the Census, 1993b, p. 13). The proximity of the United States to sev-eral Latin American countries has enabled many U. S. Latinos to keep close ties with their countries of origin by visiting frequently. This active relationship with the mother country makes it possible for many to maintain func-tional command of the Spanish language and to keep Spanish customs and traditions alive in their families sometimes for several genera-tions.

This section will examine values shared by all Latino cultures. Values and customs related to family life are discussed in greater detail in Chapter 9. Additional background information

and demographic data about U.S. Latinos are included in Chapter 4.

Family and Patriarchy

Latino cultures place central importance on the family. For the more traditional Latinos, the family represents an extended and interdependent network of blood relatives (including parents, children, grandparents, cousins, aunts, and uncles), informally adopted children (*hijos de crianza*), in-laws, godparents, and even some neighbors and close friends considered family because of their willingness to become involved in important family matters and events. Less traditional Latinos in the United States may have a more limited concept of family that includes primarily the intergenerational family—parents and children (including sometimes the parents' adult siblings on one or both sides of the family) and grandparents.

In traditional families, the father is considered the **patriarch** or offical head of the family, its chief decision maker, and its representative

in the community. At least publicly, these families emphasize the husband's role as authority figure and the wife's role as principal housekeeper and caregiver of the children, even when the actual circumstances within the family are different. U.S. Latino families with wives who work full time outside the home tend to be less patriarchal and more egalitarian, with husbands and wives sharing more in the decision making and husbands helping more with some household and child-care duties. In general, elderly members of the family are treated with respect and are more likely than the Euro-American elderly to be kept at home as part of their children's families.

Styles of Social Interaction

Latinos typically interact in a warm and personable manner and dislike the more impersonal ways of relating that are more characteristic in the Euro-American mainstream culture. This personalized mode of social interaction is called **personalismo**. Under this system, people customarily do favors for one another and, occasionally, if necessary, they may even bend the rules a little to accommodate the other person's reasonable needs. From this perspective, the impersonal inflexibility of many U.S. bureaucrats is viewed with distaste.

Because of the value placed on personal relationships, Latino clients may show interest in getting to know the practitioner as a person rather than just as a service provider. They may ask practictioners questions about personal likings, such as favorite foods or hobbies, or nonintimate details about their families. Occasionally, they may bring the worker a gift as an expression of respect and gratitude (Sandoval & de la Roza, 1986).

Closely related to the philosophy of personalismo is the high value placed by traditional Latinos on respect. The traditional culture teaches that everyone should be treated respectfully, regardless of personal accomplishments or social position, especially those who are older, more experienced, or highly educated (Mizio, 1992). As a sign of respect, many Latinos (particularly Mexicans and other Central and South Americans) address others, even members of their own families, particularly elders, by using the formal pronoun *usted* instead of the informal *tu*. Respect for deceased family members is shown by visiting the cemetery frequently and placing flowers on their graves and, in the case of Catholics, by offering masses and prayers for the repose of their souls.

In social relations, Latino cultures stress the importance of being **simpatico** (i.e., likable, pleasant, agreeable, humorous, and easy going) and of refraining from criticizing, insulting, or disagreeing with others or acting too competitively. Those who deviate from this traditional *simpatia* script may be looked down upon, unless such people happen to be authority figures, in which case they may be granted somewhat more latitude to be disagreeable (Triandis, Lisansky, Marin, & Betancourt, 1984).

The traditional culture also puts emphasis on hierarchical rather than egalitarian ways of relating. For example, first-generation immigrant young people may be expected to follow the advice and directives given by their parents, close relatives, or teachers without questioning their judgment. Similarly, traditional Latino bosses would likely expect their employees to follow orders without questioning their authority. The cultural emphasis on hierarchical relationships causes many Latino clients to expect human service practitioners to be directive in their approach and to offer advice and recommendations concerning client problems.

Religion and Folk-Healing Practices

Approximately 85 percent of U.S. Latinos are Catholic. The remainder belong to various Protestant denominations and fundamentalist sects (Medina, 1987). Many are not regular churchgoers but still pray frequently and consider religion an important part of their lives (Acosta & Evans, 1982).

In addition to conventional religion, to deal with supernatural forces, some Latinos turn to alternative folk practices, including *santeria, curanderismo,* and *espiritismo.* (These are discussed later in this chapter.) It is important to understand that participation in folk-healing rituals or belief in hexes (*mal puesto*) or in folk illnesses such as *mal de ojo* (evil eye), *susto* (fright), *empacho* (a form of indigestion), *desmayo* (fainting spells), or *decaimiento* (lack of energy) do not necessarily mean that a person is psychologically or emotional distressed. Such beliefs and the practices associated with them must be understood within the cultural context (Queralt, 1984). For example, a recent immigrant from Mexico may attribute her baby's fever to *mal de ojo,* claiming that someone looked at the child too intently or with envy. This is a common folk belief in Latin America and does not indicate that there is anything wrong with the parent's thought processes.

If the client has sought the advice of a priest or other folk healer, it may be wise for the practitioner to consult, with the client's permission, with the priest or folk healer. Similarly, for those Latino clients who pray regularly, the adjunct use of prayer in treatment (under the direction of the client's spiritual advisor) may have beneficial effects.

Cultural Traits

A fatalistic attitude is prevalent among poor and uneducated first-generation immigrants. **Fatalism** is the belief that one must accept and endure one's fate because one does not have enough control over life circumstances. According to this philosophy, a person is to accept what comes— pain, deprivation, suffering, or bad luck—because it is God's will, the "cross" one must bear, or destiny. Thus, Latinos often say, "*Sera lo que Dios manda*" ("God's will be done"). Fatalism is often accompanied by a tendency to attribute responsibility for personal problems to external causes. It is this tendency of poor recent immigrants toward external attribution that has led some helping practitioners to recommend emphasis on ecological approaches in working with this cultural group (Szapocznik, Scopetta, Aranalde, & Kurtines, 1978; Inclan, 1985; Sandoval & de la Roza, 1986). Fatalism is less prevalent among well-educated or native-born Latinos, however.

First-generation poor Latino immigrants also tend to be **present oriented**; that is, they are more concerned about day-to-day survival than about planning for the future. Typically, they seek help primarily when they are faced with a crisis, not on a preventive basis, and they are unlikely to have the opportunity to make advance provisions for the college education of their children or for the financing of their retirement. In their forced present orientation, they are not much different from other poor, uneducated persons in the United States (Queralt, 1984; Sandoval & de la Roza 1986).

Nonverbal Aspects of Culture

Those Latinos who subscribe to the traditional Spanish culture typically have a more flexible approach toward time than Euro-Americans. This is probably because in their native countries time is not considered very valuable; consequently, human activities are not strictly governed by the clock (Condon, 1988; Inclan, 1985). Traditional Latinos are particularly unlikely to be punctual for social engagements with other Latinos since they tend not to expect the other party to be on time either. For instance, they might show up for dinner half hour later than agreed upon or they might arrive at a party an hour after the designated time. Some may not even be punctual when they have an important business appointment.

When interacting socially, Latinos usually stand closer together than Euro-Americans and they tend to touch more frequently (Henderson, 1989). Female friends often kiss each other on the cheek as part of their greeting ritual or when they say good-bye. Men generally begin and end their interactions with a handshake. Male friends or relatives may embrace when they meet again after not having seen one another for some time, to offer support at difficult times, to offer congratulations or condolences, or when they bid farewell to someone who is going away.

Some Latino Contributors to the U.S. Mainstream Culture

Many U.S. Latinos have made important contributions to U.S. culture. Mentioned here as examples are Nobel Prize-winning geneticist Baruj Benacerraf and Nobel prize-winning biochemist Severo Ochoa; jurist Jose Cabranes; radiologist Manuel Viamonte; Pulitzer prize-winning writer Oscar Hijuelos; writers/poets, Isabel Allende; Edwin Torres, Barry Lopez, Eugenio Florit, and Judith Ortiz Cofer; educators/scholars Jaime Escalante, David Hayes-Bautista, Fernando Torres-Gil, Alejandro Portes, Amado Padilla, and Jorge Dominguez; architect Cesar Pelli; labor leader Cesar Chavez; U.S. Representative Henry Gonzalez; musicians Carlos Montoya, Claudio Arrau, and Jose Feliciano; and business leaders Roberto Goizueta (CEO, Coca-Cola), Joseph Unanue (CEO, Goya), and Arthur Martinez (CEO, Sears).

Additional Observations Pertaining to Latino Cultures

The previous section explored some of the more salient traditions shared by Latino cultures. In addition to partaking of the Spanish language and heritage, the three main Latino groups in the U.S.—Mexican Americans, mainland Puerto Ricans, and Cuban Americans—have distinctive values and customs. This section focuses on some additional characteristics of each of these cultures.

Mexican-American Culture

Some 60 percent of U.S. Latinos are Mexican, with some having lived in the United States since the seventeenth century. Very few Euro-Americans can trace their ancestry in the United States that far back. Other Mexican Americans have been here for several generations. Still others, the majority, arrived recently. Regardless of the time they have been in the United States, many Mexican Americans maintain frequent contact with relatives in Mexico and continue to identify with the Mexican culture. Because the mother country is so close and accessible, it is not difficult for them to travel back and forth and thus to retain Mexican customs, values, and the Spanish language (Bach-y-Rita, 1982).

Although the majority of Mexican Americans live in urban centers (Williams, 1990), a substantial proportion live in rural or semirural areas and in small towns in the Southwest. No other Latino group in the United States has a significant rural population. The rural Mexican-American population generally maintains much closer ties with the traditional Mexican culture than those settled in large urban areas, such as in Los Angeles or San Antonio.

Traditional Mexican-American families are typically closely knit and the majority include both parents. Husbands and wives characteristically treat one another with respect and a certain measure of formality, as the culture discourages excessive intimacy, conflict, or public displays of hostility between spouses. Typically, these families are extended, often including not only those sharing the same household (generally the nuclear or intergenerational unit) but also adult siblings and other close relatives and their respective families (Keefe & Padilla, 1987). Such families often act as important sources of support for their members (Keefe, Padilla, & Carlos, 1979).

Folk-Healing Practices. According to the Mexican folk-healing system known as **curanderismo**, illness and bad luck are the result of weakened ties with the church, the family, and the Mexican culture (Kiev, 1968).

Interestingly, for all that has been said in the literature about the importance of folk healers (*curanderos*) in the Mexican-American culture, Keefe, Padilla, and Carlos (1979) found them to be negligible sources of emotional support, at least among the Mexican Americans of southern California. Specifically, less than 2 percent of the Mexican-American participants in their study had used a curandero in the previous year. Similarly, even though urban Mexican Americans are familiar with folk beliefs, such as the belief in *mal puesto* (hexes or evil spells) and in folk illnesses such as *susto* (fright), *mal de ojo* (evil eye), and *empacho* (a form of indigestion), they seldom consult a folk healer to help them deal with such ailments (Van Oss Marin, Marin, Padilla, & De la Rocha, 1983; Martinez, 1988). When Mexican Americans have physical or mental problems, they prefer to turn to physicians, relatives, or priests than to see a curandero. However, curanderismo plays a more important role in the lives of those who live in rural areas.

Mainland Puerto Rican Culture

The Puerto Rican people have been described as friendly, gregarious, kind, sharing, hospitable, brotherly, and devoted to their families (Cordasco & Bucchioni, 1973). Like Mexican Americans, many **mainland Puerto Ricans** visit the island frequently, thus maintaining their culture and language. They travel to Puerto Rico to visit family members, to be with them when they are sick, to spend Christmas and New Year's Eve, and to attend family celebrations and life-cycle rituals, such as baptisms, graduations, funerals, and weddings (Ghali, 1977). In fact, they travel so much to and from Puerto Rico that, according to Schoch-Spana (1990, p. 270), the Puerto Rican population at any one time can be divided into three segments—a third on the island, a third on the U.S. mainland, and a third in transit between the two!

Religion and Spiritism.

Puerto Ricans are religious and spiritual, although many are not regular churchgoers. The majority are at least nominally Catholic, but a substantial proportion are Pentecostal, Seventh Day Adventists, and Jehovah's Witnesses, as well as Baptist, Methodist, Lutheran, and Episcopalian. Some favor small Protestant congregations because the minister frequently is Puerto Rican rather than foreign born (typically Iberian Spanish) and because these small churches tend to have more active ministries than the Catholic Church. In addition, these small Protestant congregations usually pay more attention to the needs of members by making home visits, caring for the ill, and offering counseling and drug rehabilitation programs, emergency financial aid, and help with housing and employment.

Many mainland Puerto Ricans, regardless of their religious affiliations, regularly consult *espiritistas* to protect themselves from evil spirits and to prevent illness. **Espiritistas** are persons believed to be able to communicate with and to have some control over the dead. They act as mediums, attempting to convince the spirits to help rather than harm their clients and prescribe ointments, herbs, sacrifices, and prayers (Delgado & Humm-Delgado, 1982). Several studies reported by Delgado (1988) indicated that in New York City, for example, the involvement of Puerto Ricans with spiritism ranged from 36 percent to 75 percent of those sampled. Some also practice *santeria*, a syncretic religion to be discussed later.

Cuban-American Culture

Cuban Americans are considered sociable, gregarious, and friendly people. Like Puerto Ricans and other Caribbean islanders, characteristically they relate informally, even to strangers. For instance, to reduce distance and to be friendly, they often address one another using the familiar pronoun, *tu*, instead of the more polite or formal *usted*, which is more frequently used by Central and South Americans (Bernal, 1982).

Like African Americans and mainland Puerto Ricans, Cuban Americans can be intense, noisy, and boisterous among themselves. The traditional culture also values sensuality, playfulness, humor, and gaiety. Cuban psychologists and anthropologists have generally attributed the peculiarities of the traditional Cuban character to a mixture of African and Iberian-Spanish (particularly Andalusian) influences (Bustamante, 1959; Valdes-Cruz, 1977; Queralt, 1984). There is a strong cultural emphasis on being *simpatico* (affable, charming, pleasant, light, and easy going). To be *antipatico* or *pesado* (disagreeable or heavy) is almost a cultural sin. Humor, in the form of *choteo* (bantering and teasing), joking, and *relajo* (an attitude of freedom to do as one pleases), is also part of the traditional Cuban national character (Manach, 1969; Queralt, 1984).

In comparison to other people from the Third World, many Cuban Americans seem to be assertive and self-confident, as if they thought they were in some way special. This characteristic may in part derive from the large number of middle-class persons in this refugee group. However, since this trait is also seen in those who are not middle class, it may partly stem from the geopolitical importance that the island of Cuba has had historically vis-à-vis powerful nations, such as Spain during the colonial period, the United States until the 1950s, and, more recently, the now extinct Soviet Union (Bernal, 1982). In other words, because "superpowers" have had a close relationship with this small island nation for their own strategic reasons, its people may have developed an inflated sense of self-importance. Regardless of the origin of this cultural trait, the traditional Cuban-American assertiveness and self-confidence is sometimes misperceived by other Latin Americans as aggressiveness, racism, classism, arrogance, or grandiosity (Chilman, 1993).

Alternative Religion. Although the majority of Cubans are Catholic, at least nominally, a small minority belong to various Protestant denominations and some also practice *santeria.* **Santeria** is a syncretic religion that combines elements of Roman Catholicism with ancient West African (Yoruba) beliefs and practices. Specifically, the central belief in santeria is that the deities, or *orishas*, take the form of Roman Catholic saints, such as Santa Barbara, to influence people, bringing them health and good fortune as well as illness and misfortune. Folk healers, or *santeros*, diagnose problems, and, through rituals and animal sacrifices, placate or thwart the deities, exorcise evil spirits, and assist in curing folk illnesses (Boswell & Curtis, 1983).

The extent of U.S. Cubans' involvement in santeria is unknown; however, Sandoval (1979) has suggested that it is widespread. It is more frequently practiced by individuals of limited educational background and low socioeconomic status as well as by some who migrated from Cuba in recent years. These individuals adopted this alternative religious belief system under the Castro regime because of the government's former opposition to traditional religion (Hallman & Campbell, 1983, p. 55).

ASIAN-AMERICAN CULTURES

"We do not even eat rice the same."
—Christine M. Chao (1992)

Asian Americans living in the United States constitute an aggregate of highly diverse people from many different countries who speak different languages, practice different religions, belong to different socioeconomic groups, and have different generational statuses (e.g., immigrants, native born, second, or third generation). Those who are recent immigrants tend to think and behave like their compatriots in their countries of origin. In contrast, their children are much more proficient in the use of the English language and acculturated to the "American way." Still, many second-generation U.S.-born Asian Americans keep their cultural heritage alive, depending on how much it is cultivated by their parents at home. Third and later generations of Asian Americans resemble Euro-Americans much more in terms of their English proficiency, professed values, and lifestyle. Notwithstanding their high levels of acculturation to the mainstream, many continue to take much pride in their ethnic heritage. Some Asian-American families are able to remain bicultural for several generations.

Because there are important cultural differences between East Asians and Asian Indians, and because space is limited, this book's coverage of Asian Americans has been restricted to East Asians, including groups such as the Chinese, Japanese, Koreans, Filipino, Vietnamese, and other Southeast Asians. This section will address fundamental aspects of East Asian cultures. (For additional details about family life, please refer to Chapter 9. For background and demographic information about Asian Americans, please consult Chapter 4.)

Language, Philosophy, and Religion

Asian Americans speak various languages, including Chinese, Japanese, Korean, and Vietnamese, among others. Within each ethnic group, people speak different dialects. Some Chinese, for instance, speak Cantonese; others speak Mandarin; and still others speak Fukienese. Despite the proliferation of languages and dialects, those who speak languages based on Chinese characters—the Chinese, Japanese, and Koreans, for example—can communicate in a rudimentary manner in writing, although not verbally since the pronunciation of each language is different (Chien & Yamamoto, 1982).

Confucianism, a highly conservative and sexist philosophy, has had tremendous influence on East Asian cultures, particularly the cultures of China, Japan, Korea, and Vietnam. Even the Filipino have been considerably influenced by this system because many Chinese people who practiced Confucianism migrated to the Philippines. Confucianism puts emphasis on a hierarchical or vertical ordering of the society on the basis of age, gender, and social position. Specifically, it confers elders, males, and individuals in high positions higher status than those who are younger, female, or in lower positions (Barnlund, 1989).

Confucianism also stresses the importance of maintaining social harmony by practicing the virtue of mutual benevolence in the five basic social relationships, including the relationship between father and son, husband and wife, older brother and younger brother, "ruler" (e.g., teacher or employer) and "subject" (e.g., student or employee), and between friends (Chien & Yamamoto, 1982; Henderson, 1989). According to this philosophy, the relationship between father and son should be governed by reverence toward the father and strictness and love toward the son, that between husband and wife by submission toward the husband and goodness and understanding toward the wife. The relationship between older brother and younger brother should be governed by wisdom and gentleness toward the younger sibling and by respect toward the older brother, that between employer or teacher and employee or student by loyalty toward the employer/teacher and benevolence toward the employee/student. Finally, the relationship between friends should be governed by mutual trust (Locke, 1992).

As far as religion, most East Asians practice Buddhism, Taoism, or Shintoism, although some are Christian, including a substantial number of Korean, Vietnamese, and Filipino (Locke, 1992). Buddhism is dominant among the Chinese, Koreans, and Southeast Asians (e.g., the Vietnamese, Laotian, Cambodians, and Thai). This religion stresses the value of self-control, humility, generosity, love, and mercy as well as the importance of education and of cultivating a correct lifestyle, including "right views, right desires, right speech, right conduct, right occupation, and right extinction of all cravings" (Henderson, 1989, p. 70). Buddhists also believe in reincarnation. According to this belief system, each person's life is determined by good or bad deeds in a previous life and the goal is to perfect oneself so as to attain liberation from rebirth cycles (Locke, 1992).

Shintoism is the national religion of Japan, although many Japanese also practice Buddhism. Shintoism stresses respect for nature and the importance of harmonious social relations (Barnlund, 1989). Taoism, an ancient philosophical-poetic system, is practiced by some Chinese, Koreans, and Southeast Asians. This religion teaches detachment and the importance of living a simple life in tune with nature and the universe. Followers practice breath control and other exercises similar to Hatha yoga and use herbal medicines (Henderson, 1989; Harrison et al., 1992; Locke, 1992).

Family Values and the Patriarchal System

Asian Americans typically maintain strong mutually helpful ties with family members. Particularly among Southeast Asian immigrants and refugees who have come to the United States recently, one frequently finds large extended-family groups living together, including parents, children, grandparents, aunts and uncles, and even friends. Such collective living arrangements, reflective of family solidarity and interdependence, allow them to save money to get started in their new lives in the United States (Nishio & Bilmes, 1987).

The father is the head of the traditional East Asian family, its principal decision maker, and chief disciplinarian (Locke, 1992). Customs are changing rapidly under the force of modernization and industrialization and as more Asian women join the work force. Traditionally, however, Asian cultures relegated women primarily to domestic duties, child care, and tilling the land (in the case of those in rural areas), expecting them to be subservient to their fathers, husbands, and male children.

Filial piety is a cardinal family value in all the East Asian cultures influenced by Confucianism. According to this doctrine, children are duty bound to respect their parents, to listen to them, and to obey them without question, regardless of how good or bad their parents may be.

Styles of Social Interaction

According to a Japanese saying, "The nail that stands out gets pounded down." This proverb conveys the value that Confucianism places on selflessness and deference to the collective unit. According to this philosophical tradition, blending in with others is important to maintain harmony and solidarity in social relationships. From a very young age, Asians are taught to subordinate their needs and desires to the family or group, to suppress and control their emotions or personal opinions, and to be sensitive to the reactions of their peers (Locke, 1992). Parents discourage children from being aggressive, boastful, disagreeable, critical, offensive, or competitive; rather, the children are taught that the way to gain social esteem and self-respect is by complying with social norms and restraining expressions of individualism. However, not all Asian groups value collectivism to the same extent. For example, Koreans and Thai place more emphasis on individualism, although always within the context of restraint, moderation, and avoidance of confrontation in interpersonal relations.

The emphasis on the group as opposed to the individual goes hand in hand with the East Asian preference for interdependency in human relations. The Japanese, for example, according to the principle of *amae*, are expected to establish mutually interdependent relationships governed by love coupled with a sense of reciprocal obligation, indebtedness, responsibility, and duty (Locke, 1992). In this context, those who strive for independence are perceived as defiant, self-centered, and inconsiderate of others (Barnlund, 1989). This is quite different from the Euro-American male emphasis on individualism and independence.

It is important to understand, however, that while the traditional East Asian cultures teach obedience and submission to the group, such as the family, work, or peer group, this solidarity and spirit of cooperation does not extend to outside groups in which the individual does not have membership. Indeed, East Asians can be distrustful, competitive, and uncooperative in their relations with those they consider to be outsiders (Goleman, 1990).

When interacting socially with a person they do not know well, East Asians characteristically stand at a greater distance than Euro-Americans. Among the Japanese or Vietnamese, for example, this custom may be related to the ritual of bowing since they must make sure to leave sufficient space for everyone to bow without bumping into anyone else. The Japanese bow is done in accordance with the social position of the person who is being greeted—the higher the person's position, the deeper and slower the bow the person is due. To greet someone they have not seen in a long time, Japanese bow repeatedly (Furuto, Biswas, Chung, Murase, & Ross-Sheriff, 1992; Locke, 1992).

Physical contact among adults is usually limited in public, particularly among opposite-sex adults; for instance, the Japanese people who subscribe to the traditional culture are much less likely to touch, kiss, caress, or hug in public than Euro-Americans. Yet, East Asian mothers (including the Japanese) are very demonstrative physically with their young children, and in some East Asian cultures same-sex close friends may walk hand-in-hand in public, a behavior that has no connotation of homosexuality (Barnlund, 1989; Furuto et al., 1992).

It is not customary for East Asians to invite others to their homes. This practice is a function of the very compact living arrangements typical throughout Asia that are not conducive to entertaining others comfortably. Under such conditions, home hospitality is rare and reserved for relatives or very close friends and for the most special of occasions. However, homes in the United States are more spacious; therefore, Asian Americans are less observant of this custom.

Communication Styles

In accordance with their cultural traditions, many East Asians value silence and reservation and prefer to communicate indirectly, subtly, and nonverbally rather than openly and straightforwardly, as is more characteristic of Euro-Americans (Furuto et al., 1992; Locke, 1992). In Japan, for example, it is considered wise to speak as little as possible because "it is the shallow water that makes noise" (Haglund, 1988, p. 91). Typically, traditional Asians speak softly and maintain low levels of eye contact because they are taught that speaking in a loud voice or maintaining too much direct eye contact with a person of higher status is impolite and disrespectful (Henderson, 1989; Furuto et al., 1992; Locke, 1992). Table 2.3 shows some expressions that are representative of differing views of East and West.

Unlike Euro-Americans who favor direct communication, those who adhere to the traditional East Asian cultures prefer to convey negative messages subtly or indirectly. For example, instead of outright saying "no," culturally it is more acceptable for East Asians to say "yes" in such a manner that the person spoken to gets the message that it actually means "no" or, at best, "perhaps." Similarly, anger or disgust are not usually expressed openly; rather, there is a preference for conveying these feelings more subtly, such as by a narrowing of the eyes or by using other indirect means (Argyle, 1988). It is also considered improper to embarrass or to be impolite toward another person, even if slightly. For instance, if another person were to ask, "Did I make myself clear?" the proper response would be, according to the traditional East Asian cultures, "Yes, of course," even if what the other person said was not at all clear (Henderson, 1989).

Cultural Values: Honor, Moderation, Self-Effacement, Fatalism

Traditional East Asian cultures teach that it is the duty of each family member to preserve the family's dignity and honor. The entire family—living members, ancestors, and future generations—loses face, for example, if one of its members does poorly at work or in school, has mental or emotional problems, becomes an alcoholic, is unemployed, or has trouble with the law. Consequently, family members are expected to function in society and to interact with others in a manner that protects and enhances the family name and honor and to avoid discussion of personal or family problems with outsiders because this may bring shame to them (Ho, 1976). In extreme cases, individuals who have brought shame to their families (or other collective units to which they

TABLE 2.3   Expressions Representative of the Differing Views of the East and West

THE EAST	THE WEST
What is possible depends upon the circumstances.	All things are possible.
One does not make the wind but is blown by it.	Where there is a will, there is a way.
	I am the captain of my soul, captain of my fate.
	The word *impossible* is only in the dictionary of fools.
The greatness of a person may be measured by one's humility, not by one's assertiveness. "Quiet waters run deep."	The squeaky wheel that gets the oil.
	You have to blow your own horn.
	Faint heart never won fair maiden.
	Nice guys finish last.
The nail that stands above the board gets nailed down.	He who travels fastest travels alone.
	Two roads diverged in a wood And I—I took the one less traveled by And that has made all the difference
	If a man does not keep pace with his companions, perhaps it is because he hears a different drummer.

Source: "Japan: Cultural Considerations" by F. E. Haglund in *Intercultural Communication: A Reader* (p. 92) by L. A. Samovar and R. E. Porter (Eds.), 1988, Belmont, CA: Wadsworth. Copyright 1988 by Wadsworth Publishing Co. Reprinted by permission.

belong, such as the work organization) may commit suicide to show the depth of their regret. In Asian cultures, killing oneself is considered an honorable way of dealing with one's problems (Ryan, 1985).

Among other things, Confucianism stresses the value of the "middle way" or moderation (Ryan, 1985; Ho, 1976). According to this philosophy, people are expected to control any extremes of feeling or behaving (e.g., conceit or excessive pride, anger, frustration, excessive enthusiasm, indifference, disappointment, or feelings of inferiority) and to pursue pleasure with moderation, being neither self-denying nor overly self-indulgent. The ideal is to stay neither ahead nor behind others but in step with the group.

From an early age, traditional East Asians learn to be modest and to avoid calling attention to themselves. By avoiding extremes of feeling and behaving, they are able to keep a low profile and to pass inconspicuously. This self-effacement is considered important in preserving group harmony. The thousands of Asians who have entered the United States illegally through the years have learned to appreciate the value of maintaining low visibility (Ho, 1992).

Buddhism, Confucianism, and Taoism also teach the value of calmly accepting one's situation and fate rather than attempting to change or control the environment (Henderson, 1989; Ho, 1992). Followers of these philosophical systems tend to develop a fatalistic attitude characterized by resignation and adeptness at making the most of existing situations. Such attitudes of acceptance and resignation, coupled with the cultural emphasis on preserving the family honor, make traditional East Asians reluctant to seek out help from human service agencies.

Some Asian-American Contributors to U.S. Culture

Many Asian Americans have made substantial contributions to the U.S. culture. Consider, for example, Nobel prize-winning physicists Chen Ning Yang and Tsung-Dao Lee; Nobel prize-winning chemist Yuan T. Lee; scientists/scholars Stephen Chu, James Fujimoto, Patrick Lee, H. T. Kung, Calvin Lin, Meng-yuan Wang, Woodward Yang, and Jin-Au Kong; economist Takeshi Amemiya; musicians Seiji Ozawa, Yo-Yo-Ma, and Midori; writers/poets Amy Tan and Maxine Hong Kinston; architect I. M. Pei, figure skater Kristi Yamaguchi; Senator Samuel Hayakawa; and media personality Connie Chung.

GAY AND LESBIAN CULTURES

The terms *gay culture* and *lesbian culture* are used here to refer to attitudes, common experiences, lifestyles, behaviors, artistic productions and other activities, and a sense of shared history common to gays and lesbians in the United States (Cruikshank, 1992, p. 119). Traditionally, social scientists have attributed the development of gay and lesbian cultures that are separate and distinct from the U.S. mainstream culture to discrimination and oppression. That is, they have suggested that the societal condemnation and exclusion of gays and lesbians forced them to lead an underground existence and to create a separate world where they could satisfy their need for love and friendship, support and belonging, and sexual partners.

To be sure, the gay/lesbian cultures have developed, in part, as a result of societal dis-

approval of homosexuality that served to accentuate the sense of separateness from the mainstream among gays and lesbians and the need for them to unite and collaborate. However, societal stigmatization probably has not been the only force or even the main impetus in shaping the gay and lesbian cultures. That is, even if the society were to drop completely its opposition to homosexuality, gays and lesbians would likely continue to have a separate and distinct community out of a sense of commonality, not just out of a feeling of social rejection (Cruikshank, 1992). In addition, it should be noted that the inclination of many gay men, for example, toward certain fields of endeavor, such as literature and the arts, is often evident early in their lives before they have suffered any major societal reaction as **homosexuals.** This indicates that the determinants of certain special inclinations or sensibilities and the related choice of occupations that facilitate their cultivation are probably as least in part intrinsic rather than the result of societal labeling (Whitam & Mathy, 1986).

The gay and lesbian cultures in the United States in the mid-1990s represented the values, lifestyles, and behaviors of a relatively small but growing proportion of gays and lesbians who were open about their sexual orientation, at least within some social circle, and actively pursued a gay lifestyle (Dynes, 1990). A large proportion of gays and lesbians were probably not participating to any significant extent in the gay or lesbian communities for a variety of reasons. Perhaps some did not pursue an open gay or lesbian lifestyle because they preferred to keep their sexual orientation private in fear that it might cause problems for them at work or with family or friends. Others perhaps did not participate because they did not know about the existence of a gay or lesbian community in the localities where they resided or because they lived in small towns or isolated areas with no appreciable gay life. Due to the selective nature of their participation, the gay and lesbian cultures of the mid-1990s were unlikely to represent the actual values, behaviors, and lifestyles of the gay and lesbian population in the United States.

It is also important to keep in mind that there is no such thing as a monolithic gay or lesbian culture anymore than there is a single "straight" or heterosexual culture in the United States. People vary in their value systems, behaviors, and lifestyles according to many factors, such as race, gender, ethnic origin, level of education, socioeconomic status, religion, societal position, occupation, generation, and sexual orientation, among other things. Thus, sexual orientation is only one of the many variables that determine human behavior. Practically speaking, this means that a native-born, middle-class, Catholic, suburban Euro-American who happens to be gay or lesbian may have more in common with a native-born, middle-class, Catholic, suburban Euro-American who happens to be heterosexual than with a working-class, Pentecostal, Puerto Rican immigrant or an inner-city, Baptist, African American, both of whom happen to be gay or lesbian. Moreover, there is a big gap between the older and the younger generations of gays and lesbians (Summer, 1993). The point is that a person's sexual orientation is important, but other personally defining characteristics are equally important in determining values, behaviors, and lifestyle preferences.

Surviving in the Underground

Old Meeting Places

Until recently, gays and lesbians were kept "underground," so to speak, by society; that is, they were given little opportunity by the society to congregate and fraternize openly. It was under these repressive circumstances that the gay bar culture emerged, as bars were among the very few places where homosexuals could meet. Bars served not only as the main establishments where homosexuals and some lesbians (particularly those of lower socioeconomic status) met other gay and lesbian friends and

potential sex partners but as centers of entertainment and social activity (Majors, 1988; Dynes, 1990).

Notwithstanding the important functions they have traditionally served, gay bars contributed to the high rates of alcoholism among urban gays and lesbians, to the overconsumption of drugs, and to the spread of acquired immune deficiency syndrome (AIDS) among gay men (Dynes, 1990). These unfortunate consequences, coupled with the recent emphasis in the U.S. culture on self-restraint and commitment, prompted many gay persons to give up alcohol, drugs, and recreational sex in favor of abstinence, exercise, healthy nutrition, and the establishment of longer-term relationships (Yankelovich, 1984; Herdt, 1992). Consequently, since the 1980s, as the mainstream society has become somewhat more accepting of gays and lesbians, fewer have been using bars as their principal meeting places or centers of activity.

In the 1960s and 1970s, sometimes referred to as the "golden age" of impersonal gay male sex, bathhouses were also important institutions in the underground gay culture. Despite their name, these establishments were not primarily health clubs but places where gay men met to have quick, consensual, and often anonymous sex. This part of the old gay culture is now practically extinct, as the majority of bathhouses in the United States closed their doors in the 1980s after the AIDS epidemic outbreak, and the few remaining establishments became physical fitness clubs.

Traditionally, gay beaches were also important meeting places for gays. Many still exist but their significance in the rapidly evolving gay culture is now more limited. For the most part, gay beaches are located in remote and difficult-to-reach waterfront areas to discourage heterosexuals from wandering in. In large urban communities, sometimes a portion of a public beach is designated as gay territory and gays are allowed to meet in these areas without constant police harassment. Traditionally, lesbians have been less likely to establish and hold any territory as their own because women have had limited power in this society; however, in some localities they have established lesbian enclaves within gay beaches (Dynes, 1990).

Old Ways of Identifying One Another

For as long as society has prohibited homosexual behaviors and pushed gays and lesbians underground, every generation has been forced to develop certain behaviors and signs by which they can recognize others with similar inclinations. However, given the traditional societal stigmatization of same-sex relationships, many gays and lesbians have kept their sexual orientation private and have chosen not to publicize it in any way.

In the more sexually active days prior to the AIDS epidemic, some gays would regularly go out searching for sexual partners at gay bars, gay beaches, bathhouses, favored streets and parks, and adult movie theaters. This ritual was known as **cruising** and included various ways of calling attention to oneself, such as by staring intensely at another individual or by wearing a visible key ring or a colored bandanna hanging from a rear pocket (Dynes, 1990). With the advent of AIDS, the sexual signaling aspects of cruising became less important, for the most part, and the cruising ritual evolved into subtle behaviors and symbols by which gays and lesbians made themselves known to others with similar inclinations. For example, among men, these more subtle behaviors have included the skilled use of eye contact, certain mannerisms, body postures, facial gestures, ways of dressing, and use of proximity and touch in social interaction (Majors, 1988).

Some heterosexuals think that gay men can be recognized by their effeminacy and imitation of women in their sex-role playing. Similarly, they tend to stereotype lesbians as mannish women. The reality is often contradictory. Regardless of sexual orientation, men's and women's sex-role playing and outward behaviors range from what traditionally has been considered "masculine" to "feminine." In other words, men who look "masculine" may be gay, bisexual, or heterosexual, and men who look "effeminate" may be heterosexual, bisexual, or gay. Similarly, some "feminine"-looking women are lesbians, whereas others are bisexual or heterosexual; and some "masculine"-looking women are heterosexual, whereas others are bisexual or lesbian. Research has not yet established if among "effeminate" males those who are gay are over-represented vis-à-vis those who are heterosexual; similarly, it remains to be determined systematically if lesbians are overrepresented among "masculine" women.

Effeminacy, lisping, and a special voice inflection were cultivated by some gays in the past as a way of signaling their sexual orientation to others like them within a society that prevented them from being themselves openly. However, the younger generation is much less likely to play the so-called **faggot** role. In fact, in trying to shed their traditional effeminate reputation, in the 1980s, some gay men went overboard in the development of a hypermasculine image, including pumped-up muscles, mustaches, and beards. This macho style has lost popularity as gays have become more comfortably themselves in physique, behavior, and attire (Levine, 1992; Murray, 1992).

Like gays, many lesbians nowadays do not play stereotypic sex roles. In the past, however, some lesbians known as **butches** made themselves obvious to other women by wearing "masculine" attire and by adopting traditionally "masculine" mannerisms. Such stereotyped role playing is less common now. However, some women, both lesbian and heterosexual, are naturally "masculine" in physical characteristics or demeanor. Many lead an active and athletic lifestyle and feel more comfortable in pants rather than wearing skirts and blouses or dresses. Similarly, many active women prefer to wear simple, short hairstyles rather than long hair or complicated hairdos, flat footwear rather than high heels, and little or no makeup.

As noted earlier, gays and lesbians have traditionally used various concrete symbols to signify their sexual orientation so that they can be recognized by others like them. These have changed from generation to generation, sometimes from year to year. For example, some lesbians, particularly those from the 1960s generation, favored the use of pinky rings,[2] heavy silver jewelry, or keys hanging from the belt (Grahn, 1984). The younger generation of gays and lesbians tend to use other symbols, such as earrings worn asymmetrically (e.g., in only one ear or different numbers in each ear) or special tattoos. Some of these fads, such as the use of asymmetrical earrings and pinky rings, have become so popular with heterosexuals that they do not necessarily suggest anything about sexual orientation anymore (Hall, 1991). Other symbols used by gays and lesbians are less likely to appeal to the wider culture, such as necklaces with pendants in the shape of the lower-case Greek letter lambda, which is the traditional symbol of gay liberation, or with a double women's symbol. In the United States, the color lavender—a blend of pink/red (associated with females) and blue (associated with males)—has been the most persistently associated with the gay culture (Jay & Young, 1978; Grahn, 1984; Dynes, 1990).

Coming Out

The most significant right of passage or life crisis for many gays and lesbians is a process referred to as coming out, an experience shared widely regardless of race, ethnicity, socioeconomic status, or age. **Coming out** involves a change in self-concept and in the nature of the individual's relations with others.

It is the culmination of a gradual internal and external transformational process that may stretch over several years during which the individual goes through several stages in the development of his or her identity as gay or lesbian (Coleman, 1982; Herdt, 1992). Coming out means different things to different gays and lesbians. For those who are older, it may refer to their first homosexual experience or to finding gay and lesbian friends or discovering the gay life. To some people, coming out means coming to accept their gay identity (Cruikshank, 1992). To others, it means becoming more open (less secretive) about their sexual identity. Nowadays, the term is used often to refer to the act of *telling* someone else (usually a friend or family member who assumed the person was "straight" or heterosexual) about one's same-sex sexual orientation. It also includes making some public acknowledgment of one's sexual orientation, such as going to a meeting of a gay organization, attending a gay party, or attending services at a gay church, with a feeling of commonality with other gays there rather than just as an observer (Murray, 1992). People of color may find it especially difficult to reveal their gay or lesbian identity because they, perhaps more than those who are white, value the support and allegiance of their families and racial/ethnic community in dealing with a white-dominated society. By coming out, they risk rejection or retaliation from their own group (Cruikshank, 1992).

Culturally, as well as psychologically, coming-out experiences are important to gays and lesbians; consequently, they frequently share their own stories with friends and significant others (Dynes, 1990).

Gay Liberation and Gay Rights

The gay liberation movement emerged in the early 1970s fueled by the antiwar movement, the civil rights movement, and the women's liberation movement. The protest movements of the 1960s showed that ingrained ideas, such as the need to wage war against another nation or the belief in the inferiority of blacks or women, could be exposed for what they were—prejudices fostered by the dominant group for their own self-interest rather than self-evident truths. This emergent national climate of anti-authoritarianism and nonconformity also made it possible for gays and lesbians to question the damaging labels previously applied to them, such as "sick" and "sinful." Societal injustices perpetrated against them gave them a righteous cause to pursue and the civil rights and antiwar mass demonstrations provided a model of activism to follow (Cruikshank, 1992).

Although lesbian groups in the United States existed prior to the early 1970s, they did not thrive before the women's liberation movement because of strong societal taboos against homosexuality coupled with lack of power among women. It was not until large numbers of women came together to challenge the male-dominated society that lesbian liberation began to take hold largely within the women's movement. Feminism, as a liberation ideology, became central to the lives of many lesbians who embraced it with zeal and determination, and lesbians became highly influential within the women's movement (Cruikshank, 1992).

Large numbers of gays and lesbians did not embrace the gay liberation movement until after Stonewall. The Stonewall Inn was a Greenwich Village (New York City) gay bar that was raided by the police in 1969. Thousands of gay bars had been raided routinely by the police before, but the fear of exposure had always kept gays and lesbians quiet. What made Stonewall different was that, for the first time, they fought back and rioted. Thus, Stonewall came to symbolize the end of the gay and lesbian willingness to be victimized. It was after Stonewall that the era of gay power began with the formation of the Gay Liberation Front and the Gay Activist Alliance (Cruikshank, 1992).

An important victory for the gay rights movement came in 1973 when, after years of discussion and pressure from gay activists, the American Psychiatric Association declassified homosexuality as a mental disorder, stating that there was no scientific basis for it. This eliminated the stigma of "mental illness" that had been so detrimental to many gays and lesbians. Another incident that prompted many gays and

lesbians to collaborate and join the gay liberation movement was the Save Our Children campaign of Anita Bryant in 1977, which aimed to repeal gay rights previously granted in several U.S. cities. In 1978, the Briggs initiative in California, which if successful would have required schools to fire homosexual teachers, also mobilized more gay and lesbians into coming out of the **closet** and joining the gay rights movement. Finally, the killing of San Francisco city supervisor Harvey Milk in 1978, the first gay person elected to office in a major city and a campaigner against the Briggs initiative, brought even more people into the gay rights movement. With the infusion of people, the movement became less radicalized and more mainstream.

Many important gains in the quest for civil rights were made by gays and lesbians in the 1970s. For example, some of the more blatant forms of discrimination against gays (e.g., bar raids and police harassment) were stopped or at least reduced, some states began to decriminalize private homosexual acts between consenting adults, dozens of cities began to pass legislation protecting the civil rights of gay people, and the federal government started to dismantle its antihomosexual civil service regulations. However, the civil rights gains of the 1970s could not be consolidated due to the emergence of AIDS, which required a sudden redirection of energies within the gay community toward the new life-and-death and discrimination issues brought to the fore by this deadly disease that generated considerable antihomosexual public sentiment (Cruikshank, 1992).

Today, the gay rights agenda is pursued by well-financed gay and lesbian organizations engaging in sophisticated lobbying and other political activities. Its general aim is to do away with all laws and practices in U.S. society that still discriminate against gays and lesbians and to extend to gay people the protections of the Civil Rights Act, thus making them full and equal citizens under the law. High on the gay rights agenda are the goals of (1) ending housing and job discrimination on the basis of sexual orientation; (2) repealing the remaining sodomy laws; (3) stopping discrimination against gays and lesbians in the military, in federal security clearances, and in areas of family law, such as custody, visitation, adoption, and foster care; (4) ending the remaining traces of police harassment; (5) stopping antigay violence; and (6) ending AIDS-related discrimination (Cruikshank, 1992).

New Meeting Places and Organizations

Today, there is considerable emphasis within the gay and lesbian communities and within the wider society on healthier ways of satisfying basic human needs for sociability and connectedness. This has resulted in the proliferation of gay and lesbian leisure-time meeting places and activities, such as restaurants, coffee houses, bookstores, choral ensembles, musical festivals, athletic teams and tournaments, leisure clubs that sponsor sport and recreational activities, cooking clubs, and movie groups that cater primarily to the gay/lesbian communities. In addition, there is a variety of gay churches (e.g., the Metropolitan Community Church) and gay subgroups within traditional churches (e.g., Dignity within the Catholic Church). There are also volunteer service agencies and various twelve-step programs designed especially for gays and modeled after the twelve-step system of Alcoholics Anonymous to deal with problems of alcoholism, drug addiction, codependency, and sexual addiction. Gays and lesbians in the United States have established many organizations and voluntary associations through which they pursue a large variety of interests and goals—civil rights, business, professional, political, family, racial/ethnic, generational, campus related, and educational. They also have started a large number of business establishments. The annual *Gayellow Pages* in its national, regional, and city editions includes information about gay/lesbian establishments and organizations.

Among activist and political organizations concentrating on civil rights at the national level are the National Gay and Lesbian Task Force, the Lambda Legal Defense and Education Fund, the Human Rights Campaign Fund, and the International Gay and Lesbian Human Rights Commission. There are also a variety of racial/ethnic national organizations, such as the Black Gay and Lesbian Leadership Forum, the National Latino/ Lesbian & Gay Organization, and the Gay Asian Pacific Alliance. Examples of other national organizations include the National Federation of Parents and Friends of Gays, the Gay and Lesbian Parents Coalition International, Children of Lesbians and Gays Everywhere, the Gay Parents Custody Fund, the National Gay Alliance for Young Adults, the National Gay Youth Network, and the National Committee on Lesbian and Gay Issues of the National Association of Social Workers.

Literature and Music

Literature has always been an important vehicle for self-expression and for building solidarity among gays and lesbians, and poetry has held a special place in lesbian culture. However, until recently few publishing houses, except small outfits and gay and lesbian presses, published works with homosexual themes. The new receptiveness of several major U.S. mainstream publishing houses in the 1990s to the works of gay and lesbian writers has led to an explosion of publications. Some writers have gained national recognition. For example, in 1992, gay writer Paul Monette won a National Book Award for his book *Becoming a Man: Half a Life Story* (Harcourt Brace Jovanovich) and Pulitzer Prize-winning lesbian poet Mary Oliver won a National Book Award for her *New and Selected Poems* (Beacon Press).

In addition, several recent books by gays and lesbians have climbed onto national and regional bestseller lists, such as Randy Shilts's *Conduct Unbecoming: Gays and Lesbians in the U.S. Military* (St. Martin's Press), Michelangelo Signorile's *Queer in America: Sex, the Media and the Closets of Power* (1993, Random House), Martin Duberman's *Stonewall* (1993, Dutton), and Frank Browning's *The Culture of Desire: Paradox and Perversity in Gay Lives Today* (1993, Crown).

Gays and lesbians have also established a number of magazines and newsletters. These publications help them to keep up with the latest happenings within the gay and lesbian communities and to stay in touch with their rapidly evolving cultures and with the gay and lesbian points of view on social and political issues. For example, *The Advocate* is the most widely read gay and lesbian serial publication. Other newer gay and lesbian magazines were struggling to become established in the mid-1990s, such as *Out, Genre*, and *QW* (Matthews, 1992).

Musical choruses have become important vehicles to promote gay pride while members engage in a wholesome and enjoyable social and musical activity. Many gay and some lesbian choral ensembles are in existence, with several having attained a high enough level of professionalism to perform in major concert halls, singing under renowned conductors and with famous guest artists. Some gay choruses receive small subsidies from city governments or other local and state agencies and even from the National Endowment for the Arts (Gordon, 1990).

Some Gay and Lesbian Contributors to U.S. Culture

Gays and lesbians have made worthy contributions to U.S. culture in all areas of endeavor. In some fields, their legacy has been very significant. Lesbians, for example, have devoted substantial efforts to the women's liberation movement, feminism, and women's rights. The gay men's contributions have been most obvious and impressive in literature, music, the arts, and the entertainment world. (Because sexual orientation is still a private and sensitive matter in U.S. society, the list of contributors that fol-

lows is less "current" and more historical than other lists in this chapter.) Some of the major gay and lesbian contributors to U.S. literature include Oscar Wilde, Tennessee Williams, W. H. Auden, Gertrude Stein, Walt Whitman, James Baldwin, and Truman Capote. Among social/political leaders are Susan B. Anthony, Florence Nightingale, and Harvey Milk. Among artists, musicians, and movie stars are Cole Porter, Leonard Bernstein, K. D. Lang, Rock Hudson, Montgomery Clift, and Andy Warhol.

THE CULTURE OF AMERICAN JEWS

A detailed examination of Jewish culture is beyond the scope of this chapter; however, basic information about some of the religious customs associated with Judaism may be useful to those of you who are unfamiliar with the Jewish tradition. Judaism is one of the oldest religions in the world and the first to teach about the existence of one God as opposed to many different deities. It is the foundation from which Christianity and Islam later developed.

Ashkenazic and Sephardic Jews

Jews are divided into two major groups—Ashkenazim and Sephardim—each with its distinct origins and traditions. (A third smaller group is composed of the Mizrachi or Arab Jews [Soifer, 1991].) The Ashkenazim are the most populous group in the United States. **Ashkenazic** (i.e., European or German) Jews or their foreparents came to the United States from Central and Eastern Europe, whereas the **Sephardic** (i.e., Spanish) Jews or their ancestors came from the Mediterranean, from places such as Turkey, Palestine, Egypt, North Africa, Spain, and Italy (Schiffman, 1986). As a rule (with many exceptions), the Sephardim can be distinguished from the Ashkenazim by their darker complexion, hair, and eyes.

Both Jewish groups originally spoke different languages. The Ashkenazim spoke (and some still speak) Yiddish, a dialect similar to

German. In contrast, the Sephardim spoke Ladino, an ancient language resembling Spanish. The two groups also differ in terms of food preferences. The Sephardim cuisine is Mediterranean, including foods similar to those you would find in a Greek or Lebanese restaurant, for example. In contrast, the Ashkenazim cuisine is composed of foods usually served in the United States at Jewish delicatessens, such as matzoh ball soup, bagels, borscht, lox, gefilte fish, blintzes, corned beef, and pastrami.

Orthodox, Conservative, and Reform Jews

In terms of their religious practices and traditions, some American Jews are Orthodox, whereas others are Conservative or Reformed.[3] In addition, there are secular Jews who maintain a Jewish identity even though they do not practice any religion. **Orthodox Jews** show the highest degree of adherence to the original Jewish faith and traditions. For example, they strictly observe the Sabbath from sundown on Friday until sundown on Saturday as a time of prayer, enjoyment, and rest from work. During the Sabbath, Orthodox Jews refrain from engaging in many activities besides work, such as writing, shopping, or using money (Schneider, 1989). Men must wear black garments and hats and cannot shave their beards. Married women are required to cover their hair when they go out; thus, many wear wigs. Orthodox religious services are held in Hebrew, and the men and women attend separately. Prayers must be recited in Hebrew, every day in the morning, afternoon, and evening.

Orthodox Jews strictly observe Jewish dietary laws and only eat **kosher** foods—that is, foods prepared in accordance with these laws. For example, they are not allowed to eat pork or shellfish or to mix milk and meat products at the same meal or to use the same utensils and dishes to cook or serve milk and meat product. Beef can be eaten only if it comes from a healthy animal killed quickly and painlessly under religious supervision and if the flesh has been salted and drained of all the blood (Schiffman, 1986; Bennett, 1988). **Conservative Jews** are less strict than the Orthodox in their observance of the Jewish dietary laws. Many follow dietary laws at public functions at the synagogue, but they may or may not keep a kosher kitchen at home. **Reformed Jews** are the least likely to eat kosher.

In their religious observances, Conservative Jews and particularly Reformed Jews make more use of English than the Orthodox, allow men and women to worship together, and, unlike the Orthodox, have identical religious roles for both sexes, including the ability of women to become cantors or rabbis. Conservative Jews tend to go to synagogue services regularly, but Reform Jews usually go to the "temple" (as they call it) only on High Holy Days. Of all three Jewish groups, those who are reformed are the most likely to marry non-Jews and the only ones of the three groups to accept the children of Jewish fathers and non-Jewish mothers as Jews, if they demonstrate a commitment to Judaism. The Orthodox and Conservative only accept as Jews the children of Jewish mothers (Schiffman, 1986).

Major Jewish Holy Days and Festivals

Rosh Ha-Shanah and Yom Kippur are the best known of the Jewish High Holy Days. **Rosh Ha-Shanah** is the New Year festival celebrated for one or two days (depending on the congregation) in September or October. The central ritual at the synagogue is the blowing of the *shofar*, or ram's horn, 100 times to remind worshipers of the need to atone for their misdeeds. It is celebrated with one or two consecutive evening festive meals (Schneider, 1989). The New Year marks the beginning of the penitential season that extends up to **Yom Kippur**, or the Day of Atonement, the most solemn day of the Jewish year. Yom Kippur is observed 10 days after Rosh Ha-Shanah. This is a day typically spent at the synagogue fasting and praying for God to forgive one's sins against Him.

In the Jewish tradition, transgressions against others can only be atoned by making restitution or by asking for the forgiveness of the person who was wronged. This is why during the period between Rosh Ha-Shanah and Yom Kippur, some Jews traditionally send notes to friends and acquaintances apologizing for their misdeeds and asking for their forgiveness (Schiffman, 1986; Schneider, 1989).

Two other well-known Jewish festivals are Hanukkah and Passover. **Hanukkah** (or Chanukah) (meaning dedication) is an eight-day festival celebrated sometime in December to commemorate the victory of the Jewish Maccabees over the Syrian-Greeks who occupied Jerusalem and the rededication of the Jewish Temple after the pagans were expelled. The main ritual during this festival is the daily lighting of the Menorah (an eight-branch candelabrum), one candle every evening, in commemoration of the Jewish victory. Children par-

ticularly like this holiday because it is traditional to give them small gifts on each of the eight nights.

Passover is celebrated sometime in March or April for seven days in Israel and for eight days in the Jewish communities outside Israel (called the Diaspora) in commemoration of the liberation of the Jews from slavery and their exodus from Egypt. In many Jewish congregations today, Passover is celebrated for only one or two days. On the first day, sometimes on the first two days, a special meal and worship service, known as a *seder*, is held to commemorate the liberation and to tell the story using special foods to illustrate it, such as matzoh (unleavened bread), bitter herbs, chopped apples, nuts, cinnamon, wine, and a roasted bone. The unleavened bread is a reminder of the departure from Egypt, so swift that the Jews could not wait for the bread to rise. The bitter herbs are a symbol of the Egyptian bondage. The chopped apples and

nuts, cinnamon, and wine represent the mortar used by the Jews to make bricks for the construction of the Pharaoh's cities. The roasted bone is used to commemorate the paschal lamb offering (a lamb that was slaughtered and eaten by the ancient Hebrews at Passover) whose blood is said to have marked Jewish doorposts on the night of the last plague in Egypt, thus sparing them from it (Schneider, 1989).

All Jewish Holy Days and festivals begin in the evening of the previous day rather than at daybreak and fall on different dates each year according to the civil calendar. This is because the dates are computed according to an ancient method of measuring time also used to compute the date for Easter, which takes into consideration the lunar as well as the solar cycles.

Jewish Life-Course Ceremonies

The most important life-course rituals of the Jewish tradition are the bris, the bar and bat mitzvah, and the marriage and death ceremonies. The **bris** is a religious circumcision used to welcome a newborn male to the Jewish community. Baby boys are circumcised on the eighth day after birth by a person trained in this religious ritual and surgical procedure. Typically, family and friends are invited to witness the ceremony and to partake of the festive meal that follows. The birth of a baby girl is announced by the father at the synagogue where he names her before the Torah. A get-together with family and friends usually follows (Schneider, 1989).

The **bar** (male) and **bat** (female) **mitzvah** are rituals performed when girls are 12 or 13 and when boys are 13 to mark their entrance to religious majority age. At the bar or bat mitzvah, youngsters are expected to demonstrate ability to recite certain prayers in Hebrew and knowledge of the Bible and of Jewish history. From that point on, they share the same religious obligations and privileges as any other Jewish adult (Schiffman, 1986; Schneider, 1989).

Jewish weddings are also rich in ritual. Before the ceremony, the couple must enter into a marriage contract that spells out their obligations and agreements. The wedding itself takes place under a canopy held above the couple's heads. Sometimes a prayer shawl is used to cover them, often held in place by family members or friends. At the end of the ceremony, the groom breaks a glass as a reminder of the destruction of the Temple in Jerusalem.

Death brings about the last set of rituals in the Jewish tradition. Traditionally, the dead person's body is not left alone until it is buried, usually within 24 hours, and there is no public viewing because embalming is prohibited. Before burial, the body is washed ritually, clothed in a plain linen shroud, and placed in a simple wooden coffin symbolic of the basic equality of death. At the funeral, it is traditional for the mourners to tear an article of clothing to signify their bereavement. This torn garment (usually a black ribbon) is worn during the mourning period. Following the burial, the mourning ritual, or *shivah* (meaning seven), dictates that the bereaved should remain at home for three or seven days, usually sitting on low stools and wearing only nonleather footwear as a sign of their sorrow. Traditionally, men do not shave during this period, mirrors are covered, and a candle is kept burning. Meals are usually cooked by friends and brought to the mourners as an act of kindness and as part of the religious observance. For 30 days following the burial, the mourners are not supposed to participate in festive activities. The period of mourning is longer for the children of the deceased and, according to tradition, they are expected to go to the synagogue daily during mourning to pray for their parent (Schneider, 1989).

The Holocaust

The term **Holocaust** refers to the systematic mass killing of German (European) Jews in Nazi concentration camps during World War II. Approximately six million Jews were exterminated by the Nazis, representing one-third of the world's Jewish population and 60 percent of the European Jewry (Schiffman, 1986; Bennett, 1988). The holocaust is a haunting memory for the majority of American Jews because many are either concentration camp survivors, children or relatives of a survivor, or refugees or their descendants forced to migrate to escape the Nazi persecution. The experience of the Holocaust is central to many people's lives, often acting as a lens through which they filter day-to-day and other events (Soifer, 1991). Therefore, it is important for practitioners to be sensitive to their clients' personal experiences with respect to the Holocaust.

Unlike some other social groups that have become increasingly conservative as they have climbed the socioeconomic ladder, American Jews have remained liberal in philosophy and deeply committed to civil rights. This characteristic is undoubtedly related to their long history of discrimination and persecution (Bennett, 1988).

Some Contributions of American Jews to U.S. Culture

Many American Jews have made impressive contributions to culture in the United States. Only a few will be mentioned here: scientists Albert Einstein and Jonas Salk; Nobel prize-winning writers Isaac Singer and Saul Bellows; poets Edna Ferber, Arthur Miller, and Emma Lazarus; musicians Leonard Bernstein, George Gershwin, Yehudi Menuhin, Beverly Sills, and Bob Dylan; civic and political leaders Samuel Gompers, Henry Morgenthau, Bella Abzug, and Henry Kissinger; and Supreme Court Justices Benjamin Cardozo, Arthur Goldberg, and Ruth Bader Ginsburg.

A lot of ground has been covered in this chapter. One of the best ways to maintain and expand cultural learnings is to immerse yourself in other cultures by becoming a participant observer. You can do this in many ways. For example, when you get an invitation to visit with, dine with, or share a special celebration or life-course ritual with a family or friend of a different cultural background than yours, seize the opportunity as a learning experience. Visit the communities where members of the group you want to learn about live and congregate—eat at their restaurants, attend their church services, go to their barbershops or beauty salons, and attend their festivals. Read their newspapers and magazines, watch their TV programs, visit their bookstores, and listen to their radio programs. It is also helpful to take language courses to improve your ability to communicate and to deepen your understanding of other cultures. At every opportunity, practice speaking the new language with native speakers. In the case of Native-American cultures, visit the reservations and attend rodeos, powwows, and dances. If invited, do not miss the opportunity to attend Native-American religious ceremonies.

If you are trustworthy and accepting of diversity, in most cases you will be able to communicate with people from other cultures and to develop a good relationship with them, even if at first you do not speak their language or know much about their values or way of life.

ENDNOTES

1. However, this is not to say that there is no elitism in the U.S. Some mainstream Americans are as socially distant and disengaged from the concerns of the common person as any aristocrat from another country (Yankelovich, 1984).
2. Since antiquity, the little finger has been associated with special spiritual and transformational powers and with wit, science, and communication (Grahn, 1984, p. 15)
3. Besides the three major groups—Orthodox, Conservative, and Reform—there is also a small offshoot of the Conservative movement known as the Reconstructionist movement, which is more liberal and flexible than the Conservatives (Schneider, 1989).

GLOSSARY

Acculturation: Also known as *cultural assimilation*, the process by which individuals learn the behaviors, values, and customs of a cultural group other than their own. Acculturation differs from *assimilation* in that it does not imply total integration into the new cultural group or loss of one's original cultural heritage.

African Americans: The descendants of black African slaves (or, in some cases, indentured servants) brought to the United States in the colonial period.

American Indians: See **Native Americans**.

American Jews: Persons permanently residing or born in the United States whose religion is Judaism or who trace their descent from the Israelites of the Bible.

Ashkenazim: Jews of Central or Eastern European origin.

Asian Americans: Persons living in the United States, born in a Pacific-Asian country, or whose ancestors came from a Pacific-Asian country, such as China, Japan, Korea, Vietnam, the Philippines, Thailand, Cambodia, Laos, Indonesia, Samoa, Guam, and other countries in the Indian subcontinent, such as India, Pakistan, and Ceylon. In this book, the term is restricted to East Asians; that is, it does not include persons from the Indian subcontinent (Indians, Pakistanis, and Ceylonese) because their cultures are different from the East Asians', and therefore cannot be treated together.

Assimilation: The process by which persons of diverse backgrounds give up their original cultural identity and merge into another group.

Bar and Bat Mitzvah: A ritual performed at age 12 or 13 (bat = girls) and at age 13 (bar = boys) to mark the young lady's or young man's entrance to religious majority age in Judaism. From that point on, the individual shares the same religious obligations and privileges as any other Jewish adults.

Bicultural: Persons who can function competently in two different cultures.

Bilingual: Able to speak two languages.

Bris: A religious circumcision to welcome a newborn boy to the Jewish community.

Butch: A lesbian who wears men's clothes and has mannish mannerisms.

Clan: Among Native Americans, extended families—including parents, children, grandparents, aunts, uncles, and cousins—generally spread over several households that trace their lineage to a common ancestor.

"Closet": Repression and stigmatization of gays and lesbians in most societies have forced many of them to keep their homosexuality "in the closet"—that is, secret. The term probably derives from the common expression that an individual has "a skeleton in the closet," meaning some closely guarded secret, with the skeleton in this case being the person's homosexuality.

Coming Out: An important right of passage or life crisis in the lives of many gays and lesbians. It is a transformational process consisting of several stages that may stretch over several years through which most individuals pass to develop their identity as gays or lesbians. Coming out usually involves telling someone else (generally a friend or family member who assumed the person was "straight" or "heterosexual") about the individual's gayness.

Conservative Jews: Jews that are neither as liberal as the Reformed Jews nor as strictly traditional as the orthodox. For example, they allow men and women to worship together at the synagogue, make more use of English in religious services, and are less strict than the Orthodox in their observance of the Jewish dietary laws.

Cruising: Within the gay subculture, the rituals involved in searching for sexual partners, including various ways of calling attention to oneself, such as the use of visible symbols such as a key ring or colored bandanna hanging from a rear pocket to indicate preference for specific sexual activities. After the AIDS crisis, the sexual signaling aspects of cruising within the gay community became less important, and, for the most part, the cruising ritual evolved into more subtle behaviors and symbols by which gays and lesbians communicate their sexual orientation, such as skilled use of eye contact, mannerisms, body postures, and facial gestures.

Cuban Americans: Persons permanently residing in the United States who were born in Cuba or whose parents or ancestors were born in Cuba, as compared to Cuban citizens living in Cuba who are referred to as Cubans.

Cultural Assimilation: See **Acculturation**.

Cultural Pluralism: A theoretical perspective that recognizes the strengths and merits of the cultures of each social group and supports each group's right to retain its cultures.

Culture: A society's or a group's way of life, including its customs, beliefs, values, language, accumulated knowledge, artifacts, and symbols.

Curanderismo: A Mexican-American folk-healing system that considers illness and bad luck the result of weakened ties with the Catholic Church, the family, and the Mexican culture.

Diversity Perspective: As understood in this book, a perspective that reinforces each social group's right to retain its culture and distinctiveness but that also expects them to participate in and to contribute to the overall culture of the society.

Dominant Culture: See **Mainstream Culture**.

Dominant Group: The social group in power in the society; that is, the group that controls its institutions and resources and makes the major decisions. Also referred to as *the establishment*.

Dual Perspective: The idea that many people live simultaneously in two or more cultures—the mainstream culture of the society and their own culture(s)—and must learn to negotiate these different worlds, each with its own set of values, beliefs, lifestyles, and behavioral expectations.

Espiritistas: Persons believed to be able to communicate with the dead who are consulted frequently by persons of Puerto Rican extraction as well as others. They act as mediums, attempting to convince the spirits to help rather than harm their clients and prescribe ointments, herbs, sacrifices, and prayers.

Ethnocentrism: Belief in the superiority of one's own ethnic group, culture, or way of life, as compared to others.

Faggot: An effeminate male homosexual; an obviously gay man.

Fatalism: Acceptance of one's situation and fate because of the belief that one does not have much control over life circumstances.

Fictive Kin: In some ethnic groups, persons without blood or legal ties to the family who nevertheless act as if they were relatives.

Filial Piety: A fundamental value in Asian cultures requiring that children (including adult children) treat their parents with the highest respect and obedience simply because they gave

them life and raised them, even if the parents do not "deserve" such treatment.

Folkways: Norms governing everyday behaviors and conventions that are enforced informally because their violation is unlikely to cause major concern.

Gay: A term derived from the name of Gaia, the earth goddess of Ancient Greece, generally used to refer to a homosexual person, although in recent years it has been used more specifically to refer to male homosexuals.

Hanukkah: A Jewish festival sometime in December that commemorates the victory of the Jewish Maccabees over the Syrian-Greeks and the rededication of the Jewish Temple. The main ritual during Hanukkah is the daily lighting of the Menorah (an eight-branch candelabrum). Also known as *Chanukah*.

Holocaust: The systematic mass killing of German (European) Jews held in concentration camps by the Nazis during World War II.

Homosexual: A person attracted primarily to same-sex sexual or affectional partners.

Immigrant: An individual who migrates willingly from one country to another, usually looking for better economic opportunities or a better life.

Kosher: Foods prepared in accordance with Jewish dietary laws.

Language: The verbal, nonverbal, and written symbols that enable people to communicate their meanings and experiences, to talk about the past and the future, and to pass on their heritage from generation to generation.

Latinos: Spanish-speaking people born in Latin America or the Caribbean and living in the United States or descendants of Spanish-speaking people from Latin America or the Caribbean living in the United States.

Lesbian: Originally, a person from the island of Lesbos, from which came the woman-loving poet/pristess Sappho. Today, the term is used to refer to a female homosexual.

Linguistic-Relativity Hypothesis: The thesis that the language of each culture determines how its people interpret reality by guiding their perceptions and attention. Also known as the *Sapirworf Hypothesis*.

Machismo: A doctrine that gives precedence to males as authority figures, providers, and protectors of women and children and that dictates that they should be dominant, aggressive, just, honorable, courageous, and sexually experienced.

Mainland Puerto Ricans: Persons residing in the continental United States who were born in Puerto Rico or whose parents or ancestors were born in Puerto Rico, as compared to Puerto Rican citizens living in the island who are referred to as Puerto Ricans.

Mainstream Culture: The culture of the dominant group in the society—that is, of the "establishment." In the United States of the 1990s, this was the culture of the white European-American middle class, composed primarily of Anglo-Americans, German Americans, and Irish Americans as well as of many other native-born U.S. citizens of European extraction, such as Italian Americans, French Americans, and Polish Americans. Also referred to as the *dominant culture*.

Marital Assimilation: A level of assimilation into another cultural group attained by intermarriage with members of the other group.

Material Culture: The people-made objects of a society or group, such as its cities, highways, cars, garments, schools, churches, factories, books, and electrical appliances.

Melting Pot Theory: A theory of acculturation that suggests that it is in the interest of individuals of diverse cultural backgrounds to adopt the mainstream culture and to get rid of any vestiges of their own cultures.

Mexican Americans: Persons residing in the United States who were born in Mexico or whose parents or ancestors were born in Mexico, as compared to Mexican citizens living in Mexico who are referred to as Mexicans. Mexican Americans are sometimes referred to as *Chicanos*, although not all Mexican Americans consider themselves to be Chicanos.

Mores: Social norms that are strictly enforced and that carry serious negative consequences for those who violate them because they are considered vital to the welfare of a society or community.

Namesake: Literally, someone who has the same name as another. In the Native-American cultures, a person who assumes responsibility to help to rear a child and to act as a role model.

Native Americans: Strictly speaking, according to the Bureau of Indian Affairs (BIA), a registered member of a Native-American tribe or a person whose blood quantum is one-fourth or more Native American. Also known as American Indians.

Nondominant Group: A social group that has low standing in the stratification system of the society and that is the recipient of inequitable and discriminatory treatment.

Nonmaterial Culture: All the human creations of a society or group that are not part of its material culture, including its language, values, beliefs, norms, laws, customs, mores, and folkways.

Orthodox Jews: Jews who show the highest degree of adherence to the original Jewish faith and traditions. For example, they strictly observe the Sabbath, attend sex-segregated religious services in Hebrew, say their prayers in Hebrew several times per day, and only eat kosher foods.

Passover: A Jewish festival in March or April commemorating the freedom of the Jewish people from slavery and their exodus from Egypt.

Patriarchy: A form of social organization in which the father is the head of the family or clan, descent is traced through the male line, and men exercise dominance or control.

People of Color: Members of nonwhite racial/ethnic groups, also known as *minorities of color*, including African Americans, Native Americans, Asians and Pacific Islanders, and many Latino groups with high proportions of nonwhites.

Personalismo: A Latino cultural value stressing the importance of warm and personable social interactions.

Present Orientation: Being more concerned about present goals or day-to-day survival than about planning for the future.

Reformed Jews: The most liberal of the Jews who profess to be religious. They are the least likely to eat kosher, the most likely to marry non-Jews, and the only ones of the Jews who practice religion willing to accept the children of Jewish fathers and non-Jewish mothers as Jews.

Refugee: An individual forced to leave his or her country out of fear of persecution due to his or her political opinions or actions, race, religion, nationality, sexual orientation, or membership in a particular social group.

Rosh Ha-Shanah: The Jewish New Year festival celebrated in September or October.

Santeria: A syncretic folk religion that combines elements of Roman Catholicism with ancient African Yoruba beliefs and practices. The central belief is that the African deities, or *orishas*, take the form of Roman Catholic saints and exercise influence over people, bringing them health and good fortune as well as illness and misfortune.

Sapir-Worf Hypothesis: See **Linguistic-Relativity Hypothesis**.

Sephardim: Jews of Mediterranean origin, including those originally from Turkey, Palestine, Egypt, North Africa, Spain, and Italy.

Simpatico: A person who is likable, pleasant, charming, easy going, respectful, and harmonious in his or her interpersonal relations.

Social Norms: Widely shared rules or guidelines that prescribe appropriate behavior generally and in specific situations.

Structural Assimilation: A level of assimilation into another cultural group that requires participation in the primary groups and institutions (e.g., peer groups, close friendships, private clubs) of the other social group.

Values: Socially shared assumption about what is good, right, moral, or desirable, or, conversely, what is bad, wrong, immoral, or undesirable.

Yom Kippur: Ten days after Rosh Ha-Shanah, the Jewish Day of Atonement; a day typically spent at the synagogue fasting and praying for God's forgiveness for one's sins against Him.

REFERENCES

Abercrombie, N., Hill, S., & Turner, B. S. (Eds.). (1990). *Dominant ideologies*. Cambridge, MA: Unwin Hyman.

Acosta, F. X., & Evans, L. A. (1982). The Hispanic-American patient. In F. X. Acosta, J. Yamamoto, & L. A. Evans (Eds.), *Effective psychotherapy for low-income and minority patients* (pp. 51—61). New York: Plenum Press.

Acosta, F. X., Yamamoto, J., & Evans, L. A. (1982). *Effective psychotherapy for low-income and minority patients*. New York: Plenum Press.

Arensberg, C. M., & Niehoff, A. N. (1964). *Introducing social change*. Chicago: Aldine.

Argyle, M. (1988). Intercultural communication. In L. A. Samovar & R. E. Porter (Eds.), *Intercultural communication: A reader* (5th ed., pp. 31–44). Belmont, CA: Wadsworth.

Astin, A. W., Green, K. C., & Korn, W. S. (1987). *The American freshman: Twenty year trends*. Los Angeles: Cooperative Institutional Research Program, University of California at Los Angeles.

Astin, A. W., Korn, W. S., & Berz, E. R. (1990). *The American freshman: National norms fall 1989*. Cooperative Institutional Research Program, University of California at Los Angeles.

Attneave, C. L. (1982). American Indians and Alaskan Native families: Emigrants in their own homeland. In M. McGoldrick, J. Pearce, & J. Giordano (Eds.), *Ethnicity and family therapy* (pp. 55–83). New York: Guilford Press.

Bach-y-Rita, G. (1982). In R. M. Becerra, M. Karno, & J. I. Escobar (Eds.), *Mental health and Hispanic Americans: Clinical perspectives* (pp. 29–40). New York: Grune & Stratton.

Barnlund, D. C. (1989). *Communicative styles of Japanese and Americans: Images and reality*. Belmont, CA: Wadsworth.

Bellah, R. N., Madsen, R., Sullivan, W. M., Swidler, A., & Tipton, S. M. (1985). *Habits of the heart: Individualism and commitment in American culture*. Berkeley, CA: University of California Press.

Bennett, C. I. (1988). *Comprehensive multicultural education: Theory and practice*. Boston: Allyn and Bacon.

Bernal, G. (1982). Cuban families. In M. McGoldrick, J. K. Pearce, & J. Giordano (Eds.), *Ethnicity and family therapy* (pp. 187–207). New York: Guilford Press.

Berry, J. W., Kim, U., Mind, T., & Mok, D. (1987). Comparative studies of acculturative stress. *International Migration Review, 21,* 491–511.

Booth, C. (1992, June 8). Send 'em back! *Time,* 43.

Boswell, T. D., & Curtis, J. R. (1983). *The Cuban-American experience: Culture, images, and perspectives*. Totowa, NJ: Rowman & Allanheld.

Boykin, A. W., & Toms, F. D. (1985). Black child socialization: A conceptual framework. In H. P. McAdoo & J. L. McAdoo (Eds.), *Black children: Social, educational, and parental environments* (pp. 33–51). Beverly Hills, CA: Sage.

Bureau of Indian Affairs. (1988). *American Indians today*. Washington, DC: Bureau of Indian Affairs.

Bustamante, J. A. (1959). *Raices psicologicas del Cubano*. Havana, Cuba: Impresora Modelo.

Carrier, J. (1992). Miguel: Sexual life history of a gay Mexican American. In G. Herdt (Ed.), *Gay culture in America: Essays from the field* (pp. 202–224). Boston: Beacon Press.

Champion, D. J., Kurth, S. B., Hastings, D. W., & Harris, D. K. (1984). *Sociology*. New York: Holt, Rinehart and Winston.

Chandler, C. R. (1979). Traditionalism in a modern setting: A comparison of Anglo- and Mexican-American value orientations. *Human Organization, 38*, 153–159.

Chao, C. M. (1992). The inner heart: Therapy with Southeast Asian families. In L. A. Vargas & J. D. Koss-Chioino (Eds.), *Working with culture: Psychotherapeutic interventions with ethnic minority children and adolescents* (pp. 157–181). San Francisco: Jossey-Bass.

Chau, K. L. (1990). A model for teaching cross-cultural practice in social work. *Journal of Social Work Education, 26*, 124–133.

Chestang, L. W. (1972). *Character development in a hostile environment*. Occasional Paper No. 3. Chicago: School of Social Service Administration, University of Chicago.

Chestang, L. W. (1976). Environmental influences on social functioning: The black experience. In P. S. J. Cafferty & L. Chestang (Eds.), *The diverse society: Implications for social policy* (pp. 59–74). Washington, DC: National Association of Social Workers.

Chestang, L. W. (1977). *Achievement and self-esteem among Black Americans: A study of twenty lives*. Doctoral dissertation, University of Chicago.

Chien, C., & Yamamoto, J. (1982). Asian-American and Pacific-Islander patients. In F. X. Acosta, J. Yamamoto, & L. A. Evans (Eds.), *Effective psychotherapy for low-income and minority patients* (pp. 117–123). New York: Plenum Press.

Chilman, C. S. (1993). Hispanic families in the United States. In H. P. McAdoo (Ed.), *Family ethnicity: Strength in diversity* (pp. 141–163). Newbury Park, CA: Sage.

Clark, R. L., & Passel, J. S. (1993, September 3). Immigrants: A cost or a benefit. Studies are deceptive. *The New York Times*, page A23.

Cole, J. B. (1970). Culture: Negro, black, and nigger. *Black Scholar, 1*, 40–44.

Coleman, E. (1982). Developmental stages of the coming out process. *Journal of Homosexuality, 7*, 31–43.

Condon, J. (1988). "...So near the United States": Notes on communication between Mexicans and North Americans. In L. A. Samovar & R. E. Porter (Eds.), *Intercultural communication: A reader* (5th ed., pp. 110–118). Belmont, CA: Wadsworth.

Cordasco, F., & Bucchioni, E. (1973). *The Puerto Rican experience: A sociological sourcebook*. Totowa, NJ: Littlefield, Adams, & Co.

Cortes, C. E. (Ed.). (1980). *The Cuban experience in the United States*. New York: Arno Press.

Cruikshank, M. (1992). *The gay and lesbian liberation movement*. New York: Routledge.

Crystal, D. (1989). Asian Americans and the myth of the model minority. *Social Casework, 70*, 405–413.

Davenport, D. S., & Yurich, J. M. (1991). Multicultural gender issues. *Journal of Counseling & Development, 70*, 64–71.

DeAnda, D. (1984). Bicultural socialization: Factors affecting the minority experience. *Social Work, 29*, 101–107.

Delgado, M. (1988). Groups in Puerto Rican spiritism: Implications for clinicians. In C. Jacobs & D. D. Bowles (Eds.), *Ethnicity and race: Critical concepts in social work*. Silver Spring, MD: NASW.

Delgado, M., & Humm-Delgado, D. (1982). Natural support systems: Source of strength in Hispanic communities. *Social Work, 27*, 83–89.

Devore, W., & Schlesinger, E. G. (1991). *Ethnic-sensitive social work practice* (3rd ed.). New York: Macmillan.

Dynes, W. (Ed.). (1990). *Encyclopedia of homosexuality*. New York: Garland.

Everett, F., Proctor, N., & Cartmell, B. (1983). Providing psychological services to American Indian children and families. *Professional Psychology, 14*, 588–603.

Fabric of a nation, The. (1992, June–July). *Modern Maturity, 35*(3), 24–25.

Fallows, J. (1983, November). Immigration: How it is affecting us. *The Atlantic Monthly*, 45–68, 85–106.

Foster, S., & Little, M. (1987). *The book of the vision quest: Personal transformation in the wilderness*. New York: Prentice Hall.

Furuto, S. M., Biswas, R., Chung, D. K., Murase, K., & Ross-Sheriff, F. (Eds.). (1992). *Social work practice with Asian Americans*. Newbury Park, CA: Sage.

Gann, L. H., & Duignan, P. G. (1986). *The Hispanics in the United States: A history*. Boulder, CO: Westview.

Gelfand, D. E., & Fandetti, D.V. (1986). The emergent nature of ethnicity: Dilemmas in Assessment. *Social Casework, 67*, 542–550.

Ghali, S. (1977). Culture sensitivity and the Puerto Rican client. *Social Casework, 58*, 459–474.

Gibbs, N. (1994, October 3). Keep out, you tired, you poor.... *Time*, 44–47.

Gold, S. J. (1992). *Refugee communities: A comparative field study*. Newbury Park, CA: Sage.

Goleman, D. (1990, December 30). Other nations don't reflect Americans' cult of individualism. *The Miami Herald*, pp. 1I, 5I.

Gonzalez, J. A. (1985). Undocumented Mexican laborer contribution to the American economy. *Free Inquiry in Creative Sociology, 13*(1), 60–62.

Goodman, W. (1992, June 19). The American melting pot is still simmering nicely. *The New York Times*, p. B4.

Gordon, E. A. (1990, April). The lesbian and gay community of song. *Choral Journal, 30*(9), 25–32.

Gordon, M. M. (1964). *Assimilation in American life*. New York: Oxford University Press.

Grahn, J. (1984). *Another mother tongue: Gay words, gay worlds*. Boston: Beacon Press.

Haglund, E. (1988). Japan: Cultural considerations. In L. A. Samovar & R. E. Porter (Eds.), *Intercultural communication: A reader* (5th ed., pp. 84–94). Belmont, CA: Wadsworth.

Haile, B. J., & Johnson, A. E. (1989). Teaching and learning about black women: The anatomy of a course. *Sage, 6*, 69–73.

Hall, T. (1991, May 19). Piercing fad is turning convention on its ear. *The New York Times*, Campus Life section, p. 38.

Hallman, C. L., & Campbell, A. (1983). *Cuban value orientations*. Cultural Monograph No. 1. Bilingual Multicultural Education Training Project for School Psychologists and Guidance Counselors. Washington, DC: United States Department of Education, Office of Bilingual Education and Minority Languages Affairs. (Eric Reproduction Service No. ED 269 484).

Hallman, C. L. et al. (names not specified). (1983). *U.S.-American Value Orientations*. Cultural Monograph No. 4. Bilingual Multicultural Education Training Project for School Psychologists and Guidance Counselors. Washington, DC: United States Department of Education, Office of Bilingual Education and Minority Languages Affairs. (ERIC Document Reproduction Service No. ED 269 534)

Hanna, J. L. (1984). Black/white nonverbal differences, dance and dissonance: Implications for desegregation. In A. Wolfgang (Ed.), *Nonverbal behavior: Perspectives, applications, intercultural insights*. Lewiston, NY: C. J. Hogrefe.

Harrison, D. F., Wodarski, J. S., & Thyer, B. A. (Eds.). (1992). *Cultural diversity and social work practice*. Springfield, IL: Charles C. Thomas.

Harrison, L. E. (1992, February 2). Is immigration policy a factor in our economic woes? *The Miami Herald*, p. 6C.

Hatchett, S. J., & Jackson, J. S. (1993). African American extended kin systems. In H. P. McAdoo (Ed.), *Family ethnicity: Strength in diversity* (pp. 90–108). Newbury Park, CA: Sage.

Heinrich, R. K., Corbine, J. L., & Thomas, K. R. (1990). Counseling Native Americans. *Journal of Counseling and Development, 69*, 128–133.

Henderson, G. (1989). *A practitioner's guide to understanding indigenous and foreign cultures*. Springfield, IL: Charles C. Thomas.

Herdt, G. (Ed.). (1992). "Coming out" as a rite of passage: A Chicago study. In G. Herdt (Ed.), *Gay culture in America: Essays from the field* (pp. 29–67). Boston: Beacon Press.

Herdt, G. (1992). *Gay culture in America: Essays from the field*. Boston: Beacon Press.

Herskovits, M. J. (1972). *Cultural relativism: Perspective in cultural pluralism*. New York: Random House.

Ho, M. K. (1976). Social work with Asian Americans. *Social Casework, 57*, 195–201.

Ho, M. K. (1987). Family therapy with American Indians and Alaskan Natives. In M. K. Ho (Ed.), *Family therapy with ethnic minorities* (pp. 69–83). California: Sage.

Ho, M. K. (1992). Social work practice with Asian Americans. In A. T. Morales & B. W. Sheafor (Eds.), *Social work: A profession of many faces* (6th ed., pp. 535–554). Boston: Allyn and Bacon.

Holloway, J. E. (1990). *Africanisms in American culture*. Bloomington: Indiana University Press.

Huddle, D. L. (1993, September 3). Immigrants: A cost or a benefit? A growing burden. *The New York Times*, p. A23.

Inclan, J. (1985). Variations in value orientations in mental health work with Puerto Ricans. *Psychotherapy, 22*, 324–334.

Jackson, G. G. (1986). Conceptualizing Afrocentric and Eurocentric mental health training. In H. P. Lefley & P. B. Pedersen (Eds.), *Cross-cultural training for mental health professionals* (pp. 131–149). Springfield, IL: Charles C. Thomas.

Jay, K., & Young, A. (1978). *Lavender culture*. New York: Jove Publications.

Jones, J. M. (1991). Racism: A cultural analysis of the problem. In R. L. Jones (Ed.), *Black psychology* (3rd ed., pp. 609–635). Berkeley, CA: Cobb & Henry.

Jones, N. S. C. (1990). Black/white issues in psychotherapy: A framework for clinical practice. *Journal of Social Behavior and Personality, 5*, 305–322.

Keefe, S. E., & Padilla, A. M. (1987). *Chicano ethnicity*. Albuquerque, NM: University of New Mexico Press.

Keefe, S. E., Padilla, A. M., & Carlos, M. L. (1979). The Mexican-American extended family as an emotional support system. *Human Organization, 38*, 147–148.

Kellen, H. M. (1956). *Cultural pluralism and the American idea*. Philadelphia: University of Philadelphia Press.

Kiev, A. (1968). *Curanderismo*. New York: Free Press.

Kim, K. C., Kim, S., & Hurh, W. M. (1991). Filial piety and intergenerational relationship in Korean immigrant families. *International Journal of Aging and Human Development, 33*, 233–245.

Kim, Y. Y. (1988). Communication and acculturation. In L. A. Samovar & R. E. Porter (Eds.), *Intercultural communication: A reader* (5th ed., pp. 344–354). Belmont, CA: Wadsworth.

Kochman, T. (1981). *Black and white styles in conflict*. Chicago: University of Chicago Press.

Kochman, T. (1988). Black style in communication. In L. A. Samovar & R. E. Porter (Eds.), *Intercultural communication: A reader* (5th ed., pp. 130–138). Belmont, CA: Wadsworth.

LaFrance, M., & Mayo, C. (1976). Racial differences in gaze behavior during conversation. *Journal of Personality and Social Psychology, 33*, 547–552.

Lasch, C. (1992, Fall). Is progress obsolete? A noted historian argues that the dream has become far too exclusive, *Time*, 71.

Lasch, C. (1992). The culture of narcissism. In R. Wilkinson (Ed.), *American social character: Modern interpretations from the '40s to the present* (pp. 241–267). New York: HarperCollins.

Levine, M. P. (1992). The life and death of gay clones. In G. Herdt (Ed.), *Gay culture in America: Essays from the field* (pp. 68–86). Boston: Beacon Press.

Lewis, R., & Ho, M. (1989). Social work with Native Americans. In D. Atkinson, G. Morten, & D. Sue (Eds.), *Counseling American minorities* (pp. 51–58). Dubuque, IA: William C. Brown.

Light, D., Keller, S., & Calhoun, C. (1989). *Sociology* (5th ed.). New York: Knopf.

Lipset, S. M. (1990). *Continental divide: The values and institutions of the United States and Canada*. New York: Routledge.

Lipset, S. M. (1992). A changing American character? In R. Wilkinson (Ed.), *American social character: Modern interpretations from the '40s to the present* (pp. 98–133). New York: HarperCollins.

Locke, D. C. (1992). *Increasing multicultural understanding: A comprehensive model*. Newbury Park, CA: Sage.

Longres, J. F. (1991). Toward a status model of ethnic sensitive practice. *Journal of Multicultural Social Work, 1*, 41–56.

Lum, D. (1986). *Social work practice and people of color: A process-stage approach*. Monterey, CA: Brooks/Cole.

Lustig, M. W. (1988). Value differences in intercultural communication. In L. A. Samovar & R. E. Porter (Eds.), *Intercultural communication: A reader* (5th ed., pp. 55–61). Belmont, CA: Wadsworth.

Majors, R. (1988). The non-verbal elements of a gay culture. In L. A. Samovar & R. E. Porter (Eds.), *Intercultural communication: A reader* (5th ed., pp. 163–171). Belmont, CA: Wadsworth.

Majors, R. (1991). Nonverbal behaviors and communication styles among African Americans. In R. L. Jones (Ed.), *Black psychology* (3rd ed., pp. 269–294). Berkeley, CA: Cobb & Henry.

Manach, J. (1969). *Indagacion del choteo* (2nd ed.). Miami: Mnemosyne.

Margolick, D. (1992, June, 12). A mixed marriage's 25th anniversary of legality. *The New York Times*, p. B7.

Markus, H. R., & Kitayama, S. (1971). Culture and the self: Implications for cognition, emotion, and motivation. *Psychological Review, 98*, 224–253.

Martinez, C. (1988). Mexican-Americans. In L. Comas-Dias & E. E. H. Griffith (Eds.), *Clinical guidelines in cross-cultural mental health* (pp. 182–203). New York: Wiley & Sons.

Matheson, L. (1986). If you are not an Indian, how do you treat an Indian? In H. P. Lefley & P. B. Pedersen (Eds.), *Cross-cultural training for mental health professionals* (pp. 115–130). Springfield, IL: Charles C. Thomas.

Matsuoka, J. K. (1990). Differential acculturation among Vietnamese refugees. *Social Work, 35*, 341–345.

Matthews, J. (1992, June 1). From closet to mainstream: Upscale gay magazines flood the newsstand. *Newsweek*, 62.

McAdoo, H. (1978). Factors related to stability in upwardly mobile black families. *Journal of Marriage and the Family, 40*, 762–778.

McNeely, R. L., & Badami, M. K. (1984). Interracial communication in school social work. *Social Work, 29*, 22–26.

Medina, C. (1987, January–February). Latino culture and sex education. *Siecus Report, 15*(3), 1–4.

Mizio, E. (1992). The impact of macro systems on Puerto Rican families. In A. T. Morales & B. W. Sheafor, (Eds.), *Social work: A profession of many faces* (6th ed., pp. 491–515). Boston: Allyn and Bacon.

Murray S. O. (1992). Components of gay community in San Francisco. In G. Herdt (Ed.), *Gay culture in America: Essays from the field* (pp. 107–146). Boston: Beacon Press.

National Association of Social Workers. (1990, March). *Fact sheet on refugees*. Silver Spring, MD: Child and Family Well-Being Development Education Program.

Newman, K. S. (1991). Uncertain seas: Cultural turmoil and the domestic economy. In A. Wolfe (Ed.), *America at century's end* (pp. 112–130). Berkeley: University of California Press.

Nishio, K., & Bilmes, M. (1987). Psychotherapy with Southeast Asian American clients. *Professional Psychology: Research and Practice, 18*, 342–346.

Norton, D. (1978). *The dual perspective: Inclusion of ethnic minority content in the social work curriculum*. New York: Council on Social Work Education.

Packard, V. (1957). *The hidden persuaders*. New York: David McKay.

Perry, R. B. (1992). The American cast of mind. In R. Wilkinson (Ed.), *American social character: Modern interpretations from the '40s to the present* (pp. 33–49). New York: HarperCollins.

Peterson, J. L. (1992). Black men and their same-sex desires and behaviors. In G. Herdt (Ed.), *Gay culture in America: Essays from the field* (pp. 147–164). Boston: Beacon Press.

Pierson, G. W. (1992). The m-factor. In R. Wilkinson (Ed.), *American social character: Modern interpretations from the '40s to the present* (pp. 180–200). New York: HarperCollins.

Portrait of America: A time of great change and growing poverty. (1992, May 29). *The New York Times*, p. A12.

Potter, D. M. (1954). *People of plenty: Economic abundance and the American character*. Chicago: University of Chicago Press.

Potter, D. M. (1992a). American individualism in the twentieth century. In R. Wilkinson (Ed.), *American social character: Modern interpretations from the '40s to the present* (pp. 159–179). New York: HarperCollins.

Potter, D. M. (1992b). American women and the American character. In R. Wilkinson (Ed.), *American social character: Modern interpretations from the '40s to the present* (pp. 134–158). New York: HarperCollins.

Queralt, M. (1984). Understanding Cuban immigrants: A cultural perspective. *Social Work, 29*, 115–121.

Ramos-McKay, J. M., Comas-Diaz, L., & Rivera, L. A. (1988). Puerto Ricans. In L. Comas-Dias & E. E. H. Griffith (Eds.), *Clinical guidelines in cross-cultural mental health* (pp. 204–232). New York: Wiley & Sons.

Reich, C. (1992). The greening of America. In R. Wilkinson (Ed.), *American social character: Modern interpretations from the '40s to the present* (pp. 219–240). New York: HarperCollins.

Rich, A. L. (1974). *Interracial communication*. New York: Harper & Row.

Richardson, E. H. (1981). Cultural and historical perspectives in counseling American Indians. In

D. W. Sue (Ed.), *Counseling the culturally different: Theory and practice* (pp. 216–255). New York: Wiley & Sons.

Riesman, D. (1992). From inner-direction to other-direction. In R. Wilkinson (Ed.), *American social character: Modern interpretations from the '40s to the present* (pp. 50–69). New York: HarperCollins.

Robertson, I. (1989). *Society: A brief introduction.* New York: Worth.

Rokeach, M. (1973). *The nature of human values.* New York: Free Press.

Rubin, L. B. (1992). *Worlds of pain: Life in the working class family.* New York: Basic Books.

Rumbaut, R. G. (1991). Passages to America: Perspectives on the new immigration. In A. Wolfe (Ed.), *America at century's end* (pp. 208–244). Berkeley: University of California Press.

Ryan, A. S. (1985). Cultural factors in casework with Chinese-Americans. *Social Casework, 66,* 333–340.

Sandoval, M. C. (1979). Santeria as a mental health care system: Historical Overview. *Social Science and Medicine B, 13*(2B), 137–151.

Sandoval, M. C., & de la Roza, M. C. (1986). A cultural perspective for serving the Hispanic client. In H. P. Lefley & P. B. Pedersen (Eds.), *Cross-cultural training for mental health professionals* (pp. 151–181). Springfield, IL: Charles C. Thomas.

Sapir, E. (1929). The status of linguistics as a science. *Language,. 5,* 207–214.

Schaefer, R. T., & Lamm, R. P. (1992). *Sociology* (4th ed.). New York: McGraw-Hill.

Schiffman, L. H. (1986). *Judaism: A primer.* New York: Anti-Defamation League of B'nai B'rith.

Schneider, B. (1989). *A guide to Jewish holidays and special days.* New York: Anti-Defamation League of B'nai B'rith.

Schoch-Spana, M. (1990). Es como si fuera la casa de uno: The role of the community church in maintaining Puerto Rican ethnicity. In P. L. Kilbride, J. C. Goodale, & E. R. Ameisen (Eds.), *Encounters with American ethnic cultures* (pp. 268–292). Tuscaloosa: University of Alabama Press.

Seigel, J. (1992, March 29). Possessed: The bumper sticker says, "He who dies with the most toys wins"—but researchers say don't bet on it. *The Chicago Tribune*, p. B1.

Silber, J. (1989). The pursuit of fairness. In J. Silber (Ed.), *Straight shooting: What's wrong with America and how to fix it* (pp. 185–196). New York: Harper & Row.

Sirianni, C., & Walsh, A. (1991). Through the prism of time: Temporal structures in postindustrial America. In A. Wolfe (Ed.), *America at century's end* (pp. 421–439). Berkeley: University of California Press.

Smith, E. (1981). Cultural and historical perspectives in counseling blacks. In D. W. Sue (Ed.), *Counseling the culturally different: Theory and practice* (pp. 141–185). New York: Wiley & Sons.

Soifer, S. (1991). Infusing content about Jews and about anti-semitism into the curricula. *Journal of Social Work Education, 27*, 156–167.

Sontag, D. (1993, June 13). Reshaping New York City's Golden Door. *The New York Times*, pp. 1, 18.

Sowell, T. (Ed.). (1978). *Essays and data on American ethnic groups* (pp. 7–64). Washington, DC: The Urban Institute.

Sue, D. W., & Sue, D. (1990). Counseling American Indians. In D. W. Sue & D. Sue (Eds.), *Counseling the culturally different* (2nd ed., pp. 175–188). New York: Wiley.

Summer, B. (1993, June 7). The paradox of success. *Publishers Weekly, 240*(23), 36–40.

Szapocznik, J., Scopetta, M. A., Aranalde, M. A., & Kurtines, W. (1978). Cuban value structure: Treatment implications. *Journal of Consulting and Clinical Psychology, 46*, 961–970.

Triandis, H. C. (Ed.). (1976). *Variations in black and white perceptions of the social environment.* Urbana: University of Illinois Press.

Triandis, H. C., Lisansky, J., Marin, G., & Betancourt, H. (1984). Simpatia as a cultural script of Hispanics. *Journal of Personality and Social Psychology, 47*, 1363–1375.

Tropman, J. E. (1989). *American values and social welfare: Cultural contradictions in the welfare state.* Englewood Cliffs, NJ: Prentice Hall.

Tropman, J. E., & Cox, F. M. (1987). Society: American values as a context for community organization and macro practice. In F. M. Cox, J. L. Erlich, J. Rothman, & J. E. Tropman (Eds.), *Strategies of community organization: Macro practice* (4th ed., pp.213–231). Itasca, IL: F. E. Peacock.

U.S. Bureau of the Census. (1993a). *Population profile of the United States: 1993*. Current Population Reports, Series P23-185. Washington, DC: United States Government Printing Office.

U.S. Bureau of the Census. (1993b). *Hispanic Americans today*. Current Population Reports, Series P23-183. Washington, DC: U.S. Government Printing Office.

Valdes-Cruz, R. (1977). The Black man's contribution to Cuban culture. *The Americas: A quarterly review of inter-American cultural history, 34*, 244–251.

Van Oss Marin, B., Marin, G., Padilla, A. M., & De la Rocha, C. (1983). Utilization of traditional and nontraditional sources of health care among Hispanics. *Hispanic Journal of Behavioral Sciences, 5*, 65–80.

Veciana-Suarez, A. (1993, April 16). Leaving home: Hispanic family ties tough to loosen for college. *The Miami Herald*, pp. 1E, 3E.

Wattenberg, B. J. (1991). *The first universal nation: Leading indicators and ideas about the surge of America in the 1990s*. New York: Maxwell Macmillan International.

Whitam, F. L., & Mathy, R. M. (1986). The homosexual subculture. In F. L. Whitam & R. M. Mathy (Eds.), *Male homosexuality in four societies: Brazil, Guatemala, the Philippines, and the United States* (pp. 83–105). New York: Praeger.

White, J. L., & Parham, T. A. (1990). *The psychology of blacks: An African-American perspective* (2nd ed.). Englewood Cliffs, NJ: Prentice-Hall.

Whyte, W. H. (1992). The organization man. In R. Wilkinson (Ed.), *American social character: Modern interpretations from the '40s to the present* (pp. 70–86). New York: HarperCollins.

Wilkinson, R. (Ed.). (1992). *American social character: Modern interpretations from the '40s to the present*. New York: HarperCollins.

Williams, N. (1990). *The Mexican American family: Tradition and change*. New York: General Hall.

Williams, R. M., Jr. (1970). *American society* (3rd ed.). New York: Knopf.

Wolfe, A. (Ed.). (1991). *America at century's end*. Berkeley: University of California Press.

Wolfe, T. (1976). The me decade and the third great awakening. In *Mauve gloves and madmen, clutter and vine*. New York: Farrar, Straus & Giroux.

Yankelovich, D. (1981). *New rules: Searching for self-fulfillment in a world turned upside down*. New York: Bantam.

Yankelovich, D. (1984). American values: Changes and stability. *Public Opinion, 6*, 2–9.

SUGGESTIONS FOR FURTHER READING

Agbayani-Siewart, P. (1994). Filipino American culture and family: Guidelines for practitioners. *Families in Society: The Journal of Contemporary Human Services, 75*, 429–437.

American South, The. (1994, December 10). *The Economist*. (Special report, pages 1–16.)

Asante, M. K. (1987). *The Afrocentric idea*. Philadelphia: Temple University Press.

Axtell, R. E. (Ed.). (1990). *Do's and taboos around the world* (2nd ed.). New York: John Wiley & Sons.

Barnlund, D. C. (1989). *Communicative styles of Japanese and Americans: Images and reality*. Belmont, CA: Wadsworth.

Bellah, R. N. (1985). *Habits of the heart: Individualism and commitment in American culture*. Berkeley, CA: University of California Press.

Berry, J. (1993, July 26). Culture of complaint. *Brandweek*, 32–43.

Betancourt, H., & Lopez, S. R. (1993). The study of culture, ethnicity, and race in American psychology. *American Psychologist, 48*, 629–637.

Bond, M. H. (Ed.). (1986). *The psychology of the Chinese people*. New York: Oxford University Press.

Borjas, G. J. (1994, December). *The economic benefits from immigration*. Boston, MA: National Bureau of Economic Research Working Paper #4955.

Braithwaite, D. O. (1988). Viewing persons with disabilities as a culture. In L. A. Samovar & R. E. Porter (Eds.), *Intercultural communication: A reader* (5th ed., pp. 147–153). Belmont, CA: Wadsworth.

Brislin, R. (1993). *Understanding culture's influence on behavior*. New York: Harcourt Brace.

Brookhiser, R. (1991). *The way of the WASP: How it made America, and how it can save it, so to speak.* New York: Free Press.

Castex, G. M. (1994). Providing services to Hispanic/Latino populations: Profiles in diversity. *Social Work, 39,* 289–296.

Cohen Publishers, Inc., & Collins, C. (1993). *The African Americans.* New York: Viking Studio Books.

Cruikshank, M. (1992). *The gay and lesbian liberation movement.* New York: Routledge.

DiStasi, L. (Ed.). (1990). *The big book of Italian American culture.* New York: Harper Perennial.

Dolnick, E. (1993, September). Deafness as culture. *The Atlantic Monthly,* 37–53.

DuBray, W. H. (1992). *Human services and American Indians.* St. Paul, MN: West Publishing.

Dyson, M. E. (1993). *Reflecting black: African-American cultural criticism.* Minneapolis: University of Minnesota Press.

Fierman, J. (1993, August 9). Is immigration hurting the U.S.? *Fortune,* 76–79.

Fitzpatrick, J. P. (1987). *Puerto Rican Americans: The meaning of migration to the mainland* (2nd ed.). Englewood Cliffs, NJ: Prentice Hall.

Fong, R., & Mokuau, N. (1994). Not simply "Asian Americans": Periodical literature review on Asians and Pacific Islanders, *Social Work, 39,* 298–305.

Forgotten pioneers, The. (1994, August 8). *U.S. News & World Report,* 53–55. (role of African Americans in the American frontier)

Friedman, C. G. (1990). Africans and African-Americans: An ethnohistorical view and symbolic analysis of food habits. In P. L. Kilbride, J. C. Goodale, & E. R. Ameisen (Eds.), *Encounters with American ethnic cultures* (pp. 77–98). Tuscaloosa: University of Alabama Press.

Furuto, S. M., Biswas, R., Chung, D. K., Murase, K., & Ross-Sheriff, F. (Eds.) (1992). *Social work practice with Asian Americans.* Newbury Park, CA: Sage.

Gates, H. L., Jr. (1994). *Colored people.* New York: Knopf.

Gold, S. J. (1992). *Refugee communities: A comparative field study.* Newbury Park: Sage. (Chapters 2 and 4 on Soviet Jews and Chapters 3 and 5 on Vietnamese Refugees)

Greene, B., & Herek, G. (Eds.). (1994). *Lesbian and gay psychology: Theory, research, and clinical applications.* Newbury Park, CA: Sage.

Harrington, W. (1992). *Crossings: A white man's journey into black America.* New York: HarperCollins.

Hayashi, C. (1988). *National character of the Japanese.* Tokyo: Statistical Bureau, Japan.

Hecht, M. L., Ribeau, S. A., & Collier, M. J. (1993). *African American communication: Ethnic identity and cultural interpretation.* Newbury Park, CA: Sage.

Herdt, G. (Ed.). (1992). *Gay culture in America: Essays from the field.* Boston: Beacon Press.

Hertzberg, A. (1989). *The Jews in America. Four centuries of an uneasy encounter: A history.* New York: Simon and Schuster.

Hong, M. (Ed.). (1993). *Growing up Asian American: An anthology.* New York: W. Morrow.

Keefe, S. E., & Padilla, A. M. (1987). *Chicano ethnicity.* Albuquerque: University of New Mexico Press.

Klein, M. (1993, October 17). The pious ones among us. *The Miami Herald, Tropic Magazine,* pp. 8–21. (about Orthodox Jews)

Lancaster, B. (1993). *The elements of Judaism.* Rockport, MA: Element.

Lincoln, C. E., & Mamiya, L. H. (1990). *The black church in the African American experience.* Durham: Duke University Press.

Lukes, C. A., & Land, H. (1990). Biculturality and homosexuality. *Social Work, 35,* 155–161.

Lutske, H. (1986). *The book of Jewish customs.* Northvale, NJ: Jason Aronson.

Major, R. (1992). *Cool pose: The dilemmas of black manhood in America.* New York: Lexington Books.

Martinez, K. J. (1994). Cultural sensitivity in family therapy gone awry. *Hispanic Journal of Behavioral Sciences, 16*(1), 75–89.

McCaffrey, L. J., et al. (1987). *The Irish in Chicago.* Urbana: University of Illinois Press.

Miller, N. (1989). *In search of gay America: Women and men in a time of change.* New York: Harper & Row.

Min, Pyong Gap. (Ed.). (1994). *Asian Americans: Contemporary trends and issues.* Newbury Park, CA: Sage.

Morganthau, T. (1993, August 9). America: Still a melting pot? *Newsweek*, 16–25.

Moskos, C. C. (1989). *Greek Americans: Struggle and success* (2nd ed). New Brunswick: Transaction Publishers.

Nah, Kyung-Hee. (1993). Perceived problems and service delivery for Korean immigrants. *Social Work, 38*, 289–296.

Padilla, A. M. (1994). *Hispanic psychology: Critical issues in theory and research*. Newbury Park, CA: Sage.

Paniagua, F. A. (1994). *Assessing and treating culturally diverse clients*. Thousand Oaks, CA: Sage.

Perez Firmat, G. (1987). *From ajiaco to tropical soup: Fernando Ortiz and the definition of Cuban culture*. Occasional paper: Dialogue #93. Miami, FL: Latin American and Caribbean Center.

Philips, J. E. (1990). The African heritage of white America. In J. E. Holloway (Ed.), *Africanisms in American culture* (pp. 225–239). Bloomington: Indiana University Press.

Portes, A., & Zhou, Min. (1994, summer). Should immigrants assimilate? *The Public Interest, 116*, 18–33.

Reiff, D. (1993). *The exile: Cuba in the heart of Miami*. New York: Simon & Schuster.

Riley, P. (Ed.). (1993). *Growing up Native American: An anthology*. New York: William Morrow.

Saran, P. (1985). *The Asian Indian experience in the United States*. Cambridge, MA: Schenkman.

Shneider, S. (1994, November 18). Getting past women's past. *Jewish Times*, 52–56. (About the problems of women in the Jewish culture)

Smitherman, G. (1991). Talkin and testifyin: Black English and the black experience. In R. L. Jones (Ed.), *Black psychology* (3rd ed., pp. 249–267). Berkeley, CA: Cobb & Henry.

Steinberg, S. (1989). *The ethnic myth: Race, ethnicity, and class in America*. Boston: Beacon Press.

Storti, C. (1994). *Brief encounters with cultural difference: 74 cross-cultural dialogues*. Yarmouth, ME: Intercultural Press.

Talese, G. (1992). *Unto the sons*. New York: Knopf. (About Italian immigration around the turn of the century)

Tan, A. (1989). *The joy luck club*. New York: Putnam. (About Chinese Americans)

Tropman, J. E. (1989). *American values and social welfare: Cultural contradictions in the welfare state*. Englewood Cliffs, NJ: Prentice Hall.

Wilkinson, R. (Ed.) (1992). *American social character: Modern interpretations from the '40s to the present*. New York: HarperCollins.

Williams, N. (1990). *The Mexican American family: Tradition and change*. New York: General Hall.

Wolfe, A. (Ed.). (1991). *American at century's end*. Berkeley: University of California Press.

Yankelovich, D. (1994). How changes in the economy are reshaping American values. In H. J. Aaron, T. E. Mann, & T. Taylor (Eds.), *Values and public policy*. Washington, DC: The Brookings Institution.

Young, M. E. (1994, November 6). Strangers in their own land. *Ft Lauderdale Sun-Sentinel*. (about the Seminole Indians)

Look for articles in the following journals:

American Quarterly
Black Scholar
Ethnic and Racial Studies
Hispanic Journal of Behavioral Sciences
International Journal of Intercultural Relations
Journal of American Culture
Journal of American Studies
Journal of Black Studies
Journal of Gay and Lesbian Psychotherapy
Journal of Gay and Lesbian Social Services
Journal of Homosexuality
Journal of Multicultural Social Work
Journal of Negro Education
Signs: Journal of Women in Culture and Society

CHAPTER 3

SOCIETY AND HUMAN BEHAVIOR
THE INFLUENCE OF THE SOCIAL CLASS SYSTEM

Having gained some insight into how culture determines values, behaviors, and attitudes and having acquired knowledge about various U.S. cultures, we now turn our attention to the society that provides a context for such diverse cultures. We begin by examining in this chapter the social class system with emphasis on how it shapes the circumstances of people's lives and their behaviors.

It is because of the strong relationship between socioeconomic status and life chances that social workers and other human service practitioners need knowledge about life in different socioeconomic groups, particularly the opportunities or limitations their clients may confront as a result of their socioeconomic status and how these may affect the quality of their lives. If practitioners lack such knowledge, they are likely to intervene in ways that are insensitive or unrealistic. If so, they may offend their clients, or their attempts at offering assistance may be considered irrelevant or just plain not helpful.

In addition to the influence of socioeconomic group membership, people's life chances are substantially determined by their race, eth-

nicity, gender, and sexual orientation. These factors will be explored in the next chapter as we consider their impact on the contemporary situation of various social groups in the United States, including women, African Americans, gays and lesbians, Latinos, Asian Americans, Native Americans, and American Jews.

The ecosystems perspective reminds us that it is not possible to understand human behavior without grasping the realities of the environmental context within which people function. This suprasystem includes their culture(s), the society and communities in which they live, the workplaces and other organizations with which they come into contact, the groups in which they participate, and their families. In the previous chapter, we examined various U.S. cultures. In this and subsequent chapters, we will explore the remaining social systems, one by one.

THE SOCIETAL CONTEXT

Society refers to a group of people who partake of a common overall culture and who occupy a given territory subject to a central governmental authority (Robertson, 1989, p. 51). In the modern world, most societies are nation states, such as the United States, Canada, or Mexico on the North American continent. However, some countries contain smaller societies within their borders. For example, the United States includes many indigenous American-Indian tribes considered to be separate "nations," such as the Navajo or Cherokee nations.

The United States is a postindustrial society, like the societies of other advanced countries such as Germany, Japan, Great Britain, France, and Sweden. In a **postindustrial society** the population relies for subsistence primarily on the generation of services and information rather than on the production of food or on industrial manufacturing. That is, agriculture and manufacturing are so automated and efficient in postindustrial societies that only a small proportion of the population needs to work in such sectors of the economy.

Moreover, in postindustrial societies, industries that are not amenable to high levels of automation (e.g., the apparel industry or other manual- labor-intensive industries) tend to be moved to less advanced countries where labor is less expensive. This frees a large proportion of the population to concentrate on jobs in fields that require mental rather than physical effort and that involve the production of services or the manipulation of information, such as in science and technology, computer programming, medicine, law, teaching, social work, sales, and so on. These white-collar jobs do not require muscle power; therefore, they can be executed equally successfully by males or females. Consequently, in postindustrial societies, both sexes are potentially capable of participating equally in nearly all sectors of the labor market at all levels of expertise.

In order to survive, every society must meet the basic needs of its members. Specifically, for example, the children must be cared for and socialized into the ways of the society and its culture(s), the societal knowledge must be passed on from one generation to the next, goods and services must be produced and distributed, social order must be maintained, the society must defend itself against outside aggression, and the health and social well-being of the population must be maintained. These social functions, which are vital to the maintenance of the social system, are carried out by various social **institutions** or subsystems of the society established to respond to these specific needs. Thus, for example, the social institution known as the family provides child care and socialization and contributes to the social and emotional support of its members; schools transmit the societal and cultural knowledge; hospitals and other health care facilities maintain health; social welfare agencies and churches promote social and spiritual well-being; law-enforcement agencies maintain order; and the military defends the nation. Table 3.1 summarizes major social institutions and the social needs they address.

SOCIAL STRATIFICATION AND THE SOCIAL CLASS SYSTEM

Every society develops some system of **social stratification,** or layering, according to which it ranks its members depending on the value the society assigns to the characteristics they possess, such as wealth and income, occupation, educational attainment, race, ethnic background, age, gender, or sexual orientation. The term **social class,** in particular, refers to certain aspects of the societal hierarchical ranking system. In the United States, for example, an individual's social class ranking is determined by his or her family's wealth and income, occupational status, education, and amount of power and authority over others.

Social Class and Life Chances

The United States has never been as rigidly stratified in terms of social class as many other

TABLE 3.1 Major Social Institutions

INSTITUTION	SOCIAL NEEDS ADDRESSED
Family	Provide child care, socialization, and regulation of sexual behavior
Economic System	Produce and distribute goods and services
Education	Transmit knowledge and cultural values
Health System	Provide care of the sick
Social Welfare	Provide personal/social/economic support
Religion	Share spiritual values and beliefs
Political System	Distribute power and run the government
Legal System	Maintain social control
Military	Defend the state against aggressors

countries. However, social class is an important element to consider in the study of human behavior because it plays a fundamental role in defining the **life chances** or quality of life people face (Gerth & Mills, 1958, p. 181)—that is, the likelihood that they will have positive or negative experiences and living conditions. For instance, individuals in the lower socioeconomic classes tend to have fewer life chances. They typically have fewer opportunities to get a good education; higher levels of unemployment and underemployment; higher rates of disease and disability; greater exposure to crime, pollution, and work-related hazards; more stress; and higher mortality rates than those in the higher socioeconomic classes. In contrast, those in the top social classes tend to have enhanced life chances mostly due to higher incomes and resources, which make it possible for them to live in safer neighborhoods and to get better housing, health care, nutrition, education, and various other necessities and comforts (Kerbo, 1991; Rossides, 1990).

Because members of different social classes experience different life circumstances, some come to develop a distinct outlook. For example, research has demonstrated that individuals in the higher social classes are more likely to think that their actions can make a difference because they have had opportunities and experiences to be self-directed and to be in control of situations. On the other hand, those from lower socioeconomic groups are more likely to think fatalistically—that is, to think that they are at the mercy of forces beyond their control because usually they are not in a position to control the circumstances of their lives or to be self-directed at work (Kohn, 1969; Kohn, Naoi, Schoenback, Schooler, & Slomczynski, 1990).

Practical Issues Related to Social Class

The previous section noted that the circumstances of people's lives and their values, attitudes, and lifestyles are substantially determined by their social class status. This is why it is important for social workers and other human service practitioners to be knowledgeable about what life typically is like for clients from different socioeconomic backgrounds, particularly the opportunities or limitations they may confront and how these may affect their lives. Without such understandings, practitioners may intervene insensitively, thus perhaps offending their clients or, at least unintentionally, not being helpful. This is particularly possible if the worker and client do not share the same socioeconomic group membership.

One common area of class-based misunderstandings between clients and practitioners is parental discipline. Parents from different social class backgrounds may value and reinforce different behaviors in their children and may discipline them by using different approaches. For example, middle-class parents may be more prone to put emphasis on fostering self-control and initiative in their children, whereas working-class parents may be more likely to stress obedience and conformity. Similarly, if a child misbehaves, a working-class parent may be more inclined to respond with physical punishment, whereas a middle-class parent may be more likely to look into the child's motivation for misbehaving and to reason with the child.

Sometimes practitioners do not realize that they are challenging their clients' values, authority, and beliefs about child rearing when they tell them they must stop using physical punishment as a discipline method (Parmer Davidson & Jenkins, 1989). Although research has shown that physical punishment is often counterproductive, many parents from lower socioeconomic backgrounds honestly believe that it is an appropriate way of getting children to behave as they should. Consequently, it is important that workers not be too quick to conclude that a parent is abusive simply because the parent routinely spanks the child whenever he or she misbehaves. Practitioners must explore and accept their clients' cultural and class-based belief systems about child rearing before they attempt to show them that other forms of discipline are likely to be more effective in the long run.

Misunderstandings also may arise when the practitioner makes assumptions about a client's potential for a particular service intervention on the basis of how the client dresses or expresses himself or herself, or the neighborhood in which the client lives. The danger of these assumptions based on socioeconomic considerations is that they can easily lead to a selective consideration of alternatives that deprive some clients, particularly those of low socioeconomic background, of services that could be helpful to them. For instance, traditionally, much has been made of the differences between the verbal abilities of middle-class clients and of the poor (especially those from racial/ethnic nondominant groups), with the former routinely considered "more verbal" than the latter. Based on such dubious distinctions, practitioners often have been advised, when working with the poor, to concentrate on external-environmental problems. Specifically, it has been suggested that poor clients should be offered concrete services (e.g., assistance in obtaining financial help, food stamps, health care, or other needed services), rather than verbal interventions such as "psychotherapy" and other insight-oriented methodologies, generally used with the middle class.

Although poor clients often confront a variety of external-environmental problems and need more concrete services than middle-class clients, they are no different from middle-class clients in their need for assistance with psychological and emotional problems and their desire for advice, guidance, insight, and clarification (Frank, Eisenthal, & Lazare, 1978; Davis & Proctor, 1989, p. 338). Instead of depriving clients from lower socioeconomic backgrounds from insight-oriented interventions (e.g., individual counseling or family therapy) because of their presumed "low verbal aptitude," practitioners should learn to talk with their clients simply and straightforwardly without intellectualization or technical jargon. If they refrain from using language in an alienating manner, they will find that they can use successfully all interventive methods with all clients (Hollis, 1983, p. 637; Davis & Proctor, 1989, p. 276; Parmer Davidson & Jenkins, 1989).

Perspectives on Social Stratification

Sociologists have offered contrasting reasons for the existence of social stratification. This section reviews briefly the arguments of structural functionalist and conflict theorists.

The Functionalist Perspective

Would you spend a large amount of money and put forth a great deal of effort going to school for years, studying days, nights, and weekends to become a physician if you could make as good an income and get as much respect and social status by taking a nine-to-five job that required only a high school diploma, such as a job as day-care worker or beach lifeguard? To be sure, many people would opt to become physicians regardless of the extra costs and efforts for the challenge and intellectual stimulation of a medical career. However, according to the functionalist point of view, all other things being equal, most people would take the easiest jobs available and enjoy the extra leisure, and society would not have a sufficient number of highly trained personnel available to take care of some of its critical needs.

Because society must staff its various positions with individuals with the appropriate credentials and expertise, it becomes necessary to offer special rewards in terms of higher pay and prestige to motivate people to take the more demanding and challenging jobs (Davis & Moore, 1945; Parsons, 1953).

The Conflict Perspective

You may recall from Chapter 1 that conflict theorists (Dahrendorf, 1959, 1968; Tumin, 1985) have criticized the functionalists, pointing to the difficulty of determining what social positions are more vitally important than others. In addition, conflict theorists have questioned the argument of the functionalists that only a limited portion of the population has the capacity to acquire the knowledge and skills necessary to undertake certain complex, high-level jobs essential to the society. Instead, they have argued that the power elite prevents the development of talent in order to protect their own privileged class positions.

To some extent, the functionalists are correct in their argument that individuals who take on complex jobs that are critical to the survival of the society deserve special rewards and thus a social class system is inevitable for societies to survive. However, advanced technological societies produce a lot more goods and services than necessary to attract people to valuable

occupations. What happens under such circumstances is that excess societal resources are usually appropriated by those in power, thereby creating a highly unequal distribution of wealth that generates social unrest, as emphasized by conflict theorists. In turn, to keep social unrest under control, the dominant group is forced to share some of the wealth with the working classes while still retaining considerable power and privilege (Lenski, 1966; Lenski, Lenski, & Nolan, 1991).

THE SOCIAL CLASS SYSTEM IN POSTINDUSTRIAL U.S. SOCIETY

This section will look at what life is like in the various social classes in the United States—the upper class, the corporate class, the upper-middle class, the lower-middle class, the working class (skilled and unskilled), and the poor. Before focusing attention on these social groups, however, two related trends in the U.S. economy that are having important consequences for the social class structure will be examined.

First, in the move from an industrial to a postindustrial economy, the number of manufacturing jobs has decreased substantially, not only due to advances in automation but because many industries have been "downsizing" and relocating their manufacturing plants to areas where wages are lower—often in less-developed countries. At the same time, the advancing technology has increased the number of positions available in the professional, technical, and service sectors of the economy (Kerbo, 1991.)

As industrial and manufacturing plants located in the central cities close down or reduce personnel, many blue-collar workers are losing their previously secure jobs, and, without much education, they are having difficulty finding similarly paying jobs for which they qualify. Consequently, a large proportion of industrial workers are having to accept employment at lower pay, particularly in the service sector (e.g., in the health care industry, the hotel and restaurant industry, or construction) or as semiskilled or unskilled operators in high-technology industries. In the shuffle, some people are crossing the line from working class to working poor or even joining the ranks of the unemployed. Poorly educated young people entering the job market in the 1990s also have fewer opportunities than young people of previous generations to find jobs in the manufacturing industries. Lacking the skills required to qualify for the better-paying high-tech positions available, they are forced to accept low-wage jobs, many times on an hourly basis without fringe benefits or full-time status.

A second and related economic trend, particularly during the last two decades, has been the growth in inequality. The widening gap between the rich and the poor in the United States is of serious concern. To give you an idea of the extent to which money has become concentrated in fewer hands, the richest 10 percent of U.S. families now control more wealth than the remaining 90 percent of the population combined (Nasar, 1992). In terms of income, in 1993, the top 20 percent of U.S. households earned 48 percent of the nation's income, while the bottom 20 percent earned only 3.6 percent of the income (DeParle, 1994). Another telling example of income concentration is the average pay of chief executives of the nation's largest publicly traded companies (i.e., those that issue stock and trade in the public exchanges). This figure stood at 2.56 million dollars per year in the early 1990s, 139 times the average size of a U.S. worker's paycheck (Cowan, 1992).

Given such income disparities, the well-to-do are increasingly isolating themselves from the rest of the population and drifting closer to the "Latin-American/Caribbean model," of the rich living in the "mansions on the hills above the slums" (Henwood, 1992, p. 15). Although the U.S. rich do not yet live in mansions surrounded by slums, they are increasingly moving to walled, well-guarded exclusive enclaves where they can be insulated and protected from central- and inner-city problems.

Between the top and bottom classes in the United States there is a large middle group of Americans whose incomes have been losing ground in recent years despite steady economic growth and relatively low unemployment. For example, between 1989 and 1993, the typical U.S. household lost $2,344 in annual income (DeParle, 1994). This inability of the U.S. economy in recent years to benefit anyone but those with high incomes (particularly managers and professionals) is a matter that raises serious concerns for the future of the nation (Nassar, 1994).

The Upper Class

The upper class is made up of the old and most prestigious families—the so-called aristocracy or high society. Traditionally, its members have been white Anglo-Saxon Protestants, although some non-Protestant Euro-Americans—notably some Jews and Catholics—have recently penetrated this exclusive clique. Typically, an individual is born into this class, as upper-class status is derived from the accomplishments and money of ancestors, not of the living; in fact, in this class the "age" of an individual's wealth is more important than its "size" (O'Reilly, 1990). Normally, however, members of the upper class are affluent enough that they do not have to work for a living. Nonetheless, many work hard in the family business, pursuing careers, or overlooking investments. Typically, they are listed in the *Social Register*, live in secluded homes in the most exclusive neighborhoods, maintain summer and winter resort homes or apartments in fashionable places, send their children to elite private boarding schools and Ivy League universities, and belong to exclusive social clubs. Despite their privileged social position, however, members of the upper class are seldom ostentatious or lavish in their spending. They

Source: By permission of Johnny Hart and Creators Syndicate, Inc.

do not like to call attention to themselves. In short, old money is characteristically low key.

Volunteer and public service have been traditional endeavors for the adult members of this class. Despite busy schedules, many are volunteer members of the boards of foundations, art councils, and other committees. Others hold highly influential public service positions, such as ambassadorships, senatorships, membership in the president's cabinet, and an occasional presidency. Nonemployed spouses often are deeply involved in charity work.

For leisure, many upper-class men and women enjoy certain refined and expensive outdoor activities such as yachting, golfing, horseback riding, sailing, tennis, skiing, polo, or high-culture activities, such as attendance at art exhibits and auctions, ballets, operas, concerts, plays, and literary readings. Similar to those in the corporate and upper-middle classes, upper-class men and women tend to marry later than those of lower socioeconomic status, largely because they are expected to complete their university studies before marriage. They also tend to have fewer children (Rossides, 1990).

Although they live all over the United States, many upper-class families become acquainted because they participate in a highly exclusive and restricted circle. This makes it possible for them to maintain high class consciousness and some unity of action, particularly with respect to political and economic interests. Thus, although they represent a tiny proportion of the population—perhaps no more than 0.5 to 1 percent (Kerbo, 1991)—they exercise major influence in shaping the social, political, and economic climate of the nation.

The upper class is no longer as powerful as it was in the past. For instance, nowadays this group no longer exercises total control over the major industrial and financial corporations in the nation. However, as large stockholders and members of the boards of directors of these major corporations, they continue to have a disproportionate say on what's going on. Their influence is also limited by a federal government that has become an enormous and independently powerful machine. However, here too this class makes its influence felt through public office holding, lobbying activities, political campaign contributions, and the financing of private think-tanks that provide information and recommendations to policy-making bodies. Because the upper class no longer has absolute control over the government or the economy, it no longer can be called the "ruling class," as Domhoff (1983) used to call it; however, its influence continues to be clearly felt (Alba & Moore, 1982; Barton, 1985).

The Corporate Class

A new class has emerged in the United States in recent years composed of those who *control*, though do not necessarily *own*, the major means of production (Useem, 1984). These are the people—still almost exclusively white men—who hold key positions of authority in the top U.S. corporations, such as General Motors, American Telephone and Telegraph, Ford, General Electric, Exxon, and so on. Many of these corporate chief executive receive yearly compensation packages worth several million dollars. Like the upper class, they constitute a very select group, probably comprising no more than about 0.5 percent of the population (Kerbo, 1991, p. 272). (To give you an idea of the concentration of power in this class, consider that the top 100 U.S. corporations control more than 70 percent of all the industrial assets in the nation, the top 30 banks hold more than 50 percent of all banking assets, and a mere 8 insurance companies control over 50 percent of the total assets in this sector of the economy [Kerbo, 1991, pp. 233–238].) This small group of people (mostly Euro-American men) at the helm of enormous business conglomerates dominates the U.S. economy and consequently wields a great deal of political influence within the society.

In many ways, members of the corporate class lead lives similar to the upper class; for example, they are often members of the same exclusive social clubs, frequent many of the same resorts favored by the upper class, and send their children to the same private boarding schools and elite universities. Like the upper class, they tend to be conservative in economic and political behavior. One way in which this class is different from the upper class is that its boundaries are more permeable; that is, it is possible for someone, even occasionally a member of a nondominant social group, to attain membership in this class through sheer talent, effort, and achievement.

"Actually, Lou, I think it was more than just my being in the right place at the right time. I think it was my being the right race, the right religion, the right sex, the right socio-economic group, having the right accent, the right clothes, going to the right schools..."

Source: Drawing by W. Miller; © 1992 The New Yorker Magazine, Inc.

The Upper-Middle Class

The upper-middle class represents the top layer of the 42 percent or so of the U.S. population considered to be middle class (Kerbo, 1991). It is composed of "elite" professionals (e.g., physicians, lawyers, as well as the top talent in various other technical and professional fields, such as engineering, architecture, accounting, dentistry, and the sciences), high-level managers of major corporations (i.e., the next step below chief executive officers), high-ranking government bureaucrats, and well-educated individuals who derive high income from their businesses or investments. Most upper-middle-class individuals have university degrees, frequently including graduate degrees, and they participate extensively in community and cultural affairs, politics, and voluntary and professional associations. Like those in higher classes, they typically consider their work to be challenging, fulfilling, and autonomous in the sense that they can exercise a great deal of control over it.

Like the two higher classes previously discussed, most members of the upper-middle class tend to be conservative with respect to economic issues that affect their pockets (e.g., raising the income tax rate or giving subsidies to the poor). However, they tend to be more liberal in relation to purely social issues, such as the granting of civil rights and equal opportunities to nondominant group members (Kerbo, 1991). Their homes are usually stylish, well maintained and landscaped, and built on spacious lots in affluent neighborhoods. In rearing their children, the upper-middle class (also like the upper and corporate classes) tends to heed the advise of the experts and puts a great deal of emphasis on self-direction, self-control, initiative, and deferred gratification (Kohn, 1969; Kohn, Naoi, Schoenback, Schooler, & Slomc-

zynski, 1990). This type of training prepares their children to assume positions of authority in the society. When their children misbehave, upper-middle-class parents are likely to look into the children's motivation and to reason with them rather than to use physical punishment as a discipline method (Parmer Davidson & Jenkins, 1989).

The Lower-Middle Class

The bulk of middle America is concentrated in the lower-middle class. This social stratum includes members of "minor" professions, many of whom are women (e.g., school teachers, social workers, registered nurses, computer specialists, and librarians); small business owners (e.g., owners of corner grocery stores, electronic repair shops, beauty shops); middle- and lower-echelon business/government/sales managers; some supervisory service personnel (e.g., police, firefighting, and post-office unit supervisors, head waiters and head waitresses at upscale restaurants); high-level clerical personnel (e.g., executive secretaries, legal assistants); and highly skilled craftspeople or tradespeople (e.g., expert auto mechanics, electronic and computer repairmen/women, and some self-employed plumbers and electricians). The vast majority of the lower-middle class are white-collar workers; that is, they do mental work rather than physical labor and their work environment is clean, comfortable, and safe.

The lower-middle class constitutes the most heterogeneous group of people in any of the social classes in the United States. They have various levels of education, from trade/vocational school training to graduate degrees. Their values and lifestyles vary so widely that they are, for all practical purposes, impossible to describe without stereotyping. You can see endless characterizations of life in the middle class depicted on television soap operas and situation comedies.

The Working Class

Representing about 42 percent of the population (Kerbo, 1991), the working class traditionally has included people employed in skilled and semiskilled manual-labor occupations, such as automobile assembly-line workers, petroleum and steel workers, butchers, mine workers, welders, teamsters (truckers), bus drivers, and rank-and-file craftsmen/women (e.g., plasterers, bricklayers, plumbers, carpenters, and electricians). Because their work is frequently "dirty," manual workers are collectively referred to as **blue-collar** workers. Often, their work is dangerous, subject to injury, health hazards, and even death in the workplace. Because of the recent shift in the U.S. economy from manufacturing to high-tech and service industries, this segment of the U.S. work force has been shrinking steadily. For example, the 1990 census found, for the first time in history, that the United States had more people performing executive, professional, or technical jobs than making or transporting goods (America's blue-collar sector shrinking, 1993).

The working class also includes the vast majority of rank-and-file secretarial, retail sales, and service personnel (e.g., secretaries and other office personnel, department store salespeople, police officers, firefighters, post office clerks, and flight attendants). Traditionally, a large proportion of these workers have been females and members of nondominant racial/ethnic groups.

A third major contingent of the working class are unskilled laborers. Many make incomes below the official poverty level, even though they work part time or even full time; hence, they are often referred to as *the working poor*. Unskilled laborers are typically employed at or near the minimum wage as janitors, longshoremen, gardeners, day laborers, migrant farm workers, or domestic workers. Their work is often backbreaking and monotonous, and requires a high level of physical exertion (Terkel, 1974). A disproportionate number of the members of this group in the United States are African Americans, Latinos, or other recent immigrants.

Because the working class has greater representation of members of racial and ethnic non-dominant groups than any of the other higher social classes, anytime employment becomes scarce, they are put in a position to fight among themselves for jobs. This constant scramble for jobs generates considerable racial and ethnic friction within this class.

What is life like in the working class? Although lifestyles within the various social classes are difficult to characterize without stereotyping, particularly below the upper-middle-class level, certain experiences are fairly common among members of the working class. Working-class persons typically have a high school education or less. Their jobs are often boring, repetitive, and unfulfilling, and they are seldom allowed to exercise autonomy or authority at work or to supervise others. Instead, members of the working class often work under close supervision and have limited chances for upward mobility. Some are reasonably well paid and have fairly secure jobs with fringe benefits, such as health insurance and pension plans. Many of these more privileged individuals are unionized skilled manual workers or unionized low-echelon white-collar employees of major organizations. But only about 18 percent of U.S. workers are presently unionized, in contrast to 52 percent of workers in England, 40 percent in West Germany, and 28 percent in Japan (Kerbo, 1991, p. 300). Yet, even unionized workers are subject to layoffs and to the ups and downs of the economy. The rest of the working class tend to receive less pay, to be less secure in their employment, and to have limited work-related fringe benefits.

The ability to buy a home, so central to the traditional American dream, is becoming more difficult for working-class families to realize. This is because in the past 20 years or so, the income of working-class families has not kept up with inflation which has increased considerably the median price of a starter home. The small proportion of working-class families able to become homeowners nowadays are forced to buy small homes sometimes lacking even the comforts they had when they were growing up. These homes are nearly always located in developments built in remote locations, thus forcing many to commute long distances to go to work (Rubin, 1992a).

According to Kerbo (1991), members of the working class are less mobile and therefore more "local" in orientation than members of higher classes. This is probably because their incomes, occupations and educational levels limit their opportunities to interact with people or organizations outside the local community network of work associates, family, and friends. In addition, vis-à-vis those in higher social classes, members of the working class tend to be more liberal when it comes to economic issues (e.g., acceptability of government intervention in the economy such as by providing universal health care) but more conservative in relation to matters pertaining to religion, sexual morality, or civil rights (Kerbo, 1991).

Many working-class husbands and wives work outside the home to support their families; consequently, they have little time for leisure and social activities, particularly since members of this social group, unlike those in higher classes, tend to be unable to afford the cost of household help or child care. Particularly the women often spend most of their off-work time performing family and household tasks. Frequently, two-income families solve their child-care problems by taking jobs on different shifts, often at high cost to the marriage and family life. For these families, finding time to be with friends and relatives can be very difficult. Even finding the time and privacy to have sex on a regular basis can be a problem. At bedtime, the women, particularly, tend to be exhausted (Rubin, 1992a).

In terms of child rearing, working-class members often put emphasis on teaching their children to be obedient and to conform to rules, unlike members of higher social classes who are more likely to stress self-direction and initiative (Kohn, 1969; Kohn et al., 1990). In this manner, without much conscious awareness, they have traditionally prepared their children to assume jobs in which they will take orders from others. When children misbehave, working-class parents may be more inclined to use physical punishment than middle-class parents (Parmer Davidson & Jenkins, 1989).

Research has shown that working-class persons tend to spend more of their leisure time, compared to those of higher socioeconomic status such as the upper-middle class, watching television, participating in sports as spectators (e.g., attending football or baseball games or boxing/wrestling matches or watching sports on TV), working in their home workshops making home repairs, working on their cars, going camping or fishing, or spending the afternoon strolling with family or friends at the local mall. In contrast, they are less likely than upper-middle-class individuals to spend their leisure time reading books, attending high-culture affairs such as concerts, ballets, operas, or lectures, or participating in voluntary associations or in community service or political activities (Fussell, 1983; Gans, 1974). For the most part, these lifestyle differences are due to a combination of limited income and education, which narrow the range of leisure options available at the working-class level.

The Poor

Despite a considerable decrease in poverty from the 1930s to the 1970s, too many people in the United States are poor, compared to most other advanced nations. Specifically, in 1993, 39.3 million people in the United States were poor, representing 15.1 percent of the population—the highest poverty rate in 10 years (DeParle, 1994; Zaldivar, 1994). Even more discouraging is the fact that the poverty rates experienced by children, families headed by

women, African Americans, and Latinos were considerably higher. In 1993, the poverty rate for blacks was 33.1 percent and for Latinos 30.6 percent,[1] compared to 12.2 percent for whites (DeParle, 1994; Zaldivar, 1994). In 1991, 43.6 percent of all black children and 40.7 percent of all Latino children were poor, compared to 15.6 percent of white children (U.S. Bureau of the Census, 1992, 1993b). These figures show that the poverty rates for these groups have continued to increase since the 1990 census was taken. The 1990 poverty figures are shown in Table 3.2 below.

In 1993, the poverty rate for families headed by single mothers was 35.6 percent, compared to 6.5 percent for married-couple families (DeParle, 1994; Zaldivar, 1994). The poverty rate for black and Latino female-headed families is even more pronounced—51.8 percent and 54.8 percent, respectively, according to the 1990 census. Even among white families, the poverty rate of female-headed households is eight times higher (32.9 percent) than that of married-couple families (see Table 3.2). Since the 1970s, only the elderly have shown a continuous decrease in poverty, largely as a result of increased Social Security, pension, and Medicare benefits.

Although most of the poor are concentrated in the central areas of large cities, about 29 percent live in rural communities and in small towns and villages. Rural areas have a somewhat higher than proportionate share of poverty because they often lack resources such as stable employment or a diversified economy (Tickamyer & Duncan, 1990). Many of the rural poor are African Americans living in the South, Latino migrant workers, Native Americans living on reservations and near reservations, and out-of-work coal miners, small farmers, and farm workers (Martinez-Brawley, 1987; Ellwood, 1988).

Although poverty per se need not result in personal or family difficulties, it is a pervasive handicap that makes people vulnerable to many problems. Specifically, the conditions that tend

TABLE 3.2   The Poor by Age, Racial, Ethnic, and Gender Background According to the 1990 Census

	WHITES*	BLACKS*	HISPANIC* ORIGIN	ASIAN/ PACIFIC ISLANDERS	AMERICAN INDIAN*	TOTAL MALES	TOTAL FEMALES
Percent below poverty level:							
Individuals	10.7	31.9	28.1	14.3	26.3	11.7	15.2
Children under 18 years	15.9	39.2	31.4	17.0	34.0	20.5	20.8
Individuals 65 and over	10.1	29.5	23.5	12.1	21.6	7.6	15.4

Sources: Data taken from "1990 Census of Population, Social and Economic Characteristics, United States" (1990 CP-2-1) by U.S. Bureau of the Census, 1994. Washington, DC: U.S. Government Printing Office. "Geographic Profile of Employment and Unemployment, 1990" by U.S. Bureau of the Census, 1991. Washington, DC: U.S. Government Printing Office. "Poverty in the United States: 1990 Current Population Reports Series P-60, No. 175" by U.S. Bureau of the Census, 1991. Washington, DC: U.S. Government Printing Office. "We the American ...Asians" (WE-3) by U.S. Bureau of the Census, 1993. Washington, DC: U.S. Government Printing Office. "Statistical Abstract of the United States: 1993" by U.S. Bureau of the Census, 1994. Washington, DC: U.S. Government Printing Office.
*Terms used by the Census Bureau.

to accompany poverty—such as crowded and inadequate housing located in high-crime areas, lack of health care or inadequate health care, stress, and deficient education—are serious hazards to negotiate in life (Chilman, 1975; Davis & Proctor, 1989, pp. 298–299).

Relative versus Absolute Poverty

Relative poverty is a state of deprivation felt in comparison to others who are getting more of the societal comforts and resources. **Absolute poverty,** in contrast, is economic deprivation that prevents families from meeting their minimum requirements for food, health care, shelter, clothing, transportation, and other basic survival needs. The **federal poverty line** is the official upper-income limit for the poverty level. In the mid-1990s, it was obtained by multiplying by 3 the yearly cost of a low-priced food budget for a family of four as determined by the U.S. Department of Agriculture (USDA), with adjustments up or down for family size but without regard to differences in the cost of living in different areas of the country. It is important to note that the USDA did not consider the low-

budget food plan it developed long ago when the formula for the poverty level was established to be a nutritionally adequate diet for *long-term* use (Rubin, 1992b, p. 4). Therefore, the poverty line dollar amount is lower than it would be if it took into consideration long-term nutritional needs. The "times 3" multiplier was established in 1963 when the average low-income family spent approximately one-third of its total income on food. Thus computed, in 1994, the official poverty line was $15,141 for a family of four (Pear, 1995). Any family of four with a yearly income below this dollar figure in 1994 was officially classified as poor.

Some experts suggest that poverty is more widespread in the United States than the official rates indicate because the method used for determining the top federal income levels for poverty was developed several decades ago when life circumstances were different than they are today. For example, heat, electricity, and medical care were proportionately less expensive then than they are today. Housing costs also took proportionately less of the family income in the 1950s than today. In addition,

in the 1950s and 1960s, fewer families were headed by only one parent, and therefore fewer families needed to pay for child care than today. The poverty line figures also are considered unrealistically low for survival in high-cost urban areas and central cities where poor people often pay very high rents and are overcharged by merchants for basic necessities.

Notwithstanding the preceding arguments, there are some conservatives who insist that a substantial number of the poor are better off than official government figures reflect and that the quality of their lives is better today than it was three decades ago because some now receive certain noncash benefits that were not available before the 1960s. It is true that the poor who make use of Medicaid have better access to health care than before this program was created in 1965. Some also benefit from the food stamps program created in the 1960s and from rent subsidies (Pear, 1993b). However, even if noncash benefits were counted as part of an individual's income, the poverty rate in 1993 would have been 12.1 percent instead

of 15.1 percent (Zaldivar, 1994). This slightly lower rate would still be unacceptably high for an advanced and resource-rich nation such as the United States.

Negatives must also be considered when comparing the current standard of living of the poor with the conditions they faced 20 or 30 years ago. Their work prospects, and therefore their chances of climbing out of poverty, particularly for the less skilled, are much dimmer now, given the decline in manufacturing employment. Urban living eats up more of their meager incomes. The poor also have less physical security today than years ago, given the alarming rise in violent crime, drug dealing, and random shootings taking place in concentrated poverty areas. To say that the poor have it easier today than in the past is to be blind to the harsh realities of their lives.

Misconceptions about the Poor
There are many myths about the poor in the United States. For instance, many people believe that most of the poor are black when, in

fact, two out of every three poor people in the United States are white (Ellwood, 1988). Another common belief is that the poor are lazy and unwilling to work. In fact, about 60 percent of poor adults who are able bodied work either full time, part time, seasonally or when they find employment (O'Hare, 1988; U.S. Bureau of the Census, 1990b). The wages they earn, however, are insufficient to lift them out of poverty. The working poor are among the hardest hit of the poor because they are ineligible for most governmental benefit programs other than food stamps; for instance, most do not qualify for Aid for Dependent Children (AFDC) or medicaid. Of the 40 percent of the poor who do not work, most are children, elderly people, chronically ill or disabled, and single mothers with young children. The remainder are people discouraged in their search for work who have dropped out of the labor force and young school dropouts unable to find employment. A small minority are permanently on welfare or living off illegal activities, such as small-time burglaries, drug dealings, and prostitution.

An additional misconception about the poor is that they constitute a permanent social class—that is, a group that remains poor for life and passes on this "affliction" to their children. In fact, the majority of poor people are not poor for a long time but rather experience poverty for short intervals of a year or two. Except for their temporary financial crisis—perhaps caused by unemployment, illness, an accident, or divorce—they are not very different from the rest of the population. Only a small proportion of the poor are *persistently* or chronically *poor* (i.e., poor for eight years or more). Most of the persistently poor are elderly people, families with children headed by females, blacks living in inner cities, and people from rural areas (Duncan, 1984).

Still another myth is that nearly all poor people receive welfare, which covers their basic necessities. In reality, more than half of the poor do *not* receive welfare. Some are not eligible because they work or because they are recent immigrants. (Immigrants are ineligible for welfare assistance for the first three years after they arrive in the United States.) Other poor people do not apply for welfare, even though they may be eligible for it, due to ignorance or feelings of shame. Only about 10 to 20 percent of those on welfare remain on welfare for 10 or more years (U.S. Bureau of the Census, 1990a; Hill & Ponza, 1983).

Explanations of Poverty

There are various theories that attempt to explain why poverty still exists in U.S. society, such as conflict theory, structural functionalism, and culturalism. Other explanations are more circumscribed, such counterproductive government incentives and the dual labor market theory. Each contributes valuable insights.

Conflict theory suggests that powerful people have a vested interest in preserving poverty to keep the demand up for low-wage jobs, thus minimizing costs and maximizing profits, to ensure that the "dirty work" of the society gets done (e.g., waste disposal, mining, harvesting, and so on), to have a large supply of soldiers available to wage war, and to have a ready clientele for the goods that nobody else would want, such as imperfect apparel, second-rate foodstuffs, and deteriorating automobiles (Gans, 1972). From this perspective, poverty and the means to maintain it (e.g., low wages, unemployment, discrimination, and oppression) will continue to exist as long as they serve the interests of the affluent.

Related to the conflict theory of poverty is the dual labor market theory, which suggests that part of the poverty in U.S. society derives from the existence of a secondary sector within the labor market that includes the lowest-paying jobs with the worst working conditions. Many members of racial and ethnic nondominant groups and recent immigrants are relegated to this sector of the economy. "Undocumenteds," in particular, are the most exploited sources of labor in the secondary market because of their high vulnerability (Portes & Truelove, 1987).

Structural-functional theory considers poverty to be the result of structural and systemic factors in the society such as limited and changing employment opportunities, scarcity of child-care services (which limit the ability of some women to participate fully in the labor force), discrimination, and inadequate education of the poor (which results in their not having the skills required for the jobs that are available.) Due to the previously noted movement in the economy from manufacturing to high technology and service and the relocation of factories out of central cities, many low-skill people (mostly blacks and Latinos) have been displaced from their old jobs, particularly in the northeast and northcentral areas of the United States. According to the structural fuctionalists, if the poor were provided with better education and training, jobs, and child care, and if discrimination were eliminated, most of the poor would be able to overcome their poverty.

The third major explanation of poverty is the culture of poverty theory. Its proponents, most notably Oscar Lewis (1966), emphasize the role of certain attitudes and values in causing or maintaining poverty. According to this view, the poor develop a deep sense of hopelessness that greatly reduces their ability to plan for the future and to delay gratification. Lacking positive and successful role models, they develop the belief that it is very difficult to get ahead, no matter how hard one may try. Hence, many stop putting forth effort and become, in the eyes of others, lazy and unambitious. Some without access to legitimate employment learn to hustle or to depend on welfare. Culturalists suggest that, although the poor originally developed these problematic values and attitudes in response to situational constraints, after generations of modeling after family members and other poor people around them, these traits become a permanent part of their personality.

The culture of poverty theory has become the least favored of the explanations of poverty, at least among social scientists, because it can be used to blame the poor for their economic problems (Piven & Cloward, 1971; Ryan, 1976). In other words, this theory can be used to justify the view that poverty—being the result of having inappropriate values, attitudes, or lifestyles—is the fault of the people who experience it. This is far from the truth. As you have seen, the majority of the poor are poor due to personal impediments that make it difficult for them to work full time or to earn decent wages. Such impediments tend to be unrelated to the attitudes or values they may hold about work.

Specifically, a large proportion of the poor are children too young to work or elderly persons too frail to be in the labor force. Many uneducated or marginally educated people are poor because they cannot find a job for which they are qualified or can only get menial jobs at meager wages. Others with limited work skills are poor because they are not chosen for the few jobs for which they qualify because of discrimination based on their skin color, ethnic background, immigration status, mental handicap, or old age. Many families with young children headed by females are poor because the mother cannot seek outside employment unless day care is made available to her or unless she gets some job skills that will allow her to get a better-than-minimum-wage job. Other poor people are recent immigrants doing menial work because they cannot speak English well or because they have few if any job skills. Still others are poor because they are too ill or physically disabled to be employable. Can one blame the poverty of these people on their having the wrong values or attitudes?

There is no consistent research evidence showing that poverty or welfare dependency results from holding certain attitudes or values, or that the poor and nonpoor can be distinguished by their attitudes toward work or motivation to work or to succeed, as the culture of poverty theory has suggested (Covello, 1980; Jaynes & Williams, 1989, p. 25). However, many attitudes and values—such as feeling more or less motivated, competent, optimistic, or pessimistic about the future—appear to be influenced by events that may cause poverty, such as losing a job or, in the case of a woman with children, getting divorced (Lynn & McGeary, 1990, p. 259).

In addition, evidence has shown that when people are put in circumstances they cannot control or influence with their actions, such as persistent poverty coupled with limited education and job skills, they often respond by aggressively acting out or with learned helplessness manifested in attitudes of resignation, passivity, lack of motivation, limited effort, and nonresponsive behaviors (Kane, 1987). This is why the provision of child care training, and jobs per se as the functionalists have suggested may not be enough to solve the poverty problem. Poor people need education, job training, child care, and better jobs. But without developing a stronger sense of control over their lives and a belief in their own competence, few might seize good opportunities, if they were made available to them. In short, one need not subscribe to the culture of poverty theory to acknowledge that many poor people may need help in building a stronger sense of self-efficacy and attaining some control over their lives as much as they need job training, child care, and better employment opportunities.

Another cause of poverty postulated by Charlie Murray (1984) is the availability of government assistance. Murray has argued that the liberalization of welfare and expansion of social programs during the 1960s and early 1970s made it less worthwhile for people to work at minimum-wage jobs than to receive welfare and related benefits. Thus, he suggested, many people learned to avoid work and marriage and to have children so they could receive government entitlements. In turn, this led to an increase in poverty and in the number of female-headed families. In other words, according to Murray's thesis, people become poor and stay poor because they will not work in order to take advantage of welfare benefits

made available by the society. Although the argument is persuasive at face value and some studies have shown a weak positive relationship between welfare availability and changes in family structure in the direction Murray suggested, there is no evidence at present that welfare availability is a *major* cause of poverty or female family headship (Aponte, 1991). The clearest effect of welfare on family structure appears to be that it makes it easier for young single mothers to form separate households instead of continuing to live within other households, such as with their parents (Ellwood & Bane, 1985).

The Feminization of Poverty

Recent decades have witnessed the coming together of various social and economic forces that have resulted in a significant increase in the level of poverty among U.S. women. For example, the increase in divorce and unemployment among blue-collar workers, and pregnancies among unmarried women, and the erosion in the earnings of males have led to a significant growth in the number of poor female-headed single-parent homes. The continuing existence of a labor market that remunerates female workers at a lower rate than males also contributes to female poverty. Other factors also add to the rate of poverty among women, including a welfare system that keeps recipients below the poverty line and the continuing overinvolvement of women in unpaid domestic work (particularly child care), which limits their ability to participate fully in the labor market (Rubin, 1992b, p. 15).

Female-headed families, in particular, are economically vulnerable for many reasons. First, the majority do not get child support regularly from the children's fathers; specifically, only about half of divorced women with children receive child support payments from their ex-husbands, and only about 1 in 10 never-marrieds get any assistance from the children's fathers (Ellwood, 1988). Another problem confronted by many single parents is the difficulty in holding full-time jobs while raising young children. In the case of female heads of household, it is also hard for them to be sole providers because, on the average, they make considerably less money than men. For instance, the average income of female-headed families with no husband present is about half that of one-parent families headed by males (U.S. Bureau of the Census, 1989a). Still another difficulty faced by families headed by women is the scarcity of affordable child care, which many times prevents the mother from working outside the home and consequently makes her dependent on poverty-level public assistance at least until the children are old enough to go to school.

The preceding are some of the main social forces that have led to the **feminization of poverty** (Pearce, 1978). Specifically, according to the 1990 census, 32.9 percent of the white female-headed families, 51.8 percent of black female-headed families, 54.5 percent of Latino female-headed families, and 54.8 percent of American-Indian female-headed families were poor, compared to only 4 percent of white married-couple families (see Table 3.3). One major problem associated with poverty in female-headed families is that it is often persistent, thus

making it potentially more damaging to child development than the poverty experienced in two-parent households, which tends to be temporary (Ellwood, 1988).

The Juvenilization of Poverty
Child poverty rates were cut in half in the decade of the 1960s, from 27 percent to 14 percent, due to a combination of strong economic growth and public action to combat poverty. However, the percentage of poor children in the United States grew again in the 1980s and 1990s to the point that children have become the single largest poor group in the nation (Weill, 1991; Zaldivar, 1994) (see Table 3.4). This **juvenilization of poverty** (Wilson, 1985) is a very troubling trend, particularly when one considers that the United States is alone among advanced industrial nations in having such a high rate of child poverty. In other countries— such as Canada, West Germany, Norway, Sweden, and Switzerland—the child poverty rate is less than 10 percent (Weill, 1991). In contrast, in the United States in 1992, 22 percent of the children were poor (Pear, 1993).

Of even greater concern is the poverty rate among the children of nondominant racial and

TABLE 3.3   Poverty among Married-Couple versus Female-Headed Families According to the 1990 Census

	WHITES*	BLACKS*	HISPANIC* ORIGIN	ASIAN/ PACIFIC	AMERICAN INDIANS*
Percent below poverty level:					
Married-couple families with children under 18	4.3	11.1	17.4	10.9	15.4
Female-headed families with children under 18	32.9	51.8	54.5	35.6	54.8

Sources: Data taken from "1990 Census of Population, Social and Economic Characteristics, United States" (1990 CP-2-1) by U.S. Bureau of the Census, 1994. Washington, DC: U.S. Government Printing Office. "Geographic Profile of Employment and Unemployment, 1990" by U.S. Bureau of the Census, 1991. Washington, DC: U.S. Government Printing Office. "Poverty in the United States: 1990 Current Population Reports Series P-60, No. 175" by U.S. Bureau of the Census, 1991. Washington, DC: U.S. Government Printing Office. "We the American ...Asians" (WE-3) by U.S. Bureau of the Census, 1993. Washington, DC: U.S. Government Printing Office. "Statistical Abstract of the United States: 1993" by U.S. Bureau of the Census, 1994. Washington, DC: U.S. Government Printing Office.

TABLE 3.4 The Poor in the United States, According to the 1990 Census

GROUP	NUMBER OF POOR
Children (under 18)	11.2 million
Non-Hispanic Whites	10.9 million
Blacks	7.2 million
Latinos	4.9 million
The Elderly	3.8 million
Female-Headed Family Households with Children (under 18)	2.9 million
Asian/Pacific Islanders	962,000
American Indians	286,000

Source: Data taken from "1990 Census of Population, Social and Economic Characteristics, United States" (1990 CP-2-1) by U.S. Bureau of the Census, 1994. Washington, DC: U.S. Government Printing Office.

ethnic groups. In 1991, 43.6 percent of all black children and 40.7 percent of all Latino children were poor, compared to 15.6 percent of white children (U.S. Bureau of the Census, 1992a, 1993b). Among children living with their mothers only, the situation was even worse; in 1990, more than 65 percent of children living in female-headed black and Latino families were poor (Blank, 1992). Another highly distressing statistic is that many of our children live in *extreme poverty*. In 1989, 40 percent of poor children were living in families whose income was no more than one-half of the poverty line (Weill, 1991).

For children, the consequences of poverty can be very serious. Weill (1991, p. 343) noted that "their health and development and eventual capabilities and productivity as workers, parents, and citizens are often damaged by the deprivations of growing up poor." Specifically, poor children have higher rates of infant mortality, prematurity, low birthweight, and birth defects. They suffer more sickness from infection. They have high levels of lead in their

Reprinted with permission from the Sun-Sentinel, Fort Lauderdale, Florida.

blood. Their growth is often retarded. They suffer an excess of injuries and deaths from fires, drownings, and suffocations. And many go hungry to the point that their learning is impaired (Weill, 1991).

In large part, the increase in child poverty in recent years is a reflection of three major trends: the growth in the number of one-parent families headed by women, the growing inability of government assistance programs to raise the income of the poor above the poverty line, and the increasing economic difficulties faced by young couples with children. In relation to the financial troubles faced by young parents today, Segal (1991) noted that between 1967 and 1986, the poverty rate among families with children headed by individuals under the age of 30 almost doubled, in large part because of the increasing costs of raising children. If this growth in child poverty is not reversed, the United States must brace itself for the consequences of failing to prepare a large segment of the next generation to fully participate in society.

The Ghetto Poor

Some people confuse the poor with the ghetto poor[2]—those poor people who live in areas where at least 40 percent of the residents are poor (Jargowsky & Bane, 1990, p. 19). However, the ghetto poor constitute only about one-fourth of the nation's poor. It is alarming, though, that their ranks have risen from 5.6 million in 1980 to 10.4 million in 1990. This trend suggests that poverty in the United States is becoming more highly concentrated in certain areas, notably in the old industrial cities of the Northeast and North Central states (where about half of the ghetto poor live) and in the rural South (which is home to another 40 percent of them) (Jargowsky & Bane, 1990; Applebome, 1993).

Although the increase in ghetto poverty is a matter of serious concern, it is important to note that the majority of the poor in the United States do not live in ghetto areas (Pear, 1993b). Most of the ghetto poor are African Americans (believed to constitute two-thirds to three-fourths of this group) or Latinos (who comprise most of the rest) (Ellwood, 1988; Ricketts & Sawhill, 1988; Jargowsky & Bane, 1990; Lynn & McGeary, 1990). Only a very small proportion of poor white people live in urban ghettos; most live in suburban or non-metropolitan areas (Ellwood, 1988).

Various forces have contributed to the deterioration of life or "hyperghettoization" (Wacquant & Wilson, 1989) of inner cities. As previously noted, the shift in the economy from manufacturing to service and high technology has led to many factory closings and relocations out of central cities to places with cheaper sources of labor. In the shuffle, many inner-city residents have lost their jobs or have ended up with less well-paying positions (Billingsley, 1989). Many factory workers have had to leave central-city areas in search of job opportunities elsewhere. This has left behind in the inner city a high concentration of teenagers and young adults with few employment opportunities. The unemployment rate of these young people, particularly black males ages 20 to 24, is astronomically high (Ellwood, 1988). The concentration in one area of young individuals with poor educational and work skills, without employment correlates with many problems. Some of these problems include very high rates of violence and crime (e.g., drug dealing, homicide, aggravated assault and robbery, burglary, illegal gambling, and prostitution); early unprotected sexual activity and childbearing among teenagers; female-headed households due to the limited opportunity of women in these ghetto areas to find men with jobs to marry; and dependency on welfare as one of the few options available for families with young children to survive (Wilson, 1987; Jencks & Mayer, 1990).

Other important forces leading to the decline of the inner city include "white flight" to the suburbs, which severely curtailed the economic base of central cities, and the exodus of middle-class African Americans from the

Box 3.1

On a Harlem Block, Hope Is Swallowed by Decay

BY FELICIA R. LEE

Special to The New York Times

NEW YORK, Sept. 7—There are days that Robert LeShawn Garland, a lanky 18-year-old with a yen to fly airplanes, can look out his window and spy his father waiting in a snaking line to buy crack. Once their eyes met, and his father hung his head.

On the floor below, Donna Williams often starts her day with a beer, trying to beat the blues. She has five children, she just turned 40, and she has been on welfare for more than a decade. From her living room, she can see an empty lot and rows of boarded windows.

Two stoops away sit Mel and Dennis. Once they owned the block, these two brothers with high cheekbones and laughing eyes, counting their cash from drug dealing. Now 19-year-old Mel is in a wheelchair, paralyzed after taking seven bullets from a 9-millimeter pistol.

This is 129th Street between Malcolm X Boulevard and Fifth Avenue in Harlem. It is a block in the other America, the America of the black underclass. It is a place—and it could be in Chicago, Miami or Los Angeles—with its own values, rules and economy. While the experts debate welfare reform, education and job training, generations live and die on this block, a world apart.

The world of 129th Street is increasingly violent and dispirited. The scrappers on this block—the ones who call the police on drug dealers and who badger landlords for repairs—say the old civil-rights remedies like affirmative action do little to improve lives hobbled by a multitude of ills. While the black middle class has expanded greatly in the last 30 years, a growing number of black people have also been trapped in seemingly intractable poverty.

It is a measure of the block's isolation that when a girl from 129th Street dressed for an interview for an office job recently, she chose a black evening sheath and wobbly high-heels. Few on this block have steady jobs, creating a feeling of perpetual waiting. The hours are whiled away on stoops, basketball courts or in front of the TV.

Strivers like Robert Garland, who traveled four hours each day to attend a good city high school and is now in college, are seen by many as outsiders and face ridicule. His half-sister Nadine Allen, who became an unmarried mother at 19 and is unemployed, is the one who saunters down the street greeting friends. Ms. Allen, a former drug merchant, has her pick of suitors, but Mr. Garland was dateless on prom night.

Even the sweetness of romance is brief on 129th Street, and marriages are rare. Up and down the block are women who say they have been "dogged' by men, a term for being treated badly. They talk about being raped, beaten and abandoned. Mothers complain of men who walk by their own children as if they were invisible. The men claim the women want them only for the material possessions they can provide.

Many people talk of getting high school equivalency diplomas and jobs and moving away, but the reality is that almost no one ever does. Some, like Mel and Dennis, have tasted financial success from drug dealing. These are usually short-lived episodes of lavish spending on clothes and recreation that end in violence or an arrest.

One constant is death, taking the young and old alike. Almost everyone on this block is related to someone who has been shot, is addicted to drugs or dying of AIDS. In the last five months, four young men from the block were shot; three of them died. Here, children talk about the kind of funerals they want in the way that young people in other neighborhoods plan proms.

Few on the block believe that the American dream exists for them. The lives that flicker across their television screens remind them of what they lack and what they desire. In quiet moments, anger and disappointment can be heard.

"They say that 129th Street is a black hole," said Vikki, who is 26, lives here with her younger cousins, and like others interviewed insisted on not using her last name. "If you are born here, you die here."

inner city, particularly after the passage of Title VIII of the Civil Rights Act of 1968. The black middle class and working class used to serve as positive role models for the youths in the inner-city community, helped to maintain public order, and kept an eye on the neighborhood children. Their departure has contributed to the destabilization of the areas' traditional norms and values, to the decline of its basic institutions (e.g., churches, schools, small business enterprises, and recreational facilities), and to the increasing concentration, deprivation, and isolation of those left behind (Wilson, 1987, pp. 143–144; Ellwood, 1988). Still another factor that has added to the concentration of poverty in the inner city was the building of high-rise public housing projects in these areas (Wilson, 1987; McGeary, 1990).

Little is known at present about the dynamics of Latino poverty in the United States because most researchers have concentrated on black poverty (Aponte, 1991). But what little is known about poor Latinos in the Southwest and in California (a predominantly Mexican-American group) points to a lower rate of dysfunctional behaviors than one would expect, given their strong representation among the ghetto poor (Cuciti & Franklin, 1990; Winkler, 1990). For example, compared to other equally poor people, ghetto-poor Mexican Americans have a higher rate of participation in the labor force, although they make meager salaries. They have a higher rate of two-parent families and a lower rate of female-headed families, unwed parenthood, and welfare dependency. In part, these differences may be the result of a continuous influx of male immigrants who are highly motivated to work and who add to the stock of employed males available for marriage. Many of these immigrant males provide fairly positive role models for barrio youth (Cuciti & Franklin, 1990).

Among Latinos, the mainland Puerto Rican ghetto poor presents more serious problems than the Mexican-American ghetto poor. Because they are much more likely than Mexi-

can Americans to live in big metropolitan areas of the Northeast, particularly New York City, they have suffered more from the reduction in job opportunities for the less skilled in snow-belt industrial areas. In addition, many have been displaced from their jobs by cheaper immigrant labor, particularly by "undocumenteds." In contrast, because Mexican Americans are concentrated in the Southwest, they have benefited from the better job opportunities available for less-skilled labor in southwestern cities and suburbs, as industry has moved in that direction. Poor Mexican Americans also have been less reliant than mainland Puerto Ricans on central-city employment. It is in part for these reasons that Mexican-origin families in poverty have a rate of participation in the work force that is nearly triple that of poor mainland Puerto Rican families, who are nearly three times more likely than poor Mexican-American families to receive welfare. Proportionately, however, more Mexican Americans than Puerto Ricans hold very low-wage jobs, probably because they have lower levels of English-language proficiency and because they are concentrated in areas with high levels of immigration, particularly "undocumenteds," who provide a very cheap source of labor (Aponte, 1991).

Rural Poverty

The rural poor, like the urban poor, are a varied group composed of farmhands, factory workers, coal miners, sawmill cutters, migrant farm workers, and elderly people who have remained behind while their children have migrated to the cities in search of a better life. For a while in the 1970s, the poor living in rural areas enjoyed a better chance at employment because many low-technology and apparel factories moving out of central cities of the North relocated their plants to rural areas to take advantage of cheaper land and labor. But within a decade, these companies discovered greater savings in developing countries and the rural boom ended (Smith, 1990).

Most of the persistently poor in rural areas in the United States are in the South and are likely to be elderly people, blacks, and Latinos (Jargowsky & Bane, 1990). Living conditions among the rural poor have deteriorated considerably due to the decrease in the job base and increasing reliance on government welfare (Applebome, 1993). In Tunica, Mississippi, for example, the homes of the poor are run-down shacks often without bathroom facilities or running water. Residents must get their water from an outdoor tap and use an outhouse (Smith, 1990).

Poor families in the countryside are more likely to have both parents at home and at least one of the parents is more likely to work than the poor in central cities. Comparatively speaking, there is also less crime and drugs in rural areas, although alcohol is often abused. Work is often hazardous, involving contact with toxic agents or use of machinery capable of inflicting harm. The pay may stretch a little bit more in rural areas than in urban center, but not significantly so. Housing is less expensive though more substandard. Groceries can be pricey because of the distance from distribution centers and the lack of competition. Rural workers also may spend more on transportation to work if they have to travel long distances. For children, rural education is often abysmal; this is why the brightest tend to leave as soon as they are old enough (Smith, 1990).

What Is It Like to Be Poor?

Life in poverty takes many different forms—young families with young children, recently divorced middle-class women with children whose husbands are not contributing child support, middle-class families whose breadwinner is temporarily out of work, women and children who have had to run away from an abusive husband or father, the rural poor, the suburban poor, the poor in the inner city, the working poor, the persistently poor, those who are extremely poor, poor legal immigrants, poor undocumented immigrants, the elderly poor living on social security, the physically disabled living on disability, long-term welfare-dependent families, and so on.

Even though the face of poverty has an infinite variety of expressions, some relatively mild and others very severe, the experience of financial deprivation, particularly that which persists for some time, has serious consequences. In the area of health, for example, many of the poor are unable to eat three nutritious meals a day. Sometimes the money for food must be spent to pay for utilities or rent to avoid eviction or having services disconnected. This means that not infrequently some of the poor go hungry or eat inappropriately. They often have limited access to quality health care. Even if eligible for Medicaid, many take limited or no advantage of it due to ignorance. Many times, due to ignorance, fear, lack of time, or lack of medical insurance, they wait until health problems reach critical proportions and then seek crisis-oriented medical treatment in the emergency rooms of public hospitals. The lack of regular medical attention results in high rates of mortality from chronic diseases and from health-threatening behaviors such as smoking and alcohol consumption. Many women have no medical care during pregnancy, resulting in high rates of premature and low birthweight babies who are much more vulnerable to a variety of disabling conditions.

Often living in low-income neighborhoods and sometimes in ghetto areas, the poor are more likely to be the victims of crime and violence and to receive less police protection than the nonpoor. They are also more likely to receive discriminatory treatment by the criminal justice system, reflected in such things as higher arrest and conviction rates and longer prison sentences than the nonpoor. Their housing accommodations are apt to be substandard and run-down. Few are able to afford the convenience of having a telephone and those who do often have it disconnected for nonpayment.

Few can afford air conditioning at home, even when it gets very hot. Few have enough money for fuel to heat their homes appropriately when it is cold.

Few of the poor can afford a car, even an old jalopy, because they often do not have enough money to buy the required minimum insurance or to pay for gas or repairs; thus, typically they have to depend on public transportation. Families existing on a survival budget hardly ever go out to eat (even to fast-food places) or to a movie, ball game, or any other public or private establishment that charges admission. They have no cable television, take no vacations that involve staying at a motel or hotel, and hardly ever spend money on books or magazines. They rarely have the time or resources to plan for old age or for their children's college education. When they compare themselves to the family images that appear on TV, they are likely to feel inadequate because they can't live the American dream like everybody else (Schwarz & Volgy, 1992; Rubin, 1992b).

When poor children go to school with an empty stomach, and many do, they are unlikely to be able to concentrate on learning much of anything unless the school feeds them first. That does not always happen. On top of that, the schools they attend are unlikely to have good educational resources or well-prepared and experienced teachers. Consequently, many poor children who graduate from school or drop out are inadequately prepared for the job market. Often, they experience limited employment opportunities, part-time employment, or high rates of unemployment, and they are likely to hold back-breaking and hazardous jobs, if they can find work.

In general, the lives of the poor are more exposed to environmental health hazards, particularly high levels of lead that frequently affect the children. Divorce is much more common among the poor than among the nonpoor, probably due to the stresses associated with low income and poverty (Pear, 1993c). Because they often experience divorce, separation, and unemployment, poor families are more likely to be headed by women. Poor people of all races and ethnic backgrounds are also more likely to suffer the consequences of discrimination and oppression than the nonpoor. (More will be said about this in Chapter 4.)

What Can Be Done to Help the Poor?

Although it is unlikely that the United States or any other country will be able to eliminate poverty completely, there are concrete steps that have been taken in many places to reduce poverty considerably and to lessen its negative consequences. Many of the measures suggested in this section have been tried and adopted by other advanced and developing countries. There is no reason why the United States cannot do likewise (Ellwood, 1988; Lynn & McGeary, 1990; Rubin, 1992b).

— Provide universal health care, particularly on a preventive basis, with emphasis on prenatal care, good nutrition through food supplements for pregnant women as well as infants and children, childhood immunization, teenage pregnancy prevention, and prevention and treatment of substance abuse.

— In relation to education, it is important to provide early and intensive preschool education and compensatory basic skills education, to prevent children from dropping out of school, to offer them assistance in the transition from school to work, and to give parents more control over their children's education, such as by providing educational vouchers they can use to pay tuition in the schools of their choice.

— In the area of employment, it is important for the society to make jobs available to all able-bodied working-age adults, to offer job training, help in developing a sense of self-efficacy and control over one's lives, and assistance in finding employment. It is also important to raise wages (particularly the minimum wage) so that every person who works full time is guaranteed an income above the poverty line.

— Families need universally available day care and after-school care and parents need access to maternity and child-care leaves from work that guarantee a minimum income while caring for a newborn or newly adopted child.

— One-parent families need access to a universal system of child support assurance that guarantees a certain level of financial help, whether or not the government is able to collect child support from the noncustodial parent.

— In the area of housing, it is important to reduce barriers to residential mobility by more strict enforcement of fair housing laws. This would enable more people to leave ghettos and to move to areas of job growth and opportunity, if they chose to, particularly if they were offered housing vouchers they could use to rent an apartment of their choice in the neighborhood of their choice.

— The present welfare system as currently constituted should be eliminated; instead, it makes more sense to use the money to offer the previously mentioned social services and to create a transitional financial, educational, and social support system for people suffering temporary financial setbacks.

The reforms listed above would guarantee a minimum standard of living worthy of a great nation such as the United States. How could they be accomplished? Federal taxes would probably have to be raised to a somewhat higher level, particularly taxes on large corporations, on the rich, on liquor, and on tobacco products. Many readers may not be cognizant of the fact that the United States tax rate is much lower than that of other advanced industrialized countries, such as Sweden, Denmark, Norway, France, West Germany, and Great Britain (Rubin, 1992b, p. 220).

Having completed our journey through the U.S. class system, in the next section we will consider additional related issues, including social mobility and the role of women and

African Americans within the U.S. class system.

SOCIAL MOBILITY

Social class systems may be classified as either open or closed. In an **open class system,** individuals enjoy reasonable opportunities to advance to higher social positions in accordance with their ability, efforts, and achievements. The United States does not have an entirely open social class system, but as it continues to remove barriers to mobility for women and other nondominant group members, it comes closer to this ideal. However, as long as children born to the upper or upper-middle class enjoy special privileges and advantages passed on to them by their parents and poor children suffer deprivations and disadvantages that restrict their ability to get ahead, the U.S. class system cannot be considered to be truly open. A **closed class system,** in contrast, is one in which there is little possibility of social mobility out of the class into which one was born. The old caste system in India and the old system of apartheid in South Africa are examples of closed systems.

The term **social mobility** is used to refer to the movement from one level in the social class system to another, such as the movement from working class to middle class. This social mobility may be horizontal or vertical, as well as intragenerational or intergenerational. **Horizontal mobility** is the movement from one social position to another at essentially the same level. For example, if a social worker were to move from one family service agency to another but continued to hold the same position at both agencies, she or he would experience horizontal mobility. **Vertical mobility** is movement up or down the social class system. For instance, a person promoted from filing clerk to head secretary experiences vertical mobility—specifically, **upward mobility.** Similarly, an individual demoted from director of a social agency to unit supervisor experiences vertical mobility—specifically, **downward mobility.**

Intergenerational mobility occurs when children achieve a social position higher or lower than that of their parents. For example, a family in which the father works as a janitor and his son becomes a school teacher has experienced intergenerational upward mobility. Another family in which the mother is a nurse and her daughter becomes an operator in a garment factory has experienced intergenerational downward mobility. **Intragenerational mobility** refers to those changes in an individual's social position that occur during the course of his or her life. Examples of intragenerational mobility include a person who started as a mailroom clerk at the local newspaper and eventually became the editor of the newspaper or one who began a career as an engineer and, due to illness, ended up working as a draftsperson.

Do you think that the United States is an open society in which any intelligent, highly motivated, and hard-working individual from humble origins can realistically aspire to occupy an important position? How important a position? How frequently do you think people go from rags to riches nowadays? To be sure, many doors are open to talent and effort in the United States. Yet, several recent studies have shown that, for most people, being rich or poor at birth is the most likely personal characteristic to determine the position they will eventually attain in society and even that of their children. Although most individuals are unlikely to travel long distances in the social scale in their own lifetimes (e.g., from poverty to membership in the corporate class or vice versa), limited mobility up and down the scale is more common, such as from working class to lower-middle class or from lower-middle class to upper-middle class and vice versa (Nasar, 1992).

Large-scale studies of social mobility in the United States, notably those of Blau and Duncan (1967) and Featherman and Hauser (1978), have shown that up to the early 1970s, most Euro-American males experienced upward mobility, as compared to their fathers. However, this intergenerational upward movement generally was limited in scope, such as from one social class to the next higher class (e.g., working-class fathers/middle-class sons). Such upward movement was facilitated by large-scale immigration, which provided a continuous influx of newcomers willing to take jobs at the bottom of the scale, thus pushing more experienced workers up the job ladder. Upward mobility was also facilitated by a continuously expanding economy constantly generating new jobs, by technological progress that kept increasing the pool of middle-class jobs, and by the fact that the higher classes (e.g., the upper-middle class and the corporate class) did not produce enough children to replace themselves, thus giving individuals from below a chance to move up (Light, Keller, & Calhoun, 1989, pp. 304–305). In addition, in the old days, education beyond high school played a critical role in facilitating upward mobility.

Historically, however, upward mobility did not benefit everyone equally. Even in the period up to the early 1970s, when it was so prevalent among Euro-American males, upward mobility was less consistently characteristic of the experience of African-American males due to racial discrimination (Gintis, 1980). Women, Latinos, the poor, and other members of nondominant groups traditionally also had more limited opportunities for upward mobility than white males (Hout, 1988; Kerbo, 1991).

But even white males have found it increasingly more difficult to maintain the upward-mobility momentum in recent years because the U.S. economy is no longer growing at a fast pace. Not even those with college degrees are guaranteed upward mobility because so many individuals now entering the job market have a college education (Hout, 1988).

WOMEN AND THE U.S. CLASS SYSTEM

Until recently, social scientists assumed that a woman's place in the social class system was determined by her husband's position, as head of the household, in the occupational and property structures of the society. Feminists, however, have long argued that both spouses' positions should be taken into account (Britten & Heath, 1983). Clearly, with more than half of all married women employed outside the home, many now holding important positions, the traditional system of social class ranking has become inappropriate for a large proportion of families.

Another basic issue pertaining to the place of women in the U.S. social class system has to do with how they construct their class identities. Specifically, to what extent is the class *identity* of wives employed outside the home still primarily shaped by the class position of their husbands? To what extent do they now define their social class membership on the basis of their own jobs, income, and education, as men have always done? Data analyzed by Davis and Robinson (1988) indicate that, as a group, U.S. women have begun to attach as much weight to their own occupations and income as to that of their husbands' in defining their social class positions. However, this seems to depend on how economically dependent the wives remain on their husbands.

Specifically, according to a study by Wright (1989, p. 58), the more dependent a woman is on her husband's job for her material welfare, the more likely she is to derive her own class identification from his and the lesser the weight she is likely to assign to her own class location if different from his. This means that in many class-heterogeneous families where the husband has a substantially higher social position than the wife (still a common situation nowadays), the wife is likely to put more emphasis on her husband's position than on hers in defining her own class ranking.

For instance, many women in clerical positions married to professionals, business owners, or corporate managers have a different lifestyle as well as different economic and political values and interests than female cler-

ics who are unmarried or who are married to retail salesmen, office workers, or factory workers. Women married to men who occupy much higher positions often consider themselves to belong to a higher social class than their own occupations or incomes would indicate. Thus, because their participation in the class system is primarily mediated by their husbands' class identification, one would not be able to develop an adequate picture of their lifestyles, values, or attitudes from knowledge of their occupations or incomes independent of their husbands. However, should their marriages break up, many of these women would quickly discover the social class realities of their own occupations and incomes apart from their husbands' (Wright, 1989). Undoubtedly, as women continue to become more independent of their husbands economically, they will likely continue to move in the direction of independence in the construction of their social class identities.

AFRICAN AMERICANS AND THE U.S. SOCIAL CLASS SYSTEM

Up to some years ago, African Americans of all social class backgrounds were likely to live together in the same neighborhoods, although often on different streets. By and large, their children attended the same schools and played together in the same parks (Wilson, 1992). Today, there is less social class heterogeneity in African-American communities as the income gap between those who are doing well and those who are not becomes wider (Waldrop, 1990).[3] Many African Americans who have experienced considerable upward mobility in recent years have moved away from the inner city to the suburbs, leaving behind those of lower socioeconomic status scrambling and competing for fewer and fewer industrial and manufacturing jobs with Latinos and other recent immigrants living in the central cities.

This section will examine the African-American social class system from a historical perspective, beginning with the rise of the old mulatto elite and the subsequent development of the old middle class. It concludes with a review of the contemporary African-American class scene. African Americans are used here to illustrate the evolution of the class structure of a nondominant social group because the history and development of their class system has been recorded at least to some extent. Similar information on other nondominant groups, such as Latinos or Asians, was not available in the early 1990s.

The Old Mulatto Elite

From the beginning, the Euro-American mainstream society extended greater social and economic privileges to light-skinned African Americans than to those who were darker complexioned. As you will see later in this section, there is evidence that some of that dynamic has persisted into the present. This preference on the part of Euro-Americans for light-skinned African Americans originated during slavery times as white masters often fathered children with slave women. Their fair-skinned offsprings often were spared the harder work in the fields and were kept as house servants. Sometimes they were given the opportunity to learn a trade or to acquire an education. Some were emancipated or permitted to buy their freedom. Once free, these African Americans of mixed racial ancestry frequently were able to use their skills and kinship ties to their former white masters to gain further education or training, to access better occupations than other former slaves, and to acquire property.

Early in the history of the United States, therefore, mulattos established themselves as the elite or top class in the African-American stratification system. This *mulatto elite* was quite diverse, except for its close association with Euro-Americans through service occupations. Some became the house servants of wealthy families, others were railroad porters, headwaiters at exclusive restaurants, skilled craftsmen, barber shop owners, merchants, and small businessmen. A small number became medical doctors, lawyers, and other professionals. For generations well into the twentieth century, many passed on their "advantaged" position (relative to other African Americans of darker complexion) to their light-skinned children (Frazier, 1957; Landry, 1987).

The Old African-American Middle Class

After the United States passed the 1924 National Origins Quota Act, which restricted the immigration of Eastern and Southern Europeans, industrialists in the North began to experience a desperate need for workers. They therefore started to recruit large numbers of people, regardless of their skin color. This led to a mass migration of southern rural African Americans looking for employment in the urban North. For the first time, there was a high demand for African-American professionals (e.g., teachers, physicians, dentists, undertakers, newspaper editors) and business entrepreneurs (e.g., bankers, realtors, grocery story owners, barbers and beauticians, insurance agents) to meet the needs of the rapidly growing African-American urban population in the North. As those who were dark skinned became more educated and economically successful, they began to marry into the old mulatto aristocracy. Thus, the top African-American class became somewhat darker in its complexion. Through this merger, light skin began to lose its previous high importance as a source of status within the African-American community (Landry, 1987).

After the black nationalist and black power movements of the 1960s, light skin tone became unpopular as a basis of prestige among African Americans. However, the fact that most African Americans stopped considering skin shade a relevant characteristic in their class system did not mean that Euro-Americans ignored it also. In fact, a recent study using data from a National Survey of Black Americans showed that the fairer the pigmentation of the black person's skin, the higher was his or her educational attainment, occupation, and income, even after controlling for possible contributing factors such as parental socioeconomic status, sex, region of residence, rural or urban residence, age, or marital status. Apparently, Euro-Americans in their roles as principal gatekeepers to jobs and education in the society have continued to exercise a preference for lighter-skinned blacks, thus continuing to influence the complexion of the African-American class structure (Keith & Herring, 1991).

The New African-American Class Structure

In the late 1960s, the convergence of economic prosperity with major gains attained by African Americans through the civil rights movement and through the passage of equal rights laws created a special climate in the United States. This special climate made possible important changes in the African-American class structure (Landry, 1987). Specifically, during the late 1960s, the ranks of the African-American middle class doubled in size from about one in eight to about one in four African-Americans. Many of the sons and daughters of garbage collectors, domestic workers, gardeners, bus drivers, factory workers, and farmers, among other blue-collar workers, were able to enter a whole new spectrum of white-collar occupations—professional, technical, managerial, sales, and clerical. It was at this point in U.S. history that the African-American class structure, previously heavily anchored in the poor and working classes, began to move closer in shape to the mainstream class system as it developed a larger middle-class. Members of this new black middle class, as distinguished from members of the old middle class which was highly segregated, were much more likely to study and work in integrated environments.

Since the mid-1970s, less favorable economic conditions have slowed down the growth of the African-American middle class.

One reason has been the competition for increasingly more scarce jobs at the middle of the occupational scale, which has shifted the emphasis of affirmative action and equal opportunity programs more toward women and less toward African Americans. Another reason has been the protracted economic stagnation of the 1980s and early 1990s, which limited the ability of some African-American families to send their children to college, thus reducing their chances of getting middle-class jobs. In sum, by the early 1990s, about 20 percent of African Americans were in the professional middle class, with the highest numbers concentrated in the "minor" professions, particularly social work, school teaching, and nursing. Another 15 percent or so had nonprofessional white-collar jobs, mostly at the lower limits of the middle class. Figure 3.1 compares the black and white occupational structures.

Above the 35 percent or so African-Americans considered to be middle class, there is a very small group constituting the upper class. Landry (1987) has argued that African Americans still do not have a true upper class, based on the very small number of large-scale (*Fortune* 500) businesses owned by African Americans and their small representation in *Forbes*' list of the 400 richest persons in the United States.[4] However, the criteria Landry used may not be appropriate to determine membership in the top African-American class. Certainly the super-rich have never been guaranteed a place in the Euro-American upper class, which has traditionally controlled admission to its ranks by criteria other than the size of an individual's pocketbook. Therefore, why should multimillionaire status be requisite for admission into the African-American upper class?

Perhaps a more suitable test of upper-class status at this stage in the evolution of the African-American class structure might be outstanding achievement. There is a small but growing number of African Americans educated at the best private schools and universities in the country who have achieved high levels of prestige in

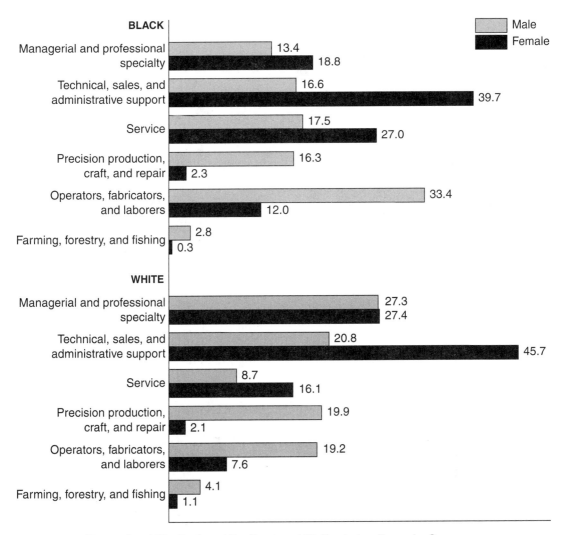

FIGURE 3.1   Occupational Distribution of the Employed Civilian Labor Force, by Sex and Race: March 1990

Source: "The Black Population in the United States: March 1990 and 1989" by U.S. Bureau of the Census, Current Population Reports, Series P-20, No. 448, 1991, page 14. Washington, DC: U.S. Government Printing Office.

the corporate world, in the professions, in academe, in the arts and letters, in government, in the military, as well as in the sports and entertainment world. Some of these outstanding achievers are from humble origins, others are the children of professionals or of families that have been wealthy and influential for generations. Like the Euro-American top two classes, this group represents a very small proportion of the African-American population, but they are in every sense of the word *upper crust.*

At the other end of the class spectrum below the middle class stand about 33 percent of African Americans classified as working class, including skilled and mostly unskilled manual laborers (Landry, 1987; Wilson, 1992). An ominous trend for this group fueled by increasing competition from displaced Euro-American blue-collar workers and cheap immigrant and third-world labor, is their increasing rate of unemployment, particularly among the unskilled, and the growing number who have become discouraged in their search for jobs and who have dropped out of the labor force to join the ranks of the poor.

Below the working class stand another one-third of African Americans who live in poverty, about half being fully destitute (Landry, 1987; Wilson, 1992; Pear, 1993a). Many of the fully destitute, the ghetto poor, are concentrated residentially in the inner cities of the northeast and northcentral industrial areas. Other poor blacks live in rural areas of the South. (The contemporary situation and demographic characteristics of African Americans will be examined in detail in Chapter 4.)

The Relative Significance
of Class versus Race

A debate has been going on for years among African-American scholars about the relative significance of race versus social class for African Americans. Probably the discussion was started formally by Wilson (1978), who argued in *The Declining Significance of Race* that the fate of African Americans was more influenced by factors related to social class (such as their level of education and occupational skills) than race. Other African-American academics disagreed with Wilson, insisting that race continued to be all-important in determining life chances.

Both Wilson and his detractors have made valid points. Pettigrew (1981) has argued, for example, that Wilson was correct in his observation that class variables (such as education) were becoming more important in defining the social class status of African Americans. But he suggested that this did not mean that race was consequently losing significance. According to Pettigrew, both race and class are important in determining the current status of African

Americans, and these two variables interact in complex and subtle ways. The author agrees with Pettigrew's position. Even though social class has become more real and important in determining the lifestyles and life chances of African Americans, race has not diminished in significance for this social group.

Pettigrew (1988, p. 26) argued, for example, that residential segregation of black people due to racial discrimination continues to cause considerable school segregation and differential levels of education, and, consequently, occupational and income differences between blacks and whites. In addition, many African Americans—regardless of their levels of education, occupation, or income—continue to suffer slights and to encounter an invisible barrier at work that is very difficult to penetrate to continue to advance occupationally. For many, therefore, skin color remains a major part of life as well as a fundamental source of identity over and above social class (Zweigenhaft & Domhoff, 1991, p. 174).

After this journey through the U.S. social class system, you may be disappointed and frustrated at the realization that U.S. society still is largely controlled by the 1 to 1.5 percent of the population who are members of the two highest classes (the corporate class and the upper class) and by the huge political/governmental machinery controlled by a small number of top politicians. This control is generally exercised with the cooperation and consent of the upper-middle class. Realistically, the bulk of the population has limited power to influence events. Yet, rather than as a source of despair, this knowledge can be taken as a challenge to exert greater influence and to help others make their influence felt too. As a human service practitioner, you can do this by participating actively in the political process, locally and at the state and national levels; by making every effort to be as fully informed as possible; by unfailingly exercising the right to vote and encouraging those around you to do likewise; by making your voice heard through participation in employee organizations, parent-teacher associations, and various other community organizations; and by speaking up against oppressive, discriminatory, unscrupulous, illegal, and unethical activities wherever they may occur, with determination to take legal action and to turn to the media if unfair and discriminatory activities go unchecked. All of us can have more say in the society if we exercise our limited influence more vigorously. Exactly the same principle applies to our clients, and we can do much to help empower them to play an active role in the social system.

ENDNOTES

1. This aggregate poverty rate for U.S. Latinos is misleading because it averages out groups doing better (e.g., Cubans) with those doing worse (e.g., Puerto Ricans). Specifically, mainland Puerto Ricans have had a poverty rate exceeding 40 percent for the last few years (Aponte, 1991).

2. The ghetto poor are frequently referred to as the "underclass."

3. To give you an idea of the widening income gap among blacks in the United States, in 1988 the highest 20 percent of black families earned half of the total income of blacks' (Wilson, 1992). In that same year, 13 percent of black families had incomes of $50,000 or more, yet 12 percent had incomes of less than $5,000 (Waldrop, 1990).

4. Several African-American business enterprises had assets of over $100 million in 1992, including TLC Beatrice International ($1.6 billion), Johnson Publishing ($274 million), Philadelphia Coca-Cola ($266 million), H. J. Russell construction ($145 million), and Anderson-Dubose food distributor ($110 million).

GLOSSARY

Absolute Poverty: A state of monetary deprivation that prevents families from meeting minimum physical necessities, such as food, shelter, and clothing.

Blue Collar: Manual labor that is often but not always "dirty," such as automobile assembly-line work, steel work, mining, bricklaying, plumbing, and so on.

Closed Class System: A social class system in which there is little possibility of social mobility out of the class into which one was born, such as the old caste system of India.

Culture of Poverty: A theory that explains poverty on the basis of certain values and attitudes held by the poor (e.g., impulsiveness, present orientation, inability to defer gratification, hopelessness) that, according to the theory, prevent them from taking advantage of opportunities available in the society.

Downward Mobility: Movement down the social class system, such as from working as a physician to working as a nurse.

Federal Poverty Line: The income level used by the government as the upper boundary for the poverty level. The figure is obtained by multiplying by 3 the yearly cost of minimally acceptable meals for a family .

Feminization of Poverty: The concentration of poverty among females, particularly female heads of household, due to their lower income in comparison to men, the fact that they are usually the custodians of their children, and the lack of affordable child care which limits their work opportunities.

Ghetto Poor: Those people whose income falls below the federal poverty level who live in census tracts where at least 40 percent of the residents are poor. They are sometimes referred to as the *underclass.*

Horizontal Mobility: The movement from one social position to another, both of which are at the same level, such as from working at one textile factory to working at another similar factory.

Institution: A social unit established to respond to specific needs of society, such as families, schools, churches, hospitals and other health care facilities, social welfare agencies, and the military.

Intergenerational Mobility: Social mobility that occurs when children achieve a social position higher or lower than that of their parents, such as when the son of a physician and a lawyer becomes a school teacher.

Intragenerational Mobility: Changes in an individual's social position that occur during the course of his or her life, such as a young man who starts as bank teller and eventually becomes a bank vice president or a young woman who starts as a concert pianist and, due to illness, becomes a welfare recipient.

Juvenilization of Poverty: An increasing concentration of poverty among children to the point that, in the mid-l990s, children constituted the single largest poor group in the nation. In part, this increase in child poverty reflected the growth in the number of families headed by women as well as the increasing economic difficulties faced by young families.

Life Chances: Opportunities to have positive or negative experiences and living conditions, depending on an individual's social class circumstances.

Open Class System: A social class system in which the individual is able, through effort and achievement, to achieve a social position higher than the one into which he or she was born.

Persistently Poor: Those who are poor for long periods of time, usually eight years or more.

Postindustrial Society: A society whose population relies for its subsistence primarily on the production of services and information rather than on the production of food or on industrial manufacturing.

Relative Poverty: A subjective state of deprivation in comparison to others who seem to be getting more of the societal comforts and resources.

Social Class: A hierarchical system of social stratification according to which people are classified (e.g., as upper class, middle class, or working class) depending on the characteristics they possess, such as education, occupation, wealth and income, and power and authority over others.

Social Mobility: The movement from one level to another in the social class system, such as the movement from working class to middle class.

Social Stratification: System by which the society assigns its members to different levels in its status hierarchy depending on the characteristics they possess, such as race, ethnic background, age, gender, social class, or sexual orientation.

Society: A group of people occupying a given territory, subject to a central governmental authority and participating in a common culture.

Underclass: See **Ghetto Poor.**

Upward Mobility: Movement up the social class system, such as from telephone operator to lawyer.

Vertical Mobility: The movement up or down the social class system, such as from computer programmer to professor of computer sciences (upward movement) or from supervisor of an auto assembly line to janitor (downward movement).

White Collar: Work that involves primarily mental work rather than manual labor and that is generally done in clean surroundings.

REFERENCES

Alba, R., & Moore, G. (1982). Ethnicity in the American elite. *American Sociological Review, 47,* 373–383.

America's blue-collar sector shrinking. (1993, January 29). *The Miami Herald,* p. 6A.

Aponte, R. (1990). Definitions of the underclass: A critical analysis. In H. J. Gans (Ed.), *Sociology in America* (pp. 117–135). Newbury Park, CA: Sage.

Aponte, R. (1991). Urban Hispanic poverty: Dissaggregations and explanations. *Social Problems, 38,* 516–528.

Applebome, P. (1993, August 21). Deep south and down home, but they're ghettos all the same. *The New York Times,* pp. 1, 6.

Bane, M. J. (1986). Household composition and poverty. In S. H. Danziger & D. H. Weinberg (Eds.), *Fighting poverty: What works and what doesn't.* Cambridge, MA: Harvard University Press.

Barton, A. (1985). Determinants of economic attitudes in the American business elite. *American Journal of Sociology, 91,* 54–87.

Batra, R. (1987, May 3). Are the rich getting richer? An ominous trend to greater inequality. *The New York Times*, Sec. 3, p. 2.

Billingsley, A. (1989). The sociology of knowledge of William J. Wilson: Placing *The Truly Disadvantaged* in its sociohistorical context. *Journal of Sociology and Social Welfare, 16*(4), 7–39.

Blank, R. M. (1992, August 5). Social scientists and the problem of poverty. *The Chronicle of Higher Education*, Section 2, pp. B1–2.

Blau, P. M., & Duncan, O. D. (1967). *The American occupational structure*. New York: Wiley.

Britten, N., & Heath, A. (1983). Women, men, and social class. In Eva Gamarmikow et al. (Eds.), *Gender, class and work*. London: Heinemann.

Bureau of the Census. (1990). *Measuring the effect of benefits and taxes on income and poverty: 1989*. Series P-60, no. 169-RD. Washington, DC: U.S. Government Printing Office.

Chilman, C. S. (1975). Families in poverty in the early 1970s: Rates, associated factors, some implications. *Journal of Marriage and the Family, 37*(1), 49–60.

Cooper, M., & Friedman, D. (1991, November 18). The rich in America: Why a populist campaign against them has its limits. *U.S. News and World Report*, 34–40.

Covello, V. T. (Ed.). (1980). *Poverty and public policy: An evaluation of social science research*. Cambridge: Schenkman.

Cowan, A. L. (1992, September 18). Coming clean on executive pay. *The New York Times*, pp. C1, C10.

Cox, O. C. (1959). *Caste, class, and race*. New York: Monthly Review Press.

Cuciti, P., & Franklin, J. (1990). A comparison of black and Hispanic poverty in large cities of the Southwest. *Hispanic Journal of Behavioral Sciences, 12*(1), 50–75.

Dahrendorf, R. (1959). *Class and class conflict in industrial sociology*. Stanford, CA: Stanford University Press.

Dahrendorf, R. (1968). On the origin of inequality among men. In *Essays in the theory of society*. London: Rutledge and Kegan Paul.

Davis, K., & Moore, W. E. (1945). Some principles of stratification. *American Sociological Review, 10*, 242–249.

Davis, L. F., and Proctor, E. K. (1989). *Race, gender, and class: Guidelines for practice with individuals, families, and groups*. Englewood Cliffs, NJ: Prentice Hall.

Davis, N. J., & Robinson, R. V. (1988). Class identification of men and women in the 1970s and 1980s. *American Sociological Review, 53*, 103–112.

DeParle, J. (1994, October 7). Census report sees incomes in decline and more poverty. *The New York Times*, pp. A1, A9.

Domhoff, G. W. (1983). *Who rules America now?* New York: Simon & Schuster.

Duncan, G. J. (1984). *Years of poverty, years of plenty: The changing economic fortunes of American workers and families*. Ann Arbor: Institute for Social Research, The University of Michigan.

Ehrenreich, B. (1989). *Fear of falling: The inner life of the middle class*. New York: Pantheon Books.

Ellwood, D. T. (1987). *Divide and conquer: Responsible security for America's poor*. New York: Ford Foundation.

Ellwood, D. T. (1988). *Poor support*. New York: Basic Books.

Ellwood, D. T., & Bane, M. J. (1985). The impact of AFDC on family structure and living arrangements. *Research in Labor Economics, 7*, 137–207.

Featherman, D. L., & Hauser, R. M. (1978). *Opportunity and change*. New York: Aeodus.

Frank, A., Eisenthal, S., & Lazare, A. (1978). Are there social class differences in patient's treatment conceptions? *Archives of General Psychiatry, 35*, 61–69.

Frazier, E. F. (1957). *The black bourgeoisie*. New York: Free Press.

Fussell, P. (1983). *Class: A guide through the American status system*. New York: Summit Books.

Gans, H. J. (1972). The positive functions of poverty. *American Journal of Sociology, 78*, 275–288.

Gans, H. J. (1974). *Popular culture and high culture: An analysis and evaluation of taste*. New York: Basic Books.

Gerth, H. H., & Mills, C. W. (1958). *From Max Weber: Essays in sociology*. New York: Galaxy.

Gintis, H. (1980, January). The American occupational structure: Eleven years later. *Contemporary Sociology, 9*, 12–16.

Henwood, D. (1992, January/February). A caste of millions. *Utne Reader, 49*, 15–17.

Hill, M. S., & Ponza, M. (1983). Poverty and welfare dependence across generations. *Economic Outlook U.S.A., 10*(3), 61–64.

Hollis, F. (1983). Casework and social class. In F. J. Turner (Ed.), *Differential diagnosis and treatment in social work* (3rd ed., pp. 628–641). New York: Free Press.

Hout, M. (1988). More universalism, less structural mobility: The American occupational structure in the 1980s. *American Journal of Sociology, 93*, 1358–1400.

Jargowsky, P. A., & Bane, M. J. (1990). Ghetto poverty: Basic questions. In L. E. Lynn & M. G. H. McGeary (Eds.), *Inner-city poverty in the United States* (pp. 16–67). Washington, DC: National Academy Press.

Jaynes, G. D., & Williams, R. M., Jr. (Eds.). (1989). *A common destiny: Blacks and American society.* Washington, DC: National Academy Press.

Jencks, C., & Mayer, S. E. (1990). The social consequences of growing up in a poor neighborhood. In L. E. Lynn & M. G. H. McGeary (Eds.), *Inner-city poverty in the United States* (pp. 111–167). Washington, DC: National Academy Press.

Kane, T. J. (1987). Giving back control: Long-term poverty and motivation. *Social Service Review, 61*, 405–419.

Keith, V. M., & Herring, C. (1991). Skin tone and stratification in the black community. *American Journal of Sociology, 97*, 760–778.

Kerbo, H. R. (1991). *Social stratification and inequality: Class conflict in historical and comparative perspective* (2nd ed.). New York: McGraw-Hill.

Kohn, M. L. (1969). *Class and conformity: A study in values.* Homewood, IL: Dorsey Press.

Kohn M. L., Naoi, A., Schoenback, C., Schooler, C., & Slomczynski, K. (1990). Position in the class structure and psychological functioning in the United States, Japan, and Poland. *American Journal of Sociology, 95*, 964–1008.

Landry, B. (1987). *The new black middle class.* Berkeley and Los Angeles: University of California Press.

Le Masters, E. E. (1975). *Blue-collar aristocrats: Lifestyles at a working-class tavern.* Madison: University of Wisconsin Press.

Lenski, G. (1966). *Power and privilege: A theory of social stratification.* New York: McGraw-Hill.

Lenski, G., Lenski, J., & Nolan, P. (1991). *Human societies: An introduction to macrosociology.* New York: McGraw-Hill.

Lewis, O. (1966, October). The culture of poverty. *Scientific American, 215*, 19–25.

Light, D., Keller, S., & Calhoun, C. (1989). *Sociology* (5th ed.). New York: Knopf.

Lynn, L. E., & McGeary, M. G. H. (Eds.). (1990). *Inner-city poverty in the United States.* Washington, DC: National Academy Press.

Martinez-Brawley, E. E. (1987). Rural social work. In A. Minahan (Ed.), *Encyclopedia of social work* (18th ed., pp. 521–537). Silver Springs, MD: National Association of Social Workers.

McGeary, M. G. H. (1990. Ghetto poverty and federal policies and programs. In L. E. Lynn & M. G. H. McGeary (Eds.), *Inner-city poverty in the United States* (pp. 223–252). Washington, DC: National Academy Press.

Murray, C. (1984). *Losing ground: American social policy 1950–1980.* New York: Basic Books.

Nasar, S. (1992, May 18). Those born wealthy or poor usually stay so, studies say. *The New York Times*, pp. A1, C7.

Nasar, S. (1994, October 17). Statistics reveal bulk of new jobs pay over average. *The New York Times*, pp. A1, C3.

O'Hare, W. (1988). The working poor. *Population Today, 16*(2), 6–8.

O'Reilly, B. (1990, July 30). How much does class matter? *Fortune*, 123–128.

Parmer Davidson, B., & Jenkins, P. J. (1989). Class diversity in shelter life. *Social Work, 34*, 491–495.

Parsons, T. (1953). A revised analytical approach to the theory of social stratification. In R. Bendix & S. M. Lipset (Eds.), *Class, status, and power.* Glencoe, IL: Free Press.

Pear, R. (1992, September 4). Ranks of U.S. poor reach 35.7 million, the most since '64. *The New York Times*, pp. A1, 12.

Pear, R. (1993a, October 5). Poverty in U.S. grew faster than population last year. *The New York Times*, p. A10.

Pear, R. (1993b, October 10). Poverty 1993: Bigger, deeper, younger, getting worse. *The New York Times*, Section 4, p. 5.

Pear, R. (1993c, January 15). Poverty is cited as divorce factor. *The New York Times*, p. A6.

Pear, R. (1995, April 30). Proposed definition of indigence could expand number of poor. *The New York Times*, pp. 1, 5.

Pearce, D. (1978). The feminization of poverty: Women, work and welfare. *Urban and Social Change Review, 11*, 28–36.

Peterson, P. E. (1991). The urban underclass and the poverty paradox. In C. Jencks & P. E. Peterson (Eds.), *The urban underclass* (pp. 3–27). Washington, DC: The Brookings Institution.

Pettigrew, T. F. (1981). Race and class in the 1980s: An interactive view. *Daedalus, 110*, 233–255.

Pettigrew, T. F. (1988). Integration and pluralism. In P. A. Katz & D. A. Taylor (Eds.), *Modern racism: Profiles in controversy*. New York: Plenum Press.

Piven, F. F., & Cloward, R. A. (1971). *Regulating the poor: The functions of public welfare*. New York: Pantheon Books.

Portes, A., & Truelove, C. (1987). Making sense of diversity: Recent research on Hispanic minorities. *Annual Review of Sociology, 131*, 359–385.

Ricketts, E. R., & Sawhill, I. V. (1988). Defining and measuring the underclass. *Journal of Policy analysis and management, 7*, 316–325.

Robertson, I. (1989). *Society: A brief introduction*. New York: Worth.

Rossides, D. W. (1990). *Social stratification: The American class system in comparative perspective*. Englewood Cliffs, NJ: Prentice Hall.

Rubin, L. B. (1992a). *Worlds of pain: Life in the working class family*. New York: Basic Books.

Rubin, L. B. (1992b). *Women and children last: The plight of poor women in affluent America*. New York: Penguin Books.

Ryan, W. (1976). *Blaming the victim* (rev. ed.). New York: Random House.

Schaefer, R. T., & Lamm, R. P. (1992). *Sociology* (4th ed.). New York: McGraw-Hill.

Schwarz, J. E., & Volgy, T. (1992). *The forgotten Americans*. New York: W. W. Norton.

Segal, E. A. (1991). The juvenilization of poverty in the 1980s. *Social Work, 36*, 454–457.

Smith, L. (1990, December 31). The face of rural poverty. *Fortune Magazine*, 100–110.

Terkel, S. (1974). *Working people talk about what they do all day and how they feel about what they do*. New York: Pantheon Books.

Tickamyer, A. R., & Duncan, C. M. (1990). Poverty and opportunity structure in rural America. *Annual Review of Sociology, 16*, 67–86.

Tumin, M. M. (1985). *Social stratification* (2nd ed.). Englewood Cliffs, NJ: Prentice Hall.

U.S. Bureau of the Census. (1989a). *Population profile of the United States: 1989*. Current population reports, series P-23, No. 159. Washington, DC: U.S. Government Printing Office.

U.S. Bureau of the Census. (1989b). *The Black Population in the United States: March 1988*. Current population reports, series P-20, No. 442. Washington, D.C: U.S. Government Printing Office.

U.S. Bureau of the Census. (1990a). *Statistical abstract of the United States, 1990*. Washington, DC: U.S. Government Printing Office.

U.S. Bureau of the Census. (1990b). *Money, income, and poverty status in the United States: 1989*. Current population reports, series P-60, No. 168. Washington, DC: U.S. Government Printing Office.

U.S. Bureau of the Census. (1991). *The Hispanic population in the United States: March 1990*. Current population reports, series P-20, No. 449. Washington, DC: U.S. Government Printing Office.

U.S. Bureau of the Census. (1992). *The black population in the United States: March 1991*. Current population reports, series P20-464. Washington, DC: U.S. Government Printing Office.

U.S. Bureau of the Census. (1993a). *Population profile of the United States: 1993*. Current population reports, series P23-185. Washington, DC: U.S. Government Printing Office.

U.S. Bureau of the Census. (1993b). *Hispanic Americans today*. Current population reports, series P23-183. Washington, DC: U.S. Government Printing Office.

Useem, M. (1984). *The inner circle: Large corporations and the rise of business and political activity in the U.S. and U.K.* New York: Oxford University Press.

Wacquant, L. J. D., & Wilson, W. J. (1989). Poverty, joblessness, and the social transformation of the inner city. In P. H. Cottingham & D. T. Ellwood (Eds.), *Welfare policy in the 1990s* (pp. 70–102). Cambridge, MA: Harvard University Press.

Waldrop, J. (1990). Shades of black. *American Demographics, 12*(9), 30–34.

Weill, J. D. (1991). Child poverty in America. *Clearinghouse Review, 25*, 337–348.

Wilson, W. J. (1978). *The declining significance of race*. Chicago: University of Chicago Press.

Wilson, W. J. (1985). The juvenilization of poverty. *Public Administration Review, 45*, 880–884.

Wilson, W. J. (1987). *The truly disadvantaged: The inner city, the underclass, and public policy.* Chicago: University of Chicago Press.

Wilson, W. J. (1991). Public policy research and *The truly disadvantaged.* In C. Jencks & P. E. Peterson (Eds.), *The urban underclass* (pp. 460–481). Washington, DC: The Brookings Institution.

Wilson, W. J. (1992, May 10). Left behind: Whole neighborhoods are cut off. *The Miami Herald,* pp. C1, 6.

Winkler, K. J. (1990, October 10). Researcher's examination of California's poor latino population prompts debate over the traditional definitions of the underclass. *The Chronicle of Higher Education,* pp. A1, A8.

Wright, E. O. (1989). Women in the class structure. *Politics and Society, 17*(1), 35–66.

Zaldivar, R. A. (1991, September 27). Bleak recession figures stir call for poverty relief. *The Miami Herald,* p. 6A.

Zaldivar, R. A. (1994, October 7). U.S. poverty rate highest in 10 years, census bureau says. *Miami Herald,* pp. A1, A6.

Zweigenhaft, R. L., & Domhoff, G. W. (1991). *Blacks in the white establishment?A study of race and class in America.* New Haven and London: Yale University Press.

SUGGESTIONS FOR FURTHER READING

Anderson, E. (1994). The code of the streets. *The Atlantic, 273*, 80–91.

Billingsley, A. (1992). *Climbing Jacob's ladder: The enduring legacy of African-American families.* New York: Simon & Schuster.

Castle, E. N. (1992). *Persistent poverty in rural America.* San Francisco: Westview Press.

Cose, E. (1994). *The rage of a privileged class: Why do prosperous blacks still have the blues?* New York: HarperCollins.

Cowley, G. (1991, Summer). Children in peril. *Newsweek,* 18–21.

DeMott, B. (1990). *The imperial middle: Why Americans can't think straight about class.* New York: William Morrow.

Duneier, M. (1992). *Slim's table: Race, respectability, and masculinity.* Chicago: University of Chicago Press.

Ehrenreich, B. (1989). *Fear of falling: The inner life of the middle class.* New York: Pantheon Books.

Ellwood, D. T. (1988). *Poor support.* New York: Basic Books.

Falcon, L. M. (1994). Poverty, migration, and the underclass. *Latino Studies Journal, 5*(2), 77–96.

Firestone, J. M., & Harris, R. J. (1994). Hispanic women in Texas: An increasing portion of the underclass. *Hispanic Journal of Behavioral Sciences, 16*, 176–185.

Gatewood, W. B. (1990). *Aristocrats of color: The black elite, 1880–1920.* Bloomington & Indianapolis: Indiana University Press.

Gibbs, J. T. (Ed.). (1988). *Young, black, and male in America: An endangered species.* Dover, MA: Auborn House.

Hilfiker, D. (1994). *Not all of us are saints: A doctor's journey with the poor.* New York: Hill & Wang.

Jencks, C., & Peterson, P. E. (Eds.). (1991). *The urban underclass.* Washington: The Brookings Institution.

Lach, M. C. (1992). Essay: an inner-city education. *Scientific American, 266*, 151.

Lamont, M. (1992). *Money, morals, and manners: The culture of the French and American upper-middle class.* Chicago: University of Chicago Press.

Landry, B. (1987). *The new black middle class.* Berkeley and Los Angeles: University of California Press.

Levitan, S. A., Gallo, F., & Shapiro, I. (1993). *Working but poor: America's contradiction* (rev. ed.). Baltimore: Johns Hopkins University Press.

Newman, K. S. (1988). *Falling from grace: The experience of downward mobility in the American middle class.* New York: Free Press.

Polakow, V. (1993). *Lives on the edge.* Chicago: University of Chicago Press.

Rubin, L. B. (1992a). *Worlds of pain: Life in the working class family.* New York: Basic Books.

Rubin, L. B. (1992b). *Women and children last: The plight of poor women in affluent America.* New York: Penguin Books.

Schwarz, J. E., & Volgy, T. (1992). *The forgotten Americans*. New York: W. W. Norton.

Steele, S. (1988). On being black and middle class. *Commentary, 85*(1), 42–47.

Whitman, D., & Friedman, D. (1994, October 17). The white underclass. *U.S. News & World Report*, 40–53.

Wilson, W. J. (Ed.). (1993). *The ghetto underclass: Social science perspectives*. Newbury Park, CA: Sage.

Wilson, J. W. (1987). *The truly disadvantaged: The inner city, the underclass, and public policy*. Chicago: University Chicago Press.

Zweigenhaft, R. L., & Domhoff, G. W. (1991). *Blacks in the white establishment? A study of race and class in America*. New Haven and London: Yale University Press.

CHAPTER 4

SOCIETY AND HUMAN BEHAVIOR
THE INFLUENCE OF RACE, ETHNICITY, GENDER, AND SEXUAL ORIENTATION

The previous chapter concentrated on the effects of societal stratification on the basis of social class. This chapter continues the study of the influence of social stratification, this time on the basis of race, gender, sexual orientation, and ethnicity. Specifically, it explores the consequences of discrimination and oppression for African Americans, women, gays and lesbians, Latinos, Asian Americans, Native Americans, and American Jews. The chapter begins by developing a general understanding of the types of discrimination and oppression faced by nondominant group members and the consequences of such unequal treatment. It then examines the contemporary situation of each of these nondominant groups.

NONDOMINANT GROUPS

There is considerable disagreement in the United States as to what constitutes a nondominant, or "minority," group. This is because whenever the society extends certain benefits or entitlements to "minorities," such as special access to opportunity structures, various groups immediately lay their claims and want to be included, whether they actually qualify for inclusion or not.

Properly speaking, a social group may be considered **nondominant** if it has low standing in the stratification system of the society. Low standing may be reflected by (1) prejudice, discrimination, subordination, oppression, or inequitable treatment directed toward the group or (2) less than proportionate participation in the social, economic, and political life of the society, given the group's numerical representation in the society.

According to the first set of criteria, a particular societal group would be considered nondominant if it did not receive the same social benefits available to the **dominant** or mainstream group (e.g., the same quality of education, health care, and housing; the same degree of access to employment and income; the same status before the law, etc.). Under the second criterion, a social group would be considered nondominant if its members did not participate proportionately in running the major institutions of the society or in making its major decisions, or if they did not hold political office to an extent proportionate to their representation in society.

Ascribed versus Achieved Membership

Generally, people attain membership in a nondominant group on the basis of certain ascribed or achieved characteristics. **Ascribed** (literally, written) attributes are those the person is born with. For example, race and gender are ascribed traits. Generally, ethnicity is also ascribed, in the sense that people are born to a particular ethnic group such as Puerto Rican or Bahamian. However, in some cases, ethnicity may be achieved, such as when someone converts to Judaism. Other characteristics that might lead to nondominant group membership are **achieved.** For example, membership in the group known as "the aged" is achieved as people become old. Similarly, a healthy person may become physically disabled or mentally ill, someone of middle-class status may become poor, and a previously heterosexual person may discover that he or she has fallen in love with someone of the same sex.

RACIAL AND ETHNIC GROUPS

An **ethnic group** consists of people who share certain commonalities that give them a sense of peoplehood, including a common history and identity, a common language, the same national background, a common culture, a common religion, or some combination of these factors (Gordon, 1988, p. 129). Ethnic groups may be dominant or nondominant, depending on their relative standing in the stratification system of the society.

Some ethnic groups in the United States have always had high standing and have always been part of the mainstream, such as individuals of English, Scottish, or Welsh ancestry (Anglos), German Americans, and Scandinavian Americans. Other more recent immigrant groups initially had low standing in the society but are now almost completely assimilated and integrated into the mainstream, such as Irish Americans, Italian Americans, Hungarian Americans, and Polish Americans. Such groups are now considered to be part of the mainstream. In contrast, other ethnic groups in the United States have not achieved integration into the mainstream. These nondominant groups are commonly referred to as **ethnic minorities.** Some continue to have low standing in the society regardless of how long their members have been in this country, such as African Americans, mainland Puerto Ricans, Mexican Americans, or Native Americans.

Strictly speaking, there are no distinctly separate racial groups in the world, as they have been so intermingled throughout history that they no longer share any unique set of genes except those that determine surface traits such as skin coloration (Cavalli-Sforza, Menozzi, & Piazza, 1994). Loosely speaking, however, one may refer to a **racial group** as one that has a common set of distinctive physical characteristics such as skin color and hair texture. All **people of color** (i.e., nonwhites) (Hopps, 1987) in the United States are considered to be nondominant group members, including African Americans, Jamaicans, Bahamians, West Indians, Haitians, Native Americans, and Asian/Pacific Americans. Latino groups with a high proportion of members of mixed racial backgrounds, such as Mexican Americans and mainland Puerto Ricans, are also classified as people of color.[1] All such people share a history of oppression and discrimination prolonged and accentuated by their physical distinctiveness which has made assimilation into the mainstream impossible for them.

PREJUDICE, DISCRIMINATION, AND OPPRESSION

Prejudice, discrimination, and oppression are the traditional weapons used by the dominant group in U.S. society to maintain its privileged position. Although most national polls conducted over the last 25 years have shown a steady reduction in the amount of prejudice and discrimination in the U.S. population, these problems are deeply rooted and continue to be a painful reality in the lives of nondominant group members.

Prejudice is a positive or negative attitude, opinion, or prejudgment concerning a person or group usually formulated on the basis of selective perception and held without sufficient evidence or justification. For example, a father may be prejudiced in favor of his son in the sense that he selectively perceives only the boy's virtues, whereas the boy's teacher may be prejudiced against him because she sees only his shortcomings. Usually, the term *prejudice* is used pejoratively to refer to a negative or hostile attitude, belief, or feeling that a person may have about others. The attitude may be justified or unjustified.

If you have a negative attitude toward someone because this person has been abusive, unfair, or injust toward you, your prejudice against this individual is justified and reality based. However, if you believe that African Americans lack motivation to work hard, that Mariel Cubans are criminals, that New Yorkers are aggressive, that old people are inefficient and incompetent, or that gays are promiscuous or immoral, your attitudes would be considered unjustified prejudices. All these stereotypes are incorrect when treated as blanket statements, even though some African Americans may lack motivation, some Mariel Cubans may have criminal records, some New Yorkers may be aggressive, certain old people may be mentally incompetent, and some gays may be promiscuous.

Prejudices share certain basic characteristics; namely, they are learned, widely shared, and long lasting. Prejudices are learned in the sense that nobody is prejudiced at birth; instead, people acquire their prejudices from others around them. Prejudices are shared by many different types of people in the society; for example, antiblack, anti-Latino, or antigay prejudices are widely shared by the poor as well as the middle class, by Protestants, Catholics, and members of other religious groups, and by people from different regions of the country, such as northerners, southerners, and westerners. It is hard to get rid of prejudices. Once they catch on, they endure, sometimes for generations and even centuries.

Discrimination, as distinguished from prejudice, is an unjustified negative or hostile *action* toward a certain group or individual. If someone insults you and you return the insult, your behavior leaves much to be desired, but it is not discriminatory because you have acted with justification. However, barring a Jew from joining a social club because he or she is Jewish, calling a black person a "nigger" or a gay person a "queer," not employing disabled people or people over the age of 50, or not renting an apartment to a Puerto Rican family because they are Puerto Rican are examples of discrimination. These behaviors are not justifiable.

There are four main types of discrimination: de jure, de facto, individual, and institutional. **De jure discrimination** is discrimination sanctioned by the law. For example, you may recall reading about the so-called Jim Crow laws in the U.S. South which, among other things, denied black persons the right to a trial, to vote, or to marry someone of the white race. It is now unconstitutional and therefore uniformly *illegal* throughout the United States to discriminate against others on the basis of their race, gender, religion, nationality, or disability. However, the Constitution remains silent with respect to discrimination on the basis of sexual orientation. As you will see later in this chapter, this allows the public as well as social institutions to discriminate openly against gays and lesbians without breaking any law in states and localities that have not specifically passed laws making discrimination on the basis of sexual orientation illegal.

De facto discrimination is discrimination that actually exists, even if it is illegal. For instance, although it is illegal to discriminate against African Americans and Latinos, they are often denied jobs and housing. However, because the practice is illegal, those who dis-/criminate against them are usually careful not to mention skin color or ethnic background as the actual bases for rejecting them. Instead, employers or property owners often make up excuses, such as that someone already took the job or rented the apartment.

Individual discrimination is discrimination perpetrated by one person against another, such as when a small business owner denies a job to a Cambodian refugee applicant because he wants a white employee. The most pervasive type of discrimination occurs at the institutional, or societal, level. **Institutional discrimination** is structural and systemic in nature; that is, it is built into the economic, educational, health, social, political, and legal institutions of the society. It is pervasive because it affects many people rather than single individuals. For instance, due to institutional discrimination, millions of children of color suffer nutritional, medical, educational, and economic disadvantages, as compared to Euro-American children.

The terms *discrimination* and *oppression* are often used interchangeably; however, they are not synonymous. Properly speaking, **oppression** is a form of discrimination that is long term, systematic, and institutionalized (i.e., embedded within key social structures such as the educational system, the health care system, and the criminal justice system). The traditional unfair and unjust treatment African Americans have received in U.S. society, as well as the treatment of women under the patriarchal system that has relegated them to less well-paid occupations and professions and that has expected them to perform unpaid labor at home, are examples of oppression.

Several factors facilitate discrimination and oppression. The more easily identifiable a group is, the more vulnerable it is to discrimination and oppression. Also, the more immutable its characteristics, the greater the likelihood

that such treatment will persist. In other words, discrimination and oppression are easier to accomplish if the group or persons toward whom they are intended have easily distinguishable physical characteristics, such as a particular skin color, gender, hair texture, facial features, or advanced age. It is also easy to discriminate against people who can be identified because they speak a foreign language, speak English with an accent, or have different customs or behaviors. However, a person's command of the English language, customs, values, and behaviors can be modified over time, so these are less effective markers for discrimination and oppression than immutable physical characteristics such as race or gender.

Discrimination and oppression are more likely to occur when the target group is perceived as a threat or when it lacks the power to retaliate. For example, gays and lesbians are seen as a threat to moral or religious values by some people. Because in many localities they do not have the same civil rights as other people, they become easy targets for the moral or religious right. Similarly, in a tight labor market, illegal immigrants are perceived as a threat by other workers. Because they have no legal status, they are often scapegoated (Turner, Singleton, & Musick, 1984, pp. 4–6).

Various terms are used to describe specific types of prejudice and discrimination. These include *racism, sexism, ageism, classism, antisemitism, ethnocentrism,* and *homophobia.*

The term **racism** is used to refer to prejudice, discrimination, or oppression based on race. It also encompasses various racial stereotypes. (A *stereotype* is a widely held idea that oversimplifies and distorts, such as the belief that blacks are more athletic or less intelligent.) Racism is usually based on a belief in the cultural or biological (innate) superiority of a particular race as compared to another race.

The most pervasive and damaging form of racism operates at the **institutional** level. For instance, many poor blacks in the United States are ill prepared for complex high-technology jobs because the system has given them an inferior education. In addition, lack of equal access to the job market has kept them poor and living in substandard housing that is often located in crime-infested neighborhoods. The perpetrators of this widespread racial oppression are not just certain individual teachers or employers who discriminate against blacks, but the whole society that treats people of color unequally through its institutions. Individual instances of racism, unlike institutional racism, are less pervasive because they affect nonwhites one by one rather than as a group.

Still another form of racism is **cultural racism**, or the belief in the superiority of the accomplishments of one race as compared to another. For example, a history textbook that focuses on the experiences and accomplishments of Euro-Americans and systematically ignores the role played by African Americans or American Indians in American history suffers from cultural racism.

Sexism, ageism, and classism consist of stereotyping, prejudice, discrimination, or oppression on the basis of gender, age, or socioeconomic status, respectively. **Sexism** is usually based on two main stereotypes: (1) Men are biologically superior, and therefore women should be subordinated to them, and (2) a woman's principal role is to take care of the family, and therefore everything else in her life (e.g., education or employment) should be subordinated to her roles as wife and mother. **Ageism** is often based on the stereotype that younger people are more competent and efficient than older people, therefore, it is justifiable to treat older people as second-class citizens. **Classism** is usually based on the stereotype that the poor have inferior traits and values (e.g., laziness, lack of motivation tendency toward immediate gratification) that cause their disadvantaged social circumstances.

Antisemitism is stereotyping, prejudice, discrimination, or oppression directed against Jews. Although it declined significantly after the atrocities perpetrated by the Nazis during World War II became known, antisemitism is reportedly on the rise again in the United States, partly at the instigation of the Ku Klux Klan and the American Nazi Party. **Ethnocentrism** consists of considering one's ethnic group or culture superior to others. For example, it is ethnocentric for Euro-Americans to think that their values and way of life are superior to those of other ethnic groups in the United States, and therefore all other groups should adopt the mainstream culture and drop their own original cultures. It is also ethnocentric to use the word *America* to refer to the United States of America because the United States is not the only country in the American continent. Canada, Mexico, and all of the countries in Central and South America and in the Caribbean are as much a part of America as the United States of America. In the extreme, ethnocentrism encompasses the attitude that it is appropriate for one's ethnic group, because it is "better" than others, to exert social, political, or economic domination over other groups. When the United States sends troops to another country "to preserve democracy," for example, it is acting ethnocentrically.

Homophobia belongs in the same category as the preceding "isms" and consists of intolerance of gays and lesbians, irrational fear of homosexuality, or prejudice or discrimination directed against gays and lesbians (Woodman, 1987; Gramick, 1983; Cummerton, 1982). It includes seemingly innocuous but prejudicial jokes about "faggots," pejorative name calling (e.g., "queer" or "dyke,"), fears of being "seduced" or "converted" if one fraternizes with gays, discrimination against gays and lesbians in employment and housing, hostility directed toward them, and even violent acts against gays and lesbians.

Factors That Contribute to Prejudice, Discrimination, and Oppression

Currently there is no all-encompassing theory or explanation for the kinds of prejudice,

Box 4.1

Victims of Gender in Asia: 60 Million Women "Missing"

BY NICHOLAS D. KRISTOF

New York Times Service

BEIJING—Little girls in China no longer have their feet crushed by binding, and widows in India are no longer supposed to be roasted alive on the funeral pyres of their husbands.

But a stark statistic testifies to women's continuing unequal status: At least 60 million females in Asia are missing and feared dead, victims of nothing more than their sex.

Worldwide, research suggests, the number of missing females may top 100 million.

A traditional preference for boys translates quickly—in China, India and many other developing countries—into neglect and death for girls.

While the discrimination is widely seen as a relic of outdated attitudes, in fact the problem appears to be getting worse in Asia.

Recently released census data in China and India show that in both countries the sex ratio of the population became more skewed over the course of the past decade.

The tens of millions of missing include females of all ages who are aborted or killed at birth or who die because they are given less food and medical treatment than males.

APPROACHES TO SICKNESS

"If a boy gets sick, the parents may send him to the hospital at once," acknowledged Li Honggui, an official in China's State Family Planning Commission. "But if a girl gets sick, the parents may say to themselves, 'Well, we'll see how she is tomorrow.'"

Remarkably little research has been conducted on the plight of the missing women, and even their disappearance is discernible merely as a shadow on the census data and mortality statistics.

"It's shocking that so little is known," said Amartya Sen, a Harvard economist who has tried to call attention to the issue. Sen estimates that considerably more than 100 million females are missing around the world, and he asserts that the reason the shortfall is getting worse is that girls are not allowed to benefit as much as boys from improvements in health care and nutrition in developing countries.

Any investigation into the case of the missing women begins with one fact: 5 or 6 percent more boys are born than girls, but in normal circumstances males die at higher rates at every age thereafter.

RATIOS IN THE WEST

In the West, children are disproportionately male, the number of men and women evens out by the time people are in their 20s or 30s, and the elderly are disproportionately female. In countries such as the United States, Britain and Poland, there are about 105 females for every 100 males.

In India, however, a census this year found only 92.9 females for every 100 males, down from 93.4 in the 1981 census and 93.0 in the 1971 census.

And in China, the 1990 census found just 93.8 females for every 100 males, compared with 94.1 at the time of the 1982 census.

By a conservative calculation there are 30 million females missing in China, about 5 percent of the national total and more than are missing in any other country.

discrimination, and oppression that exist in society. However, knowledge of important contributing factors can provide greater insight into the problem. This section examines how the socialization process as well as sociostructural, psychological, and historical variables contribute to prejudice and discrimination.

The Socialization Process and Conformity

Probably the most common explanation for the prejudice and discrimination shown by most individuals in U.S. society is learning through observation. Traditionally, children learn prejudicial attitudes and discriminatory practices from the example set by parents, grandparents, teachers, peers, babysitters, television, church representatives, and so on, and they gradually internalize these attitudes and behaviors as their own. To the extent that adults continue to show prejudice or to engage in discriminatory practices, youngsters around them learn to view these attitudes and behaviors as normal and natural. For example, if parents do not mix socially with people who are of a different color or ethnic background or if they tell their children that it is best to avoid such people, the children are likely to develop prejudicial attitudes and to view these attitudes as normal because they come from their parents. Similarly, some people may feel no particular prejudice against certain other people, but if those around them are prejudiced or routinely engage in discriminatory behaviors, they may go along with it because they find it easier to conform than to cause dissension by disagreeing.

Sociostructural Factors

An important explanation of institutional discrimination is the theory of *differential power* (Lenski, 1966). Applied to dominant/nondominant group relations, this theory means that the dominant group uses prejudice and oppression as weapons in the struggle for control over societal resources. That is, the dominant group protects its economic and political interests by fostering prejudices and by keeping various nondominant group members disadvantaged and deprived so that they cannot become effective competitors. As long as nondominants are deficient in their knowledge and skills, the dominant group can pay them less for their work and can get them to accept the less desirable jobs.

The need to compete for scarce societal resources can also increase prejudice and discrimination. Racism, for instance, rises during periods of scarcity. This is because in bad economic times there are not enough resources to go around, and people become concerned that someone will take away what they consider to be rightfully theirs. For example, during the Depression, the positive attitudes of U.S. citizens toward Chinese immigrants quickly soured. The Chinese were prohibited from coming to the United States for many years because the mainstream group felt that their jobs were threatened by the presence of these foreign workers who would work hard for low wages. More recently, in the 1990s, the public sentiment became strongly antiimmigrant in many parts of the nation as the economy lost steam.

Psychological Factors

Some prejudice and discrimination may be the result of pent-up frustration, hostility, and resentment that is displaced onto a substitute object. Sometimes one sees this dynamic operating in individuals raised by authoritarian parents—that is, parents who are rigid, highly controlling, punitive, and not willing to allow their children to express negative emotions. Their children, afraid to retaliate against their parents, often take out their hostility and resentment on a less threatening substitute object, which becomes the **scapegoat** (i.e., the one who bears the blame). For example, instead of attacking their parents, such children may pick a fight with a classmate at school. Because members of nondominant groups often are not in a position to retaliate effectively, they make excellent scapegoats for frustrated people.

Some people have a built-in propensity toward prejudice and discrimination by virtue of their personalities. For example, those who are authoritarian (i.e., power oriented, controlling, and preoccupied by rank and status) need to exert power and control over others. Nondominant group members, by nature of their low status in society, are easy targets. Similarly, some people with feelings of inferiority and insecurity tend to feel more important and better about themselves when they are able to look down on someone else.

Another psychological explanation of discrimination involves the mechanism of projection. Many people have traits that they cannot accept in themselves. Without realizing it, they go around blaming others for the very characteristics or tendencies that they fear or cannot accept in themselves. Members of nondominant groups, because of their limited social power, make particularly good targets because they are reluctant to retaliate. For example, some of the most fanatical antihomosexuals are people frightened of possible homosexual tendencies in themselves. By attacking gays or lesbians, they reassure themselves that they are not like them.

Historical Factors

Certain nonmainstream groups in society have been conquered, enslaved, colonized, or permitted to enter the United States specifically to play a subordinate role. For example, African Americans were brought in as slaves, Native Americans were conquered by the colonists, and many Mexican Americans entered the United States primarily to work the fields seasonally or to be short-term contract laborers, or *braceros.* Members of the dominant group have enjoyed for a long time a privileged position in society in comparison to the descendants of these formerly colonized and enslaved people. Having grown accustomed to these circumstances, they are having trouble accepting these nondominant group members as equals and sharing resources with them on an equitable basis (Zastrow, 1988). The same sort of thing has happened in most other countries that have former slaves, conquered natives, citizens of former colonies, or imported laborers.

Consequences of Discrimination and Oppression

Discrimination on any basis negatively affects people's life chances (opportunities and quality of life) as well as their behaviors, attitudes, values, personality traits, beliefs, customs, and roles. If the discrimination lasts long, the person may suffer multiple deprivations. For example, those who are persistently poor suffer inadequate medical care, malnutrition, substandard housing, inferior education, marginal employment or unemployment, unequal treatment by the criminal justice system, and various psychological and emotional problems. It is important to understand, however, that not all nondominant group members suffer the same types or degrees of oppression.

In general, the greater the number of the nondominant groups to which an individual belongs (e.g., poor, nonwhite, female, homosexual, physically or mentally disabled, elderly), the greater the potential damage to the individual. For example, poor people of color, such as poor African Americans or Native Americans, suffer social disadvantages due to their poverty status and race. If, on top of that, they are female, disabled, gay/lesbian, or elderly, they are at even greater risk. To be sure, their potential degree of oppression is greater, for example, than that of middle-class Euro-American women. Although middle-class Euro-American women suffer many types of oppression (which will be detailed later in this chapter), at least in their roles as daughters, wives, and mothers of men who are members of the dominant group, they enjoy some reflected power and get to share material resources with the men. In this sense, women members of the dominant group are better off because they have a closer relationship with the power structure (Hopps, 1987, p. 162).

This section begins by reviewing the major consequences of societal oppression. It will then examine the current situation of various oppressed groups in the United States, in addition to the poor whose plight was considered in the previous chapter. The groups to be covered in this chapter include African Americans, Latinos, Native Americans, Asian Americans, women, and gays and lesbians.

Nutritional Deficiencies

As a result of institutional discrimination principally in the form of economic and educational deprivation, some people in the United States are malnourished or lack a nutritionally balanced diet. They tend to overconsume foods that provide the cheapest sources of energy— such as fats, sugars, and simple starches—and to overuse salt to flavor their food because it is the most inexpensive seasoning available. They eat insufficient amounts of vegetables, fruits, and low-fat protein (e.g., fish, lean white meats) because these sources of energy are expensive.

In adults, poor diets can result in various health problems, including obesity, cholesterol problems, high blood pressure, and higher rates of diabetes. In pregnant women, poor nutrition can result in miscarriages, stillbirths, premature births, and babies of low birth weight who have a high risk of mental retardation, learning disabilities, and behavioral disorders (Citizens Commission on Hunger in New England, 1984). Because the human brain grows to 80 percent of its adult size during this period, children who are extremely deprived of protein during this period may suffer stunted brain development and irreversible retardation. Less dramatically but more commonly, the diets of economically deprived children are often deficient enough to interfere with learning and to cause the children to be inattentive, apathetic, irritable, easily fatigued, and unable to concentrate or sustain prolonged mental effort (Birch, 1972).

Inadequate Medical Care

There are many reasons why members of nondominant groups, particularly those who are poor, often go without medical care. These include lack of money, lack of insurance, fear and ignorance, lack of time, and "cooling out." Many poor people go to public hospitals and clinics because they do not qualify for Medicaid, do not know about Medicaid, or do not know that some private practitioners are Medicaid providers. Generally, they do not get the same quality and continuity of care as the middle class. They tend to be shuffled from one doctor to another and from one facility to another until some get the distinct feeling that they are just getting the run-around. They have to get on long waiting lists and when they finally get a medical appointment, they are made to wait for hours on end, sometimes only to be told at the end of the day that they must return the following day or the following week. The medical personnel at public facilities, usually overwhelmed by an excessive number of patients, frequently relate to patients in an impersonal and hurried manner, give them unclear instructions or insufficient feedback about their problems, or use "professional" language that their patients cannot understand. This treatment often turns patients off or "cools them out" so that they become reluctant to return for services.

In part because of inadequate preventive care, insufficient medical care, and a propensity to seek treatment when medical problems reach an advanced stage, poor people suffer higher rates of infant mortality, disability, and death from major diseases, as well as have as a shorter life span, than middle-class persons. The situation is even worse for people of color, particularly those groups with high rates of poverty. Black babies, for example, are twice as likely to die before their first birthday and twice as likely to be born at low birthweight as white babies, and black adults are more likely to become sick and to die from cancer, heart disease, stroke, and diabetes than whites of the same age (Rubin, 1989; Rubin, 1992b). Similarly, black males have a life expectancy of 65 years, compared to 72 years for white males;

and black females have a life expectancy of 73 years, compared to 79 years for white females (U.S. Bureau of the Census, 1990, p. 72).

Women also have suffered discrimination in their medical care. Often, they have been subjected to unneeded operations such as hysterectomies, radical mastectomies, and caesarean sections. Their physical problems have been neglected in medical research, which, until recently, was conducted mainly on males. Consequently, they have been subjected to treatments designed for males and adapted to them without a sound research basis. Many times, women's symptoms have been ignored by their physicians due to widely held stereotypes such as that they are not as prone to heart disease as males.

Substandard Housing

Many nondominant group members suffer various kinds of housing discrimination. Those who are poor often must live in deteriorated private or publicly subsidized housing projects. Their living quarters are typically ill-repaired, poorly heated and ventilated, and infested with rats and roaches. Sometimes they even lack basic necessities such as running water because the plumbing has been out of order for weeks or months and the property owner takes forever to get it repaired. They may have to live with roof leaks for months or with a collapsed ceiling in some part of the apartment because of the delay in repairing the roof. Sometimes their children get lead poisoning from eating the paint that is peeling off the walls or from inhaling the paint dust. Oppression in housing often means having to live in dangerous, filthy, overcrowded, crime-ridden, inner-city neighborhoods.

Housing segregation is a major problem for many people of color. Those with money to rent or buy in desirable neighborhoods are often told by property owners that the unit they want is no longer available when the truth is that the owner does not want to rent or sell to them. Real estate agents also sometimes contribute to the housing segregation problem in the United States, particularly by *steering* people of color to nonwhite or integrated neighborhoods. Consequently, many are forced to live in decaying inner-city areas or in less desirable segregated or integrated suburban neighborhoods than their money can afford. Some gays and lesbians who are open about their sexual orientation also sometimes suffer various degrees of housing discrimination because some property owners are reluctant to rent or sell to them. Particularly affected by discrimination in housing are those suspected of having acquired immune deficiency syndrome (AIDS).

Unequal Education

Most nondominant group members in U.S. society do not attain the same level of education as the mainstream group. Upon entering school, poor children, and even more markedly poor children of color, are typically behind middle-class children in terms of English-language proficiency, vocabulary, conceptual development, and fine motor skills. This is probably due to insufficient intellectual stimulation at home and in their immediate social environments. Although many of these children are deficient in verbal and conceptual areas, they are often more competent than middle-class youngsters at other skills, such as riding their bicycles in city traffic to go to school, running errands for their parents, or helping adults with meal preparation, housework, grocery shopping, and babysitting younger brothers and sisters.

The problem is that the competencies often exhibited by non-middle-class children are not usually taken into consideration by schools in placing them (White, 1984, p. 88). Consequently, a large proportion of these children end up in remedial classes or in special education classes for the mildly retarded because they are deficient to various extents in measurable intellectual areas (Richardson, 1994). Once placed in special classes, teachers assume these children are slow; therefore, they lower their expectations and do not challenge these students to the extent that they would challenge "regular" students. The result is that these children often do little school work, become bored, and eventually may become discipline problems. Many develop low levels of aspiration and poor self-concepts and drop out of school early because they do not see the relevance of school to their lives. Consequently, many never finish high school or go on to college. With little education, they tend to end up with menial jobs at minimum wages or they become subject to irregular employment or unemployment. Even among those who stay in high school until graduation, their schooling is often so deficient that a substantial proportion are functional illiterates unprepared for work in a technological society. In short, the often inferior educational experience of nondominant group members perpetuates their disadvantaged status in the society.

One of the major educational problems confronting children of color is the continuing segregation in public schools despite years of desegregation efforts through busing. This has been the result of "white flight" from public schools to private schools or to the suburbs where white children are able to attend better public schools in more affluent districts. This has left many poor children of color behind in central cities with a dwindling economic base to support education. Often, these children must attend poorly equipped, dilapidated schools where maintaining some semblance of order and dealing with shootings and stabbings becomes more important than learning and where the teachers tend to be less experienced and less well trained than those hired in more affluent suburban areas.

Women, including those who are members of the Euro-American middle class, also have suffered some level of educational oppression. Many have not achieved to capacity because their parents, teachers, and society in general have had lower educational expectations for them than for males. Another factor that has militated against the full educational develop-ment of women has been the traditional societal tendency to steer them toward "sex-appropriate" but lower-status and lower-paid occupations than those men have been traditionally encouraged to pursue. This will be discussed in greater detail later in this chapter in the section on women.

Unequal Access to Jobs and Income

A disproportionate number of nondominant group members, particularly people of color, suffer economic deprivation due to high rates of unemployment or relegation to low-paying jobs. This is in large part the result of having an inferior education coupled with employment discrimination. An additional problem non-whites frequently confront at work is lack of seniority: Having been among the last to be hired, when cutbacks become necessary, they are among the first to be let go.

Women, even those who are white and middle class, also suffer discrimination in employment. Studies have shown that they make significantly less income than men, even when they have the same years of education and job experience and work the same number of hours as men (Cherry, 1989). Some of the elderly also suffer economic and employment discrimination. Those over age 65 who cannot make ends meet with their retirement pensions or social security encounter great difficulty finding employment, particularly jobs that are not menial or at minimum wage. The physically disabled also have suffered much discrimination in employment. Despite federal laws prohibiting discrimination in hiring and requiring employers to make modifications in the work environment to accommodate the disabled, few businesses, particularly small enterprises, are willing to hire people with disabilities. Thus, a large proportion of such people, even those who are well educated, must live on disability income. This deprives them of the sense of accomplishment and self-efficacy associated with having the opportunity to work and to associate with others in the workplace.

Gays and lesbians also suffer employment discrimination in some fields. For example, in the mid-1990s, they still were barred from military jobs or jobs requiring federal government security clearance unless they kept their homosexuality carefully under wraps. In many localities, they were barred from most religious ministries and had trouble getting or retaining teaching jobs unless they were willing to keep their sexual orientation hidden. Some "obvious gays" (i.e., effeminate looking) also encountered employment discrimination due to the fear of AIDS in the workplace, and those afflicted with AIDS suffered serious economic problems because few places were willing to hire them.

Inequality Before the Law

The poor, particularly those who are not white, experience difficult life circumstances that often generate high levels of frustration, stress, and anger; some act out these frustrations by committing criminal or violent acts or by rioting. In addition, in order to survive, some people who live in the toughest and poorest areas of the inner city and who have few job skills or opportunities for employment may turn to street crime, such as drug dealing, prostitution, breaking and entering, robbing and stealing, and illegal gambling.

Given their bleak life circumstances, it is understandable that some nondominant group members, particularly those who are poor and nonwhite, turn to crime to survive. But, in good measure, their overinvolvement with the criminal justice system is due to prejudice and discrimination on the part of the establishment. This unfair societal treatment causes these people to be more frequently arrested, jailed while awaiting trial (since few can post bail), convicted and sentenced to longer prison terms than middle-class Euro-Americans who have committed similar though more often white-collar as opposed to street crimes. In contrast, the latter are more likely to receive probation, parole, community service, or suspended sentences.

Sometimes the poor (especially those who are not white) end up having a criminal record and serving long prison sentences simply because they cannot afford good lawyers to defend them. The court-appointed public defenders and volunteer lawyers often assigned to them seldom have the time or resources to conduct the kinds of extensive, in-depth investigations necessary to provide an adequate defense. In addition, those who are jailed before trial may find that their pretrial detention interferes with their ability to prepare an effective defense due to many barriers such as limited visitation hours and a lack of privacy. Once these people are released from prison, their criminal record makes it difficult for them to reenter the work force, as few employers are willing to hire ex-convicts (Kornblum & Julian, 1989).

Psychological and Emotional Consequences

Discrimination and oppression can lead to negative psychological and emotional reactions. Sometimes people who could be the targets of discrimination cope by escape or avoidance. For instance, in the past, some light-skinned blacks passed for white, and some Jews passed for Gentiles, usually by changing their names. Many gays and lesbians still pass for straight. By passing, they can avoid discrimination and rejection, but they do this by denying or hiding an important part of their identities. Others avoid discrimination by withdrawing as much as possible from contact with the dominant group and by leading separate though often disadvantaged or restricted lives within their racial/ethnic, age group, or gay/lesbian communities. Still others attempt to escape oppression by anesthetizing their feelings with alcohol or other drugs (Simpson & Yinger, 1985).

Many people respond to discrimination and oppression with anger, rage, hostility, resentment, bitterness, aggression, and sometimes antisocial or violent acts. Some individuals who have been oppressed displace these actions onto others; for instance, they may abuse their spouses or children (Strauss, 1980). Others full of anger and rage may participate in riots in their own neighborhoods or they may commit violent crimes (Merry, 1981). Sometimes aggression is expressed passively, such as when, to get back at an oppressive employer, a person works slowly or carelessly or calls in sick at critical times when his or her presence at work is most needed.

Other psychological and emotional reactions common to victims of societal discrimination and rejection include (1) feelings of hurt for being unappreciated, considered less capable, and treated with disrespect; (2) confusion ("What have I done to deserve this treatment?"); (3) depression and, in extreme cases, suicide; (4) feelings of helplessness, hopelessness, impotence, and despair (Chestang, 1972); (5) attitudes of distrust and paranoia toward the oppressor(s); (6) overcompensation, or a never-ending need to prove one's qualifications and credentials (Cobbs, 1988); and (7) relativistic morals and situational ethics—a feeling that one is not required to give full allegiance to the laws of the society, to institutional policies, or to the members of the dominant group if one is oppressed by them. Chestang (1972), who has written eloquently about the consequences of oppression on character development, noted, for example, that it can be difficult for a person subjected to societal injustice and personal unfairness to be just and fair toward members of the oppressive class.

Affluent people of color and other well-to-do members of nondominant groups (e.g., African Americans, Latinos, or women) are not necessarily exempt from the negative psychoemotional effects of societal oppression. Despite their economic and occupational successes, many frequently feel that they are accorded "token" high status but are not really taken seriously at work, that their competence is often questioned, and that some people automatically consider them to be intellectual lightweights,

thus putting them continually in the position of having to prove themselves.

Despite the traditional societal devaluation and rejection, many African-American children and children from other ethnic minority groups are able to develop strong feelings of confidence and self-worth because they are nurtured, protected, loved, accepted, supported, and given affirmation by their families, peers, friends, and community. As they grow up, they become increasingly more aware of how the dominant system devalues them, but if those nearest them continue to provide love, acceptance, and support, this nurturance acts as a buffer against the societal devaluation, offering various degrees of protection against its negative consequences (Chestang, 1976; Norton, 1978; White, 1984).

In the face of societal rejection, some gays and lesbians do not have the above-mentioned benefit of continuing love, acceptance, and support from family and friends. As soon as their sexual orientation becomes known, their parents, brothers, sisters, and some of their friends may withdraw their approval and support. Most compensate to various degrees for these losses by reaching out to the gay and lesbian communities and building new support networks that act as emotional buffers. Others protect themselves from possible rejection by remaining "in the closet," even though they may still experience some negative psychological and emotional reactions if they feel that significant others would reject them if they knew about their homosexuality.

Euro-American women (regardless of socioeconomic status) also have suffered negative psychological and emotional consequences as a result of societal discrimination. Many have suffered from low self-esteem and low self-confidence, a normal consequence of having occupied less desirable social positions and having had less well-paying jobs than men. Until recently, most were expected to relinquish their own last names upon marriage, a practice still common today, which has made some women feel like appendages of men rather than separate individuals. Moreover, due to the traditional social tendency to tie women's worth to their looks and ability to bear and raise children, many women have felt depressed when no longer young or beautiful, when their children did not turn out well, or when they were left by their husbands for a younger or prettier woman.

Some disabled or elderly people suffer psychologically and emotionally in U.S. society because they are often considered superfluous, incompetent, or inefficient. Many have suffered anger, depression, and much hurt as a result of being treated like second-class citizens.

Perhaps the most insidious effect of prejudice, discrimination, and oppression is the vicious circle that is generated (see Figure 4.1). Oppression causes various deprivations and negative consequences in people. These, in turn, often make the oppressed more deficient or disadvantaged than those unaffected by it. Because they do not measure up, the society feels justified to continue to discriminate against them, thus making them even more disadvantaged. In this manner, the cycle repeats itself again and again.

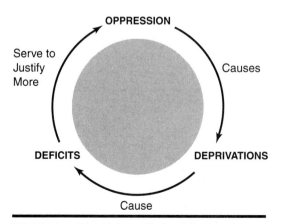

FIGURE 4.1 The Vicious Circle of Oppression

THE CONTEMPORARY SITUATION OF MAJOR U.S. NONDOMINANT GROUPS

African Americans

The 1990 census counted 30.5 million non-Latin blacks in the United States, constituting 12.3 percent of the population (Stone & Castaneda, 1991). The vast majority of these blacks were African Americans.

Up to the 1960s, most African Americans had few options as to places to work, live, eat, shop, or spend their leisure time. They attended separate schools and had to use segregated public facilities (Jaynes & Williams, 1989, pp. 1–3). Since then, their social and economic circumstances have improved dramatically. Segregation is now illegal, and many African Americans are well educated, have achieved middle-class status, and hold professional and managerial jobs in integrated settings. However, too many are still struggling under conditions of poverty and inequality.

African Americans are moving in two significantly different directions, and this is causing a deepening social and economic schism within this community (Wilson, 1978; Landry, 1987). A fast-growing group, now numbering over one-third of all African Americans, are doing well socioeconomically and have joined the ranks of the middle class or higher socioeconomic groups. But there is also a large and growing underprivileged group, representing about one-third of all African Americans, whose earning are below the poverty level. Within this group, there is a substantial and growing segment, referred to as the *ghetto poor,* who live in neighborhoods with high concentrations of poverty. These individuals, persistently poor, mostly unemployed, and living in deteriorated, crime-ridden inner cities seem to be caught in a downward spiral. To them, the future looks hopeless.

Income and Employment

Despite the tremendous growth of the African-American middle class, the income gap between white and black families remains considerable. For example, as you can see in Table 4.1, at the time of the 1990 census the median income (the family income halfway down the scale between the top and the bottom) for black families was only 57 percent of the median income for white families ($23,161 versus $40,370). In addition, there continues to be a great disparity between whites and blacks (as well as between whites and Latinos) in terms of accumulated wealth. According to the Bureau of the Census, in 1988, the median white household had a net worth (i.e., assets minus debts) about 10 times higher than the median African-American or Latino household (Census: Whites 10 times richer than minorities, 1991).

Perhaps the greatest problem that keeps the income of African Americans down is the shockingly high rate of unemployment of black men. Nobody knows for sure how many are without a job. In 1991, unemployment was officially twice higher for black Americans (12.4 percent) than for whites (6 percent) (U. S. Bureau of the Census, 1992). However, it is widely known that unemployment rates are nearly meaningless because these often-quoted official figures do not include those individuals who have dropped out of the labor force and are no longer looking for a job. According to the 1990 census, approximately 42 percent of African American males 16 years of age and older (those of working age) were either unemployed or not participating in the "official" labor force, compared to 28 percent of working-age white males. This figure is the highest for males of any racial group in the United States (U.S. Bureau of the Census, 1993e). How can so many black men without regular jobs live up to their roles as fathers and heads of household if they cannot live up to their roles as breadwinners? Given this situation, it is not difficult to understand why such a high proportion of black homes are headed by females. Black adolescents also have an unemployment rate that is officially triple that of white teenagers (U.S.

Bureau of the Census, 1989b). This means that a significant number of African-American youths are entering adulthood without the benefit of having had some work experience.

Despite these difficulties, African Americans have made significant occupational gains since the 1970s. For instance, during the past 20 years, their representation increased substantially in the fields of medicine, law, engineering, accounting, and management and administration, and the number of businesses owned by African Americans has doubled (Cannon, 1991). Yet, in 1991, African Americans were still only half as likely as whites to hold a managerial or professional job (13.9 percent versus 27.3 percent) and considerably more likely to be employed in service, factory, and other low-paying manual occupations (U.S. Bureau of the Census, 1992). Moreover, African-American professionals remained disproportionately concentrated in the less well-paying "minor" professional fields, such as primary and secondary school teaching and administration, government service, and the social services. The more prestigious professions (e.g., medicine and law) remained difficult for them and other nondominant group members to penetrate.

African Americans from the inner city, in particular, have had considerable difficulty finding employment. In part, this is due to the lack of appropriate education and skills. But it is also because of the reluctance of many employers to hire people who have a different dialect, who dress unusually by mainstream standards, and who have had little or no previous work experience (Ellwood, 1988, p. 210).

Poverty Rate

As previously noted, in 1993, one-third of black Americans were poor, compared to 12.2 percent of whites (DeParle, 1994; Zaldivar, 1994). Thus, the poverty rate of blacks was almost three times higher than that of whites. Black children had an even higher poverty rate; as you can see in Table 4.1, at the time of the 1990 cen-

TABLE 4.1   Social and Economic Characteristics of the U.S. Black* Population versus the White* Population According to the 1990 Census

SOCIAL AND ECONOMIC CHARACTERISTICS	PERCENT WHITES	PERCENT BLACKS
Married-couple families w/children under 18 as % of all households	25.7	17.8
Children living with both parents	79.0	38.0
Children living with mother only	16.0	51.0
Female-headed families w/children under 18 as % of all households	4.7	19.0
Educational Attainment (Ages 25 and over)		
4 years of high school or more	79.8	65.2
4 years of college or more	24.4	12.1
Below Poverty level:		
individuals	10.7	31.9
Families	6.2	25.7
Married-Couple Families with children under 18	4.3	11.1
Female-headed families with children under 18	32.9	51.8
Children under 18 years	15.9	39.2
Individuals 65 and over	10.1	29.5
Unemployment Rate (Ages 16 and over)	4.7	11.3
The following figures are in dollars:		
Family median income	$40,370	$23,161
Median Income for Female-headed families with children under 18	$16,255	$9,705
Per capita income	$17,307	$9,177

Sources: Data taken from "1990 Census of Population, Social and Economic Characteristics, United States" (1990 CP-2-1) by U.S. Bureau of the Census, 1994. Washington, DC: U.S. Government Printing Office. "Geographic Profile of Employment and Unemployment, 1990" by U.S. Bureau of the Census, 1991. Washington, DC: U.S. Government Printing Office. "Poverty in the United States: 1990 Current Population Reports Series P-60, No. 175" by U.S. Bureau of the Census, 1991. Washington, DC: U.S. Government Printing Office. "Statistical Abstract of the United States: 1993" by U.S. Bureau of the Census, 1994. Washington, DC: U.S. Government Printing Office.

*"Black" and "white" are terms used by the Census to refer to people who identify themselves as Negroid or Caucasian, regardless of ethnic background.

sus, 39 percent of black children under age 18 were poor, compared to 16 percent of white children. The incidence of poverty was also extremely high among black female-headed families with children under age 18: 52 percent of these families were poor, compared to 33 percent of similarly situated white families. Because of the high levels of poverty black children have experienced, particularly those living in one-parent families, they have been much more likely than white children to grow up subjected to all sorts of deprivations and dysfunctions associated not only with poverty but with ghetto poverty. These include high levels of long-term unemployment among adults, street crime, drug dealing, prostitution, teenage pregnancy, and welfare dependency (Wilson, 1987; Ellwood, 1988; Ricketts & Sawhill, 1988;

Tienda, 1989; Lynn & McGeary, 1990; Peterson, 1991).

Family Composition

African Americans have been experiencing an alarming decline in the proportion of married-couple families and a concomitant increase in the proportion of families headed by women. Specifically, in 1991, married couples constituted less than half (48 percent) of all African-American family households, down from 56 percent in 1980; conversely, black families headed by women constituted almost half (46 percent) of all black family households, up from 40 percent in 1980. In contrast, between 1980 and 1990, the changes in family structure among whites were much less dramatic. During this period, the proportion of married-couple family households decreased from 86 percent to 83 percent of all white family households, and the percent of white families headed by women increased from 12 to 13 percent of all white families (U.S. Bureau of the Census, 1992).

As a consequence of the dramatic changes in family structure that have taken place, slightly over one-half (51.2 percent) of the African-American children under age 18 in 1990 were living with their mothers only, versus 37.7 percent living with both parents. In comparison, 16.2 percent of white children were living with their mothers only while 79 percent were living with both parents (Usdansky, 1991).

The substantial increase in one-parent homes among African-American families has been due in large part to exceedingly high rates of unemployment and incarceration among young males, thus making them poor marriage prospects (Ellwood, 1988). This has left African-American women with little option but to become single parents. In turn, this has resulted in high rates of poverty with its attendant negative consequences for a large segment of the African-American population in the United States.

Booker T. Washington

Education

Many African Americans, particularly the poor, have been marginally educated in inner-city public schools. Some have not profited sufficiently from their educational experiences because of learning problems related to poor nutrition, inadequate prenatal and postnatal medical care, stressed parents, disorganized environments, and low expectations for educational achievement on the part of teachers (McAdoo, 1987) and on the part of the inner-city African-American community and the children's peers due to the influence of an "oppositional" cultural frame characteristic of "involuntary" minorities (Ogbu, 1994).

According to Ogbu (1994), members of "voluntary" immigrant groups—such as Asian Americans, West Indians, or Punjabis—are able to overcome their school difficulties after a reasonable period of time in the United States because their families and ethnic communities reinforce school learning as critical to their advancement and success in the world of work. However, "involuntary" minorities (e.g., those with a history of enslavement, conquest, or colonization, such as African Americans and American Indians) have shown a tendency to develop values and behavioral styles "in opposition" to the mainstream to assert their separate social identities and maintain boundaries. Among the poor in these groups, school learning often has been seen as learning the culture and language of whites—their traditional enemy and oppressor. Specifically in the black ghettos, school learning is often considered an act of Uncle Tomism or of disloyalty to the black cause or as a foolish way to spend one's energies, since those who successfully learn may not be given an opportunity for advancement in the job market. Under these negative conditions, school learning often has been rejected in favor of acceptance by and popularity within one's peer group.

Despite the preceding limitations, which are considerable, African Americans as a group have made good educational progress in terms of high school completion rate. In 1991, two thirds (67 percent) of those 25 years of age and older had a high school diploma, compared to 80 percent of whites—a rate substantially higher than in 1980. If the current rate of educational progress is maintained, black Americans will achieve parity with whites in terms of high school completion rate by the year 2000 (Dewart, 1991, p. 190).

Even in terms of college completion rates, progress was good up to 1980, as the proportion of black college graduates doubled from 1960 to 1970 and again from 1970 to 1980. However, governmental policies that greatly restricted postsecondary financial aid in the 1980s and early 1990s have hampered further progress in this area. Black Americans also remain significantly underrepresented in graduate education.

Housing
Considering that the first federal law against housing discrimination was not passed until 1968, the United States has made steady though slow progress in terms of housing integration. However, even though many African Americans and Euro Americans now work together and have lunch together, most still head for separate residential worlds at the end of the work day (Gelman, Springen, Brailsford, & Miller, 1988).

African Americans remain highly segregated residentially. Due to continuing discrimination, many remain concentrated in the least desirable neighborhoods of central cities as well as in separate and unequal suburbs where many overpay for substandard housing. In 1990, 30 percent still lived in neighborhoods that were at least 90 percent black, down slightly from 34 percent in 1980 (Doig, 1991). Some real estate agents hinder the housing integration process by illegally channeling people of color to black or integrated neighborhoods, instead of showing them properties in "white" areas.

Participation in the Political Process
The number of public officials who are African American has grown significantly in the past decade. Specifically, the United States now has various high government officials who are African American, including U.S. cabinet members, governors, representatives to the U.S. Congress, large-city mayors, state legislators, and judges. However, this social group still remains underrepresented among the nation's elected officials, particularly at top levels. For example, in 1993, there was only one African-American U.S. Senator out of the 100 U.S. senators, and only 8 percent of U.S. Representatives were black (U.S. Bureau of the Census, 1994, p. 281).

Criminal Justice System
Even though African Americans constitute 12 percent of the U.S. population, they make up nearly half (47.3 percent) of the state prison inmates (U.S. Bureau of the Census, 1994, p. 215). Black Americans are also twice as likely as whites to be victims of robbery, vehicle theft, and aggravated assault, and six to seven

times more likely to be victims of homicide (Jaynes & Williams, 1989). In part, the African-American overinvolvement with crime and violence may stem from the frustrations, stresses, and anger associated with an inability to make a decent living through legal means. However, another reason for their overrepresentation in jails and prisons is discrimination, which, as previously noted, causes poor people, particularly those that are not white, to be more frequently arrested and convicted, and to be sentenced to longer prison terms than whites committing similar crimes.

Latinos

The 1990 census counted 22.4 million Latinos living in the United States, comprising 9 percent of the population—up substantially from 14.6 million in 1980 (U.S. Bureau of the Census, 1993b). There are likely to be several million more Latinos who eluded the 1990 census workers because they were undocumented. The tremendous increase in the Latino population has been due to continuous migration combined with high fertility among some groups. If the present rate of growth continues, Latinos will replace African Americans by about the year 2010, perhaps even earlier, as the nation's largest racial/ethnic minority group (U.S. Bureau of the Census, 1993b).

Why do so many Latin Americans choose to come to the United States? Many are attracted to this country because of its high standard of living. The living conditions of U.S. central cities and even the inner cities look affluent to some Latinos in comparison to the conditions the poor must endure in most of Latin America.

Mexican Americans, Mainland
Puerto Ricans, and Cuban Americans
As noted in Chapter 2, Latinos come from over 20 different countries in Central and South America and the Caribbean basin. The three largest groups in the United States in 1990 were Mexican Americans (64 percent), mainland

Puerto Ricans (10.5 percent), and Cuban Americans (4.9 percent) (U.S. Bureau of the Census, 1991) (see Figure 4.2). Included under the Latino designation are individuals whose ancestors have lived in the United States for centuries, as well as others who have recently come to our shores; professionals and entrepreneurs along with migrant farm laborers and unskilled factory workers; whites, blacks, mulattos, and mestizos; U.S. citizens and illegal aliens; and those who came searching for a better economic future as well as those who were running away from political persecution in their own countries (Portes & Truelove, 1987, p. 360). Given such a widely disparate population, any generalization about this group is bound to be misleading.

Although there are Latinos living in every state of the union, the highest concentrations reside in California, Texas, New York, and Florida. About 90 percent are urban residents (compared to 76 percent of the U.S. population), with a majority living in central cities (U.S. Bureau of the Census, 1993b). Each major Latino group occupies a different geographic area. The vast majority of Mexican Americans

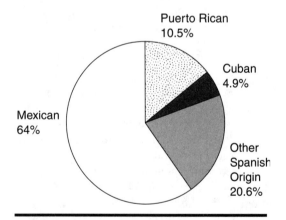

FIGURE 4.2   Percentage Distribution of Hispanic Americans by Type of Spanish Origin (1990 Census)

Source: "The Hispanic Population in the United States: March 1990" by U.S. Bureau of the Census, Current Population Reports, Series P-20, No. 449, 1991. Washington, DC: U.S. Government Printing Office.

live in the Southwest, particularly in California (Los Angeles has the largest concentration of any city in the nation), Texas, Arizona, Colorado, and New Mexico. In addition, there are large numbers of Mexican Americans in the Midwest, with the city of Chicago having the second largest concentration after Los Angeles (Martinez, 1988). Most mainland Puerto Ricans are concentrated in New York (particularly New York City) and New Jersey (Ramos-McKay, Comas-Diaz, & Rivera, 1988). The majority of Cuban Americans reside in southern Florida, principally in Miami (Queralt, 1984).

The ancestors of some Mexican Americans always lived in the Southwest, which was Mexican territory until it was lost to the United States in the Mexican-American War of 1848. Many Mexican Americans living in the Southwest lost their lands to early Spanish conquistadors and colonists, and later to other white Europeans moving into the area. The first wave of Mexican immigrants, as opposed to those who were native to the Southwest, came after the Mexican revolution of 1910. This original group of newcomers included middle-class and upper-class refugees from the revolution as well as manual laborers looking for better economic

opportunities. Some of the more recent arrivals, many of low socioeconomic origins and limited education, have entered illegally and have become important sources of low-wage labor.

As noted in the previous chapter, because Mexican Americans are concentrated in the Southwest, they have benefited from better job opportunities available for less-skilled workers in that area of the United States, compared to other areas where employment opportunities for blue-collar workers have been shrinking, such as the snowbelt. They also have been less reliant than mainland Puerto Ricans upon central-city employment and more dependent on suburban employment—another segment of the economy that has been growing. In good part, it is for these reasons that Mexican-origin families have a high rate of employment and a low rate of welfare dependency. However, a high proportion are poor because they hold very low-wage jobs due to competition from other immigrants in the areas in which most live, particularly competition from illegal aliens who provide the cheapest source of labor (Cuciti & Franklin, 1990; Aponte, 1991).

Large numbers of Puerto Ricans migrated to the United States in the years between the end of World War II and 1964 because of limited job opportunities on the island of Puerto Rico. They settled mainly in New York City and New Jersey, where many became employed in the garment industry and as service workers. Because they had U.S. citizenship, they were initially better able to enter higher-paying, highly unionized labor markets than most other immigrants from Latin America. However, employer preferences in the Northeast gradually shifted toward less-expensive newcomers and illegals, such as Salvadorans and Dominicans. Also, many industries closed, downsized, or moved elsewhere, leaving behind a large proportion of mainland Puerto Ricans to experience high levels of unemployment and poverty (Bean & Tienda, 1987; Portes & Truelove, 1987; Cuciti & Franklin, 1990; Rodriguez, 1992).

Today, the socioeconomic situation of Puerto Ricans in New York has become as precarious or more precarious than that of African Americans (Tienda, 1989). The high level of residential segregation experienced by this group, surpassed only by that of African Americans, further contributes to their deteriorating social situation, as housing barriers prevent many from access to quality schools and better job opportunities (Santiago, 1992, p. 109).

Most Cuban Americans are recent immigrants, having come to the United States as refugees after the 1959 communist takeover of Cuba. Many are white, relatively well-educated, middle-class persons of Iberian Spanish extraction displaced by Castro's revolution, although refugees arriving after the 1970s have belonged to increasingly lower socioeconomic classes (Queralt, 1984). Officially classified as refugees from communism, they have traditionally received government aid during their initial period of entry to the United States. In addition, after the first decade of migration, as a large south Florida–Cuban community became established, a good number of new refugees were able to obtain employment within the Cuban community. Therefore, many were able to put their knowledge and expertise to work immediately upon arrival rather than having to remain unemployed or to work at menial jobs until they were reasonably adapted and able to speak English. Few other Latin American immigrants have had these advantages.

On average, the socioeconomic status of Latinos in the United States is substantially inferior to that of the U.S. population. As this section will show, a disproportionate number suffer high levels of poverty, very low wages, and substandard housing. In addition, their educational attainment is lower than that of African Americans. Those Latino groups with large numbers of people of color, such as mainland Puerto Ricans, face levels of oppression similar to those suffered by African Americans. However, groups that are predominantly white, such as Cuban Americans, fare much better, though they are not exempt from prejudice and discrimination.

Despite the disadvantages they confront, Latinos in the United States may be doing better than expected in a number of areas. For example, using 50 years of U.S. Census data, Hayes-Bautista and associates at the Chicano Studies Research Center (1992) found that Latinos in California, while they have the fewest years of education and the highest rates of poverty of any group in California (including "Anglos," African Americans, and Asians), had the highest labor-force participation rate, the lowest rate of participation in welfare programs, and the highest proportion of married-couple families with children. They also found that, compared to "Anglos" and African Americans, Latinos in California had a longer life expectancy at birth, the lowest proportion of low-birthweight babies, the lowest infant mortality rate, and the fewest babies damaged by drugs. Latino women, in particular, were found to smoke, drink, and use drugs the least when compared to women and men in any of the comparison groups. The reasons for these advantages are not clear. Hayes-Bautista suggested that they may be due in part to cultural values, such as the emphasis on respect, family, and spirituality. But other ethnic minority groups have similar cultural values. Another possible hypothesis is that people who migrate from one country to another in search of a better life are a selective group that may be physically healthier. But other racial/ethnic groups are also composed of immigrants. Research is needed to confirm and clarify these unusual findings.

Employment and Income

Despite the fact that 80 percent of Latino men in the United States participate in the U.S. labor force, compared to 75 percent of non-Latin white men, they have higher unemployment and much lower income because many can only hold nonskilled jobs that are not a stable source of income and that pay meager wages (Poverty takes its toll on U.S. Hispanics, 1993). Newly arrived immigrants and refugees are easy targets for exploitive employers because, in the immigrants' need to survive and eagerness to get ahead, they are willing to take the dirtiest and most hazardous jobs at the lowest wages.

In 1992, 11.4 percent of Latinos 16 years of age or older were unemployed, compared to 6.5 percent of non-Latin whites (U.S. Bureau of the Census, 1993a). Unemployment rates were highest among mainland Puerto Ricans and lowest among Cuban Americans. In 1992, the largest proportion of Latinos were employed as factory operators, manual laborers, craft and repair workers, and in low-paying service occupations. In contrast, except for Cuban Americans who have a large professional class, their participation in professional or managerial occupations was substantially lower than that of non-Latin whites (U.S. Bureau of the Census, 1993b).

The 1990 median family income for Latinos was 62 percent of the median family income for white non-Latin families ($25,394 versus $40,370) (See Table 4.2). Family incomes are particularly low for mainland Puerto Rican and Mexican-American families. For example, in 1989, the median income for mainland Puerto

Rican families was $19,900 and for Mexican-American families $22,200, as opposed to $31,300 for Cuban-American families (U.S. Bureau of the Census, 1991). This low family income was reduced even further by the high cost of living in urban areas as well as by a large family size in the case of mainland Puerto Ricans and Mexican Americans (Estrada, 1987).

Poverty Rate, Family Composition, and Housing

A larger proportion of U.S. Latinos are poor today than the proportion who were poor 15 years ago. Specifically, in 1978, the poverty rate for Latinos in the United States was 21.6 percent (Cuciti & Franklin, 1990). In contrast, in 1993, 30.6 percent of Latinos were poor, compared to 12.2 percent of whites (DeParle, 1994; Zaldivar, 1994). Among the three large groups of Latinos, the highest rates of poverty were suffered by mainland Puerto Ricans and Mexican Americans. The situation of Latino children is even more serious. In 1990, 31.4 percent of Latino children under age 18 were poor, compared to 15.9 percent of white children. (See Table 3.2 in Chapter 3.) Given the aggregate data available from the Bureau of the Census at present, it is not possible to tell whether the increasing poverty rate among Latinos is primarily indicative of increasing economic need among established residents or reflective of increasing numbers of impoverished recent immigrants and refugees.

Despite considerable poverty, the Spanish-origin population (except for mainland Puerto Ricans) has a fairly high level of two-parent families. Specifically, in 1990, 72 percent of Mexican-American families and 77 percent of Cuban-American families were married-couple families, compared to 79.9 percent of non-Latin white families and 57 percent of mainland Puerto Rican families (U.S. Bureau of the Census, 1991, and 1992). However, the proportion of female-headed families has been increasing among Latinos at a faster pace than among non-Latin whites. As you can see in Table 4.2, when the 1990 census was taken, 27 percent of Latino children under age 18 lived with their mothers only (up from 19.8 percent in 1980), compared to 16 percent of white children (U.S. Bureau of the Census, 1993d). Possible reasons for the increase in female-headed families among Latinos include increases in the rate of divorce and separation, in the rate of unwed parenthood, and in the number of Latin American women migrating to the United States without husbands (perhaps because they hear that it is easier for women than for men without job skills to find employment, usually as domestic workers).

Substandard housing is another problem afflicting recent immigrants and refugees and Latino groups with large proportions of poor people (e.g., mainland Puerto Ricans and Mexican Americans), particularly those who cannot afford to live anywhere but in old, deteriorated areas of central cities. Some of these Spanish-speaking barrios, or poor neighborhoods in large central cities (e.g., Los Angeles, New York, Miami, Union City, and San Antonio), have become ghettoized.

Education

Latinos made modest educational gains during the 1980s, despite the masses of poor and uneducated refugees and immigrants that came to the United States from Latin America during the last decade. By 1990, 50.8 percent (about one-half) of those 25 years of age or older had completed four years of high school or more, ranging from 44 percent of Mexican Americans, 55 percent of mainland Puerto Ricans, and 63.5 percent of Cuban Americans, compared to 80 percent of non-Latin whites. About 9 percent had completed four of more years of college, ranging from 5.4 percent of Mexican Americans, 9.7 percent of mainland Puerto Ricans, and 20.2 percent of Cuban Americans, compared to 22.2 percent of non-Latin whites (U.S. Bureau of the Census, 1991).

Although U.S. Latinos have made some educational progress throughout the years, their educational levels remain low compared to African Americans. The majority (about 56 percent) are considered to be functionally illiterate in English, compared to 44 percent of African Americans and 16 percent of whites (Anderson, 1990). They also have the highest proportion of youngsters of high school age not enrolled in school of any of the major U.S. non-dominant groups. In 1992, 35.3 percent of Latino youths of high school age were out of school—nearly three times the rate for African Americans (U.S. Bureau of the Census, 1990a, p. 150; Poverty takes its toll on U.S. Hispanics, 1993). Although these youths, mostly between the ages of 16 and 18, are officially classified as "dropouts," it is likely that many never enrolled in school when they migrated to the United States because they began to work to help support their families.

Participation in the Political Process

An extension of the Voting Rights Act of 1975 mandated the use of bilingual ballots for elections held in cities with a large language minority, but this law does not affect municipalities with smaller numbers of non-English-speaking residents. This means that some Latinos, including a large proportion of the Latino elderly, and other racial and ethnic groups who do not speak English, are unable to participate in elections because the ballots are not available in their native language in their communities.

Despite the limitations noted above, the number of Latinos elected to public office has grown in the past decade. As in the case of African Americans, there are now various Latino representatives to the U.S. Congress, U.S. cabinet members, city mayors, state legislators, and judges. However, this social group continues to be significantly underrepresented, particularly at high levels. For example, in 1993, there was no U.S. Senator of Spanish origin and only 3 percent of U.S. Representatives were

TABLE 4.2   Summary of Social and Economic Characteristics of the Hispanic Origin* versus the White** Population in the U.S. According to the 1990 Census

SOCIAL AND ECONOMIC CHARACTERISTICS	PERCENT WHITES	PERCENT HISPANIC ORIGIN
Married-couple families w/children under 18 as % of all households	25.7	35.5
Children living with both parents	79.0	67.0
Children living with mother only	16.0	27.0
Female-headed families w/children under 18 as % of all households	4.7	11.6
Educational Attainment (Ages 25 and over)		
4 years of high school or more	79.8	50.2
4 years of college or more	24.4	9.4
Below Poverty level:		
individuals	10.7	28.1
Families	6.2	22.0
Married-Couple Families with children under 18	4.3	17.4
Female-headed families with children under 18	32.9	54.5
Children under 18 years	15.9	31.4
Individuals 65 and over	10.1	23.5
Unemployment Rate (Ages 16 and over)	4.7	8.0
The following figures are in dollars:		
Family median income	$40,370	$25,394
Median Income for Female-headed families with children under 18	$16,255	$9,636
Per capita income	$17,307	$8,506

Sources: Data taken from "1990 Census of Population, Social and Economic Characteristics, United States" (1990 CP-2-1) by U.S. Bureau of the Census, 1994. Washington, DC: U.S. Government Printing Office. "Geographic Profile of Employment and Unemployment, 1990" by U.S. Bureau of the Census, 1991. Washington, DC: U.S. Government Printing Office. "Poverty in the United States: 1990 Current Population Reports Series P-60, No. 175" by U.S. Bureau of the Census, 1991. Washington, DC: U.S. Government Printing Office. "Statistical Abstract of the United States: 1993" by U.S. Bureau of the Census, 1994. Washington, DC: U.S. Government Printing Office.

*"Hispanic Origin" is used by the Census to refer to people of Latin American or Iberian Origin.

**People of any background (including Hispanics) who are Caucasian.

Latinos (U.S. Bureau of the Census, 1994, p. 281).

Asian Americans

Many Asians came to the United States during the 1980s, making this diverse racial/ethnic group the fastest-growing nondominant group in the nation. Specifically, between 1980 and 1990, the U.S. Asian population almost doubled in number, from 3.8 million to 7.2 million, representing about 3 percent of the U.S. population. The increase was largely due to the migration of people from mainland China, Taiwan, Hong Kong, Vietnam, Cambodia, Laos, the Philippines, Japan, South Korea, Micronesia, and the Indian subcontinent (Barringer, 1990; Stone & Castaneda, 1991). So many Asians were able to enter the United States in the 1980s because a large proportion had refugee status and therefore came outside the immigration quota of 20,000 persons per country per year.

Many Asian Americans are driven by a strong work ethic and a great reverence for learning. They are a highly communal people who often pool their resources for housing and other needs with relatives, particularly during their initial years in the United States. In large part, these three factors—hard work, high motivation to learn, and interdependence—account for their accomplishments. In addition, a substantial proportion of those who came to the United States during the 1980s had high professional and educational qualifications, including many with college degrees and career experience. Well educated and hard working, they are generally known as America's "model minority." However, it would be a mistake to assume that Asian Americans are uniformly successful. They also suffer problems of underemployment, poverty, discrimination, and acculturation, particularly the refugees from Southeast Asia (Patel, 1988; Chua-Eoan, 1990).

Despite their consistently good performance in the United States (see Table 4.3 for details about their social and economic characteristics), few immigrant groups were subjected to as much discrimination as the Asians in the early years of their migration. For many years, they were forbidden from entering the United States and were not allowed to become U.S. citizens, to marry persons of other races, or to use public facilities. Some of these constraints were not removed until the 1960s (Kitano, 1987).

The three largest Asian groups in the United States today are the Chinese, Filipino, and Japanese.

Chinese

The Chinese are the largest Asian group in the United States. The first wave of Chinese immigrants came in the 1800s, looking for better economic opportunities. Many found jobs building railroads and in mines and farms. Eventually, whites developed considerable hostility against them, particularly during difficult economic times, because they were willing to work hard for low wages. (The harsh treatment the Chinese received in their early period in the United States is reflected in the still-common expression, "not a Chinaman's chance," indicating that they were prevented as much as possible from attaining success [Brieland, Costin, & Atherton, 1985, p. 199].) The anti-Chinese sentiment grew so strong that they were barred from entering the United States from 1881 until 1943. After the Immigration Act of 1965, which widened the yearly quota of immigrants to 20,000 persons from each country, many well-educated Chinese, particularly from Hong Kong and Taiwan, once again began to migrate to the United States (Kitano, 1987).

Chinese Americans, on average, are doing quite well socially and economically. For example, they exceed the record of the total U.S. population in terms of high school and college completion rate, percentage of married-couple families, and median family income. In addition, compared to the total U.S. population, they have a lower level of unemployment and of female-headed households (U.S. Bureau of the Census, 1990a, p. 39). However, their poverty level is slightly higher than that of the total U.S. population because, unlike the Japanese, they have a large underprivileged class, mostly segregated in the Chinatowns of major U.S. cities. In these Chinese ghettos, wages are low, few people speak English well, and housing tends to be inadequate and overcrowded.

Filipino

The Filipino are the second largest Asian group in the United States. They were able to enter this

TABLE 4.3   Social and Economic Characteristics of the U.S. Asian/Pacific Population versus the White* Population in the U.S. According to the 1990 Census

SOCIAL AND ECONOMIC CHARACTERISTICS	PERCENT WHITES	PERCENT ASIAN/ PACIFIC ISLANDER
Married-couple families w/children under 18 as % of all households	25.7	39.2
Children living with both parents	79.0	81.2
Children living with mother only	16.0	12.2
Female-headed families w/children under 18 as % of all households	4.7	4.8
Educational Attainment (Ages 25 and over)		
4 years of high school or more	79.8	77.6
4 years of college or more	24.4	36.9
Below Poverty level:		
individuals	10.7	14.3
Families	6.2	11.7
Married-Couple Families with children under 18	4.3	10.9
Female-headed families with children under 18	32.9	35.6
Children under 18 years	15.9	17.0
Individuals 65 and over	10.1	12.1
Unemployment Rate (Ages 16 and over)	4.7	5.5**
The following figures are in dollars:		
Family median income	$40,370	41,258
Median Income for Female-headed families with children under 18	$16,255	$15,912
Per capita income	$17,307	$13,624

Sources: Data taken from "1990 Census of Population, Social and Economic Characteristics, United States" (1990 CP-2-1) by U.S. Bureau of the Census, 1994. Washington, DC: U.S. Government Printing Office. "Geographic Profile of Employment and Unemployment, 1990" by U.S. Bureau of the Census, 1991. Washington, DC: U.S. Government Printing Office. "Poverty in the United States: 1990 Current Population Reports Series P-60, No. 175" by U.S. Bureau of the Census, 1991. Washington, DC: U.S. Government Printing Office. "We the American ...Asians" (WE-3) by U.S. Bureau of the Census, 1993. Washington, DC: U.S. Government Printing Office. "Statistical Abstract of the United States: 1993" by U.S. Bureau of the Census, 1994. Washington, DC: U.S. Government Printing Office.

*Caucasians of any ethnic background.

**Asian only.

country freely during the years that the Phillipine Islands belonged to the United States. In those years, many came to work for Hawaiian plantations and in the agricultural fields of California. Others came to study at U.S. colleges and universities. The immigrants who have come after the Immigration Act of 1965 are mostly young professionals and technicians in occupational fields where there is a shortage of personnel in the United States. Because of this selective migration, the U.S. Filipino, on average, are doing better socially and economically than the U.S. population (U.S. Bureau of the Census, 1990a, p. 39).

Japanese

Perhaps the darkest chapter in the history of Japanese Americans took place after the Japanese attack on Pearl Harbor during World War II. As a result, 110,000 Japanese—mostly U.S.-born citizens of Japanese origin—were forced to sell their properties and were detained in relocation camps. This action on the part of the U.S. government was particularly oppressive because other Americans of German or Italian descent were not segregated and detained during the war, even though Germany and Italy, like Japan, were at war with the United States. It took until the late 1980s for the U.S. government to officially apologize for this act of oppression and to provide some financial compensation to the evacuees.

Today, the Japanese constitute the third largest Asian group in the United States. Some refer to them as America's "most successful minority." To be sure, their socioeconomic record is impressive. Japanese Americans are firmly established in the fields of banking, commerce, finance, real estate, medicine, and engineering. On average, they are doing better than the total U.S. population in terms of high school completion rate, college completion rate, percent of married-couple families, and median family income. In addition, compared to the total U.S. population, they have lower levels of unemployment, single parenthood, female-headed households, and poverty (U.S. Bureau of the Census, 1990a, p. 39). In fact, their visible success has triggered a backlash largely based on jealousy and resentment, generally referred to as *Japan bashing.*

Other East Asian Groups in the United States: Koreans and Southeast Asians

Most Koreans came to the United States after the Korean War and after passage of the Immigration Act of 1965. As a group, they are predominantly urban, highly educated, and middle class. Consequently, like the Japanese, Chinese, and Filipino in the United States, on average, they are doing well socially and economically.

Most of the Indochinese or Southeast Asians—those primarily from Vietnam, Cambodia, and Laos—came to the United States as refugees from wars, dictatorships, natural disasters, and communist regimes (Kitano, 1987). Although the Bureau of the Census has not provided separate statistics for these groups, it is known that their situation in this country is not at all like that of the previously mentioned Asian groups. For example, the majority of recent Vietnamese, Chinese-Vietnamese, Laotian, Cambodian, and Hmong refugees have incomes below the poverty line and a high welfare dependency rate (U.S. Bureau of the Census, 1990a, p. 39; Chua-Eoan, 1990; Rumbaut, 1991, p. 228).

Native Americans

In the fifteenth century, when Columbus and other European explorers found their way to America, there were many Native Americans living in the area that later became known as the United States. The white European invaders and settlers took the natives' lands and killed many of them. The Europeans' ruthless behavior had disastrous effects on the American Natives, and the diseases brought from Europe proved fatal for many of the native people who had developed no immunity for such diseases. Demoralized and highly reluctant to join the invading society, Native Americans developed a persistent state of anomie that tragically affected their well-being for centuries thereafter (Jones, Gallagher, & McFalls, 1988, p. 323). To this day, they remain one of the most disadvantaged groups in the United States in terms of income, education, and standard of living (Locke, 1992).

On top of the experience of being conquered and dispossessed, American Indians have also suffered due to various misguided policies of the federal government. These include the old practice of removing Indian children from their families and reservations at very young ages and forcing them to attend boarding schools established by the federal government to "help" them become "assimilated" into the mainstream. The old policy of the Bureau of Indian Affairs of relocating the unemployed from reservations to urban areas to "help" them find employment was also harmful. It uprooted people from their familiar environment, weakened their ties to the extended family, and left them isolated in unfamiliar urban settings, where many became chronically dependent on government welfare programs (Blanchard, 1987).

The American-Indian population is small, representing less than 1 percent of the population, but it is one of the fastest growing groups in the United States (Locke, 1992). In 1990, the U.S. census counted 1.9 million American Indians living in the United States, up from 1.4 million in 1980 (John, 1988; Stone & Castaneda, 1991). This population growth has been due in part to a high birth rate and in part to the increasing willingness of individuals of mixed heritage to identify themselves as American Indian, probably because of rediscovered roots and increased ethnic pride. Nowadays, approximately half of American Indians live in rural areas, with half of this group (one-fourth of Native Americans) residing on over 200 reservations. No other racial/ethnic group in the United States has a higher incidence of rural residence. The remainder live in urban areas. Nearly half of all American Indians (47 percent) are concentrated in four states—California, Oklahoma, Arizona, and New Mexico. More than 50 percent are currently married to non-Indians (Blanchard, 1987; Red Horse, 1988; John, 1988; Thomason, 1991; Locke, 1992).

Although the social and economic status of Native Americans has improved considerably since the 1960s, they remain burdened with many problems. As shown in Table 4.4, a reasonable percentage of those 25 years of age and over have a high school diploma, compared to whites (71 percent vs. 80 percent). However,

their education is often deficient, in part due to the underfinancing and poor staffing of reservation and other rural and central-city schools and in part due to the influence of an "oppositional" cultural frame characteristic of "involuntary" minorities that has discouraged them from learning the "white man's" knowledge (Ogbu, 1994).

At the time of the 1990 census, 41 percent of American-Indian males 16 years of age and older were either unemployed or not part of the labor force, compared to 28 percent of white males. Only black males had a slightly higher rate (42 percent) of joblessness (U.S. Bureau of the Census, 1993e). As shown in Table 4.4, the median family and per capita income of American Indians in 1990 was about 50 percent that of U.S. whites, and their poverty rate was more than twice that of the white population. Their arrest rate is considered to be 10 times higher than that of whites and 3 times higher than that of blacks. Their rates of alcoholism and suicide are the highest in the nation (John, 1988; Heinrich, Corbine, & Thomas, 1990; Locke, 1992; Rubin, 1992b). The social and economic circumstances of American Indians living on reservations in 1990 were particularly bleak (Indian Health Service, 1994).

American Jews

The first group of Jewish immigrants—the **Sephardim**—came to various countries on the American continent from Spain and Portugal. Prior to the Inquisition, they were doing quite well in Spain and Portugal, having attained more freedom, wealth, and power there than anywhere else in Europe. In fact, they were affluent enough to help finance the explorations of Columbus in the New World. The situation changed suddenly in 1492 when King Ferdinand and Queen Isabella of Spain ordered the Jews to convert to the Catholic faith or leave. Some converted or pretended to convert. Others fled to the eastern Mediterranean. A few came to America (Bennet, 1988).

TABLE 4.4   Summary of Social and Economic Characteristics of the American Indian*
versus the White* Population in the U.S. According to the 1990 Census

SOCIAL AND ECONOMIC CHARACTERISTICS	PERCENT WHITES	PERCENT AMERICAN INDIANS
Married-couple families w/children under 18 as % of all households	25.7	28.1
Children living with both parents	79.0	55.4
Children living with mother only	16.0	n/a
Female-headed families w/children under 18 as % of all households	4.7	13.3
Educational Attainment (Ages 25 and over)		
4 years of high school or more	79.8	70.6
4 years of college or more	24.4	11.7
Below Poverty level:		
individuals	10.7	26.3
Families	6.2	22.8
Married-Couple Families with children under 18	4.3	15.4
Female-headed families with children under 18	32.9	54.8
Children under 18 years	15.9	34.0
Individuals 65 and over	10.1	21.6
Unemployment Rate (Ages 16 and over)	4.7	8.0
The following figures are in dollars:		
Family median income	$40,370	$24,798
Median Income for Female-headed families with children under 18	$16,255	$9,183
Per capita income	$17,307	9,685

Sources: Data taken from "1990 Census of Population, Social and Economic Characteristics, United States" (1990 CP-2-1) by U.S. Bureau of the Census, 1994. Washington, DC: U.S. Government Printing Office. "Geographic Profile of Employment and Unemployment, 1990" by U.S. Bureau of the Census, 1991. Washington, DC: U.S. Government Printing Office. "Poverty in the United States: 1990 Current Population Reports Series P-60, No. 175" by U.S. Bureau of the Census, 1991. Washington, DC: U.S. Government Printing Office. "Statistical Abstract of the United States: 1993" by U.S. Bureau of the Census, 1994. Washington, DC: U.S. Government Printing Office. U.S. Bureau of the Census (1994). 1990 Census of Population. Characteristics of American Indians by Tribe and Language (1990 CP-3-7) Washington, DC: Government Printing Office.

*"American Indian" and "white" are terms used by the Census to refer to people who identify themselves as Caucasian or Native American.

Much after the initial group of Sephardic Jews migrated to various countries in the American continent, the **Ashkenazim** (i.e., those from Central and Eastern Europe) began to arrive, initially from Germany. By the late nineteenth century, German Jews predomi- nated among Jews in the United States. Then, between the late nineteenth century and the beginning of World War I, the third and largest group of Jewish immigrants, also Ashkenaz- ims, arrived from Eastern Europe, particularly from Russia, where Jews were the victims of

Russification (i.e., the attempt to protect Russia from "foreign" influences) and of peasant massacres, or pogroms.

Unlike earlier Jewish immigrants, many of whom had money and were well educated, most of the people in this third wave of immigration were economically destitute and had little education (50 percent could not read or write) and peasant manners. This wave of Eastern European Jewish immigrants spoke Yiddish—a European folk dialect that was looked down upon by the more refined Jews who preferred to use the language of their countries of origin or classical Hebrew (Sowell, 1981). Most of the Eastern European Jews started their lives in the United States doing manual labor, particularly in the sweatshops maintained by the garment industry. They lived together in overcrowded ghettos because of the need for kosher foods, a synagogue to practice their Orthodox religion, and employers that would allow them to observe the Sabbath.

Still another major wave of Jewish immigration came to the United States when they were forced to flee Europe to escape Nazi persecution and concentration camps. This migration wave included a greater proportion of well-educated persons who belonged to higher socioeconomic classes.

Today, American Jews represent about 2.6 percent of the U.S. population. As a group, they are doing very well socioeconomically. Indeed, they reportedly have the highest family income of any major ethnic group in the U.S. society. However, despite greatly exaggerated claims that Jews control the nation's businesses, banks, and finance centers, very few occupy top executive positions or top positions of political power. Most American Jews are middle class (Bennett, 1988).

Women

Of the total U.S. population of 248.7 million according to the 1990 census, 127.4 million, or 51 percent, were women (U.S. Bureau of the Census, 1994). Despite their numerical majority, women have traditionally had low status in the society compared to men; therefore, women constitute the nation's largest nondominant group. Women's inequality resulted in large part from their small physical size and lesser strength, compared to men, as well as from their reproductive and nursing functions, which, in the past, kept them busy bearing and raising children for most of their fertile years due to the lack of contraception and high level of infant mortality. Although in past times these differences between men and women were decisive in determining sex roles, they are of little or no consequence today.

Women have made considerable progress in their quest for equality. Fifty-eight percent were part of the labor force in 1993 (compared to 75.2 percent of males), up from 38 percent in 1960 (U.S. Bureau of the Census, 1994). They are now entering many formerly male occupations, and the number serving in elected positions at local communities has more than tripled since 1975 (Wallis, 1989, p. 82). To be sure, women have achieved substantial gains in the past few years, but they are still far from attaining parity with men. This section will examine their current situation.

Legal Status

Legislation has helped women to make inroads toward equality with men, but its impact has been limited. For instance, the Civil Rights Act of 1964 prohibited racial and gender discrimination; yet, in spite of it, much discrimination still exists. The Equal Pay Act of 1963 prohibited the payment of different wages to men and women for the same jobs; yet, notwithstanding this law, women's earnings continue to be significantly lower than men's.

The Equal Employment Opportunity Act of 1964 prohibited job discrimination on the basis of race, national origin, gender, or religion. Through its enforcement arm, the Equal Employment Opportunity Commission (EEOC), which administers affirmative action programs,

Look guys...Why don't we just say that all men are created equal...and let the little ladies look out for themselves?

Source: Reprinted by permission, Tribune Media Services.

this law has removed many employment barriers for women, African Americans, and other nondominant groups. However, since the 1980s, its enforcement has become more lax. Similarly, although the Equal Credit Opportunity Act of 1977 prohibits credit discrimination on the basis of gender, many women remain unable to get credit due to limited income or limited employment experience. Another problem women face that complicates their credit situation after divorce is the lack of a credit record under their name rather than under their husband's name.

Women still lack constitutional assurance of equal rights. The Equal Rights Amendment (ERA) to the Constitution, passed by Congress in 1972 and sent to the states for ratification, would have eliminated all the remaining discriminatory state, federal, or municipal laws and regulations on the books. However, when it was finally put to a vote by the states 10 years later (in 1982), it was defeated because it fell 3 states short of the 38 needed for ratification. Apparently, many men and women in 1982 still believed that equal rights would be more detrimental than beneficial to women!

Political Participation

Women did not attain the right to vote until passage of the Nineteenth Amendment to the Con-

stitution in 1920. Considering their late arrival into the political arena, they have made reasonable progress in local and state politics. However, their current share of national elective positions is very inadequate. For example, in 1993, women constituted only 11 percent of U.S. Representatives and 7 percent of U.S. Senators (U.S. Bureau of the Census, 1994, p. 281). This is a "token" level of representation for the largest social group in the nation.

Education

As to educational attainment, the records of young men and women ages 25 to 29 are equal in terms of high school and college completion. Specifically, in 1991, 80 percent of young men and women were high school graduates and 23 percent had completed four or more years of college (U.S. Bureau of the Census, 1993a). However, there is still a gender difference in doctoral education; in 1991, women received only 37 percent of the U.S. doctorates awarded that year (U.S. Bureau of the Census, 1994, p. 190).

Income and Employment

Since the 1950s, U.S. women have been entering the work force in increasing numbers. Specifically, in 1950, only about one-third worked outside the home; by 1993, 58 percent of all women 16 years of age and over were part of the civilian labor force, versus 75 percent of males. Among young women, the proportion who work is much higher. For example, in 1992, about 68 percent of families with school-age children had a mother employed outside the home. Among families with preschoolers, 53 percent had mothers employed outside the home (U.S. Bureau of the Census, 1993a, 1994). Even among mothers with babies, in 1990, 53 percent were returning to work within one year of the child's birth (Chira, 1994).

Women have entered the "elite" professions and they play a significant role in the world of business as company executives and entrepreneurs. They now hold blue-collar jobs once considered taboo for females, such as truck driving, auto mechanics, and carpentry. They are making headway through the military, the police, the FBI, and other bastions of male dominance. The income they bring home is seldom discretionary anymore—in most cases, it is needed as much as the man's to cover family expenses. This is because men's earnings in the past 20 years or so have been losing ground when measured in constant dollars, so the women's wages have become necessary to support the family (Rubin, 1992a, 1992b).

Income and employment discrimination against women are substantial and take many forms (see Figure 4.3). On average, they receive lower pay than men, are relegated to lower-status occupations and professions, and are promoted more slowly and to a more limited extent. A concrete illustration of their lower status in the workplace is that, according to government figures, working women in 1993 earned only about 71 cents for every dollar earned by men, up from 61 cents in 1978 (Lewin, 1994). Even those women in the same occupations as men with equal years of experience and working for the same number of hours make less money than men (Cherry, 1989). In addition, women face other employment problems, such as more frequent sexual harassment than men.

The gender gap in income is due to many factors. By far, the most fundamental cause is the continuing sex segregation of occupations and professions (Jones, 1987). For the most part, men and women have been steered toward different types of jobs, and this occupational segregation has made it easy to pay men more than women for the work they do. Specifically, a high proportion of noncollege women traditionally have been encouraged to take jobs as secretaries and clerks, retail salespersons, dental assistants, child-care workers, bank tellers, and private household workers, for instance. The problem with these predominately female occupations is that they pay substantially lower salaries than the salaries noncollege men have made in traditionally male occupations as auto mechanics, electricians, plumbers, carpenters, truck drivers, and so on. Even college-educated females traditionally have been channeled toward low-paying fields, such as preschool and elementary school teaching, nursing, social work, and library science, as compared to men who have been encouraged to choose better-paying careers in business, accounting, the sciences, medicine, law, and engineering (U.S. Bureau of the Census, 1990a; Kilborn, 1994).

Another important reason for the pay differential between males and females is that women are frequently unfairly passed over for promotions and raises in favor of men. This is done, in part, on the assumption that women are likely to be less dedicated to their jobs than men and are likely to have more job/career interruptions than men in order to bear and raise children and take care of the ill in the family. Even in "female" occupations, women are grossly underrepresented at the supervisory and middle-management level. As an illustration, consider the situation of women in social work or in nursing. The majority of social workers and nurses are female, yet in these two fields, males earn several thousand dollars more per year, on average, than females. This is because the few men who enter these professions are given preference over women when it comes to promotions to administrative and supervisory positions that pay better (Jones, Gallagher, & McFalls, 1988). At higher than first-level supervisory or middle-management levels, the work situation of women is dismal. In the nation's *Fortune* 500 companies, for instance, women hold a tiny fraction of the top-management positions, and even those few at the top get paid substantially less than similarly situated males (Wallis, 1989).

The occupational advancement of women also has been slowed down considerably by traditional expectations. For example, wives have been expected to give higher priority to child care and other family matters than to their jobs,

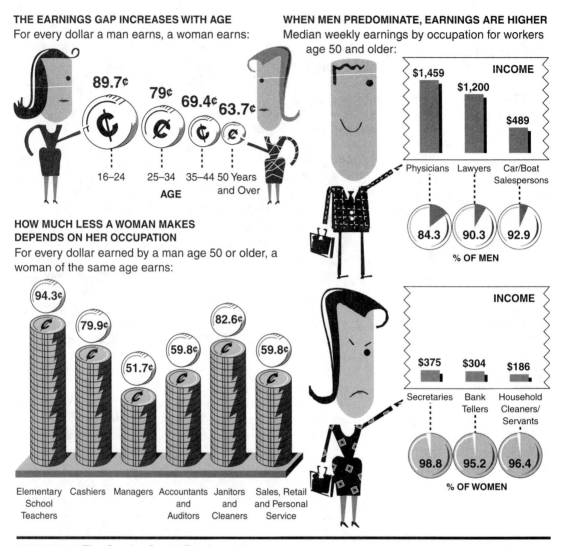

THE EARNINGS GAP INCREASES WITH AGE
For every dollar a man earns, a woman earns:

89.7¢ — 16–24
79¢ — 25–34
69.4¢ — 35–44
63.7¢ — 50 Years and Over

AGE

WHEN MEN PREDOMINATE, EARNINGS ARE HIGHER
Median weekly earnings by occupation for workers age 50 and older:

INCOME
$1,459 — Physicians
$1,200 — Lawyers
$489 — Car/Boat Salespersons

84.3 / 90.3 / 92.9
% OF MEN

HOW MUCH LESS A WOMAN MAKES DEPENDS ON HER OCCUPATION
For every dollar earned by a man age 50 or older, a woman of the same age earns:

94.3¢ — Elementary School Teachers
79.9¢ — Cashiers
51.7¢ — Managers
59.8¢ — Accountants and Auditors
82.6¢ — Janitors and Cleaners
59.8¢ — Sales, Retail and Personal Service

INCOME
$375 — Secretaries
$304 — Bank Tellers
$186 — Household Cleaners/ Servants

98.8 / 95.2 / 96.4
% OF WOMEN

FIGURE 4.3 The Gender Gap in Earnings
Source: "Gender Gap at a Glance" by American Association of Retired Persons Journal, November 1991, *32*(10), pp. 10–11. © 1991 AARP Bulletin. Reprinted with permission. All figures based on median weekly earnings of full-time workers, 1990, per U.S. Department of Labor.

and husbands have been encouraged to concentrate primarily on their jobs for the welfare of the family since the men have been able to command a higher income. This social custom of letting the husbands concentrate on their jobs and assigning more generous incomes to them has left many women and children financially vulnerable at divorce—a transition that currently affects nearly 50 percent of couples at some point in their lives. Given that marriage is no longer considered a life bond, it seems much wiser and more equitable for men and women to be paid equally for comparable jobs and for husbands and wives to share equally their investment on the family, which comes at considerable cost in terms of earnings.

Other reasons why women's earnings are lower than men's include (1) because of traditional role expectations, women are more likely than men to work part time or to take time off from work to raise their children; (2) older men have greater work experience and education than older women; (3) employers tend to assume that women's salaries are "supplementary" and therefore not as critical to the family budget as the men's salaries; and (4) women lack experience and assertiveness compared to men in salary negotiations, which often results in women accepting without question whatever salary is offered to them and in their not asking often enough for a raise or for a review of their salary as compared to that of similar male employees. Also, as more women have entered the labor force, competition among themselves for a limited number of "pink-collar" (female-segregated) jobs becomes stiffer and wages are pushed down in these occupations and professions (Gilbert & Kahl, 1987, p. 194).

Earning disparities between men and women at work have important repercussions at home. As long as husbands bring in substantially more money than wives, even if both spouses are employed outside the home on a full-time basis, husbands can find justification for not sharing equitably household tasks and child-care responsibilities. In other words, as long as the husband makes more money in his 40-hour-week job than his wife makes in her 40-hour-week job, he may feel he deserves to relax and watch TV, at least some of the time, while his wife keeps on washing dirty clothes, cooking the evening meal, cleaning and ordering the house, and so on. The reality is that as long as the husband contributes more to home finances, he has the upper hand and his wife is likely to think twice before confronting him about inequities in the division of labor at home, in fear that she may put the family in financial jeopardy if he should decide to leave (Rubin, 1992a).

The following sections examine two issues of vital concern to working women—equal pay for equal work and sexual harassment.

Achieving Pay Equality. One solution to achieve equal pay for men and women would be to integrate all occupations and professions so that there is roughly an equal amount of men and women in each. This is very difficult to accomplish because cultural dispositions toward "sex-appropriate" occupations are difficult and slow to change. Specifically, occupational choices are often made early in life with considerable influence from older significant others (e.g., parents, school counselors, teachers, grandparents) who may have very traditional ideas about what is proper for males and females to do at work.

Given the cultural inertia in changing occupational sex roles, some social scientists have suggested that the only way to close the earnings gap between the sexes without requiring the majority of people to change occupations and professions is to offer *equal pay for jobs of comparable worth.* In other words, jobs that are comparable in terms of education, skill, effort, and responsibility should command equivalent salaries. For example, there is no reason why a male forklift operator with an eighth-grade education should make considerably more money than an executive secretary with a college degree (Rubin, 1992a, p. xxiii). Under the equal pay for comparable jobs model, such gender-based differences would be eliminated.

Opponents of the comparable worth concept claim that in a capitalist system, salaries traditionally are set by market forces (i.e., supply and demand). To institute the system of equal pay for comparable work would require interference with this fundamental economic mechanism (Jones et al., 1988). This might have negative consequences, according to the opponents of this concept. In addition, it would be extremely costly for society to implement this system because the majority of salaries would have to be raised considerably to achieve parity, since it would be unrealistic to attempt to adjust men's salaries down to the level of women's salaries. For these reasons, the (male) establishment prefers the equal pay for equal work strategy. The problem with this strategy is that it has resulted in very slow progress for females because, as previously noted, occupations are highly segregated by sex and cultural ideas about sex-appropriate choices change very slowly.

Sexual Harassment.   Although pay inequity is without doubt the biggest occupational problem women confront, sexual harassment is one of the most heart wrenching. The term **sexual harassment** refers to an abuse of power consisting of sexual behavior by one person toward another that is unacceptable to the latter and that creates an intimidating or offensive work or educational environment for the victim. Sexual harassment includes unsolicited and unwelcome flirtations and sexual propositions, touching or fondling, and requests for sexual favors on the part of a person who often has power over the other person's conditions of employment or educational record.

Sexual harassment in the workplace and in educational institutions also includes displays of sexually suggestive pictures that are offensive to a worker or student, intrusive questions about an individual's personal life, offensive dirty jokes and gestures, and even use of familiarities or diminutives when these are unwelcome, such as when a male boss, professor, or colleague calls a woman employee/student "honey," "sweetheart," or "baby." Even though the Equal Employment Opportunity Commission (EEOC) prohibits sexual harassment at work and in educational institutions, the problem afflicts a substantial number of working women and female students.

The majority of victims of sexual harassment are women because they are often in positions of lesser power and authority than men. Yet not all acts of sexual harassment against women are perpetrated by males who have power and authority over them at work. For example, female physicians are not only sexually harassed by the male establishment in the field of medicine but sometimes by their male patients (Begley, 1994). To be sure,

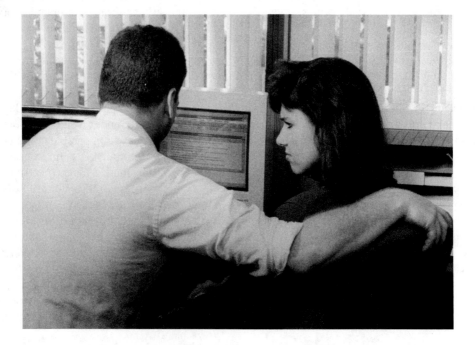

men are not the only perpetrators of sexual harassment; sometimes women in positions of power and authority sexually harass men or women.

Victims of sexual harassment can suffer a great deal of stress, anger, fear, shame, sleeplessness, and impaired job or school performance. They are often afraid to complain because they tend to be in positions subordinate to those of their harassers and because, traditionally, when the complainants are women, there is a tendency on the part of the male establishment not to take their complaints seriously and even to make the victim feel guilty for having supposedly "invited" the alleged advances. Following the confirmation hearings of Supreme Court Justice Clarence Thomas in 1991, increasing attention has been paid to this workplace issue.

What steps can be taken when one is being sexually harassed? The EEOC recommends that one immediately and unequivocally tell the harasser to stop. If the situation persists, the individual should report it to her (or his) supervisor or to the supervisor of the harasser. If that does not bring an end to the harassment, the person should begin to keep a written record while continuing to report the harassment to a supervisor. If none of these actions stops the harassment, the person can file a formal complaint within the organization. If that does not end the situation, a complaint should be filed with the EEOC or legal action should be taken, preferably with the help of an attorney specializing in sexual harassment cases. Unfortunately, if the person being harassed is in a subordinate position, these actions can be risky. That is why so many harassers continue to act with impunity.

Gays and Lesbians

Sexual orientation refers to the inclination of an individual toward sexual and affectional partners of a particular sex, whether it be toward partners of the same sex, the opposite sex, or both sexes. The term *sexual orientation*

is preferred over *sexual preference* because the latter connotes *choice,* and there is no convincing evidence at present that people deliberately choose their sexual proclivity. Individuals attracted to opposite-sex partners are called **heterosexual.** Those attracted to members of both sexes are called **bisexual.** Those attracted to same-sex partners are referred to as **gay** or **lesbian**, depending on whether they are male or female.

It is very difficult to ascertain how many people in the United States are gay or lesbian. One problem has been the lack of systematic studies of sexual behavior. Most previous studies, including the Kinsey reports of the 1940s, the Masters and Johnson study of the 1960s, and more recent popular studies such as the Hite report and other surveys conducted by various magazines, have relied on information provided by volunteers. Such information is likely to be biased in various ways. Another problem in getting an accurate estimate of the gay and lesbian population in the United States is that self-identification as gay or lesbian is not the same as having had sex with a person of the same sex or having felt sexual attraction toward persons of the same sex. Still another problem with research about sexual practices is that, because of its sensitive nature, some people may lie because they may be afraid or embarrassed to reveal the information.

Given the preceding limitations, we must be careful not to take the data emerging from any single study as accurate. However, the better the quality of the research, the greater the chances that it may provide a fair estimate. A recent study of U.S. sexual practices conducted by a team of researchers based at the University of Chicago is considered to be the most authoritative to date, because, unlike previous studies, it was based on a random though small (3,432 participants) national survey. The study found that 9 percent of the men and 5 percent of the women reported having had at least one homosexual experience since puberty, and 6 percent of the men and 5.5 percent of the women said that the idea of having sex with someone of the same gender seemed somewhat or very appealing. However, only 2.8 percent of the men and 1.4 percent of the women identified themselves as homosexual or bisexual (Gagnon, Laumann, Michael, & Michaels, 1994).

Sexual orientation is only one of many personal attributes; therefore, to think of gays and lesbians primarily in terms of their homosexuality is narrow-minded and prejudicial. Like heterosexuals and bisexuals, gays and lesbians are sons and daughters, fathers and mothers, brothers and sisters, grandfathers and grandmothers, close friends, churchgoers and worshipers, and workers engaged in the full range of occupations and careers. Like everyone else in society, they have different racial, ethnic, and socioeconomic backgrounds, attitudes and values, goals, spiritual needs, interests, and hobbies.

It is also important to keep in mind that, as previously noted, having a same-sex sexual experience (or several) is not the same as having an *identity* as gay or lesbian. As revealed by the 1994 Chicago study, only a small proportion of people who have had sex with others of the same gender consider themselves to be gay or lesbian. Instead, it appears that sexual orientation in humans occurs on a continuum extending from those who are exclusively homosexual to those who are exclusively heterosexual, with a substantial number of people falling somewhere between

the two extremes (Kinsey, Pomeroy, & Martin, 1948).

There are various popular misconceptions or stereotypes about gays and lesbians (Berger, 1987). One myth is that it is easy to tell who is gay or lesbian and who is not just by looking at the way people dress and act. In fact, as previously noted in this book, most gays and lesbians play sex-appropriate roles and are indistinguishable from the rest of the population. Only some gays are flamboyant, swishy, or effeminate looking. The same applies to lesbians, many of whom do not look or act like "dykes" or "butches." Because most gays and lesbians reveal their sexual orientation to only a handful of intimate friends or family members, the public tends to be familiar only with the minority who are open about their sexual orientation. This group is not representative of all gays and lesbians.

Some people have the misconception that gays are child molesters. The evidence shows, however, that the majority of adults who sexually molest children are heterosexual men whose victims are young girls, or, less frequently, primarily heterosexual men who molest girls and boys indiscriminately. To be sure, some child molesters are gay, but their number appears to be proportionate to the incidence of male homosexuality in the population. The incidence of heterosexual women or lesbians engaging in child molestation appears to be much lower.

Another myth about gays and lesbians is that, given the chance, they will try to convert others to their cause, so to speak. Again, there is no evidence that proselytizing is a common practice among gays and lesbians. Still another myth is that gays and lesbians would like to switch their sex; in other words, that gays would prefer to be females and lesbians would be happier as males. In actuality, most gays and lesbians have normal sexual identities. They feel comfortable with themselves as men and women and would not want to change their sex. Finally, some people have the misconception

that homosexuality is a mental illness, probably because it was classified as a mental disorder by the American Psychiatric Association until 1974. However, studies have not shown homosexuality to be linked to either mental health or mental illness (Gonsiorek, 1982).

Gays and lesbians suffer many kinds of social oppression. For instance, gay couples are denied most of the family rights heterosexual couples have. Specifically, in 1994, uniformly throughout the United States, they were not legally allowed to get married; consequently, they could not collect benefits from their mate's social security and had no legal right to inherit from their loved one, unless the inheritance was specified in a written will. A growing number of U.S. municipalities now recognize "domestic partnerships" and confer on the gay partners of city employees certain limited benefits (Gross, 1994). However, in the mid-1990s, the majority of gays and lesbians still were not covered by their partner's medical insurance and were not permitted to take sick leave to provide care for an ill or hospitalized mate (see Box 4.2). In fact, if their mate was hospitalized with a critical illness, they could legally be denied visitation rights unless they were formally designated in writing as health care surrogates or unless they tried to "pass" for a close family member, such as a brother or sister, as long as this behavior was not challenged by the biological family.

Few openly gay or lesbian individuals are granted custody of their children. Those who do have custody often feel in danger of losing it, simply because they live with a person of the same sex. Some even have trouble obtaining the right to visit with their children because they are gay or lesbian and the court does not consider their homosexuality to be a good influence on their children. Few are allowed to adopt children.

Gays and lesbians also suffer other kinds of civil rights violations. In 1994, they were not protected by antidiscrimination laws in most states in the United States. Also, they did not

City Won't Pay Lesbian Caregiver

BY ALAN GOTTLIEB

Denver Post Staff Writer

Two Denver mayoral administrations, outspoken in their support of gay rights, have refused to pay sick leave to a lesbian city worker who took three days off last winter to care for her critically injured lover.

Mary Ross, a social worker with Denver Health and Hospitals Psychiatric Services, appealed the December decision by her supervisor and took the case before Career Services Authority hearing officer Margot Jones yesterday.

Jones didn't reach a decision, and isn't expected to rule for at least two weeks.

Ross claims that Jeannie DiClementi, her "life partner" for the past 3½ years, is a family member, just as a spouse of the opposite sex would be. City policy allows workers to take sick leave to care for sick or injured family members.

By refusing to give Ross sick leave, the city has violated its own 1988 regulation—an executive order signed by Mayor Federico Peña prohibiting discrimination against gays, said Ross' lawyer, Lino Lipinsky De Orlov. The case began last year, while Peña was still mayor.

Assistant City Attorney J. Wallace Wortham argued yesterday that a Career Services Authority policy written in the early 1980s clearly delineates what constitutes a family member, and live-in lovers are not included. That regulation was applied fairly to the Ross case, he said, so no discrimination took place.

Even if the regulation had a discriminatory effect, Wortham said, "they'd have to prove it was written with discriminatory intent" to prevail.

At yesterday's hearing, University of Denver sociology professor Anne Rankin Mahoney, an expert in family structures, testified that Ross, 29, and DiClementi, 41, met current definitions of a family unit. Ross is actively involved in raising DiClementi's two children, a 10-year-old daughter and an 18-year-old son, and helps pay their school tuitions.

Lipinsky de Orlov said the city's arguments were absurd. "It's like reading 'Alice in Wonderland' to hear the agency say she has not been discriminated against," he said. "If this had been a man and woman, she would have been allowed to use sick leave. The only reason she was denied is because she is a lesbian."

Mayor Wellington Webb, who campaigned this spring on a pro-gay rights platform, couldn't be reached for comment late yesterday.

DiClementi was injured last Dec. 5 when she passed out from an allergic reaction, fell down a flight of stairs and hit her head on a concrete wall. She remained "gravely ill" for two days, so Ross stayed at her bedside. Several weeks later, Ross took another day off when DiClementi had to return to the hospital for neurological tests. Her sick-leave requests were turned down.

"I've had them (supervisors) tell me to say I was sick, not Jeannie, so that they could approve the sick leave," Ross said yesterday. "I refused to do it. I wasn't sick—my life partner was. It would have been dishonest to say anything else."

DiClementi said she found it "ironic but not surprising" that a city government supposedly committed to gay rights is strongly opposing the sick-leave request.

have the constitutional protection against discrimination granted to women and members of racial, ethnic, or religious minorities. Only the states of California, Hawaii, Minnesota, Wisconsin, Vermont, Massachussets, Connecticut, and New Jersey, and the District of Columbia had passed laws prohibiting discrimination based on sexual orientation (Gross, 1994). This situation left their protection in most states up to individual municipalities, many of which were reluctant to extend civil rights to gays and lesbians because of political, religious, or "moral"considerations. As a consequence, the majority of gays and lesbians were denied full civil rights in the society. Most employers were free to fire them simply because they were gay or lesbian, no matter how outstanding their work record might have been.

In every state with antisodomy laws (laws prohibiting oral or anal sexual activity), and there were 23 such states in the United States in 1994 (Gross, 1994), gays and lesbians risk criminal prosecution every time they have sex. If prosecuted, many would risk losing their employment and the custody of their children. Everywhere they risk **gay bashing**, which has worsened since the advent of the AIDS epidemic, perhaps because the latter has given bigots an excuse to act out their hatred of gays (Goleman, 1990). Specifically, three out of four gays report that they have been harassed by people calling them names, and as many as one in four admits to having been physically assaulted simply because he was perceived to be gay.

Lesbians are particularly disadvantaged. They are vulnerable not only to the types of discrimination just discussed but they also suffer economic discrimination because of the pay disparity between men and women, which makes their combined incomes substantially lower than the earnings of heterosexual couples or gay (male) couples. Nonwhite lesbians, particularly, are triply oppressed—by racism, sexism, and homophobia—not only from the dominant group but from their own racial/ethnic group and even from white gays and lesbians. Finally, gays infected with AIDS tend to experience the highest levels of discrimination.

AIDS has created many new problems for gays infected with this disease. Many suffer loneliness and isolation due to the unfounded fear others have of catching the disease if they have close physical contact with someone infected, such as by holding their hand, hugging them, or kissing them on the cheek. Gays with AIDS sometimes receive poor health care from personnel in hospitals and clinics who actively try to avoid working with them. Many

lose the support of friends and family who abandon them. Some suffer a loss of housing and employment due to the prejudices of landlords and employers (Berger, 1987). Although those with AIDS are now legally protected against housing or employment discrimination, the reality is that employers and property owners often find veiled ways of getting rid of them without violating the law.

Gays and lesbians are far from achieving full civil rights in the United States. However, they have made some progress. In the political arena, for example, every year there are more openly gay elected officials around the country. Also, the Human Rights Campaign Fund, a gay lobbying group, has become one of the largest independent political action groups (PACS) in the nation (Salholz et al., 1990). As they gain more political power, they are likely to attain a higher level of accommodation by the society.

Another sign of progress toward civil rights is the concept of *domestic partnership,* which is emerging in some localities. In San Francisco, for instance, unmarried couples of any sex can register as domestic partners if they have entered into an intimate and committed relationship. The purpose of registering domestic partners is to eventually extend to them some of the benefits accorded to married couples, such as health insurance, pension rights, property and life insurance rights, family sick leave, and bereavement leave. At present, however, the issue of what rights should be extended to unmarried couples, if any, is being hotly debated in many communities (Seligmann, 1990, p. 38). Some inroads are being made in a few places. In Madison, Wisconsin, the city government has approved the granting of sick leave and bereavement leave to domestic partners of city employees, and in New York City, the State Court of Appeals ruled in 1989 that a gay couple who had lived together for 10 years could be considered a family under the city's rent-control regulations. Although such progress is encouraging, it can be painfully slow for those who are suffering daily the effects of discrimination.

COMBATTING DISCRIMINATION AND OPPRESSION

This chapter has explored the deeply rooted problems of prejudice, discrimination, and oppression, and the contemporary situation of major nondominant groups in the U.S. society—African Americans, women, Latinos, gays and lesbians, Asian Americans, Native Americans, and American Jews. A few of these groups—such as American Jews, gays, Chinese Americans, and Japanese Americans—are doing well economically compared to the mainstream group, although they are still subject to various types of social prejudice, discrimination, and oppression. For most nondominant groups, however, much remains to be accomplished to bring them to socioeconomic parity or to ensure their civil rights. Particularly in the areas of health care, education, income and employment, housing, and the criminal justice system, there are serious inequities in the United States that must be addressed more effectively if we are to give all our children a fair chance to grow up into healthy and competent adults.

There are no simple solutions for problems such as discrimination and oppression. However, there are some things that human service practitioners and private citizens can do to contribute toward the effort to eradicate these social evils.

Civil Rights Legislation and Affirmative Action

As practitioners and private citizens, we can help to protect the civil rights of *all* people in the United States by actively supporting continued enactment of antidiscriminatory laws and antidiscriminatory institutional policies. We can also contribute to the fight against discrimination by insisting that every piece of legislation enacted and every policy developed be consistently enforced. Although feelings and attitudes cannot be mandated or legislated, they do change as people develop the habit of behaving in nondiscriminatory ways.

Housing segregation remains a major problem. Many children from nondominant groups are prevented from attending good schools, and this perpetuates their educational deficiencies and limits their employment opportunities. Consequently, the antidiscrimination laws in housing and lending laws must be vigorously enforced.

The violation of the civil rights of gays and lesbians must be stopped. As full members of the U.S. society, they deserve to be treated equitably. Their sexual orientation in and of itself should not be grounds to deny them employment, custody of their children, security clearance, or housing. Thus, the remaining antisodomy laws should be taken off the books, and gays and lesbians should be protected by antidiscrimination laws uniformly in every state in the union. It is unfortunate that so many social groups have to be singled out for special protection against discrimination, but when discrimination is an indisputable reality in their lives without such protection, there is no other choice.

Although controversial in some quarters, **affirmative action** has been effective in opening up the job market and educational institutions to nondominant group members. It is still necessary in many fields where the representation of nondominant groups remains significantly below their representation in the society. Established in 1965 through Executive Order 11246, affirmative action consists of programs to actively recruit qualified members of nondominant groups (e.g., women and racial and ethnic minorities) into various educational fields and occupations from which they were formerly excluded or not given the same opportunity to enter as males. When recruitment goals are not reached, the federal government has the right to withhold grants and other federal contracts from the noncomplying organizations or institutions.

As a method to combat discrimination and oppression, affirmative action has become increasingly unpopular among Euro-American males. This is understandable, since they have been the most negatively affected by it. The main problem is that affirmative action sometimes leads to discrimination, usually against qualified Euro-American males, in order to give priority to qualified women or other non-dominant group members. This situation is called **reverse discrimination.**

Social Programs

Much remains to be done in the areas of health, education, income, and employment to fight societal discrimination and oppression effectively. It is no secret that current social programs have not worked well; therefore, considerable reform is needed if we are serious about creating a more just and equitable society. A small set of *universal* programs may work better and be more cost effective, in the final analysis, than a large number of entitlement programs targeted to special groups. To be sure, universal programs are preferred by the mainstream group, which usually pays the largest chunk of the bill.

Many of the programs needed are the same as those needed to fight poverty:

— Universal health care with emphasis on prevention, nutrition, and prenatal care
— Quality universal preschool programs such as Head Start to ensure that all children will be on an equal footing as far as language, conceptual, and fine motor skills by the time they enter school
— An educational system (private, public, or a combined private/public effort) that guarantees that all children will graduate with a minimum set of competencies geared toward employment in our complex technological society

— Universal free breakfast and lunch programs for children at school
— Guaranteed child support for all single parents with custody of their children, with the IRS or other federal entity collecting from noncustodial parents their fair share
— Universal quality day care and after-school care for all children so that their parents can be employed or can receive training for employment
— Drug and alcohol detoxification and treatment available to all who need it
— Guaranteed job skills training, job placement, and employment with wages above the poverty level for all able-bodied people
— Flexible work hours for working parents and guaranteed parental leaves to take care of newborns and sick children
— Universal sex education, family planning, adolescent pregnancy prevention, and parenting education.

These programs would cost more money than we are presently spending in social entitlement programs, but they are essential to build a more just, equitable, and humane society. As noted in the previous chapter, other advanced industrial nations are more generous with their people, particularly with their children. There is no reason why the United States cannot rise to the standard of the advanced world in terms of its concern for human dignity. If it doesn't act preventively, it will pay the consequences later, as shown in Figure 4.4.

Personal Involvement, Advocacy, and Social Action

Another way of helping is to become advocates for the oppressed, serving as their supporters, advisers, champions, and representatives (Briar, 1967, p. 28; Piven & Cloward, 1971). African-American and Latino practitioners and well-established, successful members of non-dominant groups can help to empower their less fortunate brethren in a number of ways: by mentoring boys and girls in their communities and serving as positive role models; by showing care and willingness to spend time with them; by helping them to avoid adolescent pregnancy and to stay in school; and by helping teenagers already with children to be good parents and to get a good education. There is also much need to assist poor families to better negotiate the system to get the services they need; to work together to eradicate the criminal element and drug dealers from poor neighborhoods; to teach the illiterate to read and write; and to help the unemployed find work, develop greater self-confidence, and focus on their strengths. We can also help by showing faith, by teaching responsibility and hard work, by having high expectations rather than by patronizing, and by offering moral support.

Other ways of helping others in our society to achieve equality include getting involved in consciousness-raising efforts (i.e., making people aware of how society creates barriers that keep back some groups, such as women, and prevent them from developing and using their talents); lobbying for needed programs and services; and organizing, coalition building, and helping nondominant group members to establish their own networks, support systems, and self-help groups.

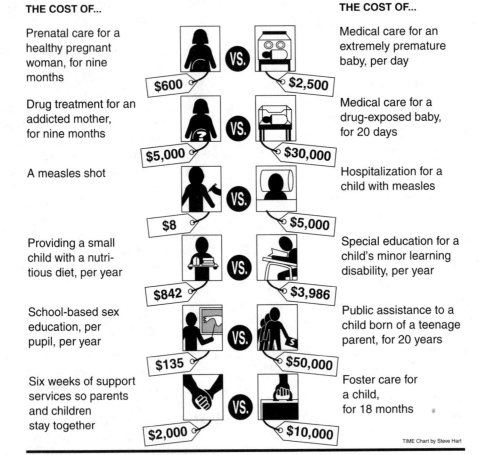

THE COST OF...

Prenatal care for a healthy pregnant woman, for nine months — $600

Drug treatment for an addicted mother, for nine months — $5,000

A measles shot — $8

Providing a small child with a nutritious diet, per year — $842

School-based sex education, per pupil, per year — $135

Six weeks of support services so parents and children stay together — $2,000

THE COST OF...

Medical care for an extremely premature baby, per day — $2,500

Medical care for a drug-exposed baby, for 20 days — $30,000

Hospitalization for a child with measles — $5,000

Special education for a child's minor learning disability, per year — $3,986

Public assistance to a child born of a teenage parent, for 20 years — $50,000

Foster care for a child, for 18 months — $10,000

TIME Chart by Steve Hart

FIGURE 4.4 Pay Now...Or Pay Later

Source: Time, October 8, 1990, p. 45. © 1990 Time Inc. Reprinted by permission.

We can take a stand against discriminatory policies and practices in our workplaces by bringing them to the attention of our colleagues and supervisors. This is not always done without some personal grief, but the satisfaction that we can feel from acting with integrity and eventually seeing the fruit of our labor often will outweigh the pain that is always involved in trying to change the status quo. Some of us can also help social groups to overcome barriers and to reach just and equitable goals by assisting them in organizing various nonviolent acts of protest, such as boycotts of certain exploitative businesses or employers or rent strikes directed at property owners that ignore requests for needed repairs. Prudent media involvement in these attempts to redress injustices is often useful. Finally, we can help to raise the consciousness of our friends, family, and those we come in contact with by letting them know, kindly but firmly, that we find their prejudicial remarks or jokes inappropriate and that we disapprove of their discriminatory practices.

Another important strategy to reduce discrimination and oppression is to be constantly vigilant to make sure that we do not pass on to our children the prejudices that we have been burdened with and to do everything we can to prevent other socialization agents (e.g., grandparents, relatives, teachers, day-care workers, the church, and television) from working at cross-purposes with our efforts. It is also important to make sure that we do not teach our daughters to play the sex roles that have traditionally kept women dependent and subordinated.

Increased Contact

Increased contact between members of social groups can help to reduce prejudice and discrimination so long as the association involves individuals whose socioeconomic status is not too dissimilar and so long as the contact is voluntary and directed toward a mutually beneficial goal. If these basic principles are violated, efforts to reduce prejudice by increasing contact may backfire. School busing, for example, has been unsuccessful in many communities as an integration strategy because it has been forced on some parents without providing them with good reasons why this effort could benefit their children. Also, it frequently brought together children and parents from widely divergent socioeconomic backgrounds, thus leading to considerable hostilities and tensions and racial misunderstandings based on class differences.

ENDNOTE

1. For example, many Mexican Americans and other Central Americans are of mixed Indian and white European descent, and a large proportion of Puerto Ricans have mixed Indian, African, and white European ancestry.

GLOSSARY

Achieved Trait: A characteristic that is attained by an individual rather than assigned or inherited. For example, an able-bodied person may become disabled due to an accident.

Affirmative Action: A program to actively recruit qualified members of nondominant groups, including women and racial and ethnic minorities, into various educational fields and occupations from which they were formerly excluded or not given the same opportunity to enter as white males.

Ageism: Stereotyping, prejudice, discrimination, or oppression based on age, usually arising from the belief that younger people are more competent and efficient than older people.

Antisemitism: Stereotyping, prejudice, discrimination, or oppression directed against Jews.

Ascribed Trait: A characteristic that is inherited or assigned to the person at birth. For example, gender is an ascribed trait because people are born either male or female.

Bisexual Orientation: An individual able to satisfy his or her affectional and sexual needs with males or females is considered to have a bisexual orientation.

Classism: Stereotyping, prejudice, discrimination, or oppression usually based on the belief that those in the lower classes have inferior characteristics and social values that account for their disadvantaged social circumstances.

Cultural Racism: Belief in the superiority of the cultural accomplishments of one race as compared to another.

De Facto Discrimination: Discrimination that actually occurs. For example, even though it is illegal to discriminate against Latinos or African Americans, they are often denied jobs.

De Jure Discrimination: Discrimination that is sanctioned or permitted by law, such as discrimination against gays and lesbians in localities that have not enacted laws forbidding such discrimination.

Discrimination: An unjustified or unfounded negative or hostile action taken against a certain group or individual—for example, denying admission to a social club to a person simply because he is an African American.

Dominant Group: The social group in power in the society; the group that controls its institutions and resources and makes the major decisions—the "establishment."

Ethnic Group: A group of people who share a common history and identity, a common language, national background, religion, racial ancestry, or some combination of these factors that gives them a sense of peoplehood.

Ethnic Minority Group: An ethnic group that is not part of the mainstream—for example, Native Americans.

Ethnocentrism: Belief in the superiority of one's own ethnic group or culture, as compared to others.

Gay Bashing: An extreme form of discrimination against homosexuals involving physical injury.

Gay Sexual Orientation: Men attracted primarily to other men as affectional and sexual partners are considered to have a gay sexual orientation.

Heterosexual Orientation: An individual attracted primarily to sexual or affectional partners of the opposite sex is considered to have a heterosexual orientation.

Homophobia: Intolerance or irrational fear of homosexuals and homosexuality sometimes resulting in discrimination and oppression directed toward gays and lesbians.

Homosexual: A person attracted primarily to same-sex sexual or affectional partners. Because this term has negative connotations, the terms *gay male* and *lesbian* are preferred.

Institutional Discrimination: Discrimination that is built into the social structure—that is, into the economic, educational, health, social, and political institutions of the society. It causes multiple disadvantages to whole categories of people, such as the poor or children of color.

Institutional Racism: Institutional discrimination directed at people of color.

Lesbian Sexual Orientation: Women attracted primarily to other women as sexual partners are considered to have a lesbian sexual orientation.

Minority of Color: See **Racial Minority Group.**

Nondominant Group: A social group that has low standing in the stratification system of the society and that is the recipient of inequitable and inferior treatment.

Oppression: Systematic and long-term action by a social group, usually institutionalized within the key social structures of the society, to prevent another social group from attaining access to the scarce and valued resources of the society. See **Institutional Discrimination**.

People of Color: See **Racial Minority Group.**

Personal Discrimination: An individual act of discrimination, as opposed to institutional discrimination, which is much more pervasive.

Prejudice: A prejudgment about a person or group based on selective perception and not supported by factual evidence. Usually, the term is used pejoratively to refer to a negative or hostile attitude, belief, or feeling held without sufficient justification—for example, the belief that women are bad drivers.

Racial Group: A group that has a common set of distinctive physical characteristics, such as skin color and hair texture.

Racial Minority Group: A nondominant, racial group, also known as **Minority of Color**. All nonwhite racial/ethnic groups in the United States are considered to be racial minority groups, including African Americans, Native Americans, Asians and Pacific Islanders, and most Latino groups with large numbers of nonwhites.

Racism: Stereotyping, prejudice, discrimination, or oppression based on race. It is usually based on the belief in the cultural or biological (innate) superiority of a particular race as compared to another race.

Reverse Discrimination: This term refers to discrimination, usually against white males, in order to give preference in hiring or educational recruitment to qualified women and other nondominant group members.

Scapegoat: A person, usually in an inferior or subordinate position, who is made to bear the blame for others.

Sexism: Stereotyping, prejudice, discrimination, or oppression on the basis of gender usually stemming from either the belief that men are biologically superior to women or that a woman's primary roles are those of wife and mother and everything else in her life should be subordinated to these roles.

Sexual Harassment: An abuse of power consisting of unwelcome sexual behavior by one person toward another that results in an intimidating, hostile, or offensive work or educational environment.

Sexual Orientation: The inclination of an individual toward sexual and affectional partners of the same sex (homosexual), opposite sex (heterosexual), or both sexes (bisexual).

Stereotype: A widely held idea that oversimplifies or distorts its referent—for example, the belief that fat people are jolly.

REFERENCES

Adorno, T. W., Frenkel-Brunswick, E., & Levinson, D. J. (1950). *The authoritarian personality*. New York: Harper.

Allport, G. W. (1954). *The nature of prejudice*. Reading, MA: Addison-Wesley.

Anderson, P. (1990, July 17). Gap grows for Hispanics in school, study says. *The Miami Herald*, pp. 1A, 8A.

Aponte, R. (1991). Urban Hispanic poverty: Dissagregations and explanations. *Social Problems, 38*, 516–528.

Barringer, F. (1990, March 2). Asian population in U.S. grew by 70% in the 80s. *The New York Times*, p. A14.

Bean, F. D., & Tienda, M. (1987). *The Hispanic population of the United States*. New York: Russell Sage Foundation.

Begley, S. (1994, January 31, 1994). Hey doc, you got great legs. *Newsweek*, 54.

Belle, D. E. (1983). The impact of poverty on social networks and supports. In L. Lein & M. B. Sussman (Eds.), *The ties that bind: Men's and women's social networks*. New York: Haworth.

Bennett, C. I. (1988). *Comprehensive multicultural education: Theory and practice*. Boston: Allyn and Bacon.

Berger, R. M. (1987). Homosexuality: Gay men. In A. Minahan (Ed.), *Encyclopedia of social work* (18th ed., pp. 795–805). Silver Spring, MD: National Association of Social Workers.

Billingsley, A. (1989). The sociology of knowledge of William J. Wilson: Placing The *Truly Disadvantaged* in its sociohistorical context. *Journal of Sociology and Social Welfare, 16*(4), 7–39.

Birch, H. G. (1972). Malnutrition, learning, and intelligence. *American Journal of Public Health, 62*, 773–784.

Blanchard, E. L. (1987). American Indians and Alaska Natives. In A. Minahan (Ed.), *Encyclopedia of social work* (18th ed., pp. 142–150). Silver Spring, MD: National Association of Social Workers.

Briar, S. (1967). The current crisis in social case-work. In National Conference on Social Welfare (Ed.), *Social work practice.* New York: Columbia University Press.

Brieland, D., Costin, L. B., & Atherton, C. R. (1985). *Contemporary social work: An introduction to social work and social welfare* (3rd ed.). New York: McGraw-Hill.

Cannon, C. M. (1991, January 1). Improving status of blacks shifts civil rights focus. *The Miami Herald,* Section A.

Cavalli-Sforza, L., Menozzi, P., & Piazza, A. (1994). *The history and geography of human genes.* Princeton, NJ: Princeton University Press.

Census: Whites 10 times richer than minorities. (1991, January 11). *The Miami Herald.*

Cherry, R. (1989). *Discrimination: Its economic impact on blacks, women and Jews.* Lexington, MA: Lexington Books.

Chestang, L. W. (1972). *Character development in a hostile environment.* Occasional Paper No. 3. Chicago: School of Social Service Administration, University of Chicago.

Chestang, L. W. (1976). Environmental influences on social functioning: The black experience. In P. Cafferty & L. Chestang (Eds.), *The diverse society: Implications for social policy.* New York: Association Press.

Chira, S. (1994, April 12). Study confirms worst fears on U.S. children. *The New York Times,* pp. A1, A11.

Chua-Eoan, H. G. (1990, April 9). Strangers in paradise. *Time,* 32–35.

Citizens Commission on Hunger in New England. (1984). *American hunger crisis.* Boston: Harvard School of Public Health.

Cobbs, P. M. (1988). Critical perspectives on the psychology of race. In J. Dewart (Ed.), *The state of black America 1988* (pp. 61–70). New York: National Urban League.

Cuciti, P., & Franklin, J. (1990). A comparison of black and Hispanic poverty in large cities of the Southwest. *Hispanic Journal of Behavioral Sciences, 12*(1), 50–75.

Cummerton, J. M. (1982). Homophobia and social work practice with lesbians. In A. Weick & Susan T. Vandiver (Eds.), *Women, power and change* (pp. 105–113). Washington, DC: National Association of Social Workers.

DeParle, J. (1994, October 7). Census report sees incomes in decline and more poverty. *The New York Times,* pp. A1, A9.

Dewart, J. (Ed.). (1991). *The state of Black America: 1990.* Washington, DC: National Urban League, Inc.

Doig, S. K. (1991, April 9). Neighborhoods show small gains in integration. *The Miami Herald,* pp. 1A, 13A.

Dollard, J., Doob, L. W., Miller, N. E., Mowrer, O. H., Sears, R. R., et al. (1939). *Frustration and aggression.* New Haven, CT: Yale University Press.

Ellwood, D. T. (1988). *Poor support.* New York: Basic Books.

Estrada, L. F. (1987). Hispanics. In A. Minahan (Ed.), *Encyclopedia of social work* (18th ed., pp. 732–739). Silver Spring, MD: National Association of Social Workers.

Folb, E. A. (1988). Who's got the room at the top? Issues of dominance and nondominance in intracultural communication. In L. A. Samovar & R. E. Porter (Eds.), *Intercultural communication: A reader* (5th ed., pp. 121–129). Belmont, CA: Wadsworth.

Frazier, E. F. (1962). *The black bourgeoisie.* New York: Crowell, Collier, and Macmillan.

Gagnon, J. H., Laumann, E. O., Michael, R. T., & Michaels, S. (1994). *The social organization of sexuality.* Chicago: University of Chicago Press.

Gelman, D., Springen, K., Brailsford, K., & Miller, M. (1988, March 7). Black and white in America. *Newsweek,* 18–23.

Gilbert, D., & Kahl, J. A. (1987). *The American class structure: A new synthesis* (3rd ed.). Belmont, CA: Wadsworth.

Goleman, D. (1990, July 10). Studies discover clues to the roots of homophobia. *The New York Times,* pp. B1, B9.

Gonsiorek, J. C. (1982). Results of psychological testing on homosexual populations. In W. Paul, J. D. Weinrich, J. C. Gonsiorek, & M. E. Hotvedt (Eds.), *Homosexuality: Social, psychological, and biological issues* (pp. 71–80). Beverly Hills, CA: Sage.

Gordon, M. M. (1988). *The scope of sociology.* New York: Oxford University Press.

Gramick, J. (1983). Homophobia: A new challenge. *Social Work,* 28, 137–141.

Gross, J. (1994, April 25). After a ruling, Hawaii weighs gay marriages. *The New York Times,* pp. A1, C12.

Hayes-Bautista, D. E. (1992, October 28). Academe can take the lead in binding together the residents of a multicultural society. *The Chronicle of Higher Education,* pp. B1–2.

Heinrich, R. K., Corbine, J. L., & Thomas, K. R. (1990). Counseling Native Americans. *Journal of Counseling and Development, 69,* 128–133.

Hopps, J. G. (1987). Minorities of color. In A. Minahan (Ed.), *Encyclopedia of social work* (18th ed., pp. 161–171). Silver Spring, MD: National Association of Social Workers.

Indian Health Service. (1994). *1993 Trends in Indian health.* Washington, DC: U.S. Dept. of Health and Human Services, Public Health Service, Office of Planning, Evaluation & Legislation, Division of Program Statistics.

Jaynes, G. D., & Williams, R. M., Jr. (Eds.). (1989). *A common destiny: Blacks and American society.* Washington, DC: National Academy Press.

John, R. (1988). The Native American family. In C. H. Mindel, R. W. Habenstein, & Wright, R., Jr. (Eds.), *Ethnic families in America: Patterns and variations* (3rd ed., pp. 325–363). New York: Elsevier.

Jones, B. J., Gallagher, III, B. J., & McFalls, J. A. (1988). *Social problems: Issues, opinions, and solutions.* New York: McGraw-Hill.

Jones, L. E. (1987). Women. In A. Minahan (Ed.), *Encyclopedia of social work* (18th ed., pp. 872–881). Silver Spring, MD: National Association of Social Workers.

Kane, T. J. (1987). Giving back control: Long-term poverty and motivation. *Social Service Review, 61,* 405–419.

Kilborn, P. T. (1994, March 13). More women take low-wage jobs just so their families can get by. *The New York Times,* p. A11.

Kinsey, A. C., Pomeroy, W. B., & Martin, C. E. (1948). *Sexual behavior in the human male.* Philadelphia: W. B. Saunders.

Kitano, H. H. L. (1987). Asian Americans. In A. Minahan (Ed.), *Encyclopedia of social work* (18th ed., pp. 156–171). Silver Spring, MD: National Association of Social Workers.

Kornblum, W., & Julian, J. (1989). *Social problems* (6th ed.). Englewood Cliffs, NJ: Prentice Hall.

Krakinowski, L. (1991, August 9). Study shows widening chasm between rich, poor blacks. *The Miami Herald,* p. 8A.

Landry, B. (1987). *The new black middle class.* Berkeley: University of California Press.

Lenski, G. (1966). *Power and privilege.* New York: McGraw-Hill.

Lewin, T. (1994, October 15). Working woman say bias persists. *The New York Times,* p. 8.

Locke, D. C. (1992). Native Americans. In D. C. Locke (Ed.), *Increasing multicultural understanding: A comprehensive model* (pp. 46–61). Newbury Park, CA: Sage.

Lynn, L. E., & McGeary, M. G. H. (Eds.). (1990). *Inner-city poverty in the United States.* Washington, DC: National Academy Press.

Male sex survey stalled 19 years. (1989, January 20). *The Miami Herald,* section A.

Marden, C. F., & Meyer, G. (1961). *Minorities in American society.* New York: American Book.

Martinez, C. (1988). Mexican-Americans. In L. Comas-Dias & E. E. H. Griffith (Eds.), *Clinical guidelines in cross-cultural mental health* (pp. 182–203). New York: John Wiley & Sons.

McAdoo, H. P. (1987). Blacks. In A. Minahan (Ed.), *Encyclopedia of social work* (18th ed., pp. 194–206). Silver Spring, MD: National Association of Social Workers.

Melville, M. B. (1988). Hispanics: Race, class, or ethnicity? *The Journal of Ethnic Studies, 16*(1), 67–83.

Merry, S. (1981). *Urban danger: Life in a neighborhood of strangers.* Philadelphia: Temple University Press.

Merton, R. I. (1949). Discrimination and the American creed. In R. H. MacIver (Ed.), *Discrimination and national welfare.* New York: Harper & Row.

Montague, A. (1964). *Man's most dangerous myth: The fallacy of race* (5th ed.). Cleveland: World.

Norton, D. (1978). *The dual perspective: Inclusion of ethnic minority content in the social work curriculum.* New York: Council on Social Work Education.

Ogbu, J. U. (1994). Understanding cultural diversity and learning. *Journal for the Education of the Gifted, 17*(4), 355–383.

Patel, D. I. (1988). Asian Americans: A growing force. *The Council of State Governments, 61*(2), 71–76.

Pear, R. (1992, September 4). Ranks of U.S. poor reach 35.7 million, the most since '64. *The New York Times,* pp. A1, A12.

Pear, R. (1993, October 5). Poverty in U.S. grew faster than population last year. *The New York Times,* p. A10.

Peterson, P. E. (1991). The urban underclass and the poverty paradox. In C. Jencks & P. E. Peterson (Eds.), *The urban underclass* (pp. 3–27). Washington, DC: The Brookings Institution.

Piven, F. F., & Cloward, R. A. (1971). *Regulating the poor: The functions of public welfare.* New York: Pantheon Books.

Portes, A., & Truelove, C. (1987). Making sense of diversity: Recent research on Hispanic minorities. *Annual Review of Sociology, 131,* 359–385.

Poverty takes its toll on U.S. Hispanics. (August 27, 1993). *The Miami Herald,* p. 16A.

Queralt, M. (1984). Understanding Cuban immigrants: A cultural perspective. *Social Work, 29,* 115–121.

Ramos-McKay, J. M., Comas-Diaz, L., & Rivera, L. A. (1988). Puerto Ricans. In L. Comas-Dias & E. E. H. Griffith (Eds.), *Clinical guidelines in cross-cultural mental health* (pp. 204–232). New York: John Wiley & Sons.

Red Horse, J. (1988). Cultural evolution of American Indian families. In C. Jacobs & D. D. Bowles (Eds.), *Ethnicity and race: Critical concepts in social work* (pp. 86–102). Silver Spring, MD: National Association of Social Workers.

Richardson, L. (1994, April 6). Minority students languish in special education system. *The New York Times,* p. B8.

Ricketts, E. R., & Sawhill, I. V. (1988). Defining and measuring the underclass. *Journal of Policy Analysis and Management, 7,* 316–325.

Rodriguez, H. (1992). Household composition, employment patterns, and income inequality: Puerto Ricans in New York and other areas of the U.S. mainland. *Hispanic Journal of Behavioral Sciences, 14*(1), 52–75.

Rubin, L. B. (1992a). *Worlds of pain: Life in the working-class family.* New York: Basic Books.

Rubin, L. B. (1992b). Women and children last: The plight of poor women in affluent America. New York: Penguin Books.

Rubin, R. (1989, February 22). Health disparity between the races. *The Miami Herald,* p. 2E.

Rumbaut, R. G. (1991). *Passages to America: Perspectives on the new immigration.* Berkeley: University of California Press.

Salholz, E., et al. (1990, March 12). The future of gay America. *Newsweek,* 20–25.

Santiago, A. M. (1992). Patterns of Puerto Rican segregation and mobility. *Hispanic Journal of Behavioral Sciences, 14*(1), 107–133.

Seligmann, J. (1990, Winter–Spring). Variations on a theme: Gays, single mothers, and grandparents challenge the definition of what a family is. *Newsweek,* 38–43.

Simpson, G. E., & Yinger, J. M. (1985). *Racial and cultural minorities* (5th ed.). New York: Plenum Press.

Sowell, T. (1981). *Ethnic America: A history.* New York: Basic Books.

Stone, A., & Castaneda, C. J. (1991, June 12). Vietnamese set pace for ethnic growth/How the USA has grown. *USA Today,* pp. 1A, 3A.

Strauss, M. (1980). Social stress and marital violence in a national sample of American families. *Annals of the New York Academy of Science, 347,* 229–250.

Thomason, T. C. (1991). Counseling Native Americans: An introduction for non-Native American counselors. *Journal of Counseling and Development, 69,* 321–327.

Tienda, M. (1983). Nationality and income attainment among native and immigrant Hispanic men in the United States. *The Sociological Quarterly,* Spring, 253–272.

Tienda, M. (1989). Puerto Ricans and the underclass debate. *Annals of the American Academy of Political and Social Sciences, 501,* 105–119.

Turner, J. H., Singleton, R., Jr., & Musick, D. (1984). *Oppression: A socio-history of black-white relations in America.* Chicago: Nelson-Hall.

U.S. Bureau of the Census. (1989a). *Population profile of the United States: 1989.* Current population reports, series P-23, No. 159. Washington, DC: U.S. Government Printing Office.

U.S. Bureau of the Census. (1989b). *The Black population in the United States: March 1988.* Current population reports, series P-20, No. 442. Washington, DC: U.S. Government Printing Office.

U.S. Bureau of the Census. (1989c). *Money, income, and poverty status in the United States: 1989.* Current population reports, series P-60, No. 166. Washington, DC: U.S. Government Printing Office.

U.S. Bureau of the Census. (1990a). *Statistical abstract of the United States, 1990.* Washington, DC: U.S. Government Printing Office.

U.S. Bureau of the Census. (1990b). *Money, income, and poverty status in the United States: 1989.* Current population reports, series, P-60, No. 168. Washington, DC: U.S. Government Printing Office.

U.S. Bureau of the Census. (1991). *The Hispanic population in the United States: March 1990.* Current population reports, series P-20, No. 449. Washington, DC: U.S. Government Printing Office.

U.S. Bureau of the Census. (1992). *The black population in the United States: March 1991.* Current population reports, P20-464. Washington, DC: U.S. Government Printing Office.

U.S. Bureau of the Census. (1993a). *Population profile of the United States: 1993.* Current population reports, series P23-185. Washington, DC: U.S. Government Printing Office.

U.S. Bureau of the Census. (1993b). *Hispanic Americans today.* Current population reports, series P23-183. Washington, DC: U.S. Government Printing Office.

U.S. Bureau of the Census. (1993c). *Statistical abstract of the U.S.: 1992.* Washington, DC: U.S. Government Printing Office.

U.S. Bureau of the Census. (1993d). *We the American...children.* Washington, D.C: Government Printing Office.

U.S. Bureau of the Census. (1993e). *1990 census of population and housing. Summary tape file 3C. United States summary* (CD 90-3C-1). Washington, DC: Bureau of the Census.

U.S. Bureau of the Census. (1994). *Statistical abstract of the United States: 1994* (114th ed.). Washington, DC: U.S. Government Printing Office.

U.S. Department of Labor, Women's Bureau. (1990, September). *Facts on working women* (pp. 1–4). Washington, DC: U.S. Government Printing Office.

Usdansky, M. L. (1991, September 20). Black women see dreams die. *USA Today,* p. 3A.

Wacquant, L. J. D., & Wilson, W. J. (1989). Poverty, joblessness, and the social transformation of the inner city. In P. H. Cottingham & D. T. Ellwood (Eds.), *Welfare policy in the 1990s* (pp. 70–102). Cambridge, MA: Harvard University Press.

Wallis, C. (1989, December 4). Onward, women! *Time,* 80–89.

White, J. L. (1984). *The psychology of blacks: An Afro-American perspective.* Englewood Cliffs, NJ: Prentice-Hall.

Willie, C. V. (1978). *The inclining significance of race.* Society, 15, 10–15.

Wilson, W. J. (1973). *Power, racism, and privilege: Race relations in theoretical and sociohistorical perspectives.* New York: Free Press.

Wilson, W. J. (1978). *The declining significance of race.* Chicago: University of Chicago Press.

Wilson, W. J. (1987). *The truly disadvantaged: The inner city, the underclass, and public policy.* Chicago: University of Chicago Press.

Wilson, W. J. (1991). Public policy research and *The truly disadvantaged.* In C. Jencks & P. E. Peterson (Eds.), *The urban underclass* (pp. 460–481). Washington, DC: The Brookings Institution.

Winkler, K. J. (1990, October 10). Researcher's examination of California's poor latino population prompts debate over the traditional definitions of the underclass. *The Chronicle of Higher Education,* pp. A1, A8.

Woodman, N. J. (1987). Homosexuality: Lesbian women. In A. Minahan (Ed.), *Encyclopedia of social work* (18th ed., pp. 805–812). Silver Spring, MD: National Association of Social Workers.

Zaldivar, R. A. (1994, October 7). U.S. poverty rate highest in 10 years, Census Bureau says. *Miami Herald,* pp. A1, A6.

Zastrow, C. (1988). *Social problems: Issues and solutions* (2nd ed.). Chicago: Nelson-Hall.

Zastrow, C., & Kirst-Ashman, K. (1990). *Understanding human behavior and the social environment* (2nd ed.). Chicago: Nelson-Hall.

SUGGESTIONS FOR FURTHER READING

Addelton, J. (1993). Hate crimes against lesbians and gay men. *The American Psychologist, 44,* 948–956.

Bean, F. D., & Tienda, M. (1987). *The Hispanic population of the United States.* New York: Russell Sage Foundation.

Bernal, G., & Gutierrez, M. (1988). Cubans. In L. Comas-Dias & E. E. H. Griffith (Eds.), *Clinical guidelines in cross-cultural mental health* (pp. 233–261). New York: John Wiley & Sons.

Betancourt, H., & Lopez, S. R. (1993). The study of culture, ethnicity, and race in American psychology. *American Psychologist, 48,* 629–637.

Brimmer, A. (1993). The economic cost of discrimination. *Black Enterprise, 24,* 27.

Card, C. (1994). Hate crimes: Confronting violence against lesbians and gay men. *The Journal of Sex Research, 30,* 287–297.

Cohen Publishers, Inc., & Collins, C. (1993). *The African Americans.* New York: Viking Studio Books.

Cose, E. (1994). *The rage of a privileged class: Why do prosperous blacks still have the blues?* New York: HarperCollins.

Ellwood, D. T. (1988). *Poor support: Poverty in the American family.* New York: Basic Books.

Fish, S. (1994). Reverse racism or "how the pot got to call the kettle black." *The Atlantic Monthly, 274*(3), 34–39.

Fitzpatrick, J. P. (1987). *Puerto Rican Americans: The meaning of migration to the mainland* (2nd ed.). Englewood Cliffs, NJ: Prentice Hall.

Fong, R., & Mokuau, N. (1994). Not simply "Asian Americans": Periodical literature review on Asians and Pacific Islanders, *Social Work, 39,* 298–305.

French, M. (1992). *The war against women.* New York: Simon & Schuster (Summit Books).

Gagnon, J. H., Laumann, E. O., Michael, R. T., & Michaels, S. (1994). *The social organization of sexuality.* Chicago University of Chicago Press.

Gann, L. H., & Duignan, P. J. (1986). *The Hispanics in the United States: A history.* Boulder: Westview Press.

Gibbs, J. T. (Ed.). (1988). *Young, black, and male in America: An endangered species.* Dover, MA: Auburn House.

Hacker, A. (1992). *Two nations: Black and white, separate, hostile, unequal.* New York: Charles Scribner's Sons.

Harrington, W. (1992). *Crossings: A white man's journey into black America.* New York: HarperCollins.

Hummer, R. A. (1993). Racial differentials in infant-mortality in the United States: An examination of social and health determinants. *Social Forces, 72,* 529–554.

Jaynes, G. D., & Williams, R. M., Jr. (Eds.). (1989). *A common destiny: Blacks and American society.* Washington, DC: National Academy Press.

Landry, B. (1987). *The new black middle class.* Berkeley: University of California Press.

McCall, N. (1994). *Makes me wanna holler: A young black man in America.* New York: Random House.

Min, P. G. (1994). *Asian Americans: Contemporary trends and issues.* Thousand Oaks, CA: Sage.

Onell, T. D. (1994). Telling about whites, talking about Indians: Oppression, resistance, and contemporary American-Indian identity. *Cultural Anthropology, 9,* 94–126.

Pinderhughes, E. (1989). *Understanding race, ethnicity, and power.* New York: Free Press.

Portes, A., & Rumbaut, R. G. (1990). *Immigrant America: A portrait.* Berkeley: University of California Press.

Riley, P. (Ed.). (1993). *Growing up Native American: An anthology.* New York: William Morrow.

Rodgers, H. R., Jr. (1990). *Poor women, poor families: The economic plight of America's female-headed households* (rev. ed.). Armonk, NY: M. E. Sharpe.

Rodriguez, C. E. (1991). *Puerto Ricans Born in the U.S.A.* Boulder, CO: Westview.

Shaefer, R. T. (1988). *Racial and ethnic groups* (3rd ed.). Glenview, IL: Scott, Foresman.

Stanfield, J. H., II, & Dennis, R. M. (Eds.). (1993). *Race and ethnicity in research methods.* Newbury Park, CA: Sage.

Staples, B. (1994). *Parallel time: Growing up in black and white.* New York: Pantheon Books.

Steele, S. (1990). *The content of our character: A new vision of race in America.* New York: St. Martin Press.

Steinberg, S. (1989). *The ethnic myth: Race, ethnicity, and class in America.* Boston: Beacon Press.

Stockard, J., & Johnson, M. M. (1992). *Sex and gender in society* (2nd ed.). Englewood Cliffs, NJ: Prentice Hall.

Takaki, R. (1994). *From different shores: Perspectives on race and ethnicity in America* (2nd ed.). New York: Oxford University Press.

Terkel, S. (1994). *Race: How blacks and whites think and feel about the American obsession.* New York: Anchor (Doubleday).

Van Dyk, S. (1993). The evaluation of race theory: A perspective. *Journal of Black Studies, 24,* 77–87.

Vaz, K. M. (Ed.). (1994). *Black women in America.* Thousand Oaks, CA: Sage.

Whetstone, M. (1993, December). The story behind the explosive statistics: Why blacks are losing ground in the workforce. *Ebony,* 102–106.

Wilson, W. J. (1987). *The truly disadvantaged: The inner city, the underclass, and public policy.* Chicago: University of Chicago Press.

Wilson, W. J. (Ed.). (1993). *The ghetto underclass: Social science perspectives.* Newbury Park, CA: Sage.

Look for articles in the following journals:

Affilia: Journal of Women and Social Work
Black Scholar, The
Ethnic and Racial Studies
Hispanic Journal of Behavioral Sciences
Journal of Black Studies
Journal of Gay and Lesbian Psychotherapy
Journal of Gay and Lesbian Social Services
Journal of Homosexuality
Journal of Multicultural Social Work
Signs: Journal of Women in Culture and Society
Women's Studies Quarterly

Chapter 5

COMMUNITIES

Many people who live on the same block in the same neighborhood have never met. Some do not even know the name of their next-door neighbors and have seen them only at a distance, even though they may have resided in the same house or apartment for years. This lack of "community" among neighbors is particularly prevalent in large cities where people's lives usually do not center around the residential neighborhood. In fact, some sociologists argue that the basic attributes of community—close, face-to-face relationships, enduring ties, and a sense of "we-ness"—no longer exist in densely populated urban areas. Yet others maintain that one can find thriving communities in the neighborhoods of many metropolitan areas. Still others contend that advances in transportation and communication have given rise to an entirely different type of community—the social network—which is no longer tied to any particular geographic location.

Obviously, the term *community* means different things to different people. Some of you may associate the community with the neighborhoods in which you grew up or where you now reside. Others may not think that the places where you have lived can be considered communities because they are too impersonal, and you may instead associate the term with the small towns with the proverbial white picket fences and smiling faces in which your parents and grandparents used to live. Still others may feel that you belong to a different sort of community; you may experience a sense of community in relation to those with whom you share the same ethnic or racial background, profession or occupation, sexual orientation, avocation, or religious way of life.

No matter how they are construed, communities are part of our immediate environment and thus have significant impact on the quality of our lives, for better or for worse. Consequently, it is essential for social workers and other human service practitioners to have a good understanding of community systems and how they operate. This knowledge will help you to improve social conditions and services in the communities with which you will be working. It will also help you to assist your clients so that they may take an active role in changing their own communities and neighborhoods to make them more responsive to their needs and interests. Frequently, this requires that, as a practitioner, you assume various *activist* roles, such as advocate, legislative lobbyist, expert witness, organizer, educator, broker and negotiator, enabler, social planner, and sometimes even the roles of politician, confronter, and protester.

This chapter explores various conceptions of community—locality based and sociopsychological. It examines some of the insights derived from the ecosystems perspective that have proven useful in analyzing communities. The central focus will be the study of the structure and dynamics of U.S. local communities—including cities, neighborhoods, suburbs, small towns, and rural communities—with particular attention to issues pertaining to power, politics, decision making, and conflict.

The two previous chapters examined major aspects of U.S. society's system of social stratification, including socioeconomic status, race, ethnicity, gender, and sexual orientation. We need not explore such factors again at the community level. However, before immersing ourselves in the study of communities, we should note that they can differ substantially depending on the demographic mix of each community. Some are very affluent; others are primarily middle class, working class, or poor. Some have large numbers of African Americans, Latinos, Asians, or other nondominant racial and ethnic groups; others are composed primarily of Euro-Americans. Some residential communities are composed mainly of traditional families—married couples with children; others have large proportions of singles, elderly people, or gays and lesbians. The demographic characteristics of a community play an important role in defining its character and flavor in terms of the values, customs, lifestyles, and behaviors of its residents.

CONCEPTS OF COMMUNITY

After studying 94 different definitions of *community*, Hillery (1955) concluded that most shared three basic elements: a common locality, social interaction among members, and common ties. In accordance with this early analysis, a *community* may be defined as a locality in which people share common ties and engage in interrelated activities. Community members develop common ties as they participate in various community institutions (e.g., school, church, the workplace), share the use of public services (e.g., public transportation, streets, water and sewer, garbage collection), consume local goods and services, and have common interests in various aspects of the community such as the job market, the quality of housing and schools, property values, the physical and cultural environment, and so on (Reitzes, 1986).

Warren (1978, p. 9) introduced a new concept of community by arguing that to be a community, a social system must perform the major societal functions, including production/distribution/consumption, socialization of its members, social control, provision of opportunities for social participation and interaction, provision of health care, and social support of its citizens. This has become the most common definition of **locality-based communities**, such as cities, towns, and villages. However, a good number of neighborhoods and suburbs that would qualify as communities under Hillery's criteria of locality, common ties, and social interaction, would not qualify under Warren's definition because they seldom perform the full range of societal functions.

Although Hillery's and Warren's concepts of community are useful constructs, they do not cover all possible types of communities. For example, they do not apply to **nonplace or sociopsychological communities**, such as religious or ethnic communities, because such communities are not necessarily attached to a specific locality. Rubin (1969) was one of the first social theorists to argue that a community need not provide for the daily needs of its members and therefore need not contain a cross-section of the major institutions in society. He also argued that the concept of community should not be tied to any particular locality, given the increased mobility characteristic of modern societies and the advances in communication and transportation that make possible frequent contact across great distances.

According to Rubin (1969), the community is an intermediary structure between family and society that serves to connect people to society. He argued that, to fulfill this mediating function, communities must possess certain characteristics; namely, they should be neither too big nor too small, they should be involved in some vital concern, and they should be relatively enduring. Specifically, he suggested that communities must be small enough to allow people to interact formally and informally but large enough to give them a feeling of incorporation into the larger society—a feeling not attainable simply by participating in a small friendship circle. A community should concern itself with some vital aspect of life (e.g., race, ethnicity, religion, profession or occupation, political concerns, sexual orientation, etc.) and not just some inconsequential or passing interest of its members. Finally, a community should exist for a reasonable period of time so that members can develop a sense of belonging.

Following the newer tradition of separating community from locality, Wellman (1988) defined the community as a **social network**. From his perspective, any group of people who actively share some interest about a social issue, personal characteristic, or organizational/associational tie (to mention a few of the possible links or connections that bring people together) can be considered a community, no matter whether this social network exists within a given locality. Examples of nonplace communities or social networks would include the African-American community, the gay and lesbian community, the Mexican-American community, the Chinese-American community, the American Jewish community, the women's rights movement, computer networks, the right-to-life movement, the social work profession, the democratic party, the banking community, and so on.

PERSPECTIVES ON AMERICAN COMMUNITIES

One of the most basic and persistent sociological debates is whether communities continue to exist today or have become the casualties of urbanization, industrialization, and bureaucratization. This controversy, to which we turn our attention briefly, is often referred to among sociologists as *the* community question.

The Community Lost Argument

According to Stein (1960), the forces of urbanization, industrialization, and bureaucratization acting in unison have created a "mass society" that has eclipsed the distinctiveness of U.S. local communities and decreased their importance by increasing their dependence on the larger society. In addition, according to Packard (1972), the high rate of geographic mobility in the United States has left many people feeling lonely and unconnected (Packard, 1972).

Urbanization

Over the years, a large proportion of the U.S. population migrated from rural communities and small towns to metropolitan areas in search of a better life. In some ways, city life represented an improvement over life in the country or in a small town because cities offered greater educational and job opportunities as well as increased opportunities to participate in cultural and intellectual activities and to enjoy a broader range of products and services. According to Tonnies (1887, 1963), the shift from rural to urban living led to a decreasing sense of community as people's relationships changed from **gemeinschaft** (i.e., close, face-to-face interactions characterized by long duration, commitment, trust, and mutuality) to **gesellschaft** (i.e., more impersonal, segmental, superficial, and contractual relationships).

Tonnies was not the only one to suggest that urbanization had a negative impact on community life. Simmel (1950) argued that the continuous sensory bombardment to which people are subjected in a noisy and crowded urban environment and the constant need to interact with strangers forced city people to adopt an attitude of indifference and insensitivity toward others to screen out excess stimulation and prevent overload. For instance, it is not unusual in a large city for an individual to drive past an injured pedestrian lying on the street or for a pedestrian to look the other way when he or she sees an elderly person apparently lost and walking aimlessly.

Wirth (1938) suggested that three features of urban environments are responsible for the reduced ability of city dwellers to maintain close personal relationships: large size, high density or crowding, and heterogeneity of the population. Specifically, he reasoned that a large population tends to maintain impersonal, superficial, and segmental relations because it becomes impossible for each individual to know well the large number of others with whom he or she must interact daily on a face-to-face basis. In addition, he suggested that crowding interfered with personal relationships because it fostered tension, irritation, conflict, and competition for space and privacy. Finally, Wirth argued that the diversity of a large urban population interfered with the development of close personal relations because people from different backgrounds (e.g., racial, ethnic, or socioeconomic) do not share the same values, norms of behavior, attitudes, or traditions.

Even though the arguments for the loss of community sentiment due to increasing urbanization appear compelling, the causal relationships suggested have not been confirmed by research (Warren & Lyon, 1988, p. 28).

Industrialization and Bureaucratization

In addition to urbanization, community theorists saw industrialization and bureaucratization as important forces leading to a loss of community. The early studies of Middletown (Muncie, Indiana) by Lynd and Lynd (1929, 1937) documented a loss of local community

sentiment as the United States became more industrialized and bureaucratized. As long as local business and industry were the center of Middletown's economy, townspeople had a strong sense of autonomy and self-sufficiency and a concomitant sense of community. But as outside enterprises took over business and industry, the townspeople became increasingly aware that they were only a small cog in a much larger business/industrial wheel over which they had little influence or control. With the influx of outside influences, the sense of community became weaker.

Warner (1963) documented a similar decline of community sentiment in Yankee City (Newburyport, Massachusetts), as the local family-owned factories were bought by regional and national corporations and thus became branch plants of large absentee organizations. Because the absentee owners and the managers that represented them in the community had primary allegiance not to the well-being of the community but to their business organizations, they were often perceived by local workers as unconcerned about worker needs and interests.

The Community Saved Argument

So that you do not develop the notion that community theorists consistently insisted that the forces of modernity effectively destroyed the possibility of community in the United States, we now shift the focus to contrary opinions.

A series of case studies of primarily low-income, working-class ethnic communities in older urban areas of U.S. cities, such as Boston and Chicago, provided early evidence that residents of these ethnic neighborhoods had a strong sense of loyalty to one another and maintained close relationships with extended kin and neighbors (Whyte, 1955; Gans, 1962; Suttles, 1968). Apparently, according to these studies, local community sentiments had been kept alive in these sections of the city despite urbanization, industrialization, bureaucratization, and the growth of mass society. Other early studies of suburban communities such as Levittown in Philadelphia (Gans, 1967) corroborated the findings that urbanization and industrialization had not destroyed community sentiments. In these suburban communities, neighbors had formed informal and formal associations centered around their children and their homes. The "quasi-primary" relationships they established, although more transient and less binding than those between friends and kin, were significant in generating community sentiments.

More recently, research has shown that large numbers of people in the United States turn to their neighbors for support and friendship. For example, according to a 1989 national survey by the University of Chicago's National Opinion Research Center, two out of three respondents reported that they socialized with neighbors and 50 percent reported that they spent a social evening with neighbors several times per month. In many cases, children foster strong ties among neighborhood parents who must organize to take turns carpooling them to school, to various recreational programs, or to the shopping center or nearby hamburger or pizza place (Rubenstein, 1993). Particularly now that most parents work, sharing the transportation and supervision of children among neighbors is becoming more and more important, and this causes neighbors to get to know one another and to interact more closely. Community residents are also becoming increasingly involved in their localities in relation to quality-of-life issues (Naisbitt, 1992).

These sociological findings about the preservation of community sentiments among city residents and suburbanites considerably weakened the original argument that urbanization, industrialization, and bureaucratization were destroying the sense of local community in the United States.

Community of Limited Liability

Although the local community or neighborhood may no longer be considered by most people to be their most important source of close relationships and social ties, studies have documented that it continues to play a role in people's lives. The concept of **community of limited liability** (Greer, 1962; Kasarda & Janowitz, 1974; Hunter, 1978) suggests that the local community (e.g., the neighborhood) continues to serve important though limited functions. For example, in an emergency, a neighbor is usually a more readily available source of assistance than a close friend or relative who lives or works a distance away. Similarly, when you go on vacation, it is usually more practical to ask a neighbor to look after your home than to ask more distantly located friends or relatives.

The concept of community of limited liability also suggests that neighborhoods and local communities continue to play an important role in the lives of *some* people at least *some* of the time. How much of a role depends on a variety of factors, such as how long an individual has resided in a particular community. Consequently, the question is not whether or not local community ties remain important but for whom and under what circumstances (Kasarda & Janowitz, 1974). For instance, some people maintain close relations with their neighbors because they share the same ethnic/racial background or sexual orientation and happen to be part of the same social circle. Others are closely tied to the local community because they lack other options due to limited mobility, such as in the case of children, the elderly, or homemakers without transportation. From a social exchange perspective (Blau, 1967), one may predict that the more a local community meets a resident's needs, the more this individual will be willing to become socially and emotionally involved in the community's internal affairs.

Defended neighborhoods (Suttles, 1972) provide still another example of communities of limited liability. In this instance, community members develop a high degree of solidarity and cooperation and engage in concerted actions because they feel that their neighborhood is being threatened by crime, racial/ethnic invasion, or changes that they consider not in the best interest of the area. For example, residents may close ranks because they fear the neighborhood will be invaded by an "undesirable" group; or because they oppose a school busing plan, the projected building of an expressway cutting through the neighborhood, or the placement of a halfway house for the retarded or the mentally ill in the neighborhood; or because they fear displacement by an urban renewal program. *Conscious communities* provide another example of community of limited liability (Hunter, 1978). These are neighborhoods, often suburban, that have made an effort to define their central values and concerns and that have established resident associations to encourage the formation of close bonds among neighbors.

The Community Liberated Argument: Social Networks

The third and final position that theorists have taken on the community question is to argue that community ties continue to exist but are seldom linked to any specific locality. The point made by those who sponsor this argument is that communities have been freed from territorial confinement by advances in transportation (e.g., superhighways, jet travel) communications (e.g., low-priced long distance telephone, electronic connectivity to country-wide and global networks through computers and cable/video interactive systems), and other technological advances. These developments have enabled people to maintain ties with others regardless of distance.

The community liberated position emphasizes that people maintain membership in various social networks, such as kin networks, work-related networks, professional networks, computer networks (e.g., discussion groups within the Internet), racial and ethnic networks, avocational networks, associational networks, gay/lesbian networks, church-related networks, and so on (Wellman & Leighton, 1979). These social networks have taken the place of local communities in our lives and they allow us to remain closely tied to a wide range of people that provide us with many of the things we need—love, companionship, someone to talk with, opportunities to pursue hobbies and interests and to socialize, help with problems, assistance in an emergency, emotional support, recognition, understanding, knowledge and information, favors, advice, financial aid, and so on (Wellman, 1988). Social networks do not necessarily perform positive or socially desirable functions. Networks such as the Mafia, various drug cartels, and gangs perform socially undesirable or illegal functions.

Social network theory, a relatively new but growing field, studies the regularities in the pattern of ties linking people. These network ties may be strong or weak, sparsely knit or densely knit. For example, most people maintain strong ties with their immediate families and close friends. If they get together with them frequently, their ties are also densely knit. In contrast, relations with extended kin and co-workers are characteristically weaker for most people. If they see relatives infrequently, the ties that unite them are also loosely knit. In contrast, ties with co-workers, though weak, may be more densely knit than those with the extended family, particularly for individuals who work closely with others.

We can turn to some of the members of our social networks under practically any circumstance. For example, chances are that you would not hesitate to call on your parents or your children to help out in all sorts of situations. However, the majority of our network ties are more limited in purpose. For instance, you might ask a neighbor or co-worker to help out in an emergency or with some small matter, but you would be unlikely to ask this person to lend you a substantial sum of money or to stay at your bedside at the hospital over a period of several days while you recover from a major operation.

Although the majority of an individual's social ties may be weak and loosely knit, their power and importance should not be discounted. Having a large network of contacts and relations, even if they are mostly casual, provides a person with indirect access to a greater variety of resources than if he or she were to rely exclusively on a small number of strong ties. Also, weak ties between two individuals may serve as a bridge between two groups or other collectivities, such as two communities that might otherwise remain unconnected (Granovetter, 1973).

To be sure, not many people are able to maintain a large network of ties, weak or strong. Studies have shown that, on average, the affluent maintain more social connections than the poor (Fischer, 1982; Auslander & Litwin, 1988). This is probably because it takes money to transport oneself to visit with others, to call long distance to keep in touch, to go out to dinner or to some social function, to entertain at home, or to connect with others via computer or fax. Another reason why individuals of higher socioeconomic background tend to have larger social networks than those who are poor is that they tend to be more educated. Education facilitates the development of social ties because it provides the person with skills and increasing self-confidence to reach out and join a variety of social networks outside the family, the neighborhood, and the workplace (Wellman & Leighton, 1979; Eckenrode, 1983).

Consider a popular way of connecting with others these days—computer "networking." To participate in a computer network, an individual needs to be literate, since most communication through the computer is in writing. The person also needs to have computer skills, access to a computer system as well as a telephone and modem, a subscription to an on-line computer service, and knowledge of how to access others via E-mail, bulletin boards, discussion groups, and so on. Despite assertions that computer networks are highly democratic because they allow people to socialize without regard to race, culture, sexual orientation, or socioeconomic status, most people in the mid-1990s, let alone the poor, did not have the education, skills, or resources to network with others via the computer (Markoff, 1993; Rheingold, 1993).

THE ECOSYSTEMS APPROACH TO THE STUDY OF LOCAL COMMUNITIES

We now turn to the study of local communities, beginning in this section by examining some of the conceptual contributions of the ecosystems perspective. The possibility that a comprehensive theory of community will evolve in the near future is practically nil (Warren, 1988). However, a number of principles derived from ecology and from the open systems perspective provide some helpful insights.

Let us begin by examining some of the contributions of human ecology to the study of communities. Park (1936) developed the concept of the **web of life** to refer to the binding together of all living organisms within a common habitat in a relationship of mutual interdependence. This concept reminds us that human communities maintain a mutually interdependent relationship with the physical and social resources in their habitats, thus keeping their biotic and social steady states.

In attempting to understand a given community, ecology reminds us of the importance of paying close attention to the physical aspects of the environment, such as the way the community is laid out, the degree of crowding the population experiences, the noise levels and amount of pollution to which community members are subjected, the quality of the housing stock, and the level of public sanitation. These characteristics of the habitat can enhance or limit the health and social functioning of community members. With respect to physical layout, for example, if low-income housing is located far from sources of public transportation or if public transportation is lacking in some areas, these deficiencies would limit access to work, health care, social services, and shopping, particularly for the poor and the elderly (Germain, 1985).

Another important concept contributed by ecology is competition. According to Park (1936), the community's natural areas (e.g., central business district, industrial areas, residential neighborhoods) are likely to have come into being through **competition** over land use, the process by which some establish dominance over others. For example, in your community, the strongest commercial and financial interests have probably secured the most strategic locations for their businesses, and residents with the most money have probably selected the most attractive surroundings for their homes.

Succession is another basic ecological principle that enhances our understanding of communities (Park, 1936). It consists of the process by which one social group invades an area, competes with its current occupants, and eventually wins out and takes control of the territory. For example, a working-class neighborhood formerly occupied almost exclusively by native-born Italian Americans may begin to experience an influx of recent immigrants from Vietnam. This may happen because, as the neighborhood starts to deteriorate, the value of homes declines to the point that they become accessible to the new immigrant group. As more Italian Americans sell their homes to Vietnamese immigrants, property values continue to decline and the process of exodus of Italian Americans and influx of Vietnamese Americans accelerates. Hacker (1992) has noted that the tipping point in the succession process occurs much earlier than common sense would indicate—when the invading group controls 8 percent of the neighborhood. At this point, the old group begins to leave steadily and the community is on its way to becoming predominantly composed of the new group.

Ecology teaches us to pay attention to the distribution of the population throughout the community in terms of salient demographic features, such as race, ethnicity, and socioeconomic status. Information about the location and size of various social groups within a community, which is easily obtainable from U.S. census tract statistics, is vital to determine the degree of need for and strategic location of various health and social services (Fellin, 1995). The ecological perspective also stresses the importance of considering other characteristics of the community population, such as size, density, and heterogeneity. As previously noted in this chapter, these factors may have significant consequences for community members.

From a systems theory perspective, we may think of communities as social systems composed of interdependent units, many with ties to other systems outside the locality. These subsystems that comprise the community—particularly the economic, governmental/political, educational, health and social welfare, and religious—provide for the fulfillment of critical social functions, such as production/distribution/consumption of goods and services, socialization, social control, social participation, and mutual support.

Production/Distribution/Consumption of goods and services is the community function carried out by the economic system through a complex of business, industrial, technological, service, and other organizations that provide for the employment, income, and sustenance needs of the population. The **socialization** function involves the transmission of knowledge, values, attitudes, and behaviors, and the teaching of social roles. Many social institutions play a role in the socialization of community members, particularly the schools, families, churches, and the media. **Social control** involves formal and informal means of regulating behavior so that community members will behave in accordance with family, community, and societal values, standards, and laws. This function is carried out informally by families and religious organizations and formally by the legal system, law enforcement agencies, and the courts.

Social participation refers to opportunities for social interaction provided by the family and various informal groups as well as by religious organizations, recreational facilities, social clubs, and professional, voluntary, and service associations. Various means of communication—such as radio, television, newspapers, and telephones—facilitate social participation and interaction. **Mutual support** encompasses the formal and informal efforts of the community to provide health care and assistance with personal, family, financial, and other problems. Health care is provided formally through hospitals, health maintenance organizations, and private physicians and informally through family and friends who take care of us when we are sick. Social support is provided formally by a variety of social welfare agencies and private practitioners and informally by family, friends, neighbors, co-workers, and self-help groups (Warren, 1978; Fellin, 1987).

Boundaries are important to separate the internal subsystems of the community and their functions; however, most community functions overlap and so do the boundaries of the institutions responsible for the fulfillment of these functions. For example, you may easily be able to distinguish the physical boundaries of the homes and schools in your community from those of its churches, newspapers, and television stations, but it is much more difficult to draw a line where the socialization function of the family ends and that of the schools, the church, or the media begins.

Boundaries are also important to separate the community system from its surrounding environment. In the case of a central city, for example, the environment includes the larger metropolitan area, the city's suburbs, nearby municipalities with which the city interacts frequently, the state in which it is located, the region, and the nation. But these boundaries, like the boundaries separating community subsystems, are often blurred due to their permeability. Permeability is important to facilitate the influx of inputs (e.g., information and human and material resources) and the outflow of outputs (e.g., community products and services). However, permeability makes it difficult to tell where one city ends and an adjoining municipality begins or where one suburb ends and another begins.

To keep a steady state, communities must be able to meet the basic needs of their members. They must also be at least minimally able to meet the accountability requirements of their suprasystems, such as county, state, and federal government agencies that provide resources or national/regional headquarters of businesses and professional associations established within the community. Meeting intrasystem and suprasystem needs requires countless adaptations and effective management of conflict and competition. Communities that fail at these efforts are likely to lose population and resources and to have difficulty surviving.

THE STRUCTURE AND DYNAMICS OF U.S. LOCAL COMMUNITIES

Types of Locality-Based Community Systems

Metropolitan and Megalopolitan Areas
This section takes a look at various locality-based community systems, including metropolitan areas, central cities, neighborhoods, suburbs, edge cities, and small towns.

The U.S. Bureau of the Census (1992, p. 896) uses the term *Metropolitan Area*, variously referred to as *Metropolitan Statistical Area (MSA)* or *Consolidated Metropolitan Statistical Area (CMSA)*, to refer to a cluster of one or more central cities and surrounding suburbs with a population of more than one million inhabitants. Some metro areas have sprawled so much that their outer boundaries have merged with the boundaries of neighboring metropolitan areas, forming vast urban stretches sometimes referred to as a **megalopolis,** a Greek term meaning great city (Gottman, 1961). For example, the California coastal strip from north of San Francisco south to San Diego, the southeastern coastal area from Palm Beach to Miami, and the huge urban belt stretching from north of Boston to south of Washington are considered megalopolitan areas (Light, Keller, & Calhoun, 1989, pp. 239–240).

One of the biggest problems faced by U.S. metropolitan areas today, unique among urban-industrial nations, is the proliferation of independent government units within their boundaries. This metropolitan fragmentation is problematic because, as will become clearer later in this chapter, it cuts off financially strong areas from areas with heavy doses of social problems.

Another consequence of fragmentation is that it creates overlapping, competing, and duplicative political/governmental units that are often too small to support the necessary range of public services in the community. This arrangement is wasteful and inefficient and makes it virtually impossible for the metropolitan area to tackle its more serious problems (Newton, 1975). Community members who are financially well off can always buy solutions for the problems left unsolved by local governments (e.g., they can send their children to private schools if the public schools are substandard, they can hire private security guards for their neighborhoods if the police protection provided is inadequate, or they can go to private health and social service providers if the public system is inferior). But the poor have no recourse and suffer the brunt of the social problems created and exacerbated by metropolitan fragmentation.

Many metropolitan areas lacking consolidated governments often deal with the need to provide basic services to the population—such as utilities (e.g., water, sewage disposal), police protection, public health, and transportation—by creating a variety of special purpose districts or areawide departments and agencies dedicated specifically to the provision of each service. Such piecemeal approach to the provision of metropolitan services is counterproductive because, by taking care of the essential services that small but affluent independent communities would find difficult or impossible to provide, the metropolitan government removes much of the incentive for these small financially secure areas to consolidate with other areas (Williams, Herman, Liebman, & Dye, 1965).

Central Cities

A **central city** is that part of a city that comprises and immediately surrounds the "downtown" commercial, financial, and industrial districts. One important trend in the United States in the post-World War II era has been the movement of much of the middle-class population, especially the white middle-class, away from central cities to the suburbs.

As the white middle-class left the cities, other groups came in to take their place. Attracted by the availability of industrial jobs, many rural African Americans from the South and various other racial and ethnic minorities settled in the aging and deteriorating central-city areas, particularly those in the Northeast and Great Lakes regions vacated by the white middle class (Mohl, 1990). Unbeknownst to these newcomers, however, the industrial job market in central cities was beginning to con-

tract because the U.S. economy was entering a postindustrial phase and many major industries were downsizing and beginning to move their operations to other areas of the country and abroad in the search for cheaper space and labor.

As the industrial base of central cities decreased, job opportunities for blue-collar workers also decreased. This led to high unemployment and exacerbated many social problems, such as crime, violence, drug and alcohol abuse, teenage unwed parenthood, homeless-ness, welfare dependency, and poor health. Many central cities have been pushed to the brink of bankruptcy by the decreased tax base experienced as a result of the middle-class, industrial, and business exodus (Mohl, 1990). This financial crunch has caused additional problems, suchas inferior schools, substandard municipal services, and an increasingly more deteriorated physical environment.

Due to the preceding developments, many central cities in the United States have lost their former leadership in relation to other units in the metropolitan area. Their job markets have become increasingly polarized, with expanded work opportunities at the high and low ends of the occupational scale but few jobs in between. Specifically,people in high-level professional and technical occupations as well as those with expertise in finance and corporate management can usually find employment in central cities. Central cities also offer a good selection of low-income jobs in the areas of information and data processing, service, and nonunion, low-skill manufacturing. But, typically, they do not offer a good selection of middle-range jobs. Given the polarized job market, central-city residential neighborhoods have developed similar disparities. Next to fashionable areas with upscale apartment complexes one can find a variety of slowly deteriorating working-class neighborhoods and low-income **ghettos** (Logan, 1988; Sassen, 1990).

A way of infusing some life back into decaying central- and inner-city areas is to declare them enterprise or empowerment zones. These two government initiatives, if well carried out, have the potential to make a significant contribution to the economic revival of urban America (Bergman, 1992). However, to date, they have had limited impact.

The **enterprise zone** initiative, which has been used to a limited extent by the federal government in recent years, grants tax breaks and other incentives to businesses that locate in economically distressed urban areas and that offer employment opportunities to disadvantaged residents of these areas (Council of Economic Advisers, 1993). Some state and local governments provide additional incentives to businesses owned by women and nondominant group members locating within an enterprise zone. To date, thousands of areas have been designated enterprise zones nationwide but less than a third of these are "active" or developing to any extent. This government program has had limited impact so far because, to a large extent, it has granted benefits to already estab-

lished businesses rather than recruited new ones and because often it has not included job training programs and investment in infrastructure.

In 1993, only a handful of areas in the United States had been declared **empowerment zones.** These areas were receiving large federal grants for social services and employers established there were given subsidies for salaries paid to employees who were residents of these areas (Stanfield, 1993).

Gentrification is another way of reviving central cities. This is the conversion of working-class, often run-down districts into upscale neighborhoods through the purchase and renovation of older homes and rowhouses (Light, Keller, & Calhoun, 1989). It has been prompted by the desire of some upper-middle-class people to live close to their work and to places of entertainment (e.g., theaters, concert halls, and restaurants) and to avoid the long commutes to the suburbs. However, this revival of decaying areas of the central city often has been achieved at the price of displacing low-income and elderly residents, many from nondominant racial and ethnic groups, who often end up paying higher rents that they can ill afford in other decaying areas of the inner city.

To make gentrification less of a burden on the poor and working-class people who are displaced, perhaps a better solution would be to establish an urban homesteading program. Under this program, those displaced by urban renewal would be granted abandoned homes acquired by the cities through foreclosure and would be given low-interest loans to rehabilitate them. This would be good for cities too because it would restore abandoned and delinquent properties to the tax roles, thus increasing the tax base.

One example of urban homesteading is the Philadelphia model developed at the instigation of the Acorn squatters' campaign. This homesteading program restricts eligibility to low- and moderate-income families and gives them low-interest rehabilitation loans and reasonable time (i.e., one to two years) to complete the renovations. Programs following the Philadelphia model have been instituted in several major cities, such as Detroit, St. Louis, Pittsburgh, Columbus, and Brooklyn (Borgos, 1988). Unfortunately, however, this practice is not widespread.

Neighborhoods

Neighborhoods are usually understood to be residential subunits of the larger local community that can be distinguished from one another according to various resident characteristics such as socioeconomic status, stage in the life cycle (e.g., singles, families with children, retirees), racial/ethnic background, or sexual orientation. Thus, a neighborhood may be primarily white, working class, Italian American, gay and lesbian, or composed of retirees, to mention a few examples. Ideally, neighborhoods should be small enough that their residents can walk their boundaries within a reasonable period of time and can become acquainted with one another if they have the inclination to do so.

Many neighborhoods are "functional" to various extents, in the sense that they provide not only housing but education, shopping, recreational opportunities, and various services. Within their boundaries are various social institutions and establishments, such as elementary schools, churches, grocery stores, social and athletic clubs, dry cleaners, hardware stores, retail stores, medical and other professional offices, and sometimes police and fire stations, hospitals, and health and social service agencies.

Neighborhoods provide opportunities for their members to engage in **neighboring** activities. That is, they provide opportunities for residents to engage in informal interactions with neighbors, sometimes in passing, as they come and go from home, across the backyard fence, on the front porch, through borrowing food, exchanging tools and services, sharing newspapers and magazines, and by participating in neighborhood associations, occasional neighborhood initiatives, and block parties (Keller, 1968; Fellin, 1987).

Neighborhood boundaries are not easy to specify because they tend to be drawn differently by various social institutions, local government units, and residents. For instance, the boundaries established by the school district, the municipality, the county, the state, health and social service agencies, and churches seldom coincide. In addition, residents often define the boundaries of their neighborhoods in different ways by using as demarcation points certain physical markers such as highways, major streets or rivers, as well as points where the social character (e.g., race, ethnicity, sexual orientation, or socioeconomic status) of the population changes.

Social workers and other human service practitioners sometimes are called to work with neighborhoods to help them function more effectively so that they may better fulfill the needs of residents. It is useful for community practitioners to have a conceptual understanding of various types of neighborhoods, their strengths, and weaknesses. Based on a study of 59 different neighborhoods, Warren and Warren (1977) identified various common types, including the integral, parochial, diffuse, stepping-stone, transitory, and anomic neighborhoods (see Table 5.1). Even though you may not be familiar with these terms, you are likely to have come across neighborhoods that illustrate each of these prototypes. Over time, neighborhoods naturally evolve from one type to another. For example, homes become older and deteriorated or as residents undergo normal life-cycle changes (e.g., retirement), the likelihood of succession increases and this may change the neighborhood's character (Choldin, Hanson, & Bobrer, 1980).

Overall, the most effective neighborhood is the **integral neighborhood**. Its residents interact actively, identify with the neighborhood, and relate to the larger community. This gives the neighborhood a high capacity to identify its

TABLE 5.1 Types of Neighborhoods

Integral: A cosmopolitan as well as a local center. Individuals are in close contact. They share many concerns. They participate in activities of the larger community.

Parochial: A neighborhood having a strong ethnic identity or homogeneous character. Self-contained, independent of larger community. Has ways to screen out what does not conform to its own norms.

Diffuse: Often homogeneous setting ranging from a new subdivision to an inner-city housing project. Has many things in common. However, there is no active internal life. Not tied into the larger community. Little local involvement with neighbors.

Stepping-Stone: An active neighborhood. A game of "musical chairs." People participate in neighborhood activities not because they identify with the neighborhood but often to "get ahead" in a career or some other nonlocal point of destination.

Transitory: A neighborhood where population change has been or is occurring. Often breaks up into little clusters of people—frequently "oldtimers" and newcomers are separated. Little collective action or organization takes place.

Anomic: It's really a nonneighborhood. Highly atomized; no cohesion. Great social distance between people. No protective barriers to outside influences making it responsive to some outside change. It lacks the capacity to mobilize for common actions from within.

Source: From *The Neighborhood Organizer's Handbook* by Rachel Warren. © 1977 by the University of Notre Dame Press. Used by permission.

problems and to take appropriate action. The **parochial neighborhood** also functions well internally, with residents showing strong social ties, loyalty to the neighborhood, and participation in neighborhood, activities. But this neighborhood tends to be insulated from the larger community, often due to language barriers or by choice of the residents. This insulation serves to protect the neighborhood from outside influences that would violate its traditional norms, but it keeps it too disengaged from the surrounding municipality and this can be detrimental. Some neighborhoods with a strong ethnic identity, such as immigrant communities, are of this type.

Diffuse neighborhoods have little active internal life and few connections with the larger community, but they have the potential to quickly become internally organized and externally linked, should circumstances require it. Their members generally identify with the neighborhood and may take considerable pride in their homes, but their social lives do not center around the neighborhood. Many affluent suburbs or areas with luxury condos fit this mold. Under normal circumstances, residents are little involved in neighborhood activities, perhaps because their social network and contacts are outside the neighborhood and local community. However, should there be any sudden external threat to the neighborhood or any internal problem that affects the residents, they can quickly become engaged, cooperative, and well organized to deal with the situation. When the crisis is over, they are likely to go back to the same old benign indifference.

Residents of **stepping-stone neighborhoods** usually are highly mobile occupationally, socially, and residentially. They are active participants in neighborhood affairs and keep the neighborhood well linked to the outside community, but they quickly move on and similar others take their places, like a game of musical chairs. The result is that few residents stay long enough in the neighborhood to develop strong ties. Consequently, although stepping-stone neighborhoods usually function efficiently, they are not the best places for people who are looking to establish long-term close ties with neighbors. **Transitory neighborhoods** are those undergoing succession. Residents are often segmented into clusters, with the old-timers and the newcomers usually keeping a distance. Finally, **anomic neighborhoods** are perhaps the type of communities with which practitioners are most likely to be called on to work. They are also the most challenging because they tend to lack a leadership structure and usually have few residents who care about the neighborhood; consequently, anomic neighborhoods have little capacity to engage in collective action, at least initially. They are often found in areas with a concentration of low-income public housing projects, although anomie can afflict any neighborhood.

According to Warren and Warren (1977), neighborhoods can fulfill important functions for their residents, including sociability, interpersonal influence, mutual aid, organizational base, reference group, and status arena (see Table 5.2). These benefits are especially important for residents who have limited access to other social networks. Community practitioners can assist by enhancing these functions in the neighborhoods in which they work.

As sociability arenas, neighborhoods provide opportunities for neighboring activities. In their role as interpersonal influence centers, they serve as places where neighbors can act as referral agents for one another and can exchange information and experience about a variety of things such as childrearing and child care, jobs, investments, and political issues. Neighborhoods also facilitate mutual aid, such as helping out in an emergency, doing the cooking or grocery shopping for a sick neighbor, or exchanging goods and services (e.g., helping neighbors with a plumbing problem in exchange for their giving you a hand with child care or babysitting). By providing opportunities for involvement in local activities and organizations—such as the PTA; neighborhood crime watch; neighborhood beautification program; the local chapters of the Boy Scouts, Big Brothers, Big Sisters, or the residents' association—neighborhoods act as organizational power bases and leadership training grounds for their residents. Many well-functioning neighborhoods also act as reference groups or bases for identification. This is evident when the residents take pride in their neighborhood and show commitment to it.

Suburbs, Exurbs, and Outer or Edge Cities

A **suburb** is a residential area within the metropolis that lies outside the central city (Fava, 1975; Lyon, 1987). An **exurb** is a residential community adjacent to *but outside* metropolitan areas. Since the 1970s, exurbs have been growing even faster than suburbs, aided by the decentralization of manufacturing, the extension of highway systems into outlying areas, the development of more flexible working hours, and the trend toward early retirement (Fava, 1975). In this chapter the author will use the term *suburb* to refer to both suburbs and exurbs.

The shift of the U.S. population from central cities to suburbia increased dramatically after World War II to the point that today about half of the population, including the majority of Euro-Americans, lives in the suburbs and exurbs and only one-quarter lives in central cities (Lacayo, 1992). The racial difference between central city and suburbs/exurbs in the United States is so striking that some people

TABLE 5.2 The Functions of Neighborhoods

1. **As a Sociability Arena**
   Refers to "informal neighboring," "back-fence" chatting, coffee klatches, and front-porch visiting.
2. **As an Interpersonal Influence Center**
   Refers to neighbors sharing opinions, asking for advice, offering suggestions, and influencing each other's behavior and thoughts about many issues—everything from raising children to getting a new job or voting in the next election.
3. **Mutual Aid**
   Refers to the exchanges of goods and services, such as helping out in an emergency, collecting money for a bereaved family or for graduation or birthdays, watching each other's homes when the neighbor is on vacation, or helping a neighbor build a garage in exchange for his help in fixing your car.
4. **As an Organizational Base**
   Refers to local groups and associations such as block clubs, PTAs, and local branches of larger organizations such as girl scouts and political groups, etc. These local groups can become a power base for people in the neighborhood.
5. **As a Reference Group**
   The idea that a neighborhood is a basis of group identity may be reflected in a name residents use to refer to themselves, in a commitment to stay in the neighborhood, or a pride in the neighborhood.
6. **As a Status Arena**
   Provides a place to show personal achievements and well-being—includes parking the new car in front of the house for all the neighbors to see, or decorating the front lawn with gas lamps, grill work, and birdbaths, etc.

Source: From *The Neighborhood Organizer's Handbook* by Rachel Warren. © 1977 by the University of Notre Dame Press. Used by permission.

call this separation the U.S. version of *apartheid* (Quindlen, 1992; Rusk, 1992).

Beginning after World War II and spurred by the development of highways and other federal programs aimed at increasing the supply of single-family homes and residential mortgages, many people (largely a white group prior to the 1960s) moved to the suburbs (Wood, 1989). They were seeking a better education for their children, a safer environment in which to raise their families, and some distance from urban riots and an increasing concentration of poor people, people of color, and recent immigrants and refugees who became trapped in the central-city's low-income ghettos. Government assistance in the form of highway construction and maintenance, low-interest government-insured home mortgages, and income tax breaks for home mortgage interest and property taxes—public handouts more costly that those given to welfare recipients—enabled the predominantly white middle class to leave the central cities. By creating their own independent suburban governments, many were able to cut themselves off legally, politically, socially, and financially from the cities (Newton, 1975; Lazare, 1990).

This trend toward suburban independence from central cities has led to a proliferation of local governments; for example, Greater Los Angeles includes over 100 independent communities and Metropolitan Atlanta comprises over 40 (Leinberger & Lockwood, 1986). The problem with this arrangement, as noted

previously in this chapter, is that the affluent or middle-class suburbs that have become independent from central cities have taken a large chunk of the cities' financial base, leaving behind most of the social problems.

It is easy to understand why the suburban population is reluctant to allow their governments to consolidate with central-city governments, as long as the metropolitan government provides them with basic services (e.g., water, sewerage, public transportation, and public health) and as long as they can afford the remaining expenses of being independent. Why not take advantage of the free lunch, so to speak, if it is available? The result is that many suburbanites earn a living in the city and, while they are there, use its public services (e.g., fire and police protection, streets, traffic control, transportation system, libraries and museums, parks, water, sewerage, sanitation), eating establishments, and places of entertainment (e.g., concert halls, theaters). After using the central city's resources, they retreat to their suburban bedroom communities where they can keep the social problems and financial strains of "the other America" out of sight and out of mind. By living in an unincorporated dis-

trict, they do not have to pay taxes to support central city services and facilities. The problem with this cozy arrangement is that it makes central cities bear the lion's share of the burden of public services while simultaneously depriving them of the fiscal resources needed to cope with the human problems that remain (Slovak, 1985).

The most widely advocated solution to the problem of unequal distribution of resources and services between central cities and suburbs, difficult as it may be for many suburbanites to accept, is to consolidate entire metropolitan areas into one district so that revenues and services can be distributed more equitably. So far, only a few large U.S. metropolitan areas have consolidated governments (Rusk, 1993). Probably this is because the idea is not only unpalatable to the suburban population but also to the established central-city politicians who do not want to lose their power enclaves, particularly African Americans and Latinos who have gained in political power under this arrangement and who fear the dilution of power that comes with consolidation (Smothers, 1993).

In the last few decades, many suburbs and exurbs have transformed themselves from mere bedroom communities into full-fledged **edge cities** (or **outer cities**) as they have become increasingly more self-contained and self-sufficient. In fact, these newest of U.S. cities are well on their way to achieving "urban" dominance (Leinberger & Lockwood, 1986; Muller, 1989; Garreau, 1991). They have developed their own downtowns—including office parks, shopping malls, and high-technology business parks—that have become important sources of employment for the community and providers of a wide range of products and services. In fact, job opportunities in many edge cities are getting to be so good that each morning there are more people coming into them than leaving (Muller, 1989; Garreau, 1991). The problem, however, is that such expanding job opportunities are often inaccessible to low-income people because of poor public transportation linking the central cities with the booming edge cities (Barringer, 1992).

To complement the office, business, and light-industrial base, some of these new mostly middle- and upper-middle-class edge cities have developed multifamily housing in some areas to accommodate the needs of low-income employees. However, low-income housing is scarce in most edge cities, even though it is needed for many clerical, light-manufacturing, maintenance, and service employees, many of whom are members of racial and ethnic minority groups. Low-income housing is usually kept out of edge cities by zoning laws that prohibit high-density housing. Consequently, most low-wage employees are forced to commute daily, if they can find transportation, from the central city or from outlying areas where they can afford to live.

In addition to work opportunities, many edge cities offer a good selection of recreational, eating, lodging, health care, and entertainment facilities. In short, many such cities have become so complete in terms of the community functions they fulfill that their residents can conduct their social, civic, and work lives almost entirely away from central cities, seldom having to interact with immigrants and refugees, the poor, and members of nondominant racial and ethnic groups (Lacayo, 1992). This almost complete isolation makes it possible for a large segment of the U.S. population to be fairly unaware and unconcerned about the plight of "the other America."

Suburban African Americans and Other Members of Racial/Ethnic Nondominant Groups. Mostly since the 1960s, African Americans, Latinos, and Asians, particularly the middle class, have joined Euro-Americans in the migration from central cities to the suburbs in search of better housing and schools and less crime. Specifically, more than 25 percent of African Americans and more than 40 percent of Latinos in metropolitan areas now reside in the suburbs (Massey & Denton, 1988, p. 622). The proportion of Asians living in the suburbs is even higher.

Only a small proportion of African-American suburbanites live in mixed-race or predominantly white suburbs. The majority continue to confront a high degree of housing segregation, although less severe than that experienced by their counterparts living in central cities. Many remain residentially segregated in older suburban neighborhoods vacated by the Euro-American middle-class or in new residential neighborhoods built especially to attract African Americans and other blacks (Massey & Denton, 1988). This is in part due to the traditional practice of some realtors of "steering" people of color away from white neighborhoods. Sometimes continued segregation is reinforced by overt and covert acts of harassment against people of color when they move into white neighborhoods, which can discourage other people of color from taking similar steps.

According to Logan (1988) and Massey and Denton (1988), many of the suburbs in which African Americans live are not a great deal better than the central-city neighborhoods left behind. These suburban communities are often fiscally stressed and crime-ridden and they tend to have predominantly black schools, less satisfactory housing than predominantly white suburbs, and poor municipal services. Those that have independent governments have little to tax but their own homes to fund essential services. Many of these suburbs have fallen deeply into debt or have become dependent on funds from the state and federal governments.

Suburban Women.   When families are unable to make affordable arrangements for extended day care for the children or for the children's participation in after-school recreational programs, suburban mothers (much more so than their husbands) traditionally have ended up taking jobs with flexible hours near home so they can be available to transport and supervise the children after school. The problem is that most such jobs in suburbia offer low wages and are not particularly challenging or promising; consequently, they typically limit considerably the women's personal and professional development (Fellin, 1987; Semyonov & Lewin-Epstein, 1991; England, 1993). As the workplace follows the flow of people out of the city and as men assume greater responsibility for housekeeping and child care, suburban mothers should be able to enjoy a wider range of occupational options.

Rural Communities and Small Towns

According to the U.S. Bureau of the Census (1991), the urban population consists of people living in metropolitan areas, cities, and urbanized areas adjacent to cities with a combined population of at least 50,000, as well as of those living in villages, towns, or other places with populations of 2,500 or more inhabitants. The remaining population not classified as urban is considered rural. In 1990, 25 percent of the U.S. population was rural and was spread out over 97 percent of the nation's land (Luloff & Swanson, 1990; U.S. Bureau of the Census, 1992b).

Today, small towns and rural communities are much influenced by the larger society (Vidich & Bensman, 1968). For example, people living in small towns and rural areas depend heavily on national television for entertainment and on newspapers from nearby cities for information, and they are continually exposed to the mass culture through these media. This constant media bombardment has accentuated the desire among the young to leave and move to the city.

Rural communities are highly dependent on the outside world for practically everything. They depend on outside businesses and industries for the majority of goods and services they consume. The curriculum in rural schools is influenced by the instructional standards prescribed by state departments of education. They are also influenced by many national and state government policies, programs, and subsidies. Even the Sunday school instruction in rural churches is largely prescribed by national religious denominations. This constant bombardment of rural communities by the institutions of mass society and their representatives (e.g., church ministers, physicians, lawyers, teachers, accountants, and field representatives of state and federal agencies) has contributed to the increasing standardization of community life throughout the United States.

Despite the standardization of community life in the United States, many differences still exist between people from rural and urban areas. For example, in rural areas, the levels of malnutrition, maternal and infant mortality, unemployment, underemployment, and poverty are higher than in urban areas (Coward & Jackson, 1983). Educational attainment and income are lower. Housing is less adequate. Particularly the differences in education explain many of the variations in values, attitudes, and behaviors between the urban and rural populations—for instance, the often greater conservatism of rural people in relation to moral, religious, and political issues. Rural communities also differ from urban areas in

Box 5.1 _____

It's Not Hip to Stay, Say Small-Town Youth

BY DIRK JOHNSON

Special to The New York Times

BROKEN BOW, Neb.—The city boy visiting this little central Nebraska town had delivered the insult with a laugh. "You're a hick," he told Tressa Baxter.

Growing up on Rural Route 3, on a farm embraced by wheat fields and cattle rangelands, Miss Baxter, 18, had spent many blue-sky mornings galloping in the saddle atop her paint mare, Angel. She had also played trumpet in the high school marching band and french horn in the concert band. She was a member of the Spanish club, the volleyball team, the track and field team and, when she had the time, the cheerleading squad.

But she responded to the taunt with little more than an awkward shrug, as if to acknowledge the embarrassment of being rural.

Young people in remote pockets of America have always got the message that rural translates to backward, something to be hidden or overcome, and harbored dreams of setting out for brighter lights.

But today, the hankering to move away seems to have become a virtual imperative. At Broken Bow High School here, all but 5 of this year's 75 graduating seniors are going off to college or military service, and the school's principal, Don Vanderheiden, estimates that no more than 1 in 10 will ever return to put down roots.

The exodus has hastened the decline of hundreds of little towns across the plains. In Nebraska, for example, about 90 percent of the state's counties lost population in the 1980's. In dozens of these towns, the average age now hovers near 65.

"Too often, you're considered a loser if you don't leave," said Janet Larreau, the secretary of the Chamber of Commerce in Arnold (population 679), who returned several years ago from Denver. "If these small towns are going to survive, we've got to change that way of thinking."

A FEELING OF SHAME

The attitude was illustrated at a Rotary dinner in Arnold two years ago when that town's 13 graduating seniors were invited to stand and announce their plans. Twelve of the young people said proudly that they were leaving for college.

One young man simply stared at the floor, shuffled his boots and said, with a note of apology, "I'll just be staying here to farm with my dad."

The speaker at the dinner was Mick Jensen, the vice president of Great Plains Communication, a telephone company based in Blair (population 6,800) that serves rural Nebraska. He was appalled that the young farmer would seem so ashamed.

Civic and education leaders in small towns say that they try to encourage young people to consider coming home after college, but that their words often fall on deaf ears.

"You'll tell kids that there are plenty of good reasons to stay in a small town—lack of crime, the friendliness, lower cost of living—and they look at you like you've got rocks in your head," said Louis Stithem, the principal of the elementary school here who in 1961 turned down a job offer in San Francisco to return to his home town.

Donna Headrick, who chose to take a counter job in a fast-food restaurant here after graduating from Broken Bow High School last spring, said some friends had told her, "We think you're crazy to stay here—but we'll support you."

She said it was easy to be one of the few left behind. "You get sad, sometimes, thinking about the way it was when everybody was together, cheering for Bow at the football game," she said. "Everybody else seems to think things are better in the bigger towns."

For Miss Baxter, life in a small town is simply too limiting.

"We're smack in the middle of the country, and by the time it gets to us, it's old," she said, just before packing her suitcases and moving to a dormitory at the University of Nebraska at Kearney (population 24,000), where she will study psychology. "There's just nothing for me here."

Jacque Davenport is the youngest of nine children on a farm outside Arnold. None of her brothers or sisters have stayed here in Custer County, and neither will she.

"There's so little going on here, that people have to make up stuff for entertainment," said Miss Davenport, sitting on the hood of a car to watch the annual "mud surfing" contest, in which contes-

(continued)

Box 5.1 *(continued)* _____

tants stand atop bales of hay being dragged through the mud by a tractor. "We've got to drive 45 miles just to see a movie."

Many of the young people from the small Nebraska towns said they felt sure that people in bigger towns and cities were more open-minded and tolerant. Not a single black person lives in Broken Bow or Arnold.

"I don't think you'd find people being prejudiced in Chicago or New York," Miss Baxter said.

But some experts on the rural West said they believed that young people in places like Broken Bow simply adopted a view often found on television, in the movies and in the national press that small towns were bigoted.

"A view is transmitted by the media elite that

small-town America is hicksville, and that affects the way young people view their surroundings," said Philip M. Burgess, president of the Center for the New West, a policy research group in Denver.

He said too much was made of the desire of young rural people to break away, noting that "bad-mouthing your town" was a rite of adolescence, even if they lived in prestigious suburbs near exciting big cities.

Indeed, several natives of Custer County have returned from big cities in recent years, weary of hassles and looking for a simpler way of life for their children.

"The lights of the big city," Mr. Burgess said, "get dimmer the closer you get to them."

Source: "It's Not Hip to Stay, Say Small-Town Youth" by Dirk Johnson, September 5, 1994, *The New York Times,* pp. 1, 8. Copyright © 1994 by The New York Times Company. Reprinted by permission.

---

terms of generally having less adequate public services (e.g., fire protection, schools, road maintenance, hospital and medical services) but lower crime, pollution, and noise levels (Reid, 1984; Fellin, 1987).

Rural employment in the United States traditionally revolved around extractive activities, such as farming, fishing, logging, and mining. As these industries became increasingly more automated and consolidated, many local small entrepreneurs were pushed out of business by big agribusiness enterprises. Faced with a reduction in employment opportunities, many people abandoned rural areas in search of a better life in the city. Most of the remaining rural population has experienced downward mobility as previously independent farmers were put out of business and forced to take employment at low wages (Luloff & Swanson, 1990; Swanson & Luloff, 1990).

Particularly since 1973, many people in rural communities have grown dependent on wages from manufacturing industries that relocated near them. In fact, some small communities, both near major metropolitan areas and in

more remote locations, enjoyed what some referred to as a "boom" in the 1973–1983 decade, as major industries opened up plants, offices and research parks near them. This led to an instantaneous increase in employment opportunities and an increase in the amount of money circulating through the local economy.

The rural industrialization "boom" seldom resulted in reduced unemployment for the traditionally rural population, however (Summers & Branch, 1984). This is because the best of the new factory jobs often went to applicants from outside the local community who were better qualified in terms of skills and experience or to union members displaced from their jobs when their plants shut down elsewhere. Frequently barred from the best of the blue-collar jobs, few of the locals were sufficiently qualified to aspire to the professional or managerial positions that were often filled with outsiders. In addition, the increased revenues the rural communities got from industrial development and the accompanying population expansion seldom paid for their increased costs because the new industries that settled in these localities often received considerable tax breaks. Consequently, many industries did not have to pay property taxes for several years while the small communities in which they settled incurred considerable immediate expenditures to provide services to the new residents, such as water, garbage removal, schools, police, and fire protection (Light, Keller, & Calhoun, 1989).

Not all rural areas have fared poorly with the new industrial influx. Those areas that have been able to attract recreational and retirement industries have generally done well. Those near metropolitan areas that have been able to benefit from the city's outward growth also generally have done well. It is the more distant communities that attracted primarily manufacturing, service, and extractive industries that have lost ground (Swanson & Luloff, 1990).

Community Structure: Vertical and Horizontal Patterns

Warren (1978) identified two sets of relationships that are crucial in understanding the behavior of local communities. One is the ties or linkages that the community maintains with extracommunity systems. Referred to as the community's **vertical pattern,** these external connections increase the uniformity of standards and practices from community to community. One significant change that has taken place in recent decades in U.S. communities is the strengthening of this vertical pattern of linkage, leading to a much greater orientation of the community toward the outside world (Warren, 1988, p. 142).

Most of the decisions that affect local communities nowadays are not made by local residents but by outsiders. For example, local branches of national chain stores, restaurants, or banks answer to their regional or national headquarters. Many health and social welfare agencies must follow state and federal government regulations because their programs are funded by these sources and they must also ful-

fill the requirements of their national professional accrediting bodies. Local chapters of labor unions answer to state or national union headquarters. Many local newspaper publishers and editors respond to national newspaper publishing organizations. The local offices of the telephone and power and light companies follow procedures set at headquarters outside the community. The teachings of local churches must be in line with the policies of their national denominational boards. Local schools must follow the dictates of state departments of education. Branch industrial plants answer to their main headquarters. And so on and on.

Although the strongest ties of the majority of local community subunits today are vertical and external, they must remain sensitive to local issues to remain viable. For example, if outside businesses want competent employees in the various localities where they are established, they must be responsive to the local employees' basic needs, such as quality education, good housing, clean and attractive environment, availability of health and social support services, availability of day care, adequate police protection to keep crime under control, good recreational opportunities, and so on. Accordingly, for instance, some outside businesses try to influence the quality of local educational institutions by donating money, equipment, and volunteer services to local schools and colleges. Similarly, they often contribute to the financing of health and social agencies that provide critical assistance to employees by donating to the Community Chest or United Way (Fellin, 1987).

The need for internal integration and cooperation has prompted communities to develop various agencies whose function is to structure rationally and deliberately the relationship among various community subunits. These internal relationships constitute the community's **horizontal pattern.** For instance, the local chamber of commerce provides local businesses an opportunity to communicate and coordinate efforts by participating in its activities, the school board oversees the public schools, Protestant churches participate in the local federations of churches, and health and social welfare agencies plan and coordinate their efforts through participation in health and social welfare councils and coordinate their financial campaigns through participation in a community chest or united fund. Moreover, community relations boards, composed of representatives from as many sectors of the community as possible, are usually created to deal with community problems and conflicts. Still another way by which communities strengthen horizontal relationships is by organizing special events, such as arts and crafts festivals, sports tournaments, music festivals, and cultural activities that foster participation of residents and cohesion (see Table 5.3).

As already noted, most subsystems within contemporary U.S. communities have stronger vertical than horizontal relationships. For example, any local branch of a national or state organization is likely to pay closer attention to the dictates of its regional or national headquarters than to other units within the local community. Yet, some have a stronger horizontal pattern. Some locally owned businesses, community relations boards, or public/community relations departments within various business organizations function primarily within the community. Most community units, however, must maintain both vertical and horizontal relationships to remain viable. This means that any serious case study of a community must explore both its complex vertical linkages to the outside and the horizontal dimension of internal structures and dynamics (Lewis, 1974).

Community Dynamics

This section will explore three key areas of community functioning: the economy; power, politics, and decision making; and community conflict.

The Economy

The economy is the sector of the community in which goods and services are produced, distributed, and marketed and where people earn a living. The more diversified the community

TABLE 5.3 Schematic Analysis of Major Locality-Relevant Functions

MAJOR LOCALITY-RELEVANT FUNCTION	TYPICAL COMMUNITY UNIT	TYPICAL UNIT OF HORIZONTAL PATTERN	TYPICAL SUPERIOR UNIT OF VERTICAL PATTERN
Production-distribution-consumption	Company	Chamber of Commerce	National corporation
Socialization	Public school	Board of Education	State Department of Education
Social control	Municipal Government	City Council	State government
Social participation	Church	Council of churches	Denominational body
Mutual support	Voluntary health association	Community welfare council	National health association

Source: From *The Community in America* by R. L. Warren. Copyright 1978, 1972, 1963 by Houghton Mifflin Company. Reprinted in 1987 by University Press of America. Permission granted by University Press of America.

economy, generally the better it can weather "bad" economic times. The economic sector of the community is composed of the recorded market economy, the home economy, and the underground economy.

The *recorded market economy* includes large and small businesses; industrial, techno-logical, and service enterprises; financial institutions; public service agencies; and professionals in private practice. The *home economy* includes all the unremunerated activi-ties performed at home by family members who clean and maintain the home, cook, and care for the children. The *underground econ-omy* includes all market activities that are not officially reported to the Internal Revenue Ser-vice, whether legal or illegal, such as lawn maintenance services, home repairs, bartering of goods and services, informal child care, cash transactions "under the table," prostitution, drug dealing, and gambling (Case & Fair, 1994; Simon & Witte, 1982).

Family members who work exclusively at home cleaning, cooking, and caring for the children (a predominantly female group) are excluded from the market economy because even though they perform a critical economic role, they do not receive any monetary remu-neration. Also excluded from the official mar-ket economy of the community are the nonmonetary exchanges among friends and neighbors—for example, one neighbor provid-ing free babysitting in exchange for some help with landscaping from the other neighbor. These informal exchanges of goods and ser-vices occur through what Lowenthal (1975) has called the "social economy."

Generally, the greater the power held by members of the recorded market economy of the community, the more emphasis the commu-nity will place on growth (Molotch, 1976). Population growth is desirable for business because it yields concrete advantages, such as more customers for products and services, more potential workers for local industries, and greater demand for property causing property

values to rise. However, growth is rarely bene-ficial to the residents of a community because they must suffer the overcrowding in the schools, the traffic jams, the crowded buses, the road deterioration, the air and water pollution, and the increased tax burden resulting from higher property values, among many other inconveniences.

Community Power, Politics, and Decision Making

Who has the power in a community; that is, who pulls the strings? This generally depends on the nature of the decisions to be made. According to Hunter's (1953) classic study of the power structure in Atlanta (Georgia), when significant local issues are at stake, decisions are usually controlled by the major economic powers in the community (e.g., industrialists, bankers, and top executives of large business enterprises). These people who pull the strings in relation to important matters often are not recognized by most community members as key decision makers. When the community decisions to be made are of a routine nature, however, they tend to be made by bureaucrats without the involvement of economic influen-tials (Lyon & Bonjean, 1988).

Particularly when the economic elite of the community develops a working relationship or a unified front, often through participation in several key community boards and councils (e.g., business councils, planning and zoning commissions, chamber of commerce, boards of education, and so on), they can be a formidable force with which to contend (Lyon & Bonjean, 1988). Yet, they are not the only sources of influence in the community.

Dahl (1961) took a different approach than Hunter in his study of New Haven (Connecti-cut). Instead of interviewing community "knowledgeables" to determine the power structure, as Hunter had done, Dahl looked at who actually made community decisions. He found a more pluralistic power structure with more people than just the economic elite involved, most notably government officials, particularly the city mayor. He also found that influence was often specialized; those individuals who were influential in one sector of the community usually were not influential in another sector (p. 169). Other researchers have criticized Dahl's methodology, suggesting that one can easily overestimate the role of certain public officials in the formal decision-making process of the community if one looks only at those who *officially* make the decisions. This is because public officials play a more visible role, whereas the influence of the economic elite tends to be exercised "behind the scenes" (Miller, 1958, 1970; Presthus, 1964).

The argument that influence is often applied surreptitiously makes Dahl's finding of a more heterogeneous power structure less compelling. Yet, his point that community power is not held *exclusively* by the economic elite is probably accurate and descriptive of the situation in most contemporary U.S. communities. Economic elites undoubtedly exert great influence. But elected officials, top government bureaucrats, and strong interest groups (e.g., labor unions, civil rights groups, and consumer groups) also exert considerable pressure.

It is interesting to observe the high degree of subtlety with which important community decisions are often made. Usually, elected officials (e.g., the mayor or council/commission members) or high-level politically appointed personnel (e.g., city or county manager) will consider a range of suggestions and opinions offered by influential individuals and groups, taking into account the players' potential to control the outcome. Many experienced politicians become so skillful at assessing the potential coalitions that may be formed by different community players and the resources that may be mobilized, that the politicians often make the "right" decisions without even "testing the waters." Successful community influentials are also highly skilled at getting the decisions they want from public officials without having to mobilize their resources—

that is, simply by making evident to the officials in charge their ability to control the outcome, if they so choose. As long as government bureaucrats and politicians maintain a reasonable record of making decisions that are "acceptable" to influentials, these powerful interests quietly stay on the sidelines (Galaskiewicz, 1979).

After analyzing the existing research on community power, Lyon (1987, p. 200) concluded that the degree to which power is concentrated in a few hands or distributed more broadly in a given community depends on three factors: the size of the community, its degree of economic diversification, and the strength of its vertical links.

1. Generally, the larger the community, the more pluralistic the power structure. This is because large communities are more likely to have multiple groups with opposing interests competing for power than smaller communities; hence, it becomes difficult for any one pressure group to dominate the decision-making process.

2. The greater the economic diversification of the community, the more pluralistic the power structure. This is because an economically diversified community is more difficult to control by any one interest group than a community with only a few businesses or industries that can easily develop a unified front.

3. As the community subunits become more strongly linked with state and national systems, making its vertical ties more dominant, the power structure becomes more pluralistic. This is what has been happening in U.S. communities as they have developed stronger ties with the outside. The reason is that it is harder for externally controlled units to develop a unified front at the local level

Community Conflict

As noted in previous chapters, conflict is a natural phenomenon that should not be suppressed because it can serve positive functions. In the community, conflict with outsiders often serves to strengthen ties between residents by making them more aware of their similarities and by highlighting differences with outsiders. Open conflict within the community also provides an opportunity for opposing sides to vent their hostilities, and this debate is often necessary for people to resolve their differences (Coser, 1956).

Many different community issues can generate conflict; for example, disputes between labor and industry over working conditions, salaries, or benefits; abortion; bilingual education; illegal immigration; school busing; gay rights; claims of discrimination by nondominant groups; scarce job opportunities; neighborhood opposition to the location of a residential drug treatment facility or group home for the mentally retarded; opposition to an urban renewal project that would displace some residents or to the construction of an expressway that would split a neighborhood in two; or church opposition to the distribution of condoms or other birth control devices in the schools. Despite the wide range of issues capable of causing community conflict, once conflict has been generated, the processes that ensue are similar in many respects.

James Coleman (1957) suggested that conflict is a good indication that community members consider their community life important enough to argue about. Based on his analysis of a large number of reports of community conflicts, he noted various fundamental similarities in the manner in which conflict develops.

Most conflicts, Coleman observed, start over specific issues and then escalate to more general issues. For example, a complaint about sloppy garbage collection in one neighborhood may quickly snowball into a formal charge of mayoral incompetence. Apparently, the initial charge acts as the spark that sets off a chain reaction of other complaints, which lead to a redefinition of the issue on a much broader basis.

Characteristically, as the community controversy deepens, new and different issues emerge. On the subject of garbage collection, one neighbor may start complaining to another neighbor across the back fence about the sloppiness of the sanitation workers that pick up her garbage. In response, the other neighbor may bicker about the unrepaired potholes on the street. After church on Sunday, more people may jump on the discontent, complaining about the state of disrepair of streetlights and the luxurious new furnishings at the mayor's office. Before long, it may seem like there is an all-out war going on. Apparently, once the ice is broken by the person who throws the first stone, the issues can multiply quickly and the dispute may escalate rapidly. Typically, issues and complaints proliferate and diversify as new players are admitted into the fray. Thus, two months after the initial conversation between neighbors across the fence concerning the sloppy sanitation workers on the block, a large group of citizens may be accusing the mayor of corruption and asking for his or her resignation at the town hall meeting. At some point in the process, the media jumps into the fray and the rumor mill activates to fill the information gaps.

Another common characteristic of community controversies, according to Coleman, is the progression from disagreement to antagonism. Community conflict usually starts with disagreement over ideas, attitudes, or proposed courses of action, such as whether the community should offer protection against discrimination in housing and employment to gays and lesbians. Typically, as people voice their differences of opinion, each side (in this case, those pro gay rights and those against extending civil rights to gays) paints a more sinister image of the other, thus fostering antagonism. This process of personalization turns the original differences of opinion into personal accusations. Now the ill will generated between the two sides becomes capable of keeping the conflict going. To move more quickly from intellectual disagreement to open battle, sometimes the players deliberately personalize the debate.

As the controversy continues, Coleman noted that community relations typically become polarized. Separate camps develop, sometimes led by organizations newly formed to conduct the dispute, and the people within each camp begin to associate less and less with those on the opposing side. With the emergence of new partisan organizations leading each side of the controversy, many times new more extremist leaders are imported from the outside to take over the dispute. The advantage of bringing in outsiders is that, being unattached to the community, they are free to wage the "war" without feeling pressured to act one way or another by local church leaders, educational leaders, business leaders, and other concerned citizens who usually try to influence the outcome.

As the conflict grows deeper, Coleman observed that many of the community's major organizations/institutions may be forced to officially enter the controversy by joining one of the sides. The Catholic Church, for example, may join forces with those opposing the granting of gay rights, or the public school system may be forced to take a position on the employment of gays and lesbians. Yet, community institutions often struggle to remain neutral to safeguard their standing with all groups within the community.

In sum, major community controversies often start with a small incident that sets off a chain reaction leading to a redefinition of the problem on a much broader basis. As more people jump into the fray, the initial differences of opinion turn into personal accusations and the community becomes polarized. As opposing camps become entrenched, professional leaders may be brought in from the outside to take over the dispute so that the battle can be fought relatively independently from internal community pressures and influences.

COMMUNITY PRACTICE AND THE CONCEPT OF THE GOOD COMMUNITY

If you were to ask an ordinary person on the street for his or her conception of a good community, the individual might reply that it would be a place with safe neighborhoods and comfortable homes, a clean and attractive environment, good schools, good employment opportunities, quality health care, nice places for recreation, and few serious social problems, such as poverty, crime, and drugs. Beyond such basic positive attributes, each person you asked would likely include additional specifications for his or her ideal community, depending on individual characteristics such as age, gender, racial or ethnic background, sexual orientation, social class, and religious affiliation, among others. If you were to ask the same question of an open systems theorist, the answer might be something along the lines that a good community is one whose subsystems or social institutions (the economy, government, education, health and social welfare, and recreation) operate interdependently and in a cooperative manner to fulfill effectively major societal functions and benefit community members.

Although stated at different levels of abstraction, the two conceptualizations would guide community practitioners toward similar goals. Such goals might include helping the community to improve its housing stock, clean up and beautify the environment, reduce crime and other social problems, improve the quality of education, provide better employment opportunities and job training, improve the health care system, and provide outlets for recreation.

This last section explores the characteristics of good communities. The aim is to make you, the reader, more sensitive to some of the issues that must be thought through in attempting to develop a model of the good community to guide community practice efforts. It must be kept in mind, however, that it is not easy to improve the quality of life in a given community because it does not exist in a vacuum. Communities exist in a larger environmental context that influences many of the problems they experience (e.g., unemployment, pollution, a scarcity of adequate low-cost housing, crime, delinquency, alcohol and drug addiction, teenage parenthood, welfare dependency, and discrimination, to mention a few). These problems can be alleviated through community efforts, but they can seldom be reduced significantly without a concerted effort at the state or national level.

In "The Good Community—What Would It Be?" Warren (1970) explored some basic issues that confront anyone seeking to formulate a model of the good community. These give us food for thought. One issue to consider in developing a model of the good community concerns the degree of closeness in interpersonal relationships that is desirable among community members. Would a community be better off if its members had close ties? In other words, would things be better if local residents knew the school teachers, the physicians, the ministers, the grocers, the mail carriers, and so on, not only in their official roles but also as individuals?

At first thought, you might conclude that a closely knit community would be preferable because people would feel more connected and safer than when surrounded by strangers. But there is a trade-off between close ties and privacy/freedom—the more you have of one, the less you get of the other. Specifically, people who live in small towns often complain that they know one another *too well*, meaning that they tend to pay a price for close relations and greater personal security in terms of loss of privacy and freedom to be themselves. In larger communities, people generally maintain more distant relations and are better able to "mind their own business," but they are likely to feel more insecure and disconnected and less able to get help and support.

A second issue to consider when thinking about what makes a community more or less good, according to Warren, is the degree of autonomy, that is desirable from external systems or, in the case of neighborhoods, from the larger community. Some people are of the opinion that a good community makes its own decisions and solves its own problems rather than have things decided for it or acted upon by external forces, such as city hall, the state government, federal officials, or the out-of-town headquarters of national business organizations. But autonomy is not without drawbacks. To be truly autonomous, a community would have to turn down most of the financial aid it receives from the outside (e.g., the municipality in the case of a residential neighborhood or the state in the case of a city), since aid often comes with many strings attached. Yet, turning down outside assistance would likely mean losing vital services and resources.

How would a community be able to get by without outside businesses if they are critical sources of local employment or important providers of goods and services? In the case of a neighborhood, would it be able to do without the services that the larger municipality provides, such as water and sewers, transportation, hospitals, schools, and police and fire protection? It is easy to favor autonomy, but one must consider its hard consequences in terms of the viability or capacity of the community to confront its needs and problems.

Cottrell (1976, p. 403) maintained that no viable community can be entirely autonomous. Instead of favoring autonomy, he emphasized the importance of community competence or the ability of the community members to collaborate in identifying problems and needs, decide which priorities to pursue, and implement the required actions. He suggested that community competence depends on certain conditions—notably, high commitment and participation on the part of residents, open communication, ability to manage relations with the larger society, and ability to manage conflict.

Competent communities are particularly adept at maintaining strong external relations so as to get the resources and supports they need from the outside. For example, such communities typically become involved in the shaping of state and national social and economic policies and rules and regulations about resource distribution plans to make sure that they are in line with the community's needs and priorities. But they also remain on guard against excessive external controls or interference that would rob them of too much autonomy (Warren, 1975).

Still another consideration to keep in mind in developing a model of the good community to guide community practice is the issue of how power should be distributed (Warren, 1970). Most studies have found that power is typically distributed unevenly; that is, a relatively small minority of people in the community usually exercise an excessive amount of influence over community decisions. Many people would agree that power should be shared more broadly. But how broadly? Should everyone in the community have equal power? What about those who are disinterested in the affairs of the community? Should they have the same influence as those who work hard on community problems?

This brings up the issue of the extent to which it is desirable for community members to participate in community affairs. It is easy to say that communities would be better off if their members were more actively involved in community affairs. But many people do not have the time or inclination. Given that advances in communication and transportation have made it possible for people to belong to many different social networks, who is to say that their local community should have precedence over the other communities to which people belong?

How homogeneous or heterogeneous should the ideal community be? For example, should those involved in community development work actively toward the goal of making every area within the community as integrated as possible in terms of income levels, racial/ethnic backgrounds, age structure, and other stratification variables? This appears to be a very worthy ideal to pursue. However, there are consequences when highly diverse people are brought close together, and the community must be prepared to face such consequences. For instance, in the initial phases of integration, there is likely to be a lot of friction and controversy and, consequently, considerable difficulty in achieving close ties and positive feelings among community members. Although in the long run such conflict is likely to produce positive changes, it may feel very uncomfortable in the short term.

Can we improve the quality of life in our communities? Can we make them better places to live, to work, to raise children, and to retire? Given so many issues to keep in the balance, you can readily see that coming up with a model of the good community to guide community practice is no easy task. To improve our communities, many hard choices must be made, and community members must be prepared to live with the implications of such choices.

APPLICATIONS: PREPARING A PROFILE OF A LOCAL COMMUNITY

What would you do if you were asked to prepare a report detailing the major characteristics of a given community? One way to deal with this assignment would be to study the local economy (i.e., the business, industry, and labor market), the local government, the way community decisions are made, how conflicts are handled, the educational system, the media, the church organizations, the health and social services system, and the community's recreational facilities. Also, you might want to gather demographic data about the local population to find out about the community's social stratification system. If the community to be studied is larger than a very small town or neighborhood, this would be a big project requiring considerable work. You would probably need to be given some resources, human and financial, to be able to complete the assignment in a timely fashion.

Sanders (1960) recommended that one good way for project participants to start preparing a community profile is to ask knowledgeable informants or individuals occupying key positions in the community to name the people they consider to be important local leaders. After questioning a few such individuals, it will become clear to you who the main players in the community are because their names will be mentioned by several informants. You can then question the identified leaders about what they see as the main problems, issues, and changes taking place in the community's main institutional areas. They can also refer you to well-informed representatives from each sector who can provide additional details.

Your interview findings can then be combined with additional data that can be collected from other sources, such as local newspaper articles, radio and television news reports, local surveys and studies, and, most importantly, statistics from the U.S. Bureau of the Census. From the census reports, you can derive much demographic information about the community such as the age structure of the population, their educational level, marital status, family structure, individual income, family income, occupational structure, unemployment rate, housing conditions, percent of the population receiving public assistance, and the percentage of the population belonging to various racial/ethnic nondominant groups, including the degree to which they are segregated residentially.

By following this practical method, you should be able to derive considerable knowledge and understanding of the community you have chosen to study.

GLOSSARY

Anomic Neighborhood: A neighborhood that lacks a leadership structure and whose residents don't care much about it; consequently, it shows, at least initially, little capacity to engage in collective action. Neighborhoods with a high number of low-income public housing projects are sometimes anomic, although anomie can afflict any neighborhood.

Central City: That part of a city comprising and surrounding the "downtown" commercial, financial, and industrial districts.

City: A settlement populated by people who live primarily off trade and commerce rather than agriculture.

Community (Locality Based): Any locality shared by people who maintain common ties and who are engaged in interrelated actions. More specifically, a local social unit or system (e.g., city, town, or village) that performs the major social functions, such as production/distribution/consumption, socialization of its members, social control, social participation and interaction, health care, and social support of its citizens in times of trouble.

Community (Nonplace or Sociopsychological): Any intermediary structure through which individuals can feel meaningfully attached to society; a social network, such as the scientific community, the social work profession, the African-American community in Little Rock, and so on.

Community of Limited Liability: The concept that some local community ties persist at least for *some* people *some* of the time and play an important role in their lives, even though the local community or neighborhood may no longer be considered by most people to be their most important social connection.

Competition: The process by which some sectors or groups in the community establish their dominance over others. For example, in a city, the strongest commercial and financial interests generally secure the most strategic locations for their purposes, and the wealthy select the most attractive settings for their residences.

Defended Neighborhood: A neighborhood whose members develop a high degree of solidarity, cooperation, and concerted action because they feel that it is being threatened by some external force, such as crime, racial/ethnic invasion, or any other change they consider not to be in the best interest of the community.

Diffuse Neighborhood: A neighborhood that, under normal circumstances, has little active internal life and few connections with the larger community, but that has the potential to quickly become internally organized and externally linked if circumstances, such as an external threats, warranted it. Some affluent suburbs or luxury highrises fit this mold.

Edge City: A suburb or exurb that has grown from a mere bedroom community into a full-fledged, self-sufficient, self-contained city offering its residents work and shopping opportunities as well as a good selection of recreational, entertainment, eating, and lodging facilities. Also referred to as Outer City.

Empowerment Zone: A government initiative to increase the employment opportunities of the disadvantaged whereby businesses receive tax breaks and other incentives to locate in poor areas.

Enterprise Zone: See **Empowerment Zone**.

Exurb: A small, generally prosperous community adjacent to *but outside* metropolitan areas.

Gemeinschaft: Relationships characterized by close social and emotional bonds, durability, commitment, trust, mutuality, and face-to-face interactions, such as the relationship between family members or close friends.

Gentrification: The conversion of working-class, often run-down districts into upscale neighborhoods through the purchase and renovation of older homes and rowhouses, usually prompted by the desire of some upper-middle-class people to live close to work and to places of entertainment and to avoid the long commutes to the suburbs.

Gesellschaft: Impersonal, segmental, superficial, and contractual relationships people engage into in order to barter or exchange one thing for another. Thus, for example, the relationship between a buyer and a seller or between an employer and an employee are typically gesellschaft.

Ghetto: A residential neighborhood in which a certain racial or ethnic group is forced to live (Choldin, 1985, p. 236). Usually, ghetto residents have low incomes, although not all do.

Horizontal Pattern: Internal linkages or interrelationships maintained by local community units, such as the communication between local businesses maintained through participation in the local chamber of commerce or between health agencies through participation in the health planning council.

Integral Neighborhood: A neighborhood in which residents show a good deal of interaction and participation, identification with it, and linkage with the larger community. This gives the integral neighborhood a high capacity to deal with its problems and needs.

Locality-Based Community: See **Community (Locality Based)**.

Megalopolis: A collection of metropolitan areas that have sprawled so much that their outer boundaries have merged with the outer boundaries of neighboring metropolitan areas, forming vast urban stretches—for example, the huge urban belt stretching from north of Boston to south of Washington, DC.

Metropolitan Area: According to the Bureau of the Census, a large population nucleus, together with adjacent communities that have a high degree of economic and social integration with that nucleus.

Mutual Support: A basic social function encompassing the formal and informal community efforts to provide health care and assistance with personal, family, economic, or other concerns.

Neighborhood: A residential subunit of the larger local community into which community members sort themselves on the basis of various factors such as socioeconomic status, stage in the life cycle, racial/ethnic background or sexual orientation.

Neighboring: Informal interactions among neighbors, such as backfence or front-porch visiting, food borrowing, exchanging tools and services, participating in neighborhood associations, and holding block parties.

Nonplace or Sociopsychological Community: See **Community (Nonplace or Sociopsychological)**.

Outer City: See **Edge City.**

Parochial Neighborhood: A neighborhood whose residents show a good deal of identification with it, interaction, participation, and commitment but that is insulated from the outside community. Neighborhoods with a strong ethnic identity usually are of this type.

Production/Distribution/Consumption: A basic social function carried out by the economic sector of the community through a complex of business, industrial, and service organizations that provide for the employment, income, and sustenance needs of the population.

Slum: A dirty, unsanitary, deteriorated, and run-down urban area having high rates of crime and of social or family disorganization.

Social Control: A social function consisting of the regulation of behavior through formal and informal means so that people will behave in accordance with family, community, and societal standards. This social function is carried out informally by the family as it disciplines its members and by religious organizations and formally by the legal system, law enforcement agencies, and the courts.

Social Network: Any set of people who actively share some link or connection, such as an interest, hobby, work role, organizational or associational tie, personal trait, or blood relationship, no matter whether this network exists within a given locality or is nationwide or worldwide in scope. A nonplace or sociopsychological community. Examples include the gay and lesbian, African-American, or Latino communities; the civil rights movement; the women's liberation movement; the right-to-life movement; the social work, medical, or legal professions; the democratic party; the banking community; and so on.

Social Participation: A social function consisting of providing community members with opportunities for social interaction. It is carried out by the family and peer groups as well as by religious organizations, recreational facilities, social clubs, and professional, voluntary, and service associations.

Socialization: The transmission of knowledge, values, attitudes, behaviors, and the teaching of social roles. Many social institutions play a role in socialization, particularly the schools, the family, and the media.

Stepping-Stone Neighborhood: Its residents tend to be highly mobile, occupationally, socially, and residentially. They are active participants in neighborhood affairs and keep the neighborhood well linked to the outside community, but they quickly move on and similar others move in. The result is that few stay long enough to develop strong ties to the neighborhood.

Suburb: Any territory within a metropolitan area that lies outside the central city.

Succession: The process by which one social group invades an area, competes with its current occupants, and eventually wins out and takes control of the territory.

Transitory Neighborhood: A neighborhood undergoing a change of population with residents often segmented into clusters and old-timers and newcomers usually keeping a distance.

Urbanization: The migration of the population from the countryside and small towns to metropolitan areas.

Vertical Pattern: The ties or linkages that some community units have to extracommunity systems, such as the relationship of the local Wal-Mart or McDonald's to their national offices or the relationship of the community's public schools to the state department of education.

Web of Life: The binding together of all the living organisms within a common habitat in a relationship of mutual interdependence.

REFERENCES

Auslander, G. K., & Litwin, H. (1988). Social networks and the poor: Toward effective policy and practice. *Social Work, 33*, 234–238.

Barringer, F. (1992, December 4). Hire cities' poor in the suburbs, report advises. *The New York Times*, p. A10.

Bergman, D. (1992). Enterprise zones: A cure for urban America? *National Civic Review, 81*, 186–187.

Blau, P. (1967). *Exchange and power in social life.* New York: John Wiley & Sons.

Borgos, S. (1988). The ACORN squatters' campaign. In R. L. Warren & L. Lyon (Eds.), *New perspectives on the American community* (5th ed., pp. 358–365). Belmont, CA: Wadsworth.

Burgess, E. (1925). The growth of the city. In R. Park, E. Burgess, & R. D. McKenzie (Eds.), *The city*. Chicago: University of Chicago Press.

Case, K., & Fair, R. (1994). *Principles of economics*. Englewood Cliffs, NJ: Prentice-Hall.

Choldin, H. (1985). *Cities and suburbs*. New York: McGraw-Hill.

Choldin, H., Hanson, C., & Bobrer, R. (1980). Suburban status instability. *American Sociological Review, 45*, 972–983.

Coleman, J. S. (1957). *Community conflict*. New York: Free Press.

Collins, G. (1984, July 30). A study of blacks in white suburbia. *The New York Times*, p. A16.

Coser, L. (1956). *The functions of social conflict*. Glencoe, IL: Free Press.

Cottrell, L. S. (1976). The competent community. In B. H. Kaplan, R. N. Wilson, & A. H. Leighton, (Eds.), *Further explorations in social psychiatry*. New York: Basic Books.

Council of Economic Advisers. (1993). *Economic report of the president*. Washington, DC: U.S. Government Printing Office.

Coward, R. T., & Jackson, R. W. (1983). Environmental stress: The rural family. In H. I. McCubbin & C. R. Figley (Eds.), *Stress and the family* (pp. 178–200). New York: Brunner/Mazel.

Curtis, R. F., & Jackson, E. F. (1977). *Inequality in American communities*. New York: Academic Press.

Dahl, R. (1961). *Who governs*. New Haven, CT: Yale University Press.

Eckenrode, J. (1983). The mobilization of social supports: Some individual constraints. *American Journal of Community Psychology, 11*, 509–528.

England, K. V. L. (1993). Suburban pink color ghettos: The spatial entrapment of women. *The Annals of the Association of Amereican Geographers, 83*, 225–226.

Fava, S. F. (1975, November). Beyond suburbia. *The Annals of the American Academy of Political and Social Science, 422*, 11–24.

Fellin, P. (1987). *The community and the social worker*. Itasca, IL: F. E. Peacock.

Fellin, P. (1995). *The community and the social worker* (2nd ed.). Itasca, IL: F. E. Peacock.

Fischer, C. S. (1982). *To dwell among friends: Personal networks in town and city*. Chicago: University of Chicago Press.

Galaskiewicz, J. (1979). *Exchange networks and community politics*. Beverly Hills, CA: Sage.

Gans, H. J. (1962). *The urban villagers: Group and class in the life of Italian-Americans*. New York: Free Press.

Garreau, J. (1991). *Edge city: Life on the new frontier*. New York: Doubleday.

Germain, C. B. (1985). The place of community work within an ecological approach to social work practice. In S. H. Taylor & R. W. Roberts (Eds.), *Theory and practice of community social work* (pp. 30–55). New York: Columbia University Press.

Gottman, J. (1961). *Megalopolis, the urbanized northeastern seaboard of the United States*. New York: The Twentieth Century Fund.

Goudy, W. J. (1990). Community attachment in a rural region. *Rural Sociology, 55*, 178–198.

Granovetter, M. S. (1973). The strength of weak ties. *American Journal of Sociology, 78*, 1360–1379.

Greer, S. (1962). *The emerging city*. New York: Free Press.

Hacker, A. (1992). *Two nations divided: Black, white, separate, hostile, & unequal*. New York: Scribner's.

Hillery, G. A., Jr. (1955). Definitions of community: Areas of agreement. *Rural Sociology, 20*, 111–123.

Hunter, A. (1978). Persistence of local sentiments in mass society. In D. Street et al. (Eds.), *Handbook of contemporary urban life*. San Francisco: Jossey-Bass.

Hunter, F. (1953). *Community power structure: A study of decision makers*. Chapel Hill: University of North Carolina Press.

Kasarda, J. D., & Janowitz, M. (1974). Community attachment in mass society. *American Sociological Review, 39*, 328–339.

Keller, S. (1968). *The urban neighborhood: A sociological perspective*. New York: Random House.

Lacayo, R. (1992, May 18). This land is your land. *Time*, 28–33.

Lazare, D. (1990, October 23). Planes, trains, and automobiles. *Village Voice, 35*, 39–41.

Leinberger, C. B., & Lockwood, C. (1986, October). How business is reshaping America. *Atlantic Monthly*, 43–52.

Lewis, G. F. (1974). Sociological study of communities: Is there still a role for microcosmic analysis? *Journal of the Community Development Society, 5*(1), 10–18.

Liebow, E. (1967). *Tally's corner.* Boston: Little, Brown.

Light, D., Keller, S., & Calhoun. (1989). *Sociology* (5th ed.). New York: Alfred A. Knopf.

Logan, J. R. (1988). Realities of black suburbanization. In R. L. Warren & L. Lyon (Eds.), *New perspectives on the American community* (5th ed., pp. 231–241). Belmont, CA: Wadsworth.

Long, N. E. (1958). The local community as an ecology of games. *American Journal of Sociology, 64*, 251–261.

Lowenthal, M. D. (1975). The social economy in urban working-class communities. In G. Gappert & H. Rose (Eds.), *The social economy of cities.* Beverly Hills, CA: Sage.

Luloff, A. E., & Swanson, L. E. (Eds.). (1990). Introduction. In A. E. Luloff & L. E. Swanson (Eds.), *American rural communities* (pp. 1–6). Boulder: Westview Press.

Lynd, R. S., & Lynd, H. M. (1929). *Middletown: A study in contemporary American culture.* New York: Harcourt, Brace, Jovanovich.

Lynd, R. S., & Lynd, H. M. (1937). *Middletown in transition.* New York: Harcourt, Brace, Jovanovich.

Lyon, L. (1987). *The community in urban society.* Chicago: Dorsey Press.

Lyon, L., & Bonjean, C. M. (1988). Community power and policy outputs: The routines of local politics. In R. L. Warren & L. Lyon (Eds.), *New perspectives on the American community* (5th ed., pp. 303-314). Belmont, CA: Wadsworth.

Markoff, J. (1993, August 31). The keyboard becomes a hangout for a computer-savvy generation. *The New York Times*, pp. A1, C5.

Massey, D. S., & Denton, N. A. (1988). Suburbanization and segregation in U.S. metropolitan areas. *American Journal of Sociology, 94*, 592–626.

McIntyre, E. L. G. (1986). Social networks: Potential for practice. *Social Work, 31*, 421–426.

Michelson, W. (1973, October). *Environmental change.* Centre for Urban and Community Studies, Research Paper no. 60. University of Toronto.

Miller, D. C. (1958). Decision-making cliques in community power structures. *American Journal of Sociology, 64*, 299–310.

Miller, D. C. (1970). *International community power structures.* Bloomington: Indiana University Press.

Mills, C. W. (1956). *The power elite.* New York: Oxford University Press.

Mohl, R. A. (1990). The transformation of urban America since the second World War. In R. B. Fairbanks (Ed.), *Essays on sunbelt cities and recent urban America.* College Station: Texas A&M University Press.

Molotch, H. (1976). The city as a growth machine. Toward a political economy of place. *American Journal of Sociology, 82*, 309–332.

Muller, P. O. (1989). The transformation of bedroom suburbia into the outer city: An overview of metropolitan structural change since 1947. In B. M. Kelly (Ed.), *Suburbia re-examined* (pp. 39–44). New York: Greenwood Press.

Naisbitt, J. (1982). *Megatrends: Ten new directions transforming our lives.* New York: Warner Books.

Newton, K. (1975). American urban politics: Social class, political structure, and public goods. *Urban Affairs Quarterly, 11*, 243–264.

Packard, V. (1972). *A nation of strangers.* New York: McKay.

Park, R. E. (1936). Human ecology. *American Journal of Sociology, 62*(1), 1–15.

Park, R. E. (1952). *Human communities: The city and human ecology.* New York: Free Press.

Presthus, R. (1964). *Men at the top: A study in community power.* New York: Oxford University Press.

Quindlen, A. (1992, May 20). Suburbs have power, funds to rebuild the cities. *The Miami Herald*, p. A15.

Reid, J. N. (1984). *Availability of selected public facilities in rural communities.* Washington, DC: U.S. Department of Agriculture.

Reitzes, D. C. (1986). Alinsky in the 1980s: Two contemporary Chicago community organizations. *Sociological Quarterly, 28*, 265–283.

Rheingold, H. (1993). *The virtual community: Homesteading on the electronic frontier.* Reading, MA: Addison-Wesley.

Rubenstein, C. (1993, January 17). Increasingly, we're turning neighbors into friends. *The New York Times*, pp. 1G, 9G.

Rubin, I. (1969). Function and structure of community: Conceptual and theoretical analysis. *International Review of Community Development, 21–22*, 111–119.

Rusk, D. (1992, May 21). America's urban apartheid. *The New York Times*, p. A15.

Rusk, D. (1993, September 8). Suburban renewal. *The New York Times*, p. A19.

Sanders, I. T. (1960). The community social profile. *American Sociological Review, 25*(1), 75–77.

Sassen, S. (1990). Economic restructuring and the American city. *Annual Review of Sociology, 16*, 465–490.

Semyonov, M., & Lewin-Epstein, N. (1991). Suburban labor markets, urban labor martkets, and gender inequality in earnings. *The Sociological Quarterly, 32*, 611–620.

Simmel, G. (1950). The metropolis and mental life. In K. H. Wolff (Ed.), *The sociology of George Simmel* (pp. 409–424). New York: Free Press.

Simon, C. P., & Witte, A. D. (1982). *Beating the system: The underground economy*. Boston: Auburn House.

Slovak, J. (1985). City spending, suburban demands, and fiscal exploitation: A replication and extension. *Social Forces, 64*, 168–190.

Smothers, R. (1993, October 18). City seeks to grow by disappearing. *The New York Times*, p. A8.

Stanfield, R. L. (1993, May 22). Zoning dispute: Criticism of Clinton's empowerment zones. *National Journal, 25*, 1260.

Stein, M. R. (1960). *The eclipse of community: An interpretation of American studies*. Princeton, NJ: Princeton University Press.

Summers, G. F., & Branch, K. (1984). Economic development and community social change. *Annual Review of Sociology, 10*(1), 41–166.

Suttles, G. D. (1968). *The social order of the slum: Ethnicity and territory in the inner city*. Chicago: University of Chicago Press.

Suttles, G. D. (1972). *The social construction of communities*. Chicago: University of Chicago Press.

Swanson, L. E., & Luloff, E. E. (1990). Barriers and opportunities for community development: A summary. In A. E. Luloff & L. E. Swanson (Eds.), *American rural communities* (pp. 228–234). Boulder: Westview Press.

Taylor, R. (1979). Black ethnicity and the persistence of ethnogenesis. *American Journal of Sociology, 84*, 1401–1423.

Tonnies, F. (1887, 1963). *Community and society*. (C. P. Loomis, Trans.). New York: Harper & Row.

U.S. Bureau of the Census. (1991). *Statistical abstract of the United States: 1991* (111th edition.) Washington, DC: U.S. Government Printing Office.

U.S. Bureau of the Census. (1992a). *Statistical abstract of the United States: 1992* (112th edition). Washington, DC: U.S. Government Printing Office.

U.S. Bureau of the Census. (1992b, February). *1990 census of population and housing summary tape file 1C, CD 90-1C, United States summary*. Washington, DC: U.S. Government Printing Office.

Vidich, A. J., & Bensman, J. (1968). *Small town in mass society: Class, power, and religion in a rural community* (rev. ed.). Princeton, NJ: Princeton University Press.

Warner, W. L. (1963). *Yankee city*. New Haven, CT: Yale University Press.

Warren, R. B., & Warren, D. I. (1977). *The neighborhood organizer's handbook*. Notre Dame, IN: University of Notre Dame Press.

Warren, R. L. (1970). The good community—What would it be? *Journal of the Community Development Society, 1*(1), 14–23.

Warren, R. L. (1975). External forces affecting local communities—Bad news and good news. *Journal of Community Development Society, 6*(2), 5–14.

Warren, R. L. (1978). *The community in America* (3rd ed.). Chicago: Rand McNally.

Warren, R. L. (1988). Observations on the state of community theory. In R. L. Warren & L. Lyon, (Eds.), *New perspectives on the American community* (5th ed., pp. 84–86). Belmont, CA: Wadsworth.

Warren, R. L., & Lyon, L. (1988). *New perspectives on the American community* (5th ed.). Belmont, CA: Wadsworth.

Weber, M. (1958). *The city*. Translated and edited by D. Martindale & G. Neuwirth. New York: Free Press.

Wellman, B. (1988). The community question re-evaluated. In M. P. Smith (Ed.), *Power, community and the city* (Vol. 1, pp. 81–107). New Brunswick: Transaction Books.

Wellman, B., & Leighton, B. (1979). Networks, neighborhoods, and communities: Approaches to the study of the community question. *Urban Affairs Quarterly, 14*, 363–390.

Whyte, W. F. (1955). *Street corner society: The social structure of an Italian slum*. Chicago: University of Chicago Press.

Williams, O. P., Herman, H., Liebman, C. S., & Dye, T. R. (1965). *Suburban differences and metropolitan policies: A Philadelphia story*. Philadelphia: University of Pennsylvania Press.

Wirth, L. (1938). Urbanism as a way of life. *American Journal of Sociology, 44*, 1–24.

Wood, R. C. (1989). Rethinking the suburbs. In B. M. Kelly (Ed.), *Suburbia re-examined* (pp. 223–228). New York: Greenwood Press.

SUGGESTIONS FOR FURTHER READING

Choldin, H. M. (1985). *Cities and suburbs*. New York: McGraw-Hill.

Duneier, M. (1992). *Slim's table: Race, respectability, and masculinity*. Chicago: University of Chicago Press.

Fellin, P. (1995). *The community and the social worker* (2nd ed.). Itasca, IL: F. E. Peacock.

Garreau, J. (1991). *Edge city: Life on the new frontier*. New York: Doubleday.

Ginsberg, L. (Ed.). (1994). *Social work in rural communities* (2nd ed.). Alexandria, VA: Council on Social Work Education.

Hallman, H. W. (1984). *Neighborhoods, their place in urban life*. Beverly Hills, CA: Sage.

Hart, J. F. (Ed.). (1991). *Our changing cities*. Baltimore: Johns Hopkins University Press.

Hay, F. J. (1991). *African-American community studies from North America: A classified, annotated bibliography*. New York: Garland Publishing.

Jones, S. G. (Ed.). (1994). *Cybersociety: Computer-mediated communication and community*. Thousand Oaks, CA: Sage.

Luloff, A. E., & Swanson, L. E. (Eds.). (1990). *American rural communities*. Boulder: Westview Press.

Martinez-Brawley, E. E. (1990). *Perspectives on the small community: Humanistic views for practitioners*. Silver Springs, MD: National Association of Social Workers.

Moore, G. (1990). Structural determinants of men's and women's personal networks. *American Sociological Review, 55*, 726–735.

Norman, A. J. (1994). Managing ethnic conflict within a community context: Black-Korean relations in an American city. *Community Development Journal, 29*, 169–176.

Portes, A., Castells, M., & Benton, L. A. (Eds.). (1989). *The informal economy: Studies in Advanced and less developed countries*. Baltimore: Johns Hopkins University Press (Two chapters: "New York City's informal economy" by Saskia Sassen-Koob [pages 60–77] and "Miami's two informal sectors" by Alex Stepick [pages 111–134]).

Portes, A., & Stepick, A. (1993). *City on the edge: The transformation of Miami*. Berkeley: University of California Press.

Rheingold, H. (1993). *The virtual community: Homesteading on the electronic frontier*. Reading, MA: Addison-Wesley.

Rusk, D. (1993). *Cities without suburbs*. Baltimore: Johns Hopkins University Press.

U.S. Bureau of the Census. *County and city data book*. Washington, DC: U.S. Government Printing Office. (Look for the most recent issue available at your library for current information about counties, cities, and small towns of 2500 inhabitants or more.)

Warren, R. L. (1965). *Studying your community*. New York: Free Press. (This is an old book, but it still provides a wealth of practical guidance to those interested in studying local communities.)

Warren, R. L., & Lyon, L. (1988). *New perspectives on the American community* (5th ed.). Belmont, CA: Wadsworth.

Wolf, D. G. (1979). *The lesbian community*. Berkeley: University of California Press.

Zukin, S. (1991). The hollow center: U.S. cities in the global era. In A. Wolfe (Ed.), *America at century's end* (pp. 245–261). Berkeley: University of California Press.

Look for articles in the following journals:

American Journal of Sociology

American Sociological Review

Journal of the Community Development Society

Journal of Community Practice

Journal of Urban Affairs

Rural Sociology

Social Networks

Urban Affairs Quarterly

Urban Studies

CHAPTER 6

ORGANIZATIONAL BEHAVIOR

Consider the many organizations and institutions that have played and continue to play a vital role in your life. You have attended primary and secondary school and college at several educational institutions. You may have served in the military. If you work, you are likely to be employed by a for-profit or nonprofit organization, big or small. There are likely to be several churches in your community; perhaps you attend services or participate in activities sponsored by one of these religious organizations. Your entertainment is provided by organizations such as cinemas, clubs, restaurants, or theaters. The food that you eat is processed, distributed, and sold by various organizations. The clothes that you wear are manufactured, wholesaled, and retailed by organizations. Look and you will see scores of organizations all around you—

the neighborhood supermarket, the child day-care center, the department stores and small shops at the nearby shopping center, the offices at the office park, the community mental health center, the local hospital, the neighborhood church or temple, the family service agency, the police and fire departments, the social security office, the welfare department, and the county correctional facility, to mention but a few.

An **organization** is a social unit composed of two or more people engaged on a relatively continuous basis in a specialized and interdependent activity aimed at accomplishing a common goal or mission (Robbins, 1989, p. 4; Gortner, Mahler, & Nicholson, 1987, p. 2). Like families, organizations have considerable influence on our behavior and on the quality of our lives because we spend most of our lives in them, particularly as students and later as working people. We also continually interact with organizations as customers, patrons, parishioners, clients, recipients, patients, or perhaps even as inmates. It is therefore important to understand these social units with which we constantly interact, their impact on us, and the influence we have on them.

This chapter will explore the major conceptual models that aim to explain behavior within organizations. It will also examine organizational structure and dynamics, the influence of the external environment on organizations, and organizational culture. Finally, the chapter will look at the relationship between individuals and their work organizations and will consider significant issues of concern to women and other organizational members belonging to nondominant social groups. The goal is to give you basic knowledge about organizations that will help you to better understand the human service organizations with which you will be associated in your professional career and to function effectively within them in the front-line, supervisory, and managerial positions that you will likely occupy during the course of your professional life. The knowledge that you will gain in this chapter will also help you to understand better all the other organizations that are a part of your daily life.

HUMAN SERVICE ORGANIZATIONS

Human service organizations are those organizations whose principal function is to protect, maintain, or enhance the welfare of the people they serve (Hasenfeld, 1983, p. 1). They include many of those just mentioned, such as schools, social service agencies, hospitals, churches, law enforcement agencies, colleges and universities, and correctional facilities. They may be government run, private nonprofit, or business ventures.

Types of Human Service Organizations

Hasenfeld (1983, p. 4) classified human service organizations according to two basic dimensions: the type of clients they serve and the techniques they use to work with clients. As shown in Table 6.1, clients can be divided into two groups: (1) those who function normally, such as regular school children or retirees on social security; and (2) those who are dysfunctional, such as criminal offenders or mental patients.

Techniques used to work with clients can be classified into three categories: (1) **people processing**—that is, technologies aimed at conferring a social label such as patient suffering from diagnosis of heart disease or mental disorder; (2) **people sustaining**—that is, technologies whose purpose is to prevent or retard

TABLE 6.1 A Typology of Human Service Organizations

TYPE OF CLIENT	PEOPLE PROCESSING	PEOPLE SUSTAINING	PEOPLE CHANGING
Normal functioning	*Type* I College admissions office Credit rating bureau	*Type III* Social Security Retirement home	*Type V* Public school YMCA
Malfunctioning	*Type II* Juvenile court Diagnostic clinic	*Type IV* Public assistance Nursing home	*Type VI* Hospital Residential treatment center

Source: From Yeheskel Hasenfeld, *Human Service Organizations*. Copyright © 1983. Reprinted by permission from Allyn and Bacon.

functional deterioration or to maintain health and well-being such as the care of the elderly in intermediate care facilities or of the chronically mentally ill in community group homes and income-maintenance programs such as the Supplementary Security Income program (SSI) or Aid for Dependent Children (AFDC); and (3) **people changing**—that is, technologies that attempt to alter the personal characteristics of the client or to enhance the person's well-being such as medical treatment, education, and psychotherapy.

Human service organizations can also be classified as public, nonprofit or voluntary, and for-profit agencies. **Public service organizations** are government funded and usually government run and provide services mandated by legal statute. **Nonprofit or voluntary organizations** are not established by mandate but rather are created voluntarily to provide on a continuing basis a needed social service to a clientele in the community. They are governed by a volunteer board of directors and may depend on public or private funding (McMurtry, Netting, & Kettner, 1990). Any "profits" they make must be reinvested in the agency. **For-profit organizations** are privately run money-making operations. In practice, the lines between these three basic types of organizations are somewhat blurred. For instance, nonprofit (voluntary) agencies may provide publicly mandated services paid by public funds and private for-profit agencies may offer essential community services.

Human Service Organizations and Their Clients

As service recipients or product consumers, clients play an important role in all organizations. The clients of human service organizations in particular play an even more crucial role within these organizations because they constitute the very "raw material" with which practitioners work. In this sense, clients become "quasi-members" of human service organizations (Hasenfeld, 1983, p. 177). They acquire official

status within the organization when they become officially associated with it. For example, a small boy becomes a student upon enrollment in kindergarten.

Once given official status, clients are deeply affected by the human service organizations with which they become associated. Some statuses are positive, such as student, although many variations are not positive, such as failing student, truant student, or special education student. Other statuses conferred by human service organizations are inherently negative, such as mental patient, inmate, or welfare recipient, and these may affect the client's reputation profoundly. For instance, a label of *mental patient* or *criminal offender* may change the course of a person's entire life because it can alter the way in which people relate to the individual, his or her own self-concept, and life opportunities, particularly employment chances.

Some clients have good leverage in their relationships with human service organizations. Specifically, when they control certain resources needed by the organization (such as when they pay high fees), they have a power advantage, particularly if the organization has few alternative sources of funding. Such clients are in a good position to make their needs and demands heard and to obtain as efficient and competent services as the organization is able to offer. If the organization does not respond, they can take their business elsewhere. However, not all clients are so fortunate. If the organization provides a service or resource that is not readily available from any other source, such as a welfare check or food stamps, the organization has the power advantage over the individual. This power advantage of the organization over the client sometimes results in insensitivity to the client's needs or excessive intrusion by some workers into the client's life.

One major dilemma in the relationship between clients and human service organizations is the frequent dependence of the organization on client performance for continued funding and survival. For example, a drug rehabilitation program's future funding potential may depend on its success rate in treating patients. Such situations foster a tendency on the part of some human service organizations to get rid of the very clients that need their services the most because these clients may be considered "failure prone." Agencies get rid of unwanted clients in various ways. For example, some require applicants to fill out lengthy and complicated application forms that discourage many who are not sufficiently persistent. Others make clients wait for a long time on waiting lists and in waiting rooms, treat them disrespectfully, conveniently do not speak the client's language, or give them the "run around" by referring them to other organizations or departments rather than taking care of their needs. Some drop certain clients for lack of "motivation" or "uncooperative" behavior, and so on. These are just a few examples of the many unfortunate ways in which human service agencies sometimes drop "undesirable" clients to maintain an image of success.

MAJOR ORGANIZATIONAL PERSPECTIVES

Currently there is no comprehensive theory of organizational behavior. However, there are several conceptual models that aim to explain various aspects of behavior in organizations. These include the rational or bureaucratic model, the human relations model, the ecosystems model, and the political model.

The Rational or Bureaucratic Model

Most of us spend a good deal of our lives interacting with or working for bureaucracies, whether they be schools, government agencies, large business enterprises, or the U.S. military, to mention but a few. **Bureaucracies** are rational structures designed to attain organizational goals (Weber, 1947). An example would be the local office of the Department of Health and Human Services, the public health department, or the central office of the school district. Bureaucracies have a clear division of labor that lets employees know exactly where they fit in the organizational chart and what tasks they are supposed to perform. Typically, employees are expected to give precedence to rules and procedures over individual needs. This tends to create an impersonal climate. Large bureaucracies often have a multilevel chain of command with each level being under the control and supervision of a higher one. Decisions many times have to be cleared through the chain of command and are supposed to be made rationally on the basis of what is most effective and efficient in terms of organizational goals. Personnel decisions are ideally to be based on technical qualifications and performance rather than on subjective criteria.

In the minds of some members of the public, bureaucracies are large, inefficient organizations whose employees, referred to as *bureaucrats*, appear to be primarily concerned with following rules inflexibly and watching the clock to close shop as the clock strikes the designated closing time, whether they are finished with their work or not. Although there is an element of truth in this characterization, many bureaucrats are hardworking and conscientious and well-run bureaucracies can be efficient and effective. Nevertheless, certain characteristics of bureaucracies may be responsible for some of the negative connotations associated with this form of organization. For example, some bureaucracies are overloaded with rules and procedures and have an unwielding chain of command. This fosters an inflexible, impersonal, and dehumanizing environment and causes much unnecessary red tape. This situation is descriptive of many of the large social service agencies, such as the agencies that dispense public assistance.

The bureaucratic model is not appropriate for professional human service organizations whose work is not of a routine nature. This is because professionals need to exercise their judgment with relative freedom from hierarchical authority and from rigid rules.

The Human Relations Model

The **human relations model** of organization, exemplified by McGregor's Theory Y and Likert's "System 4" organizations (McGregor, 1960; Likert, 1967), is characterized by employee participation in organizational problem solving, decision making, and goal setting; minimum hierarchical or status differences among employees; open communication at all levels of the organization; and democratic and considerate leadership.

Although these human relations principles are admirable and likely to result in high employee satisfaction, they do not guarantee organizational effectiveness unless they are accompanied by a competent technology (Perrow, 1965). Specifically in relation to human service organizations, this means that a human relations approach in and of itself cannot be expected to improve the treatment outcome for clients. For instance, a public assistance agency that is human relations oriented might be more polite and empathetic toward clients, but it would be unlikely to be more efficient or effective in its eligibility determinations simply because of its human relations orientation. Some suggest that to treat clients more humanely, human service agencies need to institute certain specific measures, such as reducing the size of the facility and the client-to-staff ratio or caseload, improving salaries to be able to hire better- trained personnel, using more effective interventions, and having routine monitoring by external agencies (Hasenfeld, 1983, p. 28). Such reforms would be more helpful than simply following a human relations approach. This is not to say that a human relations approach is not a good organizational model—quite the contrary. But we must be reminded that good relations *by themselves* seldom get the job done well.

The Ecosystems Model

The systems perspective views organizations as social systems composed of interdependent units interacting within a constantly changing environment (Katz & Kahn, 1978). From an **ecosystems model** perspective, one important organizational goal is to achieve a good fit internally (in terms of structure, patterns of authority, communication, decision-making styles, technology, and the needs, values, and abilities of employees) and externally in relation to the environment. One of the major tasks facing the leadership of an organization is to achieve this internal and external balance, or steady state, that keeps the organization attuned to and ready to meet emerging challenges.

Organizations have various overlapping subsystems, including the technical, structural, supportive, psychosocial, maintenance, adaptive, and managerial subsystems (Kast & Rosenzweig, 1973; Katz & Kahn, 1978; Gummer, 1987). The job of the *technical subsystem* is to take resources from the environment and transform them by means of some technology into products or services that are sent back to the environment (see Figure 6.1). **Technology** (another term for *throughput*) refers to the procedures whereby the organization transforms its inputs (e.g., raw materials or clients) into outputs (e.g., products or better functioning individuals).

The organizational technology may be routine or nonroutine (Perrow, 1967). **Routine technologies** are generally (though not always) applied to inanimate objects, such as auto parts or construction materials. Because such raw materials tend to be stable, the technology can be specified in advance, such as in a blueprint for building a house. The more routine the technology of an organization, the more directions can be followed word for word and the lesser the autonomy or flexibility required by those who process inputs into outputs. Therefore, organizations with routine technologies can function well under a bureaucratic model.

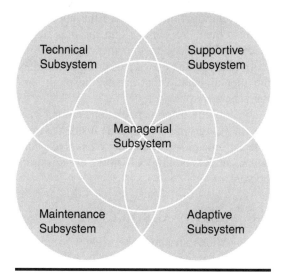

ENVIRONMENTAL SUPRASYSTEM

Technical Subsystem

Supportive Subsystem

Managerial Subsystem

Maintenance Subsystem

Adaptive Subsystem

FIGURE 6.1   The Systems View of Organizations

Nonroutine technologies, on the other hand, are more appropriate for living things, such as human beings. Because people are changeable and lacking in uniformity, it is very difficult to standardize the way in which they should be processed. Due to lack of standardization, organizations specializing in nonroutine technologies (e.g., teaching and psychotherapy) must grant their front-line staff discretion to exercise judgment in determining appropriate courses of action. This means that the staff must have a considerable amount of education and experience. Thus, organizations with nonroutine technologies usually employ professionals and generally function with a fairly simple organizational structure since much of their work takes place at the direct service level.

The *structural subsystem* distributes the technical tasks so that they can be accomplished, and sets forth role descriptions, rules and procedures, and patterns of authority and communication. (Organizational structure will be discussed in detail later in this chapter.) The *supportive subsystem* function is to transact with the environment to ensure that there is a steady supply of resources (e.g., money, clientele, facilities), support, and consumers for the organization's products. The *psychosocial subsystem* consists of the individual behaviors and motivations of the organization's members, their group dynamics, and influence systems (e.g., leadership, power, and political behaviors). (Many of these processes will be explored later in this chapter.)

The *maintenance subsystem's* function is to keep the steady state and to ensure the continuing existence of the organization by enforcing its rules and regulations, seeing to it that the organizational structure remains relevant to its tasks and that the behavior of its members is appropriate. The *adaptive subsystem* ensures that the organization remains responsive to changes within its environment, such as political or economic shifts or emergence of other competing organizations. Formally, the adaptive function is performed by employees with responsibility for collecting information about the organization and its environment and for carrying out research, planning, and development programs.

The *managerial subsystem* is composed of various department and division managers. It plans, organizes, and controls the organizational endeavor, seeing to it that no subsystem becomes unduly dominant to the detriment of the other subsystems, that subsystem functions are carried out in an integrated and coordinated fashion, and that conflict is dealt with.

Like all social systems, organizations eventually move toward disorganization and death (entropy). However, as long as they are able to bring in more energy from the environment than is needed to operate, they grow (negative entropy) and become more differentiated, vertically and horizontally. (The process of vertical and horizontal differentiation will be covered later in this chapter.)

The Political Model

The **political model** rests on the premise that self-interest is a fundamental motivator of organizational behavior. It views organizations as political arenas within which different internal and external interest groups compete for attention to their concerns and interests (Zald, 1970; Hasenfeld, 1983, p. 44). Thus, a family service agency may be pushed in one direction by its professional staff with their own interests and concerns, in another direction by the institutions it serves (e.g., schools, juvenile court), and in still other directions by the clientele, the board of directors, and various advocacy groups representing family, children, or mental health concerns.

The relative influence that each of the preceding interest groups may have on the organization depends on the importance of the resources they can make available to it and the extent to which the organization can obtain such resources elsewhere. Specifically, the greater the importance to the organization of the resources a particular group has to offer, the greater influence the group is likely to have on the organization. The greater the availability of these resources elsewhere, the lesser the group's power to shape the organization (Emerson, 1962). For instance, families in need of assistance are a critical resource for family service agencies because without clients these agencies cannot operate, but their influence on a particular agency would be limited if there were an excess of families in need of the agency's services and no other agencies available to serve them. By the same token, funding sources usually have major power over most social agencies because they provide financial resources difficult to obtain elsewhere.

Within the organization, the distribution of power and authority depends on the importance of the contribution of each unit or individual member to the attainment of organizational goals. For example, departments or individuals that bring in large extramural financial grants tend to have considerable power. Similarly, in an outpatient mental health clinic staffed with psychiatrists, psychologists, and social workers, psychiatrists usually have the upper hand because their credentials lend the most legitimacy and prestige to the agency's activities, particularly in the eyes of insurance providers, the mental health community, hospitals, and the general public.

By looking at power relations among various interest groups within and outside the organization, the political model helps us to gain a better understanding of how organizations operate.

ORGANIZATIONAL STRUCTURE

Organizations structure themselves to coordinate their activities, control the behavior of their employees, and adapt to the external environment. To accomplish these objectives, they typically become differentiated horizontally, vertically, and spatially into various sub-units and become formalized and centralized to various extents.

Horizontal Differentiation

Typically, an organization divides its work among different units or departments, each specializing in different tasks or client characteristics or serving different geographic areas. For example, a county department of human services may have several divisions, such as children, youth, and family services; developmental disabilities services; mental health services; public health services; vocational rehabilitation services; and aging services. Within each division there may be several more specialized programs. For example, under the division of children, youth, and family services, there may be several programs such as protective services, adoptions, economic services, delinquency and adolescent pregnancy prevention, and so on. This permits each program unit to be staffed with employees specialized in each area of expertise. Such division of labor is referred to as **horizontal** or **lateral differentiation**. Figure 6.2 shows the organizational chart of a county department of human services.

Some organizations divide their tasks to such an extent that each worker becomes excessively specialized. For example, in a factory, an employee may be in charge of tightening a couple of bolts on every picture tube of every TV set on the assembly line. Such extreme division of labor can make the job very boring and unfullfilling, even though it may be efficient and profitable economically for the organization, as it may allow it to rely on a largely unskilled labor force.

Vertical and Spatial Differentiation

An organization is usually differentiated vertically into a number of hierarchical levels. For example, a county department of human services may have direct-service practitioners working in various program units, each reporting to a program supervisor who reports to a division manager. Each division manager, in turn, reports to the agency's director. Therefore, this particular agency has a four-level **chain of command**: the direct-service practitioners, the program supervisors, the divisional managers, and the director.

Some organizations are *tall* (i.e., they have many hierarchical levels); others are *flat* (i.e., they have a short chain of command). Tall organizations with a long chain of command are slow to adapt to their environments because changes must be approved at many levels before they can be implemented. Also, when organizations are very tall, lower-level employees may feel detached and isolated, particularly if they are left out of the decision-making process. However, tall organizations often enhance the job satisfaction of higher ups, probably because they give them high status and pay and greater autonomy than those at lower levels (Robbins, 1989).

Those in the direct line of command of the organization—that is, those with decision-making authority and leadership responsibility—are referred to as **line personnel.** In the department of human services example, these include the director, the division managers, and the program supervisors. The rest of the employees are classified as **staff.** The staff includes the direct–service professionals, the secretaries, and the support personnel at each level, including the assistants to the division managers and the associate directors in charge of planning, development and evaluation, finance, personnel, and in-service training.

If the organizational arrangement is such that each employee receives commands from and is responsible to only one supervisor, then the organization is said to function under the principle known as **unity of command** (March & Simon, 1958). This system helps to avoid confusion, multiple and conflicting expectations, divided loyalties, and uncoordinated action.

Span of control is another important concept describing vertical differentiation. It refers to the number of employees under the direction and supervision of a higher officer. For example, if there are six employees in each service unit of the department of human services reporting to each supervisor, the span of control of the supervisors is six. It is generally assumed that five or six is an ideal number of employees to supervise (March & Simon, 1958). However, Argyris (1957) has argued against the close supervision inherent in small spans of control because it can reinforce dependency and passivity on the part of employees. If employee autonomy is important, large spans of control are probably better.

If an organization has offices and personnel in various locations, it is **spatially differentiated** For example, if the county department of human services had a headquarters office downtown and two suburban branches, it would be spatially differentiated.

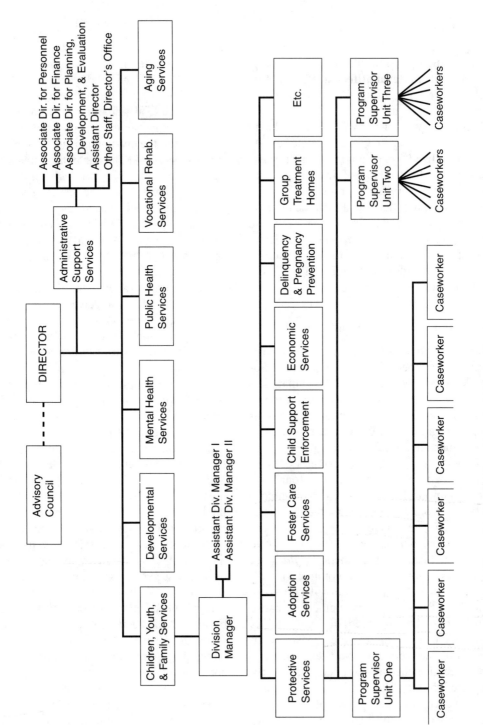

FIGURE 6.2 Organizational Chart of a County Department of Human Services

Complexity, Formalization, and Centralization

Together, the horizontal, vertical, and spatial differentiation of an organization define its degree of complexity. The more **complex** the **organization,** the more difficult the task of integrating or coordinating all its activities. This integration must be accomplished by various means, such as the communication system (e.g., memos, staff meetings), plans, and schedules.

Another structural aspect of organizations is their degree of **formalization**. In some organizations, jobs are highly formalized in the sense that employees must do things exactly as specified. For example, in an automobile assembly line, each worker must do exactly what he or she is supposed to do without deviating from the specifications, since all the car models produced must be identical. Eligibility workers in a public assistance agency also have highly formalized roles, as they are expected to follow eligibility policies and procedures exactly as specified in the agency manual. In contrast, human service agencies employing professionals such as mental health or family service clinics tend to grant their professional employees considerable autonomy to exercise their judgment; thus, they have lower levels of formalization. One advantage of less formalized organizations is that they are better able to adapt to environmental changes.

Still another aspect of organizational structure besides complexity and formalization is **centralization**—the degree to which decision-making authority is concentrated in the higher echelons of the organization. If higher-level administrators make decisions with little input or participation from those below, the organization is centralized. The more the lower-echelon personnel participate in decision making or the greater the discretion they are given to make decisions, the more **decentralized** the organization.

There is evidence that employee performance and job satisfaction are higher in decentralized than in centralized organizations (Robbins, 1989). Other advantages of decentralized organizations include greater responsiveness to clients, more employee autonomy, greater flexibility in dealing with external demands, and faster decision making. These are all features that can add to the effectiveness of human service organizations. However, decentralization per se is not a panacea. If overdone, it can result in inconsistencies and poor control, with individual units developing duplicative services or conflicting policies, procedures, and operating systems. Excessive decentralization can also lead to an inability of the organization to respond to environmental demands as a single entity (Gortner, Mahler, & Nicholson, 1987). Therefore, the organization must be able to keep an appropriate centralization/decentralization balance to match the requirements of its technical and environmental situation.

The main purpose of a given organizational structure is to help organizational members achieve organizational objectives. Therefore, as the organization's objectives change, its structure needs to be modified accordingly. Many organizations naturally become increasingly more differentiated horizontally, vertically, and, perhaps, spatially as they grow and expand their activities. Structural changes are also made sometimes for political reasons. For example, public agencies under political fire may embark in "total reorganizations" to placate the public and the legislature, although the changes they often make are more cosmetic or symbolic than real.

Loosely Coupled Organizations

Organizations such as universities, hospitals, and other professional agencies frequently are loosely coupled (Weick, 1976). **Loosely coupled organizations** have staff members who exercise substantial discretion in the work they do. Their tasks are typically loosely coordinated, with one staff member usually not knowing exactly what others in the same unit may be doing, even in relation to the same clients, students, or patients. That is, unless there is a deep commitment to teamwork on the part of the staff, the activities of various work units and specialties within the loosely coupled agency are usually so insulated that nurse X may not know what social worker Y is doing with respect to patient Z, and psychiatrist A may not know what either one is doing. Or professor A may not know what professor B or professor C are teaching, even though all three teach different sections of the same course. The control system is also characteristically weak in loosely coupled organizations. In a psychiatric hospital, for example, the nurses, social workers, psychologists, and psychiatrists have considerable latitude to decide how they will work with patients, and hospital administrators and department supervisors have little control over the way the staff practice their professions due to confidentiality and autonomy issues. Similarly, at a university the administration has limited authority over the manner in which professors conduct their work. Of course, the entire organization is seldom loosely coupled. Universities, which are classic examples of loosely coupled organizations, have some departments, such as registration and records and personnel, that are much more tightly coupled than others.

The danger of excessively loose coupling, like excessive decentralization, is that it can result in a disjointed and even contradictory service delivery process. Hasenfeld (1983, p. 158) noted, for example, the confusion that patients may experience in some psychiatric hospitals when attendants reward patients for being passive and compliant while social workers encourage them to be assertive, or when psychiatrists prescribe and nurses administer psychotropic drugs to the patients while psychotherapists may be advising them against drug dependency.

ORGANIZATIONAL PROCESSES

This section will discuss the basic activities of the organization, including communication, leadership, decision making, power, politics, and conflict.

Communication Processes

Communication is an interactive process between the sender and receiver of a message whereby one influences the other. In organizations, communication is the most important means of achieving integration and coordination across units and divisions as well as up and down the chain of command. This section deals with issues pertaining to communication in organizations. (Other more general aspects of the communication process, verbal and nonverbal, will be discussed in Chapter 7.)

Communication Networks
Organizational communication flows through various networks, or channels. Some of the most commonly used channels are the chain, the wheel, and the all-channel system. In the **chain** network, each link represents a level in the organizational hierarchy, and communication flows upward or downward along the chain of command. For example, in our county department of human services example, communication flows up and down through a four–level chain—from the direct-service workers to their supervisors to the division managers to the director.

The **wheel** represents a work situation in which the team leader or supervisor has a certain number of subordinates who report to him or her with no formal interaction required among members of the staff. Of course, the staff members are likely to engage in much informal interaction at work, but under this arrangement their formal work roles would not require that they communicate. The person in the middle of the wheel—the team leader or supervisor—is the most central member of the communication network. If too many people report to this individual, he or she may suffer from saturation or communication overload (Shaw, 1981, pp. 158–159). However, this person also has the potential to be the most satisfied member of the group because he or she is in control of the situation (Bavelas, 1950). The wheel network may be a more appropriate work arrangement for assembly-line jobs in the manufacturing industries than for professional jobs in agency settings where formal interaction between staff members is necessary and expected.

In an **all-channel** communication network, everyone communicates with everyone else. Under this arrangement, team members interact among themselves and with their leader or supervisor in order to fulfill their work roles. For example, when three or four different professionals—physician, nurse, and social worker, for instance—are working as a team with the same client or when several employees are working on the solution of a complex problem, the all-channel system would be the most appropriate communication network.

Informal Communication Network. In addition to the official communication system, each organization has several informal communication channels variously referred to as the *grapevine* or the *rumor mill.* These informal networks may be radial, interlocking, or combination radial-interlocking (see Figure 6.3). In a **radial network**, a person communicates with a number of others and the others, in turn, talk with still others. But the members of this type of network are not directly connected; that is, they do not interact with one another. For example, one employee in one unit of the department or human services may speak to another employee in another unit about rumors concerning layoffs. The person he spoke to then tells others in other departments who, in turn, tell several of their friends throughout the

organization. Before long, news about the impending layoffs has reached every unit of the organization. In an **interlocking network**, the people with whom an individual interacts also interact with one another. In real situations, personal communication networks are likely to be both radial and interlocking (Gortner, Mahler, & Nicholson, 1987, p. 159). For example, among those you interact with at work, you are likely to have some who communicate regularly with one another and others who do not.

The organizational **grapevine** carries information and rumors about many different things, from the sexual indiscretions of organizational members to concerns with anticipated cutbacks in funding, layoffs, or branch agency closings. Higher-ups in the organization usually try to keep up with the rumor mill indirectly, sometimes through a trusted secretary or assistant who is well connected informally or through direct communication with employees at lower levels in the organization. "Keeping an ear to the ground," so to speak, helps them to pick up early signs of misinformation or issues of concern that need to be clarified through the formal communication system.

Higher-ups in the organization sometimes purposely "float" ideas through the grapevine to get informal feedback on actions they may be contemplating. If the grapevine brings strongly negative feedback, they know they must work harder on selling the concept; if, on the other hand, the idea is well received informally, they can implement it with greater assurance that the road ahead will be fairly smooth. The grapevine is sometimes used for ill purposes. For example, members of the organization sometimes purposely inject falsities into the rumor mill to create havoc or to further their personal interests.

Some informal networks extend beyond the organization, linking it with external groups such as the media, the legislature, or various interest groups. Public service organizations

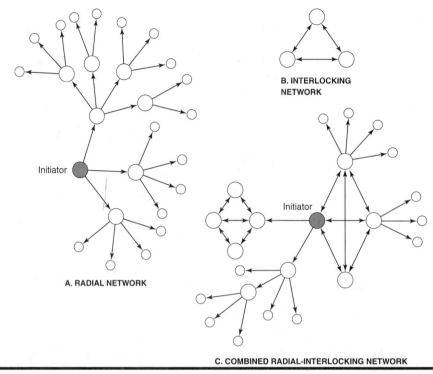

FIGURE 6.3 Informal Communication Networks in Organizations

often attempt to restrict such external contacts by requiring that employees clear them in advance.

Internal Communication Roles

Various organizational members play important internal communication roles, such as gatekeeper and liaison or linking pin. The **gatekeeper** is the person through whom messages must pass to get from source to destination. For example, an agency director may have an administrative assistant who acts as gatekeeper intercepting all communications addressed to the director. Some messages may be passed on directly to the director, others may be grouped and summarized for action, and still others may be delegated to other employees or may be acted on by the assistant.

Another important communication role within the organization is that of **liaison** or **linking pin**. This is the individual who serves as connector between various subdivisions. For example, unit supervisors act as liaisons or linking pins when they serve as representatives to departmental or divisional meetings or to coordinating councils.

The Flow of Communication

Organizational communication flows vertically up and down the chain command, horizontally between co-workers, units, or divisions, and externally to and from environmental entities.

Vertical Communication.
Vertical communication flows in a downward or upward direction along the chain of command. **Downward communication** moves from a higher level to a lower level—for example, from the agency director's level to the various work units. By means of formal staff meetings, memoranda, training sessions, and procedural

manuals, the agency director and other administrators and supervisors make assignments, set standards, give job instructions, keep employees informed about agency policies, procedures, and goals, and provide performance feedback.

Communication is seldom restricted to a downward flow, however. Particularly in democratically run organizations, communication flows in all directions. **Upward communication** serves to provide feedback to higher-ups about problems the staff may be experiencing, to offer employee suggestions for improving policies and practices, and to relay employee opinions and attitudes. Different organizations use different methods of collecting upward communication. Most require units to file regular reports. Some also conduct attitude surveys or have an open-door policy, a formal grievance procedure, informal "gripe" sessions, suggestion boxes, and so on. Organizations that emphasize upward communication show respect for their employees by giving them a chance to express their ideas (Planty & Machaver, 1984).

Although almost always beneficial, upward communication is not entirely free of potential drawbacks. Sometimes the problem is simply that it is not allowed to get very far. For instance, upward communication may go as far as the next immediate supervisor, who may decide not to transmit the message upward because he or she disapproves of its content. Even if the information is relayed to the next higher level, it may be condensed or modified. Upward communication is also frequently distorted due to the reluctance of lower-level employees to tell their bosses things they think their bosses do not want to hear or due to the fear of providing bosses with information that may have negative consequences for the staff (Katz & Kahn, 1978). Another problem with upward communication is that employees may quickly lose faith in its value if management fails to act on matters brought to their attention (Planty & Machaver, 1984).

Horizontal or Lateral Communication. Communication between peers in the same work unit or in similar positions in different units within the organization is called **horizontal** or **lateral communication.** This type of communication is crucial to integrate and coordinate the work of the organization. Because it is less likely to be concerned with performance than vertical communication, it tends to be more open and informal, less threatening, and less prone to distortion.

External Communication. **External communication**—communication between the organization and other individuals, groups, and organizations in its environment—is particularly critical for human service organizations. Such organizations need to keep in touch with environmental entities to remain accountable, to provide more comprehensive or effective services to clients, to establish legitimacy, and to obtain external support.

Leadership Processes

A leader is someone in the organization who influences, motivates, or empowers others to pursue the organizational goals. Individuals heading an organization or its various units or divisions hold institutionalized positions of leadership. Although usually they are expected to exercise leadership within the organization, they may or may not function as leaders. Sometimes they act as **figureheads,** and others in the organization or unit exercise the leadership.

Leadership plays a central role in organizational efforts to influence, motivate, direct, control, and integrate the activities of employees and to maintain a network of contacts with other organizations and important players in the external environment. This section focuses primarily on aspects of a contingency theory of leadership that are directly relevant to leadership at the supervisory level in organizations. Chapter 7 examines the concept of leadership, factors facilitating the emergence of leaders in

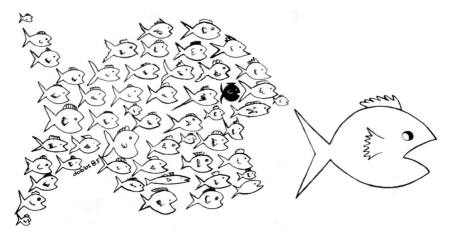

Source: Reprinted with the permission of Simon & Schuster, Inc. from the Macmillan College text *Introduction to the Human Services 2/e* by Barbara Schram and Betty Reid Mandell. Copyright © 1994 by Macmillan College Publishing Company, Inc.

groups, basic leadership styles, and situational variables that influence a leader's effectiveness.

Theories of Organizational Leadership

Fiedler's Contingency Theory of Leadership. No one leadership style is effective in all situations. Recognition of this fact has led to the formulation of several contingency models. One of the most popular and widely tested is that developed by Fred Fiedler (1978) on the basis of research conducted on over 1,000 different groups. His theory suggests that leader effectiveness depends on several factors, such as the style of the leader and the organizational situation. The person who emerges as a leader in one situation may not be an appropriate leader in another situation.

Fiedler recognizes the basic distinction made between task-centered and relationship-centered leadership styles. Namely, **task-oriented** leaders concentrate primarily on establishing operating procedures, initiating action, providing expert information, motivating organizational members toward goal achievement, and evaluating movement toward goals. They are not necessarily inattentive to group member relations, but getting the job done is their pri-

mary goal. In contrast, **relationship-oriented leaders** put emphasis on support functions such as encouraging open communication and participation, providing encouragement, showing concern for organizational members, and seeking to maintain strong and positive interpersonal relations. Although they are not necessarily disinterested in meeting organizational goals and activities, they put primary emphasis on relationships.

In addition, Fiedler has identified three basic situational factors: (1) leader/member relations, which may range from good to poor; (2) task structure, which may range from clear and concrete to ambiguous; and (3) the leader's position power, which may range from high to low.

Fiedler's research has shown that the quality of the relations between leader and members is the most important of the three situational factors to consider in deciding which of the two basic leadership styles (task oriented or relationship oriented) is likely to be more effective. Organizational members are deemed to have good relations when they show loyalty, positive affect, and acceptance toward one another and toward the leader. Their relations are considered to be poor if they show little loyalty, negative affect, or low acceptance toward one another.

The second situational determinant of leadership style, according to Fiedler, is the nature of the task at hand. In some work situations, employees work on relatively straightforward problems following a clearly delineated procedure. For example, welfare eligibility workers follow clearly spelled-out rules. Other employees have more ambiguous assignments with no agreed-upon rules to be followed. For instance, if the secretary of health and human services were asked by the president to appoint a task force to propose a national policy to deal with adolescent pregnancy, the task force members would likely have few guidelines to follow.

The third situational factor to consider in deciding which is the most appropriate leadership style, according to Fiedler, is the leader's power over other organizational members. Leaders who hold an important position in the organization and who have control over the organizational members' material and nonmaterial rewards, punishments, evaluations, and task assignments have strong position power. Those who do not have an important position or who have little control over the salaries and other aspects of the job situation of other organizational members have weak position power.

On the basis of the three situational factors delineated here, Fiedler identified eight different leadership situations ranging from most favorable to least favorable. The most favorable leadership situation would be one in which the leader/member relations are good, the task is unambiguous, and the leader's authority is unquestioned. The least favorable would be a situation in which the leader/member relations are bad, the task is ambiguous, and the leader has little power.

As shown in Figure 6.4, Fiedler's research has shown that task-motivated leaders will be most effective in highly favorable or highly unfavorable situations, whereas relationship-motivated leaders will be most effective in middle-range situations. The reason for this finding is likely to be that task and relationship leaders have different motivational priorities.

As you may recall, relationship-oriented leaders give highest priority to the establishment and maintenance of satisfying interpersonal relations, whereas task-oriented leaders concentrate on task completion. In a very unfavorable work situation, the task-motivated leader pushes the group toward task completion without investing much time trying to improve member relationships. In contrast, the relationship-oriented leader focuses on attempting to improve interpersonal relations. But since the interpersonal situation is rather hopeless, the relationship-oriented leader is likely to make little progress in terms of improving relations or getting the task done, whereas the task-oriented leader at least will make some progress toward task completion.

In very favorable work situations, the task-motivated leader can afford to relax and be considerate and pleasant. The strong task emphasis of this type of leader, coupled with the individual's increased supportiveness made possible by the favorableness of the situation, enhance his or her leadership effectiveness and usually give this leader an edge over the relationship-motivated leader. However, in all intermediate situations, and the majority of work situations fall in the intermediate range, a relationship-oriented leader has the advantage, according to Fiedler's research.

Many different programs developed to "train" effective leaders have generally shown disappointing results. The reason for their frequent inability to change people's leadership styles, according to Fiedler, is that such styles are deeply rooted and therefore difficult to modify. In other words, people who are primarily task oriented cannot easily become primarily relationship oriented, or vice versa. Accordingly, Fiedler has suggested that it is better to engineer the situation to fit the supervisor's style or to place the supervisor in a situation that fits his or her behavioral style rather than to attempt to change the individual's

SITUATIONAL FACTORS

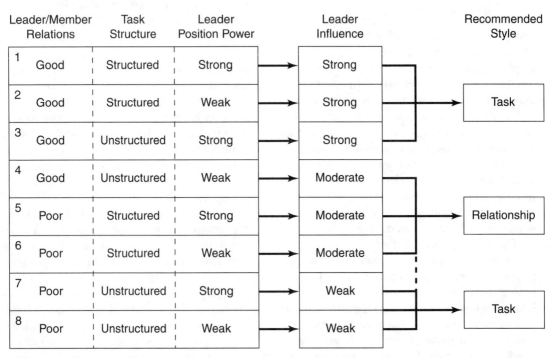

	Leader/Member Relations	Task Structure	Leader Position Power	Leader Influence	Recommended Style
1	Good	Structured	Strong	Strong	
2	Good	Structured	Weak	Strong	Task
3	Good	Unstructured	Strong	Strong	
4	Good	Unstructured	Weak	Moderate	
5	Poor	Structured	Strong	Moderate	Relationship
6	Poor	Structured	Weak	Moderate	
7	Poor	Unstructured	Strong	Weak	
8	Poor	Unstructured	Weak	Weak	Task

FIGURE 6.4 Fiedler's Contingency Model of Leadership Style

Source: From *Understanding Organizational Behavior: A Managerial Viewpoint* (p. 178) by R. E. Callahan, C. P. Fleenor, and H. R. Knudson, 1986, Columbus, OH: Charles E. Merrill. Adapted from *A Theory of Leadership Effectiveness* (p. 37) by F. E. Fiedler, 1967, New York: McGraw-Hill. Used by permission.

approach. For example, the organization may put its task-oriented supervisors in charge of the most favorable or unfavorable work units, reserving the middle-range situations for primarily relationship-oriented supervisors. In engineering the organizational situation to fit the supervisors, many adjustments can be made, such as the following:

1. *Changes in leader/member relations.* If it were necessary to improve leader/member relations to fit the needs of a particular supervisor, the work unit could be made more homogeneous by transferring out employees who increase its diversity and replacing them with others who are similar to the remaining group in terms of race, gender, culture, or socioeco-

nomic background, or the work unit could be reassembled by selecting a group of employees who work together well. If another supervisor were capable of handling a more difficult interpersonal situation, this person could be assigned a more diverse work unit in terms of race, gender, cultural, or socioeconomic background, among other possible factors, or the supervisor could be given a group of problematic employees with whom to work.

2. *Changes in task structure.* Task structure can easily be increased by giving a particular supervisor clear-cut job assignments or precise instructions. To decrease structure for another supervisor, the person could be given only a general statement of the problems to work on,

then shouldn't supervisor be transferred?

leaving the individual free to develop possible ways of dealing with them.

3. *Changes in the leader's position power.* Position power can also be adjusted as needed. For example, if the organization needed to increase the position power of one of its supervisors, it might assign this person to work with employees of clearly lower rank, or it might give the supervisor tasks that would not require any approval other than his or hers so as to grant the person sole authority to take action. In contrast, if the organization needed to decrease the position power of another supervisor, this person could be assigned to work with people of similar or equal rank, or the organization could assign his or her work unit tasks that require approval at higher levels prior to taking action.

Fieldler's contingency theory has been strongly validated in laboratory situations; however, field experiments have thus far yielded support only for categories 2, 5, 7, and 8 in Figure 6.4 (Brown, 1988, pp. 75–80; Peters, Hartke, & Pohlmann, 1985). Even though we must keep in mind that field validation is limited, this conceptual model remains one of the more useful currently available for analyzing leadership effectiveness.

Other Theories of Organizational Leadership. The path-goal theory of leadership (House, 1971; House & Mitchell, 1974) has also developed a solid empirical foundation, although research on this theory has not been nearly as extensive as on Fieldler's theory. In essence, path-goal theory proposes that effective leaders are those able to help their followers achieve their work goals by helping them see the path(s) to follow and by reducing barriers.

The leader participation theory developed by Vroom and Yetton (1973) is one of the most elaborate. It is based on limited but generally positive research findings (Field, 1982). This model uses a decision tree to consider various possible contingencies in the process of deciding which of several alternative leadership styles best fits a situation. It is based on the idea that leaders do not have a fixed behavioral style (primarily task centered or relationship centered) but are flexible enough to be able to switch if the situation warrants it. Depending on the results obtained by using the decision tree, the leader can switch from one style of leadership to another, as needed. To be sure, some people are better than others at switching styles. Many everyday organizational problems would not merit using decision trees to determine which decision-making style to assume. However, when dealing with major issues, this highly rational method may be useful.

Leadership in Public Organizations

Leadership in public organizations can be particularly challenging because public managers tend to have much less power and flexibility than their counterparts in the private sector. For example, public administrators frequently face severe limitations in terms of the motivational devices they can use in hiring, promoting, rewarding, and disciplining employees, since these decisions are largely governed by system-wide policies. More so than private-sector executives, administrators in public service agencies must be sensitive to the forces affecting the larger environmental context they serve so as to run the organization in a manner that is congruent with the external climate. In addition, leaders of public service agencies must deal with the external environment with considerable political savvy to represent the agency's interests, to protect it from cutbacks, and to help it to take advantage of emerging opportunities (Gortner, Mahler, & Nicholson, 1987). (We will come back to the issue or organizational politics later in this chapter.)

Transformational Leadership

The kinds of leaders we have been discussing so far are generally referred to as *transactional* leaders—that is, leaders that guide or motivate their followers to keep the organization functioning in accordance with its goals. Another type is the **transformational leader.** These are individuals who are able to have a profound effect on their followers by inspiring them to aim toward higher goals (Burns, 1978; Bass, 1985). Such leaders are especially needed by organizations whose work has an ideological component, such as social service agencies, religious institutions, and the military (House, 1977).

Research has shown that *transformative* leaders share certain characteristics—namely: (1) a vision or clear sense of purpose; (2) persistence; (3) awareness of their strengths and abilities and how to maximize them; (4) a strong desire to learn; (5) enjoyment of their work without feeling obsessed about it or controlled by it; (6) ability to engage or motivate others; (7) relations to group members characterized by maturity, acceptance, respect, and appreciation of their contributions; (8) willingness to take risks to reach their goals; (9) ability to see mistakes as necessary for growth rather than as indicative of failure; and (10) a sense of the public need (Bennis & Nanus, 1985; Conger & Kanungo, 1988).

Leadership as Empowerment

In recent years, power sharing, or empowerment, has gained importance as a leadership function not only in the field of social work where it has long been a popular concept but in other fields as well. To **empower** is to increase the power of others to do things by themselves and for themselves. This is done by teaching people the skills to accomplish their goals and by giving them confidence that they can do it. To empower their employees, supervisors and other managers must be willing to delegate and grant autonomy to subordinates in accordance with their ability and responsibility. This is an important way of fostering the development of leadership in others. One advantage of empowering employees is that it frees the leader to concentrate on the most important activities of the organization (McClelland, 1975; Hollander & Offerman, 1990).

Decision-Making Processes

People are constantly making decisions, ordinary and vital. For example, as you read this chapter, you may be thinking about going to the movies or to the beach rather than completing the chapter in one sitting. Someone else may be trying to decide whether he or she should file for divorce or attempt once again to work out seemingly insurmountable marital differences. At work, we also constantly face alternatives. For example, social agencies often face the choice of opening before 8:30 A.M. or staying open beyond 5:30 P.M. or on Saturdays to accommodate the needs of their working clientele. Some agency directors may be contemplating right now if they should go through the trouble of computerizing client records, start a new group for divorced parents or pregnant teens, or close a branch office to reduce expenses.

Optimizing and Satisficing Decision Making

Sometimes a person's goal is to make the best possible decision he or she can make. If this is the case, it may pay to follow certain rational decision-making steps. For example, one may start by defining the problem, generating alternatives, evaluating the alternatives, making a choice, and implementing and evaluating the decision. (These steps are examined in detail in Chapter 7.) Such an approach to decision making is generally known as the **optimizing** model, and it is a fine ideal to strive for when making important decisions or when there is enough time, energy, and resources to dedicate to the process of decision making. However, the reality is that only very occasionally would one be able to use the elaborate method just described or other highly sophisticated methods of decision making that have been developed within the rational tradition, such as decision trees, cost-benefit analyses, planning charts, and so forth. Sometimes decision makers use these methods to justify their decisions or to create some semblance of order and structure in otherwise turbulent organizational environments.

In everyday work situations, employees are more likely to follow a **satisficing** model of decision making—that is, they tend to choose solutions that satisfy their purposes, even though they may not be the best possible decisions that could be made (Simon, 1976). Frequently, they make decisions intuitively and automatically without much deliberation (Mitchell & Beach, 1990).

Incrementalism

Those who work for public service agencies with scant resources often have very limited opportunities to optimize their decisions, particularly everyday decisions. Besides, the climate in such organizations tends to be too political for truly open consideration of the few alternatives available. Under such conditions, decisions are often made incrementally (Hickson, 1987). **Incremental** decisions are usually made on the basis of successive approximations to a desired goal and characteristically produce small changes that avoid major conflict. Such decisions are frequently guided by persuasion, negotiation, and debate, not rational analysis.

The incremental model of decision making often deals with problems as they arise rather than by taking a long-term perspective (Gortner, Mahler, & Nicholson, 1987). For example, if a child protective services worker was unable to properly investigate a home due to excessively high caseloads, and subsequently the child is battered to death by her parents, the media may publicize the child's tragic death enough to cause a public uproar. As a result, the department of health and human services may quickly reshuffle some funds to add two or three more workers to the protective services

unit—hardly enough to make a difference, but at least a move in the right direction.

Garbage Can Decision Making

Another common way of making organizational decisions is known as the **garbage can** method. This method is frequently seen in operation in organizations with unclear goals, ambiguous technology, fluid participation of members in organizational activities, and turbulent environments (Cohen, March, & Olsen, 1972; Cohen & March, 1986). Such organizations are often called *organized anarchies*.

Many human service organizations fit the description of organized anarchy, such as universities, therapeutic communities, and some innovative treatment and community-based programs (Hasenfeld, 1983, pp. 31–32). In such organizations, decisions many times result from the juxtaposition of relatively independent problems, solutions, and participants that are simultaneously thrown together into the same decision-making arena or choice opportunity— "a garbage can," so to speak—where they all get blended. Under this system, a "decision" is said to be made when an independent "problem" and "solution" get paired up at a decision-making forum. For example, university faculty members (participants) come to faculty meetings (choice opportunities) with a collection of wants, needs, and pet projects—a bag of possible "solutions." In the course of a meeting, several issues (problems) may arise and they somehow may get matched up by the participants with the "solutions" in their agendas.

Power Processes

Many people feel uncomfortable when they have to exercise power over others. Some see the exercise of power as a threat to autonomy and as a potentially corrupting and destructive force. Yet, when power is exercised judiciously, the results are often beneficial. For example, when one uses influence to mobilize resources to help others in need, such as when advocating for the rights of clients, the use of power is legitimate and constitutes an important part of the role of social workers and other human service practitioners. This section examines the major sources of power and some basic principles related to its use.

Sources of Power

Power is the potential of one person to influence the behavior of another. French and Raven (1959) identified five basic sources of power: legitimate authority, reward, coercion, expertise, and attractive personal attributes.

Authority or Legitimate Power.

Authority, also called **legitimate power,** is derived from the position one occupies. A welfare worker has authority to determine if clients are eligible to receive public assistance. A teacher has authority over his or her students in matters pertaining to school learning. Those in authority usually have at their disposal certain reward and coercive powers.[1]

Reward Power.

Reward power is the ability of one person to influence the behavior of another through reinforcement. In an organization, individuals with the power to grant financial awards (such as wage increases, financial aid, or aid for dependent children) as well as those in a position to provide regularly other social reinforcers (e.g., recognition, support, grades, and praise) have reward power.

Coercive Power.

Coercive power is the ability to influence another through coercion or punishment. For example, those individuals who can threaten or intimidate others and those who can give undesirable assignments, cut salaries, terminate or lay off, demote, reprimand, cut public assistance, suspend, fail, give tickets, arrest, or sentence to prison have coercive power. The use of coercion in dealing with employees in work organizations has declined considerably in recent years not only because there is little psychological evidence that it is effective in inducing compliance and increasing productivity but also due to the protections gained by employees through labor unions and the civil service system.

Expert Power.

Expert power is the ability to influence others through one's knowledge, expertise, or persuasive skills. For example, human service practitioners usually have expert power over their clients due to their knowledge and expertise regarding human problems. Many social agencies value employees who can develop and implement innovative programs as well as those who can secure external funds through grant writing, public relations, or fund-raising efforts. Their expert power within the agency is usually considerable. Similarly, articulate and outspoken employees who can present clear, lucid, and persuasive arguments can also exert much influence, particularly if they are politically astute and develop good intra- or extramural connections.

Referent Power.

Referent power, sometimes called *charisma*, is influence that is based on the attraction or admiration an individual is able to generate or on the person's ability to serve as a role model. Many people are attracted to those who are energetic, friendly, positive, good looking, reliable, good humored, and emotionally stable. Individuals with such characteristics often can influence others. People whom others respect and look up to and those with vision, strong ideals and convictions also have the power to influence the behavior of others, even if their position power within the organization is not high.

Basic Power Principles

To have power over someone else, one must possess or control something that is important to the other, that the other cannot readily obtain elsewhere (something scarce), and that cannot be easily substituted (Mintzberg, 1983). For example, if you were seeking a promotion at a particular social agency, and you could obtain this promotion only through the recommendation of your immediate supervisor, then your supervisor would have considerable power over your work behaviors—particularly if the agency for which you work is the only agency of its kind in the locality where you live and you are not able to relocate. By the same principle, people who can bring in large amounts of public or private funds to cash-strapped organizations can usually "call the shots," so to speak, because they can provide the organization with something important to it, scarce, and not easily substituted.

In contrast, things that are plentiful do not give power to those who possess even large quantities (Emerson, 1962). Take the case of a student who is as smart and knowledgeable as her classmates in the honors program at a university. It would be difficult for her to gain influence within this group on the basis of intelligence or knowledge because her classmates have plenty of it themselves. However, she might have a greater chance of influencing them with charm, humor, or good looks.

The amount of power that an individual or group has within an organization is often reflected by the amount of resources such person or group controls. These resources may be money (direct budgetary allocations or funds from external grants), number of staff members, office space, equipment, desirable location, furniture, or clientele, for example. In turn, the more resources an individual or group has, usually the more resources they can get. That is, once one is in control of certain resources, the resources themselves generate opportunities to obtain even more resources. For example, after an agency has been able to enlarge its staff and services through financial grants or other means, it has increased opportunity to apply for more grants, to increase the clientele even more, to conduct research, to participate in powerful community committees, and therefore to continue to increase its power base.

Political Processes

Any behaviors that attempt to manipulate the distribution of advantages or disadvantages within a social group are considered political (Farrell & Petersen, 1982). Employees often engage in **political behaviors** in organizations that have limited resources to distribute and unclear rules about how these resources should be allocated. Social service agencies are a good example (Gummer, 1990). Political behaviors are also common in an organizational environment of dwindling resources or when resources are to be redistributed within an organization (Hardy, 1987). In such circumstances, employees feel pressed to fight for their fair share. Politicking is also commonplace in organizations characterized by low trust, lack of clarity in the definition of employee roles, use of subjective and unclear criteria for employee appraisal, and zero-sum allocation practices (i.e., every gain of an employee or unit must come at the expense of another) (Vredenburgh & Maurer, 1984; Madison et al., 1980).

Political behaviors are evident in practically all organizations. If you are currently employed, you are likely to find examples of political behaviors all around you. For example, you may have a co-worker who seems to spend more time promoting herself and talking about her accomplishments than working, another who is always buttering up the boss, and still another who always seems to be campaigning for or against something. Some people are more likely to engage in political behaviors than others. For example, those with a high need for power or status generally engage in more political behaviors than those who have a lesser need (Madison, Allen, Porter, Renwick, & Mayes, 1980).

Political Tactics
Some people shrink at the thought of politicking, as if this were one of the most disagreeable things one could possibly do. However, so long as one's political behaviors are ethical and

aimed at good purposes, one should not refrain from engaging in them.

One of the most basic political tactics is to develop the habit of being helpful and friendly, not only because these are good traits to have but because such behaviors build up goodwill with others from which one can borrow when one needs to ask for a favor. Another important political tactic is to develop the habit of being reasonable—that is, to habitually argue one's ideas not by force or coercion but on the basis of solid facts and rational arguments.

Good politics frequently requires coalition formation, bargaining, or cooptation. A **coalition** involves the temporary coming together of several individuals or groups that put their differences (if any) aside to achieve a common objective. **Bargaining** is the skillful use of negotiation to share benefits. Through bargaining or compromise, neither party obtains exactly what it wants, but none loses out completely. Both sides usually give ground on some matters but hold the line on issues considered critically important. **Cooptation** is a political tactic whereby a person or other entity is invited to join in a project primarily not because the other's input is particularly valued but so that the individual will not sabotage or challenge the effort.

It is also politically important to maintain as good relations as possible with powerful people (as long as ethical principles are not compromised) and to have an extensive network of contacts. It is also advantageous to make a good impression and to project a positive image. This involves things like dressing appropriately, being on time, speaking clearly and to the point, acting confidently and decisively, and even occasionally making others aware of one's important achievements that might otherwise not be noticed. Politics sometimes extends to purely procedural issues, such as rearranging the order of items in the agenda of a meeting. For example, politically "savvy" people usually avoid the first spot in the agenda of a meeting because the first issue discussed is usually

treated in excessive detail and can be torn apart by so much attention. Very late placement in the agenda typically is also avoided because items that come up at the end may be treated too superficially or may be postponed for lack of time (Selznick, 1949; Brager, 1968; Kipnis, Schmidt, & Wilkinson, 1980; Martin & Sims, 1980).

Conflict Processes

The last of the organizational processes that will be considered in this chapter is conflict. As noted previously, **conflict** is natural and unavoidable in human interaction and can be a positive force as long as it is not excessive. For instance, conflict is constructive and invigorating when it stimulates people to be creative or innovative or to gather as much knowledge as they can in an attempt to find mutually satisfying solutions to their problems. It is also constructive when it leads to selfassessment or to openly airing differences. In fact, lack of conflict can cause boredom, complacency, and little motivation to change or improve (Robbins, 1989). The problem is that most of us have been inculcated ideas at home, at school, or at church that conflict is bad and should be avoided. Therefore, we tend to feel uncomfortable when it arises.

The Nature and Sources of Conflict in Organizations

Conflict arises in an organization when a person or group engages in behavior that another individual or group perceives as interfering with the attainment of their goals. For example, if management attempts to reduce health insurance benefits due to increased costs, employees may respond by threatening to go on strike if their benefits are reduced.

Many factors contribute to organizational conflict. Perhaps the most common is scarce resources or inequitable allocation of resources (Pondy, 1980). For instance, if two or three units within an agency have need for additional office space or support personnel but the budget can only provide for one additional part-time secretary or if all the space available is allocated to one of the units, conflict is likely to erupt. Another common source of conflict is the divergence of goals among various units in the organization (Pondy, 1980). This is to be expected, particularly when there is a proliferation of units with divergent goals. For example, in the county department of human services, the division of children, youth, and family services has very different needs and goals than the division of vocational rehabilitation, the public health division, or the division of aging services. Even the use of a participative administrative style is likely to foster conflict. This is because when there is a high level of employee participation and interaction, they are more likely to discover differences and to argue about these differences (Robbins, 1974, pp. 11–25).

Common Ways of Dealing with Conflict

Ways of dealing with conflict include competition, avoidance, accommodation, compromise, and collaboration (Thomas, 1976, 1977). **Competition** involves two or more parties seeking to achieve their goals by winning the contest among them, regardless of the effect success may have on the losing sides. This type of win/lose method of settling conflicts may be appropriate when the issue is vital to all sides and collaboration is not possible or when each side is convinced that it is right and the others are wrong. For example, two practitioners at the same social agency may decide to compete for the same federal grant by proposing diametrically opposed intervention approaches if each believes that his or her proposed program is the appropriate way of dealing with the problem.

Avoidance consists of one or all parties to the conflict withdrawing from it. It may be appropriate when the issue is not important enough to fight over, when there are more pressing matters to attend to, when there is no chance of winning, or when the parties are too angry to act. For example, two secretaries may

suddenly find themselves involved in a monumental fight over whether the copying machine should or should not be moved away from the water cooler. In the heat of the argument, they may decide to call it off because the issue is not worth it, as far as they are concerned.

In **accommodation**, one party sacrifices its own interests on behalf of another party. It may be appropriate when the issue is of much greater concern to one side than to the other, so the other side prefers to give in to build social credits to trade on later. For instance, a unit that could use but does not really need more office space may not press for its fair share when a new wing of the building is inaugurated. This is an accommodation to the other units that have greater need for additional space so that they will be more compelled to give the accommodating unit precedence in the future in relation to something else, such as equipment.

Compromise consists of each party giving up something and getting something in return. Under this system, nobody wins, but nobody comes out empty handed either. Compromise may be the only approach possible when there are time constraints or when collaboration has been tried unsuccessfully. For instance, if, in the middle of a very busy morning, two secretaries were to find themselves in conflict over who should take lunch hour first, they might settle the issue quickly by deciding that they will take turns weekly. Neither may be completely satisfied with this arrangement since they both want the early slot, but at least they will get it half of the time.

Collaboration is a particularly desirable conflict-resolution method because it requires that all parties to the conflict find a mutually rewarding (or "win-win") solution. It is indicated when each side is committed to its position, when the issue is vital, when there is interest on all sides to find a solution that takes every perspective into consideration, or when commitment to the solution is important. For instance, if the department of human services were to decide to revamp the way it delivers a critical service, such as public health, it would be important to undertake a collaborative effort, including key players from the community as well as representatives from within the organization.

ORGANIZATIONAL CULTURE

Organizations have personalities, like people. Some are warm, informal, and supportive of their employees and clients, whereas others are formal, cold, and unfriendly. Some are flexible and progressive, whereas others are rigid and conservative. Some are highly conflictual; others are characterized by a polite and cordial environment. Some look full of excitement and seem to be bustling with activity, with groups of employees sometimes working on their projects until late at night; others appear full of nine-to-fivers, bored, and waiting for the clock to strike five to call it a day. These characteristics are part of the culture of the organization.

Organizational culture is the system of shared meanings and values held by members of an organization that distinguishes it from other organizations (Schein, 1985, p. 168). Most large organizations have a *dominant culture* that expresses those central values that define the organization. Organizations likewise have various *subcultures,* or minicultures, that typically reflect additional values held by employees of different subunits or departments or by members of diverse groups within the organization.

Some organizations have strong cultures and others have weak cultures. If organizational members strongly agree about what the organization stands for and its core values are deeply held and widely shared, the organization is said to have a *strong culture*. Military organizations such as the Navy, the Marines, or the Air Force are good examples of organizations with strong cultures. Organizations that do not have such a distinctly defined culture are said to have *weak cultures* (Schein, 1990; Robbins, 1989).

Culture is important to an organization because it conveys its identity, guides and shapes employee attitudes and behaviors, decreases the need for formal rules and regulations, and holds the organization together. However, culture can become a liability for an organization when its values no longer serve the organizational goals. This can happen when the environmental situation changes radically and requires a major adaptation on the part of the organization. If the organizational culture is entrenched and inflexible, it may become a liability (Robbins, 1989).

An organization uses a variety of means to maintain its culture. For example, when searching for new employees, it can make sure that those who are hired fit in in terms of values, attitudes, and behaviors. It can also establish performance criteria, reward systems, and codes of behavior that are consistent with its values and goals. Another way by which an organization sustains its culture is by indoctrinating new employees—a process called *organizational socialization*. Sometimes socialization is formal, involving special training sessions, retreats, briefings, handbooks, or an apprenticeship program. Other times socialization is accomplished more informally through coaching by co-workers and supervisors and through stories and jokes that teach about the folklore of the organization.

The organizational culture is also maintained by means of rituals, material symbols, and a specialized language. Organizational rituals are regular practices that express and reinforce the key values and goals of the organization (Robbins, 1989). For example, a social agency may distribute holiday gifts and food baskets to poor families in the community for Thanksgiving and Christmas, it may hold an annual charity ball, it may honor each retiring employee at a banquet luncheon, and so on. Many material symbols also serve to reinforce the organization's values. For instance, a public assistance agency may have small work cubicles for offices, discarded furniture, and an unpretentious facility to stress its public service mission. Finally, the organization may reinforce its culture through the development of a specialized language. For example, employees of drug rehabilitation agencies or of social service units at hospitals often communicate using jargon that only they can understand.

THE ORGANIZATION AND THE ENVIRONMENT

Organizations have considerable impact on their environments. For instance, business organizations influence the level of employment of the communities in which they are located, the distribution of wages, the tax revenue base, and the quality of life (DavisSacks & Hasenfeld, 1987). The environment also has much impact on organizations. In fact, it would be very difficult for organizations to survive if they are not sensitive to their environments. For instance, a social agency located in a neighborhood that has become primarily African American would have a very hard time surviving if it does not have African Americans on the staff or if it does not welcome them as clients. Given the importance of the organization/environment transaction, it is essential that organizations develop a good sensing apparatus with which to learn about their environments and a good action apparatus with which to respond to it (Leavitt, Dill, & Eyring, 1980). This section will examine the organizational environment and its influence on the organization.

The General External Environment

Organizations need to function in accordance with the value systems and norms of behavior of their surrounding communities and of the larger society. Those organizations that ignore or deviate significantly from community and societal values and accepted social conventions risk censure, legal action, boycott, or failure. If they want to survive, they must also be mindful of the racial, ethnic, socioeconomic, and age composition of the surrounding community, as these factors determine the attributes of clients, their product and service preferences, the effectiveness of the technology used by the organization, and their acceptance within the community. For instance, to be effective, a social agency serving poor central-city Latino immigrants would need to use a significantly different approach than an agency serving a suburban middle-class Euro-American community.

Economic conditions also greatly influence organizations. For instance, during economic downturns, the resources of social agencies typically dwindle while the demand for services increases. This puts considerable strain on practitioners whose caseloads increase significantly. In addition, the political climate of the nation plays a significant role in the lives of organizations, particularly human service organizations. It is common knowledge, for example, that liberal or democratically controlled legislatures tend to increase the funding for social services while conservative or republican legislative bodies are more likely to cut back on social programs. Finally, individual pieces of legislation can also have a profound effect on organizations. For instance, the civil rights act with all its ramifications has had a profound effect on organizations in terms of opening them up to previously excluded groups and has led to the creation of many public agencies to enforce its mandates.

The Task Environment

In addition to having to adapt to general external environmental conditions, organizations must also interact with many external entities that monitor their activities or with which they exchange resources and services. These form the **task environment** of the organization (Thompson, 1967; Hasenfeld, 1983). Specifically, human service organizations must interact with the following:

1. Providers of financial resources such as private charities and foundations, community chests, county agencies, state agencies or federal agencies, fee-paying clients, and health insurance companies
2. Providers of legitimation and authority such as the legislature, city and county commissions, accrediting bodies, and professional associations
3. Client referral sources such as the schools and the courts
4. Other human service agencies providing complementary services such as employment agencies in the case of a vocational rehabilitation agency or hospital detoxification units in the case of a drug rehabilitation agency
5. Clients and consumers of the organization's products, such as colleges and universities in the case of high schools
6. Various entities that monitor agency activities such as federal and state regulatory agencies, the media, and various interest groups (supportive and nonsupportive)

Placid and Turbulent Environments

The external environment of an organization is rarely stable, calm, or placid. **Placid environments** are occasionally found in small, homogeneous, conservative, relatively isolated, and self-sufficient communities, but they are rare today. Most organizational environments are characterized by multiple, changing, and often incompatible community values and interests and a constantly changing configuration of resources and social and economic conditions. These are generally referred to as **turbulent environments** (Emery & Trist, 1968) and are typically the environments of those human service organizations that must deal with frequent shifts in public opinion and in the demands of interest groups as well as changes brought about by new political administrations and public officials.

The external environment, with its often conflicting values, sometimes pulls human service organizations simultaneously in different directions, making it difficult for them to respond to their clientele effectively. For example, the juvenile court system must often contend with police and public demands for the removal of troublesome delinquents from the community; child advocacy groups insisting that these children receive community treatment, not incarceration; the media looking to expose improper behavior on the part of court and social service employees; and government officials insisting on cutting corners to keep costs down (Hasenfeld, 1983, p. 9). Under such conflicting conditions, it is difficult for social agencies to operate effectively.

Environmental Links

Most organizations maintain regular contact with certain groups or individuals in their environments. The greater the number of entities in the external environment with which they must transact, the greater the number of linkages the organization must maintain. The organizational members in charge of relating the organization to its environment are called **boundary spanners**. They function as ambassadors and sensory organs, representing the organization in the environment and the environment within the organization. Top officials of the organization frequently act in this capacity as well as practitioners through their contacts with fellow practitioners in their fields and through membership in professional organizations. In addition, large organizations usually have personnel with official external liaison roles, such as public information and public relations officers, congressional liaisons, and lobbyists. Direct practitioners and other organizational personnel directly dealing with clients and the public also occupy boundary-spanning positions (Gortner, Mahler, & Nicholson, 1987).

THE INDIVIDUAL AND
THE WORK ORGANIZATION

The work organization influences the behavior and well-being of its employees in innumerable ways. For example, the wages it pays have a direct bearing on the type of housing, residential neighborhood, and leisure activities workers can afford. The degree of employment security it offers helps determine the employees' psychological security. The quality of its health care benefits and the safety standards it maintains in the work environment influences employee physical well-being. The quality of its pension plan determines in part the employees' economic security in their old age. The work roles the organization assigns have an impact on the employees' social status, job satisfaction, work motivation, feelings of self-worth, sense of identity, and opportunities for self-actualization. The organization's system of rewards and punishments, its interpersonal climate, and its working conditions, particularly the level of work stress, also in part determine the level of psychological well-being of its employees (Davis-Sacks & Hasenfeld, 1987, pp. 217–218). These are but a few of the ways in which the work organization influences the staff.

This section will first take a look at three fundamental factors in the relationship between individuals and their work organizations: job satisfaction, job stress, and work motivation. We will then examine some of the problems nondominant group members face in work organizations.

Job Satisfaction

People spend a very significant portion of their lives at work; therefore, it is very important to derive satisfaction from the things they do on the job. Employers are also concerned about job satisfaction not only because it is important to the employees but because they generally assume that satisfied workers are more productive.

Job satisfaction is a global attitude that includes the employee's feelings about many different aspects of the job. Research indicates that it is largely determined by extrinsic variables such as having the right amount of challenge, an equitable system of rewards, supportive working conditions, and a supportive social climate at work (Locke, 1976). Specifically, people tend to be satisfied with their jobs when the work is neither too challenging (which can be stressful) nor too easy (which can be boring), when the pay and promotion system is considered fair, when the work environment is safe and comfortable, and when they have helpful supervisors who listen and show interest and friendly and cooperative co-workers. Job satisfaction also depends a great deal on the employee's personality and general disposition (positive or negative) toward work (Feldman & Arnold, 1985; Staw, Bell, & Clausen, 1986). Some people have very positive dispositions toward work and are able to see the good side of most job situations; others have negative attitudes toward work in general and specifically toward their jobs, no matter what.

Employers are interested in job satisfaction primarily because they believe that it will have a positive effect on performance and that it will reduce absenteeism and turnover. However, the correlation between job satisfaction and productivity, although consistently positive, is not strong (Iaffaldano & Muchinsky, 1985). The correlation is stronger for higher-level employees—such as those in professional, supervisory, and managerial positions—than for rank-and-file members of an organization. Interestingly, research indicates that in many cases productivity leads to satisfaction—not the other way around, as generally assumed. Therefore, it may be more accurate to characterize the correlation between job satisfaction and productivity by saying that when people do a good job, they tend to feel good, rather than that, when they feel good, they do a good job (Petty, McGee, & Cavender, 1984). The implication of this finding is that to increase job satisfaction, employers would do well to help employees do the best job they can.

The correlation between job satisfaction and absenteeism is consistently negative; that is, the higher the satisfaction experienced by an employee, the fewer the absences from work. But this inverse relationship is not strong (Hackett & Guion, 1985). On the other hand, the relationship between job satisfaction and turnover is strong and consistently negative; that is, the less satisfied people are with their jobs, the more likely they are to change jobs. However, other factors also contribute to the decision to leave one's job besides dissatisfaction, particularly whether or not one has alternative job opportunities, how good these are, and the number of years one has been with the organization (Hulin, Roznowski, & Hachiya, 1985; Carsten & Spector, 1987). To be sure, a person may be highly dissatisfied with his or her job, but if the individual has no alternative job opportunities, if the alternatives are worse, or if the person is close to retirement, he or she is unlikely to change jobs.

Job satisfaction is also important to employers and employees because it is related to employee health. Namely, there is evidence that people who are dissatisfied with their jobs are more susceptible to health and stress problems, from headaches to heart disease. For the employer, therefore, a satisfied work force translates into savings in medical insurance and life insurance (Robbins, 1989, p. 139).

Job Stress

Just as work can be an important source of satisfaction and fulfillment, it can also be a major source of stress in people's lives. Some jobs are inherently stressful, such as emergency room physician or nurse, rescue or ambulance paramedic, crisis intervention worker, police officer, child protective services investigator, or air traffic controller. In general, any job that involves constant time pressures, threatening physical conditions, or major responsibility for the money or the lives of others is inherently stressful (Cooper & Payne, 1978).

Sometimes people suffer job stress during economic recessions due to their fear of being temporarily laid off or of becoming unemployed. Others suffer work stress because they fear that they are going to be replaced by a machine or that their skills are becoming obsolete. During difficult economic periods when many people have lost their jobs or have felt insecure about their chances of remaining employed, certain trends are evident. There is usually a rise in the number of admissions to mental hospitals; more arrests; greater incidences of alcohol and drug abuse, anxiety, depression, and spouse and child abuse; and more deaths from heart disease, stroke, cirrhosis of the liver, suicide, accidents, and homicides (Brody, 1992).

Various organizational factors can also generate stress, such as excessive caseloads, conflicting demands, demands that exceed the individual's skills or capacity, not knowing what one is supposed to do (role ambiguity), a disagreeable, controlling, and demanding boss, uncooperative and unfriendly co-workers, capricious firings or routine layoffs of employees, office temperature that is persistently excessively hot or cold, excessive noise, overcrowding, and constant interruptions (Parasuraman & Alutto, 1984).

It is important to realize that stress is a highly personal experience and that people vary tremendously in terms of their stress perception and tolerance. What one person may perceive as threatening or intolerable another may see as a challenge. Stress is not altogether bad, however. Some stress, such as a reasonable deadline or having somewhat more work than one is able to accomplish each day, is good because it keeps you "on your toes" and stimulates higher levels of performance. In fact, if the work environment were totally devoid of stress, most people would slow down, get bored, or become disinterested. But too much stress or even moderate amounts of unrelenting stress result in lower performance and may cause **burnout**—that is, physical, psychological, and emotional exhaustion. Job-related stress can also lead to job dissatisfaction, tension, anxiety, irritability, procrastination, frequent absences from work, and a decision to leave the job (Beehr & Newman, 1978; Robbins, 1989).

Job stress can be reduced by improving working conditions. This may call for defining tasks and standards of performance more clearly so that employees know exactly what they are expected to do, providing more supervisor support, involving workers in the decisions that affect their work lives, and giving them some control over their jobs (e.g., in matters pertaining to working conditions or the way in which their work is done). Another important way of reducing occupational stress is by promoting the development of meaningful social relationships at work—for example, by valuing and supporting teamwork efforts and by providing social and recreational facilities for employees and their families to use during breaks, at lunch time, and after work hours (Taylor, 1991).

Work Motivation

People usually put forth effort when they are motivated to do so. For a work endeavor to be motivating, however, it must have the potential to fulfill one's needs or desires in some way. Employers knowledgeable about the psychology of motivation try to enhance the **work motivation** of their employees—that is, their willingness to put forth effort toward organizational goals, by arranging the work situation so that it provides goals and incentives that are personally satisfying. At present, there is no overall theory of work motivation, although a number of discrete and intuitively logical mod-

els have been developed, each with various degrees of research validation. This section will review some of the better-established models.

ERG Theory

According to **ERG theory** (Alderfer, 1969), which borrows heavily from Maslow's hierarchy of needs model (Maslow, 1954), people are motivated by *existence*, *relatedness*, and *growth* needs (hence, the term *ERG*). *Existence* needs are those that have to do with the basic physical and material requirements of human beings, such as the need for food, shelter, clothing, and health care. These parallel Maslow's physiological and safety needs. *Relatedness* refers to the basic human need for interpersonal relationships, including the need for affection, acceptance, love, friendship, and recognition by others. These needs are equivalent to Maslow's love and external esteem needs. The *growth* needs represent the desire for personal development and parallel Maslow's self-esteem and self-actualization needs.

Like Maslow's theory, ERG theory argues that when lower-order needs (such as the existence needs) are satisfied, the person becomes interested in pursuing higher-order needs, such as relatedness and growth. However, ERG theory also maintains that multiple needs can act as motivators at any one time. In other words, the fact that a person may be considerably driven by existence needs does not preclude his or her need for relatedness or growth. In this respect, ERG theory differs from Maslow's self-actualization theory, which postulates that higher-order needs (e.g., the need for growth or self-actualization) do not become significant motivators of behavior until the lower-order needs have been satisfied to a reasonable extent.

According to ERG theory, jobs should be designed to appeal to a broad spectrum of human needs in the areas of existence, relatedness, and growth. For example, employers can appeal to existence needs by offering such things as fair salaries, salary increases, and benefits; a safe and comfortable work environment; child care; and some degree of employment security. Ways of satisfying relatedness needs include things such as worker participation in decision making, recognition of achievements, and a caring and supportive work environment. Employers can appeal to their employees' growth needs by offering opportunities for further education and training, as well as progressively more challenging work assignments and, if completed successfully, increasing levels of autonomy and responsibility.

Employers would do well to appeal not only to a broad spectrum of employee needs but also to the specific needs of individual workers in order to elicit their best performance. For example, some employees may prefer material reinforcers, such as higher pay, bonuses, or a shorter work week. Others give higher priority to security, preferring to opt for a more generous package of benefits than extra money in hand. Some respond particularly well to social reinforcers, such as recognition and increased participation in decision making. Still others are most inclined toward growth motivators, such as increased autonomy and responsibility. To be sure, not all employers have the wherewithal to be able to tailor reinforcers to the individual needs of their employees. Employers in the public sector are especially limited in terms of the financial reinforcers they are able to offer.

McClelland's Theory of Social Motives

McClelland (1961, 1975) suggested that there are three basic human needs important to the understanding of work motivation: achievement, power, and affiliation. *Achievement* is the drive to excel or to do things as well as one can. *Power* is the need to influence others—that is, to have impact. *Affiliation* is the need to be liked and accepted, to cooperate, and to be friendly.

Although most people have at least some need for achievement, affiliation, and power, each person has a different configuration of these needs. Those who are primarily achievement oriented, for example, prefer to concentrate on their work rather than on social relations. Those with strong affiliation needs prefer to emphasize the interpersonal aspects of work, and therefore enjoy taking on collaborative tasks or supervisory, public relations, or other positions that allow them to be helpful and supportive. Individuals with a strong need to influence and control might do best in supervisory and management positions, provided that their need for power is properly socialized (i.e., aimed primarily at benefiting others) rather than mostly self-interested (McClelland, 1970). Given that people have different need configurations, you can readily see that it would be to the advantage of a work organization to encourage its employees to pursue work roles that best allow them to fulfill their basic needs.

Goal Theory

Another powerful work motivator is to have a specific and challenging work goal (Mento, Steel, & Karren, 1987; Tubbs, 1986). Research has shown that having a specific goal, such as "I will complete five case histories today" leads to greater productivity than a generalized goal such as "I will do my best at work today." Also, the more ambitious the goal, generally, the higher the level of performance. That is, if your goal is to write five case histories, generally you will get further along in your recording than if your goal is to complete three.

Reinforcement Theory

Many work organizations make use of a wide range of positive reinforcers to motivate employees. **Positive reinforcers** are positive consequences made contingent on performance, including such things as praise, recognition, approval, support, pay increases, promotions, or various perquisites such as awards, bonuses, a larger office, time off, a paid vacation, and so on.

Public agencies usually have limited leeway in administering material reinforcers and must depend more on nonmaterial reinforcers to motivate employees. Private organizations tend to have greater flexibility to offer a wider range of reinforcers to their employees than public organizations. This is because public agencies are generally governed by policies and procedures that set salary ranges for yearly salary increases for each job classification with limited flexibility left to supervisors to grant additional monetary awards. Similarly, promotions in public agencies are many times dependent not only on qualifications but also on seniority and are frequently limited because of low turnover and few openings.

Equity Theory

Organizations interested in motivating employees to be as productive as they can be (and what organization would not be?) must be keenly sensitive to equity issues. **Equity theory** (like exchange theory) suggests that employees weigh the benefits they get from their jobs against what they put in and then compare their input/outcome ratio with that of others similarly experienced or educated or with the input/outcome ratios of alternative jobs or jobs they have previously held (Adams, 1965; Ronen, 1986). If they perceive inequity—that is, if they think that they put more into the job than what they get out of it—they will likely act to reduce the imbalance in some manner, such as by working less.

This exchange dynamic is often seen in many high-volume/low-pay jobs. For example, in many service units of various departments of health and human services, you are likely to find a good number of staff members with low wages, unrealistically high caseloads, little supervisory support, and few advancement opportunities. To make the situation more equitable, some workers limit the amount and quality of work they produce to a level concomitant with their poor working conditions. Other possible ways of dealing with perceived inequities

at work would be to ask for a raise (if this is perceived as a possibility) or, if the worker has other employment prospects, to change jobs.

Expectancy Theory

Still another widely accepted theory of work motivation is **expectancy theory** (Vroom, 1964; Lawler, 1973). According to this theory, people will exert themselves at work if they believe that their efforts will lead to success and if they think that successful performance will be reinforced, providing that the reinforcements available at work are personally satisfying. In other words, most people will work hard if they think that by working hard they will be able to get the job done and that their work will be rewarded in ways that are personally appealing.

Some work organizations miss opportunities to increase the productivity of employees and the quality of their work when they provide reinforcements that are not made contingent on individual performance. Examples of this are when organizations give across-the-board pay increases rather than bonuses tied to specific and measurable levels of performance, or, in educational institutions, when organizations offer teaching awards that are tied to inappropriate criteria such as number of students or number of courses taught rather than other more qualitative measures of performance.

Problems Faced by Members of Nondominant Groups in Work Organizations

Although progress is being made slowly in the fight against discrimination by work organizations, many women, African Americans, Latinos, Asian Americans, Native Americans, gays and lesbians, and other nondominant group members still face an inhospitable climate at work. This section will examine some of the major problems they face, including hiring biases, promotional difficulties, channeling into "minority" positions, tokenism, less challenging assignments, inadequate feedback on performance, limited access to training and development programs, scarcity of role models and mentors, and sexual harassment. The special workplace problems of gays and lesbians will also be addressed.

Persisting Hiring Biases

Since the advent of affirmative action, many people think that it is easier for members of nondominant groups to get jobs than for Euro-American whites. This is not true. Research shows that Euro-Americans, particularly the men, are more likely to be favored in the hiring process than African Americans or Latinos. For example, as part of a study involving 476 advertised entry-level job openings in Chicago and Washington, DC, the Urban Institute sent white and black pairs of equally qualified male college students posing as job applicants. Some 15 percent of the non-Latin white students posing as job seekers received a job offer, compared to only 5 percent of blacks. A similar study conducted by the Urban Institute in Chicago and San Diego showed discriminatory treatment of Latinos in 31 percent of tested workplaces and discriminatory treatment of blacks in 20 percent of the workplaces examined (Epstein, 1991).

Difficulties Attaining Promotions

Affirmative action has increased entry-level opportunities for women and other nondominant group members at many organizations. Since the 1980s, however it has lost momentum and its enforcement has become lax. This is probably because, as noted in Chapter 4, this program has become unpopular with many Euro-American males as a method to combat discrimination and oppression as it sometimes results in discrimination against white males in order to give access to qualified nondominant group members. This situation is called **reverse discrimination**.

Undoubtedly, progress has occurred as a result of Affirmative Action in terms of the number of nondominants who have reached middle-management positions, but the movement up the ladder to high-level positions has been limited (Kanter, 1988). For example, a study of nine *Fortune* 500 companies found that women and other nondominants typically got stuck in lower-management to middle-management positions, with racial and ethnic minorities often reaching a plateau in their careers even earlier than women (Zaldivar, 1991).

Women and other nondominant group members do not seem to get the same chances at promotions to supervisory, middle-management, and higher administrative positions as Euro-American men of equal abilities (Loden, 1986; Rubin, 1992). Some have been reaching the vice presidential level or higher, but according to the Glass Ceiling Commission, a bipartisan federal panel, white men still hold 95 percent of the senior management (i.e., vice president and above) positions in the United States (Kilborn, 1995).

Even in the U.S. government bureaucracy, just a few years ago women held only 8.6 percent of the senior executive service positions (U.S. Office of Personnel Management, 1989). The employment situation of women at U.S. colleges and universities is also quite disadvantaged; for instance, Sandler (1986) found only 1.1 women per institution of higher education at the rank of dean or higher. African Americans, Latinos, and Asian Americans do not fare any better proportionately (Jones, 1986; Knouse, Rosenfeld, & Culbertson, 1992; Dickens & Dickens, 1982). Asian Americans, for example, are often not perceived as management or leadership material because they are stereotyped as not sufficiently assertive (Louie, 1993).

The barrier that separates some nondominant group members, particularly women, from the top of organizations is so subtle in some cases that it seems transparent, but, at the same time, it is so strong that it effectively prevents them from moving up any further in the organizational hierarchy. The term **glass ceiling** is often used to refer to this situation (Morrison & Von Glinow, 1990). Faced with a formidable barrier at the top, some nondominants are becoming discouraged and are opting to leave major organizations to establish their own firms (Christie, 1991).

In the field of social work, the advancement of women has been very limited. In fact, women are less likely to be social work supervisors or managers today than they were 30 years ago. Although three-fourths of the members of the National Association of Social Workers (NASW) are females, only about 18 percent of the female membership list administration as their primary occupation. In contrast, men, who make up only 27 percent of the membership of NASW, hold 37 percent of the administrative jobs. In short, even though men are a small minority in social work, they are twice as likely as women to hold the higher and better-paying positions in the profession (Gummer, 1990, p. 79).

Channeling into "Minority" Positions

A related problem that limits the advancement possibilities of nondominants in organizations is that they tend to be employed in positions that are not part of the hierarchy or "line" of command; that is, they are often hired to play staff or support roles. Some of the positions available to highly educated nondominants carry impressive titles, such as director of personnel, vice president for public or community relations, assistant or associate director, coordinator, technical assistant, affirmative action or equal opportunity officer, or project director. These job titles "window dress" the organization by showcasing the diverse backgrounds of their incumbents and may help it to comply with affirmative action policies. However,

Source: Jim Morin's View in the *Miami Herald*, April 29, 1993, p. 24A. Copyright 1993 The Miami Herald. Reprinted with permission.

these lofty-sounding titles often do not grant much authority or possibilities for further advancement.

Of course, in a large organization it is possible to make a reasonably good career out of a collection of progressively higher staff and support positions, and some women have traditionally followed these paths outside the often all-white-male line of command. But the pay for these support positions is often considerably lower than the pay for jobs that are part of the line of command. No matter how impressive the titles may sound, these positions carry low prestige within the organization and lie outside the power structure.

An important drawback of "minority" positions is that usually they are not perceived to be training grounds for other positions in the power structure. For example, just because a woman or an African American has been director of personnel, vice president for public relations, and even associate vice president of an organization, these positions and the experiences they provide are not considered to qualify the individual who has held them for any of the positions in the line of command, such as department or division head, vice president, or president.

Tokenism Combined with Low Status

We have seen that at high organizational levels, Euro-American males predominate and females and other nondominants are scarce. Work groups with a large majority of members of one type (e.g., Euro-American males) over another are called *skewed*. The few individuals who are different in a skewed group are called **tokens**.

According to Kanter (1977), tokenism generates visibility, polarization, and role entrapment. Visibility makes the token individual stand out from the rest of the group. This extra attention may have advantages, but it often results in performance pressures. For instance, it makes the person's mistakes or shortcoming stand out more. Also, some token individuals

feel as if they are constantly on display, constantly having to perform for an audience or pressured to act as ambassadors for their own group. For example, if an African American is the only African American in his or her work unit, this person may be expected to provide the "African-American point of view" at meetings.

Tokens must also learn to deal with the problem of being used to "window dress" meetings, committees, and task forces that require a diverse representation. Although this may give the token representatives increased visibility and access to powerful people that they might not otherwise have, their competence is often suspect in the eyes of others typically because it is assumed that they were included in the group to fulfill a quota, not because of their competence. Consequently, their contributions may not be taken seriously enough. Similarly, visibility may help a nondominant group member to rise quickly within the organization, particularly if the individual is charming or agreeable, but if his or her ascent is not built on competence and a sound background of experience, it may lead to a swift descent as soon as a more interesting token comes along.

Tokenism also may result in polarization or an accentuation of differences within the organization. Kanter (1977) noted that the presence of an outsider in a work unit may cause a group to close ranks—that is, to exaggerate their commonalities and to accentuate the outsider's differences. This sudden burst of camaraderie among insiders may increase the feelings of isolation and discomfort of the token individual.

A third major drawback of tokenism is that the token individual may be forced into playing stereotypical roles. This may work to the advantage of a token individual who happens to be a white male but against women and other nondominants because of their lower social status. For example, a Euro-American male nurse at a hospital talking with a group of female nurses may be taken by others to be "the doctor" in the group. This stereotype works to the advantage of the male nurse by elevating his prestige. In contrast, at a meeting of social agency directors that includes only a couple of women, there may be a tendency on the part of the men to expect the women members to make arrangements for the food and decorations. This time, the stereotype works to the disadvantage of the token women if they accept the charge because it dissipates their energies in tasks that are not considered important.

The example of the male nurse who is taken for a physician shows that the effects of tokenism are attenuated when the token has higher social status in comparison to the rest of the group (Fairhurst & Snavely, 1983). In other words, if you are the only one of your kind in a group but you also happen to have higher social status than the rest of the group (e.g., a male among females, an Anglo among Latinos), the token status could actually work to your advantage. This is probably one of the reasons why Euro-American males are frequently elevated by women to positions of leadership within the professions women dominate in terms of numbers, such as social work, teaching, and nursing (Crocker & McGraw, 1984). This suggests that the problem that many women and other nondominants confront in work organizations is not so much tokenism as the vulnerability that results from *a combination of low status and low numbers*. If they had higher status in society, their low numbers might not be a problem; in fact, the scarcity might make them valuable commodities.

Less Challenging Assignments and Inadequate Feedback on Performance

Nondominant group members are often presumed to have limited expertise, probably because most organizational members assume that they were given preferential treatment in hiring. The consequence of such presumption of limited skills or knowledge is that their supervisors many times shy away from giving them the most challenging assignments or refrain from giving them honest feedback on their job performance in fear that any constructive criticism may be misinterpreted as prejudicial. This combination of unchallenging assignments and inadequate feedback works against nondominants because it does not prepare them adequately for increasingly more complex tasks within the organization; consequently, they are less likely to be chosen when better opportunities come along (Pettigrew & Martin, 1987).

Limited Access to the Informal Network

Many middle- and higher-level managers play golf or tennis or regulary engage in social activities after work. These informal contacts outside the work environment often serve as arenas where important decisions are made. The "buddy" network also acts as an important source of information, tactical assistance, advice, role models and sponsors, contacts, informal feedback on performance, and emotional support. The problem is that women and other nondominants often have difficulty becoming full members of these managerial social networks because many are still dominated by Euro-American males. Some such groups may accommodate nondominants by inviting them to participate in certain informal social activities, but they may keep them out of more "sensitive" transactions by moving these activities to more private settings.

Scarcity of Role Models and Mentors

Cross-sex mentor relationships are frequently subject to sexual innuendo, and cross-race mentorships are difficult to initiate and maintain (Thomas, 1986). The reality is that the power elite in work organizations, still mostly Euro-American men, prefer to mentor and sponsor other Euro-American males because they feel more comfortable working closely with others like them. This puts nondominants at a disadvantage in finding a good mentor or sponsor.

Sexual and Racial Harassment

Sexual harassment, which was discussed in detail in Chapter 4, involves unwelcome sexual advances, requests for sexual favors, or other conduct of a sexual nature that affects job performance or that creates an intimidating or offensive work environment. This is a problem that touches a large proportion of working women. It can be particularly painful when a woman feels powerless to fight back because the man accosting her has more power within the organization (Gutek, 1985).

Formal complaints of racial harassment in the workplace, filed with the Equal Employment Opportunity Commission, have been on the rise since 1990, apparently due to the increased hirings of nonwhites often at the expense of Euro-American males. This trend has coincided with a cut in personnel by many corporations to preserve profitability, which has further threatened the job security of Euro-American males and has led to a backlash against nonwhite workers. The problem of racial harassment is not limited to work organizations that employ manual workers. It exists wherever there is a diverse workforce and fewer jobs, be it in professional organizations, in government service, or in universities (Janofsky, 1993).

Special Workplace Problems of Gays and Lesbians

Perhaps the most persistent problem that lesbians and gay men face in the workplace is how to manage their sexual identities (Schneider, 1987). The decision to come "out of the closet" at work can have serious consequences, even though it is generally accepted that it is better for gays and lesbians to be open about their sexual orientation. Openness promotes better mental health, results in improved interpersonal relations, provides other gays and lesbians with positive role models, and furthers civil rights.

One problem with being openly gay or lesbian at work is that a substantial proportion of the public still favors keeping gays and lesbians out of certain fields—most notably fields in which they would work closely with children. Consequently, those who are openly gay or lesbian risk exclusion from a number of occupations. Many gays and lesbians are unwilling to accept such restriction as the price to pay for being open. In addition, some gays and lesbians are reluctant to be open at work about their sexual identity because they fear hitting a "glass ceiling" that prevents their rise in the organization beyond a certain point. Many also fear retaliation such as exclusion from the informal network, avoidance by co-workers, disapproval, offensive jokes, disrespectful treatment, or even harassment.

Perhaps the most serious potential consequence of disclosure of a gay or lesbian orientation at work is the possibility of job loss (Levine & Leonard, 1982; Schneider, 1984). This is possible as long as gays and lesbians do not have the same constitutional protections against discrimination as other nondominant group members. A nationwide survey of 145 businesses conducted by the Society for Human Resource Management revealed that 9 out of 10 of the businesses surveyed did not have an explicit policy against discrimination on the basis of sexual orientation and only 62 percent had an unwritten policy against discrimination on the basis of sexual orientation. This means that in many places, people can reasonably fear that they can be fired simply because their sexual orientation is offensive to their employer or because the employer thinks it might be offensive to the clientele (Fields, 1993).

Given all the potential disadvantages of disclosure, it is understandable that a sizable proportion of gays and lesbians choose to remain in the closet at work. In the past, some have dealt with the need to preserve secrecy by not getting too close or friendly with anyone at work lest they get nosy about their private life or by projecting a front of heterosexuality or sexlessness (Schneider, 1984). Those with high positions or high incomes potentially have more to lose, and consequently have been less likely to reveal their sexual orientation at work than those who have less at stake (Schneider, 1987).

We have navigated through considerable human behavior and social environment terri-tory in our exploration of organizations. Hope-fully, this knowledge will make you a more effective member of the organizations that are part of your life.

ENDNOTE

1. Of course, rewards and punishments are also fre-quently administered, appropriately or inappropri-ately, by "unauthorized people." For example, some people threaten or bully others without having any right to do so.

GLOSSARY

Accommodation: A conflict-resolution method consisting of one party sacrificing its own inter-ests on behalf of another party.

All-channel: A decentralized communication net-work in which everyone communicates with everyone else in the group; that is, everyone is connected with everyone else.

Authority: See **Legitimate Power**.

Avoidance: A conflict-resolution method whereby one or all parties to the conflict retreat.

Bargaining: The use of negotiation to exchange benefits and reach a compromise. Through bar-gaining, every party to the negotiation gets something, even though no one obtains exactly what he or she wants.

Boundary Spanners: Organizational members in charge of relating the organization to its environ-ment, such as public information and public rela-tions officers or congressional liaisons.

Bureaucracy: A highly rational organizational structure with a clear division of labor, clearly specified roles, a multilevel hierarchy of posi-tions, highly formalized rules and procedures, impersonal climate, personnel decisions suppos-edly based on qualification and performance rather than on subjective criteria, and clear sepa-ration of the members' work and personal lives.

Burnout: Physical, psychological, or emotional exhaustion that workers sometimes experience as a result of having too much job-related stress.

Centralization: The degree to which decision-making authority is concentrated in the higher echelons of an organization. When higher-level managers make decisions with little input or par-ticipation from those below, the organization is centralized.

Chain: A communication network in which each link of the chain represents a level in the organi-zational hierarchy, with communication moving up or down the chain of command.

Chain of Command: The number of hierarchical levels of authority in an organization. Also referred to as the *line of command* or *vertical dif-ferentiation*.

Coalition: A group formed usually on a tempo-rary basis to facilitate the attainment of a goal that could not be reached if individual group members tried to achieve it independently. It sometimes includes adversaries who choose to ignore their differences temporarily so they can attain their goals.

Coercive Power: The potential to influence another through coercion or punishment such as threats, reprimands, or undesirable assignments.

Collaboration: A method of conflict resolution that requires that all parties to the conflict find a mutually rewarding solution.

Communication: The exchange of verbal and nonverbal messages between a sender and a receiver.

Competition: A win/lose method of conflict reso-lution in which each party seeks to achieve its goal by winning, regardless of the effect its suc-cess will have on the others.

Complex Organization: An organization that is differentiated horizontally, vertically, and perhaps also spatially. See **Horizontal Differentiation, Spatial Differentiation, Vertical Differentiation**.

Compromise: A conflict-resolution method whereby each party gives up something and gets something in return.

Conflict: When a person or group engages in behavior that another individual or group perceives as interfering with the attainment of one of its goals.

Cooptation: A political tactic that involves inviting a potential competitor to participate in a project in the hope that he or she will lend support rather than challenge or subvert the effort.

Decentralization: The degree to which lower-level personnel are allowed to participate in decision making or are given discretion to make organizational decisions.

Downward Communication: Communication that flows from a higher level to a lower level along the organizational chain of command—for example, from a vice president to a unit supervisor.

Ecosystems Model of Organizations: This perspective characterizes organizations as social systems composed of interdependent subsystems interacting in a constantly changing environment. The aim of the organization is to achieve a good fit internally in terms of its structures and functions and externally in relation to the environment.

Empower: To increase the power of others to do things by themselves, teaching them how to accomplish their goals, giving them autonomy, and showing confidence that they can do it.

Equity Theory: When applied to work motivation, this theory suggests that employees weigh the benefits they get from a job against their costs or what they put into it and compare their input/outcome ratio with that of others. If they perceive that there is inequity, they will likely act to reduce it—for example, by working less.

ERG Theory: A theory of work motivation that borrows heavily from Maslow's conceptualization of a hierarchy of needs and that maintains that people are motivated by **E**xistence, **R**elatedness, and **G**rowth needs. Jobs should therefore be designed to appeal to these basic human needs.

Expectancy Theory: A work motivation theory that suggests that people will work hard if they think that by working hard they will be able to accomplish whatever they are trying to accomplish, and if they believe that their accomplishments will be reinforced at work in personally satisfying ways.

Expert Power: The ability to influence others through one's knowledge, expertise, or persuasive skills. A physician, for example, has expert power over his or her patients in matters pertaining to their health.

External Communication: Communication between the organization and other individuals, groups, and organizations in its environment.

Figurehead: Persons who have a leadership position but act "ceremonially" only—that is, they do not exercise leadership functions.

Formalization: The degree to which organizational roles are specified by detailed job descriptions. In highly formalized organizations employees must do things exactly as specified.

For-Profit Human Service Organization: A human service organization that is privately run for business purposes.

Garbage-Can Decision Making: Under this system, common in organized anarchies, decisions are the outcome of the mixture of relatively independent problems, solutions, participants, and choice opportunities that somehow get connected because they simultaneously tumble into the same decision-making arena or garbage can, so to speak.

Gatekeeper: A person in the communication system through whom messages must pass to get from source to destination.

Glass Ceiling: A barrier that separates some non-dominant group members from the top of organizations, so subtle that it seems transparent but so strong that it effectively prevents them from moving up any further in the organizational hierarchy.

Grapevine: An informal communication network that carries information and rumors about many things that are going on in a social system.

Horizontal Communication: Communication among peers in the same work unit or in similar positions in different units or divisions. Also referred to as *Lateral communication*.

Horizontal Differentiation: The division of labor in an organization by units or departments, each specializing in a different function. Also known as *lateral differentiation.*

Human Relations Model: An organizational model characterized by employee participation in organizational problem solving, decision making, and goal setting; minimum hierarchical or status differences; open communication at all levels of the organization; and democratic and considerate leadership.

Human Service Organization: An organization whose principal function is to protect, maintain, or enhance the welfare of the people it serves, such as a school, social service agency, hospital, church, law enforcement agency, college, university, or correctional facility.

Incrementalism: A decision-making model that uses persuasion, negotiation, and debate to achieve small and gradual changes from the status quo to avoid major conflict.

Interlocking Network: An informal communication network that connects all participating members so that everyone interacts with everyone else.

Job Satisfaction: A global attitude that includes the employee's feelings about many different elements of his or her job, largely determined by extrinsic factors such as having the right amount of challenge, an equitable system of rewards, supportive working conditions, and a supportive social environment.

Lateral Communication: See **Horizontal Communication**.

Lateral Differentiation: See **Horizontal Differentiation**.

Leadership: A reciprocal process in which a person (the leader) is permitted by the group members to influence, motivate, or empower them so that they may be better able to attain their goals.

Legitimate Power: Power to influence others that derives from the position one occupies. Parents, for example, have legitimate power over their children. Also known as *authority.*

Liaison: A person in a social system who serves as connector between various subsystems or between the system and its environment. Also known as *linking pin.*

Line of Command: See **Chain of Command**.

Line Personnel: Organizational members in the direct chain of command—that is, those with decision-making authority and leadership responsibility.

Linking Pin: See **Liaison**.

Loosely Coupled Organization: Organizations such as universities, hospitals, and other professional agencies that have staff members who exercise substantial discretion in the work they do. Their tasks are typically loosely coordinated, with one staff member usually not knowing what others in the same unit may be doing.

Nonprofit (or Voluntary) Human Service Organization: A human service organization that is established on a voluntary basis to provide a continuing social service to a clientele in the community. It is governed by a volunteer board of directors and depends on public or private funding. Any "profits" it makes must be reinvested in the agency.

Nonroutine Technology: A technology that cannot be standardized because its raw materials are changeable and lacking in uniformity. An example would be psychotherapy.

Optimizing Decision Making: A rational decision-making model that strives to make the best possible decision that can be made.

Organization: A social unit composed of two or more people engaged on a relatively continuous basis in a specialized and interdependent activity aimed at accomplishing a common goal or mission.

Organizational Culture: A system of shared meanings and values held by members of an organization that distinguishes one organization from another—the character of an organization, so to speak.

People-Changing Human Service Organization: A Human service organization whose aim is to alter the personal characteristics of clients or to enhance their well-being, such as a hospital, school, or mental health agency.

People-Processing Human Service Organization: A human service organization whose principal function is to confer a social label, such as a diagnosis of physical or mental disorder.

People-Sustaining Human Service Organization: A human service organization whose purpose is to prevent or retard the deterioration of its clients or to maintain their well-being, such as a nursing home, an institution for the chronically mentally ill, or an income-maintenance agency such as the department of public welfare or the food stamps office.

Placid Environment: An environment external to the organization that is relatively stable and calm. Such environments are not common but may occasionally be found in small, conservative, relatively isolated, and self-sufficient communities.

Political Behavior: A behavior that attempts to influence the distribution of advantages or disadvantages in a social system.

Political Model of Organization: This perspective views the organization as an political arena in which different external and internal interest groups vie for attention to their concerns and interests.

Positive Reinforcer: A positive consequence, such as a pat on the back or praise, given after a specific behavior, which strengthens the behavior it follows.

Power: The potential of one person to influence another.

Public Service Organization: A human service organization that is government funded and provides services mandated by statute.

Radial Network: An informal communication network consisting of a person interacting with a number of others who, in turn, interact with still others, and so on.

Referent Power: Potential influence over others that is based on attraction or admiration or on one's ability to serve as a role model.

Reinforcement Theory: The theory that states that administration of a positive reinforcer strengthens the rate of emission of the behavior it follows, whereas administration of a negative reinforcer decreases the rate of emission of the behavior it follows.

Relationship-Oriented Leadership: Leadership that, although not necessarily oblivious to the task at hand, puts primary emphasis on facilitating open communication and interaction, providing support and encouragement, and showing concern for organizational members.

Reverse Discrimination: Usually understood to be discrimination against Euro-American males that sometimes occurs in affirmative action efforts to provide educational or job opportunities to members of formerly excluded groups or members of groups that formerly were not given the same employment opportunities as white males.

Reward Power: The ability of one person to influence the behavior of another through the use of reinforcement such as salary raises, recognition, praise, and support.

Routine Technology: A technology that follows procedures specified in advance. An example would be the technology of a factory assembly line.

Satisficing Decision Making: A decision-making model that aims at making decisions that satisfy one's purposes, even though they may not be the best possible.

Sexual Harassment: An abuse of power consisting of unwelcome sexual behavior by one person toward another which results in an intimidating, hostile, or offensive work or educational environment or which links the recipient's response to her or his terms or conditions of employment (e.g., determines whether the person is promoted, retained, or fired).

Span of Control: The number of employees under the control and supervision of a higher officer.

Spatial Differentiation: An organization that has offices and personnel in various locations.

Staff: All the employees of an organization that are not part of the chain of command.

Task Environment: A collection of external environmental entities with which an organization exchanges resources and services or which monitor its activities. For example, in the case of human service organizations, the task environment includes providers of economic resources, providers of legitimation and authority, client referral sources, clients and consumers of the organization's products, federal and state regulatory agencies, the media, and various interest groups.

Task-Oriented Leadership: Leadership that places primary emphasis on processes that facilitate task completion, such as establishing operating procedures, initiating action, providing expert information, motivating members toward goal achievement, and evaluating movement toward goal achievement.

Technology: The procedures whereby an organization transforms its inputs (e.g., raw materials, clients) into outputs (e.g., products or services).

Tokens: The few members of one type in a skewed group, compared to a much greater number of members of another type who are called dominants. If there is only one token in the group, the person is referred to as a "solo" member.

Transformational Leader: A leader able to have a profound effect on his or her followers by inspiring them to transcend their self-interest and to achieve higher goals.

Turbulent Environment: An environment that is characterized by multiple, changing, and often incompatible values and a constantly changing configuration of resources, interests, and general conditions.

Unity of Command: An administrative principle that states that each employee should report to only one supervisor to avoid confusion, unfair expectations, divided loyalties, and uncoordinated action.

Upward Communication: Communication that flows from a lower level to a higher level along the organizational chain of command—for example, from a staff member to a supervisor.

Vertical Communication: Communication that flows in a downward or upward direction along the chain of comman of the organization. See **Downward Communication, Upward Communication**.

Vertical Differentiation: See **Chain of Command**.

Wheel: A centralized communication network in which each member of the group officially communicates only with the group leader.

Work Motivation: The relative willingness of employees to put forth effort toward the achievement of organizational goals.

REFERENCES

Adams, J. S. (1965). Inequity in social exchanges. In L. Berkowitz (Ed.), *Advances in experimental social psychology* (pp. 267–300). New York: Academic Press.

Alderfer, C. P. (1969). An empirical test of a new theory of human needs. *Organizational Behavior and Human Performance, 4,* 142–175.

Argyris, C. (1957). The individual and the organization: Some problems of mutual adjustment. *Administrative Science Quarterly, 2*(1), 1–24.

Bass, B. M. (1985). *Leadership and performance beyond expectations.* New York: Free Press.

Bavelas, A. (1950). Communication patterns in task-oriented groups. *Acoustical Society of America Journal, 22,* 727–730.

Beehr, T. A., & Newman, J. E. (1978). Job stress, employee health, and organizational effectiveness: A factor analysis, model, and literature review. *Personnel Psychology, 31,* 665–699.

Bennis, W., & Nanus, B. (1985). *Leaders: The strategies for taking charge.* New York: Harper & Row.

Brager, G. A. (1968). Advocacy and political behavior. *Social Work, 13*(2), 5–15.

Brody, J. E. (1992, March 25). Overcoming the traumas of losing your job. *The New York Times,* p. B7.

Brown, R. (1988). *Group processes: Dynamics within and between groups.* Oxford: Basil Blackwell, Ltd.

Burns, J. M. (1978). *Leadership.* New York: Harper & Row.

Bush, J. A. (1977). The minority administrator: Implications for social work education. *Journal of Education for Social Work, 13*(1), 15–22.

Carsten, J. M., & Spector, P. E. (1987). Unemployment, job satisfaction, and employee turnover: A meta-analytic tests of the Muchinsky model. *Journal of Applied Psychology, 72,* 374–381.

Christie, R. (1991, June 16). A harder climb. *The Miami Herald,* pp. 1k, 3k.

Cohen, M. D., & March, J. G. (1986). *Leadership and ambiguity* (2nd ed.). Boston: Harvard Business School Press.

Cohen, M. D., March, J. G., & Olsen, J. P. (1972). A garbage can model of organizational choice. *Administrative Sciences Quarterly, 17,* 1–25.

Conger, T. A., & Kanungo, R. N. (1988). *Charismatic leadership: The elusive factor in organizational effectiveness.* San Francisco: Jossey-Bass.

Cooper, C. L., & Payne, R. (1978). *Stress at work.* London: John Wiley.

Croker, J., & McGraw, K. M. (1984). What's good for the goose is not good for the gander: Solo status as an obstacle to occupational achievement for males and females. *American Behavioral Scientist, 27,* 357–369.

Davis-Sacks, M. L., & Hasenfeld, Y. (1987). Organizations: Impact on employees and community. In A. Minahan (Ed.), *Encyclopedia of social work* (18th., ed., pp. 217–228). Silver Springs, MD: National Association of Social Workers.

Dickens, F., Jr., & Dickens, J. B. (1982) *The black manager: Making it in the corporate world.* New York: AMACOM.

Emerson, R. M. (1962). Power-dependence relations. *American Sociological Review, 27,* 31–41.

Emery, F. E., & Trist, E. L. (1968, August). The causal texture of organizational environments. *Human Relations, 18,* 20–26.

Epstein, A. (1991, May 15). Tests by black-white pairs show hiring bias persists. The *Miami Herald,* pp. 1A, 13A.

Fairhurst, G. T., & Snavely, B. K. (1983). Majority and token minority group relationships: Power acquisition and communication. *Academy of Management Review, 8,* 292–300.

Farrell, D., & Petersen, J. C. (1982). Patterns of political behavior in organizations. *Academy of Management Review, 7,* 403–412.

Feldman, D. C., & Arnold, H. J. (1985, June). Personality types and career patterns: Some empirical evidence on Holland's model. *Canadian Journal of Administrative Science,* 192–210.

Fiedler, F. E. (1978). The contingency model and the dynamics of the leadership process. *Advances in Experimental Social Psychology, 11,* 59–112.

Field, R. H. G. (1982). A test of the Vroom-Yetton normative model of leadership. *Journal of Applied Psychology, 67,* 523–532.

Fields, G. (1993, March 15). Ambitious, corporate and gay. *The Miami Herald,* Business Monday, pp. 26–27.

French, J. R. P., Jr., & Raven, B. (1959). The bases of social power. In D. Cartwright (Ed.), *Studies in social power* (pp. 150–167). Ann Arbor, MI: Institute for Social Research.

Gortner, H. F., Mahler, J., & Nicholson, J. B. (1987). *Organization theory: A public perspective.* Chicago: Dorsey Press.

Grant, J. (1988). Women as managers: What they can offer to organizations. *Organizational Dynamics, 16,* 56–63.

Gummer, B. (1987). Organization theory for social administration. In F. M. Cox, J. L. Erlich, J. Rothman, & J. E. Gropman (Eds.), *Strategies of community organization* (4th ed., pp. 427–449). Itasca, IL: F. E. Peacock.

Gummer, B. (1990). *The politics of social administration: Managing organizational politics in social agencies.* Englewood Cliffs, NJ: Prentice-Hall.

Gutek, B. A. (1985). *Sex and the workplace.* San Francisco: Jossey-Bass.

Hackett, R. D., & Guion, R. M. (1985). A reevaluation of the absenteeism-job satisfaction relationship. *Organizational behavior and human decision processes, 35,* 340–381.

Hardy, C. (1987). The contribution of political science to organizational behavior. In J. W. Lorsch (Ed.), *Handbook of organizational behavior.* Englewood Cliffs, NJ: Prentice Hall.

Hasenfeld, Y. (1983). *Human service organizations.* Englewood Cliffs: NJ: Prentice Hall.

Hersey, P., & Blanchard, K. H. (1982). *Management of organizational behavior.* (4th ed.). Englewood Cliffs, NJ: Prentice Hall.

Hickson, D. J. (1987). Decision-making at the top of organizations. *Annual Review of Sociology, 131,* 165–192.

Hollander, E. P., & Offerman, L. R. (1990). Power and leadership in organizations: Relationships in transition. *American Psychologist, 45,* 179–189.

House, R. J. (1971). A path-goal theory of leader effectiveness. *Administrative Science Quarterly, 16,* 321–338.

House, R. J. (1977). A 1976 theory of charismatic leadership. In J. G. Hunt & L. L. Larson (Eds.), *Leadership: The cutting edge* (pp. 189–207). Carbondale: Southern Illinois University Press.

House, R. J., & Mitchell, T. R. (1974). Path-goal theory of leadership. *Journal of Contemporary Business, 3,* 81–95.

Hulin, C. L., Roznowski, H. M., & Hachiya, D. (1985). Alternative opportunities and withdrawal decisions: Empirical and theoretical discrepancies and an integration. *Psychological Bulletin, 97,* 233–250.

Iaffaldano, M. T., & Muchinsky, P. M. (1985). Job satisfaction and job performance: A meta-analysis. *Psychological Bulletin, 97,* 251–273.

Janofsky, M. (1993, June 20). Race and the American workplace. *The New York Times,* Sec. 3, pp. 1, 6.

Jones, E. W., Jr. (1986, May–June). Black managers: The dream deferred. *Harvard Business Review,* 84–93.

Kanter, R. M. (1977). Numbers: Minorities and majorities. In R. M. Kanter (Ed.), *Men and women of the corporation* (pp. 206–242). New York: Basic Books.

Kanter, R. M.(1979). Power failure in management circuits. *Harvard Business Review, 57,* 65–75.

Kanter, R. M. (1988). Ensuring minority achievement in corporations: The importance of structural theory and structural change. In D. E. Thompson & N. DiTomaso (Eds.), *Ensuring minority success in corporate management* (pp. 331–346). New York: Plenum Press.

Kast, F. E., & Rosenzweig, J. E. (1973). *Contingency views of organization and management.* Chicago: Science Research Associates.

Katz, D., & Kahn, R. L. (1978). *The social psychology of organizations* (2nd ed.). New York: John Wiley & Sons.

Kelborn, P. T. (1995, March 16). Women and the minorities still face "glass ceiling." *The New York Times,* p. C22.

Kipnis, D., Schmidt, S. M., & Wilkinson. (1980). Intraorganizational influence tactics: Explorations in getting one's way. *Journal of Applied Psychology, 65,* 440–452.

Knouse, S. B., Rosenfeld, P., & Culbertson, A. L. (Eds.). (1992). *Hispanics in the workplace.* Newbury Park, CA: Sage.

Kravetz, D., & Austin, C. B. (1984). Women's issues in social administration: The views and experiences of women administrators. *Administration in Social Work, 8*(4), 25–38.

Lawler, III, E. E. (1973). *Motivation in work organizations.* Monterey, CA: Brooks/Cole.

Lawler, III, E. E., & Suttle, J. L. (1972). A causal correlational test of the need hierarchy concept. *Organizational Behavior and Human Performance, 7,* 265–287.

Leavitt, H. J., Dill, W. R., & Eyring, H. B. (1980). Strategies for survival: How organizations cope with their worlds. In H. J. Leavitt, L. R. Pondy,

& D. M. Boje (Eds.), *Readings in managerial psychology* (3rd ed., pp. 720–731). Chicago: University of Chicago Press.

Levine, M. P., & Leonard, R. (1982, September). *Discrimination against lesbians in the workforce.* Paper presented at the Annual Meeting of the American Sociological Association.

Likert, R. (1967). *The human organization.* New York: McGraw-Hill.

Locke, E. A. (1976). The nature and causes of job satisfaction. In M. D. Dunnette (Ed.), *Handbook of industrial and organizational psychology* (pp. 1319–1328). Chicago: Rand McNally.

Loden, M. (1986, February 9). Disillusion at the corporate top: A machismo that drives women out. *The New York Times,* Business Section.

Louie, V. (1993, August 8). For Asian-Americans, a way to fight a maddening stereotype. *The New York Times,* p. 9.

Madison, D. L., Allen, R. W., Porter, L. W., Renwick, P.A., & Mayes, B. T. (1980). Organizational politics: An exploration of manager's perceptions. *Human Relations,* 33, 79–100.

March, J., & Simon, H. (1958). *Organizations.* New York: John Wiley & Sons.

Martin, N. H., & Sims, J. H. (1980). Power tactics. In H. J. Leavitt, L. R. Pondy, & D. M. Boje (Eds.), *Readings in managerial psychology* (3rd ed., pp. 365–372). Chicago: University of Chicago Press.

Maslow, A. (1954). *Motivation and personality.* New York: Harper & Row.

McClelland, D. C. (1961). *The achieving society.* New York: Van Nostrand Reinhold.

McClelland, D. C. (1970). The two faces of power. *Journal of International Affairs, 24*(1), 29–47.

McClelland, D. C. (1975). *Power: The inner experience.* New York: Irvington.

McGregor, D. (1960). *The human side of enterprise.* New York: McGraw-Hill.

McMurtry, S. L., Netting, F. E., & Kettner, P. M. (1990). Critical inputs and strategic choice in non-profit human service organizations. *Administration in Social Work, 14*(3), 67–82.

Mento, A. J., Steel, R. P., & Karren, R. J. (1987). A meta-analytic study of the effects of goal setting on task performance: 1966–1984. *Organizational Behavior and Human Decision Processes, 39,* 52–83.

Merton, R. K. (1940). Bureaucratic structure and personality. *Social Forces, 18,* 560–568.

Mintzberg, H. (1983). *Power in and around organizations.* Englewood Cliffs, NJ: Prentice Hall.

Mitchell, T. R., & Beach, L. R. (1990).... Do I love thee? Let me count... Toward an understanding of intuitive and automatic decision making. *Organizational Behavior and Human Decision Processes, 47,* 1–20.

Morrison, A. M., & Von Glinow, M. A. (1990). Women and minorities in management. *American Psychologist, 45,* 200–208.

Parasuraman, S., & Alutto, J. A. (1984). Sources and outcomes of stress in organizational settings: Toward the development of a structural model. *Academy of Management Journal, 27,* 330–350.

Perrow, C. (1965). Hospitals: Technology, structure, and goals. In J. G. March (Ed.), *Handbook of organizations* (pp. 910–971). Chicago: Rand McNally.

Perrow, C. (1967). A framework for the comparative analysis of organizations. *American Sociological Review, 32,* 194–208.

Peters, L. H., Hartke, D. D., & Pohlmann, J. T. (1985). Fiedler's contingency theory of leadership: An application of the meta-analysis procedures of Schmidt and Hunter. *Psychological Bulletin, 97,* 274–285.

Pettigrew, T. F., & Martin, J. (1987). Shaping the organizational context for black American inclusion. *Journal of Social Issues, 43,* 41–78.

Petty, M. M., McGee, G. W., & Cavender, J. W. (1984). A meta-analysis of the relationship between individual job satisfaction and individual performance. *Academy of Management Review, 9,* 712–721.

Planty, E. G., & Machaver, W. (1984). Stimulating upward communication. In J. L. Gray & F. A. Starke (Eds.), *Organizational behavior: Concepts and applications* (3rd ed., pp. 229-241). Columbus, OH: Charles E. Merrill.

Pondy, L. R. (1980). Organizational conflict: Concepts and Models. In H. J. Leavitt, L. R. Pondy, & D. M. Boje (Eds.), *Readings in managerial psychology* (3rd ed., pp. 473–492). Chicago: University of Chicago Press.

Robbins, S. P. (1974). *Managing organizational conflict: A nontraditional approach.* Englewood Cliffs, NJ: Prentice Hall.

Robbins, S. P. (1989). *Organizational behavior: Concepts, controversies, and applications* (4th ed.). Englewood Cliffs, NJ: Prentice Hall.

Ronen, S. (1986). Equity perception in multiple comparisons: A field study. *Human Relations, 39,* 333–346.

Rubin, L. B. (1992). *Worlds of pain: Life in the working class family.* New York: Basic Books.

Rudolph, B. (1990). Why can't a woman manage more like...a woman? *Time, 136*(9), 53.

Sandler, B. R. (1986, October). *The campus climate revisited: Chilly for women faculty, administrators, and graduate students.* Washington, DC: The Project on the Status and Education of Women, Association of American Colleges.

Schein, E. H. (1985). *Organizational culture and leadership.* San Francisco: Jossey-Bass.

Schein, E. H. (1990, February). Organizational culture. *American Psychologist, 45,* 109–119.

Schneider, B. E. (1984). Peril and promise: Lesbians' workplace participation. In T. Darty & S. Potter (Eds.), *Women-identified women* (pp. 211–230). Palo Alto, CA: Mayfield.

Schneider, B. E. (1987). Coming out at work. *Work and Occupations, 13,* 463–487.

Selznick, P. (1949). *TVA and the grass roots.* Berkeley: University of California Press.

Shaw, M. (1981) *Group dynamics: The psychology of small group behavior* (3rd ed.). New York: McGraw-Hill.

Simon, H. A. (1976). *Administrative behavior* (3rd ed.). New York: Free Press.

Smith, D. E. (1965). Front-line organization of the state mental hospital. *Administrative Science Quarterly, 10,* 381–399.

Staw, B. M., Bell, N. E., & Clausen, J. A. (1986). The dispositional approach to job attitudes: A lifetime longitudinal test. *Administrative Science Quarterly, 31,* 56–77.

Taylor, S. E. (1991). *Health psychology* (2nd ed.). New York: McGraw-Hill.

Thomas, D. A. (1986). *An intra-organizational analysis of black and white patterns of sponsorship and the dynamics of cross-racial mentoring.* Unpublished Ph.D. dissertation, Yale University.

Thomas, K. W. (1976). Conflict and conflict management. In M. D. Dunnette (Ed.), *Handbook of industrial and organizational psychology* (pp. 889–935). Chicago: John Wiley & Sons.

Thomas, K. W. (1977). Toward multidimensional values in teaching: The example of conflict behaviors. *Academy of Management Review, 2,* 484–490.

Thompson, J. D. (1967). *Organizations in action.* New York: McGraw-Hill.

Tubbs, M. E. (1986). Goal setting: A metaanalytic examination of the empirical evidence. *Journal of Applied Psychology, 71,* 474–483.

U.S. Office of Personnel Management. (1989). *Report on minority group and sex by pay plan and appointing authority* (EPMD Report No. 40, March 31, 1989). Washington, DC.: U.S. Office of Personnel Management.

Von Glinow, M. A., & Krzyczkowska-Mercer, A. (1988, Summer). Women in corporate America: A caste of thousands. *New Management, 6,* 36–42.

Vredenburgh, D. J., & Maurer. (1984) A process framework of organizational politics. *Human Relations, 37,* 47–66.

Vroom, V. H. (1964). *Work and motivation.* New York: John Wiley.

Vroom, V. H., & Yetton, P. W. (1973). *Leadership and decision-making.* Pittsburgh: University of Pittsburgh Press.

Weber, M. (1947). *The theory of social and economic organizations.* (T. Parsons Ed., A. M. Henderson & T. Parsons, Trans.). New York: Free Press.

Weick, K. (1976). Educational organizations as loosely coupled systems. *Administrative Science Quarterly, 21,* 1–19.

Women in corporate America faring better, survey shows. (1993, June 30). *The Miami Herald,* p. 3C.

Zald, M. N. (1970). Political economy: A framework for comparative analysis In M. N. Zald (Ed.), *Power in organizations* (pp. 221–261). Nashville, TN: Vanderbilt University Press.

Zaldivar, R. A. (1991, August 9). Women, minorities face obstacles to executive suites, study finds. *The Miami Herald,* pp. 1A, 8A.

SUGGESTIONS FOR FURTHER READING

American Psychologist. (1990, February). Volume 45. (This whole issue is dedicated to organizations; highly sophisticated treatment for advanced readers.)

Banner, D. K., & Gagne, T. E. (1994). *Designing effective organizations: Traditional and transformational views.* Thousand Oaks, CA: Sage.

Bowman, P. J. (1991). Organizational psychology: African American Perspectives. In R. L. Jones (Ed.), *Black psychology* (pp. 509–531). Berkeley, CA: Cobb & Henry.

Curtis, R. L. (1989). Leadership decision making in a service organization: A field test of the Vroom-Yetton model. *Human Relations, 42,* 671–689.

Davis, G., & Watson, G. (1982). *Black life in corporate America: Swimming in the mainstream.* Garden city, NY: Anchor Press/Doubleday.

Dickens, F., Jr., & Dickens, J. B. (1982). *The black manager: Making it in the corporate world.* New York: American Management Association.

Frost, P. J., & Moore, L. F. (1991). *Reframing organizational culture.* Newbury Park, CA: Sage.

Gardner, J. W. (1990). *On leadership.* New York: Free Press.

Hasenfeld, Y. (Ed.). (1992). *Human services as complex organizations.* Newbury Park, CA: Sage.

Haynes, K. S. (1989). *Women managers in human services.* New York: Springer.

Holland, T. P., & Petchers, M. K. (1987). Organizations: Context for social service delivery. In A. Minahan (Ed.), *Encyclopedia of social work* (18th ed., pp. 204–217). Silver Spring, MD: National Association of Social Workers.

Karasek, R., & Theorell, T. (1990). *Healthy work: Stress, productivity, and the reconstruction of working life.* New York: Basic Books.

Kenney, G. M., & Wissoker, D. A. (1994). An analysis of the correlates of discrimination facing young Hispanic job-seekers. *American Economic Review, 84,* 674–683.

Knouse, S. B., Rosenfeld, P., & Culbertson, A. L (Eds.). (1992). *Hispanics in the workplace.* Newbury Park, CA: Sage.

March, J. G. (1994). *A primer on decision making: How decisions happen.* New York: Free Press.

McNaught, B. (1993). *Gay issues in the workplace.* New York: St. Martin's Press.

Mills, A. J., & Tancred, P. (1992). *Gendering organizational analysis.* Newbury Park, CA: Sage.

Muczyk, J. P., & Reimann, B. C. (1987, November). The case for directive leadership. *Academy of Management Executive*, 301–311.

Smith, P. B., & Peterson, M. F. (1988). *Leadership, organizations, and culture.* Newbury Park, CA: Sage.

Wernet, S. P., & Austin, D. M. (1991). Decision making style and leadership patters in nonprofit human service organizations. *Administration in Social Work, 15*(3), 1–17.

Woods, J. D., & Lucas, J. (1993). *The corporate closet: The professional lives of gay men in America.* New York: Free Press.

Yukl, G. A. (1989). *Leadership in organizations.* Englewood Cliffs, NJ: Prentice Hall.

Look for articles in the following journals:

Academy of Management Journal
Academy of Management Review
Administrative Science Quarterly
Administration in Social Work
Human Relations
Organizational Behavior and Human Decision Processes
Organizational Dynamics
Strategic Management Journal

CHAPTER 7

HUMAN BEHAVIOR
IN SMALL GROUPS

Four clients who do not know one another and who are sitting in separate waiting rooms at the local social service agency would hardly be considered a group. But if the agency created the potential for them to interact—for example, by encouraging them to talk among themselves while waiting for services—these four individuals might become a group. A **group** consists of two or more persons interacting in such a manner that each influences and is influenced by every other (Shaw, 1981, p. 8).

According to this definition, groups can range in size from dyads, or two-person systems, to large crowds. Many examples of dyads come to mind: couples, parent and child, best friends, practitioner and client, nurse and patient, and so on. At the other end of the spectrum, large crowds or mobs can also behave as groups under some circumstances. This chapter will not examine these two extremes of the group spectrum. Instead, the focus will be on the study of groups ranging in size from 3 to 12 or 15 members. They are generally referred to as *small groups*.

Among the most important characteristics of small groups are interaction, structure, a common purpose, goals, and dynamics. By definition, all groups must engage in some sort of **interaction**, the most fundamental of all group processes. Interaction refers to the patterns of mutual influence—verbal, nonverbal, or physical—that exist in groups. All groups also develop a certain **structure** or stable pattern of behavior exhibited by group members as they interact repeatedly in their characteristic ways. As you will see, roles, norms, statuses, and subgroups are important aspects of group structure. In addition, all groups have some **purpose** or function (i.e., the reason they were created, such as to accomplish a task, to assist members in their growth, or to provide leisure activities), as well as **goals** or specific objectives instrumental to the group purpose (e.g., a visit to the countryside organized by a leisure group).

Finally, all groups are **dynamic** in the sense that they are active, they have energy, they engage in a number of activities such as decision making and communication, and they go through various developmental stages.

An important aspect of the role of social workers and other human service practitioners is to work with groups within their employing agency and in the community. Even those who do not conduct treatment groups must participate in a large number of task groups, such as staff meetings, interdisciplinary teams, committee meetings, board of directors meetings, task forces, delegate councils, labor unions, professional organizations, and so on. In addition, practitioners and clients are influenced by many groups outside the work environment, such as their families and social networks, the religious and political groups to which they belong, and various leisure and support groups in their neighborhoods and communities. In short, all human service practitioners need to have a good understanding of small group behavior, particularly knowledge that is applicable to the range of task groups in their work environments.

This chapter will discuss the types and functions of groups you are likely to encounter at work and in the community and the major theories that attempt to explain behavior in small groups. We will examine structural aspects of groups, such as roles, norms, subsystems, and group composition effects. We will consider issues relevant to the inclusion of women, African Americans, Latinos, and Asian Americans in small groups. And we will learn about the processes of communication, leadership, problem solving, and decision making and about the stages small groups go through as they develop.

Given the important role that groups play in people's occupational and personal lives, it is unfortunate that research on small groups has been limited in recent years. After the explosion of knowledge about small groups that took place in the 1950s (Toseland and Rivas, 1984), the field has been unusually quiet. Garvin

(1987) and Ephross & Vassil (1988), among other group experts in social work, have noted the dearth of small-group research in recent decades, in comparison to other areas of inquiry. However, interest in the study of small groups appears to be resurging (Garvin, 1987b, Paulus, 1989), with the bulk of the research nowadays being conducted by organizational psychologists (Levine & Moreland, 1990, p. 620). Social workers recently have begun to play a role in the generation of knowledge about groups (Feldman, 1987).

Until recently, a good portion of the research on small groups was conducted using groups of college students put together especially for the purpose of studying them and with a majority having Euro-American males as leaders or members. This research focused primarily on training or experiential learning groups (Ephross & Vassil, 1988; Garvin & Reed, 1983). Now those who study small groups are developing a more practical orientation, seeking to base their theories on natural rather than laboratory groups (Levine & Moreland, 1990). Still, there is a dearth of studies focusing on groups with memberships that are more reflective of the diversity of U.S. society.

TYPES AND FUNCTIONS OF GROUPS

There are various ways of classifying the many groups we come across in our daily lives. An important distinction is between primary and secondary groups. A **primary group**, first defined by Cooley (1909), is a small group of people whose relationships are characterized by intimacy, frequent interaction, strong interdependence, and group identification. Although a close relationship among members is necessary for a group to be considered primary, this closeness need not be expressed by positive emotions, such as love and affection; sometimes, it is expressed through anger, hatred, jealousy, fights, and even violence. Good examples of primary groups are families, close friends, and *some* sports teams, military platoons, peer groups, work groups, or rock bands. Primary group interaction is usually face to face, although some primary groups are able to maintain close ties over long distances by communicating through letters, phone calls, videos, E-mail, or faxes. Any group that cannot be classified as primary is a **secondary group.**

We may also differentiate between natural and formed groups. A **natural group** is one that already exists, such as a family or peer group. A **formed group** is constituted for a specific purpose, such as an athletic team, a rehabilitation group for drug addicts, a group for prospective foster parents, an interest group, or a committee.

There are also open-ended and closed groups. An **open-ended group** is one that keeps adding members to the group regularly—for example, a support group for recently divorced single parents that is run continuously by an agency and that new members may join at any time. One important disadvantage of open-ended groups is the instability that is generated by the constant turnover in membership. A **closed group** is one whose membership does

not change after it is constituted, except through natural attrition; the U.S. Supreme Court is an example of a closed group because its members usually serve for life or until they retire.

Another important distinction that may be made among groups is between those whose membership is voluntary and those whose membership is nonvoluntary. A **voluntary group** consists of members who have willingly chosen to participate in the group. A **nonvoluntary group** consists of members who have no choice regarding their participation—for instance, drug offenders, sexual abusers, wife batterers or drunk drivers who have been court-ordered to undergo group treatment. The distinction is important because in nonvoluntary groups, members tend to show a higher level of distrust and lower levels of commitment, cooperation, and self-disclosure than in voluntary groups (Napier & Gershenfeld, 1989, p. 74).

Groups may be classified by the purpose or type of activity in which they engage. Two basic purposes are task achievement and personal growth. **Task groups** are primarily for the purpose of getting a job done, whether it be to

solve a problem, make a decision, develop a policy, provide a service, or create a product. Committees, task forces, work teams, court juries, meetings of professional organizations, and advocacy groups are examples of task-oriented groups. **Growth groups** aim primarily at helping members in their personal development. Examples include groups that focus on developing interpersonal skills, encounter and sensitivity groups, human relations groups, and various treatment, counseling, support, and consciousness-raising groups. **Treatment groups** are a type of growth group focusing on helping members to change or to overcome personal problems or deficits, such as a group of people who want to stop smoking or who want to cope more effectively with divorce or depression.

The classification of groups into task or growth covers a lot of ground, but it is not exhaustive or mutually exclusive. Many groups combine both purposes, although generally there is greater emphasis on one purpose or the other. Examples of groups that focus on both task and growth include families, students attending the same class section, empowerment groups, social skills training groups, self-help groups, and athletic teams. Some groups are primarily neither task nor growth oriented. A good example is a leisure-time group, such as a bridge club. Another example of a group that is neither task nor growth oriented is a **reference group**—a group that an individual uses as his or her frame of reference for self-evaluation and comparison.

THEORETICAL CONTRIBUTIONS TO THE UNDERSTANDING OF GROUP BEHAVIOR

There is no theory capable of explaining all the complexities and subtleties of group behavior; however, some provide worthwhile insights into some small-group processes. This section will consider concepts derived from various perspectives such as ecosystems, symbolic interactionism, social exchange theory, field theory, behavioral theory, and psychoanalytic theory.

Ecosystems Perspective

Chapter 1 detailed the ecosystems perspective and its parent theory, structural functionalism. This is probably the most comprehensive and most widely utilized framework for organizing knowledge about small groups. From this perspective, groups are seen as open social systems composed of interdependent members engaged in transactions aiming toward specific goals. Group members are constantly influencing and being influenced by one another's actions and by the environment. Because they depend on one another and on the environment, they are usually motivated to work cooperatively, at least to some extent, and to keep a steady state—that is, some degree of order, stability, cohesion, and continuity. When conflict arises, the group attempts to deal with it by calling into play its stabilizing forces.

Groups exist within specific social, political, economic, cultural, and physical environments and are in continuous transaction with these external forces. These outside systems may act as resources that help group members meet their needs and goals or as barriers that interfere with the attainment of their objectives. To maximize external supports or resources or to modify unsupportive or detrimental external forces, group leaders often must intervene in the community on behalf of the group or of individual group members (Vinter & Galinsky, 1985). For example, the leader of a group of acting-out teenagers may need to meet with their parents, teachers, and other school personnel to enlist their cooperation and to work on problematic aspects of their attitudes or approach toward the teens.

Groups depend on a variety of inputs from the environment. These include a supply of members, information, resources (e.g., released time to work on the group task, space to accommodate the group, money to pay consultants or to pay for staff help), direction (e.g., a charge to a committee or task force that details its task), and constraints (e.g., organizational policies or funding agency regulations). They act on and transform the inputs they get into outputs, which they send back to the environment in the form of better-functioning citizens, recommendations, products, or services. Permeable boundaries allow groups to seek and receive inputs, including positive and negative feedback from environmental suprasystems. For example, group leaders get periodic feedback on their performance through supervisory conferences, information they use to adjust their functioning within the group. Feedback prevents entropy from setting in and ensures continued growth and development.

Symbolic Interactionism

You may recall from Chapter 1 that, according to symbolic interaction theory, human beings do not merely respond or react to each other's actions or to environmental stimuli but assign meanings to these events and act on the basis of these perceptions. Thus, a symbolic interactionist approach to group work would stress the importance of entering the private world of meanings of group members to understand their group behaviors. One way to achieve movement and to bring about change in the group from this perspective would be to negotiate new meanings among members by looking at situations and responses from a different vantage point (Ephross & Greene, 1991, pp. 222–223).

Because of its emphasis on the transfer of meaning among people, symbolic interactionism is particularly relevant to interpersonal communication, probably the most fundamental of all small group processes. Communication in groups takes place through language but also through other means of expression, such as gestures, voice tone, and body movements. These components of the communication process will be explored later in this chapter.

The concept of labeling developed by Erving Goffman (1959, 1961, 1974) is an important derivative of symbolic interactionism. Many of the clients seen by group practitioners have been assigned various labels, such as *depressed, spouse abuser, drug addict, school dropout, criminal offender*, or *child abuser*. According to Goffman, once assigned a label, clients often act in accordance with the label's expected roles, altering their behavior and eventually their self-concepts and fates to fit the label they have been assigned.

Social Exchange Theory

As discussed in Chapter 1, social exchange theory suggests that social interaction is like economic activity in that people make decisions concerning its desirability on the basis of a cost-benefit analysis. Thus, in deciding whether to join a group or to continue to participate in it, an individual may engage in a cost-benefit analysis, no matter how informally it may be carried out. If membership is thought to offer more rewards than costs, the person will likely favor the association with the group, whereas if joining is thought to involve more costs than benefits, he or she may decide against it.

For example, in deciding whether or not to join an Alcoholics Anonymous (AA) group, Mr. Suarez may first attempt to enumerate the positive and negative outcomes that might result from membership in the group. He may think of several possible advantages if he decides to participate, such as having access to people who care about what happens to him; being able to share his experiences with people with similar problems; getting understanding, encouragement, and support; and having something safe to do in the evenings. On the negative side, he may consider the time and effort involved in attending meetings three nights per week and all the enjoyable activities he'd have to give up to attend. He may dread the tension and anxiety of having to admit to being an alcoholic in front of others and of having to disclose his personal problems. If he concludes that the potentia! benefits outweigh the possible costs, he will likely join the group.

A fundamental tenet of exchange theory is the principle of fair exchange. According to fair exchange, we would expect that if a group member consistently takes more from the group than she contributes to it, the other group members are likely to confront her, get angry with her, put her down, make her feel guilty, or ask her to leave the group. But if she contributes to the group in a different way, perhaps by facilitating access to resources not otherwise available to it, or if she happens to be a high-status person and her association with the group adds prestige to it, the group may consider the exchange fair regardless of whether or not she actually contributes during group sessions.

Field Theory

Perhaps the greatest contribution of Kurt Lewin's field theory (1951) to small group theory was his insistence that human behavior cannot be considered apart from its environmental context. Behavior, he noted, is a function of person and environment, both of which are interdependent. He suggested that person and environment make up an indivisible unit, or gestalt, which he called the *lifespace* or subjective world of experience. Therefore, to understand what is happening in a group, it is necessary to understand not only its internal social interactional field but the external environment within which the group operates and the subjective perceptions of its members. As you can see, Lewin's ideas are compatible with both the ecosystems perspective and symbolic interactionism.

The Behavioral Approach

Over the past 20 years or so, the behavioral approach has been increasingly applied to group work with diverse memberships and problems. This approach is based on radical behavioral and cognitive behavioral theories. Basically, the behavioral method as applied to group work requires precise definitions and assessments of the problems and concerns of group members as well as intervention plans that are directed toward the achievement of specific and measurable objectives. This approach has been found to be useful with a wide range of groups, including groups of individuals who would be difficult to work with using other perspectives, such as psychiatric clients with severe impairments or clients who are mentally retarded (Sundel & Glasser, 1985). A variety of procedures are used to modify the behavior of group members including modeling, behavioral rehearsals, assertiveness training, social skills training, cognitive restructuring structured discussion groups, programmed instruction, relaxation training, behavioral assignments, and systematic desensitization. Probably the principal proponent of behavioral group work within the field of social work has been Sheldon Rose (1977, 1989).

Psychoanalytic Theory

Freud wrote a book entitled *Group Psychology and the Analysis of the Ego* (1922) in which he set forth his theoretical ideas about groups and their influence on human behavior. Although he did not practice group treatment, many of his followers have adapted psychoanalytic theory to group work (e.g., Bion, 1961; Yalom, 1985). According to this perspective, the group becomes a reenactment of the family situation, with the group leader acting as the parent figure and group members representing the children/ siblings. Members form transference reactions to the group leader and to one another on the basis of their early life experiences. In turn, the group leader interprets these transference reactions to help members work through unresolved conflicts and develop insight into their behaviors.

Other Group Theories

Many other group theories have been formulated. Although discussion of them is beyond the scope of this chapter, interested readers may wish to pursue some. William Schutz (1958), in his fundamental interpersonal relations orientation theory (FIRO), hypothesized that people join groups to satisfy three basic needs—inclusion, control, and affection. Jacob Moreno (1953) was one of the first theorists to explain group behavior through the use of diagrams, which he called *sociograms*, to represent the interpersonal relationships among group members. Robert Bales (1968, 1983; Bales, Koenigs, & Roman, 1987) has concentrated on the analysis of internal functions of small groups, such as their task and social activities, phases of development, and roles played by members. Based on observation and analysis of hundreds of groups, he and his colleagues developed two systems, one called Interaction Process Analysis (IPA) and the most recent one called SYMLOG (a system for the multiple-level observation of groups). Both of these systems are often used today in the analysis of small-group behavior.

GROUP STRUCTURE

As people form a group and begin to interact, typically they establish common rules of behavior or norms and begin to play different roles. Some become quite active and talkative in the group and enjoy throwing around their influence. Others are more quiet and passive and prefer to sit on the sidelines. This section will look at the most basic aspects of **group structure:** roles, norms, subgroups, and the status of the individual within the group.

Roles

A **role** is a set of expectations that group members share concerning the behavior of a person who occupies a certain position in the group. Group roles become differentiated over time. Typically, when the group starts, all the participants consider themselves "members." Gradually, however, various other roles emerge. Probably the first level of role differentiation is reached when the majority of the group members recognize one of them as the group leader. The leader guides the group toward goal attainment and provides support. In many instances, one group leader is not enough; consequently, separate specialists may emerge, one leading the group toward task completion while another, the socioemotional specialist, attempts to maintain harmony and peace. As the group evolves, more specialized roles emerge along the task and maintenance dimensions.

As noted previously in this book, the concept of role was borrowed by social scientists from the theater, where it is used to refer to the part an actor plays. Although actors must perform certain behaviors as part of their roles, they can offer their own interpretations of the role by speaking in an original way or by changing their stage behaviors somewhat. However, they cannot diverge too much from the script, lest the rest of the cast find itself unable to adapt to the changes. Similarly, roles in groups are somewhat flexible but within limits. Interactions among group members would become chaotic if each one were to enact his or her role in a manner that failed to meet the basic expectations of the position.

Almost half a century ago, Benne and Sheats (1948) provided what is still considered one of the most complete and succinct descriptions of the various task, socioemotional, and individual roles performed by group members. The task and socioemotional roles are summarized in Table 7.1. Many of these roles will be familiar to you regardless of your experience with task or growth groups because they are often played out within the family. Additional roles commonly played out in groups include that of the *joker*, or *clown*, who looks at things differently and injects humor; the *nag*, who complains about everything, the *troublemaker*,

TABLE 7.1   Task Roles and Socioemotional Roles in Groups

ROLE	FUNCTION
Task Roles	
1. Initiator contributor	Recommends novel ideas about the problem at hand, new ways to approach the problem, or possible solutions not yet considered
2. Information seeker	Emphasizes "getting the facts" by calling for background information from others
3. Opinion seeker	Asks for more qualitative types of data, such as attitudes, values, and feelings
4. Information giver	Provides facts and data for forming decisions
5. Opinion giver	Provides opinions, values, and feelings
6. Elaborator	Gives additional information—examples, rephrasings, implications—about points made by others.
7. Coordinator	Shows the relevance of each idea and its relationship to the overall problem
8. Orienter	Refocuses discussion on the topic whenever necessary
9. Evaluator-critic	Appraises the quality of the group's efforts in terms of logic, practicality, or method
10. Energizer	Stimulates the group to continue working when discussion flags
11. Procedural technician	Provides operational details such as rules of order, materials, and so on
12. Recorder	Provides a secretarial function
Socioemotional Roles	
1. Encourager	Rewards others through agreement, warmth, and praise
2. Harmonizer	Mediates conflicts among group members
3. Compromiser	Shifts his or her position on an issue in order to reduce conflict in the group
4. Gatekeeper and expediter	Smooths communication by setting up procedures and ensuring equal participation from members
5. Standard setter	Expresses, or calls for discussion of, standards for evaluating the quality of the group process
6. Observer and commentator	Informally points out the positive and negative aspects of the group's dynamics and calls for change if necessary
7. Follower	Accepts the ideas offered by others and serves as an audience for the group

Source: From "Functional Roles of Group Members" by K. D. Benne and P. Sheats, 1948, *Journal of Social Issues,* 4(2). Copyright 1948 by the Society for the Psychological Study of Social Issues. Reprinted by permission.

or *provocateur*, who is always looking for trouble; the *scapegoat*, who is made to bear the blame for the group whenever something goes wrong; the *attention seeker*, who likes to draw attention to himself or herself; the *silent member*, who is reluctant to speak up or to interact; the *newcomer* (new group member); and the *deviant*, who stands in opposition to the values, norms, and goals of the group and often is rejected by group members.

Group members often play several roles simultaneously. When a person discovers that the behaviors associated with one role she must play are incompatible with those associated with other roles she must also play, she suffers **interrole conflict.** For example, it is difficult (though not impossible) to be both task and socioemotional leader because the demands associated with getting the job done and controlling the behavior of group members often clash with the need to harmonize and offer support. **Intrarole conflict** results, you may recall, from opposing demands from a single role. Frequently this happens when a role occupant and the group differ in their interpretation of the role. For instance, a group member may interpret his role as *gatekeeper* to mean that he is to prevent "ordinary" group members from talking too much so as to allow the more influential people in the group to dominate the discussion. Other members of the group, however, may want the gatekeeper to act more democratically.

Norms

Norms are the rules or standards that regulate the behavior of group members. They serve as the primary means of control within the group, pressuring members toward uniformity and conformity. Norms reach the group from various sources, such as the members' cultural values and the norms and values of the sponsoring organization and surrounding community. Through confrontation and negotiation within the group, as well as sometimes by external mandate, these diverse values get translated into a common system or group culture that governs the behavior of the group participants.

Norms may be prescriptive or proscriptive, explicit or implicit. **Prescriptive norms** describe the kinds of behaviors that should be performed; for example, treatment group members are generally expected to maintain confidentiality. **Proscriptive norms** articulate the behaviors that are forbidden; for instance, members may not be permitted to smoke or drink alcohol during group sessions. **Explicit norms** are those regulations that are clearly spelled out, such as the group's bylaws.

Implicit norms are rules that are presumed but unspoken; for instance, although there may be no assigned seats at meetings, members of a particular committee may consistently leave the head of the table open for the chairperson.

One of the most important tasks of the group practitioner is to facilitate the development and enforcement of ethical group norms. Among the most fundamental of these ethical norms is the acceptance of diversity among group members and respect for the worth of each individual, regardless of race, gender, national origin, cultural background, social class, sexual orientation, religious creed, age, or disability. Other important humanistic values that the group worker is expected to enforce are fairness in dealing with one another, responsibility for one's actions, freedom to express one's thoughts and feelings, cooperation, mutual aid, and the right of each group member to participate in the decision-making process of the group (Konopka, 1983; Northen, 1988; Ephross & Vassil, 1988). Additional ethical values to be maintained in treatment groups include confidentiality, self-determination or the right to take part in decisions involving one's treatment course, the right to have one's problems and concerns addressed by the group to which one belongs, and the right to be protected from psychological and physical harm inflicted by other group members.

Subgroups

As groups increase in size, members begin to form subgroups and alliances based on common interests, concerns, and feelings. These subgroups facilitate work on specific subtasks and, particularly in large groups, they help members to meet their needs for intimacy, control, and affection. As pairs, triads, and other cliques come into being, they combine to form a pattern, often called the *interpersonal structure of the group* (Hartford, 1971; Northen, 1988).

One special type of subgroup—the **coalition**—arises, usually temporarily, to facilitate the attainment of a goal that could not be reached if the individual group members acted independently. Coalitions sometimes include adversaries who choose to ignore their differences for a limited period of time so they can better accomplish a goal. Once the goal is attained, differences among the coalition members may surface again and may make continued cooperation difficult.

Status within the Group

Group members may start off on an equal footing, but after a few group sessions, some group members will have gained more ascendancy than others either because they have personal characteristics that the group values (e.g., intelligence or expertise) or because they have made special contributions, such as taking on responsibilities, providing guidance, obtaining resources for the group, or offering support. These group members are accorded higher **status** and, therefore, more power, influence, and control. In this manner, a hierarchical system of statuses emerges (Northen, 1988) with some group members becoming more highly valued than others.

GROUP COMPOSITION EFFECTS

In putting together a group, it is important to consider the impact of a number of structural variables, such as the ideal group size for the purpose one has in mind, the gender of the potential group members, and their racial and ethnic backgrounds.

Group Size

The optimum size for a group varies, depending on its purpose and task; however, most group dynamicists would agree that five to seven persons is the ideal size for group discussion. This size is small enough to permit a high level of participation, and the odd number prevents a deadlock, which is an important feature

in making decisions. This is also a good size in terms of member satisfaction. As the size of the group increases, group members often feel more anxious and hesitant to speak up and therefore tend to participate less often. Consequently, in larger groups, a few members often dominate the discussion and the rest of the group membership may feel less satisfied and may interact less (Levine & Moreland, 1990, p. 593).

Gender of Group Members

Cultural values concerning the role of women in society are changing rapidly; consequently, research findings about gender differences in small group behavior may not accurately represent reality by the time they are published.

The only fairly well-established biologically based difference between males and females that may have some repercussions on group participation is that males are bigger, stronger, and more aggressive than females (McLoughlin, Shryer, Goode, & McAuliffe, 1988; Maccoby, 1990). The greater aggressiveness of men may hold women back in their verbal participation and may be a reason why male group members are often perceived as more influential than female group members.

Other possible differences in the behaviors of men and women in groups are likely to be primarily related to social factors. For example, since women still have lower status and prestige than men in U.S. society, they may be more inclined, on average, to be submissive or deferential toward male group members, particularly older women who are likely to be more traditional in their sex role-playing.

The ratio of males to females in the group appears to determine at least in part how well women fare in them. Females are often negatively evaluated in groups in which males predominate, particularly in skewed groups in which females are solo members or "tokens." This appears to hold even when the women have some influence on the group decision

(Martin & Shanahan, 1983). As the proportion of females in mixed-gender groups increases, their performance is enhanced. For example, in a study of human relations training groups (T-groups) with a college student membership of 60 percent male and 40 percent female, Mabry (1989) found that, proportionately, women participated more than men both in terms of instrumental and expressive behaviors and showed a significant degree of verbal dominance. Still, the female group members were perceived as less competent and less powerful leaders than the males (Morrison & Stein, 1985).

Martin and Shanahan (1983) recommended that practitioners become actively involved in helping group members to overcome the undesirable effects of sex composition. Perhaps the most important strategy is to compose mixed-sex groups so that they are balanced in terms of male and female members, whenever this is possible. When the group's representation of males and females is about equal, members are more likely to be viewed as individuals, sex stereotypes are less likely to operate, and the influence of female members is enhanced. In addition, groups that are balanced as to the sex of their participants have a positive effect on men; specifically, in such groups men become more personable, less competitive, and less aggressive and controlling. Mixed-sex groups that cannot be balanced should have a minimum of two females to attenuate the negative effects of tokenism.

Another useful strategy to reduce the undesirable effects of sex composition is to legitimize the right of women to assume leadership and task-related roles in groups. Sometimes this can be accomplished by holding elections for the key positions in the group, such as chairperson. If a female wins the election fair and square, her role has been legitimized by the group members. The practitioner can also encourage women members not to shy away from demonstrating their competence relative to the group task and their willingness to assist the group in accomplishing its tasks. Research shows that competent and highly motivated females can be influential in mixed groups.

Racial and Ethnic Background of Group Members

Race and ethno-cultural background are among the most prominent characteristics that individuals bring into the group; therefore, it is important that the practitioner be especially sensitive to their potential effects. For example, many Native Americans do not like to be given advice, help, or opinions unless they ask for them. Consequently, the group worker or group members who volunteer unsolicited assistance risk alienation, regardless of how good their intentions may be. This section will consider some of the issues and challenges faced by small groups with African American, Latino, and Asian American members. Next, some of the strategies that have been found to be effective in including members from diverse groups will be discussed.

African Americans

It is difficult for some African Americans and Euro-Americans to have meaningful interactions individually or in groups because of mutual suspicion, discomfort with one another, or a lack of knowledge of one another's historical background and social circumstances. Consequently, running a racially mixed group often is a challenging task for the practitioner. If the group worker is Euro-American and the group members are African American, the members may resist, challenge, or reject the worker not only because he or she may be perceived as insufficiently knowledgeable about or insensitive to issues of concern to African Americans but because they may be reluctant to accept Euro-American leadership. If the group membership is racially mixed, some may never have had intense or close contact with persons of a different race. Under such circumstances, interactions may be anxiety producing for some African Americans and Euro-Americans, but particularly for Euro-Americans since African Americans, as a group, usually have had more exposure and contact with Euro-Americans (Davis, 1984).

In creating a mixed-race group, the ratio of African-Americans to Euro-Americans is an important consideration. According to Davis (1984), African Americans tend to prefer to participate in racially balanced groups—that is, groups with about an equal number of African Americans and Euro-Americans. Euro-Americans, on the other hand, appear to prefer groups in which they predominate and may be reluctant to participate in groups in which they are in the minority. Any significant departure from whatever racial mixture is comfortable for group members is bound to produce some discomfort, dissatisfaction, and perhaps even some defections from the group. At a minimum, all groups should include at least two members of any one race to reduce the possibility of tokenism and scapegoating and to provide each member with a second opinion by which to check his or her perception of social reality.

Davis (1984) suggested that group members in a racially mixed group get into an early discussion of the group's racial composition so that they may have an opportunity to express any concerns they might have about it and to give sanction to race as a legitimate topic for group discussion. There is always some danger of heightening racial tensions in the group if the group worker introduces race as a topic, but the probability of relieving tension by openly acknowledging the racial dimension is usually greater.

Trust is another basic issue in racially mixed groups to which group workers must be sensitive. Some African-American group members, in particular, may feel, at least initially, that the nonblack group participants have insufficient understanding of the realities of their lives or that the nonblack members are insensitive about their concerns. They may show distrust by not engaging in self-disclosure or in-depth discussions, by remaining silent, by participating superficially or infrequently, by skipping sessions, by coming late or leaving early, or by dropping out from the group. Davis (1984) suggested that some of the distrust may disappear in time, if the group stays together long enough and if the group worker consistently encourages the development of trust.

In interracial groups, the worker must also be attentive to status and role issues. Due to the lower social status and subordinate roles that were assigned to African Americans in the United States until recently, older blacks in racially mixed groups may participate less than they might if they were in an all-black group. Another possible reason for the lower rate of participation of some African-American group members might be a feeling that their contributions are not appreciated or that they are considered less important than Euro-American group members. This might cause black group members to feel alienated. In either case, the group worker must remain vigilant to make sure that African-American group members are encouraged to participate in the group and that their attempts at participation are not thwarted or ignored.

Latinos

In forming and conducting groups with Latinos, language is a fundamental consideration. Some Latinos cannot express themselves well in English; others speak English well but not well enough to talk about their personal problems or feelings in English. If the group is conducted in Spanish or if members are allowed to express themselves in either language, Spanish or English, group cohesion and communication is usually enhanced. This flexibility is possible only if the group members and the practitioner are bilingual.

When composing a group, practitioners, out of necessity, many times tend to lump together persons of different Spanish origins, such as Mexicans, Puerto Ricans, Cubans, Nicaraguans, and Colombians, to mention a few. It is important to keep in mind that clients who come from different countries have distinct cultures. Although this diversity may not necessarily present a problem to the group (Acosta & Yamamoto, 1984), the practitioner should be cautious not to assume that group members are more similar than they actually are simply because they speak the same language and are familiar with the Hispanic culture to various degrees (Davis & Proctor, 1989). Another common problem in composing groups of Latinos is that of putting together persons of different ages. This should be avoided as much as possible since it can create a communication gap between older and younger participants who tend to have different perspectives and levels of acculturation to the U.S. culture (Delgado & Humm-Delgado, 1984).

Because traditional Latinos, particularly recent immigrants, tend to be more hierarchical in their relationships than non-Latins, they may expect the group leader to act as an authority figure, actively providing advice, interpretations, and suggestions to deal with problems (Delgado, 1981). An action orientation rather than a strictly talk-oriented approach often works well with recent immigrants, with emphasis on finding concrete solutions to current problems. Structured activities, such as role-playing and modeling, bringing foods and eating them together, and invitational lectures often work well also. Frequently, an important aspect of the group worker's role with Latinos and other group members of low socioeconomic status is to act as advocate and service broker, intervening in the community on behalf of the group members and teaching them to negotiate the system (Delgado, 1981; Delgado & Humm-Delgado, 1984).

Asian Americans

Given their cultural backgrounds, Asian Americans are often reluctant to engage in self-disclosure or to share their feelings with strangers. Many consider it inappropriate to call attention to themselves by discussing their personal prob-

lems in a group and think it is impolite to interrupt others. Because of their preference for indirect forms of communication, Asians often consider open confrontation and criticism, which are common in groups, to be offensive and impolite. Therefore, they may be reluctant to participate in groups, particularly treatment groups. Yet, Asians can be excellent group members because of the value they place on interdependence and cooperation; therefore, they can be expected to be supportive of one another and to work jointly on common goals (Chu & Sue, 1984; Ho, 1984).

For those who have migrated to the United States recently, racially and ethnically homogeneous groups (e.g., all Cambodian, all Vietnamese, or all Hmong) may be more appropriate than racially or ethnically mixed groups, at least initially (Chu & Sue, 1984). This is because in mixed groups, particularly those including non-Asian members, some Asian participants may be even more reluctant to speak up, to interrupt, or to take the lead. Similarly, because of pronounced status differences between the sexes in various Asian cultures, Asian females who have recently arrived in the United States may feel uncomfortable in a group with men or in a group led by a man.

In working with Asians, often it is important for the group practitioner to be directive in a nonthreatening, nonconfrontational way. For example, it may be necessary for the group leader to encourage the group members to speak up and to ask specific questions in order to get group members to talk about themselves (Chu & Sue, 1984). Structured discussions of various topics (e.g., how to balance family and work or how to be more assertive) may help to make group members feel more comfortable. Modeling and role-playing can also be effective to show group members how to be more assertive and more open in expressing feelings.

In summary, group practitioners working with clients from diverse racial and ethnic groups, particularly clients of lower socioeconomic status and recent immigration, should put emphasis on delivering concrete services, providing active leadership, paying immediate attention to problem solving, recognizing the environment as a contributing factor to the clients' problems, facilitating empowerment, and acting as brokers and advocates (Garvin, 1987; Davis & Proctor, 1989, p. 115).

The Assembly Effect

Individuals contribute differently to the group, depending on their own characteristics and the particular others with whom they are assembled. Therefore, in composing a group, it is important to consider the effects of putting together a particular configuration of potential members. For example, if you put four aggressive people in one group, you are going to get a different kind of group dynamic than if you combine two passive and two aggressive people or four quiet and shy people. Similarly if you assemble four men and one woman, you are going to get a different group dynamic than if you compose an all-female group. The term **assembly effect** is used to refer to the consequences on group behavior of putting together a particular collection of individuals versus another potential set.

Cohesiveness

One possible assembly effect is **cohesiveness,** or the degree to which group members like one another and the group as a whole and desire to remain a part of it. A cohesive group has a sense of community and solidarity, a "we-feeling" that prompts members to get together and stay together and to enjoy one another's company. Some of the factors that foster group cohesiveness are similarity of members in terms of various characteristics such as race, gender, nationality, cultural/ethnic background, age, common interests, skills or type of problems experienced; an atmosphere of open communication and noncompetitiveness; relatively small size of the group;

and the group's ability to meet the needs and expectations of its membership (Shaw, 1981; Toseland & Rivas, 1984).

Group cohesiveness is important because it is associated with positive results such as active participation, willingness of members to engage in self-disclosure, mutual liking, cooperativeness, and friendliness toward other group members. In turn, these factors promote achievement of group goals and greater enjoyment and satisfaction (Shaw, 1981; Levine & Moreland, 1990).

Cohesiveness has some potential disadvantages, however. One possible problem is groupthink (Janis, 1982). **Groupthink** refers to certain defective group processes that occur when there is too much pressure toward uniformity and conformity in highly cohesive groups. These defective group processes include the tendency to make decisions without evaluating their possible consequences, to disregard ethical considerations, to fail to get sufficient information, to ignore discrepant information, and to fail to fully consider alternatives. Groupthink may lead members to censor themselves so as not to disagree, keeping silent about their misgivings and doubts. If they momentarily express concerns about the group's shared illusions, they are likely to be censored by the other group members and pressured into agreement.

To prevent groupthink, Janis (1982) recommended that groups encourage their members to be critical, to play the devil's advocate, to air openly any disagreements, objections, or doubts, and to search for a wide range of alternatives without prematurely taking sides or stating preferences. In addition, it often pays to invite outside experts to express their opinions and to encourage group members to challenge one another's views.

Homogeneity/Heterogeneity

A fundamental assembly effect to consider when putting together a group is its degree of homogeneity or heterogeneity. A group may be homogeneous with respect to a single trait—for example, a group of unwed mothers—or it may be homogeneous with respect to a number of characteristics, such as gender, race, cultural background, social class, and age. Groups that are homogeneous in terms of several member characteristics are called *profile* homogeneous. For example, a group of African-American, teenage mothers on Aid to Families with Dependent Children (AFDC) conducted by a family service agency in an inner-city area is profile homogeneous, at least in terms of race, gender, ethnic background, age, economic status, and residence.

Task groups that are profile heterogeneous in terms of characteristics *relevant* to the group task usually perform more effectively than groups that are profile homogeneous. This is because when group members have varied opinions, abilities, skills, and perspectives, there is greater chance that the group as a whole will possess the characteristics and skills necessary for efficient group performance (Hoffman & Maier, 1961). However, when profile heterogeneity includes diversity in terms of race, ethnicity, or socioeconomic background, there are likely to be some differences in values, lifestyles, modes of expression, and expectations among the group members that may generate conflict and feelings of discomfort and distance. These discrepancies must be addressed within the group. To be sure, leading a profile heterogeneous group is more demanding and challenging than leading a homogeneous group.

GROUP DYNAMICS

This section will examine several major group processes, including communication, leadership, problem solving, and decision making. Other processes that also operate in groups—such as power and authority relations, conflict, and politics—were discussed in Chapters 5 and 6 on communities and organizations.

The Communication Process

Communication, or the exchange of verbal and nonverbal messages, is the most basic of all group interaction processes. It begins when an individual (the sender) wishes to convey some message, verbal or nonverbal, to another individual (the receiver). The material to be shared must be **encoded,** or placed in understandable form for transmission. To this end, the sender carefully selects words or nonverbal symbols that will convey the meanings in a manner that the receiver will understand. Then the sender transmits the message to the receiver through one or more channels. For example, the sender may speak to the receiver, thus transmitting the message through the auditory channel, or the message may be sent through the visual channel if it is written (see Figure 7.1).

Once received, the message must be **decoded**, or interpreted by the receiver. Suppose that the sender conveyed two messages, one verbally and the other through gestures, and that the two messages were contradictory. The meaning would differ greatly, depending on whether the receiver focused on what was said or on the body language. Let us assume, however, that the message sent was not particularly inconsistent. Still, it might have been distorted to some extent by the receiver due to selective perception. Based on socialization into a particular cultural group, past experiences, and personal likes and dislikes, each communicator has a unique system of personal meanings through which the individual filters all incoming and outgoing messages. Therefore, to fully understand what the sender is trying to communicate, the receiver would have to be able to enter the sender's private world of meanings. This is seldom completely possible.

In addition to the misunderstandings that may arise from selective perception, communication may be distorted by various types of **noise,** or interference. For example, there may

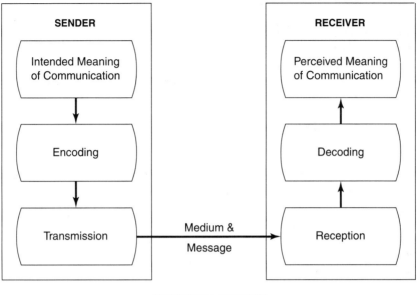

FIGURE 7.1   Components of the Communication Process

Source: Reprinted with the permission of Simon & Schuster, Inc. from the Macmillan College text *Understanding Organizational Behavior* by Robert E. Callahan, Patrick C. Fleenor and Harry R. Knudson. Copyright ©1986 by Merrill, an imprint of Macmillan College Publishing Company, Inc.

be interference due to language barriers or other obstacles, such as hearing impairments or speech impediments, or another conversation taking place close by may interfere with reception. All this means that communicators usually work under conditions of less than perfect understanding.

Another basic component of the communication process is feedback. **Feedback** is the reaction or response of the receiver to the sender's message. It provides information to the sender about how well the message was understood or accepted. Thus, if necessary, other messages can be sent until, through the feedback loop, the sender is fairly certain that the message has been properly understood.

Verbal Forms of Communication

Verbal communication takes place primarily through two channels—hearing and sight—depending on whether the message is oral or written. Oral communication frequently involves additional channels besides the auditory. When a person talks, we attend to his or her facial expression, tone of voice, eye contact, gestures, body movements, and other nonverbal clues. In contrast, written communication depends strictly on what is recorded on paper. No other clues are usually available to help us decode the written message.

This section focuses on oral communication because it is the usual method of communication in small face-to-face groups. Its major components are language and paralanguage. Communication through **language** involves words that are supposed to have standard meanings. But even when people speak the same language and share the same culture, socioeconomic circumstances, gender, and age, they frequently hold different meanings for the same words because their life experiences have not been identical.

Paralanguage includes the optional vocal effects that accompany an utterance and make it less monotonous and more meaningful. These include voice tone, inflection, speed, volume, and use of silence and pauses. Voice *tone* offers some indication of the speaker's attitude; for example, a group member may talk with a decisive, angry, or tentative tone. *Inflection* is a change of tone normally accomplished by changing the voice pitch from high to low or vice versa. *Volume* can be used to emphasize certain points; for instance, some people develop the habit of raising their voices to stress a point or to get someone's attention, while others prefer to lower their voices to almost a whisper to draw attention to what they are saying. Similarly, sometimes people change the *speed* with which they speak, depending on the importance of the message being conveyed; for instance, they may speak slowly when going over important points and move quickly over less important material.

Silence also can be used effectively in oral communication. Sometimes it means that the receiver is listening attentively. In the form of long *pauses*, a lack of response, or a blank stare, it may be used to convey various messages. For example, if a group member wishes to stress a point, she may choose to pause right before it to attract the listener's attention. Or, if one member speaks to another and the other does not respond, the silence may indicate distractibility, acceptance of what was said, disrespect, disagreement, or anger, depending on how it is interpreted.

Nonverbal Communication

When people speak, they usually emit certain body cues, such as gestures and facial expressions. To communicate effectively, group members must pay attention to these nonverbal messages. Nonverbal communication includes body language (e.g., facial expression, eye contact, hand gestures, and body posture) as well as other factors such as physical distance and physical contact people maintain when they communicate. The meaning of many forms of nonverbal communication varies from culture to culture. This is one of the reasons why there is often confusion and misunderstanding in groups that include people from diverse cultures.

Facial Expression. Without saying a word, just by your facial expression, you can convey many different feelings, such as disagreement or agreement, happiness or sadness, approval or disapproval, anger or happiness, fear, surprise, or disgust. Some people are very good at reading faces. For example, a group member may be particularly adept at detecting the disapproval behind a smile, the reservations behind a gesture of agreement, or the anger or hostility behind a joke. Others may be particularly good at controlling their facial expressions. A group can function with greater sensitivity and effectiveness when its members are competent at reading the facial expressions, including the masked facial expressions, of its members.

Eye Contact. Eye contact may be used in a group setting to invite interaction. If a group member seeks to establish eye contact with another and the other avoids the individual's gaze, this can be interpreted to mean that interaction is not desired. Eye contact also serves to convey trustworthiness and self-confidence. Group members who look at others in the eye while speaking to them are usually regarded as more believable and self-assured than those who do not (Argyle & Dean, 1965). However, one must be careful in the use and interpretation of eye-contact behavior because it varies from culture to culture. For example, people from various Arab countries and from France traditionally maintain high levels of eye contact in their social interactions. In contrast, Native Americans and many Asians often consider high levels of eye contact to be rude and disrespectful.

Body Movement. People communicate their attitudes and feelings through various body movements. For instance, a person who is constantly changing posture may be conveying boredom, tension, nervousness, or impatience. Group members usually nod or shake their heads to indicate agreement or disagreement since they are unable to react by emitting the usual "mm-hum" or "I see" response that is frequently used in two-person transactions. Sometimes they lean back on their seats, moving away from the group; this may be indicative of relaxation in an informal setting, but in a formal meeting it might be taken as indication of lack of involvement or boredom. As with other forms of nonverbal communication, cultural differences often confound the interpretation of body movements. Asian Indians, for example, move their heads up and down to signify no and from side to side to indicate yes.

Territory and Personal Space. The amount of space separating two people in a group is a function of many different factors, such as their cultural background, the setting, the space available, the nature of the task, the members' gender, their degree of acquaintantship, and the status and respect they accord to one another. For instance, female group members tend to sit closer to one another than to male group members, and males usually keep greater distance among themselves than females. Group members who dislike or do not know one another usually sit further apart than those who like each other or who are well acquainted. If the task is informal, group members may feel more comfortable sitting closely together than if they are having a business meeting. Interpretations of spatial behavior become more complicated if the group members are culturally diverse because space is used differently in various cultures. By U.S. standards, for example, men in Arab countries sit uncomfortably close together.

Touching. Group members rely primarily on language to communicate, but they sometimes touch to reinforce verbal comments or to communicate encouragement or emotional support. For instance, a group member may touch another's shoulder while verbally expressing congratulations or sympathy. Although touch may be more effective than words in some situations, it may be detrimental if the person who is touched is not receptive to it. Group practitioners should always keep in mind that touch is an invasion of the personal space of another person and that some people react to it with anxiety, anger, or feelings of threat. Therefore, much sensitivity and caution are needed in communicating through touch. Norms for touching also vary from culture to culture. For example, as a group, Asians would be less receptive to touch than Latinos.

Personal Appearance as Nonverbal Communication. Group members make inferences about one another on the basis of their appearance. For instance, a social service agency director who comes to a board of directors meeting wearing jeans and a loud shirt when everyone else is wearing business attire may be perceived as rebellious, off-beat, or ultraliberal. This may not be an accurate representation of the individual, but it is the impression some people might get. Once formed, these initial stereotypical impressions are difficult to modify.

A group member's physical appearance may also affect his or her self-image and group interactions. For example, if an individual feels that he looks well groomed, he may participate more actively and confidently and be more tolerant of the opinions of others in the group than if he were feeling self-conscious or dissatisfied about his appearance.

Communication Networks

Some groups have highly centralized **communication networks,** such as the *wheel* in Figure

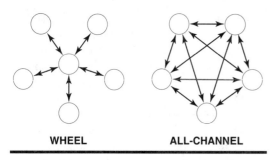

WHEEL   **ALL-CHANNEL**

FIGURE 7.2   Common Communication Networks

7.2. In this type of arrangement, the group leader communicates freely with every member, but the members can communicate with each other only through the leader. Some formal group meetings and classroom activities are conducted in this fashion: The leader speaks to the group, and the participants respond when recognized by the leader, but they are discouraged from carrying on individual conversations with one another while the group is in session. Such highly centralized networks can be efficient if the task is simple or if the principal objective of the meeting is to disseminate information.

When the group task is complex, a decentralized network, such as the *all-channel* system in Figure 7.2, is superior to the wheel. This is because, in order to deal effectively with a complex problem, the group needs to integrate a much greater amount of information, and this can be accomplished better by open communication. The all-channel communication network is also the appropriate communication system for growth and treatment groups because a high level of interaction among members is desirable in such groups. Cohesiveness, morale, and satisfaction are also higher in decentralized systems such as the all-channel system (Shaw, 1964; Fisher & Ellis, 1990).

In reality, most groups often shift from one communication pattern to another, depending on the circumstances. For example, a group may occasionally meet for informational or consultative sessions that are held following the wheel arrangement and yet at other times, it may engage in free discussions using the all-channel pattern.

Barriers and Gateways to Communication

One of the greatest barriers to effective communication is the natural tendency to evaluate and pass judgment on what others say. Even positive judgments can be threatening because the person receiving them is put on notice that his or her utterances are being evaluated and that approval can turn into criticism at any point.

One way to improve communication in groups is to get in the habit of withholding judgment and listening with understanding. This requires that group members be able to assume one another's points of view. One way is to respond only after having restated the thoughts and feelings of the previous speaker to the person's satisfaction (Rogers & Roethlisberger, 1977). Communication in groups can also be improved by insisting that members send specific and clear messages, that the group members focus on issues and not on personalities, that each member makes an effort to balance negative comments with positive ones, and that good timing is employed (Haslett & Ogilvie, 1988, p. 397).

Leadership

Leadership is a reciprocal process whereby the leader is allowed by the group members to influence, motivate, or empower them to pursue the group's goals. Several key features of this definition should be noted. First, it emphasizes that the relationship between group leader and members is mutual. The leader directs, guides, empowers, or facilitates the group members' behavior, and the members accept the guidance and assistance of the leader. Second, it represents leadership as a process of legitimate influence rather than as a characteristic inherent in any one individual. Third, it stresses that leadership cannot be imposed; it must be accepted voluntarily by the group members.

Factors Affecting Leadership

Various factors help in attaining leadership of a group, including central location, active participation, and expertise in the group task. Specifically, the person who holds a central position in the group's communication network and who sits in a location providing maximum eye contact with group members increases his or her likelihood of emerging as group leader (Shaw, 1981, p. 319). For instance, the person sitting at the head of the table has an initial advantage. Active participation is another important factor that facilitates the attainment of leadership. The person who participates the most in the group has the highest probability of becoming the leader (Stodgill, 1974), as long as he or she speaks sensibly and does not overtalk to the point of antagonizing the group members.

Apparently, quantity of participation gives the person the right to influence the group because it is often perceived by group members as an indication of interest and involvement in the group's task and willingness to work toward its accomplishment. Quality of participation, per se, appears to be less associated with the attainment of leadership in the group. However, if the group members know that a given individual is a recognized expert in their task, this person need not be overly participative in order to be offered the leadership of the group (Sorrentino & Boutillier, 1975).

Some group leaders are more effective than others, depending on their leadership style. Various basic styles have been identified such as task- or relationship—centered and directive or nondirective. You may recall from Chapter 6 that **task-oriented leaders** are those who concentrate on establishing operating procedures, initiating action, providing expert information, motivating members toward goal achievement, and evaluating movement toward goals. In short, although they may not necessarily be inattentive to group maintenance functions, their primary goal is to get the job done. In contrast, **relationship-oriented leaders** put primary emphasis on group maintenance functions, such as facilitating open communication and participation of group members in the group's activities, providing support and encouragement, showing concern, and seeking to establish strong interpersonal links. Although not necessarily disinterested in the group task, they put emphasis on maintenance functions. Perhaps the most effective group leaders are those who can use a **coaching style**—that is, those who can simultaneously focus on the group task and on member relationships (Blake & Mouton, 1964; Stogdill, 1974; Sorrentino & Field, 1986).

Many studies have shown that the effectiveness of a leadership approach depends on different factors. One important factor is the level of *maturity* of the group members or the extent to which they can responsibly and confidently perform their task and pursue their goals without active direction from the group leader. According to Hershey and Blanchard (1977), immature group members (e.g., chronic mental patients or the mildly retarded) do best under task-oriented leaders. Group members at medium levels of maturity (and the majority of group members fall in this category) do better under leaders who concentrate primarily on relationship behaviors, alternating between being more or less task oriented as needed. Mature group members function best when given maximum latitude by the group leader. For example, when working with a subcommittee of a professional organization or with the board of trustees of a public hospital, the group leader generally would do best to be **nondirective,** assuming a staff function and allowing the group to conduct itself.

The effectiveness of a leadership style also depends on the purpose or function of the group. For example, if the group's purpose is remedial (e.g., a treatment group aiming to habilitate or rehabilitate individuals suffering from chronic mental disorders), an active, **directive** leadership style may be the most indicated. Here, the practitioner offers group members feedback, advice, interpretations, suggestions, information, and even tells them what to do or not to do (Garvin, 1987; Rose, 1989). In general, the more deteriorated the social health or competence of the group members, the more active and directive the group worker should be (Heap, 1985). On the other hand, if the function of the group is mutual aid, such as in the case of various self-help groups, the leader would be expected to act as a resource person, mediating and facilitating interaction and using a coaching style.

In the section entitled Leadership Processes in Chapter 6, we considered other important factors that determine what leadership style works best under various group situations, such as the quality of the leader/member relations, the degree of structure of the group task, and the amount of power the leader has within the group. You may want to review this section again.

Problem Solving and Decision Making

Social service practitioners spend a considerable amount of time working in groups. In their work roles and as community members, they attend many different meetings and participate in a large variety of staff meetings, committees, interdisciplinary teams, conferences, and task forces. In these task groups they work on many projects from reorganizing their work unit so that it is more efficient and responsive to its clientele to developing services to individuals with drug problems, developing a program to prevent adolescent pregnancy, or a program to provide a safe place for victims of family violence or shelter for the homeless, just to mention a few possible endeavors. They can be more effective participants in task groups if they have a clear understanding of the processes of **problem solving** and **decision making.**

Individual versus Group Problem Solving and Decision Making

Groups generally produce more and better solutions to problems than individuals. Probably this is because groups often have more information available to them and more people to contribute to the solution and to correct possible errors. Specifically, with few exceptions, groups tend to develop better solutions to problems than individuals when the problem is highly complex, when it requires information gathering, when the problem is additive (i.e., when it can be solved by pooling individual contributions), and when the work can be divided up so that each person can concentrate on a part of the overall project (Shaw, 1981).

In terms of judgment, groups are usually at least as accurate as, and often better than individuals working alone. This is probably because there are more individual judgments contributing to the group judgment and the range of knowledge and experience of the group as a whole is usually greater than that of any individual member (Shaw, 1981; Fisher & Ellis, 1990).

Although groups generally solve problems better than individuals working alone, there are always some disadvantages to working in groups. For instance, group members tend to lose time organizing and coordinating their efforts, establishing procedural rules, and socializing. Individuals generally can work faster.

Various factors facilitate group problem solving or decision making—such as working conditions, including proper lighting, good ventilation and temperature, sound proofing, and pleasant wall colors. Other factors conducive to problem solving or decision making are a sitting arrangement that permits easy eye contact and communication, group size appropriate to the task, group members who get along well and who have diverse competencies, and good leadership. In contrast, pressures toward uniformity and conformity, uneven participation of group members, and status differences interfere with problem solving or decision making. As previously noted, pressures toward uniformity sometimes result in groupthink. Uneven participation is always a possibility as the group size increases because some group members feel uncomfortable when they have to speak before a large group. In addition, there is always the danger that those who talk the most may not have the best ideas or solutions or that they may prevent the group from utilizing all the information available. When such is the case, uneven participation can hurt the group. Similarly, status differences can be problematic when the higher-status group members prevent the group from fully utilizing its human resources (Shaw, 1981).

The Problem-Solving and Decision-Making Process

Many different approaches to problem solving and decision making have been suggested. The *rational* approach generally includes steps such as identification and definition of the task or problem, generation of alternative solutions, selection of the best solution, implementation of the decision, evaluation, and implementation of modifications, if needed. These steps do not necessarily have to take place in the sequence in which they are listed here.

In real life, groups seldom solve problems or make decisions in a structured, rational, or step-by-step manner. Sometimes group solutions and decisions *emerge* spontaneously without the group having followed any particular process (Fisher & Ellis, 1990, p. 153). For example, one of the practitioners at the local family service agency may mention during a staff meeting that she has heard that another agency handles a particular problem they are experiencing in such and such a manner. That may be

enough for the group to jump on that "solution" without any consideration as to whether or not it fits the rather different situational circumstances at their own agency. Other times, decisions are made outside the group and the group is used merely to window dress them, thus lending them an "air" of democratic process (Napier & Gershenfeld, 1989, p. 321). Still other times, groups make seat-of-the-pants or chaotic decisions with total disregard for process.

Cohen, March, and Olsen (1972) describe a "garbage can" model of decision making that one can often see in operation. According to this model, choices are made, as it were, by throwing problems and possible solutions in a can and shaking them up so that a problem gets randomly matched up with a solution without any logical relationship between the two. One group member may have been putting pressure on others to pay attention to her pet problem while another group member may have been attempting to sell one of his ideas. At a meeting, the group may well take the two issues and reframe them as "problem" and "solution."

This goes to show that some of what passes for problem solving or decision making is a sham. Therefore, it pays to have a good understanding of the rational aspects of these processes so that you may be in a better position to spot the phony, to resist manipulation, and to do a better job as a member or leader of a problem-solving or decision-making group. It is essential to keep in mind, however, that in most real-life situations, logic and rationality, in and of themselves, are not necessarily the most desirable approaches. The best problem solving and decision making often occur when groups are able to blend logic and rationality with intuition, imagination, and attention to the total situation including emotional and nonverbal aspects (Siebold, 1988).

Step 1. Problem Identification.   Before trying to solve any problem or to make a decision,

group members must understand and agree on what the problem is. Problem identification is the most critical, yet the most often neglected, part of the decision-making process (Boje, 1980). One of the most difficult tasks for the group at the problem identification stage is to separate the problem from its many symptoms, consequences, and even potential solutions. Consider, for example, a social agency director who wants to increase staff productivity and believes that the way to do this is to eliminate or limit personal telephone calls. She concentrates on thinking of ways to limit the employees' use of the telephone for personal calls, losing sight of the original goal of improving productivity. In this case, one possible solution—to limit personal telephone calls—becomes confused with the problem and, in pursuing it, the director loses the opportunity to consider better alternatives to increase productivity.

An important dictum for problem-solving groups to keep in mind is that "the starting point of a problem is richest in solution possi-

bilities" (Maier, 1979, p. 368). This means that if a group is truly interested in finding good solutions or in making good decisions, it must be willing to spend sufficient time analyzing the issue. The discussion leader can help by encouraging "problem-mindedness" and holding the group back from moving too quickly toward thinking about solutions. This can be difficult at times because some group members have "hidden agendas" and are more interested in lobbying on behalf of their pet solutions rather than in having the group carefully analyze the problem. The group leader and members must be alert to catch these manipulators and to ask them politely to withhold from offering suggestions until later (Boje, 1980).

Step 2. Generating Alternatives. Having agreed on the nature of the problem, the group can begin to think of alternative solutions. To this end, it is important that all criticisms or evaluations of the proposed alternatives be withheld during the process of generating ideas because evaluation inhibits free thinking (Maier, 1979,

Major business corporations give large amounts of money to community agencies that provide needed support services to their employees and families. These corporate executives are using problem-solving/decision-making methods to decide how to apportion the year's corporate giving budget.

p. 372). The group members may wish to brainstorm, particularly if the problem they face has no "correct" solution, such as when the group is to decide on the theme for a national child welfare conference or if the group has been empowered to reorganize a public assistance agency so it can offer better services to its clientele. In **brainstorming,** criticism, judgment, and evaluation are suspended and every member of the group is encouraged to offer as many ideas as possible, no matter how wild or crazy, and to combine and improve on one another's contributions.

In terms of quantity and quality of ideas generated, the **nominal grouping** technique may actually work better than brainstorming (Diehl & Stroebe, 1987). Under this system, group members independently list their suggested solutions without discussing them with others in the group. Then, all the written comments are read aloud and discussed, without identifying their authors. In a variation of this approach, referred to as *ringi* by the Japanese, the anonymous written suggestions are sent around the group to be edited and elaborated upon as many times as necessary (Zander, 1982, p. 23).

Throughout this stage, some group members may attempt to "hard sell" their ideas or to kill someone else's ideas by insisting that they will never work. It is the role of the group leader to keep these individuals in line by reminding them that challenging or promoting ideas must be saved for the evaluation phase.

Perhaps at some point during this second stage or at any other point during the problem-solving process, the group may realize that it has overlooked some important issues in defining the problem. Members must feel free to go back to the drawing board to redefine the problem as many times as necessary (Boje, 1980).

Step 3. Evaluating Alternatives. Having identified several alternatives, the group is ready to consider in detail the main strategies that have been generated. If the group members have come up with too many possible options, the group may want to rank order them and to limit its assessment of pros and cons to the top five choices. The assessment may be done by the entire group or by the members working individually to develop independent lists of pros and cons that can be combined later. The important thing is to give each of the alternative choices a complete hearing. This is why the list should not be too long.

To contribute their best thinking, members should feel free to disagree. In this respect, it is important to keep in mind that disagreements sometimes make people feel uncomfortable, angry, or hurt and often generate defensive responses or counterattacks (Maier, 1979). To avoid discomfort, many group members would rather conform than disagree, but by so doing they compromise the problem-solving process. One of the most important tasks of the group leader during the assessment stage is to protect diverse opinions and to encourage group members to be less defensive and more respectful of differences of opinion.

Some group members get their egos tied up with their own ideas and take it personally when they are criticized. When this occurs, the group leader would do well to remind the group that personal ownership of ideas interferes with good problem solving and should be avoided. In fact, it may be best for the group leader to warn group members in advance about this and other common pitfalls in the process of problem solving/decision making.

Another possible problem the group may experience while evaluating alternatives is groupthink. Members may place such high value on getting along that they may pressure one another to agree on a given choice, perhaps that which is favored by the more powerful member(s) of the group. To counter this tendency, as previously noted, it is advisable that as many group members as possible play the role of critical evaluator. Group leaders would also do well to refrain from stating their opinions or passing judgment concerning the alternatives being considered. This is due to the fact that because of the leaders' central position in the group, their ideas tend to be given more or less weight than those of other group members, depending on whether they are liked, disliked, or feared by the membership (Boje, 1980).

Step 4. Making a Decision.   Groups need not always use the same decision-making method, such as taking a vote. Different methods are appropriate under different circumstances. For instance, when member support for the decision or their involvement in its implementation is important or when a high-quality decision is needed to avoid potentially harmful consequences, it is best to decide by **consensus**—that is, by the unanimous agreement of all group members. Sometimes, however, the decision is less momentous or the group does not have sufficient time to work toward consensus since this process takes a long time. In such cases, the group members may decide to vote and let the majority win. **Rank ordering** is a variation of this approach. In rank ordering alternatives, the group members rate them independently and reach a decision on the basis of their combined rankings.

One danger during the decision stage is the rush to finish (Boje, 1980). If group members are tired and hurrying to end the session, it may be better, if possible, to postpone decision making until they are rested and have more time available. Another pitfall to avoid at this stage is the member who pushes for a particular decision, suggesting that there is more agreement around it than there is in actuality. The group leader can usually counter this pressure by checking with members to ascertain their degree of agreement or disagreement with the proposed solution.

Step 5. Implementation, Evaluation, and Adjustment.   Before implementing a decision, it is advisable for the group to do a reality check (Boje, 1980). Does the proposed solution actually solve the problem? Sometimes group members get carried away and build "lead balloons." Therefore, before implementation, members should have a chance to reflect about the chosen strategy and to think through its implications. It is also good practice to consult the people who will be affected and to have them criticize the solution. The point is that if the solution does not seem to fit the situation well, a lot of aggravation can be avoided if possible problems are identified and addressed in advance of implementation.

Having settled on a particular plan of action, the group is finally ready to work out the details of how the plan will be put into practice. If the group does not work out the details of how its decision will be implemented and how to monitor its implementation, there is a high probability that the decision will be shelved and forgotten. In fact, one of the biggest disappointments associated with task groups is that after all their work and effort, often nothing is done to implement the decisions and recommendations made by the group. To give the chosen plan a better chance of being put to practice, it is advisable for committee members to break it down into action steps to be implemented by certain target dates, with individual group members taking responsibility for seeing that each step is accomplished.

After implementation, it is important to follow up and to get feedback as to whether the plan is working. Sometimes strategies that appear well suited to the circumstances fail to work because of contingencies that were not anticipated; in such cases, it becomes necessary to make adjustments.

STAGES IN GROUP DEVELOPMENT

Various theories have been formulated to account for the developmental changes that groups undergo during their life span.

Recurring Phase Theories

According to recurring phase theories, different issues tend to be central to a group at various phases of development. These issues often emerge without following any consistent order and often resurface at various points in the life of the group. For example, according to Robert Bales's equilibrium or balance theory of group development (1955), task groups strive to maintain a balance between task-oriented actions and emotionally expressive behaviors, sometimes focusing on relationships and sometimes shifting back toward a greater concentration on the task. Similarly, studies have shown that therapeutic groups tend to fluctuate between various basic themes, such as confrontation and evasion of problems (Bennis & Shepard, 1956).

Sequential Stage Theories

Sequential stage theories specify the typical phases a group goes through during its life. However, it is important to stress that these stages seldom unfold neatly along a linear continuum. Instead, groups often move back and forth between stages in response to changes in membership or to various problems and conflicts that arise during their life. When a group revisits previously experienced issues or goes back to themes characteristic of an earlier stage, this does not necessarily mean that the group is regressing. Rather, it may be reworking or consolidating matters that previously it had not settled completely (Ephross & Vassil, 1988).

Having reviewed many studies of laboratory, natural, and therapy groups, Tuckman and Jensen (1977) suggested five basic stages in the development of a group: forming, storming, norming, performing, and adjourning. During the *forming* stage, the group is constituted and its members begin to relate to one another, initially in a tentative and often polite manner. Conflict usually arises during the second phase (*storming*) as group members begin to disagree, to compete, and to criticize one another's ideas. Eventually, during the *norming* stage, the group becomes more cohesive as members begin to feel they belong together, they develop operating procedures, and, they begin to play different roles, with some members developing

higher status than others within the group. During the *performing* stage, group members reach the peak of their cooperative effort, engage in less conflict, and concentrate on working on their task. In the *adjourning* phase, the group's work is completed, some members express regret and sadness at having to separate, and the group comes to an end. Northen's (1988) conceptualization of group development is similar, including the stages of orientation-inclusion, dissatisfaction and power conflict, mutuality-work, and separation-termination.

Blending the Two Models

Both recurring phase and sequential stage models provide useful concepts for understanding group development. Other conceptualizations of group development include a blending of the two approaches—for example, that of Sarri and Galinsky (1985) and of Balgopal and Vassil (1983) in the field of social work. The following is a synthesis of the group developmental process that takes into account both its recurring and sequential dimensions.

Phase 1. Constituting the Group. During phase 1, the group is put together, taking into consideration the types of problems that clients are experiencing as well as compositional variables such as ideal group size, age of the potential participants, gender, ethnicity, and type of participation (voluntary vs. involuntary). Agency characteristics that will support or constrain the group experience—such as fees, time constraints, and facilities available—are also considered. In task groups, this is the time when group members and a chairperson are appointed and a charge is prepared for the group.

Phase 2. Normative Phase. During phase 2, members cautiously begin to participate and to form relationships. Initially, the members may be considerably dependent on the leader, frequently silent, self-conscious, and looking for one another's reactions. Soon, they begin to form interpersonal ties and to develop a quasi-structure as they begin to play different roles, such as leader and member (the former played by the most assertive and aggressive group participants and the latter by the rest of the group membership). Members also begin to define the group's basic norms on the basis of their common values and attitudes and to make up rules concerning behaviors that are acceptable and unacceptable. Some begin to test boundaries and to challenge rules. Members also begin to get into pairs and other subgroups to address their interests and needs and to manage tension and conflict.

Phase 3. The Middle Phase: Conflict, Mutuality, and Work. During the intermediate phase, members develop a closer relationship and begin to get involved in goal-directed activities. Specialized roles become more clearly differentiated, such as the roles of task and socioemotional leaders. Cliques and subgroups also become more apparent. Group members develop additional norms and social control mechanisms that they begin to apply as members deviate from the established rules. Pressures toward uniformity and consensus become apparent. Because members have experienced some events in common, they begin to build a common tradition and common values.

Sometimes during the middle phase there is a challenge to and revision of the previous leadership structure and of the norms and goals the group has developed. It happens most often when the group leader is aggressive and attempts to prevent other members from engaging in leadership activities. Generally, as a result of the revisions that take place, more group members begin to assume leadership functions in their areas of competence and roles become increasingly more differentiated. Norms, values, purposes and goals, and traditions of the group may be changed in varying degrees during this stage, or, if they are not changed, at least they are clarified further by the group members. Not all groups experience an

identifiable challenge or revision; however, almost all experience some structural modifications as a more complex division of labor emerges and roles become more differentiated.

As members establish closer interpersonal ties, and the group becomes better integrated and more cohesive, they become increasingly involved in goal-related activities. Roles become more specialized, and subgroups, norms, values, and traditions become more firmly established. With increasing interaction, group members develop more intense feelings and reactions, positive or negative, toward each other. Conflicts and crises may emerge at this or any other point due to internal or environmental issues, and the group must address these challenges.

Once the group has reached full maturity, it can focus most productively on its work. Successful groups reach maturity and are able to remain at this stage until their goals are attained. Others disintegrate before they reach this point or revert to more primitive stages.

Phase 4. Termination Phase. The final phase of a group comes when its goals are attained, the allotted time has elapsed, or the group disintegrates due to maladaptation. Few groups reach the end with perfect composure and only positive feelings.

Typically, during the termination phase, members engage in a recapitulation of the group experience and a review of its accomplishments. In treatment groups in particular, members may express anger toward other members or toward the group practitioner, feelings of uncertainty about the future, and concern as to whether they will continue to receive support from group members, if needed, after the group is dissolved. As the separation becomes imminent, some members may express feelings of loss, mourning, or abandonment, feelings of regret that not all the group's goals were accomplished, or envy that other members accomplished more than they did.

Sometimes the final group meeting is memorialized by a party, the taking of pictures, and an exchange of addresses and telephone numbers. Some members leave with feelings of sadness that the group has ended, others and with anticipation about new beginnings.

One important aspect of your job in the human services will be to work with task and treatment groups within your agency and in the community. In this chapter, you have learned about theories of small-group behavior and about many aspects of group structure and function, such as roles and norms, group composition effects, communication, leadership, problem solving and decision making, stages groups undergo as they evolve, and issues relating to the inclusion of members from diverse social groups. The knowledge and understanding about small group behavior you have gained should serve as a sound foundation upon which to build your group work skills.

ENDNOTE

1. Those interested in exploring the characteristics of the professional/client dyad may want to consult Martin and O'Connor (1989).

GLOSSARY

Assembly Effect: The consequences for group behavior of combining a particular set of individuals versus another potential group of people. For example, if you put five African Americans in a group, you are going to get a different assembly effect than if you put together five Latinos, or five Asian Americans, or two African Americans, two Latinos, and one Asian American.

Brainstorming: In problem solving, a method of generating as many ideas as possible by encouraging free thinking while delaying criticism or evaluation until a later time so that group members will not be inhibited.

Closed Group: A group whose membership does not change after it is constituted, except through natural attrition—for example, a grand jury.

Coaching Style: A style of leadership that emphasizes attention to the group task and to member relationships.

Coalition: A special type of subgroup, usually temporary, that is formed to facilitate the attainment of a goal that could not be reached if individual group members tried to achieve it independently. It sometimes includes adversaries who choose to ignore their differences temporarily so they can attain their goals.

Cohesiveness: The degree to which group members like one another and the group as a whole and desire to remain a part of it.

Communication: This most basic of all aspects of group interaction consists of the exchange of verbal and nonverbal messages between a sender and a receiver.

Communication Network: The structure of linkages among group members—such as the wheel or all-channel network—that illustrates the pattern of transmitting and receiving messages in the group.

Consensus: A judgment or decision arrived at by general agreement or unanimity of those involved.

Decision Making: The process of choosing among a series of alternatives by using some method, such as considering the pros and cons of each alternative and then taking a vote.

Decoding: The part of the communication process during which the receiver interprets the message.

Directive Leadership: An active leadership approach in which the leader offers other group members advice, suggestions, and information, and may even tell them what to do or not to do.

Dynamic: Anything (in this case, a group) that is active and energized and therefore constantly changing and evolving.

Dynamics: See **Group Dynamics.**

Encoding: An aspect of the communication process consisting of the selection of words or nonverbal symbols by the sender to convey meaning in a manner that will be understandable to the receiver.

Explicit Norms: Group norms that are clearly spelled out. For example, in a college course, the requirements specified in the syllabus.

Feedback: In the communication process, it refers specifically to the response by the receiver to the message transmitted by the **sender**. It provides information about how well the message was understood or accepted.

Figurehead: A person who heads in name only but who does not exercise leadership.

Formed Group: A group constituted for a specific purpose, such as a self-help group, a bridge group, or a treatment group.

Goal: In a group, a specific objective that is instrumental to the group's purpose—for example, to increase the frequency at which members speak up in an assertiveness training group.

Group: Two or more individuals interacting so that each one influences and is influenced by the other.

Group Dynamics: The major processes or patterns of interaction in a group, such as communication, leadership, problem solving, and decision making.

Group Norms: The rules or standards that regulate the behavior of group members. They serve as the primary means of control within the group.

Group Structure: A stable pattern of behavior that develops in a group as its members interact. Roles, norms, and subgroups are important aspects of group structure.

Groupthink: The pressure in certain highly cohesive groups toward excessive conformity and uniformity resulting in group members making decisions without thinking critically, without regard for ethical consequences, without sufficient information or regard for discrepant information, and without full consideration of alternatives.

Growth Group: A group aiming primarily to help members in their personal development—for example, a training group (T-group), encounter, or sensitivity group, as well as treatment, counseling, support, self-help, and consciousness-raising groups.

Implicit Norms: Norms that are presumed but unspoken. For instance, vulgar language may be considered inappropriate when addressing a church congregation, even though there may be no regulation that explicitly prohibits it.

Interaction: The patterns of mutual influence—verbal, nonverbal, or physical—that exist in all social systems, including groups.

Interrole Conflict: The conflict experienced when a person discovers that the behaviors associated with one role he or she plays are incompatible with those associated with his or her other roles. For example, having to be both leader and recorder in a committee.

Intrarole Conflict: Conflict experienced as a result of the opposing demands of a single role. For instance, a group leader may want to provide support at a particular time but has to be directive with a disruptive member.

Language: Communication by using words supposed to have a fairly standard meaning.

Leader: A person who exercises leadership.

Leadership: In a group, a reciprocal process in which a person (the leader) is permitted by the group members to influence, motivate, or empower them so that they may be better able to attain their goals.

Natural Group: A group that already exists, such as a family or peer group.

Noise: Interference during the communication process due to a variety of reasons, such as a competing conversation nearby.

Nominal Grouping: In problem solving, a method of producing as many alternative solutions as possible by having group members independently list their suggested solutions to be discussed by the group later without identifying individual authors.

Nondirective: An approach fairly common in counseling or treatment groups whereby the group leader creates a warm, permissive, nonjudgmental, and accepting atmosphere to encourage clients to discuss problems freely. Also, an approach whereby the person managing the group stays on the sidelines, letting the group conduct itself.

Nonvoluntary Group: A group composed of members who had no choice regarding their participation, such as court-ordered drug offenders or juvenile delinquents.

Norms: See **Explicit Norms; Group Norms, Implicit Norms; Prescriptive Norms; Proscriptive Norms.**

Open-Ended Group: A group that keeps adding members regularly—for example, a weight-watchers group that is run continuously and that new members may join at any time.

Paralanguage: Various vocal effects that accompany an utterance, such as voice tone, inflection, speed, volume, and use of silence.

Power: See **Social Power.**

Prescriptive Norms: Group norms that describe the kinds of behaviors that are expected; for example, most treatment groups require members to maintain confidentiality.

Primary Group: A small group of people whose relationship is characterized by intimacy, frequent interaction, and strong interdependence and identification. Good examples are families and close friends.

Problem Solving: The process involved in solving a problem, generally including such steps as identification and definition of the task or problem, generation of alternative solutions, selection of the best solution, implementation of the decision, and follow up.

Proscriptive Norms: Group norms concerning behaviors that are not permitted; for instance, some teachers do not allow personal conversations while class is in session.

Purpose: The function or end to be attained by the group, or the reason it is created for, such as leisure, task, or treatment.

Rank Order: A decision-making method in which the group members independently rate the alternatives numerically from most to least preferred and reach a decision on the basis of the combined numerical ranks.

Reference Group: A group used by an individual as a frame of reference for self-evaluation or comparison purposes.

Relationship-Oriented Leader: A leader who, although not necessarily oblivious to the task at hand, puts primary emphasis on group maintenance functions, such as facilitating open communication and interaction, providing support and encouragement, and showing concern for members.

Role: In a group, a set of expectations that group members share concerning the behavior of a person who occupies a certain position in the group.

Role Collision: The conflict that arises when different individuals hold overlapping roles and disagree about them. For instance, various members of a treatment team at a social agency—such as the psychiatrist, psychologist, and social worker—may have ambiguously defined roles that frequently collide.

Secondary Group: Any group that does not qualify as a primary group.

Social Power: The ability of one person to influence or control another in some way. It may be based on ability to control rewards and punishments, position authority, expertise, or personal attributes.

Status: The relative power, influence, and control that certain group members have relative to other members depending on many internal and external factors. Some of the internal factors that determine the status of group members include their willingness and ability to take on responsibility to coordinate activities, provide guidance, obtain resources, offer support, or relay communication.

Structure: See **Group Structure.**

Task Group: A group convened primarily for the purpose of getting a job done, whether it be to solve a problem, make a decision, develop a policy, provide a service, or make a product. Examples are committees, work teams, or juries.

Task-Oriented Leader: In a group, a leader who places primary emphasis on processes that facilitate task completion, such as establishing operating procedures, initiating action, providing expert information, motivating members toward goal achievement, and evaluating movement toward goal achievement.

Transmission: The part of the communication process that involves the transfer of a message over one or more of the available channels—the senses—and through some medium. For example, if the sender communicates in writing, the channel is visual and the medium is paper or computer.

Treatment Group: A type of growth group focusing on helping members to change or to overcome intrapersonal or interpersonal problems or deficits—for example, a group for persons suffering from depression.

Voluntary Group: A group consisting of members who have willingly chosen to participate in it.

REFERENCES

Acosta, F., & Yamamoto, J. (1984). The utility of group work practice for Hispanics. In L. Davis (Ed.), *Ethnicity in social group work practice.* New York: Haworth Press.

Argyle, M., & Dean, J. (1965). Eye contact, distance, and affiliation. *Sociometry*, 28, 289–304.

Bales, R. F. (1955). The equilibrium problem in small groups. In E. Borgatta & R. F. Bales (Eds.), *Small groups: Studies in social interaction.* New York: Knopf.

Bales, R. F. (1968). Interaction process analysis. In D. L. Sills (Ed.), *International encyclopedia of the social sciences* (Vol. 8, pp. 465–471). New York: Crowell, Collier, and Macmillan.

Bales, R. F. (1983). SYMLOG: A practical approach to the study of groups. In H. H. Blumberg, A. P. Hare, V. Kent, & M. Davis (Eds.), *Small groups and social interaction* (Vol. 2, pp. 499–523). New York: Wiley & Sons.

Bales, R. R., Koenigs, R. J., & Roman, P.D. (1987). Criteria for adaptation of SYMLOG rating items to particular populations and cultural contexts. *International Journal of Small Group Research, 3,* 161–179.

Balgopal, P., & Vassil, T. V. (1983). *Groups in social work: An ecological perspective.* New York: Macmillan.

Bennis, W., & Nanus, B. (1985). *Leaders: The strategies for taking charge.* New York: Harper & Row.

Bennis, W. G., & Shepard, H. A. (1956). A theory of group development. *Human Relations, 9,* 415–437.

Benne, K.D., & Sheats, P. (1948). Functional roles of group members. *Journal of Social Issues,* 4(2), 41–49.

Bion, W. R. (1961). *Experiences in groups* (2nd ed.). New York: Basic Books.

Blake, R., & Mouton, J. (1964). *The managerial grid.* Houston: Gulf.

Boje, D. M. (1980). Making a horse out of a camel: A contingency model for managing the problem-solving process in groups. In H. J. Leavitt, L. R. Pondy, & D. M. Boje (Eds.), *Readings in managerial psychology* (3rd ed., pp. 445–470). Chicago: University of Chicago Press.

Brower, A., Garvin, C. D., Hobson, J., Reed, B., & Reed, H. (1987). Exploring the effects of leader gender and race on group behavior. In J. Lassner, K. Powell, & E. Finnegan (Eds.), *Social group-work: Competence and values in practice* (pp. 129–148). New York: Haworth Press.

Brower, A. M. (1989). Group development as constructed social reality: A social-cognitive understanding of group formation. *Social Work with Groups,* 12(2), 23–41.

Brown, R. (1988). *Group processes: Dynamics within and between groups.* Oxford: Basil Blackwell.

Campbell, D. T. (1958). Common fate, similarity, and other indices of the status of aggregates of persons as social entities. *Behavioral Science, 3,* 14–25.

Chu, J., & Sue, S. (1984, Fall). Asian/Pacific Americans and group practice. *Social Work with Groups,* 7(3), 23–36.

Cohen M. D., March, J. G., & Olsen, J. P. (1972). A garbage can model of organizational choice. *Administrative Sciences Quarterly,* 17, 1–25.

Cooley, C. H. (1909). *Social organization.* New York: Schocken.

Davis, L. (1984). Essential components of group work with black Americans. *Social Work with Groups, 7,* 97–109.

Davis, L., & Proctor, E. (1989). *Race, gender, and class: Guidelines for practice with individuals, families, and groups.* Englewood Cliffs, NJ: Prentice Hall.

Delgado, M. (1981). Hispanic cultural values: Implications for groups. *Small Group Behavior, 12,* 69–80.

Delgado, M., & Humm-Delgado, D. (1984). Hispanics and group work: A review of the literature. *Social Work with Groups, 7,* 85–96.

Diehl, M., & Stroebe, W. (1987). Productivity loss in brainstorming groups: Toward the solution of a riddle. *Journal of Personality and Social Psychology, 53,* 497–509.

Ephross, P. H., & Greene, R. R. (1991). Symbolic interactionism. In R. R. Greene & P. H. Ephross (Eds.), *Human behavior theory and social work practice* (pp. 203–225). New York: Aldine de Gruyter.

Ephross, P. H., & Vassil, T. V. (1988). *Groups that work: Structure and process.* New York: Columbia University Press.

Evans, C. R., & Dion, K. L. (1991). Group cohesion and performance: A meta-analysis. *Small Group Research, 22,* 175–186.

Feldman, R. A. (1987). Group work knowledge and research: A two-decade comparison. In S. D. Rose & R. A. Feldman (Eds.), *Research in social group work* (pp. 7–14). New York: Haworth Press.

Fiedler, F. E. (1978). The contingency model and the dynamics of the leadership process. *Advances in Experimental Social Psychology, 11,* 59–112.

Fisher, B. A., & Ellis, D. G. (1990). *Small group decision making* (3rd ed.). New York: McGraw-Hill.

French, J. R. P., Jr., & Raven, B. (1959). The bases of social power. In D. Cartwright (Ed.), *Studies in social power* (pp. 150–167). Ann Arbor, MI: Institute for Social Research.

Freud, S. (1922). *Group psychology and the analysis of the ego.* London: Hogarth Press.

Garvin, C. D. (1987a). *Contemporary group work* (2nd ed.). Englewood Cliffs, NJ: Prentice Hall.

Garvin, C. D. (1987b). Group theory and research. In A. Minahan (Ed.), *Encyclopedia of social work* (18th ed., pp. 682–696). Silver Spring, MD: National Association of Social Workers.

Garvin, C. D., & Reed, B. G. (1983). Gender issues in social group work: An overview. *Social Work with Groups, 6*(3), 5–18.

Gemmill, G. (1989). The dynamics of scapegoating in small groups. *Small Group Behavior, 20,* 406–418.

Gemmill, G., & Wynkoop, C. (1991). The psychodynamics of small group transformation. *Small Group Research, 22,* 4–23.

Goffman, E. (1959). *The presentation of self in everyday life.* New York: Doubleday/Anchor.

Goffman, E. (1961). *Asylums: Essays on the social situation of mental patients and other inmates.* New York: Doubleday/Anchor.

Goffman, E. (1974). *Frame analysis: An essay on the organization of experience.* New York: Harper & Row.

Greif, G. L., & Lynch, A. A. (1983). The eco-systems perspective. In C. H. Meyer (Ed.), *Clinical social work in the ecosystems perspective* (pp. 35–71). New York: Columbia University Press.

Hardy-Fanta, C. (1986). *Social action in Hispanic groups. Social Work, 31,* 119–123.

Hare, P. (1982). Creativity in small groups (p. 141). Beverly Hills, CA: Sage.

Hartford, M. (1971). *Groups in social work.* New York: Columbia University Press.

Haslett, B., & Ogilvie, J. R. (1988). Feedback processes in task groups. In R. Cathcart & L. Samovar (Eds.), *Small group communication* (5th ed., pp. 385–401). Dubuque, IA: Brown.

Heap, K. (1985). *The practice of social work with groups.* Boston: G. Allen & Unwin.

Hershey, P., & Blanchard, K.H. (1977). *Management of organizational behavior: Utilizing human resources* (3rd ed.) Englewood Cliffs, NJ: Prentice Hall.

Hirokawa, R. Y., & Johnston, D. D. (1989). Toward a general theory of group decision making: Development of an integrated model. *Small Group Behavior, 20,* 500–523.

Ho, M. K. (1984). Social group work with Asian/Pacific Americans. In L. Davis (Ed.), *Ethnicity in social group work practice.* New York: Haworth Press.

Hoffman, L. R., & Maier, N. R. F. (1961). Quality and acceptance of problem solutions by members of homogeneous and heterogeneous groups. *Journal of Abnormal and Social Psychology, 62,* 401–407.

Homans, G. C. (1950). *The human group.* New York: Harcourt, Brace & World.

Janis, I. L. (1982). *Groupthink: Psychological studies of foreign policy decisions and fiascoes* (2nd ed.). Boston: Houghton Mifflin.

Konopka, G. (1983). *Social group work.* Englewood Cliffs, NJ: Prentice Hall.

Kornblum, W. (1991). *Sociology in a changing world* (2nd ed). Ft Worth, TX: Holt, Rinehart and Winston.

Kurtz, L. F., & Powell, T. J. (1987). Three approaches to understanding self-help groups. *Social Work with Groups,* 10(3), 69–80.

Levine, J. M., & Moreland, R. L. (1990). Progress in small group research. *Annual Review of Psychology, 41,* 585–634.

Lewin, K. (1951). *Field theory in social science.* New York: Harper & Row.

Mabry, E. A. (1989). Some theoretical implications of female and male interaction in unstructured small groups. *Small Group Behavior, 20,* 536–550.

Maccoby, E. E. (1990). Gender and relationships: A developmental account. *American Psychologist, 45,* 513–520.

Maier, N. R. F. (1979). Leadership principles for problem solving conferences. In D. A. Kolb, I. M. Rubin, & J. M. McIntyre (Eds.), *Organizational psychology: A book of readings* (3rd ed., pp. 367–376). Englewood Cliffs, NJ: Prentice Hall.

Martin, P. Y., & O'Connor, G. G. (1989). The professional-client dyad: A two-party system. In P. Y. Martin & G. G. O'Connor (Eds.), *The social environment: Open systems applications.* New York: Longman.

Martin, P. Y., & Shanahan, K. A. (1983). Transcending the effects of sex composition in small groups. *Social Work with Groups*, 6(3), 19–32.

McLoughlin, M., Shryer, T. L., Goode, E. E., & McAuliffe, K. (1988, August 8). *Men vs. women.* U.S. News and World Report, 50–56.

Milgram, S. (1963). *Behavioral study of obedience. Journal of Abnormal and Social Psychology, 67,* 371–378.

Moreno, J. L. (1953). *Who shall survive?* (rev. ed.). Beacon, NY: Beacon House.

Morrison, T. L., & Stein, D. D. (1985, February). Member reaction to male and female leaders in two types of group experience. *Journal of Social Psychology, 125,* 7–16.

Napier, R. W., & Gershenfeld, M. K. (1989). *Groups: Theory and experience* (4th ed.). Boston: Houghton Mifflin.

Northen, H. (1988). *Social work with groups* (2nd ed.). New York: Columbia University Press.

Parsons, T., Bales, R. F., & Shils, E. A. (1953). *Working papers in the theory of action.* Glencoe, IL.: Free Press.

Paulus, P. B. (1989). *Psychology of group influence* (2nd ed.). Hillsdale, NJ: Lawrence Erlbaum Associates.

Rogers, C., & Roethlisberger, F. J. (1977). In J. L. Gray & Starke, F. A. (Eds.), *Readings in organizational behavior: Concepts and applications.* Columbus, OH: Charles E. Merrill.

Rose, S. (1977). *Group therapy: A behavioral approach.* Englewood Cliffs, NJ: Prentice Hall.

Rose, S. (1989). *Working with adults in groups: Integrating cognitive-behavioral and small group strategies.* San Francisco: Jossey-Bass.

Sarri, R. C., & Galinsky, M. J. (1985). A conceptual framework for group development. In M. Sundel, P. H. Glasser, R. Sarri, & R. Vinter (Eds.), *Individual change through small groups* (2nd ed.). New York: Free Press.

Schutz, W. C. (1958). *FIRO: A three-dimensional theory of interpersonal behavior.* New York: Rinehart.

Seaman, D. F. (1981). *Working effectively with task oriented groups.* New York: McGraw-Hill.

Shaw, M. (1964). Communication networks. In L. Berkowitz (Ed.), *Advances in experimental social psychology* (Vol. 1). New York: Academic Press.

Shaw, M. (1981). *Group dynamics: The psychology of small group behavior* (3rd ed.). New York: McGraw-Hill.

Siebold, D. R. (1988). Making meetings more successful: Plans, formats, and procedures for group problem solving. In R. Cathcart & L. Samovar (Eds.), *Small group communication* (5th ed., pp. 209–224). Dubuque, IA: Brown.

Siporin, M. (1980). Ecological systems theory in social work. *Journal of Sociology and Social Work, 7,* 507–532.

Sorrentino, R. M., & Boutillier, R. G. (1975). The effect of quantity and quality of verbal interaction on ratings of leadership ability. *Journal of Experimental Social Psychology, 11,* 403–411.

Sorrentino, R. M., & Field, N. (1986). Emergent leadership over time: The functional value of positive motivation. *Journal of Personality and Social Psychology, 50,* 1091–1099.

Stogdill, R. M. (1974). *Handbook of leadership.* New York: Free Press.

Strube, M. J., & Garcia, J. E. (1981). A meta-analytic investigation of Fiedler's contingency model of leadership effectiveness. *Psychological Bulletin, 90,* 307-321.

Sundel, M., & Glasser, P. (1985). Developments influencing the Michigan group work model and future directions. In M. Sundel, P. Glasser, R. Sarri, & R. Vinter (Eds.), *Individual change through small groups* (2nd ed., pp. 562–573). New York: Free Press.

Thibaut, J. W., & Kelley, H. H. (1959). *The social psychology of groups.* New York: Wiley.

Toseland, R. W., & Rivas, R. F. (1984). *An introduction to group work practice.* New York: Macmillan.

Tuckman, B. W., & Jensen, M. A. C. (1977). Stages of small group development revisited. *Group and Organizational Studies, 2,* 419–427.

Vinter, R. D., & Galinsky, M. J. (1985). Extragroup relations and approaches. In M. Sundel, P. Glasser, R. Sarri, & R. Vinter (Eds.), *Individual change through small groups* (2nd ed., pp. 266–276). New York: Free Press.

Yalom, I.D. (1985). The theory and practice of group psychotherapy (3rd ed.). New York: Basic Books.

Zander, A. (1982). *Making groups effective.* San Francisco: Jossey-Bass.

SUGGESTIONS FOR FURTHER READING

Cathcart, R. S., & Samovar, L. A. (1988). *Small group communication: A reader* (5th ed.). Dubuque, IA: William C. Brown.

Conyne, R. I. (1989). *How personal growth and task groups work.* Newbury Park, CA: Sage.

Corey, M. S., & Corey, G. (1987). *Groups: Process and practice* (3rd ed.). Pacific Grove, CA: Brooks/Cole.

Edwards, E. D., & Edwards, M. E. (1984). Group work practice with American Indians. *Social Work with Groups, 7*(3), 7–21.

Fatout, M. & Rose, S. R. (1995). *Task groups in the social services.* Thousand Oaks CA: Sage.

Fisher, B. A., & Ellis, D. G. (1990). *Small group decision making* (3rd ed.). New York: McGraw-Hill.

Garvin, C. D. (1987). Group theory and research. In A. Minahan (Ed.), *Encyclopedia of social work* (18th ed., pp. 682–696). Silver Spring, MD: National Association of Social Workers.

Johnson, D. W., & Johnson, F. P. (1987). *Joining together: Group theory and group skills* (3rd ed). Englewood Cliffs, NJ: PrenticeHall.

Knapp, M. L., & Miller, G. R. (1994). *Handbook of interpersonal communication* (2nd ed.). Newbury Park, CA: Sage.

Mullen, B., Anthony, T., Salas, E., & Driskell, J.E. (1994). Group cohesiveness and quality of decision-making: An integration of tests of the groupthink hypothesis. *Small Group Research,* 25(2), 189–204.

Napier, R. W., & Gershenfeld, M. K. (1989). *Groups: Theory and experience* (4th ed.). Boston: Houghton Mifflin.

Rose, S. D. (1989). *Working with adults in groups: Integrating cognitive-behavioral and small group strategies.* San Francisco: Jossey-Bass.

Schultz, B. G. (1989). *Communicating in the small group: Theory and practice.* New York: Harper & Row.

Toseland, R.W., & Rivas, R.F. (1995). *An introduction to group work practice* (2nd ed.). Boston: Allyn and Bacon.

Zastrow, C. (1993). *Social work with groups: Using the class as a group leadership laboratory* (3rd ed.). Chicago: Nelson-Hall.

Zastrow, C. (1990). Starting and leading therapy groups: A beginner's guide. *Journal of Independent Social Work, 4*(4), 7–26.

Look for articles in the following journals:

Group
International Journal of Small Group Research
Small Group Research (previously called *Small Group Behavior)*
Social Psychology (previously called *Sociometry)*
Social Work with Groups

CHAPTER 8

FAMILIES

The previous chapters examined many of the major social systems that influence individual development and behavior: our cultural experiences, socioeconomic circumstances, and societal institutions to which we have been exposed; our racial and ethnic backgrounds; our genders and sexual orientations; the neighborhoods and communities in which we grew up and in which we live; our work environments and the organizations and institutions with which we come in contact; and the groups to which we belong. Each of these social systems has had and continues to have profound influence on us. But none is likely to have been more influential than our families in determining the course of our development and behavior.

Families are the central units of social organization in every known human society probably because they perform major social functions without which civilizations would be difficult to sustain. This chapter will examine various concepts of family, major theoretical perspectives applicable to the study of families, and a variety of contemporary patterns of family organization.

THE MANY CONCEPTS OF "FAMILY"

What is your personal concept of "**family**"? In other words, what does the word *family* mean to you? Take a few moments to list the people you would consider to be part of your family. Did you include someone living with you who is not a blood relative? Was anyone on your list not related to you by marriage or adoption? Did you include someone not living with you? Was anyone you listed a relative other than your parents, siblings, or children? Did you leave out a stepparent, stepchild, or stepsibling with whom you live or have lived in the past? Let us now look at various definitions of family to see where your concept fits in.

Anthropologists used to define families as social units containing at least two generations: parent(s) and child(ren). According to this old idea, a married couple would not become a family until they had a child, but an unmarried woman and her baby would be considered a family. Many people today would argue that a married couple constitutes a family, regardless of whether they have children.

Another popular definition of family in Western societies is that of the traditional, or intact, family—that is, a social unit consisting of a married couple and their biological children. The problem with this definition is that it applies to only about 25 percent of the households in the United States today (U.S. Bureau of the Census, 1993c).

Many family scholars define the family as two or more persons related by birth or "blood," marriage, or adoption and usually sharing the same household. This widely accepted definition is somewhat more comprehensive than the aforementioned ones in the sense that it allows for the inclusion of relatives other than parents and their biological children, as long as they share the same home. For example, according to this definition, two sisters living together or grandparents living with their grandchildren would constitute a family. This concept also encompasses remarriage families, which are quite prevalent nowadays.

Although more comprehensive, the preceding definition of family leaves out significant relationships that are not based on blood, marriage, or adoption. For example, it excludes unmarried couples living together—opposite sex or same sex—with or without children. Yet, an increasing number of family households in the United States today fall in this category.

In primarily agricultural or semi-industrialized societies, as well as among various U.S. racial/ethnic groups, families are still understood to comprise the entire kin group. This view of the family includes relatives such as grandparents, cousins, aunts, and uncles, even if they do not share the same household. Such families are often referred to as **extended families** (Sussman, 1965). They were normative in the United States prior to the industrial revolution when the economy was primarily agrarian and large extended families were handy to get the farm work done. African Americans have retained this family form more than Euro-Americans not only because it was normative in Africa but because many lived in the rural

South until recently. An additional reason why African Americans have favored the extended family form is the cooperation, support, and mutual aid it provides, which are helpful in coping with societal oppression. Many of the recent immigrants to the United States, including many Latinos and Asians, also favor the extended family form, probably because it is still prevalent in their native countries, some of which are still primarily agricultural or semi-industrial.

Some people would argue, including the author, that we should have the right to create our own families on the basis of mutual caring and commitment, regardless of whether or not the family members we choose are related by blood, marriage, or adoption or share the household. From this flexible perspective, the family might be defined as any combination of people—male or female—who share an intimate and committed relationship of mutual caring and who choose to call one another family (Hite, 1994).

As you can see, the term *family* means different things to different people. However, the definition that a particular government unit adopts—federal, state, or local—has critical importance. Such definition determines which individuals will be recognized by the law and by the policies of most official organizations and institutions to be given the rights and benefits available to family members and which will be excluded or considered deviant. For example, in the case of a family consisting of an unmarried couple living together (heterosexual or homosexual), one partner would not be covered by the health insurance policy of the other as a legal spouse would if the government unit or work organization that offers the insurance does not include unmarried couples in its definition of family. Similarly, if an unmarried partner got seriously ill, the other would not be allowed to take sick leave to care for the sick person. Or, if one unmarried partner were to die intestate (i.e., without a will) and intended to leave the other what he or she owned, a distant relative would have a greater legal claim on the

"I'm your wife, Arthur. You talk to me. You don't touch base with me."
Source: Drawing by Joe Mirachi, © 1988 The New Yorker Magazine, Inc.

estate than the decedent's partner because the unmarried partner would not be recognized by the inheritance laws as a family member. For the same reason, even though an unmarried couple may have shared a leased apartment for 20 years, if one partner were to die, the other could be evicted, unless his or her name appeared on the lease. These are just some of the consequences that the societal or local official definition of *family* could have on people's lives.

No matter how the family is defined, it is a high-voltage emotional setting, charged with love and hatred, tenderness and spite, and at times violence (Skolnick, 1981, p. 45). Anytime there is closeness and intimacy, there is potential for conflict. This means that even so-called normal families at times can be turbulent environments for their members.

APPROACHES TO THE STUDY OF FAMILIES

Several theoretical perspectives help us to better understand the families around us. This section will examine some of the insights gained from looking at families from five different angles: structural functionalism (including the social systems and ecological perspectives), social conflict theory, symbolic interactionism, social exchange theory, and the life course approach. None of these perspectives by itself is sufficient to adequately explain family behavior. But each theory acts like an extra lens that serves to sharpen our focus, adding a new dimension to our understanding of specific families.

Structural-Functional Approach

From a structural-functional perspective, families are viewed as social systems that perform certain tasks or functions for the society and for their members. (These functions will be discussed later in this section). According to systems theory, a derivative of structural functionalism, families, like other social systems, are composed of interrelated and interdependent parts or subsystems (i.e., family members who participate in various subunits of the family and in the family as a whole). Because of the interconnectedness of family members, what happens to one member (e.g., husband, wife, or children) affects every other. Conflict is inevitable in family life, but whenever it arises, families attempt to keep it within bounds by calling into play their stabilizing forces. This is because family members depend on one another for their welfare, thus they are usually motivated to work cooperatively to maintain or to return to a steady state—that is, to keep at least some remblance of order, stability, cohesion, and continuity in the family.

Role theory, another derivative of structural functionalism, also contributes useful insights to understanding families. You may recall that role theory stresses that the way people act in a given social position is influenced by the expectations that accompany such position, as well as by their own ideas of how they should behave as occupants of the position. According to this perspective, the family is a system of roles. Family members play many different roles, such as husband, wife, lover, father, mother, breadwinner, companion, friend, son, daughter, brother, sister, grandfather, grandmother, mother-in-law, father-in-law, stepfather, stepmother, stepson, stepdaughter, stepsibling, and so on. Each family member takes on multiple roles. For example, the father may alternately act as stepfather, husband, lover, companion, friend, son, son-in-law, cook, or repairman.

Because family members play many roles, they are vulnerable to experience role conflict or role overload. **Role conflict** arises when there is a discrepancy between what others expect you to do and what you want to do or think you should do. For example, on a given day, Mrs. Gomez may be expecting her husband to come home early to fix the bedroom window, but Mr. Gomez may feel that it is more important for him to stay late at the shop to keep up with his work. His conflict may not be easy to resolve. If he goes home at 5:00, he may feel that he is missing out on his chances to get promoted. On the other hand, if he works

overtime, he will not be able to fix the window, the house will remain vulnerable to weather conditions, and his wife will be upset.

A similar type of role conflict is experienced when one feels obligated to do something one does not want to do. Mrs. Rodgers, who lives down the street from the Gomez family, felt pressured by her husband to quit work and stay home with their three small children until the children were old enough to go to school; however, she hated the daily routine of full-time housekeeping and child care and became depressed. She would have felt much better if she had chosen to go back to work, but her husband and his parents would have thought that she was not a "good enough" mother. Instead, she decided to stay home but became unhappy. No matter what she had chosen to do, she would have felt some conflict.

Sometimes the problem is **role overload,** which you may recall occurs whenever a family member tries to play too many roles at the same time. For example, Mrs. Gomez is often torn between the demands of her full-time job, the housework, and the children. She gets some help from Mr. Gomez and her elderly mother, but it is not enough. When she collapses in bed at night after working nonstop since dawn, her problem is role overload.

Analyses of families from the structural-functional perspective focus on various aspects of family structure or function. For instance, at one point, one may want to assess how a particular family is performing or failing to perform certain functions for its members or for society—for example, the extent to which the family is fulfilling its child-care functions. At another point, one may need to examine the consequences of certain structural characteristics—for example, the problems that a one-parent family may be experiencing or the extent to which members of an extended family provide or fail to provide assistance and support for its members.

In working with a particular family from a structural-functional perspective, one would carefully assess its ecological status. This would include its strengths or deficiencies in transactions with external systems (such as the school, workplace, or the social welfare system) or the environmental pressures it faces (such as economic hardship, unemployment and underemployment, racism, sexism or homophobia).

Family Structure

The classification of families according to structure was popularized by Billingsley (1968) drawing on the formulations of Parsons and Bales (1955). According to this categorization, there are three basic forms or units of family organization: nuclear, extended, and augmented. A **nuclear family** consists of a couple with or without child(ren) or one parent with her or his child(ren). Nuclear families may be traditional or intact, remarried, couple-only, or one-parent families. The **traditional or intact family** is composed of both parents and their own biological or adopted children. A **remarriage family** is created when one or two previously married people remarry. It may or may not include their children from previous marriages. The **stepfamily** is a remarriage family, including a child or children belonging to one or each of the spouses from a previous relationship. In the **couple-only family,** there are two mates without children. The **one-parent family** consists of one parent and her or his children.

Extended family households include other relatives besides the parents and children. For example, after the death of Mrs. Gomez's father, her 72-year-old mother, Doña Dora, moved in with her daughter; thus, the Gomez family became extended. Many racial and ethnic families in the United States include grandparents and other relatives, making them extended. **Augmented family** households include unrelated people considered to be members of the family. For example, some African-American families incorporate *fictive kin*—that is, unrelated people who are informally adopted

as family members, such as boyfriends or informally adopted children. Affluent families often have employees such as live-in child-care workers or long-term housekeepers who sometimes function as family members. Extended and augmented families as well as those that are both extended and augmented are generally referred to as **expanded families** (Boulding, 1972).

The Billingsley system of family classification further divides families into two major types: families of origin and families of procreation. *Families of origin* are the ones people are born into. Everyone has a family of origin. *Families of procreation* are established by getting married or by living together. Perhaps a more modern and neutral term for families of procreation would be *created families* since the latter term does not connote that couples ought to have children.

All these family categorizations are not simply an exercise to expand your vocabulary. These concepts of family structure are important because they sensitize you to the variety of family units that you will encounter as a human service practitioner. If your concept of family before starting to read this chapter was that of the traditional nuclear family, as a practitioner you might have been in danger of developing incomplete and distorted ideas about the families you encountered because many would not be traditional. To understand the dynamics of contemporary families, you must identify their members, and these members are not necessarily going to be the father, mother, and their biological children. Grandparents, boyfriends and girlfriends, stepparents and stepchildren, noncustodial parents, informally adopted children, aunts and uncles, and various other people often play significant roles in family dynamics.

Minuchin's Structural Family Theory

One of the more practical and insightful applications of structural functionalism to the analysis of families is that of Salvador Minuchin (1974). In the ecological systems tradition, he views families as open systems moving through various life stages and transitions and constantly adapting to their internal and external environment and changing circumstances. According to Minuchin, each family develops unique transactional patterns, subsystems, coalitions, and boundaries. Let us examine each of these ideas.

Transactional Patterns. **Transactional patterns** are habitual ways of interacting based on generic rules of family relationships or on idiosyncracies within particular families. Generic patterns of interaction are those derived from traditional rules governing family functioning. For instance, families traditionally have enforced a certain power hierarchy in parent/child relationships consisting of an expectation that parents will tell their children what to do and that children will obey their parents. In patriarchal families, the power hierarchy often also extends to husband/wife relations, with the husband usually making the major family decisions. Also traditionally, there has been an expectation that husband and wife will work cooperatively as a team. As a result, a particular couple may believe that they should share the job of teaching the children values and proper behaviors and that they should choose together the schools to which they will send the children, the places the family will go on vacation, and so on. Each family develops its transactional patterns in part on the basis of these generic or universal rules of operation.

Idiosyncrasies of particular families also play a role in determining transactional patterns. That is, certain ways of operating are negotiated or developed within specific families in response to special family situations. Consider the following examples of families that live in the same neighborhood as the Gomez family. At the Miller home, the eldest son acts as the head of the family apparently because his father left the family and his mother felt that a "man" should be in charge.

Down the street, Mrs. Carrillo makes the major decisions in her family apparently because she makes more money than her husband and consequently wields more power in the household.

Subsystems. **Subsystems** are important structural elements within families. Subsystems are subunits composed of certain family members. Each family member belongs to different subsystems, such as the spouse subsystem, the executive subsystem, the parental subsystem, the parent/child subsystem, and the sibling subsystems. The **spouse subsystem** consists of the couple who heads the family in their role as spouses. The **executive subsystems** is composed of those who make the decisions in the family; for instance, in a one-parent family it may comprise the mother and her eldest child. The **parental subsystem** is composed of the parent(s) or any other parent substitute, each in his or her parental role. The **parent\child subsystem** includes the parent(s) and child(ren). The **sibling subsystem** consists of various groupings of the children, such as the older children and the younger children in a large family.

Coalitions. Sometimes family members join forces to cooperate or to oppose others. For example, mother and daughter may form a temporary coalition against the father's idea to move to another state. Structurally, **coalitions** are family subsystems that form an integral part of the decision-making process and are functional as long as they do not become entrenched. However, they can be detrimental when family members form rigid alliances. For example, in a three-generational family, when the maternal grandmother and her grandson consistently align themselves against the father, no matter what the issue may be, this "triangulation" that forces the child to choose sides can seriously damage the father/son relationship. Another dysfunctional type of coalition occurs, for example, when the two oldest sisters in a family consistently align themselves against their younger brother and systematically leave him out of the sibling subgroup.

Boundaries. **Boundaries** are major structural components of families. Internal boundaries separate various subsystems within the family. External boundaries serve to differentiate families from their environment. Not all family boundaries are evident, like the skin that covers the physical body, but family members generally know where they are located, who belongs, and who does not belong. For example, a parent may spend years away from his or her family in a mental institution, in prison, or in the military and yet remain an important member of the family. Similarly, children of a first marriage who never lived with their father after he remarried may be part of what he considers his family. Yet he may not consider someone who has lived with him for years, such as his second wife's eldest son, to be part of his family. To help delineate boundaries, internal and external, families use a variety of symbols, such as the family name, the wedding band the spouses wear, a marriage certificate, the home, a hedge around the home, doors marking the entrance to various rooms (e.g., the children's, the parents'), closets and drawers to keep each family member's belongings separate, and so on.

Minuchin (1974) suggested that for proper functioning, **boundaries** in families and their subsystems must be **clear**—that is, defined well enough to allow members to carry out their functions without outside interference but sufficiently permeable to allow free exchange of inputs and outputs with outside systems. For example, as previously noted, the boundary between the children's subsystem and the parents' subsystem should be drawn clearly enough to allow the children to learn to get along, negotiate, cooperate, and compete among themselves. This often requires that parents refrain from exerting too much influence or control over their children. At the same time,

parents need to make sure that they do not deprive the children of their input and guidance.

To maintain clear boundaries, the spouse subsystem needs relative noninterference from others in the family and outside the family so as to develop skill in mutual accommodation and in working cooperatively. The parental subsystem also needs freedom from interference by the in-laws or the children's school to develop skill in nurturing, guiding, controlling, and allowing the children increasingly greater independence as they become older. Similarly, social agency practitioners should maintain clear boundaries between themselves and the families with whom they work by not interfering in aspects of family life that are not within their purview; at the same time, they should make themselves available to client families in need and should keep open the lines of communication with these families.

One extreme of boundary functioning is **enmeshment.** Family members are said to be enmeshed when their relationship is so symbiotic that it discourages the development of autonomy and competence and does not give them enough breathing space. For example, if Mrs. Gomez were to overprotect her son Charlie and do everything for him, he might become overly dependent on her, and their relationship would be considered enmeshed. The other extreme of boundary functioning is **disengagement.** When family members are excessively distant in their relations and do not have a clear sense of belonging together, of loyalty to the family, or of interdependence, their boundaries are said to be disengaged. Actually, Mrs. Gomez is more concerned about disengagement than enmeshment in relation to Charlie because he often does not want to participate in family activities and seldom takes an interest in what anyone else in the family is doing or feeling. For such a young child, he is very independent.

One useful aid in exploring the internal dynamics of a family is the **genogram** (Hartman, 1978; McGoldrick & Gerson, 1985), which is similar to a family tree except that it provides more information. As shown in Figure 8.1, the genogram depicts the family over time, usually three generations, recording basic demographic data for each member (e.g., age, date of birth, sex, marital status, occupation, and level of education) as well as significant information concerning the person's physical, social, and emotional functioning, and major life events. It can also be used to portray relationships, using various symbols to depict enmeshment, disengagement, or conflict. Detailed genograms may also help to uncover recurrent family problems (such as a history of depression, family violence, or alcoholism) when these problems recur in an intergenerational family.

The Ecological Context of Families

As previously noted, in working with families, it is important to identify the principal players and to become acquainted with their transactional patterns, the functioning and configuration of subsystems, and the quality of internal boundaries. However, to understand the dynamics of a particular family, it is not sufficient to focus on its interior. Ecosystems theory reminds us that we also must pay close attention to the family's suprasystem—its entire environmental context, particularly those extrafamilial forces that have an impact on it.

Much can be happening in the external environment (e.g., extended family, school, workplace, neighborhood) that is deeply affecting a family's ability to adapt. Maybe the family has recently added a new member (e.g., grandma or a stepdaughter) who presents new health-care or discipline problems. Perhaps the father recently lost his job because the factory that employed him relocated to Mexico. Perhaps he has become discouraged in his search for another job because he has limited education and work skills. Maybe the eldest son has begun to skip school because he feels self-conscious about lacking fashionable clothes. As a result of hanging out in the streets, he may have become involved in a youth gang. Maybe the daughter was caught stealing a wallet at the grocery store after her father lost his job. The point is this: In order to fully understand what is happening in a family, you must look at all the internal and external forces impinging on it.

A useful device for assessing the ecological context of families is the **ecomap** (Hartman, 1978). As shown in Figure 8.2, an ecomap is a pictorial representation of (1) the significant people in every key system with which a family ordinarily interacts (i.e., extended family, neighborhood, friendship circle, school, workplace, social welfare system, juvenile justice system, public hospital, church, community groups and organizations, and so on); (2) the flow of energy and resources from the family to each of these systems and from these systems to the family; and (3) the quality of the interface or relationship of the family with representatives from each of these systems (i.e., weak, strong, or stressful).

Family Functions

So far, this discussion has centered on the analysis of various structural aspects of families. A functional assessment would add to our understanding by providing indices of performance along a different dimension. Specifically, from a functional perspective, one may assess the extent to which a particular family has been fulfilling or neglecting some of its major duties. Thus, we will turn our attention momentarily to the principal tasks that families have traditionally performed for their members as well as for the society. These functions include the following:

— *Procreation or reproduction.* Most couples make a conscious decision to have or not to have children. However, some have children by accident rather than choice, and others may not be able to procreate due to infertility.

— *Socialization and control.* Socialization involves the teaching and learning of a variety of family and social roles, as well as the teach-

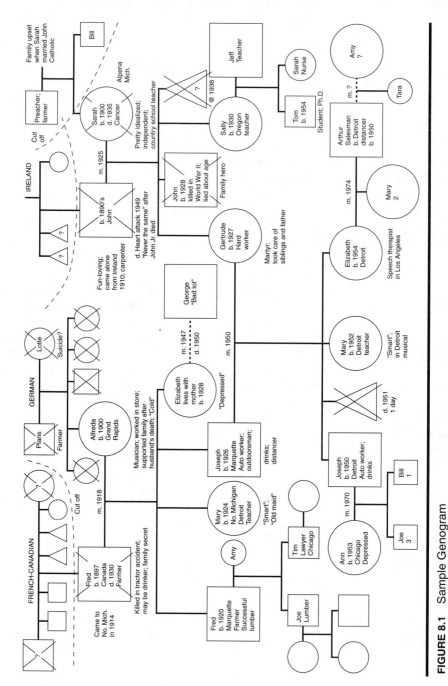

FIGURE 8.1 Sample Genogram

Source: From "Diagrammatic Assessment of Family Relationships" by A. Hartman, 1978, *Social Casework*, October. Copyright 1978 by Families International, Inc. Reprinted by permission.

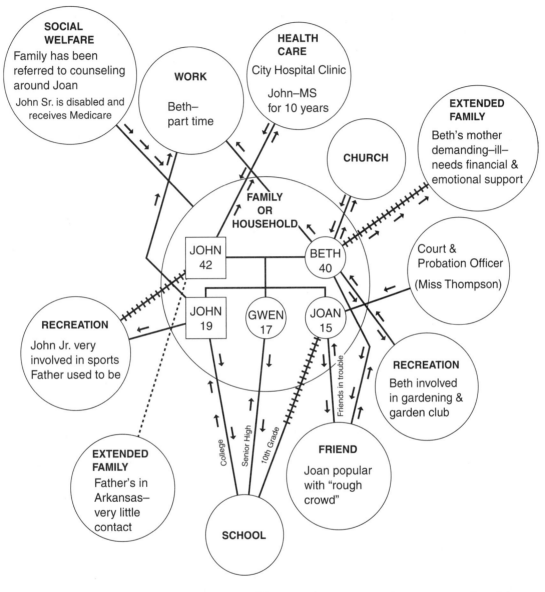

Nature of connections shown by different kinds of lines: —— strong; ----- tenuous; ++++ stressful. Arrows along lines signify flow of energy, resources, etc.

FIGURE 8.2 Ecomap

Source: From "Diagrammatic Assessment of Family Relationships" by A. Hartman, 1978, *Social Casework,* October. Copyright 1978 by Families International, Inc. Reprinted by permission.

ing and learning of ethical values, attitudes, beliefs, and behaviors in accordance with the family's racial and cultural background, and socioeconomic status. The socialization function of families is shared by various social institutions, including the schools, the church, the media (particularly TV), and day-care facilities. Society also requires that the family control its members' behaviors and keep them within acceptable limits. In recent years, the family control function has been reinforced by the authorities in some localities holding parents responsible for the behavior of their children, regarding such areas as school truancy, vandalism, use of a weapon, and drug abuse.

— *Child care.* This function includes feeding, dressing, sheltering, supervising, and making sure that children in the family have medical attention. In some families, child-care functions are shared with others, such as babysitters, day-care centers, or grandparents.

— *Care of other dependent persons.* Some families must assume primary responsibility for the care of others besides their own children, such as elderly parents who have become physically or mentally disabled.

— *Nurturance and refuge* (i.e., a safe place where family members can relax, unwind, and be themselves). Family members fulfill the nurturance function by giving and receiving love, affection, and empathy, by sharing their interests and concerns, by playing with the children, and by attending functions in which other family members participate such as a school play, graduation, a wedding, baptism, and so on. As noted by Minuchin (1974), families also nurture their members by providing support and assistance in coping with the problems they are experiencing, such as school problems, problems with peers or at work, problems at transitional points (e.g., when a child enters school or college, when the parents divorce, or when a parent changes jobs or retires) and with various idiosyncratic problems (i.e., a developmental disability or a mental disorder).

— *A home base for the family group.* This involves paying the rent or the mortgage, buying and preparing food, washing and ironing, cleaning the house or apartment, making repairs, and innumerable other household tasks. Those with ample financial resources may hire help to assist with some of these duties. Others may need public assistance to fulfill this function.

To fulfill their functions, families need considerable inputs in terms of time, energy, and financial and emotional resources from their members and from the external environment. When they do not receive enough inputs, they may have difficulty producing good outputs such as physically, socially, and emotionally healthy, well-adjusted, and competent family members.

Social Conflict Theory

Social conflict theory assumes that conflict is natural and inevitable within the family. In fact, according to this theory, competition among family members, power struggles, coercion, domination, arguments, and even chaos and violence may be more characteristic of some families than the relative harmony, cooperation, and accommodation that families supposedly try to maintain, according to structural functionalism.

Family conflict can have positive consequences. For instance, it may expose misunderstandings between family members which, once allowed to surface, can be clarified. Conflict may strengthen relationships as family members become better attuned to the things that others in the family find toxic. Consequently, conflict theorists suggest that families should allow conflict to surface and to run its course rather than suppress it. According to this view, a successful family is one that can negotiate conflict in a mutually satisfying manner rather than one that avoids it (Sprey, 1979).

Conflict frequently erupts as family members negotiate the division of labor and as they compete for access to valued resources such as affection and attention, money, sex, power and authority, and various privileges. One important source of conflict in families is the socially sanctioned patriarchal system that has kept women in a subordinate and disadvantageous position. Specifically, due to traditional sex-role assignments, women often end up assuming, without remuneration, a disproportionate amount of family labor, as compared to men, particularly the most time-consuming household maintenance chores and child-care tasks. Another frequent source of dissension in the family is the age hierarchy, which results in inequalities between the rights of children and their parents, with the children generally having less say in the decision-making process and less access to resources than their parents.

Conflictual interactions among family members can range from verbal disagreements to the use of physical force. In some cases, the use of coercion by dominant family members results in spouse, child, or elder maltreatment. When conflict cannot be resolved, many spouses opt for divorce. For a more detailed treatment of the application of conflict theory to the study of families, refer to Sprey (1979).

Symbolic Interactionism

According to **symbolic interaction theory,** social acts have no inherent meaning other than that which people attribute to them. Accordingly, family members interact or enact their family roles based on their subjective understanding of situations, what they think needs to be done, and their perception of what others expect them to do. As they relate to others, they receive feedback as to how well or how poorly they are doing, and based on their interpretation of this information, they continue to adjust their family behaviors.

Symbolic interactionists maintain that through the lifelong process of socialization, parents and others inside and outside the family pass on their meanings, values, beliefs, attitudes and norms to children, and, reciprocally, are influenced by the personalities, behaviors, meanings, beliefs, attitudes, and values of their children. Beginning in childhood, we learn to put ourselves in the shoes of others and to imagine how we affect them and how they perceive us. By assuming the other person's perspective, we learn to anticipate possible consequences of intended actions and to modify our behavior in accordance with these perceptions. Our significant others—those who are particularly close to us—greatly influence our emerging sense of self. Within the family, these significant others may be parents, siblings, various relatives, and other informally adopted family members. Readers interested in more detailed knowledge about the use of symbolic interactionism in family analysis are referred to Burr, Leigh, Day, and Constantine (1979).

Social Exchange Theory

As noted in Chapter 1, **social exchange theory** assumes that human relations are motivated by self-interest and involve a consideration of benefits versus costs of various actions. Specifically, according to the principle of fair exchange, most people expect to get out of a relationship something roughly equivalent in value to what they put into it. If the costs exceed the actual or potential benefits, they are likely to abandon the relationship.

The judgment of what constitutes a fair exchange is very subjective. For example, some parents may expect very little from their children in return for the sacrifices they make for them, whereas others may be much more demanding in their expectations. A husband may feel obligated or even glad to care for a chronically ill wife who can reciprocate only in small ways, whereas another may feel very little obligation to remain married under such circumstances or may feel that his duty as a husband is fulfilled by putting her in a nursing home.

According to Thibaut and Kelley (1959; Kelley & Thibaut, 1978), couples generally use two basic standards to assess the relative merits of their relationships: the comparison level and the comparison level for alternatives. The *comparison level* represents the degree of satisfaction that each member of a dyad feels he or she deserves out of the relationship on the basis of the individual's experiences in similar relationships and the person's perception of the rewards one should enjoy in such a relationship. The *comparison level for alternatives* is the level of satisfaction an individual believes he or she can get from other relationships or activities available as alternatives to the present relationship (including the option of being alone). When the outcome value of the cost-benefit analysis of the person's current relationship drops below that of the alternatives, the person is likely to leave and move on to another relationship or activity. But if the person believes that his or her available alternatives are worse than the present relationship, he or she will likely remain in the current relationship even if it is not gratifying.

Many people are able to wait for a considerable time, sometimes even years, to get their fair share out of a relationship, but eventually most expect to "collect" in some way. In a marriage, a wife may willingly endure her husband's near total disregard of her physical and emotional needs while he concentrates on some important work project or while he completes his studies. But if he should continue to ignore her past the completion of his special effort, she may decide that the relationship "is not worth it." In other words, when one partner of a relationship consistently and over the long run gets more out of it than he or she puts into it, the relationship becomes exploitative, and the disadvantaged party is likely to terminate it, unless the person's comparison level for alternatives

is even worse. For example, as noted previously in this book, a battered wife may continue to live with an abusive husband as long as she believes that staying with him is better for the children or for herself than having to resort to public assistance or as long as she feels that he will seriously hurt her if she attempts to leave him.

Exchange theory is simple, straightforward, and practical. For more detailed applications to family analysis, you may want to refer to Nye and colleagues (1979).

Developmental Approach:
The Family Life Course

A popular approach to the study of families is to view them developmentally as one would view an individual. Based on the assumption that there is an "average expectable" (Butler & Lewis, 1977) patterned sequence of stages of human development, one major focus of this approach is the study of the timing and order in which life events unfold within families. One of the major concepts within this tradition is the **developmental task,** a normative standard concerning what an individual is expected to be able to accomplish at a given stage in his or her life based on biological changes taking place in the body as well as on cultural norms and societal expectations (Havighurst, 1972). Developing language or increased independence from parents, learning to read and write, getting a job, and becoming sexually and intimately involved with another human being are examples of developmental tasks. Another important concept within this tradition is that development unfolds in stages often punctuated by crises and transition points as one goes from one stage to another. If these crises are resolved satisfactorily, they usher in a new, higher phase of growth and development (Erikson, 1963).

From a life-course perspective, one would look at the stages through which a family has progressed in the course of its unique existence and determine the extent to which it has accomplished successfully or failed to accomplish the developmental tasks generally associated with each stage. To be sure, these stages are *not* universally experienced by all families and they do not unfold in the same sequence or at the same pace in all families. Even well-functioning, healthy families skip some stages, sometimes moving to a new stage without having completed the tasks usually associated with the previous stage. Some families move through life stages at an unusually slow or fast pace or experience them in a different order. For example, some couples establish a separate household when they get married. Others tackle this task as roommates while going to school before becoming romantically involved. Still others continue to live with their parents for years after getting married, perhaps in order to save money to buy their own home at a future time. Similarly, some couples have children before getting married, whereas others postpone having children for several years until after they are well established financially and occupationally. Some remain childless throughout their marriage. The trajectory of a family's life is deeply affected by the timing at which various developmental stages unfold. For example, spouses who become first-time parents in their early forties follow a significantly different life course than those who become grandparents in their mid-thirties.

Every family follows a unique path and faces a different set of issues and events in the course of its life. Some issues arise unexpectedly rather than as part of the expectable developmental sequence. For example, some families must face idiosyncratic problems such as mental retardation, schizophrenic disorder, a disabling accident, or chronic physical illness of one or more members. Some families face a variety of external environmental problems and pressures such as sudden unemployment or criminal victimization. Other issues and events confronted by families are primarily related to their racial, ethnic, socioeconomic, and cultural contexts, such as discrimination, poverty, acculturation prob-

lems, or inability to speak the English language. In addition, the course of a family's life is influenced by the varied paths that individual family members follow in their own lives, such as youth gang membership, teenage pregnancy and parenthood, divorce, remarriage, graduate studies, and so on.

Because families are influenced by so many different factors, they can follow an almost infinite number of possible paths in their lives. However, for instructive purposes, it is useful to examine the *typical* life course of traditional, intact, heterosexual, two-parent, middle-class families to illustrate certain common developmental tasks that these and other families face at different points in the course of their lives. It must be understood, however, that not many *specific* families experience the same life course developmental processes. Even those families that face the same tasks to be described in this section are likely to experience them in a somewhat different order.

Mindful of the uniqueness of the trajectory of each family's life, let us examine the typical life course of traditional families. The stages delineated here are those suggested by Carter and McGoldrick (1980).

1. *Premarital phase.* The premarital phase normally starts with the development of a close friendship. As two friends explore their beliefs, values, behaviors, likes and dislikes, and affective styles, they get to know each other better. At some point in the development of a close relationship, they may become sexually or romantically involved. In time, love, caring, and intimacy may develop. Some couples may decide to become engaged or in some way formally committed to each other. For those who do, the engagement or formal commitment becomes the first rite of passage in their family's life course. Some couples may decide to live together to see how they get along. As the relationship deepens, they begin to experience conflict and to develop their own ways of managing it.

A traditional Euro-American middle-class family at play, as Grandma, who is visiting for the day, looks on.

2. *The newly married couple*. Most heterosexual couples eventually legalize their relationship by getting married. This is often a major rite of passage involving a church wedding, a wedding party, and a honeymoon. With marriage, the partnership acquires greater exclusiveness and the spouses make a longer-term commitment. They may decide to pool their resources, in which case they need to agree on how to share them. Sometimes disagreements about sharing money, possessions, decisions, or household tasks generate conflict.

For many young people, this is the first time they establish a separate household; consequently, they must develop a system to manage the housework and to pay the bills on time. They must also make innumerable compromises in order to adjust to living together, some as simple as deciding on which side of the bed each one is going to sleep or what toothpaste they are going to buy, and others more complex, such as who will go to college first while the other works if they decide that they will take turns in going to school. After marriage, most spouses also need to restructure their relationships with parents and friends, giving preference to their own mate over these other significant people in their lives who may have been given priority before.

3. *The family with young children*. Generally, the birth of a child marks the next major rite of passage for the family, as the spouses become parents. The parents now have major new responsibilities to nurture, socialize, control, and support their child. Faced with new pressures and demands, new family conflicts are likely to arise. For instance, the parents may want to continue the activities in which they engaged prior to the birth of their child, such as partying, going out to the movies and to dinner frequently, staying out late at night, and so on. But the new baby makes these frequent outings much more difficult and costly. The husband may get jealous of the attention his wife lavishes on the baby or vice versa. The child may awaken them several times during the night and one of them, whoever gets up, or both may feel groggy every morning when it is time to get up and go to work. The new expenses related to the baby may force the couple to deprive themselves of some things they previously enjoyed, such as being able to buy nice clothes or taking occasional weekend vacations.

Some families continue to expand by having or adopting additional children, thus increasing their responsibilities and pressures. As the children grow up and enter school, teachers become additional sources of influence, competing with parents for the children's attention. At home, parents and children must learn to cope with sibling rivalries and continuous invasions of privacy. Often, financial pressures mount and one or both parents may be forced to increase their work hours. Two-worker families risk role overload as they try to balance the pressures of outside work, housekeeping, and child care. These combined pressures often are felt more sharply by mothers who work full time outside the home. Some children with working parents may have to learn at a young age to take care of themselves and their younger brothers or sisters after school while their parents are at work because after-school child care can be expensive and difficult for some working parents to arrange.

4. *The family with adolescents.* Another rite of passage or test of fire for the family comes when the children become adolescents and the parents must adjust to their demands for increasing independence coupled with the growing influence of the peer group. Family boundaries may expand considerably during the adolescent years as some of the children's peers become de facto additional family members. Adolescents grow at an alarming rate, putting additional financial pressure on the family as they outgrow their clothes almost overnight and consume food faster than it can be stocked. Many families, including most middle-class families, feel the added pressures during these years associated with having to provide financial assistance for their children to go to college.

5. *Launching children.* Some time during midlife for the majority of parents, children move away from home to gain more independence and to experience what it is like to be on their own. Some parents feel a major loss over their children's departure—a phenomenon known as the *empty-nest syndrome*. However, most parents welcome their independence now that the children are grown up. This gives them a new opportunity for self-development and for espousal intimacy. Now they must learn new ways of relating to their children and lending them support appropriate to their newly gained adult status.

Another major event in the life course of families takes place when the children get married and the parents must welcome into the family a new son- or daughter-in-law and his or her relatives. When the children have children, the parents celebrate another major milestone—grandparenthood. For most people, this is a joyful new role to play but one that makes them more mindful of their own aging. During this time, many parents are beginning to lend support to their own aging parents, some of whom are becoming chronically ill or disabled.

6. *The family in later life.* The next important family developmental milestone comes when the spouses retire. With reduced income from pensions or social security, some parents must learn to accept financial assistance from their adult children. As they become older, some face new illnesses and disabilities while simultaneously having to deal with the disabilities and deaths of their own elderly parents.

7. *Death of a spouse.* The final stage in the life course of families comes when one of the spouses dies and the other must adjust to this major loss and to widowhood. Now the family is reduced to one person. She, or sometimes he, must learn to live alone or to adjust to living with children or other relatives. Widowed traditional women often must learn to manage their financial affairs on their own and to find their own means of transportation, if they depended on their husbands to pay the bills or to get around. Many widowed traditional men must develop skill in cooking and housekeeping. Both widows and widowers need to make new friends and to continue to lead an active life. Many widowers and some widows remarry and establish a new family. These remarriages involving adult children are usually less demanding developmentally than those including young children.

The next two sections will examine briefly some variations observed in the lives of poor families and some family issues of particular concern to women. Life-course matters pertaining to other contemporary family units will be examined later in the section entitled Contemporary Forms of Family Organization.

Life Course of Poor Families

As you might expect, life unfolds differently in low-income families, as compared to the middle-class families we have examined. Some of these differences are summarized in Table 8.1 below which compares the typical course of life of poor families with that of professional families.

Low-income families often experience an accelerated and truncated life, a high proportion of one-parent (mostly female-headed)

TABLE 8.1   Comparison of Family Life Cycle Stages

AGE	PROFESSIONAL FAMILIES	LOW-INCOME FAMILIES
12–17	a. Prevent pregnancy b. Graduate from high school c. Parents continue support while permitting child to achieve greater independence	a. First pregnancy b. Attempt to graduate from high school c. Parent attempts strict control before pregnancy, after pregnancy, relaxation of controls and continued support of new mother and infant
18–21	a. Prevent pregnancy b. Leave parental household for college c. Adapt to parents-child separation	a. Second pregnancy b. No further education c. Young mother acquires adult status in parental household
22–25	a. Prevent pregnancy b. Develop professional identity in graduate school c. Maintain separation from parental household. Begin living in serious relationship	a. Third pregnancy b. Marriage—leave parental household to establish stepfamily c. Maintain connection with kinship network
26–30	a. Prevent pregnancy b. Marriage—develop nuclear couple as separate from parents c. Intense work involvement as career begins	a. Separate from husband b. Mother becomes head of own household within kinship network
31–35	a. First pregnancy b. Renew contact with parents as grandparents c. Differentiate career and childrearing roles between husband and wife	a. First grandchild b. Mother becomes grandmother and cares for daughter and infant

Source: From *The Family Life Cycle: A Framework for for Family Therapy* (2nd ed.) by B. Carter and M. McGoldrick, 1989, Boston: Allyn and Bacon. Copyright 1989 by Allyn and Bacon. Reprinted by permission.

households, continuous crises and stresses, and frequent reliance on institutional/government assistance (Colon, 1980, p. 355; Hines, 1988). The concept of a truncated life course, refers to the "limited calendar time" within which various developmental stages unfold in multiproblem poor families, as compared to middle-class families (Colon, 1980). In other words, the poor tend to leave school, get married, have children, become grandparents, get old, and die faster and earlier than their middle-class counterparts. This gives them little time to deal with the developmental tasks of earlier life stages before later stages unfold. This situation often forces the members of poor families to assume new roles and responsibilities before they are developmentally ready to do so. As later life stages unfold, they become "more difficult to traverse because the solid underpinnings of previously resolved tasks are not available" (Colon, 1980, p. 355).

For example, many low-income young people face parenthood in their mid-teenage years. This makes it difficult, if not impossible, for them to deal successfully with adolescent developmental tasks, such as finishing high school or going to college, choosing an occupation they would like to pursue, and developing appropriate work skills. These teenage parents are prematurely thrust into a world of adult responsibilities for which most are poorly prepared. Before long, their children are having children and they become grandparents, thus arriving into "middle age" without having had a chance to successfully resolve basic youthful and young adult developmental tasks.

Poor families are also more likely than middle-class families to be headed by one parent due to higher rates of unemployment, unmarried pregnancy, divorce, separation, and desertion. They are also more likely to experience sudden losses of family members not only due to unemployment, separation, desertion, and divorce but also as a result of death, chemical dependency, and imprisonment. Such sudden changes in family membership require that the

remaining family members assume roles and responsibilities for which they often are not developmentally ready. For instance, a 16-year-old son may be forced to drop out of school after his father's departure to assume the role of breadwinner for the family. His 13-year-old sister may suddenly have to act as caregiver for their younger brother and sister because their mother had to increase her work hours to support the family.

The life course of poor families is often punctuated by more crises and stresses than those experienced by the middle class. The widespread problems of unemployment, poverty, divorce, desertion, and unwed and teenage pregnancies have been mentioned. In addition, poor families often face problems related to truancy and school dropout, crime and delinquency, gang involvement, incarceration, inadequate housing, substance abuse, family violence, mental disorder, infant mortality, learning disorders, physical disability, and untimely death (Hines, 1988, p. 513).

The external environment also intrudes a great deal on the lives of many low-income families. Those suffering a variety of economic and survival problems often experience repeated intrusions from various governmental and social agencies that attempt to regulate their lives—the housing authority, the welfare system, the courts, the public schools, the public health system, and so on. For example, those forced to seek Aid to Families with Dependent Children (AFDC) had their lives disrupted until recently by the public assistance rule that required fathers to be absent from the home in order for the family to qualify for needed benefits. Hines and Boyd-Franklin (1982) have suggested that one of the most useful services that practitioners can offer poor families is guidance in negotiating effectively the complexities of the bureaucratic systems with which they must contend.

Lower-income families seldom launch their children into a period of single and independent living, as their middle-class counterparts often do. This is because their children tend to quit school early, sometimes even before completing high school, and they often get married or have children at a young age. Many middle-class youths postpone marriage and a full-time job until after college. In this manner, they are able to experiment with various adult roles without having to make a lasting commitment to any of them. The early choices made by lower-income youths (e.g., having a child, dropping out of school) often have more serious or permanent consequences.

Poor families frequently have an extended childbearing and childrearing stage because, on average, they have more children over a longer period of time than middle-class families. Also, because of their tendency to have children early, they usually have more living representatives of different generations than middle-class families (Fulmer, 1988). For instance, many lower-income extended families include great-grandparents, despite their higher mortality rates and shorter life spans.

Women and the Family Life Course

Parents, grandparents, and great-grandparents were exposed to different gender-role socialization experiences than today's young people. This section examines some family life-course experiences that have been more characteristic of women than men. We should be cognizant of the fact that societal standards concerning sex roles are changing rapidly; therefore, these traditional differences between the sexes within the family will be much less pronounced among the younger generations.

Launching Stage. McGoldrick (1989, p. 207) noted that, until recently, most women went "from their families of origin to their families of procreation with no space in between to be independent." That is, the period of youthful experimentation prior to making major commitments to family and to work was, until recently, largely a male prerogative, with most daughters

having been expected to go directly from their parents' home to their husbands'. Even today, some old-fashioned or deeply religious families as well as some immigrant families, such as some Latino or Asian families, might be concerned if their daughters took "full advantage" of their youthful independence and moved out of home prior to marriage.

Combining Work, Marriage, and Children. A small but growing proportion of women today are choosing to remain unmarried (about 12 percent) or childless (about 25 percent). No doubt this is in part due to the fact that work and family life frequently create conflicting demands for women, whereas traditionally work and family have been mutually supportive for men (McGoldrick, 1989). In other words, family life constantly has intruded in the work lives of women because women traditionally have been expected to assume primary responsibility for the children and for the household. Precisely because of this traditional division of labor putting the lion's share of household and child-care chores on wives, husbands have been freer to concentrate on their work and often have found marriage to be supportive of their jobs or careers.

Divorce and Remarriage. After divorce, most women still act as the custodial parents for the children. Hence, divorce tends to increase the women's work and family responsibilities and to decrease their income. In contrast, many men actually improve their financial situation and have fewer family responsibilities after divorce. At remarriage, the women's financial situation often improves again, but family responsibilities usually increase for those women who take on (at least on a part-time basis) the role of stepparent for their new husband's children, in addition to their own parental responsibilities.

Caring for Elderly Parents. Another important difference between the course of family life for men and women traditionally has come when the parent(s) get old and begin to require assistance. Daughters have been expected to provide most of the caregiving for their parents, sometimes at the expense of their quality of life during middle age. Some wives also have had to provide care for their husbands' parents.

After the Death of a Spouse. As old age approaches, another characteristic difference between the sexes surfaces. Because husbands are likely to die first, women more often than men spend their last years of life without a spouse and frequently without sufficient income.

LIFE BEYOND THE TRADITIONAL FAMILY: CONTEMPORARY FORMS OF FAMILY ORGANIZATION

Families are undergoing rapid and dramatic changes, becoming more diverse and less durable. For example, there are fewer traditional or intact families today—that is, families composed of two parents and their biological children. Divorce has become an acceptable option for many people, and this has led to the creation of an increasing number of one-parent families, stepfamilies, and joint-custody families. Dual employment is now the standard for most families, even those with small children, and many couples are living together without legal sanction. In addition, as the society becomes more tolerant about racial intermarriage and gays and lesbians, there is an increasing number of interracial families and families headed by gays and lesbians. These are some of the realities of contemporary family life.

This section examines various contemporary forms of family organization other than the traditional family. These include one-parent families, stepfamilies, joint-custody families, dual-worker families, extended families, families headed by lesbians and gays, cohabitation, interracial families, migrant families, foster families, and child-free families.

One-Parent Families

The United States is witnessing a tremendous increase in the number of **one-parent families.** Specifically, in 1992, one-parent families constituted about 30 percent of all U.S. families with children, up from 13 percent in 1970. Their incidence varied substantially by race, gender of the head of the household, and ethnic background (U.S. Bureau of the Census, 1993b). For example, in 1990, approximately 20 percent of non-Latin white children were living with one parent only, compared to 63 percent of non-Latin black children and 36 percent of Latino children of all races (U.S. Bureau of the Census, 1993d). In 1992, 86 percent of one-parent families were headed by women and 14 percent were headed by men. Since 1980, the proportion of one-parent families headed by men has risen from 10 percent to 14 percent (Johnson, 1993). Most one-parent families are transitional, given that over 70 percent of those who divorce eventually remarry. However, a substantial proportion of these families are long term because they are headed by unwed women or by women who are less likely to remarry, such as African-American women or highly educated divorced women over 30 years of age.

Most one-parent families result from divorce, separation, or unwed pregnancies. Some are due to the death of one of the parents. A few are formed by choice, although the proportion of one-parent families created by single persons adopting children or by women deliberately choosing to have and to rear children by themselves is increasing but still very small.

One-parent families face several common challenges and problems. For example, custodial parents must often cope simultaneously with the pressures of making a living, raising the children, and maintaining the household without the help of the other parent. Many feel overloaded as they try to take care of these multiple responsibilities, particularly those who lack a good social support network. Their

situation is frequently aggravated by employers who treat them with inflexibility in relation to their conditions of employment, such as work hours.

Income is usually limited when the family has only one potential wage earner, particularly if it is a woman. (Even families headed by single fathers are not exempt from poverty; in 1992, 18 percent of one-parent families headed by men lived in poverty [Johnson, 1993].) As noted previously in this book, more than a third of female-headed homes are poor due to the women's low earnings coupled with the failure of many ex-husbands or ex-boyfriends to contribute to the support of their children on a regular basis. This problem has thrust many recently divorced women heads of household into the full-time job market for the first time since they had their children at the very same time they are suffering from a great deal of stress due to the marriage breakup.

If the family's income has decreased substantially after divorce, the single parent (usually the mother) may be forced to move to more affordable housing or sometimes to return to her (or his) parents' home. Having to move at a crisis point causes the family additional hardship. The children may have to change schools, teachers, and classmates, and everyone may have to adjust to living in a different neighborhood. Moving is sometimes aggravated by property owners and lending institutions unwilling to rent or lend money to female heads of household with children because they are considered a poor financial risk.

Some families are reduced to poverty by divorce. The single parent may have to apply for public assistance for the first time in her or his life, and the family may have to endure substandard housing, an unsafe neighborhood, and poor health due to the many pressures such families face coupled sometimes with the loss of health insurance.

Many parents raising children by themselves experience social isolation and loneliness. Married couples usually do not like to socialize with an unattached woman or man, even those who were their close friends prior to divorce, perhaps in part because the single person—the proverbial third wheel—can be perceived as a rival or a threat. Consequently, many single parents find themselves excluded from many social events except those that are child related (Brown, 1988). Some single parents may avoid social engagements even when they are invited because they feel awkward going without a partner or because they are too exhausted or depressed to engage in social activities.

Another reason why single parents often feel left out socially is that few single men or women like to socialize with or date people who have children because of the complications children inevitably create. Some single parents compensate by developing friendships with other parents in similar circumstances or by relying on their parents, siblings, close friends, or other relatives, even their ex-spouse's relatives, for social and emotional support as well as for some help with child

care, finances, and household chores. Another way of filling the gaps is to participate in support groups, such as Parents Without Partners and various other social activity groups geared to single parents.

Still another problem associated with divorce and single parenthood is that many children do not get to be with their noncustodial parent frequently enough, particularly if the noncustodial parent is the father. It appears that a substantial proportion of men in the United States are close to their children and responsible for them while they are living with them and their mother or as long as they remain unremarried; however, once those men marry someone else, they often transfer their attention and loyalties to their new family (Furstenberg, Nord, Peterson, & Zill, 1983; Lewin, 1990). Specifically, a follow-up nationwide study of a representative group of more than 1,000 children in families disrupted by divorce revealed that nearly half had not seen their fathers in the previous year, and only one in six actually saw their fathers once a week or more. Not all fathers are to blame for withdrawing from their children's lives after divorce. In some cases, both parents cause the alienation by maintaining too high a level of conflict between them. Some mothers cause the break by not allowing the fathers to visit with their children. To be sure, although many fathers practically disappear from their children's lives after divorce, some remain "active auxiliary members of the single-parent family" (Brown, 1988, p. 389).

Many single parents and their children develop a degree of closeness that exceeds that usually maintained by parents and children in two-parent families. Because of this, when the custodial parent tries to establish an intimate relationship with a new partner, the children, who have become used to having the parent's undivided attention, often react negatively. The adjustment to the parent's new romantic partner can be difficult, with the children often feeling threatened, displaced, hurt, resentful, and perhaps acting rebelliously. The children may also perceive the new person as a threat to the possibility of their parents getting back together and may therefore resent him or her (Brown, 1988).

Another characteristic of one-parent families is that the children often help out more than the children in two-parent families, both by working part-time and by doing some of the housework, shopping, chauffeuring, and caregiving of younger ones, if the single parent is willing to live with a "flexible" (occasionally abysmally lower!) performance standard. Having to help out in these various ways may pressure some of the children in one-parent families into growing up faster than the children in two-parent homes (Weiss, 1979; Hogan, Buehler, & Robinson, 1983).

One-parent families are not intrinsically deficient or dysfunctional. A study of 300 one-parent and two-parent families selected at random from the records maintained by a large southeastern school district found comparable levels of psychosocial adjustment among children coming from these two types of families (Green & Crooks, 1988). Analyses of broad-based data such as the National Survey of Families and Households and the National Survey of Children have suggested that problems previously thought to be caused by the absence of the father in one-parent families appear to be related, to a large extent, to the loss of his income (Acock & Demo, 1994). Children from intact families fare slightly better than children from one-parent families or from remarried families in terms of school achievement, high school completion rate, personal/emotional adjustment, and adult poverty rates, but the differences between the groups are small (Olson & Haynes, 1993; Acock & Demo, 1994).

Research is beginning to show that what matters most, it seems, is not the type of family unit in which children are reared but its socio-economic circumstances (at least in terms of poverty versus nonpoverty status), whether the children have a warm and nurturing home environment that teaches them values and responsi-bility, whether they have a noncustodial parent who remains involved with them, and whether or not their custodial parent is employed. Employment of the custodial parent may be important because it provides needed money, independence, and workplace-related adult friends for the single parent (Olson & Haynes, 1993; Acock & Demo, 1994).

Olson and Haynes (1993) found that the group of 29 successful single parents they studied shared the following traits: All were highly competent in the parental role and enjoyed raising their children. They nurtured their children and made them a priority in their lives. They took care of their own mental, physical, and emotional needs as well as their children's. They had a trusting relationship with the children and used consistent, nonpunitive discipline methods. They fostered their children's relationship with the noncustodial parent, when the other parent wanted to be involved. They were gainfully employed or getting further education. Although some were struggling financially, they were not poor.

One-parent families are not intrinsically harmful. In fact, getting out of a stressful two-parent home can be very relieving and positive for the healthy development of children (Wattenberg, 1987), particularly for those who are leaving behind family lives filled with violence, alcoholism, and drug abuse. But the transition can be very stressful, particularly if there is financial need after the divorce or separation. A large proportion of one-parent families suffer the consequences of poverty in addition to the challenges and stresses of single-parenthood. This is in large part the reason why such families, as a group, are more vulnerable than those headed by two adults. Therefore, their substantial growth in numbers in recent years is a social concern, as long as society does not offer adequate supports to all its families.

One important thing society can do to prevent a further increase in one-parent families is to provide disadvantaged young males with the best possible education, mentoring, role modeling, job training, job opportunities, and help toward self-sufficiency so that they will be in a better position to assume their share of responsibility for their children (Raspberry, 1989). Just as important is to find more effective ways of preventing teenage pregnancy, to increase the availability of day care and after-school programs so that more single parents will be able to hold a job, and to provide occupational training and jobs for single heads of household. It is also essential to find a way of ensuring that noncustodial parents pay their fair share of the support of their children.

Social service practitioners can assist one-parent families by becoming active in making the needs of these families known to policy makers at the national and state levels. In the community, they can assist by advocating and initiating services for them such as child care and after-school care and by working against discrimination of single parents in the workplace and in housing. One important goal for direct practitioners working with one-parent families is to help them to function more effectively without feeling that because the other parent is missing, the family is somehow deficient or incomplete. This requires, among other things, that the single parent achieve financial control, effective discipline over the children, and a viable network of social and support relationships (Brown, 1988, p. 386).

Remarriage and Stepfamilies

When people remarry, they establish a **remarriage family.** If either marriage partner brings to the newly-created family his or her own children from a former marriage, the remarriage family is generally referred to as a **stepfamily.** (The prefix *step* in the term *stepfamily*, however, may have negative connotations for some people; consequently, some families may prefer to be called *remarriage families with children*. In this section, the term *stepfamily* will be used simply because it is the most frequently encountered in the family literature). The

Bureau of the Census does not keep figures on stepfamilies; however, it has been estimated that about one in five two-parent families with children is a stepfamily and approximately one-third of all the children born in the 1980s will live in such a family unit for some time before the age of 18 (Wald, 1987; McGoldrick & Carter, 1988; Kantrowitz & Wingert, 1990).

It generally takes considerable time and effort, probably as much as five years or even longer if adolescents are involved, for the members of a stepfamily to stop feeling like a collection of people living together and to begin to feel like a real family. This is because there are many adjustments to be made and tasks to be accomplished before the group can function as a family. Consider some of the problems typically experienced by such families. Many start by having to move to a different home, a major disruption in and of itself. A study of 30 remarriage families by Dahl, Cowgill, and Asmundsson (1987, p. 41) showed that one-third had moved in the first year either to avoid the awkwardness of living "in someone else's home" or to accommodate the children's combined needs in terms of living space. The stepfamily must also discard old family rules and traditions and develop a new way of running the household that is acceptable to its members. Everything—from the time to have dinner and to go to bed to what is to be cooked for Thanksgiving dinner and who is to be invited—must be renegotiated and reimplemented.

The transformation from a group of people living together to a family whose members have a reasonable amount of trust and affection toward one another takes place slowly and painfully. Stepfamily members must learn to cope with feelings of being in competition for attention and affection or feelings of being left out. For example, the stepparent may feel excluded at times because of the strong bond between the biological parent and her or his children. Under such circumstances, some stepparents become depressed and withdrawn.

Others become jealous and competitive with their stepchildren, sometimes coming between biological parent and her or his child(ren). Similarly, the children may feel left out because of the new romantic relationship between their parent and stepparent and may also become jealous, competitive, demanding, sad, or angry. Children from a previous marriage of one parent or the other may feel like second-class citizens in relation to the remarriage children. Noncustodial children who visit occasionally may feel hurt because the children living in the household have more continuous access to their parent.

Mourning and feelings of loss are nearly universal in the transition to the stepfamily, particularly among families that plunge into remarriage before their members have been able to work through the grief and losses associated with divorce. Thus, children may be struggling to adjust to the stepparent and stepsiblings while simultaneously missing the absent parent, the old home, the grandparents, the brothers or sisters left behind with the other parent, and perhaps teachers and close friends from the old school or neighborhood. Children coming into stepfamilies from one-parent families also frequently experience the loss of their exclusive relationship with their parent. Fathers, and occasionally some mothers, must adjust to the loss of custody of the children to the ex-spouse. Not even a previously-never-married stepparent is exempt from feelings of loss in the transition to a stepfamily, as some mourn losing the chance to have a traditional family (Stanton, 1986, p. 202).

Sexual issues sometimes add to the tensions experienced in stepfamilies. Particularly delicate are situations in which teenagers of the opposite sex are suddenly thrown together and expected to relate as brothers and sisters. Similarly, stepfathers may suddenly find themselves living with young women who have become their stepdaughters and to whom they must be able to relate as fathers (McGoldrick & Carter, 1988).

We have discussed some of the problems confronted by stepfamilies as a whole. In addition, stepparents face special challenges. For example, they are expected to act appropriately in the stepparent role even though there are no clear social prescriptions for such a role. They are also expected to develop acceptable and effective discipline methods—a difficult task because they have no real kinship or legal ties to invoke when regulating their stepchildren's behavior. Child support or alimony payments are still another problem the spouses frequently face in stepfamilies. The monetary outflow can be draining on limited resources, and the new spouse may become resentful of such expenses. Ex-spouses are yet another issue. When there is shared custody of children, the remarried couple must develop a working relationship with ex-spouses. This can be difficult if conflicts remain unresolved or if the absent parent refuses to cooperate. Another challenge for some stepparents is to learn to accept that their new husband or wife may still care for his or her ex-spouse and consider this person to be family, no matter how "unreasonable" the person may be, particularly after a long marriage and when children are involved.

Stepchildren also face special challenges. They must learn to act as stepchildren and stepsiblings without having a clear idea of what is expected of them in such positions. They must get used to different methods of discipline as these are reworked by the stepfamily. Some are forced to give up their previous special positions or privileges with respect to their parent. For example, a daughter who took pride in fixing breakfast for her daddy may now have to yield to her stepmother. An only child may suddenly become a middle child in the new stepfamily configuration, or the previously youngest or eldest child may lose his or her special position to a stepsibling even younger or older. There are also new stepsibling rivalries to work through. For example, the biological son who comes to visit and finds his father playing with his new stepson is bound to feel resentful or hurt. Stepchildren may get jealous of the children born to the remarried couple—that is, of the nuclear family within the stepfamily. Loyalty conflicts are still another problem: A child may feel guilty or at least uneasy if she allows herself to have a good time with her stepmother, as she may interpret this as an act of disloyalty toward her own mother. Similarly, some children may be pressured by one or both parents into taking sides or into causing problems for the other parent or the stepparent.

No matter how hard a stepfamily tries to become a family and to function smoothly, the first year or so tends to be quite difficult, according to families that have gone through this process. Particularly difficult to manage successfully are those stepfamilies with young children who still need active parenting or those with adolescents. If both spouses are at the same life-course phase, such as when both have young children, or, even better, when both have grown children, difficulties tend to be fewer than when they are at different stages. Consider, for example, a middle-aged husband with custody of his adolescent sons who marries a previously-never-married young woman. His new wife may be unrealistically looking forward to a romantic first marriage and to having children of their own. Whereas he, overwhelmed with work pressures and the demands of his adolescent boys, does not have enough time for her and refuses to have any more children. If these things were not thoroughly discussed prior to the marriage, she may suffer a severe disappointment (Visher & Visher, 1983; Dahl, Cowgill, & Asmundsson, 1987; McGoldrick & Carter, 1988).

Instant intimacy is not possible to achieve in a stepfamily, yet stepparents and stepchildren often feel guilty because they are unable to trust, love, or feel close to steprelatives shortly after the new family is formed. However, regardless of the difficulties encountered initially, eventually many stepfamilies find an adequate level of cohesion and their members are able to form warm or at least cordial (though usually not intense) attachments with other stepfamily members. Nonetheless, stepfamilies generally remain more vulnerable than intact families. Specifically, such families are more than twice as likely as traditional families to divorce; and child abuse, including sexual abuse, also occurs more frequently in stepfamilies than in traditional families (Levine, 1990, p. 51; Kantrowitz & Wingert, 1990, p. 27). Hence, self-help support groups, such as those sponsored by the Stepfamily Association of America, as well as special instruction for stepparents and, in some cases, psychosocial intervention may be necessary for some stepfamilies.

Stepfamilies can benefit from the advise other stepfamilies can give them as well as from the knowledge and insight of practitioners who specialize in working with them. The wisdom gathered from these two sources indicates that open communication, joint decision making, the ability to negotiate and reach a compromise, and mutual respect are essential skills all families need, especially stepfamily members. It is particularly important for the stepparent to respect the special bond between the stepchildren and their biological parents, grandparents, and significant others on the paternal and maternal side. Keeping connected to their roots helps children to develop a strong sense of identity and well-being (Stanton, 1986). Similarly, it is important for the children's biological parents, particularly those who do not have custody, to allow the relationship between child(ren) and stepparent to grow without undermining it. After all, the children must live with their stepparents, so they are entitled to as comfortable a relationship as possible.

In the area of discipline, it is important for parent and stepparent to present a unified front and to avoid disagreements in front of the children so as not to undermine the authority of either parent. In this respect, stepparents may do well to limit their discipline of the other parent's children, when necessary, to enforcing the rules that have been jointly established, leaving major issues to be settled by the biological parent (Dahl, Cowgill, & Asmundsson, 1987; McGoldrick & Carter, 1988; Papernow, 1991). It is equally important for parents not to show favoritism toward their own children versus their stepchildren in terms of rule enforcement, even though they should feel free to admit that they feel different levels of love or concern for each child depending on whose child it is.

It usually pays for stepparents to go into the stepfamily with low expectations. To expect love or respect from the stepchildren from the start is to ask for too much in most cases. However, if stepparents are courteous and considerate toward their stepchildren, they should be able to expect to be treated in like manner.

Shared-Custody Families

Strictly speaking, when divorced or separated parents agree in writing to share responsibility and decision making concerning major aspects of their children's lives—such as health care, education, place of residence, or religion—they are said to have **joint legal custody.** If they also agree to share the parenting and child-rearing responsibilities, they have **joint physical custody.** If the joint custody has been ordered by the court, it is referred to as **court-ordered joint custody,** which can be stressful for many children because they are put in a situation of having to live with one parent against the strong objections of the other. In general, families that share the custody of children, legal or physical, are referred to as **shared-custody or binuclear families** (Ahrons & Rodgers, 1987).

Much of what has been said about the challenges experienced by stepfamilies also applies to joint-custody families since many joint-custody families are stepfamilies. The material that applies to the stepfamily aspects of joint-custody families will not be repeated here since it is available in the previous section. Instead, this section will concentrate on the special challenges and experiences associated with sharing the physical custody of children.

Joint-custody children often live with biological parents who occupy separate homes. (Only in one rare joint-custody arrangement, referred to as **birdnesting**, the children stay at home and the parents take turns moving in and out [Wallerstein & Blakeslee, 1989].) Living arrangements vary in joint-custody families. For instance, a child may live with one parent during the week and with the other during the weekend or the child may live with one parent for a week and move in with the other parent for the following week, and so on. Other children may change homes more or less frequently. Generally, the more frequent the required transitions from home to home, the harder it is for children to cope satisfactorily with joint-custody arrangements (Wallerstein & Blakeslee, 1989, p. 270). This is because joint-custody children experience many changes as they go from one home to the other—different disciplinary rules, lifestyles, living standards, codes of ethics, foods, and so forth. They must be flexible enough to negotiate these changes on a regular basis. Many must also adapt to changing stepparents and stepsiblings, changing schools and classmates, and varying substitute care arrangements as they shuttle from one parent to the other (Wallerstein & Blakeslee, 1989).

Although it is difficult to deal with so many changes, some children's lives may actually be enriched by such diversity (Visher & Visher, 1983). Other children, however, may be unable to handle the transitions. To be sure, the constant moving from one parent's home to the other's can leave a child feeling rootless. The shuttling back and forth is particularly difficult for adolescents who have established or are in the process of establishing their own social networks (Johnson, 1993). Although the children bear the brunt of the transitions from one home to the other, family members also must exercise considerable flexibility to conduct their lives in the midst of the expansions and contractions of family boundaries necessary to include visiting children as they come and go (McGoldrick & Carter, 1988).

It is still too early to have knowledge about the long-term effects of joint physical custody on children. Based on their studies, Wallerstein and Blakeslee (1989, pp. 269–270) concluded that there is no evidence at present that joint custody is better for children than good single custody when the noncustodial parent remains involved in the life of the children. A study by Maccoby and Mnookin (1992) of the outcome of 1,000 divorces in California found that when shared custody arrangements lasted, the consequences for the children were no worse than the consequences of single custody arrangements. The researchers therefore concluded that the welfare of children following divorce seems to depend not so much on custody arrangements as on the quality of their home life and how well the parents are able to cooperate. When it works well, joint custody enables children to remain closely related to both parents and to be part of their homes and lives. In bad situations, such as when the parents are constantly quarreling, joint custody keeps children locked into their parents' struggles. One obvious disadvantage of joint custody is that, if one parent pulls out of the arrangement, the children can easily perceive this as a personal rejection. Such a blow after divorce can be devastating for some children.

For joint-custody arrangements to succeed, both parents must be able to maintain a cordial relationship characterized by open communication and cooperation, sensitivity, and flexibility. This is because the two homes must be linked very closely for the children to be able to go back and forth regularly. Both families must know all the details of the child's daily routine, including such things as bedtime, naptime, medicines taken, doctors' appointments, school work, extracurricular activities, and much more. It is equally important for members of both families to attend major events, such as birthdays, graduations, weddings, and funerals, since both play a major role in the children's lives. For these rea-sons, joint physical custody is not indicated if the ex-spouses have a conflictive relationship.

Dual-Employment Families

In 1992, in 60 percent of all married-couple families with children under age 18, both parents were employed outside the home. Even among families with children under the age of 6, 53 percent had two parents employed outside the home (U.S. Bureau of the Census, 1993a). Consequently, **dual-employment families** have become standard. These families, particularly those with young children, experience considerable stresses due to the competing pressures of their occupational and family lives.

Dual-worker families enjoy certain advantages over families with one wage earner only, such as a higher standard of living and a higher potential for the personal fulfillment of each spouse. Parents who work outside the home also present a desirable role model for their children to emulate (Skinner, 1983). However, employed couples need cooperation, sex-role flexibility, and good coping skills to juggle the demands of job, marriage, children, and household, as well as the psychological tensions and strains arising from these pressures. For their own health and fulfillment, they must also find a reasonable amount of time to set aside for joint family activities, leisure, and relaxation.

Although nowadays men and children in dual-employment families are assuming more responsibilities, women still bear the brunt of the household and child-rearing work; consequently, the women in such families are more prone to overload. Some families can purchase goods and services to ease some of the strains, such as time-saving devices, household assistance, and child care. Others have extended-family members who help out, such as live-in or nearby grandparents. Those who are less well-off financially or who do not have relatives to help out feel the burden of dual employment most unremittingly.

Dual-career families are those with two spouses employed in professional or managerial positions. Their experiences are essentially the same as those of all dual-employment families, except that because careers are generally highly demanding in terms of time and energies, the spouses may have even less time for family life or household chores. Usually this is compensated to various extents by more ample financial resources to buy the goods and services necessary to make their family lives easier. Yet, finding suffcent time to be together can be a problem for some of these families.

Sometimes, in order to fulfill his or her career aspirations, one of the spouses accepts a position in another area of the country so far away from home that it becomes necessary to set up another household. This requires that the spouses take turns traveling to be together from time to time. These families, referred to as **dual-career commuter families,** constitute a very small but growing segment of dual-employment families. The commuter family arrangement is difficult; however, it can be manageable. Generally, those spouses with well-established marriages and careers, grown children, and frequent reunions (such as every other weekend or so) experience the least strains. Their stable marital history helps to sustain the separations (Gerstel & Gross, 1984).

Multigenerational Extended Families

Multigenerational extended families are composed of several generations of the same family and sometimes other relatives living together. Although these family units comprise a small minority of U.S. families, their numbers are on the rise. To give you an idea of the growth in the number of multigenerational families in the United States, between 1980 and 1991, the census reported that the number of children in the United States living in multigenerational households had increased from 1.3 million to 2.4 million (Ames, Lewis, Kandell, Rosenberg, & Chideya, 1992).

Part of the reason for this increase is the rise in life spans, which has caused more elderly parents to move in with their children. In addition, many adult children have contributed to the growth in intergenerational family living in recent years by returning to their parents' homes after divorce (sometimes with their own children) or when faced with unemployment, part-time employment, low wages, or inability to get adequate housing at affordable prices. Changes in the economy have hit young people particularly hard, unless they enter the job market with a high level of skills and education; in contrast, by and large their aging parents have done relatively well financially and are more likely to have a spacious home (with low mortgage payments) to accommodate their adult children (Ames et al., 1992).

New immigrants and racial/ethnic minorities with a multigenerational family tradition also have added to the growth in such families. Many racial and ethnic minority families, particularly those of recent immigrants, favor the extended family form. For example, there is a higher proportion of multigenerational extended families among Latinos, African Americans, American Indians, and Asian Americans than among Euro-Americans. For racial and ethnic minority families, the extended family has served as a protective environment and coping strategy in the face of discrimination, oppression, poverty, and various other adverse circumstances (Billingsley, 1968). To a lesser extent, immigrants who came to the United States in the first half of the twentieth century—such as many Italian Americans, Polish Americans, American Jews, and Greek Americans—also have a higher proportion of multigenerational extended families than Euro-Americans whose foreparents have been in the United States longer. Many of these ethnic families still retain, to some extent, the traditions of their countries of origin.

The multigenerational extended family unit is a good choice for those who must depend on mutual aid for survival. Its special appeal is extending nowadays to mainstream families. This is because this type of family organization lightens the burden of raising children and keeping the household, decreases the cost of living for each family member, and offers more sources of companionship and emotional support.

Families Headed by Gay and Lesbian Parents

In Norway, Denmark, and Sweden, individuals of the same sex are allowed to get married and they have all the rights of marriage, except the right to adopt children. Same-sex marriages, however, were not legal in the United States in the mid-1990s, although Hawaii was coming close to removing the last few legal barriers to same-sex marriages (Ingrassia, 1994). Because such unions are not legally recognized, the Census does not keep a count of the number of families headed by gays or lesbians. However, estimates are that there may be more than 2 million lesbian and gay families rearing several million children (Seligmann, 1990, p. 39; Hare, 1994), the vast majority having resulted from divorce or separation. A small proportion of these families have been created by adoption by one of the partners or artificial insemination. But in the mid-1990s, only a very small number of gay and lesbian couples had been allowed to adopt children jointly, since most states still prohibited adoptions by same-sex couples.

We have discussed many of the special circumstances surrounding stepfamilies and female-headed families. In many ways, lesbian-headed and gay-headed families face similar problems, with additional complications. For example, the roles and relationships of parents and children in these families lack social definition as well as social or legal sanction. Moreover, same-sex couples who try to raise children may experience difficulties specifically related to their sexual orientation. For instance, many lesbian and gay parents fear

rejection and isolation from their own parents or siblings. This problem may be less common than they fear, at least for those who are middle class and well educated. A study by Hare (1994) of 28 middle-class families headed by lesbians, most with college degrees, showed that the couples felt more accepted by their families of origin than by the lesbian community.

Another problem feared by gay and lesbian parents is rejection by heterosexual families as well as by gays and lesbians who do not have children. Some heterosexuals do not accept the gay/lesbian lifestyle and are reluctant to mix socially with them. In some cases, they may be hostile toward them. In addition, some families headed by gays and lesbians feel that they do not have much in common with childless gays and lesbians (Hare, 1994). Therefore, they may find themselves isolated and lacking a support network, particularly if they are unconnected with other families headed by lesbians or gays. Their children may have less peer support available to them than the children of heterosexuals, either because they may choose to maintain greater distance from peers in fear of being rejected or embarrassed or because some peers from heterosexual families may be taught to keep away from them in fear that they may be a "bad influence." Fear of the impact of social stigma on their children runs high among gay/lesbian parents, although there is some research evidence that overt stigmatizing experiences are not common (Hare, 1994). Lack of day-to-day access to male or female role models also may be a problem for some of the children in gay/lesbian families.

Child custody is another major concern for lesbians and gays. Until recently, only a small proportion of openly lesbian mothers were able to obtain custody of their children. Nowadays, the judicial system is somewhat more flexible in making custody determinations, considering the parent's sexual orientation not as the overriding factor but as one of several elements to be contemplated (Hare, 1994). Nonetheless,

Box 8.1

For 5-Year-Old Girl, 'Mommy, Mommy'

JOINT ADOPTION BY GAY COUPLE ALLOWED

Boston–(AP)–A state Supreme Court ruling Friday made a prominent breast cancer surgeon and her lover the first homosexual couple to win approval from Massachusetts to adopt a child.

In a 4-3 decision, the court said two unmarried women, whom it identified only as "Susan" and "Helen," may adopt "Tammy," a 5-year-old girl whom they have reared since birth.

Their attorney, Katherine Triantafillou, confirmed that the couple is breast cancer surgeon Susan Love and her lover of more than 10 years, Helen Cooksey, also a surgeon. Both are 45.

Despite the wording of the ruling, the women had no reluctance about being identified, their lawyer said. They have held positions on the Harvard Medical School faculty and now live in California, the lawyer said.

"They are like the perfect parents, and all-American, except for being lesbian," Triantafillou said. "It is an absolutely extraordinary, wonderful decision."

Dr. Love conceived Tammy through artificial insemination from Cooksey's cousin.

Although Love is the child's natural mother, joint adoption was required for both women to share parental rights. That is because Massachusetts law holds that if a child is adopted by a non-biological parent, the biological parent automatically loses parental rights.

The women's relatives, teachers, religious leaders from their church and neighbors testified that the couple were ideal parents and endorsed their adoption request. The state department of social services also recommended the adoption be approved.

Central to the case was the fact that the two women are not married. Massachusetts, like all other states, does not recognize same-sex marriages.

However, a majority of the court said there is nothing in state law that prevents joint adoption by a homosexual couple.

Two of the dissenting justices said they did not disapprove of the couple's homosexuality but interpreted state law as permitting joint adoptions only by married people. A third justice agreed with that point while also objecting to the women's lifestyle.

Triantafillou said other jurisdictions allowing such adoptions include California, Alaska, Vermont, Washington and the District of Columbia.

A similar case in Richmond had a much different outcome Tuesday when a Virginia judge ruled that a lesbian's relationship with her lover made her unfit to rear her 2-year-old son.

Source: "For 5-Year-Old Girl, 'Mommy, Mommy'" November 1993, *Miami Herald.* Reprinted with permission of the Associated Press.

many lesbians who get custody of their children still live in constant fear that their ex-husbands will use any information about their lifestyle to take the children away (Kirkpatrick, Smith, & Roy, 1981). For gay men, it has been nearly impossible to obtain custody of their children. In addition to these problems, some families headed by gays and lesbians face discrimination in housing from homophobic property owners and lenders.

One of the major dilemmas of gay and lesbian parents is whether they should tell the children about their sexual orientation, and, if so, how they should go about telling them and when. There is no easy solution and practitioners can assist by helping them weight the potential benefits and costs (Hare, 1994). It may be comforting for such parents to know that children are generally more understanding and accepting and take the news better than wives or husbands (Maddox, 1982). In fact, a study of children of lesbians by Lewis (1980) revealed that, without exception, they had found their parents' divorce more upsetting than the mother's disclosure of her sexual orientation. However, knowing that one of their parents is gay or lesbian can cause children a variety of concerns, particularly in relation to their own sexual orientation. For instance, children may worry about whether they will also be gay or lesbian when they grow up.

Not all are problems and complications, however. A study by Golombok, Spence and Rulter (1983) found that lesbian mothers and their ex-husbands maintained more cordial relations than heterosexual mothers and their ex-husbands. In addition, they found that children raised by lesbian mothers saw their fathers more frequently than those living with heterosexual mothers. Kirkpatrick, Smith, and Roy (1981) also found that lesbian mothers more frequently included male friends and relatives in their children's lives than heterosexual mothers. Lesbian couples with children often report other possible benefits from the experience of being raised in gay/lesbian family, such as tolerance for diversity, greater sensitivity to issues of discrimination, and greater probability that the children will be more androgynous and that they will have the courage of their convictions (Hare, 1994).

A review of various research projects on the mental health or adjustment of children raised by lesbian and gay parents has revealed no deficits. Moreover, none of the studies has found any effects on their sexual orientation (Patterson, 1992). In short, no strong evidence has been uncovered in the last decade that changes the general professional view that the children of gay or lesbian parents appear to be no more mixed up, disturbed, or likely to become gay or lesbian than the children of divorced parents (Maddox, 1982, p.68). The definitive answer to this question, however, will have to wait until researchers have been able to follow large numbers of children of gay and lesbian parents of various socioeconomic backgrounds over several decades (Chira, 1993).

Cohabitation

Cohabitation, or living together without legal sanction, is becoming more acceptable and prevalent as society becomes more tolerant of varying lifestyles. In 1992, 3.4 percent of U.S. households, or approximately 3.3 million households, included an unmarried opposite-sex couple with or without children (U.S. Bureau of the Census, 1993b), an increase of 500 percent over 1970 figures. (Although some people of the opposite sex living together are simply roommates or have an employer/employee relationship, a large majority are couples.) More than two-thirds of cohabiting units in 1988 consisted of the couple only; nearly one-third included children. Rates of cohabitation were higher for persons of low income living in metropolitan areas and for African Americans.

Several studies have shown that a large proportion of young people today live together before getting married (Gwartney-Gibbs, 1986; Tanfer, 1987; Thornton, 1988). Some argue that living together facilitates the process of mate selection and is an effective training ground for marriage. However, the existing evidence seems to point to the contrary. Several studies have shown that living together premaritally is associated with lower satisfaction in marriage for both spouses (DeMaris & Leslie, 1984; Booth & Johnson, 1988). Additionally, a survey of nearly 5,000 women conducted by the National Bureau of Economic Research in Sweden found that couples who had lived together before marriage had a divorce rate that was nearly 80 percent higher than those who did not (Bennett, Blanc, & Bloom, 1988). One reason for the significantly higher divorce rate among previously cohabiting couples, compared to married couples, may be that the former are more committed philosophically to personal independence and less likely to consider monogamy or a long-term relationship to be important (Eshleman, 1991, p. 284).

Regardless of its possible long-term outcomes, cohabitation serves positive immediate functions, especially for young couples. For example, it is a less expensive living arrangement for the partners than living alone and it provides a homelike atmosphere, an intimate relationship, and easy access to sex within a nonbinding union—a convenient arrangement. For these reasons, its popularity will likely continue to grow.

Interracial Families

Until recently, a large proportion of **interracial families** in the United States were established by enlisted men who met their wives, mostly Asians, while on military duty abroad. However, as society has become more tolerant and respectful of the individual freedom and personal rights of its citizens, and as children of different races spend more time together at school and develop close friendships, we are seeing many more home-grown interracial families. In 1992, 1.2 million U.S. married couples, or 2.2 percent of all married couples, were interracial, nearly four times the 1970 count (U.S. Bureau of the Census, 1993b).

Interracial marriages most commonly involve Native Americans and persons of Spanish and Asian origin. Estimates are that over half of all current marriages of Native Americans and about one-third of those of Latinos and Japanese Americans are interracial (Collins, 1984; Collins, 1986; Leslie & Korman, 1989). Interracial marriages are more likely than same-race marriages to be remarriages, and spouses belonging to different races tend to be older and better educated than their same-race counterparts (Dickinson & Leming, 1990).

Interracial families face special challenges. Most notable perhaps is the disapproval, rejection, or outright discriminatory treatment they sometimes receive not only from strangers but from those they considered friends and even from their own family. Those who lose extended-family support and acceptance because of their interracial relationships frequently establish a supportive network composed of interracial couples and other friends and relatives who approve of them. Interracial families also frequently encounter discrimination in housing—a problem sometimes dealt with by sending the spouse belonging to the "more acceptable" racial/ethnic group to inspect the property and to sign the contract. People sometimes stare at interracial families, mostly out of curiosity; this is an annoyance with which most couples learn to live.

Black/white relationships account for about one-fifth to one-fourth of all interracial marriages. Interestingly, in 75 percent of these unions, the husband is black and the wife is white. One possible reason for the greater number of black males compared to black females to marry outside their race, despite having a wide selection of black females available, is that some may prefer less independent women (Collins, 1986). Also, some black males may choose to marry white women, thinking that a white wife may contribute to their advancement in mainstream society more than a black wife. Although traditionally black/white families have been considered potentially the most problematic of all interracial families, a study by Dr. Alvin Poussaint of 37 children of black/white marriages suggested that they may be more successful than previously anticipated. Despite often feeling that they were scrutinized and sometimes teased by both black and white peers, the children Dr. Poussaint interviewed were high achievers and adept at forming friendships with black and white peers. These children also felt that they were more objective and nonjudgmental than their peers, less intimidated by the white world, and that they had benefited from the exposure to the two racial/ethnic heritages (Collins, 1984).

Migrant Families

Migrant families move from place to place as they work for large farms that hire temporary help to harvest the crops. They are largely concentrated in California, Florida, and Texas. Most of these families are very poor and belong to diverse nondominant racial and ethnic

Box 8.2

Migrant's Daughter Becomes Judge

BY SUSAN BELLIDO

Herald Staff Writer

Nancy Perez made true her farm worker parents' dream of getting ahead through education and hard work Monday when she became Palm Beach County's first Hispanic judge.

"I think it says so much that someone can work her way up the way you have, Nancy," said Gov. Lawton Chiles, who appointed Perez.

Chiles was among more than 200 people who attended the emotional ceremony in which Florida Supreme Court Justice Rosemary Barkett swore in the 37-year-old public defender.

Perez, the first-born daughter of Puerto Rican migrants who settled in the Fort Meyers area, credits her success to her parents. "They provided me with the motivation to keep on plugging, that it would all work out somehow." Perez picked fields

as a child. She remembered the pride she felt after earning $6 for seven hours of harvesting. But her parents–who left school early and met in an adult education class–encouraged her to aim for a better life.

When she was a girl, she said, many schoolmates headed north before the end of the school year. But her late father, Antonio, let his children stay behind and finish their studies. He then reurned from New York to pick them up. Her mother, Eduarda, gave birth to 11 children in 12 years, sewed and washed to help support the family, Perez said.

"Ever since she was small she was very smart," Perez's mother said. "She watched Perry Mason and said, 'I'll be better.' "

---

groups, particularly Mexican American, Puerto Rican, African American, and Haitian.

Migrant families confront many of the problems associated with poverty and racial oppression that were examined in Chapter 4. They also face problems characteristic of their migratory lifestyle, such as constant dislocation as they move from place to place and inability to establish roots anywhere. Those migrant workers who are undocumented are the most exploited by ruthless employers.

Because migrant families move so frequently, it is difficult for them to establish a social support network. It is also difficult for their children to attend school regularly. Long work hours and hard labor leave little time or energy for recreation or attention to the children. The children often begin to work in the fields at very young ages and have little chance of breaking out of the cycle of poverty since their education is typically meager.

Foster Families

Foster families are families paid to provide substitute care for children whose own parents cannot take care of them because of illness or disability or because they have been found to be abusive or neglectful. Providing foster care is often very challenging because many of the children in placement are angry, hostile, aggressive, bitter, and, in general, quite difficult to handle. Some act out in various ways. Many put little trust in adults and have difficulty forming close relationships. This is because a large proportion of these children have been abused, neglected, or rejected by their parents.

Most parents, including foster parents, are unprepared to cope with children who present serious problems. They may have been highly successful managing their own children's behavior, but the things that worked with their children or any other thing they may try may prove ineffective with a foster child. Consequently, many children in foster care fail to adjust to the homes in which they are placed or their foster parents request their removal from their home because they are unable to work with them. This constant movement from one family to another tends to aggravate the children's psychoemotional and social problems.

Although foster parents generally are carefully screened and trained and the majority do the best job they can under the difficult circumstances in which they are placed, occasionally some foster parents aggravate the problems of the children placed under their care by being abusive, neglectful, or rejecting. When this happens, it adds injury to pain.

One important priority for social service workers is to find more effective ways of working toward the rehabilitation of natural parents so they can be reunited with their children. We must also continue to improve the process by which foster families are selected, given consultation, direction, support, and training to improve their skills to care successfully for the children who temporarily cannot be maintained at home (Morrissette, 1994).

Child-Free Families

A growing proportion of married couples, many well educated and with high incomes, are choosing not to have any children. These are referred to as **child-free families.** Their voluntary childlessness may be due to a desire to commit themselves to their work, a previous unsuccessful marriage that has made them reluctant to have children, or an unwillingness to make the financial commitment necessary to have children. While in the past they may have been perceived as somewhat egotistical and self-centered, few people today would find fault with the choice to remain childless or question their right to self-determination.

Every family in the United States is vital to the character and strength of our nation, whether they be two-parent or one-parent families, nuclear or intergenerational, intact or remarried/stepfamilies, same race or interracial, headed by gay or lesbian parents or by heterosexual parents, single-provider or dual-employment families, legally married or cohabiting, single-custody or shared-custody families. All our families are fundamental social units necessary for the nurturance, socialization, control, and support of the citizenry.

We have seen that some families face formidable challenges. To produce happy, healthy, socially well-adjusted, and competent individuals, families need better societal supports, including quality health care and child care, guaranteed child support payments, equitable pay for women, maternity/paternity leaves with job security, flexible sick leave to take care of ill family members, and more flexible work hours to better accommodate the needs of children.

GLOSSARY

Augmented Family: A family unit including live-in unrelated people informally adopted as family members, such as a boyfriend or girlfriend or a nanny who has lived with the family for years.

Binuclear Families: See **Joint-Custody Families.**

Birdnesting: A rare postdivorce joint-custody arrangement whereby the children stay at home while their parents take turns moving in and out.

Blended Family: See **Stepfamily.**

Child-Free Family: A social unit composed of a couple who do not have and do not desire to have children.

Clear Boundaries: The dividing line between subsystems or between a system and its environment is defined well enough to allow system or subsystem members to carry out their functions without interference from the outside while permitting free exchange of inputs and outputs with those outside.

Coalition: Two or more persons joining forces to cooperate in a project or to oppose something.

Cohabition: Two unmarried adults sharing a household and being sexually intimate.

Conflict Theory: See **Social Conflict Theory.**

Couple-Only Nuclear Family: A social unit composed of two spouses without children.

Court-Ordered Joint Custody: The court orders the divorced or separated parents to share the physical or legal custody of the child(ren). See **Joint Legal Custody** and **Joint Physical Custody.**

Developmental Task: A normative developmental standard concerning what an individual is expected to be able to do at a given stage in his or her life based on biological changes taking place in the body as well as on cultural norms and societal expectations.

Disengagement: The members or subunits of a social system relate to one another or to their environment in an excessively detached manner—that is, without showing much loyalty, interdependence, or a sense of belonging.

Dual-Career Commuter Family: A special type of dual-career family in which the spouses practice their careers in different parts of the country and therefore must take turns traveling to be together from time to time.

Dual-Career Family: A type of dual-employment family in which both spouses hold professional or managerial positions outside the home.

Dual-Employment Family: A family in which both spouses work outside the home.

Dual-Worker Family: See **Dual-Employment Family.**

Ecomap: A pictorial representation of the significant people in every key environmental system with which a family ordinarily interacts, the relationship of the family with each of these systems, and the flow of energy and resources to and from the family.

Enmeshment: The relationship between members or subunits of a social system or between the system and its environment is so excessively close that it discourages autonomy, independence, and individual skill development.

Executive Subsystem: A subunit of a social system, in this case of the family, composed of those family members who have the authority to make decisions, such as, in a traditional family, the father and mother.

Expanded Family: See **Extended Family** and **Augmented Family**.

Extended Family: A family unit that includes live-in relatives, such as grandparents, aunts, uncles, cousins, nephews, or nieces.

Family: The term is generally understood to refer to two or more persons related by birth or "blood," marriage, or adoption who reside in the same household. Although this is a widely held definition of family, it is somewhat restrictive. A more inclusive and contemporary definition would characterize a family as two or more people who share in an intimate and committed relationship of mutual caring and who consider themselves to be family.

Family Life Course: The unique path followed by a family in the course of its life, including the developmental tasks and events it confronts.

Foster Family: A family paid to provide substitute care for children whose own parents cannot take care of them due to illness, death, disability, abuse, or neglect.

Genogram: A pictorial representation of a family system over several generations providing information concerning demographic factors as well as physical, social, and emotional functioning of its members, and major life events.

Intact Family: A family unit consisting of a married couple and their *own* biological children.

Intergenerational Family: A family including more than two generations, such as when grandparents, children, and grandchildren share the same household.

Interracial Family: A family in which the spouses belong to different races.

Joint-Custody Families: Also known as *binuclear*, families that share the legal or physical custody of children.

Joint Legal Custody: A legal arrangement whereby divorced or separated parents agree in writing to share responsibility and major decisions concerning their children.

Joint Physical Custody: An agreement by divorced or separated parents to share the parenting and rearing of their children.

Migrant Family: Mostly poor racial or ethnic minority families that move from place to place working temporarily in large farms that hire help to harvest the crops.

Modified-Extended Family: A family including relatives, such as grandparents, cousins, aunts, and uncles, as family members, even though they do not live in the same household.

Multigenerational Family: See **Intergenerational Family.**

Life Course Perspective: Looking at the stages through which a family progresses in the course of its unique existence.

Nuclear Dyad: See **Couple-Only Nuclear Family.**

Nuclear Family: A social unit consisting of a couple with or without children or a parent with children.

Nuclear Intact Family: A family composed of both biological parents and *their own* biological children.

One-Parent Family: Also known as *solo family* or *single-parent family*, a social unit consisting of one parent and her or his children.

Parent/Child Subsystem: A subunit of the family composed of the parent(s) and their child(ren).

Parental Subsystems: A subunit of the family that includes the parent or parents or any other parent substitute(s) in their parental roles.

Reconstituted Family: See **Remarriage Family.**

Remarriage Family: Also known as a *reconstituted family*, A family in which at least one of the spouses was previously married. It may or may not include their children from previous marriages.

Rite of Passage: A ceremonial observance or ritual marking an important transition in the life of an individual or family, such as a wedding marking a marriage or a funeral marking death.

Role: A pattern of behavior expected of an individual occupying a specific social position. Family roles include father, husband, sexual partner, mother, wife, son, daughter, stepfather, stepdaughter, and so on.

Role Conflict: Inner struggle arising from a felt discrepancy between what others expect one to do in a given position and what one thinks one ought to do.

Role Overload: That which occurs when a person is trying to play too many roles at the same time.

Role Theory: A theory within the tradition of structural functionalism that emphasizes that the way people act in a given position within the family is influenced by the expectations that accompany such a position, as well as by their own ideas of how they should behave.

Shared-Custody Families: See **Joint-Custody Families.**

Sibling Subsystem: A subunit of the family composed of various possible groupings of the children, such as the boys subsystem or the older children's subsystem.

Single-Parent Family: See **One-Parent Family.**

Social Conflict Theory: A sociological theory that considers conflict to be a natural and inevitable outcome of social interaction such as within the family.

Social Exchange Theory: A sociopsychological theory that assumes that human relations are motivated by self-interest. Social exchange involves a consideration of benefits to be derived from the relationship versus costs of the relationship.

Spouse Subsystem: A subunit of the family composed of the couple playing their roles as spouses.

Stepfamily: Also known as a *blended family*, a *remarriage family* composed of a biological parent and a stepparent and a child or children belonging to one or both parents.

Structural-Functionalism: A prominent sociological theory that views the family as a dynamic system of interconnected parts or structures (members), each performing certain tasks or functions.

Symbolic Interaction Theory: A sociopsychological point of view that stresses the importance of personal meanings, symbols, interpretations, and other internal processes in understanding family dynamics.

Traditional Family: See **Intact Family.**

Transactional Patterns: Habitual ways in which people interact.

REFERENCES

Acock, A. C., & Demo, D. H. (1994). *Family diversity and well-being*. Newbury Park, CA: Sage.

Ahrons, C. R. (1987). *The binuclear family: Two households, one family*. Paper presented at the sixth annual conference of the Stepfamily Association of America, Lincoln, NE.

Ahrons, C. R. & Rodgers, R. H. (1987). *Divorced families: A multidisciplinary developmental view*. New York: W. W. Norton.

Ames, K., Lewis, S., Kandell, P., Rosenberg, D., & Chideya, F. (1992, September 14). *Newsweek*, 52–53.

Bennett, N. G., Blanc, A. K., & Bloom, D. E. (1988). Commitment and the modern union: Assessing the link between premarital cohabitation and subsequent marital stability. *American Sociological Review, 53*, 127–138.

Billingsley, A. (1968). *Black families in white America*. Englewood Cliffs, NJ: Spectrum.

Booth, A., & Johnson, D. (1988). Premarital cohabitation and marital success. *Journal of Family Issues, 9*, 255–272.

Boulding, E. (1972). The family as an agent of change. *The Futurist, 6*, 186–191.

Brown, F. H. (1988). The postdivorce family. In E. Carter & M. McGoldrick (Eds.), *The changing family life cycle* (2nd ed., pp. 371–398). New York: Gardner Press.

Burr, W. R., Leigh, G. K., Day, R. D. & Constantine, J. (1979). Symbolic interaction and the family. In W. R. Burr, R. Hill, F. I. Nye, & I. L. Reiss (Eds.), *Contemporary theories about the family* (Vol. 2, pp. 42–111). New York: Free Press.

Butler, R. N., & Lewis, M. I. (1977). *Aging and mental health*. St. Louis: C. V. Mosby.

Carter, E, & McGoldrick, M. (Eds.) (1980). *The family life cycle: A framework for family therapy*. New York: Gardner Press.

Carter, E., & McGoldrick, M. (Eds.). (1988). *The changing family life cycle* (2nd ed.). New York: Gardner Press.

Cashion, B. G. (1982). Female-headed families: Effects on children and clinical implications. *Journal of Marital and Family Therapy, 8,* 83.

Chira, S. (1993, September 30). Gay parents grow more visible. *The New York Times,* pp. A1, B5.

Collins, G. (1984, June 20). Children of interracial marriage. *The New York Times*, pp. C1, C7.

Collins, R. (1986). *Sociology of marriage and the family*. Chicago: Nelson-Hall.

Colon, F. (1980). The family life cycle of the multi-problem poor family. In E. A. Carter & M. McGoldrick (Eds.), *The family life cycle: A framework for family therapy* (pp. 343–381). New York: Gardner Press.

Dahl, A. S., Cowgill, K. M., & Asmundsson, R. (1987). *Life in remarriage families. Social Work, 32,* 40–44.

DeMaris, A., & Leslie, G. R. (1984). Cohabitation with the future spouse: Its influence upon marital satisfaction and communication. *Journal of Marriage and the Family, 46,* 77–84.

Dickinson, G. E., & Leming, M. R. (1990). *Understanding families: Diversity, continuity, and change*. Boston: Allyn and Bacon.

Durkheim, E. (1964). The division of labor in society. (G. Simpson, Trans.). *New York: Free Press.*

Erikson, E. H. (1963). *Childhood and society* (rev. ed.). New York: Norton.

Eshleman, J. R. (1991). *The family: An introduction* (6th ed.). Boston: Allyn and Bacon.

Finkelstein, N. E. (1980). Children in limbo. *Social Work, 25*, 100–105.

Fulmer, R. H. (1988). Lower-income and professional families: A comparison of structure and life cycle process. In E. Carter & M. McGoldrick (Eds.), *The changing family life cycle* (2nd ed., pp. 545–578). New York: Gardner Press.

Furstenberg, F., Nord, C. W., Peterson, J. L., & Zill, N. (1983). The life course of children of divorce: Marital disruptions and parental contact. *American Sociological Review, 48,* 656–668.

Gays seek clearer image through census. (1991, June 28). *The Miami Herald*, section A.

Gerstel, N., & Gross, H. (1984). *Commuter marriage: A study of work and family*. New York: Guilford.

Golombok, S., Spence, A., & Rutter, M. (1983). Children in lesbian and single-parent households: Psychosexual and psychiatric appraisal. *Journal of Child Psychology and Psychiatry, 24,* 551–572.

Green, R. G., & Crooks, P. D. (1988). Family member adjustment and family dynamics in established single-parent and two-parent families. *Social Service Review, 62,* 600–613.

Gwartney-Gibbs, P. A. (1986). The institutionalization of premarital cohabitation: Estimates from marriage license applications, 1970 and 1980. *Journal of Marriage and the Family, 48,* 423–434.

Hampson, R. B., & Tavormin, J. B. (1980). Feedback from the experts: A study of foster care mothers, *Social Work, 25,* 108–113.

Hare, J. (1994, January). Concerns and issues faced by families headed by a lesbian couple. *The Journal of Contemporary Human Services, 27*–35.

Hartman, A. (1978). Diagrammatic assessment of family relationships. *Social Casework, 59,* 465–476.

Havighurst, R. J. (1972). *Developmental tasks and education.* New York: David McKay.

Hines, P. M. (1988). The family life cycle of poor black families. In E. Carter & M. McGoldrick (Eds.), *The changing family life cycle* (2nd ed., pp. 513–544). New York: Gardner Press.

Hines, P. M. & Boyd-Franklin, N. (1982). Black families. In M. McGoldrick, J. K. Pearce, & J. Giordano (Eds.), *Ethnicity and family therapy* (pp. 84–107). New York: Guilford Press.

Hite, S. (1994). *The Hite report on the family: Growing up under patriarchy.* London: Bloomsbury.

Hogan, M. J., Buehler, C., & Robinson, B. (1983). Single parenting: Transitioning alone. In H. I. McCubbin & C. R. Figley (Eds.), Stress and the family, Vol. I: *Coping with normative transitions* (pp. 116–132). New York: Brunner/Mazel.

Howard, T. U., & Johnson, F. C. (1985). An ecological approach to practice with single-parent families. *Social Casework, 66,* 482–489.

Ingrassia, L. (1994, June 8). Brides and brides, grooms and grooms, wedded bliss for all. *The Wall Street Journal Europe,* pp. 1, 7.

Johnson, D. (1993, August 31). More and more, the single parent is dad. *The New York Times,* pp. A1, A8.

Kantrowitz, B., & Wingert, P. (1990, Winter/Spring). Step by step. *Newsweek Special Issue,* 24–34.

Kelley, H. H., & Thibaut, J. W. (1978). *Interpersonal relations: A theory of interdependence.* New York: John Wiley & Sons.

Kirkpatrick, M., Smith, C., & Roy, R. (1981). Lesbian mothers and their children: A comparative

survey. *American Journal of Orthopsychiatry, 51,* 545–551.

Leslie, G. R., & Korman, S. K. (1989). *The family in social context* (7th ed.). New York: Oxford University Press.

Levine, A. (1990, January 29). *The second time around: Realities of remarriage.* U.S. News & World Report, 50–51.

Lewin, T. (1990, June 17). Dad disappeared: A new reality for American families. *The Miami Herald,* section I, p. 6.

Lewis, K. G. (1980). Children of lesbians: Their point of view. *Social Work, 25,* 198–203.

Maccoby, E., & Mnookin, R. (1992). *Dividing the child*: Cambridge, MA: Harvard University Rress.

Maddox, B. (1982, February). Homosexual parents. *Psychology Today, 16,* 62–69.

Martin, P. Y., & O'Connor, G. G. (1989). *The social environment: Open systems applications* (Chapters 3 and 4). New York: Longman.

McGoldrick, M. (1989). Women through the family life cycle. In M. McGoldrick, C. M. Anderson, & F. Walsh (Eds.), *Women in families: A framework for family therapy* (pp. 200–226). New York: W. W. Norton.

McGoldrick, M., & Carter, B. (1988). Forming a remarried family. In B. Carter & M. McGoldrick (Eds.), *The changing family life cycle* (2nd ed., pp. 399–429). New York: Gardner Press.

McGoldrick, M., & Gerson, R. (1985). *Genograms in family assessment.* New York: W. W. Norton.

Merton, R. (1968). *Social theory and social structure* (enlarged edition). New York: Free Press.

Minuchin, S. (1974). A family model. In S. Minuchin (Eds.), *Families and family therapy* (pp. 46–66). Cambridge, MA: Harvard University Press.

Morrissette, P. J. (1994). *Child and Adolescent Social Work Journal, 11*(3), 235–246.

Nye, F. I., et al. (1979). Choice, exchange and the family. In W. R. Burr, R. Hill, F. I. Nye, & I. L. Reiss (Eds.), *Contemporary theories about the family* (pp. 1–41). New York: Free Press.

Olson, M. R., & Haynes, J. A. (1993, May). *Successful single parents. Families in Society: The Journal of Contemporary Human Services*, May 1993, 259–267.

Papernow, P. (1991). *Stages of development in stepfamilies.* New York: Gardner Press.

Parsons, T. (1951). *The social system.* Glencoe, IL: Free Press.

Parsons, T., & Bales, R. F. (1955). *Family, socialization, and the interaction process.* Glencoe, IL: Free Press.

Patterson, C. J. (1992). Children of lesbian and gay parents. *Child Development, 63,* 1025–1043.

Raspberry, W. (1989, July 18). *A recipe for survival: Save the boys.* The Miami Herald, p. 13A.

Rich, S. (1990, June 22). *U.S. isn't the only place where modern family is being transformed.* Washington Post.

Seligmann, J. (1990, Winter/Spring). Variations on a theme: Gay and lesbian couples. *Newsweek* Special Issue, 38–40.

Skinner, D. A. (1983). Dual-career families: Strains of sharing. In H. I. McCubbin & C. R. Figley (Eds.), *Stress and the family, Vol. I: Coping with normative transitions* (pp. 90-101). New York: Brunner/Mazel.

Skolnick, A. (1981, January–February). The family and its discontents. *Society, 18,* 42–47.

Sprey, J. (1979). Conflict theory and the study of marriage and the family. In W. R. Burr, R. Hill, F. I. Nye, & I. L. Reiss (Eds.), *Contemporary theories about the family* (Vol. 2, pp. 130–159). New York: Free Press.

Stanton, G. W. (1986). Preventive intervention with stepfamilies. *Social Work, 31,* 201–206.

Sussman, M. B. (l965). Relationship of adult children with their parents in the United States. In Shanas & G. Streib (Eds.), *Social structure and the family: Generational relations.* Englewood Cliffs, NJ: Prentice Hall.

Tanfer, K. (1987). Patterns of premarital cohabitation among never-married women in the United States. *Journal of Marriage and the Family, 49,* 483–497.

Thibaut, J. W., & Kelley, H. H. (1959). *The social psychology of groups.* New York: John Wiley & Sons.

Thornton, A. (1988). Cohabitation and marriage in the 1980s. *Demography, 25,* 497–508.

U.S. Bureau of the Census (1984). Household and family characteristics: March 1984. *Current Population Reports*, Series P-20, No. 398.

U.S. Bureau of the Census. (1989). *Marital status and living arrangements,* March 1988. Current population reports, Series P-20, No. 433, Table A-7, p. 63. Washington, DC: U.S. Government Printing Office.

U.S. Bureau of the Census. (1993a). Population profile of the United States: 1993. *Current population reports, Series* P23-185. Washington, DC: U.S. Government Printing Office.

U. S. Bureau of the Census. (1993b). *Statistical abstract of the United States:* 1993 (113th edition.). Washington, DC: U.S. Government Printing Office.

U.S. Bureau of the Census. (1993c). *1990 census of population: Social and economic characteristics.* United States (1990 CP-2-1). Washington, DC: U.S. Government Printing Office.

U.S. Bureau of the Census. (1993d). *We the American... Children.* Report WE-10. Washington, DC: U.S. Government Printing Office.

Visher, E., & Visher, J. (1983). Stepparenting: Blending families. In H. I. McCubbin & C. R. Figley (Eds.), *Stress and the family, Vol. I: Coping with normative transitions* (pp. 133–146). New York: Brunner/Mazel.

Wald, E. (1987). Family: Stepfamilies. In A. Minahan (Ed.), *Encyclopedia of social work* (18th ed., pp. 555–561). Silver Spring, MD: National Association of Social Workers.

Wallerstein, J. S. & Blakeslee, S. (1989) *Second chances: Men, women, and children a decade after divorce.* New York: Ticknor & Fields, .

Wattenberg, E. (1987). Family: One parent. In A. Minahan (Ed.), *Encyclopedia of social work* (18th ed., pp. 548–555). Eighteenth edition. Maryland: National Association of Social Workers.

Weiss, R. (1979). Growing up a little faster: The experience of growing up in a single-parent household, *Journal of Social Issues, 35,* 97–111.

Wodarski, J. S., & Gordon, J. E. (1983). Juvenile recidivism, single- and two-parent families: Implications for social work practice. *Family Therapy, 10,* 69–76.

Wrigley, E. A. (1977). Reflections on the history of the family. *Daedalus, 106(2),* 71–85.

SUGGESTIONS FOR FURTHER READING

Abramovitz, M. (1991). Social policy in disarray: The beleaguered American family. *Families in Society, 72,* 483–495.

Acock, A. C., & Demo, D. H. (1994). *Family diversity and well-being.* Newbury Park, CA: Sage.

Blankenhorn, D., Bayme, S., & Elshtain, J. B. (Eds.). (1991). *Rebuilding the nest: A new commitment to the American family.* Milwaukee, WI: Family Service America.

Bozett, F. W. (Ed.). (1989). *Homosexuality and the family.* New York: Harrington Park Press.

Broderick, C. B. (1993). *Understanding family process: Basics of family systems theory.* Newbury Park, CA: Sage.

Burke, P. (1993). *Family values: Two moms and their son.* New York: Random House.

Cherlin, A. J. (1993). *Marriage, divorce, remarriage.* Cambridge, MA: Harvard University Press.

Chilman, C. S., Nunnally, E. W., & Cox, F. M. (Eds.). (1988). *Variant family forms.* Newbury Park, CA: Sage.

Conger, R. D., & Elder, G. H., Jr. (1994). *Families in troubled times: Adapting to change in rural America.* Hawthorne, NY: Aldine.

Cunningham, J. D., & Antill, J. K. (1994). Cohabitation and marriage retrospective and predictive comparisons. *Journal of Social and Personal Relationships, 11* (1), 77–93.

DeFrain, J., & Stinnet, N. (1985). *Secrets of strong families.* Boston: Little, Brown.

Dunn, J., & Booth, A. (Eds.). (1995). *Stepfamilies: Who benefits? Who does not?* Hillsdale, NJ: Lawrence Erlbaum.

Edwards, J. N. (1969). Familial behavior as social exchange. *Journal of Marriage and the Family, 31,* 518–526.

Falk, P. J. (1993). Lesbian mothers: Pyschosocial assumption in family law. *American Psychologists, 44,* 941–944.

Ganong, L., & Coleman, M. (1994). *Remarried family relationships.* Newbury Park, CA: Sage.

Garfinkel, I., & McLanahan, S. S. (1986). *Single mothers and their children: A new American dilemma.* Washington, DC: The Urban Institute Press.

Gelles, R. J. (1994). *Contemporary families: A sociological view.* Thousand Oaks, CA: Sage.

Green, R. G., & Crooks, P. D. (1988). Family member adjustment and family dynamics in established single-parent and two-parent families. *Social Service Review, 62,* 600–613.

Greif, G. (1987). A longitudinal examination of single custodial fathers: Implications for treatment. *The American Journal of Family Therapy, 15,* 253–259.

Guttmann, J. (1993). Children of divorced parents: Theoretical and research considerations. *Divorce in psychosocial perspective: Theory and research* (pp. 141–168). Hillsdale, NJ: Lawrence Erlbaum.

Handel, G., & Whitchurch, G. G. (Eds.). (1994). *The psychosocial interior of the family* (4th ed.). Hawthorne, NY: Aldine.

Harry, J. (1992). Same-sex relationships. In M. M. Henslin (Ed.), *Marriage and family in a changing society* (4th ed., pp. 82-92) New York: Free Press.

Henry, W. A., (1993, September 20). Gay parents: Under fire and on the rise. *Time,* 66–71.

Henslin, J. M. (Ed.). (1992). Marriage and family in a changing society (4th ed.) *New York: Free Press.*

Hite, S. (1994). *The Hite report on the family: Growing up under patriarchy.* London: Bloomsbury.

Kissman, K., & Allen, J. A. (1993). *Single-parent families.* Newbury Park, CA: Sage.

Laird, J. (1994). Lesbian families: A cultural perspective. *Smith College Studies in Social Work, 64*(3), 263–296.

Lewin, E. (1993). *Lesbian mothers.* Ithaca, NY: Cornell University Press.

Maddox, B. (1982). *Married and gay.* New York: Harcourt Brace Jovanovich.

Maglin, N. B., & Schniedewind, N. (Eds.). (1989). *Women and step-families: Voices of anger and love.* Philadelphia: Temple University Press.

Martin, A. (1993). *The lesbian and gay parenting handbook.* New York: Harper/Collins.

McPhatter, A. R. (1991). Assessment revisited: A comprehensive approach to understanding family dynamics. *Families in Society, 72,* 11–22.

McWhirter, D. P., & Mattison, A. M. (1984). *The male couple: How relationships develop.* Englewood Cliffs, NJ: Prentice Hall.

Mindel, C. H., Habenstein, R. W., & Wright, R. (1988). *Ethnic families in America: Patterns and variations* (3rd ed). New York: Elsevier. (Chapters on Polish, Irish, Italian, and Greek families)

Minuchin, S., & Nichols, M. P. (1992). *Family healing: Tales of hope and renewal from family therapy.* New York: Free Press.

Nichols-Casebolt, A. M. (1988). Black families headed by single mothers: Growing numbers and increasing poverty. *Social Work, 33,* 306–313.

Norment, L. (1985, September). *Children of interracial marriages.* Ebony, 158–162.

Osmond, M. W. (1987). Radical-critical theories. In M. B. Sussman & S. K. Steinmetz (Eds.), *Handbook of marriage and the family* (pp. 103–125). New York: Plenum Press. (This chapter contains a good assessment of the family from a conflict theory perspective)

Papernow, P. (1993). *Becoming a stepfamily: Patterns of development.* San Francisco: Jossey-Bass.

Patterson, C. J. (1994, April). Lesbian and gay families. *Current Directions in Psychological Science, 3,* 62–64

Procidano, M. E., & Fisher, C. B. (1992). *Contemporary families: Handbook for school professionals.* New York: Teachers College Preess.

Seligmann, J. (1992, December 14). It's not like Mr. mom. *Newsweek, 70–73.*

Seltzer, J. A. (1993). Consqences of marital dissolution for children, *Annual Review of Sociology, 20,* 97–110.

Smith College Studies in Social Work (1993). 63(3) (Entire issue is on lesbian families).

Smolowe, J. (1993, Fall). *Intermarried... with children.* Time, 64–67.

Visher, E. B., & Visher, H. S. (1988). *Old loyalties, new ties: Therapeutic strategies with stepfamilies.* New York: Brunner/Mazel.

Wallis, C. (1992, Fall). The nuclear family goes boom! *Time,* 42–44.

Wolf, P. A., & Mast, E. (1987). Counseling issues in adoptions by stepparents. *Social Work, 32,* 69–74.

Look for articles in the following journals:

American Journal of Family Therapy
Families in Society
Family Relations
International Journal of Sociology of the Family
Journal of Family Issues
Journal of Family Social Work
Journal of Marital and Family Therapy
Journal of Marriage and the Family
Journal of Marriage and Family Counseling
Stepfamily Bulletin (published quarterly by the Stepfamily Association of America, Baltimore, MD)

CHAPTER 9

FAMILIES BELONGING TO NONDOMINANT RACIAL AND ETHNIC GROUPS

AFRICAN-AMERICAN FAMILIES
  Extended Family
  Communal Emphasis
  The Role of the Aged within the Family
  The Stereotype of the Matriarchy
  One-Parent Homes Headed by Women
  Egalitarianism in Sex Roles
  Family Size
  Child-Rearing Practices
  Divorce
  The Church
  Shades of Black in the Family
  Relations with Social Service Agencies
NATIVE-AMERICAN FAMILIES
  Extended Family Tradition
  Child Rearing
  Relationship between the Sexes
  The Elderly
  *Relationship with Social
  Service Agencies*

IMMIGRANT FAMILIES
LATINO FAMILIES
  Extended and Intergenerational Families
  Respect for Elderly Family Members
  Patriarchy and Sex Roles
  Religion
  Mexican-American Families
  Mainland Puerto Rican Families
  Cuban-American Families
ASIAN-AMERICAN FAMILIES
  Emphasis on Family
  *Patriarchy and Hierarchical Family
  Roles*
  Child Rearing
  Harmony in Family Relations
  *Honor and Respect for Elderly Parents
  and Ancestors*
  *Attitude toward Involvement with Social
  Agencies*

Until the 1950s or 1960s, the research on families from nondominant racial and ethnic groups was carried out mainly by Euro-American social scientists and centered on those lower- or lower-middle-class minority families that were often seen at public agencies. There was a problem in developing an understanding of racial or ethnic families based on studies of mostly poor families, however. This practice resulted in a tendency to attribute the characteristics of these families of limited means primarily to **ethnocultural** factors without giving sufficient consideration to the effects of socioeconomic circumstances.

Another important shortcoming of much of the early research on families belonging to nondominant racial and ethnic groups was the tendency to compare the poor minority families

seen at public agencies to the Euro-American middle-class norm, and consequently the inclination to find the former "deficient" in various ways. In recent years, indigenous scholars have been more influential in the development of the literature on racial and ethnic families. This has resulted in a more balanced portrayal of their characteristics. However, still there is a lingering tendency on the part of the mainstream group to discount the writings of indigenous scholars, particularly when based on personal observation and various other accounts of experience rather than on empirical data analyzed statistically.

Based as much as possible on research and observations by scholars belonging to the various racial and ethnic groups under consideration, this chapter will examine the characteristics and family values of African-American, Latino, Asian-American, and Native-American families. Chapter 4 included demographic data reflecting the contemporary situation of the racial and ethnic families discussed in this chapter, and Chapter 2 covered other aspects of their culture.

The most prevalent characteristic of all families, including those belonging to nondominant groups, is diversity. Because families are so diverse, we must be careful not to overgeneralize or stereotype them. Thus, there is no such thing as a *typical* African-American, Latino, Asian-American, or American-Indian family. As noted throughout this book, people of all racial and ethnic backgrounds vary a great deal in terms of their values, behaviors, and lifestyles. This diversity depends on many factors, such as the number of years they have lived in the United States and their degree of acculturation, their socioeconomic status, place of birth, age, level of education, rural or urban location, and experiences with discrimination and oppression. For instance, some Mexican immigrant families have been in the United States for a short time only, whereas others have been here for many generations. Some are poor, some are middle class, and some are affluent. Some of these families are rural or migrant; others are urban or suburban. Aged family members are less acculturated to the mainstream, whereas the young are much more acculturated. Some are illiterate, others are highly educated. To be sure, the culture and lifestyle of each and every family is affected by these and many other differences.

AFRICAN-AMERICAN FAMILIES

> *It takes a village to raise a child.*
> —*An old African saying*

The African-American families that have been most frequently described in the literature are the low-income, inner-city families often seen at public agencies (Staples, 1992). It is impor-

tant to keep in mind that their values, behaviors, and lifestyles are not representative of African-American families in general, but only of low-income, inner-city, African-American families. Socioeconomic status, in particular, is an increasingly significant factor to consider in describing African-American families as well as other racial and ethnic families. Hence, it should be made clear from the start that this chapter will emphasize understandings pertinent to low-income families, which are the families most often seen by practitioners. Class variations will be noted whenever possible. Class variations pertaining to African-American families are also addressed in Chapter 3.

Extended Family

As noted previously in this book, most African Americans consider themselves to be part of an extended intergenerational family including blood relatives as well as quasi-related adults or fictive kin. These large family constellations are normally spread over several households that may be in the same neighborhood or city or scattered over various cities and various regions of the country. Intergenerational living arrangements (three or more generations living together) are common. Research has shown that even after controlling for income, African Americans have extended-family households twice as frequently as Euro-Americans (Taylor, Chatters, Tucker, & Lewis, 1990). This higher proportion of extended households is due primarily to the higher proportion of homes including grandmothers and grandchildren or grandmothers, their unmarried daughters, and their children.

In the inner city, in particular, family households expand and contract frequently. For instance, when a family is faced with an emergency or crisis, the children may be sent away to live with relatives. Or, at times, relatives may move in with extended family members for a period of time when they are having a rough time, such as when they are "between jobs" or "between relationships." Sometimes, a young pregnant teenager or a teenage parent or couple and their children may move in with a family member until they can be on their own financially. In one-parent families, boyfriends may move in and out depending on the economic or other circumstances of their lives (Willie, 1985; Boyd-Franklin, 1989b).

Communal Emphasis

The African-American cultural emphasis on kinship bonds and communal values is evident in family dynamics involving mutual aid and cooperation, reciprocity, interdependence, and responsibility for others in the family. Neighbors, co-workers, friends, and in-laws also provide assistance for many, although those who are not blood related tend to be less involved in the family informal support network (Taylor et al., 1990). Communal values continue to play an important role even in families of middle and higher socioeconomic status, probably because such values have worked well for African Americans of all income levels under the adverse circumstances they have confronted within the U.S. society (McAdoo, 1978; Taylor, 1986).

In low-income communities, relatives often live in close proximity and help to "share the burden." For example, grandmothers, great-grandmothers, or aunts often help with child care. Sometimes children are "kept" or "informally adopted" by relatives or friends who have resources not available to the parents or who can provide a more stable or wholesome environment. For instance, a child born to a young unmarried teenager may be brought up by the grandmother, aunt, or an older sister. Or, after a couple breaks up, the children may be distributed among various family members until the mother (or father) is able to resume child care (Boyd-Franklin, 1989b).

Although extended families have been a major source of strength for African Ameri-

cans, it should not be assumed that they always function as support systems. For various reasons, many African-American extended families today cannot offer the same degree of support to their members that they used to offer in years past. Nowadays, grandmothers are younger and more likely to be working; a grandmother in her thirties and working full time is not likely to be able to take a large part of the responsibility for raising her grandchild, even if her teenage daughter needs her to help out. After more than one generation of father absence in many families, there are fewer grandfathers available to offer help and support. Some family members cannot count on their extended families for support either because they do not have family living nearby, because they do not get along with family members, or because their families are burdened with too many problems of their own to be able to offer assistance. To complicate things further, the old neighborhood sense of community with everybody looking out for everybody else's kids is disintegrating in many places, particularly in the inner city (Ingrassia, 1993). Now, people are more estranged and not as likely to get involved.

The Role of the Aged within the Family

The aged normally are functional and valued members of the African-American extended family. Many grandmothers and great-grandmothers have raised not only their own children but some of their grandchildren, great-grandchildren, and other related or unrelated youngsters. In fact, some who have never had a chance to experience an "empty nest" sometimes become overloaded or burned out as a result of being too central to their families. Reciprocally, the extended family traditionally has taken care of its elderly members when they become sick or infirm or when they are in need, unless they are forced to place them in nursing homes due to a lack of resources.

Elderly members of the family are respected for the wisdom they possess that comes from having been through many hardships, having overcome adversity, and having "learned how to keep on keepin' on" (White & Parham, 1990, p. 74). In addition, the traditional cultural emphasis on oral communication has increased the value the African culture places on the elderly as keepers of the oral literature inherited from ancestors. This oral heritage includes parables, folk poetry, folktales, biblical stories, songs, and proverbs.

The Stereotype of the Matriarchy

According to most African-American family scholars, it would be inaccurate to characterize African-American families as **matriarchal** because about 4 out of 10 African-American families are two-parent units, and the available evidence indicates that these families tend to be egalitarian or patriarchal rather than matriarchal (Willie, 1985; Eshleman, 1991). Even mother-only families, as you will see later, are unlikely to be matriarchal *by choice*.

Although it is inaccurate to characterize African-American families as matriarchal, the mother has always been a very special figure in the African-American culture. Historically, motherhood has been a more important role for black women than their role as wives (Staples, 1992). The mother traditionally has been cherished and perceived as a strong, self-sacrificing, warmly loving, accepting, and emotionally supportive figure. Particularly in families with no father present at home, she takes on great significance in the lives of her children. In such families, because mother is the children's nurturer, provider, and protector, she comes to be perceived by her children as especially powerful and self-sacrificing (Chestang, 1977, pp. 128–132).

Probably because of the central position enjoyed by mothers in the African-American culture, motherhood is often seen as very

important for women to attain fulfillment in life (Davenport & Yurich, 1991). For the same reason, one of the worst offenses that can be perpetrated on an African American is to mention his or her mother's name in a disparaging way (Smith, 1981).

One-Parent Homes Headed by Women

Many African-American women are having children out of wedlock and raising them without husbands. Even women in the upper-income brackets (i.e., above $75,000 in 1993) are more than seven times more likely than white women to have children out of wedlock. According to sociologist Andrew Cherlin, the separation between marriage and childbearing among African Americans is now almost complete (Ingrassia, 1993).

Staples (1985) observed that the high incidence of single parenthood is not necessarily indicative of a devaluation of marriage. In fact, many unmarried mothers hold traditional and even conservative attitudes about marriage, parenthood, and childrearing. A fundamental reason for their single parenthood is the shortage of eligible African-American men who can be marriage partners and successful breadwinners. Other reasons for the excessive number of female-headed households in the African-American community are a high proportion of teenage out-of-wedlock births in part due to the early age at which males and females initiate sexual activity, the women's greater likelihood of not using any birth control method, and a lower probability that they will choose to have an abortion if they get pregnant (Taylor et al., 1990; Staples, 1992).

Since there is an excess of males at birth, what causes the shortage of African-American males as marriage partners? Contributing factors include higher mortality at birth, unemployment, homicides, accidents, drug overdoses, war casualties, and suicides. In addition, about 25 percent of young African-American males are unavailable as marriage partners because they are in jail or prison. Others are away serving in the armed forces. Some may still be hiding from the welfare system because until recently the system required fathers to be absent from the home in order for their families to be eligible to receive Aid to Families with Dependent Children (AFDC). Still others may have become physically disabled due to hazardous jobs (Hines & Boyd-Franklin, 1982).

Various structural conditions in the U.S. economy have contributed to the joblessness and other social ills that afflict many African-American males and to the split between African-American family values and actual family arrangements (Staples, 1985, p. 1010). As noted earlier in this book, one important structural problem that interferes with the ability of African Americans to form two-parent families is the shift that has taken place in the U.S. economy from manual labor to automation, high technology, and service. This shift has left many African-American factory operatives and unskilled laborers (mostly men) out of work. Many of the men also have been negatively affected by the industrial flight from the central cities to the suburbs and elsewhere, and by increased competition for entry-level jobs from women and immigrants (Billingsley, 1988). These factors have contributed to high levels of joblessness and underemployment for the men, criminal and violent behavior, imprisonment, homelessness, and chemical dependency. Unable to earn a living and shaken in their self-confidence, many men have become unable to form stable family unions (Ingrassia, 1993).

As the job market crashed for black men, work opportunities improved considerably for black women, many of whom had pursued an education beyond high school while the men went to war. Particularly the women armed with college degrees were aided in finding employment in corporate America by the women's movement emphasis on opening the workplace to women and the civil rights emphasis on affirmative action. With a higher level of education than the men, as a group, many African-American women were able to qualify for the new jobs in service and technology, thus gaining considerable financial independence from men (Staples, 1992). But some of the women's jobs came at the expense of their male counterparts. This is because workplaces generally found it more advantageous to hire black women than equally qualified black men, given that in hiring a black woman the organization got "double credit" (credit for hiring a black and a woman). This explains, in part, why the gap in income between white and black women has disappeared while a large gulf continues to separate the income of white and black men (Ingrassia, 1993).

Without an adequate supply of potential marriage partners, African-American women at all income levels, particularly those of low socioeconomic status, have had to raise their children by themselves. Staples (1985) noted that, because such women have been *forced by circumstances* beyond their control to assume responsibility for their families to ensure survival, outside observers may have overemphasized the role of the matriarchy in African-American family culture. In contrast, research has shown that African-American women would much prefer to have a two-parent home (Heiss, 1981).

Not only has the lack of available males created an excess of poverty and one-parent homes among African-American families, but it has contributed to the perception of African-American men as "peripheral." According to Hines and Boyd-Franklin (1982) and Boyd-Franklin (1989c), this so-called peripheralness may have been overstated. Taylor and associates (1990) suggested that this stereotype may be due to the dearth of research concerning the role of men in black families. To be sure, not all African-American men are uninvolved in family matters. Like all husbands, lovers, and fathers, they differ in their degree of involvement in the family, in part depending on their income, according to research (Taylor et al., 1990). Many are

married, live at home, and are quite involved in decision making and childrearing. Others, particularly those who are not regularly employed, may come and go, perhaps appearing when they have a job or get some money and leaving when the income ceases. Still others do not live at home but acknowledge their children and contribute financially to their support when they can. Some do not acknowledge their children and do not offer financial help.

Even when fathers are minimally involved with their children or not living at home, often there are other male models available to the children, such as grandfathers, uncles, and mothers' boyfriends. In addition, paternal mothers and sisters frequently keep in touch with their sons' and brothers' children and sometimes provide emotional or material support even if fathers do not. Male models are also available thorough the church, such as ministers, deacons, and fellow church members who take an interest in children whose fathers are absent.

There is some research evidence that African-American children living with one parent only are less likely to be in school at age 17 or to graduate from high school. Daughters of single mothers also appear to be at higher risk of becoming sexually active as teenagers, of becoming unmarried teenage mothers, and of establishing a female-headed household at an early age (Taylor et al., 1990). It is difficult to tell at this juncture whether these effects are largely the consequence of economic deprivation or whether other factors are also at play.

Although most African-American children have positive and wholesome female and male role models even if their fathers do not live with them, some do not. This is particularly true for many boys in the inner city who learn their ways from youth gangs and other undesirable elements on the street. On the street, they often learn to view women as whores, handmaidens, and sexual conquests. Typically, many get the young women pregnant to assert their masculinity and to earn respect from their peers; then they abandon their children and their children's mothers for other women (Ingrassia, 1993).

Some African-American children—particularly those living in the inner city who are the product of fleeting sexual liaisons and drug-addicted parents—end up being left without adequate supervision and care. This neglect has resulted in a large number of children placed in foster care. In fact, according to Taylor and colleagues (1990), African-American children are three times more likely to be in foster care than Euro-American children. Because they are more likely to remain in the substitute care system longer, they more often undergo multiple placements. These circumstances are not good for their development.

Egalitarianism in Sex Roles

Many African-American women have worked outside the home to support their families long before it became acceptable for Euro-American women to do so. (Even as far back as the year 1900, about 41 percent of black women in the United States were in the labor force, compared with 16 percent of white women [Staples, 1992].) African-American women have been the sole or principal wage earners in the household much more frequently than Euro-American women because they have had less difficulty than African-American men attaining and keeping jobs within the U.S. society. This has made it difficult for African-American husbands to surpass their wives in income. The greater economic parity between African-American husbands and wives compared to Euro-Americans may be a reason why the women appear to have attained somewhat greater equality within the family than Euro-American women (Staples, 1992). If African-American husbands, as a group, consistently had made more money than their wives, their families might be less egalitarian (Eshleman, 1991).

Probably due to these reasons, the relationship between the sexes within African-American families traditionally has been fairly **egalitarian,** with both spouses sharing child care and household responsibilities—such as cooking, washing, ironing, keeping house, and

shopping—earlier than Euro-Americans (Jones, 1990). According to White (1984, p. 67), a family decision may be made by husband or wife, depending on who is available at a given time, who has expertise with reference to a given problem or who has had prior experience in making that kind of decision. Although African-American husbands appear to be somewhat more likely than Euro-American husbands to share in the housework and in child-care responsibilities, African-American wives, like Euro-American wives, still do most of the cooking, cleaning, and laundering and are more likely than their husbands to feel overworked (Taylor et al., 1990).

In talking about sex roles, class differences must be considered. As is true in the case of Euro-American families, working-class African-American families are more likely than middle-class families to have more clearly differentiated sex roles. For instance, working-class wives are more likely than middle-class wives to be responsible for the cooking, cleaning, and child care while their husbands more frequently make decisions about financial expenditures, unless there is a crisis, in which case roles may change quickly (Willie, 1986). Similarly, although the double standard of sexual behavior does not appear to be as prevalent in African-American families as in other U.S. families, African-American husbands of lower socioeconomic background seem to have greater latitude than those of higher socioeconomic status to socialize and drink away from home, and to engage in extramarital relationships (McGoldrick, Garcia-Preto, Hines, & Lee, 1989).

Family Size

Similar to other racial/ethnic groups, the size of African-American families is highly dependent on socioeconomic status. Those in the poor and working classes tend to have large families, often including four or more children, perhaps

due in part to a lack of birth control information or an unwillingness to practice birth control or reluctance to have an abortion (Taylor et al., 1990). Another reason for large families is that parents of lower socioeconomic status, particularly fathers, tend to take pride in having a large number of children, as this is one of the few special contributions they can make. Another reason for large families is that African Americans of lower socioeconomic status are likely to marry young and to start having children in their teens prior to marriage. Those of higher socioeconomic standing, on the other hand, marry later and usually have no more than two children (Willie, 1985, 1986).

Child-Rearing Practices

Characteristically, African-American parents, grandparents, and children, particularly the women, relate in a close, warm, positive, and intensely loyal manner. Grandparents, particu-

larly grandmothers, take an active part in childrearing, more so than Euro-American grandparents, probably because they are more likely to live with or near their grandchildren (Taylor et al., 1990). Mothers and grandmothers raise their children, including the girls, to be assertive, independent, and emotionally expressive, and try to develop in them a strong sense of self-worth to offset the negative evaluations they may later get from the larger society (McGoldrick et al., 1989; Staples, 1992).

Many lower-income mothers are likely to use physical force rather than verbal reasoning to discipline the children. Yet, Staples (1985) noted that, even though African-American mothers, particularly those who are poor and uneducated, are more likely than middle-class Euro-American mothers to strike their children when they misbehave, they are less inclined to threaten them with withdrawal of their love. This may be one reason why the bond between mother and children remains so strong and important among African Americans through-out their lives (Taylor et al., 1990; Staples, 1992).

With respect to the use of physical punishment, Hines and Boyd-Franklin (1982) cautioned that it should not automatically be considered a sign of child abuse since it is a culturally accepted method of discipline. The practitioner can help parents who use physical punishment by suggesting more effective approaches while showing acceptance, though not approval or encouragement, of the parental physical style of discipline. At the same time, some parents who strike their children are abusive and, as practitioners, we must be able to recognize the difference. We must keep in mind that due to the stresses related to poverty and racism, child abuse is likely to be more common in African-American families than in white families (Staples, 1992).

Families with working parents or with a large number of children sometimes have a daughter or son who acts as a substitute parent or **parental child.** The system can function well, but it can run into difficulties if authority is not clearly delegated to parental children or if the parental children are developmentally unprepared for this role. Sometimes when family responsibilities conflict with the parental children's age-appropriate need to be with peers, the children may vent their frustration through delinquent acts, abuse of siblings left in their care, or sexual promiscuity (Hines & Boyd-Franklin, 1982).

Many African-American families try to inculcate in their children the value of an education as a way of attaining work security and social mobility. Middle-class parents, in particular, put a great deal of emphasis on the importance of attending college and make great efforts to send their children to college immediately after high school. Working-class parents often put pressure on their children to finish high school. Some make considerable sacrifices to send them to college. In return, older brothers and sisters may help to put a younger

sibling through school, and later, the one who benefited may contribute to the schooling of yet another child in the family.

Parents in low-income families who did not finish school sometimes hold themselves up to their children as examples of what happens when one drops out and admonish them not to commit the same mistakes. But their children, particularly those who live in inner-city ghettos, may see other relatives or people in the community having trouble attaining and maintaining employment, even those with high school diplomas, and may get a conflicting message more powerful than the parental advice about the value of an education (Hines & Boyd-Franklin, 1982; Willie, 1985).

Divorce

Despite a tradition of low social acceptance of divorce and of high tolerance of suffering within relationships (Hines & Boyd-Franklin, 1982), the divorce rate is more elevated among African Americans than among Euro-Americans. To give you an idea, among African-American women under age 30 the chances that their marriage will end in divorce are approximately two out of three, compared to a 50 percent chance for Euro-American women. It is estimated that after 10 years of marriage, only one out of every three black couples will remain married. The divorce rate of those who are middle class is lower, however (Staples, 1992).

Staples (1985, 1992) argued that African-American marriages are disrupted by the same societal conditions that limit the supply of eligible men—unemployment, underemployment, imprisonment, military service, institutionalization, or chemical dependency. Other factors that contribute to a high divorce rate include marriage and child bearing at a young age; stresses related to poverty, racism, and urban living; high competition among women for eligible males; high level of independence of the women; and high status of some wives compared to their husbands due to higher educational and income levels.

The Church

African Americans show higher levels of religiosity than Euro-Americans (Taylor et al., 1990). Therefore, the church is of central importance in the lives of many families and the bible is highly respected. Willie (1985) noted that for working-class families, the most important social activity in the community may be attending church.

Research has shown that church members often serve as important sources of support for many families (Taylor et al., 1990). For instance, ministers and their spouses, deacons, deaconesses, and other church members often make themselves available in times of need and crisis, act as substitute family for isolated and overloaded single parents, and serve as role models for young people. Boyd-Franklin (1989d) noted that many African-American churches also provide important programs for children and youth, such as day-care centers, Boy Scout units, and sponsorship of sport teams.

Shades of Black in the Family

Skin color is still a sensitive issue in some families, although it is often kept quiet or even denied. As noted previously in this book, for generations it was easier for the light-skinned person than for those with darker skin to get an education or a job and to advance in the U.S. society. Probably this is partly the reason why some African-American families still value light skin color. Other families, however, prefer dark skin and may scapegoat or reject their lighter-skinned members, seeing them as reminders of the sexual exploitation of black women by white men.

Discrepancies in skin color, which are quite common due to normal genetic variations, may create major problems in some families. For example, parents who favor their lighter-skinned or darker-skinned children may give them a strong sense of self-worth, but they may damage the children's relations with less favored siblings. Or, if the relationship between the parents is shaky, the father may question a child's paternity if the child's skin color happens to be significantly different from his. In still other cases, a child may have a difficult time getting along with parents and siblings, simply because his or her skin is of a substantially different color than that of the rest of the family (Boyd-Franklin, 1989a).

Relations with Social Service Agencies

According to Hines and Boyd-Franklin (1982), many African-American families, particularly low-income families, have strong reservations about discussing private matters with strangers. As a rule, in times of need or crisis, it is considered preferable to rely on family members, close friends, ministers, church members, or neighbors rather than on social workers or other human service practitioners. In this respect, low-income African-American families are similar to other low-income families from nondominant racial and ethnic groups.

Those who have previously experienced the intrusion of public assistance agencies in their families may be suspicious of the motives of agency personnel in asking for confidential information or permission for release of information to or from other agencies. Some are so overloaded trying to survive from day to day that they do not have time to go to a public agency to talk with a stranger unless they can clearly see the benefit. Others may consider mental health clinics as appropriate only for "crazy" people.

Besides frequently distrusting public agency practitioners or lacking time, some low-income family members may view their troubles as a burden that God has given them to carry in this life or as a consequence of failure to follow the teachings of the bible. These individuals may prefer to rely on prayer and religious faith rather than on public agencies.

Some may be afraid of being misdiagnosed or treated inappropriately. This is a well-founded concern because African-American patients traditionally have been more likely to be institutionalized for mental disorders or given medication than offered other possible interventions. Many times, lower-income families become involuntary clients as a condition imposed by public agencies (e.g., the schools, the courts, or the welfare system) and they may feel negative about being pressured into treatment. Probably the best way to engage involuntary clients is to offer short-term concrete services they agree they need and to work with them on the problems that they identify as being of concern to them.

NATIVE-AMERICAN FAMILIES

American Indians belong to several hundred different tribes with different cultural traditions. Nearly half the population is concentrated in four states—California, Oklahoma, Arizona, and New Mexico. This section will examine characteristics common to most traditional families, regardless of tribal membership. Those who intend to work with members of a particular tribe need to acquire more specific information about the tribal family customs of their clients.

It is important to bear in mind that American-Indian families do not necessarily follow traditional values and customs or follow them to various extents. According to Red Horse (1988), more than half the families in the United States reside in urban areas, not in reservations. In addition, half the marriages of American Indians today are to non-Indian spouses. Consequently, many American-Indian families have become highly acculturated to the U.S. mainstream, visit the clan infrequently, and no longer speak the tribal language. Some are part of social networks that are primarily non-Indian, have adopted non-Indian religions, and follow Westernized health care practices. The values and practices described here may not apply to such families. In addition, because there is very little research on Native-American families, the few descriptions in the literature must be taken as tentative (John, 1988). Always keep in mind that there is no such thing as a typical American-Indian family. With so many different tribes, American Indians are among the most diverse ethnic groups in the United States.

Extended Family Tradition

Many traditional families live on reservations or in rural areas near reservations, practice traditional religious rituals, speak the tribal language at home and in the village, and practice a communal family economy. These families form part of a much larger group of families, or **clan,** that trace their descent to a common ancestor (John, 1988; Locke, 1992).

Traditional American-Indian families typically are intergenerational and extended, spreading over several households and including parents and their children, grandparents, aunts, uncles, and cousins (who are considered the same as siblings) (Ho, 1987b; Locke, 1992). Sometimes, through a formal ritual, a highly trusted person who is not kin becomes a **namesake** for one of the children. By becoming a namesake, this person joins the family and helps to bring up the child, acting as a role model. If the parents should become unable to take care of the child for any reason, the namesake is obligated to take over (Red Horse, 1980).

Decision making in traditional families is often nonverbal because of the emphasis on unity, cooperation, and consensus. Family members typically think over the situation and when one of them "has the sense of the group," he or she offers a suggestion. In the context of interdependence, it is important to sense one another's needs and to respond to them. Relatives often help without being asked and elders expect assistance without having to ask for it from family or tribe members (John, 1988).

According to Red Horse (1988), as families relocate to urban areas away from the reservations, the clan and the extended family support system begin to break down, although many members try to stay in close touch by frequent mutual visits, even if they are hundreds of miles away from one another. Some families are able to develop new support networks through the integration of fictive kin into the family system and manage their isolation from the reservation by attending urban powwows.

Many parents who themselves grew up in reservations continue to speak the tribal language at home, but, being away from the reservation, their children tend to lose it as they adopt English as their primary language. After several generations living in urban areas, most American Indians lose the ability to communicate in the tribal language.

Child Rearing

In traditional families, particularly those living in reservations and rural areas near reservations, child-rearing responsibilities typically are shared by various relatives, including the grandparents, aunts, and uncles. Grandmothers, in particular, play a central role in the family network and may take primary responsibility for the rearing of one or more grandchildren (John, 1988). Older sons, daughters, and cousins also help with the care of young children. For the children, the opportunity to develop close relationships with several parental figures and to live with different extended-family members provides security, affection, and a variety of role models. Under this arrangement, parents have more freedom to enjoy a more relaxed and egalitarian relationship with their children.

Although practices vary from tribe to tribe, according to various tribal customs, husbands move in with their wives' family but maintain leadership and disciplinary roles in their families of origin. Thus, for example, a man may play an important role in raising his nephews, while at home he may remain unassertive with respect to his own children.

Compared to Euro-American families, traditional American-Indian families put less emphasis in the rearing of children on toilet training, cleanliness, punctuality, competition, or achievement (Price, 1981). Children generally learn self-discipline from same-sex parental figures and are expected to act in accordance with the values they have been taught (Attneave, 1982; Ho, 1987b; Locke, 1992). Clan members are typically tolerant with children and let them learn from the natural consequences of their actions rather than by telling them specifically what to do. Thus, children are given a great deal of freedom to explore and to be independent and are allowed to make their own decisions (even important decisions such as whether or not to attend school) without pressure, threats, punishments or bribes (John, 1988). There are no fixed schedules for children for eating or sleeping. Such disciplinary methods may be considered too lax by non-Indian standards.

Attitudes toward sex are likewise liberal, with premarital sexual experiences common in most tribes. Out-of-wedlock births are typically accepted without stigma (John, 1988; Locke, 1992). This may be one of the reasons why young teenage girls have a high rate of pregnancy. In reservations and rural areas, children born out-of-wedlock are absorbed into the extended family without stigma. In urban areas, out-of-wedlock births result in a high rate of female-headed households.

Relationship between the Sexes

The American-Indian traditional cultures generally put more emphasis on consanguineous (blood) than on conjugal (marriage) ties. This may be one reason why marriage and divorce among American Indians appear to be taken more casually than among Euro-Americans and to be less fraught with guilt or recrimination. There is little systematic knowledge about contemporary sex roles within families. Many of the old tribal cultures had rigidly prescribed roles for males and females, but this has changed considerably in the direction of the more flexible roles of the mainstream society (John, 1988).

The Elderly

Within the clan, as well as in the tribe, elders are honored and respected for their wisdom and experience and typically fill important positions on the tribal council (Lewis & Ho, 1989; Locke, 1992).

Relationship with Social Service Agencies

For help with health or emotional problems, traditional families typically turn to the extended family, to a religious or spiritual leader, to tribal elders, or to the tribal medicine person. Given the discrimination to which Native Americans have been subjected within the mainstream society, few traditional families voluntarily turn to mainstream social agencies for help (Ho, 1987b).

IMMIGRANT FAMILIES

Immigration has played a major role with important consequences in the lives of many racial and ethnic families in the United States. To be sure, it can be very stressful not only because of the losses it may involve but because it requires innumerable adjustments. For example, migrating families frequently suffer a loss of significant others left behind in the native country as well as a loss of extended family and support network, familiar environment, language, culture, home, and, in some cases, status and material possessions. While confronting these multiple losses, immigrant families must simultaneously make a living in the host country, deal with racial discrimination perhaps for the first time in their lives, and negotiate a new culture, language, physical, and social environment. The dislocation that is usually experienced can engender feelings of grief, anger, resentment, and depression (Shon & Ja, 1982; Queralt, 1984; Ho, 1987a).

Sometimes, particularly when the family is poor, the father is the first to migrate, with mother and children staying behind in the native country until he can arrange to bring them. Sometimes the reverse is true if the family believes that it would be easier for the mother to find employment in the United States as a domestic worker or child-care worker; in such cases, the mother may be the first to migrate. Separations sometimes are so prolonged that the father, the mother, and children become used to being without one another and have trouble readjusting to being together when they reunite. In any case, when mother, children, and father reunite after years of separation, the family frequently undergoes a major reorganization similar to that experienced when there is a remarriage and new family members are incorporated into the family.

Families migrating with children frequently confront the problem of differential acculturation rates. Because the parents tend to adjust to the new culture more slowly than their children, the children sometimes are placed in the position of acting as interpreters or culture brokers for their parents. This reversal of the usual power hierarchy can cause generational conflicts. Language is another area likely to generate intrafamilial conflict during acculturation. As younger family members become more proficient in the use of the English language than their parents, they may become less proficient in their native language or less inclined to speak their parents' language and therefore less willing or able to communicate with older family members at home who cannot or will not speak English (Falicov, 1982).

Still another source of acculturative conflict emerges when the parents achieve some financial stability and decide to bring the grandparents, perhaps to help with child care and supervision. This tends to exacerbate intergenerational differences, as every family member may be at a different stage of acculturation. For example, if the mother does not work outside the home, she and the grandparents may be barely beginning the process of acculturation while the father may be at an intermediate stage and the children may be progressing most rapidly (Falicov & Karrer, 1980; McGoldrick, 1988). Mothers who work outside the home acculturate at a faster pace, like their husbands, but they must often deal with the conflicts generated by their newly acquired interest in achieving more equality in relation to their husbands who sometimes become insecure or feel uncomfortable with their wives' growing autonomy and demand even greater submission from them (Ho, 1987a).

Families that migrate with adolescent children may have the heaviest burden. They, of course, must confront all the usual stresses related to migration and cope with generational conflicts engendered by different rates of acculturation within the family. In addition, they must contend with their children's rapid developmental transitions and push for independence and for adoption of the lifestyle of their peers at school.

Families are unlikely to migrate during the launching phase because their children are resistant to join their parents at that stage. Therefore, they do so mostly when forced to leave their native countries for political reasons or due to war or other catastrophes (McGoldrick, 1988). Those forced to leave their countries usually suffer particularly heavy losses, materially, socially, and emotionally. Some may become even more distressed if their sons

or daughters become romantically involved with persons from different ethnic backgrounds because of the possibility of marriage outside their ethnic group.

Many political exiles and refugees are middle aged because they tend to be among the more established members of their native societies and therefore among the most likely to be deeply affected by political changes. Because they tend to be an older group, they may have a hard time mastering the language and culture of the host society, finding employment, and connecting with a new social/emotional support network. Those too old to become fluent in the new language may find life in the new country to be very isolating.

LATINO FAMILIES

The family is an institution of central importance within Latino cultures and an important source of security, comfort, support, and identity for its members (Cortes, 1980).

Extended and Intergenerational Families

For many of those who hold on to traditional values, the concept of family refers to an extended and interdependent network of blood relatives (including parents, children, grandparents, cousins, aunts, and uncles), in-laws, godparents, sometimes informally adopted children (*hijos de crianza*), and even some neighbors and close friends considered family because of their willingness to become involved in important family issues and events. Other Latinos in the United States may have a more limited concept of family that includes primarily the intergenerational family—parents, children (including sometimes the parents' adult siblings on one or both sides), and grandparents.

Many family members feel a strong sense of family obligation and loyalty and put their family affairs ahead of other matters such as careers or personal ambitions. Thus, for example, when adult children relocate, it is not unusual for their aging parents to follow them to remain in close proximity. When the parents no longer can live independently because of illness or incapacity, often their adult children take them in, as there is a strong commitment to keeping the elderly at home, whenever possible. Similarly, many first- and some second-generation Latino college students forego educational opportunities at good universities out of the local area because their parents expect them to live at home while they attend college and until they get married (Lustig, 1988; Veciana-Suarez, 1993).

Respect for Elderly Family Members

Latino cultures put greater emphasis on respect for elderly and deceased family members than the U.S. mainstream culture. This value is common among people from nontechnologically advanced areas.

The tradition of respect for the elderly stems, in part, from the custom prevalent in agrarian and semi-industrial societies that elders retain control of the family property—such as the land, the home, or the fishing boat used by family members to make a living—until they die. This tends to keep adult children closer to their parents and promotes respect since sons and daughters often depend on their parents for their livelihood.

Patriarchy and Sex Roles

In traditional families, the father is considered the **patriarch** or head of the family, its chief decision maker, and its representative in the community. According to the traditional philosophy of **machismo**, which is part of the patriarchal ideology, men are expected to be brave and courageous, protective of women and children, and responsible providers. Reciprocally, women are expected to take primary responsibility for the home and the children and to provide their husbands with social and emotional support. At its worst, machismo involves a hypermasculinity that is expressed by some men by being tough, aggressive, and sometimes abusive and violent; by sexual conquests and extramarital affairs; or by excessive spending, gambling, or alcohol/drug use (Sandoval & de la Roza, 1986, p. 156).

Sex roles have become much less rigidly differentiated than they used to be under the traditional patriarchal system because of the high proportion of Latino women in the United States who work outside the home to support their families. Consequently, Latino women who are part of the labor force have acquired varying degrees of decision-making power and now receive various levels of housework and child-care assistance from their husbands. Notwithstanding this, traditional Latino families, many more in principle than in practice, adhere to the patriarchal ideology and to the philosophy of machismo more than U.S. mainstream families. One implication for human service practitioners is the possible reluctance of some Latino men to get involved in individual or family treatment because they might view these activities as unmanly and as an infringement on their family authority (Bach-y-Rita, 1982; Sandoval & de la Roza, 1986).

Religion

Religion plays an important role in many Latino families, particularly as a source of identification and support (Rothman, Gant, & Hnat, 1985). Therefore, in dealing with a practicing family, the helping agent may want to establish contact with their priest or indigenous religious leader (e.g., *curandero, espiritista, santero*), if this seems appropriate or desirable to the family.

Mexican-American Families

This section examines distinctive features of Mexican-American families, the largest group of Latino families in the United States. Keep in mind that the characteristics described here are more descriptive of first-generation immigrant families of lower-socioeconomic status and of rural families. These characteristics are less consistently found in families of higher socioeconomic background, urban families, or families that have been in the United States for a long time. Also keep in mind that of the Latino groups in the United States, Mexicans have been here the longest and, consequently, they are the most difficult to describe without stereotyping as some have been here for several generations while others are new arrivals from Mexico.

The Extended Family

Traditional Mexican-American families tend to be large and closely knit. A high proportion include both parents. Many have low incomes and are of mixed (Indian and Caucasian) racial background. Generally, traditional families are extended and include not only those sharing the same household (usually the nuclear or intergenerational unit) but also adult siblings and other close relatives and their respective families. Sometimes even distant relatives such as second cousins and great-aunts and great-uncles are considered part of the family. Some traditional families may take in the orphaned children of relatives or the children of divorced parents unable to keep them. Some may also include unmarried, widowed, or divorced adult relatives.

In some families, first cousins (*primos hermanos*) may be treated as siblings, and close friends of the parents may augment the family (Keefe, Padilla, & Carlos, 1979; Falicov, 1982). Traditionally, godparents (*compadres/ padrinos*) have been part of the family. However, nowadays godparents tend to have a lower level of involvement with and commitment to the family, unless they happen to be blood relatives (Williams, 1990).

Opinions vary as to the importance currently given to the extended family in the Mexican-

American culture, and research findings have not been consistent in this area (Vega, 1990). The majority of experts maintain that it continues to play an important role in the Mexican-American culture and in other Latino cultures in the United States because family members tend to live nearby and this facilitates visiting and exchange (Vega, 1990; Keefe, Padilla, & Carlos 1979; Chandler, 1979; Keefe & Padilla, 1987). For example, in a study conducted in Lubbock, Texas (population 150,000), Chandler (1979) found that 45 percent of the Mexican-American participants in the probability sample that was used were closely attached to their families and to the kin group, compared to only 3 percent of the "Anglo" participants in the study. The difference between "Anglos" and Mexicans was statistically significant, even after controlling for the effects of socioeconomic factors such as education, age, and occupation.

Nearly a decade later, Keefe and Padilla's studies (1987) of Mexican Americans in Santa Barbara, Oxnard, and Santa Paula in southern California yielded similar findings. In addition, they found that well-acculturated Mexican Americans, as well as those of higher socioeconomic status, had a stronger extended-family network than more recent immigrants of lower socioeconomic status (Keefe & Padilla, 1987, p. 134). Apparently, many immigrants lose regular contact with their extended families when they come to the United States due to the physical separation of family members between the two countries; in contrast, native-born Mexican Americans have had more time in the United States to rebuild their family networks.

Despite the emphasis on the importance of the extended family in the literature on Mexican Americans, at least one researcher recently found a decline in the level of interaction among extended-family members. Williams (1990), in an interview study of middle-class second- to fourth-generation Mexican Americans in Austin and Corpus Christi, Texas, found that most participants in her study were unable to keep in touch regularly with extended family members, mostly seeing them at family funerals and weddings. To be sure, more research is needed to throw light on the current significance of the extended family in the lives of Mexican-American families.

Compadrazgo is one traditional aspect of the Mexican-American extended family that has been losing significance in recent years. It originally consisted of the naming of friends as the baptismal godparents of a couple's children. Through this practice, friends became part of the family and pledged responsibility for the couple's children, in case the parents became unable to fulfill their parental duties. Traditionally the centerpiece of the **fictive kinship** system among Mexican Americans and other Latinos, *compadrazgo* no longer seems to play an important role. This is probably due to the increasing mobility characteristic of urban life, which makes it difficult to maintain lifelong close ties with nonrelatives (Keefe & Padilla, 1987; Williams, 1990). Thus, although Mexican-American and other Latino couples still select baptismal godparents for their children, nowadays most choose close relatives and no longer expect them to assume any additional responsibility for their godchildren beyond that which they would normally have by nature of their blood ties.

Cooperation and Emotional Support among Family Members

Traditional Mexican-American families put value on maintaining a close and cooperative family atmosphere. This requires that individual family members subordinate their needs to those of the family group and avoid confrontation and competition. They typically live near relatives and exchange many favors (Becerra, 1992). For example, extended-family members often share in the care and disciplining of children, provide temporary housing when needed, help with finances, give personal advice, nurse relatives during times of illness, and provide emotional support and companionship. Parents expect their children to take care of them in

their old age, and children usually comply. Few family members live by themselves before marriage, after divorce, or when they become widowed.

One of the important functions of traditional families is to provide members with emotional support (Keefe, Padilla, & Carlos, 1979). Even those Mexican Americans harboring mixed feelings about the advisability of confiding in a family member often prefer to turn to the family for help rather than to outsiders. To be sure, most often they rely on first-degree relatives—mothers, sisters, fathers, and brothers—with other relatives, friends, and priests being less frequently consulted. All this means that traditional families are unlikely to seek out professional mental health services except in cases of serious mental disorder. The traditional belief is that private matters should not be discussed with strangers and that the family should take care of its problems. However, the middle classes and the well educated are much more inclined to consult professionals.

In their research, Keefe and associates (1979) found that Euro-Americans, whom they loosely referred to as "Anglos," also would have preferred to rely on their families for help and emotional support, except that few had family residing in the same locality. Thus, they learned to turn to various formal and informal helping agents, such as friends, neighbors, co-workers, self-help and therapeutic groups, and individual counseling. On this issue, Mexican Americans are distinguishable from Euro-Americans only in terms of the high proportion of the former as compared to the latter who have family members nearby to offer help and support.

The strong reliance of traditional Mexican Americans on their families for emotional support would present problems for those who do not have kin in the local community, as they are not likely to have substitute sources of help available in times of stress. This can be particularly troublesome for recent immigrants and migrant workers who are the least likely to have a local kin group. Similarly, those who lack a well-integrated family may suffer stress because their family does not correspond to the normative or traditional family system in the Mexican culture. In short, because the extended family is considered an important source of emotional support for Mexican Americans who subscribe to the traditional culture, its absence or malfunction is probably more distressing to them than to Euro-Americans in similar circumstances (Keefe, Padilla, & Carlos, 1979).

Hierarchical Relationships and Sex Roles

Age and gender determine a person's status within the traditional Mexican-American family hierarchy, with older family members and males normally having higher power and authority than women and younger people. At least publicly, most Mexican-American families emphasize the husband's role as head of the family, provider, and protector and the wife's role as homemaker and child caregiver, even if the actual circumstances within a particular family are different. As is true of most families, regardless of racial or ethnic background, parent/child relationships are typically hierarchical, with children having low status compared to their parents.

Because of the father's higher official status and the cultural importance of machismo, Mexican-American families are characterized as patriarchal. However, research has shown that some families are more egalitarian than previously assumed in terms of decision making, the sharing of household tasks, and child rearing, especially urban families with wives who work outside the home, middle-class or professional families, and those headed by young couples (Staples & Mirande, 1980). But even in families with wives who are employed outside the home, the husband often continues to wield greater power and the wife continues to have primary responsibility for the maintenance of the household and for child care (Tienda & Glass, 1985; Williams, 1990). Yet even if hus-

band and wife do not have an egalitarian relationship, the stereotype of the Mexican-American husband having total control over his family is inaccurate.

Whether their relationship is more or less egalitarian, the traditional Mexican culture prescribes that husband and wife should treat one another with respect and consideration and a certain degree of formality. Too much intimacy, intense conflict, or public displays of hostility between spouses are frowned upon.

Child Rearing

In the traditional Mexican-American culture, children are considered more important than spouses, and the love of the mother (*el amor de madre*) is given precedence over the love of a spouse. In this context, having a close and warm relationship with one's children is primary and marital satisfaction assumes secondary importance.

During the first few years of their children's lives, Mexican-American parents put more emphasis on nurturing them than on encouraging autonomy or responsibility. However, although very young children tend to be infantilized and overprotected, as they grow up they are encouraged to assume greater independence and to take on family responsibilities. The traditional culture stresses respect and obedience of parents and elders and subordination of the children's needs and concerns to those of the family group. These expectations may cause problems as the children become acculturated because of the Euro-American emphasis on individualism and egalitarianism (Falicov, 1982).

During late childhood and throughout adolescence, traditional parents count on their children's help with housework, child care, and errands, usually without offering them any rewards or allowances for performing these tasks. Mothers count on their older daughters to help them to care for younger siblings, and the eldest son is generally expected to assume the role of provider in his father's absence, even if he is only 15 or 16 years old. These practices

are more commonly observed in families of low socioeconomic standing.

Parents expect their children to do well at school. However, a good number of the children—hampered by racism and ethnic discrimination, financial disadvantage, language barriers, and Spanish accents—find it difficult to fulfill parental expectations. When they speak English well, they are able to do better at school since teachers generally give higher grades to English-fluent children than to those who have language difficulties (Rothman, Gant, & Hnat, 1985).

Special Events and Milestones in the Lives of Mexican-American Families

The timing of family events and developmental milestones varies considerably from culture to culture (Falicov & Karrer, 1980). For example, females from one ethno-cultural group may, on the average, date, marry, and bear children at a younger age than those from another. There is also wide intercultural variability in the rituals families go through to mark the transition from one developmental stage to another (such as the

bar mitzvah in the Jewish culture) and in the meanings attached to certain events (such as the placement of an elderly parent in a nursing home). Although there is a good amount of writing on the life-course as it pertains to middle-class Euro-American families, the literature has been practically devoid of information concerning life-course events related to ethnic minority families, such as Latino families. However, such information is important to the many social service practitioners who come in contact with these families.

The purpose of this section is to familiarize you with some customs and patterns of behavior frequently followed at various developmental phases by first-generation Mexican-American families, particularly those that have recently migrated to the United States. Some of the observations made here may also be applicable to other Latino families of recent immigration. You can be assured, however, that you will always encounter families of Mexican origin and many other Latino families in the United States that do not exemplify the customs or patterns of behavior described here.

Premarital Phase. Before marriage, Mexican Americans who subscribe to the traditional Mexican culture engage in a long period of courtship, sometimes lasting several years. Because marriage is viewed as a lifetime commitment and a major step, parents tend to scrutinize their children's steady dates, particularly their daughters', more so than Euro-American parents (except perhaps those of high socioeconomic standing who have financial interests to protect). In the more traditional families, at all socioeconomic levels, courting couples get formally engaged prior to marriage. The engagement party is usually elaborate and functions as a means of officially bringing together the two families (Falicov & Karrer, 1980).

The Newly Married Couple with Young Children. Parents usually expect their newly married children to live near them and to visit them frequently, preferably several times a week. Mothers may not be satisfied unless their married daughters telephone them daily. Traditional couples often have children right after marriage, given that the traditional culture assigns a higher value to procreation than to marital or sexual satisfaction (Falicov & Karrer, 1980). Usually, if the maternal or paternal grandmother lives nearby, she will assist with child care, making the task of parenthood less burdensome than it can be for those without extended family members available. As the children enter school, teachers may find them to be more infantile and overdependent than usual due to the overprotectiveness of mothers and grandmothers.

Families with Adolescents. Traditional parents closely supervise and control the behavior of their adolescent daughters, allowing them as little independence as possible. One important ritual that marks the transition from early to later adolescence for girls is the quinceañera—a formal party given by the parents when their daughters turn 15 years old, which sometimes also signifies the beginning of the dating period. But even after the age of 15, the most traditional parents may not allow their daughters to go on a date without a chaperone. In contrast, they tend to be much more lax with their sons, often condoning premarital sexual experimentation, even though sex is considered taboo for unmarried daughters from traditional families.

Launching the Children. Marriage is the accepted way for children, particularly daughters, to leave their parents' home. In fact, many unmarried daughters continue to live with their parents until the parents die, at which time some may move in with a married sister or brother rather than live alone. Recently, however, more Mexican-American youths have been leaving home prior to marriage to attend an out-of-town college. Their families often find the separation more painful than Euro-American families, particularly mothers heavily invested in the maternal role. Sometimes, while the children are being launched, elderly grandparents on the mother's or father's side of the family may be moving in with the parents, thus compounding the stresses of this period (Falicov & Karrer, 1980).

The Family in Later Life. Elderly parents generally continue to center their lives around their married adult children and grandchildren, frequently helping with child care and adolescent supervision. This may be one reason why they tend to feel less superfluous or intrusive with respect to their children's families than their Euro-American counterparts.

The traditional culture expects adult children to take care of their parents when they get old. Consequently, Mexican-Americans, like most other members of nondominant racial and ethnic groups, often have strong feelings against placing their elderly parents in a nursing home or other social institution. Sometimes, however, there is no other alternative for working families without relatives nearby to care for the elderly during the day. The decision to place an elderly parent in a nursing home, no matter how justified, can generate much conflict and guilt.

Mainland Puerto Rican Families

Mainland Puerto Rican families are concentrated in metropolitan areas, particularly in central-city/inner-city areas of New York City, Newark, Hartford, and Chicago. Of the three largest Latino groups in the United States, Puerto Ricans have the highest rate of out-of-wedlock births, divorce, and female-headed families, and the lowest family income (Sanchez-Ayendez, 1988).

Much of what we know about Puerto Rican families in the United States is derived from writings based on observations of low-income families receiving services from government agencies. Little is known about the lifestyle and customs of families of higher socioeconomic status, as social-class differences have not been studied systematically among mainland Puerto Ricans (Sanchez-Ayendez, 1988). Therefore, the discussion that follows is more applicable to families of lower socioeconomic standing who stay close to the traditional cultural values.

Extended Family Tradition

Like other Latino families, the idealized traditional Puerto Rican family is extended and augmented, encompassing blood- and nonblood-related members, such as hijos de crianza (children informally adopted such as nephews and nieces, godchildren, or children from an extramarital liaison of the husband), friends who are like family (como de la familia), and godparents (compadres). Grandmothers play a special role and exert a great deal of influence within the extended family (Ramos-McKay, Comas-Diaz, & Rivera, 1988). Similar to the Mexican-American family, the Puerto Rican extended family functions as an important source of support for its members.

Puerto Rican family members living on the mainland tend to maintain very close relations with those on the island and visit them fre-quently. When problems arise, it is common for relatives on the mainland to send a child or other family member to live temporarily with a relative residing on the island, or vice versa.

In a study of 100 Puerto Rican families in New York City, Colleran (1984) found a significant decline in the importance placed on family by the young. Acculturation undoubtedly contributes to a change in values. However, the extended-family tradition and informal network of support would be difficult to maintain by the substantial number of poor Puerto Rican families randomly placed in public housing projects and thus separated from kin residing in Puerto Rican neighborhoods (Sanchez-Ayendez, 1988).

Patriarchy and Male and Female Sex Roles

For two-parent families, the traditional power structure is patriarchal, with the husband heading the family and being its main provider, protector, and authority figure. Even when the wife works outside the home, she is traditionally expected to defer to her husband, to be forbearing in her relations with him, and to take primary responsibility for the maintenance of the household and child care, and the maintenance of family unity (Sanchez-Ayendez, 1988). Because husbands customarily are not expected to help out with household tasks or child care, wives tend to depend on other women in the extended family (especially their mothers but also sisters or aunts) to assist with these responsibilities. Garcia-Preto (1982) noted that those women who are unable to get assistance from the extended family tend to become more insistent on their husbands to share the work; this may cause much friction between husbands and wives.

When wives are forced to become the primary breadwinners or the only family providers, perhaps because it is easier for them than for men to get jobs in urban centers, the sex-role reversal can generate considerable marital discord. Sometimes as the man's authority is threatened by his inability to earn a living, he may engage in excessive acts of machismo to compensate for his loss of status and power that may result in the breakdown of the marriage (Sanchez-Ayendez, 1988). These problems arise in a good number of Puerto Rican families on the mainland. In fact, as noted earlier, a larger proportion of Puerto Rican than of other families from major Latino groups in the U.S. are headed by females mostly due to divorce or separation. For the women, the ability to speak English, to work outside the home, and to receive AFDC due to their having U.S. citizenship status makes them highly independent of the men in taking care of themselves and their children, perhaps more so than any other group of Latino women in the United States (Bernal & Alvarez, 1983).

With respect to sexual conduct, the double standard remains strong. According to Garcia-Preto (1982), it is considered acceptable and perhaps even desirable in the traditional Puerto Rican culture for men to be sexually experienced. Their extramarital affairs, which are reportedly common, tend to be overlooked. In contrast, women are supposed to remain sexually inactive until marriage and, in marriage, they are expected to remain faithful to their husbands and to center their lives around their children, making every conceivable sacrifice for them (Sanchez-Ayendez, 1988). In this respect, Badillo-Ghali (1982) noted that Puerto Rican women often become less concerned about their personal appearance after motherhood, even those who previously took pride in their grooming. This may be viewed as a virtue by those who subscribe to the traditional culture—an indication of the mother's total commitment to her children.

Child Rearing and Discipline

The traditional culture values children as a sign of fertility and as an enrichment of the family, and the whole family normally pampers and enjoys them while they are young. Typically, parents strive to keep their children closely attached and discourage independence for as long as possible (Garcia-Preto, 1982; Bernal & Alvarez, 1983). Children are normally rein-

forced for being obedient, passive, submissive, and respectful. Typically, they are not permitted to question or challenge their parents' authority. These cultural values may be counterproductive in a society that frowns on passivity and expects independent thinking and behavior.

Puerto Rican parents are characteristically loving and affectionate with their young children. However, those of low socioeconomic status, like parents of low socioeconomic status from other racial and ethnic groups, often resort to physical punishment when the children do not behave as expected. Because the traditional culture considers physical punishment to be an acceptable method of disciplining children, teachers and human service practitioners should not automatically label parents who hit their children child abusers. Instead, as noted with respect to low-income African-American parents, practitioners can help by suggesting more positive disciplinary approaches while showing acceptance of the parental traditional beliefs and values.

Traditional parents commonly reward their daughters for being passive and submissive and often remind them of their weakness and inferiority as compared to men. They try to give them as little freedom as possible and carefully protect their virginity. Boys are encouraged to engage in masculine activities, scolded if they play with girls, and given greater independence; in ghetto areas many boys find friends on the streets who are bad influences and get into "trouble" (Locke, 1992).

In times of crisis, children may be transferred from one nuclear family unit to another within the extended network. For example, a child may be taken in temporarily by grandparents, aunts, godparents, or even neighbors who assume responsibility for the child as their own. Because this practice is culturally sanctioned, it is not perceived by the children or other family members as parental rejection or neglect; therefore, human service practitioners should refrain from interfering in such arrangements, unless they are regarded by the family as a problem (Garcia-

Preto, 1982). However, on the U.S. mainland, the family that has informally adopted a child is likely to encounter problems with various social institutions, such as the welfare system, the courts, or the schools, if there are no papers indicating that the child is legally theirs.

Education is valued particularly by middle- and upper-class parents who typically require their children to work hard at school and to do well. These parents often enroll the children in a variety of after-school enrichment activities, including music, dance, or art lessons and expect them to go to college (Bernal & Alvarez, 1983). Lower-income parents are less likely to stress the importance of education.

The Elderly

When parents grow old, children are expected to show gratitude by taking care of them (Sanchez-Ayendez, 1988). In the Puerto Rican culture, as well as in other Latino cultures, sons and daughters usually assume different roles with respect to their elderly parents. Typically, sons provide financial support, if needed, whereas daughters are likely to do the actual caregiving to the parents. Generally, it is the daughters who take in the parents when they can no longer live independently or their mothers after their fathers die. In turn, grandmothers help out with household chores and especially with child care, making it easier for daughters to work outside the home (Sanchez-Ayendez, 1988). The alternative of sending chronically impaired elderly parents to a nursing home is not widely accepted (Sanchez-Ayendez, 1988). It is probably somewhat more acceptable for the middle-class and for dual-employment families.

Skin Color

Many of the Puerto Rican families in the U.S. mainland are of mixed white and black racial background, including all the shades in between. Within the Puerto Rican culture, those with various degrees of black heritage are called *morenos, trigueños,* or *jabaos* as one goes from darker to lighter skin shades. Normally, on the island, persons of mixed race are not considered black, although those who are of purely European/Iberian background may subtly segregate themselves to keep their children from intermixing. In the United States, discrimination hits Puerto Ricans of mixed race doubly—because they are black and because they are Latinos. Sometimes they face racial discrimination for the first time when they migrate to the mainland, and this may create an identity crisis for some (Ramos-McKay, Comas-Diaz, & Rivera, 1988).

Relationship with Social Service Agencies

Like Mexican Americans, when faced with problems, mainland Puerto Ricans prefer to turn to their families for help, utilizing social services only as a last resort (Garcia-Preto, 1982). Particularly those of lower socioeconomic background are more likely to consult a **spiritist** than a mental health professional. Spiritists are persons believed to be able to communicate with and to have some control over the spirits of the dead. They act as mediums, trying to convince the spirits to help rather than to harm their clients. They may also prescribe ointments, herbs, massages, and prayers.

Cuban-American Families

Cuban-American families—mostly concentrated in the Miami area, New Jersey, and New York—are the third largest group of Latino families in the United States.

Intergenerational Family

Cuban-American families are characteristically small, probably for several reasons: a large proportion of persons of middle-class status in this immigrant group, a heavy emphasis on upward mobility, the women's high rate of participation in the work force, the high median age of this population group due to selective migration of older (more established) versus younger persons, and the traditionally low fertility rate of this ethnic group, which has become even lower in exile (Queralt, 1984).

Although Cuban-American family households are small and usually composed of the nuclear family group only, relations within the intergenerational family are typically strong. Grandparents frequently play an important role in helping with child care and supervision so that parents can work outside the home. They generally live close to their adult children. Some grandparents live with their children, particularly widowed mothers who often move in with their daughters or sons after the death of their husbands.

Ties with other members of the extended family—such as aunts, uncles, cousins, nephews, and nieces—are mostly evident during holidays and other special joyous occasions when the extended family may come together for celebration or during crisis periods when relatives may come forward to offer support. In this sense, they are not particularly different from mainstream Americans.

Like other Latinos, Cuban Americans give central importance to the family and show a high level of involvement with members of the intergenerational family (Bernal, 1982; Queralt, 1984). Compared to Euro-Americans, parents and children may show a tendency toward enmeshment. The same may be true of other Latino groups. Since this degree of closeness is culturally sanctioned, it should not be considered a problem unless the family considers it to be.

Child Rearing
Judged by U.S. mainstream standards, Cuban children are typically pampered, babied, overprotected, and overindulged. For example, immigrant parents often do not allow their children to go to school unless they are accompanied by an adult or to cross the street by themselves even when, by U.S. standards, the children are old enough to do so. Because this degree of overprotection is culturally based, practitioners need not be concerned about it unless it is extreme or it is viewed as a problem by the family. By and large, the excesses of overprotection and overindulgence are moderated as the children grow up.

Although the divorce rate is high among Cuban Americans, the large majority of children live with both parents. Discipline tends to be relaxed by Latin American standards, and parents and children treat one another more informally than many other Latino family members. Immigrant parents and those who are very traditional expect their daughters to live at home until marriage, even if they marry late and make good incomes at work. There is a lingering feeling that if the unmarried daughter wants to live independently, it must be for "no good reason." When daughters divorce, with or without children, often they move back with their parents (Voboril, 1991).

The Patriarchy and Sex Roles
Like other Latinos, Cuban Americans have a patriarchal tradition, although mothers are given central importance within the family. Although the typical family still subscribes to an ideology of male authority, the rhetoric may be stronger than the actual dominance practiced by males. The wives' high level of outside employment in the United States may have helped them to achieve greater equality in relation to their husbands in terms of decision-making power and even some housekeeping and child-care assistance from their husbands (Queralt, 1984); but, like other U.S. women, they still carry the lion's share of the household and child-care chores. The degree to which differential sex roles are emphasized in marriage depends particularly on the family's socioeconomic standing and level of education and acculturation (Bernal, 1982).

ASIAN-AMERICAN FAMILIES

Because there are significant cultural differences among the various Asian groups in the United States, particularly between East Asians and Asian Indians, this section, consistent with previous chapters, will be restricted to East Asian families, including particularly Chinese, Japanese, Korean, Filipino, Vietnamese, Thai, Cambodian, and Laotian families. Many of these families are concentrated in the western states in the U.S. mainland and in Hawaii. Although they come from different nations with unique customs, values, and traditions, they are similar in a number of ways.

This section will look at similarities in family structure and dynamics among East Asians. However, keep in mind that values and behaviors vary considerably according to socioeconomic status (in the country of origin as well as in the United States), nationality, place of birth (the native country or the United States), and years of residence in the United States. Also, it is important to bear in mind that the characteristics of Asian-American families to be discussed will be most applicable to traditional families of recent immigration, as well as to older, traditional, first-generation family members. The information contained in this section will be much less descriptive of second-third-, or later-generation Asian-American families whose customs may more closely resemble the U.S. mainstream.

Emphasis on Family

Eastern philosophies and religions, such as Confucianism and Buddhism, stress the precedence of the family over the individual. Personal actions reflect not just on the individual but first and foremost on the family, including all its preceding and future generations. Consequently, family members are expected to preserve the family honor and dignity and to avoid bringing shame to it (Ho, 1987a).

Among East Asians, intergenerational family relations and kin relationships are extensive and important. Among Southeast Asians, in particular, even second or third cousins may be referred to as brothers or sisters, and old friends of the family may carry the status of aunts or uncles (Chao, 1992). Ho (1987a) noted that extended family ties are often maintained by sharing the same household or by frequent visits and are aided by the stability of residence of Asian Americans who seldom move once they settle down.

Patriarchy and Hierarchical Family Roles

Traditional family relations in many East Asian cultures are influenced by Confucianism and its clearly prescribed and differentiated family roles (Shon & Ja, 1982; Ho, 1987a). Within the Confucian tradition, men are expected to provide economic support for their families, to rule over their families, and to make family decisions with unquestioned authority. In accordance with Confucian teachings, women are expected to submit to and obey men—their fathers during youth, their husbands in marriage, and after the husband's death, their eldest sons. Yet, even under this system, traditional mothers, at least in their old age, may rule their families through the influence they exert on their deeply attached and respectful sons who frequently follow their advice.

In traditional Asian cultures, sons are more highly prized than daughters. The preference for sons over daughters dates back to ancient times when males were more useful to the family because they could accomplish more heavy manual and agricultural labor. This preference is still prevalent in rural, nonindustrial areas of the world, but the ideology lingers even among technologically advanced East Asians, such as the Japanese and Koreans, for whom male physical strength no longer has much practical utility. This preference for boys over girls exists even among some of those living in the United States (Poong Ryu & Vann, 1992).

Among sons, the eldest holds a special position within the traditional family. He is expected to act as a role model and is given authority over younger brothers and sisters who are supposed to follow his guidance throughout their lives. When the father dies, the eldest son becomes the new head of the family. Should he die or abandon his role for any reason, Shon and Ja (1982) have observed that, with the recent loosening of traditional attitudes toward women throughout East Asia, a daughter may be just as likely as another son to assume the family reigns, particularly among Asian Americans.

Arranged marriages are no longer common (Ho, 1987a), but Asian families still exert considerable influence on mate selection by withholding their blessings if they do not approve of the prospective husband or bride. Marriage traditionally continues the man's family line; therefore, upon marriage, women from old-fashioned families are expected to leave their own families and to become part of their husbands' families. However, many modern East Asian families no longer expect wives to discontinue their relationships with their own families and totally transfer their allegiance to their husbands' (Shon & Ja, 1982).

Throughout Asia and in the United States, Asian women have recently attained considerable freedom to pursue a higher education or a career and to choose their own marriage partners. According to Ho (1987a), the status of contemporary Asian-American women within the family depends on many factors—such as their place of birth and that of their husbands, their level of education and degree of acculturation, and the relative scarcity or oversupply of women of marriageable age in their ethnic group.

Despite the progress toward equality made by Asian women in relation to Asian men, their relationship is far from egalitarian. For example, even today few Asian-American men would consider dating a woman who has been previously married or even engaged to another man (Ho, 1987a). Because traditional Asian cultures do not sanction divorce, many wives must suffer marital unhappiness silently. Accordingly, divorce rates remain low, although those born in the United States tend not to be as conservative with respect to divorce as their foreign-born parents. One positive outcome of the conservative sexual mores prevalent in Asian cultures is the low proportion of out-of-wedlock births among women and the high proportion of two-parent homes (Staples & Mirande, 1980).

Wives who work outside the home have made the most progress toward parity with their husbands, but Ho (1987a) observed that the responsibility for the household and children

continues to be the woman's. As more wives share wage-earning responsibilities with their husbands, Asian wives will likely gain more power and influence vis-à-vis Asian husbands (Matsuoka, 1990).

Perhaps due to the lingering inequality between the sexes, marriage to non-Asians, although still frowned upon, is common among Asian females, particularly those from families that have been in the United States for two or more generations. Some of the women are favorably inclined toward Euro-American men, in part due to their dissatisfaction with the sexist attitude Asian men often display toward them.

Child Rearing

In traditional Asian families, men normally handle the discipline of the children. Because of their role as disciplinarians, children may perceive them as somewhat distant and difficult to approach. The traditional culture expects mothers to be highly devoted, nurturant, and attached to their children. Placing the children in day-care facilities or leaving them with babysitters generally is not culturally sanctioned. Consequently, mothers who work outside the home try to leave the children in the care of close relatives (Ho, 1987a). Small children are typically pampered, protected, indulged, and showered with love and affection.

Some young Asian-American children may appear overprotected and overdependent by Euro-American standards, but this is generally not a problem as long as it remains within the limits prescribed by the culture. As the children grow up, parents express their affection toward them less openly and less physically. Children are expected to follow increasingly more rigid rules of behavior, including respect for authority, strict obedience, control of aggression, suppression of emotion, politeness, and high achievement at school.

A respectful love of parents, or **filial piety,** is probably the most fundamental value that children are taught within the family. This principle requires that children treat their parents with the highest respect and obedience simply because they gave them life and raised them, even if the parents do not "deserve" the good treatment.

Confucian teachings forbid close association between boys and girls beyond the age of 7 until marriage. This prohibition is more strict for daughters than sons (Poong Rye & Vann, 1992). Few Asian Americans would strictly enforce this separation; nevertheless, teenagers of the opposite sex do not mix as freely as Euro-American teenagers. This may be one reason why the rate of teenage out-of-wedlock pregnancies is so low. Children are expected to live with their parents until they get married and to contribute financially to the support of the family once they start working.

Harmony in Family Relations

East Asian cultures emphasize the importance of harmonious relationships and shun open disagreement, direct confrontation, and open expression of negative feelings. Hence, traditional families typically downplay problems and discuss them indirectly rather than openly. It is considered inappropriate for low-status family members to express negative feelings toward those who occupy higher roles. For instance, children are not allowed to question the authority of their parents or to talk back to them. Shon and Ja (1982) suggested that what frequently happens under such circumstances is that family members internalize their negative feelings and transform them into self-recrimination.

Honor and Respect for Elderly Parents and Ancestors

Because the parent/child relationship, or consanguine tie, is given priority in traditional Asian cultures over the marital bond, filial piety requirements extend to adult children. They are expected to continue to honor and respect their parents by maintaining upright behavior, by consulting with them about impor-

tant decisions, and by observing important family dates, such as their parents' birthdays and wedding anniversaries. Traditionally, sons and their spouses have been expected to make sacrifices to take care of the physical needs of their parents and to provide for their social, emotional, and material well-being.

In most traditional East Asian cultures, the husband's parents are given priority over the wife's parents in fulfilling filial obligations. The system of primogeniture stipulates that male children (particularly first-born males) get the largest share of the inheritance from their parents, and consequently have the main responsibility for their care. However, this custom is not prevalent in all East Asian cultures. For example, in some of the Southeast Asian countries, such as Lao, daughters are responsible for the care of elderly parents instead of sons (Crystal, 1989).

Even after migration to the United States, sons sometimes continue to live with their parents after marriage, as is customary in various Asian countries, bringing their new wives into the parents' home. However, customs are changing quickly. For example, in mainland China and in Hong Kong, filial obligation now includes the care of the wife's parents too, not just the husband's parents (Kim, Kim, & Hurh, 1991).

Many East Asian immigrants to the United States try to continue to fulfill their filial obligations, even though it is more difficult to carry out this family duty in the United States, particularly when both spouses work outside the home. However, regardless of the efforts they may make to honor and respect elderly parents, some traditional parents feel slighted and degraded when their children ask them to help with the housework or with child care. If they express a desire to move out of their children's homes, the children may be reluctant to let them go, for fear that other Asian friends and relatives may think that they are not treating their parents right (Kim, Kim, & Hurh, 1991).

The East Asian tradition of honoring and respecting the aged extends to ancestors. Ancestor worship is commonly practiced by maintaining a family altar at home. The altar may hold a variety of objects, such as incense, flowers, a Buddha, pictures of family members who have died, or food or fruit offerings (Chao, 1992). The altar's custodian (usually the eldest male in Vietnamese culture, but it may be a different family member in other East Asian cultures) makes offerings and prayers to ancestors (Gold, 1992). This custom is less common among Asian Americans, but it is still followed in some traditional homes.

Attitude toward Involvement with Social Agencies

Like other racial and ethnic families, Asian Americans strongly believe that problems should be resolved within the family. Their traditional cultures view problems as failures in fulfilling moral obligations, as resulting from circumstances over which one has no control, or as due to organic factors, such as an imbalance of the basic life forces (Ho, 1987a). According to Shon and Ja (1982), they may feel ashamed or feel that they have failed if they must turn to an outsider for help, such as a social worker or other human service practitioner. Therefore, many are not likely to seek out help from community agencies until they have exhausted all internal family resources.

Outside the family, some may prefer to consult religious figures or to turn to traditional healers, such as **herbalists** or **acupuncturists** before agreeing to seek Westernized help. When contact is established with a Western practitioner, families are likely to expect to be given guidance and direction and, typically, they will be very obedient and unquestioning concerning the practitioner's decisions and advise. This places great responsibility on the worker (Chao, 1992).

In the role of human service practitioner, you will likely work with many diverse families—African American, Latino, Asian American, and Native American, for example. The knowledge that you have acquired in this book about some of their most salient characteristics should help you to relate to these families with greater understanding of their customs and dynamics. Your chances of successfully intervening with them will be greater if they sense that you are knowledgeable about their culture and values and that you are genuinely respectful, sensitive, interested, and understanding.

Although the families we have studied in this chapter are diverse and distinct, you may have noticed they all share some common features. Among them are an excess of poverty and societal oppression, emphasis on the intergenerational extended family and on mutual aid, a closely knit family group, high respect accorded to the elderly and an important role played by grandparents, high value placed on traditional religions, and reluctance to use social and mental health services.

In working with families from diverse racial and ethnic groups, as well as with mainstream families, it is important to capitalize on their strengths rather than to focus on deficiencies. The intergenerational extended family network, in particular, can be a major source of strength and cooperation to tap when there are problems. For many, religion is another important source of strength that can be used advantageously in social interventions.

Poverty and oppression are two social conditions that have had serious negative effects on many racial and ethnic minority families. It is crucial to direct some of your interventive efforts toward a modification of the environmental and social conditions that prevent some

GLOSSARY

Acculturation: The process by which individuals learn the behaviors, values, and customs of a cultural group other than their own. Acculturation differs from assimilation in that it does not imply total immersion into the new cultural group with the loss of one's original cultural heritage.

Acupuncturist: A person trained to relieve pain or disease by inserting needles in various key points in the body.

Clan: Among Native Americans, a group of families that trace their lineage to a common ancestor.

Egalitarian Family: A family in which roles, household chores, child rearing, and power are democratically distributed between male and female members.

Ethno-Cultural Group: A group of people who share a common set of customs, values, ideology, history, national origin, race, language, sexual orientation, or religion.

Fictive Kin: In some ethnic groups, persons without blood or legal ties to the family who nevertheless exchange emotional support, concrete help, or financial assistance as if they were relatives. For example, many African Americans consider certain especially close friends, informally adopted children, or favorite preachers to be part of their families. Some of these quasi-relatives may be referred to as play "mamas," "aunts," or "uncles."

Filial Piety: A fundamental value in Asian cultures requiring that children treat their parents with the highest respect and obedience simply because they gave them life and raised them, even if the parents do not "deserve" such treatment.

Herbalist: An herb doctor or a person who helps people with various physical, emotional, or psychological complaints by prescribing various natural herbs.

Intergenerational Family: A family that includes members of several different generations, such as great-grandparents, grandparents, parents, and children.

Lineal Relatives: Direct-line ancestors or descendants of an individual—for example, grandparents, parents, children, and grandchildren.

Machismo: A doctrine that gives precedence to males as authority figures, providers, and protectors of women and children and that dictates that they should be dominant, aggressive, just, honorable, courageous, and sexually experienced.

Matriarchal Family: A family in which the power resides by choice or cultural value rather than by force of circumstance in a female head. Most African-American scholars argue that African-American families, despite the large proportion of female-headed households, are *not* matriarchal because many of the women head the family not by choice but due to circumstances in the society that render a large number of African-American males unable to assume leadership of their families.

Namesake: Someone who has the same name as another. In the Native-American cultures, a person who assumes responsibility to help to rear a child, to act as a role model, and to take care of the child if the parents become unable to do so for any reason.

Parental Child: A male or female older sibling who acts as a substitute parent. This usually happens in families with a large number of children or where the mother or both parents work.

Patriarchal Family: A family in which the power resides by choice or cultural value rather than by force of circumstance in a male head. Many Latino and Asian-American families are patriarchal. Many upper-class families of all ethnic backgrounds, including Anglos, are also patriarchal.

Spiritist: Person believed to be able to communicate with the dead. He/she acts as a medium attempting to convince the spirits to help rather than harm clients and prescribes ointments, herbs, sacrifices, and prayers.

REFERENCES

Attneave, C. (1982). American Indians and Alaskan native families: Emigrants in their own homeland. In M. McGoldrick, J. K. Pearce, & J. Giordano (Eds.), *Ethnicity and family therapy* (pp. 55–83). New York: Guilford Press.

Bach-y-Rita, G. (1982). In R. M. Becerra, M. Karno, & J. I. Escobar (Eds.), *Mental health and Hispanic Americans: Clinical perspectives* (pp. 29–40). New York: Grune & Stratton.

Badillo-Ghali, S. (1982). Understanding Puerto Rican traditions. *Social Work, 27*(1), 98–102.

Becerra, R. M. (1992). Mexican American families. In J. M. Henslin (Ed.), *Marriage and family in a changing society* (4th ed., pp. 66–75). New York: Free Press.

Bernal, G. (1982). Cuban families. In M. McGoldrick, J. K. Pearce, & J. Giordano (Eds.), *Ethnicity and family therapy* (pp. 187–207). New York: Guilford Press.

Bernal, G., & Alvarez, A. I. (1983). Culture and class in the study of families. In J. C. Hanson (Ed.) & C. J. Falicov (Vol. Ed.), *Cultural perspectives in family therapy* (pp. 187–207). Rockville, MD: Aspen Systems.

Billingsley, A. (1988). The impact of technology on Afro-American families. *Family Relations, 37*, 420–425.

Boyd-Franklin, N. (1989a). Racism, racial identification, and skin color. In N. Boyd-Franklin (Ed.), *Black families in therapy: A multisystems approach* (pp. 25–41). New York: Guilford Press.

Boyd-Franklin, N. (1989b). Black extended family patterns and informal adoption. In N. Boyd-Franklin (Ed.), *Black families in therapy: A multisystems approach* (pp. 42–63). New York: Guilford Press.

Boyd-Franklin, N. (1989c). Role flexibility and boundary confusion in Black families. In N. Boyd-Franklin (Ed.), *Black families in therapy: A multisystems approach* (pp. 64–77). New York: Guilford Press.

Boyd-Franklin, N. (1989d). Religion, spirituality, and the treatment of Black families. In N. Boyd-Franklin (Ed.), *Black families in therapy: A multisystems approach* (pp. 78–91). New York: Guilford Press.

Chandler, C. R. (1979). Traditionalism in a modern setting: A comparison of Anglo- and Mexican-American value orientations. *Human Organization, 38*, 153–159.

Chao, C. M. (1992). The inner heart: Therapy with Southeast Asian families. In L. A. Vargas & J. D. Koss-Chioino (Eds.), *Working with culture: Psychotherapeutic interventions with ethnic minority children and adolescents* (pp. 157–181). San Francisco: Jossey-Bass.

Chestang, L. W. (1977). *Achievement and self-esteem among Black Americans: A study of*

twenty lives. Doctoral dissertation, University of Chicago.

Colleran, K. (1984). Acculturation in Puerto Rican families in New York City. *Research Bulletin, Hispanic Research Center.* New York: Fordham University, 7, 2–7.

Colon, F. (1980). The family life cycle of the multi-problem poor family. In E. A. Carter & M. McGoldrick (Eds.), *The family life cycle: A framework for family therapy* (pp. 343–381). New York: Gardner Press.

Cortes, C. E. (Ed.). (1980). *The Cuban experience in the United States.* New York: Arno Press.

Crystal, D. (1989). Asian Americans and the myth of the model minority. *Social Casework, 70*, 405–413.

Davenport, D. S., & Yurich, J. M. (1991). Multicultural gender issues. *Journal of Counseling & Development, 70*, 64–71.

Eshleman, J. R. (1991). *The family: An introduction* (6th ed.). Boston: Allyn and Bacon.

Falicov, C. J. (1982). Mexican families. In M. McGoldrick, J. K. Pearce, & J. Giordano (Eds.), *Ethnicity and family therapy* (pp. 134–163). New York: Guilford Press.

Falicov, C. J., & Karrer, B. M. (1980). Cultural variations in the family life cycle: The Mexican-American family. In E. A. Carter & M. McGoldrick (Eds.), *The family life cycle: A framework for family therapy* (pp. 383–425). New York: Gardner Press.

Garcia-Preto, N. (1982). Puerto Rican families. In M. McGoldrick, J. K. Pearce, & J. Giordano (Eds.), *Ethnicity and family therapy* (pp. 164–185). New York: Guilford Press.

Gold, S. J. (1992). *Refugee communities: A comparative field study.* Newbury Park, CA: Sage.

Heiss, J. (1981). Women's values regarding marriage and the family. In H. P. McAdoo (Ed.), *Black families* (pp. 186–198). Beverly Hills, CA: Sage.

Hill, R. (1972). *The strengths of black families.* New York: Emerson Hall.

Hines, P. M. (1988). The family life cycle of poor Black families. In E. Carter & M. McGoldrick (Eds.), *The changing family life cycle* (2nd ed., pp. 513–544). New York: Gardner Press.

Hines, P. M., & Boyd-Franklin, N. (1982). Black families. In M. McGoldrick, J. K. Pearce, & J. Giordano (Eds.), *Ethnicity and family therapy* (pp. 84–107). New York: Guilford Press.

Ho, M. K. (1987a). Family therapy with Asian/ Pacific Americans. In *Family Therapy with Ethnic Minorities* (pp. 24–38). Beverly Hills, CA: Sage.

Ho, M. K. (1987b). Family therapy with American Indians and Alaskan Natives. In M. K. Ho (Ed.), *Family therapy with ethnic minorities* (pp. 69–83). Beverly Hills, CA: Sage.

Ingrassia, M. (1993, August 30). Endangered family. *Newsweek*, 17–27.

John, R. (1988). The Native American family. In H. Mindel, R. W. Habenstein, & R. Wright, Jr. (Eds.). *Ethnic families in America* (3rd ed., pp. 325–363). New York: Elsevier Science.

Jones, N. S. C. (1990). Black/white issues in psychotherapy: A framework for clinical practice. *Journal of Social Behavior and Personality, 5*, 305–322.

Keefe, S. E., & Padilla, A. M. (1987). *Chicano ethnicity*. Albuquerque, NM: University of New Mexico Press.

Keefe, S. E., Padilla, A. M., & Carlos, M. L. (1979). The Mexican-American extended family as an emotional support system. *Human Organizations, 38*, 144–152.

Kim, K. C., Kim, S., & Hurh, W. M. (1991). Filial piety and intergenerational relationship in Korean immigrant families. *International Journal of Aging and Human Development, 33*, 233–245.

Leslie, G. R., & Korman, S. K. (1989). *The family in social context* (7th ed.). New York: Oxford University Press.

Lewis, R., & Ho, M. (1989). Social work with Native Americans. In D. Atkinson, G. Morten, & D. Sue (Eds.), *Counseling American minorities* (pp. 51–58). Dubuque, IA: William C. Brown.

Locke, D. C. (1992). *Increasing multicultural understanding: A comprehensive model*. Newbury Park, CA: Sage.

Lustig, M. W. (1988). Value differences in intercultural communication. In L. A. Samovar & R. E. Porter (Eds.), *Intercultural communication: A reader* (5th ed., pp. 55–61). Belmont, CA: Wadsworth.

Matsuoka, J. K. (1990). Differential acculturation among Vietnamese refugees. *Social Work, 35*, 341–345.

McAdoo, H. (1978). Factors related to stability in upwardly mobile black families. *Journal of Marriage and the Family, 40*, 762–778.

McGoldrick, M. (1988). Ethnicity and the family life cycle. In E. Carter & M. McGoldrick (Eds.), *The changing family life cycle* (2nd ed., pp. 69–90). New York: Gardner Press.

McGoldrick, M., Garcia-Preto, N., Hines, P. M., & Lee, E. (1989). Ethnicity and women. In M. McGoldrick, C. M. Anderson, & F. Walsh (Eds.), *Women in families: A framework for family therapy* (pp. 169–199). New York: W. W. Norton.

Pinderhughes, E. (1982). Afro-American families and the victim system. In M. McGoldrick, J. K. Pearce, & J. Giordano (Eds.), *Ethnicity and family therapy* (pp. 108–122). New York: Guilford Press.

Poong Rye, J., & Vann, B. H. (1992). Korean families in America. In M. E. Procidano & C. B. Fisher (Eds.), *Contemporary families: A handbook for school professionals* (pp. 117–134). New York: Teachers College.

Price, J. A. (1981). North American Indian families. In H. Mindel, R. W. Habenstein, & R. Wright, Jr. (Eds.), *Ethnic families in America* (2nd ed., pp. 245–270). New York: Elsevier Science.

Queralt, M. (1984). Understanding Cuban immigrants: A cultural perspective. *Social Work, 29*, 115–121.

Ramos-McKay, J. M., Comas-Diaz, L., & Rivera, L. A. (1988). Puerto Ricans. In L. Comas-Dias & E. E. H. Griffith (Eds.), *Clinical guidelines in cross-cultural mental health* (pp. 204–232). New York: John Wiley & Sons.

Red Horse, J. (1980). Family structure and value orientation in American Indians. *Social Casework, 61*, 462–467.

Red Horse, J. (1988). Cultural evolution of American Indian families. In C. Jacobs & D. D. Bowles (Eds.), *Ethnicity and race: Critical concepts in social work*. Silver Spring, MD: National Association of Social Workers.

Rothman, J., Gant, L. M., & Hnat, S. A. (1985). Mexican-American family culture. *Social Service Review, 59*, 197–215.

Sanchez-Ayendez, M. (1988). The Puerto Rican American family. In C. H. Mindel, R. W. Habenstein, & R. Wright, Jr. (Eds.). *Ethnic families in America* (3rd ed., pp. 173–195). New York: Elsevier Science.

Sandoval, M. C., & de la Roza, M. C. (1986). A cultural perspective for serving the Hispanic client. In H. P. Lefley & P. B. Pedersen (Eds.), *Cross-*

cultural training for mental health professionals (pp. 151–181). Springfield, IL: Charles C. Thomas.

Shon, S. P., & Ja, D. Y. (1982). Asian families. In M. McGoldrick, J. K. Pearce, & J. Giordano (Eds.), *Ethnicity and family therapy* (pp. 208–228). New York: Guilford Press.

Smith, E. (1981). Cultural and historical perspectives in counseling blacks. In D. W. Sue (Ed.), *Counseling the culturally different: Theory and practice* (pp. 141–185). New York: John Wiley & Sons.

Staples, R. (1985) Changes in Black family structure: The conflict between family ideology and structural conditions. *Journal of Marriage and the Family, 47,* 1005–1013.

Staples, R. (1992). African American families. In J. M. Henslin (Ed.), *Marriage and family in a changing society* (4th ed., pp. 51–65). New York: Free Press.

Staples, R., & Mirande, A. (1980). Racial and cultural variations among American families: A decennial review of the literature on minority families. *Journal of Marriage and the Family, 42,* 157–173.

Szapocznik, J., & Kurtines, W. (1980). Acculturation, biculturalism, and adjustment among Cuban Americans. In A. M. Padilla (Ed.), *Acculturation: Theory, models, and some new findings.* Washington, DC: Westview.

Taylor, R. J. (1986). Receipt of support from family among Black Americans: Demographic and familial differences. *Journal of Marriage and the Family, 48,* 67–77.

Taylor, R. J., Chatters, L. M., Tucker, M. B., & Lewis, E. (1990). Developments in research on black families: A decade review. *Journal of Marriage and the Family, 52,* 993–1014.

Tienda, M., & Glass, J. (1985). Household structure and labor force participation of Black, Hispanic, and White mothers. *Demography, 22,* 381–394.

Veciana-Suarez, A. (1993, April 16). Leaving home: Hispanic family ties tough to loosen for college. *The Miami Herald,* pp. 1E, 3E.

Voboril, M. (1991, May 30). Single? You're not alone in this world. *The Miami Herald,* p. 3G.

White, J. L. (1984). Psychosocial dynamics of Black family life. In J. L. White (Ed.), *The psychology of blacks* (pp. 60–82). Englewood Cliffs, NJ: Prentice Hall.

White, J. L., & Parham, T. A. (1990). *The psychology of blacks: An African-American perspective* (2nd ed.). Englewood Cliffs, NJ: Prentice Hall.

Williams, N. (1990) *The Mexican American family: Tradition and change.* Dix Hills, NY: General Hall.

Willie, C. V. (1985). *Black and white families: A study in complementarity.* Dix Hills, NY: General Hall.

Willie, C. V. (1986). The Black family and social class. In R. Staples (Ed.), *The black family: Essays and studies* (3rd ed., pp. 224–231). Belmont, CA: Wadsworth.

Willie, C. V. (1989). The Black family: Striving toward freedom. In National Urban League (Ed.), *The state of Black America 1988.* New York: National Urban League.

SUGGESTIONS FOR FURTHER READING

Agbayani-Siewart, P. (1994). Filipino American culture and family: Guidelines for practitioners. *Families in Society, 75,* 429–437.

Aponte, R. (1993). Hispanic families in poverty: Diversity, context, and interpretation. *Families in Society, 74,* 527–538.

Becerra, R. M. (1992). Mexican American families. In J. M. Henslin (Ed.), *Marriage and family in a changing society* (4th ed., pp. 66–75). New York: Free Press.

Billingsley, A. (1992). *Climbing Jacob's ladder: The enduring legacy of African-American families.* New York: Simon & Schuster.

Eshleman, J. R. (1991). Life-styles among Chinese families. In J. Ross Eshleman (Ed.), *The family: An introduction* (6th ed., pp. 136–157). Boston: Allyn and Bacon.

Farber, M., Mindel, C. H., & Lazerwitz, B. (1988). The Jewish American family. In C. H. Mindel, R. W. Habenstein, & R. Wright, Jr. (Eds.), *Ethnic families in America* (3rd ed., pp. 400–437). New York: Elsevier Science.

Hill, R. B., Billingsley, A., Engram, E., Malson, M. R., Rubin, R. H., Stack, C. B., Stewart, J. B., & Teele, J. E. (1993). *Research on African-Ameri-*

can family: A holistic perspective. Westport, CT: Auburn House.

Ho, M. K. (1987). *Family therapy with ethnic minorities*. Newbury Park, CA: Sage.

Jarrett, R. L. (1994). Living poor: family life among single parent, African-American women. *Social Problems, 41*(1), 30–50.

Landry, B. (1987). *The new Black middle class.* Berkeley: University of California Press.

McAdoo, H. P. (Ed.). (1988). *Black families* (2nd ed.). Newbury Park, CA: Sage.

McAdoo, H. P. (1992). Upward mobility and parenting in middle-income black families. In A. K. H. Burlew, W. C. Banks, H. P. McAdoo, & D. A. Azibo (Eds.), *African American psychology: Theory, research, and practice* (pp. 63–86). Newbury Park, CA: Sage.

McAdoo, H. P. (1993). *Family and ethnicity: Strength in diversity.* Newbury Park, CA: Sage.

Mindel, C. H., Habenstein, R. W., & Wright, R. Jr. (1988). *Ethnic families in America* (3rd ed.). New York: Elsevier Science.

Rubin, L. B. (1992). *Worlds of pain: Life in the working class family.* New York: Basic Books.

Saba, G. W. (1990). *Minorities and family therapy.* New York: Haworth Press.

Sotomayor, M. (Ed.). (1991). *Empowering Hispanic families: A critical issue for the '90s.* Milwaukee, WI: Family Service America.

Staples, R. (1992). African American families. In J. M. Henslin (Ed.), *Marriage and family in a changing society* (4th ed., pp. 51–65). New York: Free Press.

Taylor, R. J., Chatters, L. M., Tucker, M. B., & Lewis, E. (1990). Developments in research on black families: A decade review. *Journal of Marriage and the Family, 52*, 993–1014.

Taylor, R. L. (Ed.). (1994). *Minority families in the United States: A multicultural perspective.* Englewood Cliffs, NJ: Prentice Hall.

Tseng, W., & Hsy, J. (1991). *Culture and family: Problems and therapy.* New York: Haworth Press.

Vega, W. A. (1990). Hispanic families in the 1980s: A decade of research. *Journal of Marriage and the Family, 52*, 1015–1024.

White, M. M. (1987). We are family!: Kinship and solidarity in the black community. In G. Gay & W. L. Baber (Eds.), *Expressively black: The cultural basis of ethnic identity* (pp. 17–34). New York: Praeger.

Williams, N. (1990). *The Mexican American family: Tradition and change.* Dix Hills, NY: General Hall.

Willie, C. V. (1985). *Black and white families: a study in complementarity.* Dix Hills, NY: General Hall.

Wilson, M. N. (1992). Perceived parental activity of mothers, fathers, and grandmothers in three-generational black families. In A. K. H. Burlew, W. C. Banks, H. P. McAdoo, & D. A. Azibo (Eds.), *African American psychology: Theory, research, and practice* (pp. 87–104). Newbury Park, CA: Sage.

Wilson, W. J. (1993). *Urban poverty and family life in the inner city.* Oxford: Oxford University Press.

Yanagisako, S. J. (1985). *Transforming the past: Tradition and kinship among Japanese Americans.* Stanford, CA: Stanford University Press.

Look for articles on families from nondominant racial/ethnic groups in the following journals:

American Journal of Family Therapy
Families in Society
Family Relations
The International Journal of Sociology of the Family
Journal of Family Issues
Journal of Family Social Work
Journal of Marital and Family Therapy
Journal of Marriage and Family Counseling
Journal of Marriage and the Family

INDEX